American College of Physicians®
INTERNAL MEDICINE | *Doctors for Adults*

MKSAP 16

Medical Knowledge Self-Assessment Program®

Cardiovascular Medicine

Welcome to the Cardiovascular Medicine Section of MKSAP 16!

Here, you will find updated information on epidemiology, diagnostic testing, coronary artery disease, heart failure, myocardial disease, arrhythmias, pericardial disease, valvular heart disease, adult congenital heart disease, diseases of the aorta, peripheral arterial disease, and other important diseases. All of these topics are uniquely focused on the needs of generalists and subspecialists *outside* of cardiovascular medicine.

The publication of the 16th edition of Medical Knowledge Self-Assessment Program heralds a significant event, culminating 2 years of effort by dozens of leading subspecialists across the United States. Our authoring committees have strived to help internists succeed in Maintenance of Certification, right up to preparing for the MOC secure examination, and to get residents ready for the certifying examination. MKSAP 16 also helps you update your medical knowledge and elevates standards of self-learning by allowing you to assess your knowledge with 1,200 all-new multiple-choice questions, including 120 in Cardiovascular Medicine.

MKSAP began more than 40 years ago. The American Board of Internal Medicine's examination blueprint and gaps between actual and preferred practices inform creation of the content. The questions, refined through rigorous face-to-face meetings, are among the best in medicine. A psychometric analysis of the items sharpens our educational focus on weaknesses in practice. To meet diverse learning styles, we offer MKSAP 16 online and in downloadable apps for PCs, tablets, laptops, and smartphones. We are also introducing the following:

High-Value Care Recommendations: The Cardiovascular Medicine section starts with several recommendations based on the important concept of health care value (balancing clinical benefit with costs and harms) to address the needs of trainees, practicing physicians, and patients. These recommendations are part of a major initiative that has been undertaken by the American College of Physicians, in collaboration with other organizations.

Content for Hospitalists: This material, highlighted in blue and labeled with the familiar hospital icon (🏥), directly addresses the learning needs of the increasing number of physicians who work in the hospital setting. MKSAP 16 Digital will allow you to customize quizzes based on hospitalist-only questions to help you prepare for the Hospital Medicine Maintenance of Certification Examination.

We hope you enjoy and benefit from MKSAP 16. Please feel free to send us any comments to mksap_editors@acponline.org or visit us at the MKSAP Resource Site (mksap.acponline.org) to find out how we can help you study, earn CME, accumulate MOC points, and stay up to date. I know I speak on behalf of ACP staff members and our authoring committees when I say we are honored to have attracted your interest and participation.

Sincerely,

Patrick Alguire, MD, FACP
Editor-in-Chief
Senior Vice President
Medical Education Division
American College of Physicians

Cardiovascular Medicine

Committee

Rosario V. Freeman, MD, MS, Editor[1]
Associate Professor of Medicine
Associate Director, Cardiology Fellowship
Medical Director, Echocardiography
Division of Cardiology
University of Washington
Seattle, Washington

Howard H. Weitz, MD, FACP, Associate Editor[1]
Professor of Medicine
Director, Jefferson Heart Institute
Director, Division of Cardiology
Jefferson Medical College of Thomas Jefferson University
Philadelphia, Pennsylvania

R. Michael Benitez, MD[1]
Professor of Medicine
Fellowship Program Director
Director, Clinical Cardiology
Interim Chief, Division of Cardiology
University of Maryland School of Medicine
Annapolis, Maryland

Heidi M. Connolly, MD[1]
Professor of Medicine
Mayo Clinic College of Medicine
Rochester, Minnesota

Andrew M. Kates, MD[2]
Associate Professor of Medicine
Director, Cardiovascular Fellowship Program
Washington University School of Medicine
St. Louis, Missouri

Jordan M. Prutkin, MD, MHS[2]
Assistant Professor of Medicine
Department of Medicine, Division of Cardiology
University of Washington
Seattle, Washington

David M. Shavelle, MD[2]
Associate Clinical Professor
Keck School of Medicine
University of Southern California
Director, Cardiac Catheterization Laboratory
Director, Interventional Cardiology Fellowship
Los Angeles County University of Southern California
Medical Center

Division of Cardiovascular Medicine
Los Angeles, California

Marcus F. Stoddard, MD[1]
Professor of Medicine
Director, Non-Invasive Cardiology
Division of Cardiovascular Medicine
Department of Medicine
The University of Louisville
Louisville, Kentucky

Andrew Wang, MD[2]
Associate Professor of Medicine
Director, Fellowship Training Program
Division of Cardiovascular Medicine
Duke University Medical Center
Durham, North Carolina

Audrey H. Wu, MD, MPH[1]
Clinical Assistant Professor
Division of Cardiovascular Medicine
University of Michigan Health System
Ann Arbor, Michigan

Editor-in-Chief

Patrick C. Alguire, MD, FACP[1]
Senior Vice President, Medical Education
American College of Physicians
Philadelphia, Pennsylvania

Deputy Editor-in-Chief

Philip A. Masters, MD, FACP[1]
Senior Medical Associate for Content Development
American College of Physicians
Philadelphia, Pennsylvania

Senior Medical Associate for Content Development

Cynthia D. Smith, MD, FACP[2]
American College of Physicians
Philadelphia, Pennsylvania

Cardiovascular Medicine Clinical Editor

Robert L. Trowbridge, Jr., MD, FACP[2]

Cardiovascular Medicine Reviewers

Robert Anderson, MD, MACP[1]
Frantz Duffoo, MD, FACP[1]
Norman Dy, MD, FACP[1]
Nora F. Goldschlager, MD, MACP[2]
Jeffrey L. Jackson, MD, MPH, FACP[2]
Lia Logio, MD, FACP[1]
Warren J. Manning, MD, FACP[2]
Asad K. Mohmand, MD, FACP[1]
Joseph J. Padinjarayveetil, MD[1]
Ileana L. Piña, MD[2]

Cardiovascular Medicine Reviewers Representing the American Society for Clinical Pharmacology & Therapeutics

Ahmed D. Abdalrhim, MD, FACP[1]
L. Amy Sun, MD[1]

Cardiovascular Medicine ACP Editorial Staff

Becky Krumm[1], Senior Staff Editor
Sean McKinney[1], Director, Self-Assessment Programs
Margaret Wells[1], Managing Editor
Linnea Donnarumma[1], Assistant Editor

ACP Principal Staff

Patrick C. Alguire, MD, FACP[1]
Senior Vice President, Medical Education

D. Theresa Kanya, MBA[1]
Vice President, Medical Education

Sean McKinney[1]
Director, Self-Assessment Programs

Margaret Wells[1]
Managing Editor

Valerie Dangovetsky[1]
Program Administrator

Becky Krumm[1]
Senior Staff Editor

Ellen McDonald, PhD[1]
Senior Staff Editor

Katie Idell[1]
Senior Staff Editor

Randy Hendrickson[1]
Production Administrator/Editor

Megan Zborowski[1]
Staff Editor

Linnea Donnarumma[1]
Assistant Editor

John Haefele[1]
Assistant Editor

Developed by the American College of Physicians

---

1. Has no relationships with any entity producing, marketing, re-selling, or distributing health care goods or services consumed by, or used on, patients.

2. Has disclosed relationships with entities producing, marketing, re-selling, or distributing health care goods or services consumed by, or used on, patients. See below.

Conflicts of Interest

The following committee members, reviewers, and ACP staff members have disclosed relationships with commercial companies:

Nora F. Goldschlager, MD, MACP
Honoraria
St. Jude Medical, Rhythm Management

Jeffrey L. Jackson, MD, MPH, FACP
Royalties
UpToDate

Andrew M. Kates, MD
Speakers Bureau
Pfizer, Merck, AstraZeneca

Warren J. Manning, MD, FACP
Research Grants/Contracts
Philips Medical Systems
Royalties
UpToDate, Saunders

Ileana L. Piña, MD
Consultantship
GE Healthcare, FDA
Speakers Bureau
Otuksu, Merck, Solvay
Research Grants/Contracts
NIH

Jordan M. Prutkin, MD, MHS
Speakers Bureau
Biotronik, Inc.

David M. Shavelle, MD
Speakers Bureau
Abbott Vascular, AbioMed
Research Grants/Contracts
CardioMems, Cordis, Abbott Vascular, St. Jude, GlaxoSmithKline, Maquet/Data Scope, Roche, AGA Medical, AbioMed

Cynthia D. Smith, MD, FACP
Stock Options/Holdings
Merck and Company

Robert L. Trowbridge, Jr., MD, FACP
Other
First Aid Board Review Book Series

Andrew Wang, MD
Research Grants/Contracts
Evalve, Inc., Edwards Lifesciences, Abbott Vascular,
 Gilead Sciences
Other
Expert reviewer for legal case of infective endocarditis

Acknowledgments

The American College of Physicians (ACP) gratefully
acknowledges the special contributions to the development
and production of the 16th edition of the Medical
Knowledge Self-Assessment Program® (MKSAP® 16)
made by the following people:

Graphic Services: Michael Ripca (Technical Administrator/
Graphic Designer) and Willie-Fetchko Graphic Design
(Graphic Designer).

Production/Systems: Dan Hoffmann (Director, Web Services
& Systems Development), Neil Kohl (Senior Architect), and
Scott Hurd (Senior Systems Analyst/Developer).

MKSAP 16 Digital: Under the direction of Steven Spadt,
Vice President, ACP Digital Products & Services, the digital
version of MKSAP 16 was developed within the ACP's
Digital Product Development Department, led by Brian
Sweigard (Director). Other members of the team included
Sean O'Donnell (Senior Architect), Dan Barron (Senior
Systems Analyst/Developer), Chris Forrest (Senior Software
Developer/Design Lead), Jon Laing (Senior Web Application
Developer), Brad Lord (Senior Web Developer), John
McKnight (Senior Web Developer), and Nate Pershall
(Senior Web Developer).

The College also wishes to acknowledge that many other
persons, too numerous to mention, have contributed to the
production of this program. Without their dedicated efforts,
this program would not have been possible.

Introducing the MKSAP Resource Site (mksap.acponline.org)

The MKSAP Resource Site (mksap.acponline.org) is a continually updated site that provides links to MKSAP 16
online answer sheets for print subscribers; access to MKSAP
16 Digital, Board Basics® 3, and MKSAP 16 Updates; the
latest details on Continuing Medical Education (CME) and
Maintenance of Certification (MOC) in the United States,
Canada, and Australia; errata; and other new information.

ABIM Maintenance of Certification

Check the MKSAP Resource Site (mksap.acponline.org) for
the latest information on how MKSAP tests can be used to
apply to the American Board of Internal Medicine for
Maintenance of Certification (MOC) points.

RCPSC Maintenance of Certification

In Canada, MKSAP 16 is an Accredited Self-Assessment
Program (Section 3) as defined by the Maintenance of
Certification Program of The Royal College of Physicians and
Surgeons of Canada (RCPSC) and approved by the Canadian
Society of Internal Medicine on December 9, 2011. Approval
of this and other Part A sections of MKSAP 16 extends from
July 31, 2012, until July 31, 2015. Approval of Part B sec-
tions of MKSAP 16 extends from December 31, 2012, to
December 31, 2015. Fellows of the Royal College may earn
three credits per hour for participating in MKSAP 16 under
Section 3. MKSAP 16 will enable Fellows to earn up to 75%
of their required 400 credits during the 5-year MOC cycle. A
Fellow can achieve this 75% level by earning 100 of the maxi-
mum of 174 *AMA PRA Category 1 Credits*™ available in
MKSAP 16. MKSAP 16 also meets multiple CanMEDS
Roles for RCPSC MOC, including that of Medical Expert,
Communicator, Collaborator, Manager, Health Advocate,
Scholar, and Professional. For information on how to apply
MKSAP 16 CME credits to RCPSC MOC, visit the MKSAP
Resource Site at mksap.acponline.org.

The Royal Australasian College of Physicians CPD Program

In Australia, MKSAP 16 is a Category 3 program that may
be used by Fellows of The Royal Australasian College of
Physicians (RACP) to meet mandatory CPD points. Two
CPD credits are awarded for each of the 174 *AMA PRA
Category 1 Credits*™ available in MKSAP 16. More information about using MKSAP 16 for this purpose is available
at the MKSAP Resource Site at mksap.acponline.org and
at www.racp.edu.au. CPD credits earned through
MKSAP 16 should be reported at the MyCPD site at
www.racp.edu.au/mycpd.

Continuing Medical Education

The American College of Physicians is accredited by the
Accreditation Council for Continuing Medical Education
(ACCME) to provide continuing medical education for
physicians.

The American College of Physicians designates this endur-
ing material, MKSAP 16, for a maximum of 174 *AMA
PRA Category 1 Credits*™. Physicians should claim only
the credit commensurate with the extent of their participation in the activity.

Up to 18 *AMA PRA Category 1 Credits*™ are available from July 31, 2012, to July 31, 2015, for the MKSAP 16 Cardiovascular Medicine section.

Learning Objectives

The learning objectives of MKSAP 16 are to:
- Close gaps between actual care in your practice and preferred standards of care, based on best evidence
- Diagnose disease states that are less common and sometimes overlooked and confusing
- Improve management of comorbid conditions that can complicate patient care
- Determine when to refer patients for surgery or care by subspecialists
- Pass the ABIM Certification Examination
- Pass the ABIM Maintenance of Certification Examination

Target Audience

- General internists and primary care physicians
- Subspecialists who need to remain up-to-date in internal medicine
- Residents preparing for the certifying examination in internal medicine
- Physicians preparing for maintenance of certification in internal medicine (recertification)

Earn "Same-Day" CME Credits Online

For the first time, print subscribers can enter their answers online to earn CME credits in 24 hours or less. You can submit your answers using online answer sheets that are provided at mksap.acponline.org, where a record of your MKSAP 16 credits will be available. To earn CME credits, you need to answer all of the questions in a test and earn a score of at least 50% correct (number of correct answers divided by the total number of questions). Take any of the following approaches:

1. Use the printed answer sheet at the back of this book to record your answers. Go to mksap.acponline.org, access the appropriate online answer sheet, transcribe your answers, and submit your test for same-day CME credits. There is no additional fee for this service.

2. Go to mksap.acponline.org, access the appropriate online answer sheet, directly enter your answers, and submit your test for same-day CME credits. There is no additional fee for this service.

3. Pay a $10 processing fee per answer sheet and submit the printed answer sheet at the back of this book by mail or fax, as instructed on the answer sheet. Make sure you calculate your score and fax the answer sheet to 215-351-2799 or mail the answer sheet to Member and Customer Service, American College of Physicians, 190 N. Independence Mall West, Philadelphia, PA 19106-1572, using the courtesy envelope provided in your MKSAP 16 slipcase. You will need your 10-digit order number and 8-digit ACP ID number, which are printed on your packing slip. Please allow 4 to 6 weeks for your score report to be emailed back to you. Be sure to include your email address for a response.

If you do not have a 10-digit order number and 8-digit ACP ID number or if you need help creating a username and password to access the MKSAP 16 online answer sheets, go to mksap.acponline.org or email custserv@acponline.org.

Disclosure Policy

It is the policy of the American College of Physicians (ACP) to ensure balance, independence, objectivity, and scientific rigor in all of its educational activities. To this end, and consistent with the policies of the ACP and the Accreditation Council for Continuing Medical Education (ACCME), contributors to all ACP continuing medical education activities are required to disclose all relevant financial relationships with any entity producing, marketing, re-selling, or distributing health care goods or services consumed by, or used on, patients. Contributors are required to use generic names in the discussion of therapeutic options and are required to identify any unapproved, off-label, or investigative use of commercial products or devices. Where a trade name is used, all available trade names for the same product type are also included. If trade-name products manufactured by companies with whom contributors have relationships are discussed, contributors are asked to provide evidence-based citations in support of the discussion. The information is reviewed by the committee responsible for producing this text. If necessary, adjustments to topics or contributors' roles in content development are made to balance the discussion. Further, all readers of this text are asked to evaluate the content for evidence of commercial bias and send any relevant comments to mksap_editors@acponline.org so that future decisions about content and contributors can be made in light of this information.

Resolution of Conflicts

To resolve all conflicts of interest and influences of vested interests, the ACP precluded members of the content-creation committee from deciding on any content issues that involved generic or trade-name products associated with proprietary entities with which these committee members had relationships. In addition, content was based on best evidence and updated clinical care guidelines, when such evidence and guidelines were available. Contributors' disclosure information can be found with the list of contributors' names and those of ACP principal staff listed in the beginning of this book.

Hospital-Based Medicine

For the convenience of subscribers who provide care in hospital settings, content that is specific to the hospital setting has been highlighted in blue. Hospital icons (🏥) highlight where the hospital-only content begins, continues over more than one page, and ends.

Educational Disclaimer

The editors and publisher of MKSAP 16 recognize that the development of new material offers many opportunities for error. Despite our best efforts, some errors may persist in print. Drug dosage schedules are, we believe, accurate and in accordance with current standards. Readers are advised, however, to ensure that the recommended dosages in MKSAP 16 concur with the information provided in the product information material. This is especially important in cases of new, infrequently used, or highly toxic drugs. Application of the information in MKSAP 16 remains the professional responsibility of the practitioner.

The primary purpose of MKSAP 16 is educational. Information presented, as well as publications, technologies, products, and/or services discussed, is intended to inform subscribers about the knowledge, techniques, and experiences of the contributors. A diversity of professional opinion exists, and the views of the contributors are their own and not those of the ACP. Inclusion of any material in the program does not constitute endorsement or recommendation by the ACP. The ACP does not warrant the safety, reliability, accuracy, completeness, or usefulness of and disclaims any and all liability for damages and claims that may result from the use of information, publications, technologies, products, and/or services discussed in this program.

Publisher's Information

Unauthorized Use of This Book Is Against the Law

MKSAP 16 ISBN: 978-1-938245-00-8
(Cardiovascular Medicine) ISBN: 978-1-938245-01-5

Printed in the United States of America.

For order information in the U.S. or Canada call 800-523-1546, extension 2600. All other countries call 215-351-2600. Fax inquiries to 215-351-2799 or email to custserv@acponline.org.

Errata and Norm Tables

Errata for MKSAP 16 will be available through the MKSAP Resource Site at mksap.acponline.org as new information becomes known to the editors.

MKSAP 16 Performance Interpretation Guidelines with Norm Tables, available July 31, 2013, will reflect the knowledge of physicians who have completed the self-assessment tests before the program was published. These physicians took the tests without being able to refer to the syllabus, answers, and critiques. For your convenience, the tables are available in a printable PDF file through the MKSAP Resource Site at mksap.acponline.org.

Table of Contents

Cardiovascular Medicine High-Value Care Recommendations

The American College of Physicians, in collaboration with multiple other organizations, is embarking on a national initiative to promote awareness about the importance of stewardship of health care resources. The goals are to improve health care outcomes by providing care of proven benefit and reducing costs by avoiding unnecessary and even harmful interventions. The initiative comprises several programs that integrate the important concept of health care value (balancing clinical benefit with costs and harms) for a given intervention into various educational materials to address the needs of trainees, practicing physicians, and patients.

To integrate discussion of high-value, cost-conscious care into MKSAP 16, we have created recommendations based on the medical knowledge content that we feel meet the below definition of high-value care and bring us closer to our goal of improving patient outcomes while conserving finite resources.

High-Value Care Recommendation: A recommendation to choose diagnostic and management strategies for patients in specific clinical situations that balance clinical benefit with cost and harms with the goal of improving patient outcomes.

Below are the High-Value Care Recommendations for the Cardiovascular Medicine section of MKSAP 16.

- Cardiac stress testing is most useful in patients with an intermediate probability of disease, in whom a positive test significantly increases disease likelihood and a negative test significantly decreases likelihood; do not perform cardiac stress testing in patients with either a low or a high pretest probability of disease (see Items 1, 82).
- Do not perform coronary artery calcium scoring in asymptomatic patients at very low or very high risk of a coronary event.
- Reserve cardiac stress tests with imaging (echocardiographic or nuclear) for patients who are unable to exercise or have abnormalities on their resting electrocardiogram that may interfere with test interpretation (see Items 28, 92, 107, and 115).
- Do not obtain echocardiography in asymptomatic patients with innocent-sounding heart murmurs, typically grade 1/6 or 2/6 short systolic mid-peaking murmurs that are audible along the left sternal border (see Item 3).
- Perform coronary angiography in patients with a history of chronic stable angina in the setting of progressive symptoms despite optimal medical therapy, difficulty tolerating medical therapy, or high-risk findings on exercise testing; there is no role for routine periodic cardiac catheterization in patients with chronic stable angina and well-controlled symptoms as it has not been shown to improve outcomes and carries risk (see Item 99).
- Do not order routine stress testing or routine electrocardiography for asymptomatic patients following successful percutaneous coronary intervention.
- Do not order serial echocardiography for the assessment of chronic heart failure unless the patient's clinical status changes.
- Reserve the B-type natriuretic peptide (BNP) test to differentiate between a cardiac and pulmonary cause of dyspnea when the diagnosis is unclear; do not routinely measure BNP in patients with typical signs and symptoms of heart failure.
- In patients who develop heart block following a myocardial infarction, delay the decision to implant a permanent pacemaker for several days to determine whether the heart block is transient or permanent.
- Do not prescribe antibiotic prophylaxis before any procedure (including dental procedures) in patients with native valvular disease unless there is a history of endocarditis.
- Perform echocardiography in patients with known mild aortic stenosis in the setting of new or progressive symptoms, but do not obtain routine periodic echocardiography in asymptomatic patients with mild aortic stenosis more frequently than every 3 to 5 years.
- Do not routinely repeat echocardiography in asymptomatic patients with mild mitral regurgitation and normal left ventricular size and function.
- Avoid combination treatment with an antiplatelet agent and warfarin for the treatment of peripheral arterial disease because it is no more effective than antiplatelet therapy alone and carries a higher risk of life-threatening bleeding.
- Treat patients with stable claudication symptoms with medical therapy and exercise and not percutaneous or surgical revascularization because the rate of progression to critical limb ischemia and limb loss is less than 5% annually (see Item 91).
- Do not refer asymptomatic patients for patent foramen ovale closure to prevent stroke because the available procedures are not effective.
- Do screen asymptomatic men aged 65 to 75 years who have ever smoked with a one-time abdominal ultrasonographic screening to look for abdominal aortic aneurysm; do not repeat this screening after a normal study.

Epidemiology of Cardiovascular Disease

Overview

Cardiovascular disease comprises several conditions that affect the cardiovascular system, including coronary artery disease (CAD), acute myocardial infarction (MI) and angina pectoris, hypertension, stroke, heart failure, atrial fibrillation, peripheral arterial disease, valvular heart disease, and congenital heart disease. More than 81 million adult Americans (1 in 3) have one or more types of cardiovascular disease. Cardiovascular disease accounts for 1 of every 2.8 deaths in the United States while CAD caused 1 of every 5 deaths in the United States in 2004. Data from the Framingham Heart Study indicate the lifetime risk for cardiovascular disease is 2 in 3 for men and 1 in 2 for women.

The percentage of deaths attributable to cardiovascular disease increases with age. In 2006, 19% of deaths in adults between the ages of 35 and 44 years were from cardiovascular disease, compared with 45% among persons aged 85 years and older. CAD is the leading cause of death in Americans aged 65 years and older and is second only to cancer for Americans between the ages of 45 and 64 years.

Approximately one in six hospital stays in the United States result from cardiovascular disease, accounting for more than 30 million days of inpatient hospital care in 2006. The total inpatient hospital cost for cardiovascular disease was $71.2 billion, about one fourth the total cost of inpatient care in the United States. In 2010, the costs of cardiovascular disease were projected to be $503.2 billion, representing $324 billion in direct and more than $160 billion in indirect costs. By comparison, the estimated cost of all cancers in 2008 was $228 billion.

One in five men and women who are aged 40 years or older will develop heart failure during the course of their lifetime. The average 1-year mortality rate for heart failure is approximately 20%. Survival is lower in men than in women. The number of hospital admissions for heart failure has increased markedly over the past decade, with more than 1.1 million Americans hospitalized for heart failure in 2006. Although the number of hospitalizations has gone up, the case fatality rate for these hospitalizations has declined over the same period. The estimated direct and indirect cost from heart failure in the United States for 2010 is almost $40 billion. Epidemiologic data from heart failure can be difficult to interpret because heart failure is the end stage of many processes, including CAD and hypertension.

Ethnicity and Cardiovascular Disease

Prevalence data from the National Health Interview Survey (NHIS) and the National Center for Health Statistics (NCHS) indicate that in the United States, 12.1% of whites have CAD, compared with 10.2% of blacks or African Americans, 8.1% of Hispanics or Latinos, 5.2% of Asians, and 12.1% of American Indians or Alaska Natives. Death rates for cardiovascular disease are higher for blacks than for whites (for males and females) and are higher for American Indians and Hispanics than for Asian Americans.

Different population risk factors around the world have been established by the INTERHEART study, a study of 30,000 persons conducted in 52 countries around the world. For example, South Asians are, as a group, at overall higher cardiovascular risk than other groups. This has been attributed to several mechanisms, including different distribution of body fat with greater central obesity, higher waist-to-hip circumference ratio, and a greater likelihood of insulin resistance in the South Asian population. Waist circumference and waist-to-hip ratio are indicators of abdominal adiposity and are positively related to coronary heart disease in men and women independently of body mass index and conventional coronary heart disease risk factors.

Mexican Americans have higher rates of CAD, attributable mainly to higher obesity rates and lower levels of physical activity. Blacks in the United States have a greater cardiovascular risk than persons of African or Caribbean descent living in the United Kingdom, a fact that might relate to greater levels of obesity, poorer socioeconomic status, and poorer access to health care among black Americans. American Indians are at higher risk of cardiovascular disease as well, although a subgroup, the Pima Indians of Arizona, have a low prevalence of CAD despite high rates of diabetes mellitus. This relatively low rate of CAD is attributed to lower cholesterol levels and the rarity of heavy smoking. The Japanese have traditionally had low rates of CAD, but now have increased rates of obesity with the adoption of a Western-style diet. This increased obesity, coupled with higher smoking rates, may result in a significant increase in CAD rates in this population.

KEY POINT

- Death rates for cardiovascular disease are higher for blacks in the United States than for whites and are higher for American Indians and Hispanics than for Asian Americans.

Chronic Kidney Disease and Cardiovascular Disease

Cardiovascular disease is the leading cause of death in patients with chronic kidney disease (CKD). Cardiovascular disease mortality is 5 to 30 times higher in dialysis patients than in the general population. Many traditional cardiovascular disease risk factors are also risk factors for CKD, including age, hypertension, diabetes, dyslipidemia, and smoking. Any degree of albuminuria is an independent risk factor for cardiovascular events, heart failure hospitalizations, and all-cause mortality. Although a number of consensus statements have suggested that persons with CKD be considered part of the highest risk group for developing cardiovascular disease as well as for all-cause mortality, shared risk factors between cardiovascular disease and CKD may be responsible for much of the association.

KEY POINT

- Any degree of albuminuria is an independent risk factor for cardiovascular events, heart failure hospitalizations, and all-cause mortality.

Systemic Inflammatory Conditions and Cardiovascular Disease

Systemic inflammatory diseases are inflammatory conditions that are associated with more than one organ system. These conditions can have various cardiac presentations, including pericarditis, myocarditis, myocardial fibrosis, coronary arteritis, endocardial disease with valvular involvement, pulmonary hypertension due to concomitant lung disease, rhythm disturbances (including both bradyarrhythmias and tachyarrhythmias), and systemic hypertension (**Table 1**). Not all conditions that present with these manifestations are systemic inflammatory diseases—the broad differential also includes infections, toxins (cocaine, amphetamines), drug-induced hypersensitivity reactions, and infiltrative processes. In a patient with a systemic inflammatory disease presenting with a cardiac condition, it is important to consider such causes in the differential diagnosis.

Atherosclerosis is a major cause of morbidity and mortality in patients with systemic lupus erythematosus (SLE) as well as other inflammatory conditions, including rheumatoid arthritis. In SLE, accelerated atherosclerosis is attributed to both an increased prevalence of traditional risk factors in this population as well as the inflammatory effect of SLE itself. The risk of MI is increased by up to 50-fold in women aged 35 to 44 years with SLE compared with age-matched Framingham controls. This premature atherosclerosis has led to evaluation of subclinical markers, including coronary artery calcification and carotid atherosclerosis in risk assessment for SLE. Notably, the recently published LAPS trial (Lupus Atherosclerosis Prevention Study) failed to show benefit of statin therapy on either progression of coronary artery calcification, carotid intima media thickness, or carotid plaque over a 2-year period in patients with SLE in comparison with placebo.

TABLE 1. Systemic Inflammatory Conditions and Associated Cardiovascular Diseases

Systemic Inflammatory Condition	Cardiac Involvement and Prevalence
Systemic lupus erythematosus	Pericarditis (25%-50%), noninfective endocarditis (22%-61%), moderate or severe valvular regurgitation (up to 20%), premature coronary artery disease
Rheumatoid arthritis	Pericardial effusion (30%-40%), coronary artery disease, leaflet fibrosis (up to 30%), left ventricular diastolic dysfunction (up to 15%)
Ankylosing spondylitis	Proximal aortitis/valvulitis (25%-60%), moderate or severe aortic regurgitation (up to 40%), conduction system disease (2%-20%), left ventricular diastolic dysfunction
Systemic sclerosis	Systemic hypertension, including scleroderma renal crisis; pulmonary arterial hypertension; myocardial fibrosis; pericardial disease
Takayasu arteritis	Arteritis, predominantly aortic (aneurysms, stenosis, occlusion); coronary arteritis (15%-25%); aortic regurgitation; pulmonary arterial stenosis or aneurysm; malignant hypertension due to renovascular involvement
Giant cell arteritis	Peripheral arterial disease, stroke, myocardial infarction
Polyarteritis nodosa	Cardiomyopathy
Kawasaki disease	Coronary artery aneurysms, occlusion
Behçet syndrome	Aortic valve regurgitation, myocarditis, pericarditis, conduction abnormalities
Sarcoidosis	Cardiomyopathy (dilated or restrictive); conduction abnormalities; ventricular arrhythmias, including sudden death

Quality Measures in Cardiovascular Disease

Multidisciplinary, evidence-based clinical guidelines for a variety of cardiovascular diseases, including CAD, valvular heart disease, heart failure, arrhythmia and device management, congenital heart disease, and vascular disease, are updated on a regular basis (generally every 2-4 years). Statements and guidelines from the American Heart Association can be accessed at http://my.americanheart.org/professional/guidelines.jsp. The Get With The Guidelines (GWTG) program from the American Heart Association was established in 2001 and has been an effective vehicle for hospitals to analyze quality of care and implement improvements through evidence-based changes. Review of data from nearly 46,000 patients from 92 hospitals from across the United States participating in the GWTG program for at least 1 year demonstrated significant improvement in 10 of 11 measures pertaining to the inpatient management of patients with an acute coronary syndrome from the first quarter to the fourth quarter. Measures that showed improvement included early aspirin for acute MI, early β-blockers for acute MI, ACE inhibitor use for acute MI, β-blocker at discharge, smoking cessation counseling, measurement of LDL cholesterol and treatment to lower LDL cholesterol to below 100 mg/dL (2.59 mmol/L), discharge blood pressure below 140/90 mm Hg, and referral to cardiac rehabilitation or exercise counseling. Additional GWTG programs focus on heart failure, stroke, and outpatient management of cardiovascular disease.

The Joint Commission core measures serve as a national standardized performance measurement system providing assessments of care delivered in specific focus areas. There are ten core measures for acute coronary syndromes, including medications prescribed at discharge (aspirin, β-blockers, and statins), ACE inhibitors or angiotensin receptor blockers for left ventricular systolic dysfunction, and primary percutaneous coronary intervention received within 90 minutes of hospital arrival. The core measures for heart failure include evaluation of left ventricular systolic function, ACE inhibitors or angiotensin receptor blockers for left ventricular systolic dysfunction, and smoking cessation advice and counseling. The hospital-based core measures are reported publicly and are utilized by organizations such as the Centers for Medicare and Medicaid Services as a means of assessing and helping improve hospital quality. These measures have also been linked to reimbursement methods, including pay-for-performance initiatives.

Appropriateness criteria for utilization of diagnostic procedures and treatment interventions published by the American College of Cardiology (and other professional societies) provide recommendations based on clinical scenarios, available data, and expert opinion. Examples to date include appropriateness criteria for usage of echocardiography; percutaneous revascularization; and cardiac imaging, including CT, MRI, and nuclear imaging. ⊞

Diagnostic Testing in Cardiology

Clinical History and Physical Examination

Most patients with significant cardiac disease manifest symptoms such as heart failure, dyspnea, decreased exercise tolerance, chest discomfort, or palpitations. Symptom recognition is critical, often determining timing of intervention.

Diagnostic testing is typically needed for initial diagnosis and subsequent clinical management of patients with suspected cardiac disease. The standard approach incorporates patient factors such as sex, age, pretest probability of disease, and likelihood of intervention when test results are known. Unless critical prognostic information is obtained, testing should not be performed if it is unlikely results will alter management.

Diagnostic Testing for Atherosclerotic Coronary Disease

Cardiopulmonary symptoms or atherosclerotic risk factors heighten suspicion for coronary artery disease (CAD). Resting electrocardiogram (ECG) findings, such as Q waves, may indicate previous myocardial infarction. With active angina, dynamic ECG changes such as conduction abnormalities or ST-T wave changes may be present (**Figure 1**). The advantages and limitations of test modalities to evaluate patients for CAD are presented in **Table 2**.

Cardiac Stress Testing

The utility of cardiac stress testing is determined in part by pretest disease probability (see Coronary Artery Disease). In patients with low CAD pretest probability, false-positive results may lead to potential downstream testing and treatment. Conversely, in patients with high CAD pretest probability, falsely negative studies lead to false security and missed diagnoses. Therefore, the greatest benefit is in patients with intermediate CAD probability, in whom a positive test significantly increases disease likelihood and a negative test significantly decreases likelihood.

The premise of stress testing is provocation of transient myocardial ischemia. Exercise is the recommended form of stress as long as an adequate workload is achieved (goal = 85% of maximum predicted heart rate [220 − patient age]). Exercise is preferred to pharmacologic stressors because it provides a gauge of functional capacity and a contextual understanding of symptoms, and it records hemodynamic response to exercise. β-Blockers should be withheld for 24 to 48 hours before testing. Variables associated with worse outcomes following exercise stress testing include poor exercise capacity, provoked angina, hypotension during exercise,

(Text continued on page 6)

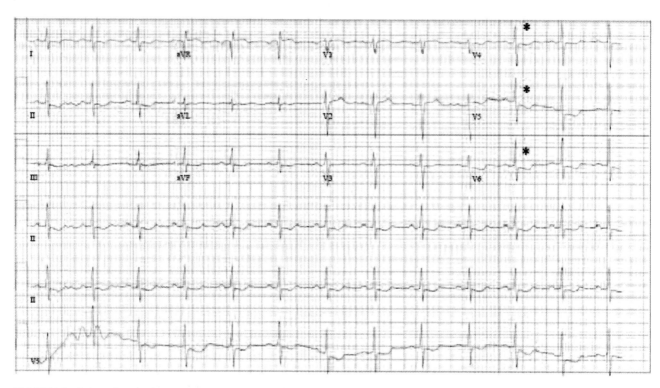

FIGURE 1. Electrocardiogram of a 44-year-old woman with a non–ST-elevation myocardial infarction presenting with exertional left arm and jaw pain. A 1-mm ST-segment depression is seen in leads V₄ through V₆ (*asterisks*) and nonspecific ST-T wave changes are seen in leads II, III, and aVF. Subsequent coronary angiography demonstrated subtotal occlusion of the first obtuse marginal artery.

TABLE 2. Diagnostic Testing for Coronary Artery Disease			
Diagnostic Test	**Utility**	**Advantages**	**Limitations**
Exercise Stress Testing			
Exercise ECG	Initial test in most patients with suspected CAD	Data acquired on exercise capacity, blood pressure and heart rate response, and provoked symptoms	Not useful when baseline ECG is abnormal (LVH, LBBB, paced rhythm, WPW syndrome, >1 mm ST-segment depression)
Stress echocardiography	Recommended when baseline ECG is abnormal or when information on an area of myocardium at risk is needed	Exercise data acquired along with imaging for wall motion abnormalities to indicate ischemia Allows evaluation of valve function and pulmonary pressures Relatively portable for lower cost than nuclear protocols Entire study is completed in <1 h	Image quality is suboptimal in some patients but can be improved with microbubble transpulmonary contrast Image interpretation is difficult when baseline wall motion abnormalities are present Diagnostic accuracy decreases with single-vessel disease or delayed stress image acquisition
Nuclear SPECT perfusion	Recommended when baseline ECG is abnormal or when information on an area of myocardium at risk is needed With LBBB, conduction delay in the septum may cause false-positive abnormality; this can be improved with the use of vasodilator stress	Technetium has less attenuation and superior images compared with thallium If improved tissue penetration is needed, technetium can be used for rest and stress images, which lengthens the test time to ensure adequate wash-out between injections If thallium is used for rest and technetium for stress images (dual-isotope), the study is shorter than with technetium only	Attenuation artifacts can be caused by breast tissue or diaphragm interference Radiation exposure
			(Continued on the next page)

4

TABLE 2. Diagnostic Testing for Coronary Artery Disease (continued)

Diagnostic Test	Utility	Advantages	Limitations
Pharmacologic Stress Testing			
Dobutamine echocardiography	Recommended in patients who cannot exercise Recommended when information on an area of myocardium at risk is needed	Images are acquired continuously, allowing the test to be stopped as soon as ischemia is evident	Dobutamine contraindications are severe baseline hypertension and arrhythmias β-Blockers must be withheld before the test
Dobutamine nuclear perfusion	Recommended in patients who cannot exercise Recommended when information on an area of myocardium at risk is needed	Diagnostic accuracy is equivalent to echocardiography Nuclear perfusion is preferred when echocardiography image quality is suboptimal	Dobutamine contraindications are severe baseline hypertension and arrhythmias β-Blockers must be withheld before the test Radiation exposure
Vasodilator nuclear perfusion (adenosine, dipyridamole, regadenoson)	Recommended in patients who cannot exercise and have contraindications to dobutamine With LBBB, a conduction delay in the septum may cause a false-positive abnormality; this can be improved with the use of vasodilator stress	Late reperfusion imaging allows evaluation of myocardial viability	Contraindications are bronchospastic airway disease and theophylline use Caffeine must be withheld 24 hours before the test Adenosine is contraindicated in sick sinus syndrome or high-degree AV block Adenosine or dipyridamole may cause chest pain, dyspnea, or flushing Radiation exposure
PET/CT	Provides best perfusion images in larger patients Provides data on myocardial perfusion and function	Study duration is shorter and radiation dose is lower than conventional nuclear perfusion imaging Absolute myocardial blood flow can be measured Can be combined with CAC scoring	Not widely available More expensive than other imaging modalities Used with pharmacologic stress only (no exercise protocol) Radiation exposure
Other Tests			
Coronary angiography	Provides definitive diagnosis of the presence and severity of CAD	Percutaneous revascularization can be performed following diagnostic study	Invasive Risks of vascular access and radiocontrast exposure (kidney dysfunction, allergy) Radiation exposure
CAC testing	CAC testing is reasonable in asymptomatic patients at intermediate risk for CAD	CAC scores are predictive of cardiovascular risk in selected patients	Does not provide data on coronary luminal narrowing Radiation exposure
Coronary CT imaging	Identifies anomalous coronary arteries Useful for selected patients with intermediate risk for CAD	Coronary artery vessel lumen and atherosclerotic lesions can be visualized in detail	Requires high-resolution (64-slice) CT instruments Does not provide detailed images of distal vessel anatomy Catheterization is still needed for intervention when disease is present Radiation and radiocontrast exposure
CMR imaging	Gadolinium-enhanced images accurately identify viable and infarcted myocardium Identifies anomalous coronary arteries	More accurate test for myocardial viability	Some patients experience claustrophobia May be contraindicated in patients with pacemaker, ICD, or other implanted devices Gadolinium is contraindicated in kidney failure Sinus rhythm and a slower heart rate are needed for improved image quality Limited availability and expertise

AV = atrioventricular; CAC = coronary artery calcium; CAD = coronary artery disease; CMR = cardiovascular magnetic resonance; ECG = electrocardiography; ICD = implantable cardioverter-defibrillator; LBBB = left bundle branch block; LVH = left ventricular hypertrophy; SPECT = single-photon emission CT; WPW = Wolff-Parkinson-White.

chronotropic incompetence, and ischemia at lower workloads. If a stress test is negative but adequate workload was not achieved, the study is submaximal or indeterminate.

For patients unable to exercise because of physical limitations or physical deconditioning, pharmacologic stressors can be used. These agents, recommended if the patient cannot achieve at least five metabolic equivalents, increase myocardial contractility and oxygen demand (dobutamine) or induce regional hypoperfusion through coronary vasodilation (adenosine, dipyridamole, regadenoson).

Exercise ECG testing is the standard stress test for CAD diagnosis in patients with a normal baseline ECG. If abnormalities limiting ST-segment analysis are present (left bundle branch block [LBBB], left ventricular hypertrophy, paced rhythm, Wolff-Parkinson-White pattern), results may be indeterminate. Additionally, exercise ECG does not accurately localize the site or extent of ischemia, which is important in patients who have undergone revascularization. Contraindications to exercise ECG testing include recent myocardial infarction (<30 days ago), uncontrolled arrhythmia, symptomatic severe aortic stenosis, acute decompensated heart failure, acute pulmonary embolism, and acute aortic dissection.

Results from exercise ECG testing allow prognostication for future cardiac events. Based on exercise duration, the degree of ST-segment deviation, and the presence or absence of exercise angina, the Duke treadmill score stratifies patients into low-, intermediate-, and high-risk categories.

Among patients with resting ECG abnormalities limiting ST-segment analysis, the addition of imaging aids diagnostic accuracy and provides improvement in localizing the site and extent of ischemia. Patients with moderate CAD risk based on exercise ECG but with normal imaging results are at low risk for cardiac events. For patients who cannot exercise, pharmacologic stressors in combination with imaging can be used. In patients with LBBB, exercise stress may result in abnormal septal motion due to conduction delay with falsely positive septal abnormalities; this abnormality is lessened with use of vasodilator stress imaging.

Stress imaging options include echocardiography and nuclear perfusion studies. Images are obtained at rest and following a stressor (**Figure 2**). Induced abnormalities in myocardial function or perfusion suggest a hemodynamically significant coronary blockage. Poor prognostic findings include large ischemic zones that cover multiple coronary territories and resting left ventricular ejection fraction below 40%. Choice of imaging modality depends on factors such as laboratory expertise or baseline patient characteristics. Both echocardiography and nuclear perfusion studies offer more accuracy than exercise ECG testing alone (**Table 3**). Imaging adds cost, time, and, in the case of nuclear studies, radiation exposure. No clinical study has compared the diagnostic accuracy of all available stress modalities in the same patient group.

With stress echocardiography, regional myocardial function is assessed in real time. Stress images are obtained at peak or immediately after stress, before cardiac function returns to

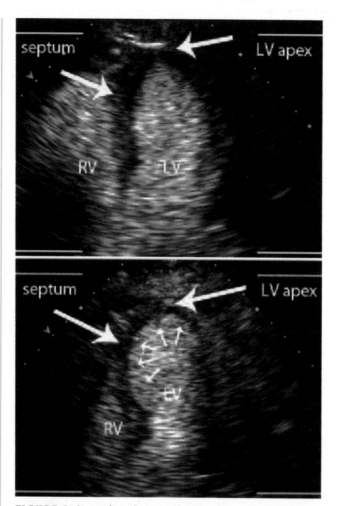

FIGURE 2. Stress echocardiogram with microbubble transpulmonary contrast. In the *top panel,* the heart is shown at baseline (rest) with the left (LV) and right (RV) ventricles opacified by echocontrast. The interventricular septum and LV apex are also indicated. Following administration of dobutamine (*bottom panel*), there is a decrease in inward systolic motion of the apex and distal half of the septum, suggestive of myocardial ischemia (*small arrows*). The remainder of the left ventricle contracts normally, with inward endocardial motion and a decrease in ventricular size.

baseline. Wall motion abnormalities indicate either infarction (seen on stress and rest images) or ischemia (seen on stress images only). Obtaining good imaging windows may be difficult in obese patients or those with chronic pulmonary disease. Diagnostic accuracy decreases with single vessel disease or with delay in obtaining stress images, because ischemic myocardium may normalize before stress images are taken. Stress echocardiography also provides evaluation of valve function and pulmonary pressures and is relatively portable, with less time commitment and a lower cost than nuclear protocols. However, image interpretation is more subjective and can be difficult when baseline wall motion abnormalities are present. Dobutamine protocols are typically used for pharmacologic stress echocardiography. Atropine is used to augment heart rate if not adequate with dobutamine alone.

For nuclear perfusion single-photon emission CT (SPECT) studies, rest images show baseline myocardial perfusion (**Table 4**). After a stressor, radioisotope uptake decreases with reduced coronary flow; relative differences between stress and rest images are compared (**Figure 3**). Two radioisotopes are primarily used, thallium and technetium. With thallium, breast tissue or obesity may lead to false-positive image artifacts because of higher photon scatter. Technetium is a newer radioisotope associated with less scatter and attenuation and superior images; however, testing takes more time (up to 2 days) because adequate wash-out is needed between injections. If thallium is used for the rest portion of the test and technetium for the stress portion (dual-isotope protocol), the study can be completed within several hours. Vasodilator agents used for pharmacologic SPECT protocols include adenosine, dipyridamole, and regadenoson. Regadenoson is a recently approved vasodilator agent with increased ease of use and an improved safety profile. In the ADVANCE trial, side-by-side interpretation of regadenoson and adenosine images showed comparable results for detecting reversible defects. Caffeine should be withheld for at least 24 hours before administration of adenosine because it is an

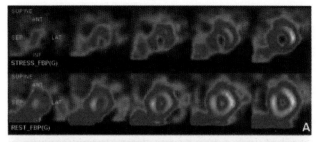
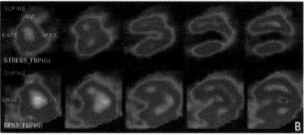

FIGURE 3. Selected images from a nuclear perfusion single-photon emission CT (SPECT) stress study. Short axis views (*panel A*) of the heart with stress (*top row*) and at rest (*bottom row*) show a radiotracer defect in the septum and inferior wall that is filled on the rest images. Long axis views (*panel B*) demonstrate an apical filling defect with stress (*top row*) that is perfused on rest images (*bottom row*).

TABLE 3. Diagnostic Accuracy of Cardiac Stress Modalities for Diagnosis of Coronary Artery Disease

Diagnostic Test	Sensitivity (%)	Specificity (%)	Number of Patients	Number of Studies in Meta-analysis
Exercise ECG	68	77	24,074	132
Nuclear SPECT perfusion	88	77	628	8
Stress echocardiography	76	88	1174	10
PET stress	91	82	206	3

ECG = electrocardiography; SPECT = single-photon emission CT.

Adapted from: Garber AM, Solomon NA. Cost-effectiveness of alternative test strategies for the diagnosis of coronary artery disease. Ann Intern Med. 1999;130(9):719-728. [PMID: 10357690]

TABLE 4. Interpretation of Nuclear Stress and Viability Studies

Stress Testing		
At Rest	**After Stressor**	**Interpretation**
Normal	Normal	Normal function, no ischemia
Normal	Perfusion defect	Normal function at rest, ischemia after stress
Perfusion defect	Perfusion defect	Infarct
Any	LV dilation	No distinct zone of ischemia, possible balanced ischemia or multivessel CAD
Viability Testing		
Initial Study (at rest)	**Rest Study Repeated After 24 h**	**Interpretation**
Perfusion defect	Perfusion defect	Infarct, no viability
Perfusion defect	Perfusion of area	Viable myocardium

CAD = coronary artery disease; LV = left ventricle.

adenosine receptor antagonist. If patients are unable to receive vasodilator agents, dobutamine can be substituted.

PET with CT is a newer cardiac stress testing modality that combines myocardial perfusion data (PET) with structural anatomic imaging (CT). PET/CT quantifies absolute myocardial blood flow with a shorter protocol time than SPECT, and it provides improved image quality. Overall accuracy of PET/CT stress testing for diagnosis of CAD is excellent, with a meta-analysis demonstrating sensitivity of approximately 92% and specificity of approximately 85%. In some studies, PET/CT performance was superior to SPECT, particularly in obese patients. However, PET/CT is more expensive and is not yet widely available.

Viability Testing

With significant coronary blockage, minimal blood flow may keep myocardium alive, but may not be adequate to generate normal contraction. With revascularization, perfusion to this region is improved, improving myocardial function. Viability testing is available with all imaging modalities by comparing two at-rest studies performed 24 hours apart (see Table 4).

Historically, treatment planning for surgical revascularization in patients with systolic dysfunction due to ischemic disease heavily utilized viability testing for decision making. However, a recent substudy of the STICH trial found that a baseline finding of substantial viable myocardium did not have a significant impact on all-cause mortality at 5 years when comparing medical therapy with bypass surgery versus medical therapy without bypass surgery, implying that viability assessment alone should not be the primary deciding factor in determining treatment strategy for these patients.

Visualization of the Coronary Anatomy

Conventional coronary angiography identifies the location and severity of blockages and allows vascular access for percutaneous intervention (**Figure 4**). CT angiography examines coronary anatomy noninvasively following intravenous injection of radiocontrast. Tomographic evaluation of coronary arteries with CT angiography or cardiovascular magnetic resonance (CMR) imaging provides improved visualization of the coronary os and very proximal vessels, which is helpful in assessing congenitally anomalous coronary arteries. CT angiography is sensitive for coronary atherosclerosis presence but is relatively limited in providing data on the hemodynamic significance of the lesions seen. Therefore, a normal CT angiogram is most effective at ruling out CAD in patients with low to intermediate pretest disease probability. If the CT angiogram is abnormal, other stress testing or angiography is typically needed. Utility of CT angiography increases if other causes for chest pain are highly suspected, such as pulmonary embolism or aortic dissection; however, discussion with the provider performing the CT angiography is often helpful because a nonstandard protocol may be needed to optimally image specific structures.

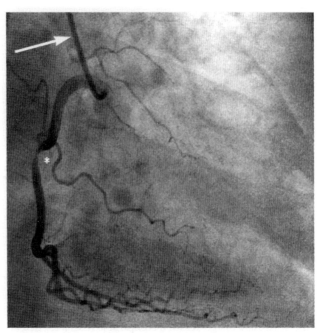

FIGURE 4. Coronary angiogram. Radiocontrast dye is injected via catheter (*arrow*) during coronary angiography, demonstrating 85% to 90% occlusion of the mid right coronary artery (*asterisk*).

Coronary Artery Calcium Scoring

Electron beam or multidetector CT quantifies coronary artery calcification (CAC) using noncontrast tomographic images. Because contrast is not used, intracoronary occlusion severity and disease progression are not evaluated. CAC scoring is sensitive but not very specific for CAD. Studies evaluating the effect of statins on CAC progression have not provided clear evidence of benefit. In asymptomatic patients at either low or high risk of a coronary event, CAC scoring does not alter the recommended intensity of risk modification per clinical guidelines and is, therefore, not recommended. A 2007 American College of Cardiology Foundation/American Heart Association Expert Consensus Panel did not recommend CAC as a screening tool for diagnosis of obstructive CAD because of low specificity and a high false-positive rate when applied to low-risk populations. However, selective use in patients at intermediate risk (10%-20% 10-year risk) may be considered if it prompts more intensive risk factor modification.

Risks of Coronary Diagnostic Testing

Major risks associated with cardiac diagnostic testing, including arrhythmia and myocardial infarction, occur in fewer than 1% of studies. Severity of radiation exposure depends on patients' body habitus, operator technique, procedure length, and imaging system. The radiation dose with CT angiography is higher than with CAC scoring because CT angiography requires a high-resolution CT scanner. Radiation exposure with nuclear SPECT is higher than with CT angiography.

Nephropathy occurs in 2% of patients exposed to radiocontrast. Peak creatinine elevation occurs 3 to 5 days after the procedure, with return to baseline several days later. Increased nephropathy risk occurs with increased contrast load, pre-existing kidney disease, diabetes mellitus, and intravascular volume depletion. Nephropathy is decreased with periprocedural hydration, use of low-osmolar contrast, decreased contrast load, and pretreatment with N-acetylcysteine. Another cause of kidney dysfunction is renal cholesterol embolism from dislodged aortic atheroma during catheter manipulation; lower extremity embolism appears as mottled skin with purple toe discoloration. Laboratory evidence of cholesterol embolism includes urine and peripheral eosinophilia. Treatment is supportive.

Vascular access complications following coronary angiography manifest following arterial sheath removal. Vascular ultrasound is diagnostic for groin hematomas; primary treatment is direct, manual pressure by experienced personnel. Arteriovenous fistula or pseudoaneurysm should be suspected if groin tenderness, a pulsatile mass, or a femoral bruit is present and can typically be treated conservatively with ultrasound-guided compression. Surgical repair is indicated if hemostasis is not obtained or femoral neuropathy from nerve compression ensues. Retroperitoneal hematoma should be suspected with hemodynamic instability or a rapidly decreasing postprocedure hematocrit; noncontrast abdominal CT is diagnostic.

KEY POINTS

- Cardiac stress testing is the preferred diagnostic test in symptomatic patients with intermediate coronary artery disease probability.

- Exercise stress testing is preferred to pharmacologic stress testing because it gauges functional capacity and provides contextual understanding of symptoms.

- Pharmacologic stressors are indicated for stress testing if the patient is unable to achieve adequate workload or if the risk for a false-positive study is increased, such as with left bundle branch block.

- Coronary artery calcium scoring should not be performed in asymptomatic patients at very low or very high risk of a coronary event.

Diagnostic Testing for Structural Heart Disease

Structural heart disease includes myocardial, pericardial, and valvular abnormalities. Physical examination findings in structural disease include signs of heart failure and abnormal cardiac auscultation. Murmurs are generated from turbulent flow through an orifice, an incompetent valve, or a congenital defect. Grade 1/6 to 2/6 midsystolic murmurs are usually benign, attributable to minor valve abnormalities or physiologic increases in blood flow. In asymptomatic patients with benign midsystolic murmurs, no further diagnostic testing is indicated, because results are unlikely to alter management.

In patients in whom pathologic structural heart disease is suspected, transthoracic echocardiography provides noninvasive, quantitative evaluation of cardiac size and function, valve morphology and function, pericardial disease, pulmonary artery pressures, and proximal great vessels (**Table 5**). Doppler echocardiography allows assessment of direction and velocity of blood flow. Two types of echocontrast are agitated saline, which opacifies the right heart with bubble transmission to the left heart in the presence of an intracardiac shunt, and microbubble transpulmonary contrast, which crosses the pulmonary circulation to enhance left ventricular endocardial borders.

Hand-held echocardiography is increasingly available for limited bedside imaging, most commonly in intensive care units and emergency departments. When used by trained providers, these devices may assist in acute triage, such as diagnosing large pericardial effusions, but do not supplant standard transthoracic echocardiography. If transthoracic echocardiography images are nondiagnostic, transesophageal echocardiography may be useful. Transesophageal echocardiography is a semi-invasive test in which the transducer is positioned in the esophagus, avoiding intervening structures such as ribs and lungs and providing clearer images, particularly of the left atrium and mitral valve (**Figure 5**). Transesophageal echocardiography is an appropriate initial test in certain clinical situations, such as detection of left atrial thrombus, evaluation of prosthetic valve dysfunction, and evaluation of aortic dissection, as well as in patients with a high pretest probability of endocarditis. Complications of transesophageal echocardiography are rare and include aspiration or esophageal injury.

Three-dimensional echocardiography is a newer modality adjunctive to standard echocardiography. Three-dimensional echocardiography has shown the most utility in visualizing the mitral valve and interatrial septum to aid catheter and device placement during percutaneous intervention, such as mitral valvuloplasty (**Figure 6**). Other advanced cardiac imaging for structural heart disease includes cardiac CT and CMR imaging (**Figure 7**).

Serial imaging is often used to follow disease progression in asymptomatic patients. Published clinical guidelines provide recommended thresholds for surgical intervention for asymptomatic or minimally symptomatic disease.

Pulmonary artery (PA) catheterization may be performed in the intensive care unit or cardiac catheterization laboratory to obtain hemodynamic information. PA catheters are useful in diagnosing the cause of hemodynamic shock and guiding therapy. PA catheter data on intracardiac pressures and blood oxygen can be used to identify the location of intracardiac shunts. Information on cardiac output, preload (pulmonary capillary wedge pressure), afterload (systemic vascular resistance), and mixed venous oxygen saturation (SVO_2) can be obtained.

PA catheters have the most utility in hemodynamically unstable patients, typically those requiring inotropic or vasopressor support. PA catheters are not indicated for continuous use in hemodynamically stable patients for monitoring purposes. Prospective cohort studies have suggested increased morbidity and mortality for patients in whom a PA catheter was used during treatment. Although subsequent prospective randomized trials evaluating PA catheter–directed clinical management have not demonstrated an increase in mortality or morbidity, a clear benefit was also not demonstrated, suggesting that PA catheters should be used judiciously with prompt removal when the data obtained are no longer needed.

KEY POINTS

- Mild midsystolic murmurs are usually benign and warrant no further testing.
- Pulmonary artery catheters are not indicated for continuous use in hemodynamically stable patients for monitoring purposes.

TABLE 5. Diagnostic Testing for Structural Heart Disease

Diagnostic Test	Major Indications	Advantages	Limitations
Transthoracic echocardiography	Heart failure Cardiomyopathy Valve disease Congenital heart disease Pulmonary hypertension Aortic disease Pericardial disease	Accurate diagnosis of presence and severity of structural heart disease Quantitation of LV size and function, pulmonary pressures, valve function, and intracardiac shunts No known adverse effects Widely available, portable, fast	Operator-dependent data acquisition Interpretation requires expertise Variability in instrumentation Image quality limits diagnosis in some patients, may require microbubble contrast agents
Transesophageal echocardiography	Endocarditis Prosthetic valve dysfunction Aortic disease Left atrial thrombus	High-quality images, especially of posterior cardiac structures Most accurate test for endocarditis evaluation, prosthetic valves, and left atrial thrombus	Requires esophageal intubation, typically with conscious sedation
Three-dimensional echocardiography	Mitral valve disease Interatrial septum (percutaneous ASD closure)	Improved tomographic imaging Used during cardiac procedures for device placement Improved assessment of LV global/regional systolic function	Adjunct to two-dimensional imaging Limited availability and expertise
Radionuclide angiography	Evaluation of LV systolic function	Quantitative ejection fraction measurements	Radiation exposure No data on other cardiac structures
Cardiac catheterization	Congenital heart disease Coronary angiography	Direct measurement of intracardiac pressures Contrast angiography provides visualization of complex cardiac anatomy Allows percutaneous intervention for structural heart disease	Invasive Radiation and radiocontrast exposure Images not tomographic, limiting evaluation of complex three-dimensional anatomy
CMR imaging	Congenital heart disease Aortic disease Myocardial viability Myocardial disease (infiltrative disease, myocarditis, hypertrophic cardiomyopathy) RV cardiomyopathy (ARVC) Quantitation of LV mass and function	High-resolution tomographic imaging and blood-flow data Quantitative RV volumes and ejection fraction No ionizing radiation or contrast Enables three-dimensional reconstruction of aortic and coronary anatomy	Limited availability and expertise Some patients experience claustrophobia May be contraindicated in patients with pacemaker, ICD, or other implanted devices Gadolinium is contraindicated in kidney failure Sinus rhythm and slower heart rate are needed for improved image quality
Chest CT	Aortic disease Coronary disease Cardiac masses Pericardial disease	High-resolution tomographic images Enables three-dimensional reconstruction of aortic and coronary anatomy	Radiation and radiocontrast exposure Image acquisition improved with sinus rhythm and slower heart rate

ARVC = arrhythmogenic right ventricular cardiomyopathy; ASD = atrial septal defect; CMR = cardiovascular magnetic resonance; ICD = implantable cardioverter-defibrillator; LV = left ventricle; RV = right ventricle.

Diagnostic Testing for Cardiac Arrhythmias

A cardiac arrhythmia is suspected when a patient presents with palpitations, dizziness, syncope, or decreased exercise tolerance. Although a resting ECG during symptoms may make the diagnosis, symptoms are often intermittent or fleeting. Occasionally, a resting ECG may provide clues to the source of an arrhythmia, such as heart block, pre-excitation, or a long QT interval. Arrhythmias typically are of greatest clinical significance if they occur in the presence of underlying structural heart disease. Therefore, echocardiography is often performed. In patients with a potentially life-threatening arrhythmia, ischemia evaluation with cardiac stress testing or angiography is also performed. Additionally, invasive electrophysiology testing may be used to provoke the arrhythmia in a controlled setting or to electrically map the arrhythmia for ablative intervention. Newer imaging modalities, such as CMR imaging, are increasingly used in conjunction with echocardiography to investigate a potential structural source of the arrhythmia, such as a cardiomyopathy or sarcoidosis.

Various rhythm recorders can be used to capture an arrhythmia; selection depends on the frequency and duration of symptoms. A continuous ambulatory ECG monitor records rhythm while worn (24-48 hours) and is used to detect asymptomatic arrhythmias or correlate rhythm with relatively frequent symptoms. With infrequent symptoms, the utility of continuous ECG monitoring is limited. Event

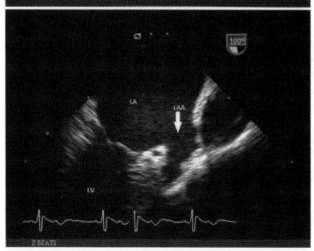

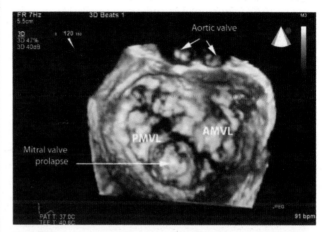

FIGURE 6. Three-dimensional transesophageal echocardiographic image of a mitral valve with prolapse of the posterior mitral valve leaflet, looking "down" on the valve from the left atrium. For orientation, a portion of the aortic valve is seen at the top of the image. A portion of the mid-posterior mitral valve leaflet (*long arrow*) prolapses into the left atrium during systole, shown by differential shadowing, providing depth perspective. AMVL = anterior mitral valve leaflet; PMVL = posterior mitral valve leaflet.

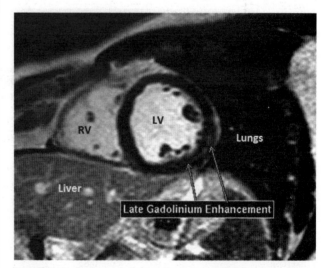

FIGURE 7. Cardiovascular magnetic resonance (CMR) image of a patient with acute myocarditis. The heart is shown in cross-section. The liver, adjacent to the right ventricle (RV) and the posterior wall of the left ventricle (LV), is seen below the heart, and the lungs are seen adjacent to the lateral wall of the left ventricle. Within the myocardium, there is late gadolinium enhancement (thin bright stripe) within the midportion of the posterolateral myocardial wall (*arrows*).

FIGURE 5. Transthoracic echocardiography in a patient with normal systolic function and atrial fibrillation (*top*) demonstrates good visualization of the left ventricle (*LV*); however, the left atrial appendage (*LAA*) is in the far field and poorly seen. With transesophageal echocardiography (*bottom*), the transducer is posterior to the heart, and the left atrium (*LA*) and left atrial appendage are more easily seen, showing absence of thrombus in the appendage.

recorders record ECG tracings only when triggered by the patient and are more useful for infrequent symptoms. Two types of event recorders are used. When the patient triggers a *looping* event recorder, a permanent recording includes several seconds of the presymptom rhythm, which is useful in patients with syncope. With a *postsymptom* event recorder, no preceding rhythm is saved when the device is triggered. The advantage of a postsymptom recorder is the lack of electrode leads, making it more comfortable to carry. For very rare symptoms, a small implantable loop recorder can be placed subcutaneously and interrogated noninvasively. These devices store up to 42 minutes of data and have a battery life of up to 3 years. More recently, mobile cardiac outpatient telemetry (MCOT) units have become available, which continuously monitor the ECG, automatically recognize an arrhythmia, and instantaneously transmit ECG recordings. A central monitoring station provides real-time rhythm analysis.

KEY POINTS

- Continuous ambulatory electrocardiographic monitors are used to detect frequent or asymptomatic arrhythmias while the device is worn.

- Event recorders are used for infrequent symptoms and record electrocardiographic tracings only when triggered.

Coronary Artery Disease

Risk Factors for Coronary Artery Disease

Numerous landmark studies have identified risk factors that independently increase the risk of developing cardiovascular disease. The INTERHEART study assessed the prevalence of nine potentially modifiable risk factors (**Table 6**) in more than 15,000 patients with first acute myocardial infarction (MI) and almost 15,000 asymptomatic age- and sex-matched controls. All of these risk factors were strongly associated with acute MI in the 52 countries included in the trial. Results of the INTERHEART study suggest that these modifiable risk factors accounted for more than 90% of the risk for acute MI.

The Framingham risk score estimates the 10-year risk of a major cardiovascular event (MI or coronary death) based on age, sex, cholesterol levels, smoking status, and blood pressure. (An online Framingham risk calculator is available at http://hp2010.nhlbihin.net/atpiii/calculator.asp?user type=prof.) One advantage of risk scores such as the Framingham score is the identification of those at risk not from a single markedly elevated risk factor but from several moderately elevated risk factors. Although this is a well-validated model, it may not be as applicable in some patient populations such as women and minorities. In addition, some patients with a low 10-year risk may have a high lifetime risk.

An optimal risk factor profile at 50 years of age in the Framingham Heart Study cohort, defined as blood pressure below 120/80 mm Hg, total cholesterol level below 180 mg/dL (4.66 mmol/L), and absence of diabetes mellitus and smoking, was associated with a significantly lower risk for developing cardiovascular disease compared with persons with three or more risk factors.

Established Risk Factors

Dyslipidemia is the most powerful modifiable risk factor for the development of cardiovascular disease. High LDL cholesterol and low HDL cholesterol are each independent risk

---

TABLE 6. Potentially Modifiable Risk Factors Associated with Myocardial Infarction

Risk Factor	Odds Ratio (adjusted for other risk factors)	Attributable Risk (%)
Cholesterol (ApoB/ApoA1 ratio)	3.25	49.2
Current smoking	2.87	35.7
Psychosocial stressors	2.67	32.5
Diabetes mellitus	2.37	9.9
Hypertension	1.91	17.9
Abdominal obesity	1.62	20.1
Moderate alcohol intake	0.91	6.7
Exercise	0.86	12.2
Vegetables and fruit daily	0.70	13.7
All risk factors	129.20	90.4

Apo = apolipoprotein.

Data from: Yusuf S, Hawken S, Ounpuu S, et al; INTERHEART Study Investigators. Effect of potentially modifiable risk factors associated with myocardial infarction in 52 countries (the INTERHEART study): case-control study. Lancet. 2004;364(9438):937-952. [PMID: 15364185]

factors for the development of cardiovascular disease. Treatment goals vary based on risk factors and 10-year risk as assessed by the Framingham risk score (see MKSAP 16 General Internal Medicine). The Framingham Heart Study found a 1% reduction of risk rate for every 1% reduction in LDL cholesterol level in middle-aged men and women over a 12-year period. Findings from Framingham and other large cohort studies have shown a 2% to 4% reduction in coronary heart disease risk for every 1% increase in HDL cholesterol level over a similar period.

Cigarette smoking results in a two- to threefold increased risk of dying of cardiovascular disease. Among modifiable risk factors, smoking ranked second only to dyslipidemia in importance for attributed risk of MI in the INTERHEART study. Most of the cardiovascular risk from smoking decreases within the first 2 years after quitting, and by 3 to 5 years, the risk for cardiovascular events is the same as for a nonsmoker. Tobacco users should be encouraged to use both counseling and medication to help them to quit (see MKSAP 16 General Internal Medicine).

Psychosocial stressors, including depression, anger, and anxiety, play an important role in cardiovascular risk. Psychosocial stressors accounted for 30% of attributable risk of acute MI in the INTERHEART study, third only to dyslipidemia and smoking in importance of modifiable risk factors. Depression is present in at least one of five patients with cardiovascular disease and is associated with poor quality of life and worse outcomes. The American Heart Association (AHA) recommends that patients with cardiovascular disease be screened periodically for depression.

Patients with diabetes are at a particularly high risk for cardiovascular, cerebrovascular, and peripheral arterial disease. Adults with diabetes have heart disease death rates and stroke risk about two to four times higher than adults without diabetes. In 2007, 7.8% of the U.S. population had diabetes; nearly a quarter of these were undiagnosed. Almost half of all patients hospitalized with an acute MI have known or previously undiagnosed diabetes. Diabetes is an independent predictor of secondary events such as reinfarction, heart failure, and death.

Hypertension affects one in three adults in the United States; of the 70% of patients who are aware they have hypertension, blood pressure is controlled in only 30%. In the INTERHEART study, hypertension accounted for almost 20% of the risk associated with acute MI. The increased risk of cardiovascular events attributable to hypertension is seen best when one considers the reduction of events observed in clinical trials. Compared with placebo, antihypertensive therapy reduces the incidence of major cardiovascular events (stroke, heart failure, MI) by 20% to 25%. Multiple medications may be required in patients to achieve their target blood pressure. Aggressive treatment is critical in those patients with comorbid conditions, including chronic kidney disease, heart failure, and diabetes.

The metabolic syndrome is a constellation of conditions characterized by the following: insulin resistance, hyperinsulinemia, hyperglycemia, dyslipidemia, and hypertension (see MKSAP 16 General Internal Medicine). Data from NHANES 2003-2006 and NCEP ATP III guidelines estimate 34% of adults older than 20 years meet the criteria for metabolic syndrome. Metabolic syndrome nearly doubles the risk for developing CAD in men and women. Those with metabolic syndrome have a risk for cardiovascular events higher than those without metabolic syndrome but lower than those with diabetes. A strong positive association exists between the number of metabolic syndrome traits and the subsequent risk for CAD, cardiovascular disease, and diabetes. Guidelines suggest that patients with one or more risk factors for metabolic syndrome should undergo testing to establish the diagnosis. The diagnosis of metabolic syndrome is not superior to risk models (such as the Framingham risk score) in predicting risk for CAD and stroke.

A family history of a premature cardiovascular event in a parent or sibling (male younger than 45 years, female younger than 55 years) is associated with an approximately doubled risk for cardiovascular disease. A family history of early-onset sudden death in a parent is associated with more than a twofold increased risk for sudden death in offspring.

Emerging Risk Factors

High-sensitivity C-reactive protein (hsCRP), a nonspecific marker for systemic inflammation, is an independent predictor for adverse cardiovascular events. Joint guidelines from the AHA and Centers for Disease Control and Prevention do not recommend routine measurement of hsCRP in the general population. For patients at intermediate risk for CAD (10% to 20% 10-year Framingham risk), however, hsCRP levels may help direct further prevention efforts. For example, an elevated hsCRP level (>0.3 mg/dL [3.0 mg/L]) in an intermediate-risk patient based on Framingham risk score would prompt more aggressive treatment. A low hsCRP level (<0.1 mg/dL [1.0 mg/L]) would permit reclassification of the same patient as low risk. hsCRP is a nonspecific indicator; thus, patients with a value above 1.0 mg/dL [10 mg/L] should have the measurement repeated after an interval of at least 2 weeks and, if still elevated, be evaluated for infection or inflammation. Although several trials have suggested that a low hsCRP level is associated with a lower risk of cardiovascular events, it remains to be seen whether therapy directed toward lowering CRP actually affects outcomes.

Improvements in imaging have enabled the detection and quantification of atherosclerotic burden before it manifests clinically, offering an assessment of cardiovascular risk. The two best-studied methods are cardiac CT to determine a coronary artery calcium (CAC) score and B-mode ultrasound for carotid intima-media thickness. Guidelines from the American College of Cardiology Foundation and the AHA suggest that CAC score screening may be appropriate in persons at intermediate cardiovascular risk based on Framingham score, but not in those at low risk or with established CAD or diabetes. Carotid intima-media thickness is an earlier manifestation of atherosclerosis than CAC, but guidelines are not yet available for screening asymptomatic patients to assess cardiovascular risk.

Although elevated homocysteine levels are associated with CAD risk, no data support the use of folic acid supplementation, which can lower homocysteine levels, to reduce the risk. Lp(a) lipoprotein is also a marker for increased cardiovascular risk and can be lowered with agents such as niacin. However, no outcome studies have demonstrated efficacy in lowering cardiovascular events by lowering Lp(a) lipoprotein level.

KEY POINTS

- Potentially modifiable risk factors associated with cardiovascular disease are dyslipidemia, smoking, psychosocial factors, diabetes mellitus, hypertension, obesity, alcohol consumption, physical inactivity, and diet.
- The Framingham risk score can be used to assess the 10-year risk of a major cardiovascular event (http://hp2010.nhlbihin.net/atpiii/calculator.asp ?usertype=prof).

Chronic Stable Angina

Diagnosis and Evaluation

Stable angina pectoris is a common manifestation of coronary artery disease (CAD) and results from an imbalance between myocardial oxygen supply and demand that usually occurs because of a fixed coronary stenosis. A variety of noninvasive stress tests are available to determine whether a patient with cardiovascular symptoms has CAD (see Diagnostic Testing in Cardiology). The decision to perform a specific test is based on the pretest probability of CAD, the patient's ability to exercise, findings on the resting electrocardiogram (ECG), and comorbid conditions, such as reactive airways disease, that may influence the choice of a pharmacologic stress agent (**Figure 8**).

The pretest probability of CAD is based on the patient's age, sex, and description of chest pain (**Table 7**). Stress testing is most useful in patients with an intermediate pretest probability of CAD. For patients with a low pretest probability of CAD, stress testing is not useful because an abnormal test is likely a false positive and a normal test only confirms the low pretest probability of CAD. For patients with a high pretest probability of CAD, stress testing is also not useful to diagnose CAD and empiric medical therapy should be initiated; in this setting, a normal stress test would likely be a false negative and an abnormal stress test would only confirm a high pretest probability of CAD. Circumstances that may warrant stress testing in a patient with a high pretest probability

of CAD for prognostic (as opposed to diagnostic) considerations include establishing the effectiveness of current medical therapy, obtaining an objective measure of exercise capacity, evaluating the extent and severity of ischemia to identify patients with surgical disease, and assessing preoperative risk in a patient undergoing noncardiac surgery.

Because of the invasive nature of coronary angiography and the inherent risks of vascular complications, it should be reserved for patients with lifestyle-limiting angina despite medical therapy or high-risk criteria on noninvasive stress testing (see Figure 8).

Cardiac CT angiography can be considered in the diagnostic evaluation of a patient with an intermediate pretest probability of CAD. Because CT angiography provides no functional information (extent of ischemia), a markedly abnormal study should be followed by coronary angiography or stress testing to delineate coronary anatomy or determine the ischemic burden.

KEY POINTS

- Pretest probability of coronary artery disease in symptomatic patients is determined by the age and sex of the patient and the description of the chest pain.
- Cardiac stress testing is most useful diagnostically in symptomatic patients with an intermediate pretest probability of disease.

Medical Therapy

Medical therapy is the cornerstone for long-term treatment of patients with chronic stable angina (**Figure 9**). The goals of medical therapy in patients with chronic stable angina are to reduce the frequency and severity of angina, thereby improving the quality of life; reduce the progression of atherosclerosis and subsequent cardiovascular events; and improve survival. In addition to medical therapy, patients should be counseled regarding the benefits of diet, exercise, smoking cessation, and weight loss.

Antianginal Medications

The three major classes of antianginal medications for stable angina are β-blockers, nitrates, and calcium channel blockers. These three classes of medications improve functional capacity, delay onset of exercise-induced myocardial ischemia, and decrease the frequency and severity of anginal episodes. Most patients with stable angina will require combination therapy to achieve effective control of anginal symptoms.

Cardioselective β-blockers reduce heart rate, myocardial contractility, and blood pressure and, therefore, reduce myocardial oxygen demand. These agents are first-line therapy in patients with chronic stable angina and are well tolerated in most patients. Dosage should be adjusted to achieve a resting heart rate of approximately 55/min to 60/min and approximately 75% of the heart rate that produces angina with

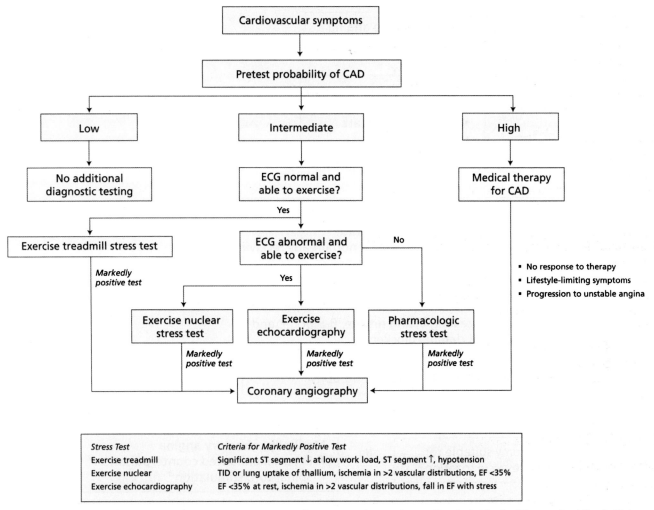

FIGURE 8. Diagnosis of coronary artery disease. CAD = coronary artery disease; ECG = electrocardiogram; EF = ejection fraction; TID = transient ischemic dilation.

TABLE 7.	Clinical Assessment of Pretest Probability of Coronary Artery Disease					
Pretest Probability						
	Nonanginal Chest Pain[a]		**Atypical Chest Pain[b]**		**Typical Chest Pain[c]**	
Age (y)	**Men**	**Women**	**Men**	**Women**	**Men**	**Women**
30-39	4	2	34	12	76	26
40-49	13	3	51	22	87	55
50-59	20	7	65	31	93	73
60-69	27	14	72	51	94	86

[a]Nonanginal chest pain has one or none of the components for typical chest pain.

[b]Atypical chest pain has two of the three components for typical chest pain.

[c]Typical chest pain has three components: (1) substernal chest pain or discomfort, (2) provoked by exertion or emotional stress, (3) relieved by rest and/or nitroglycerin.

Adapted with permission from Gibbons RJ, Abrams J, Chatterjee K, et al. ACC/AHA 2002 guideline update for the management of patients with chronic stable angina: a report of the American College of Cardiology/American Heart Association Task Force on Practice Guidelines (Committee to Update the 1999 Guidelines for the Management of Patients with Chronic Stable Angina). 2002. Available at www.cardiosource.org/~/media/Images/ACC/Science%20and%20Quality/Practice%20Guidelines/s/stable_clean.ashx. Accessed February 27, 2012.

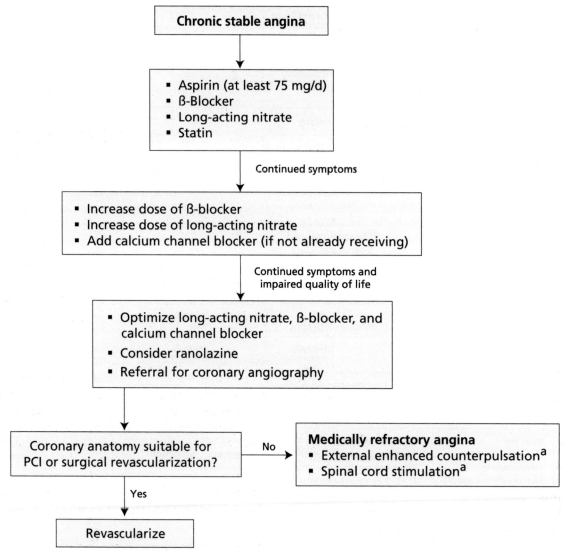

FIGURE 9. Management of chronic stable angina. PCI = percutaneous coronary intervention.

ªNot recommended by current guidelines.

exertion. Potential adverse effects include impaired sexual function, reduced exercise capacity, bradycardia, and generalized fatigue. Absolute contraindications to β-blockers include severe bradycardia, advanced atrioventricular block, decompensated heart failure, and severe reactive airways disease.

Nitrates cause coronary and systemic vasodilation, increasing myocardial oxygen supply and reducing myocardial oxygen demand. Nitrates appear to be as effective as β-blockers and calcium channel blockers in reducing angina. All patients with chronic stable angina should carry either a sublingual or a spray form of nitroglycerin for emergency use. Regardless of the agent and route used, patients using chronic nitrate therapy must be managed for nitrate tolerance. The effectiveness of nitrate therapy can be maintained by establishing a nitrate-free period of 8 to 12 hours per day (typically overnight), during which nitrates are not used. A common problem in clinical practice involves the interaction of medications used for erectile dysfunction (sildenafil, vardenafil, and tadalafil) when patients require nitrates for the relief of angina. These agents relax vascular smooth muscle cells and potentiate the hypotensive effects of nitrates. For patients using nitrates in any form, either on a daily basis or intermittently, these agents are contraindicated.

For patients with absolute contraindications to β-blockers, calcium channel blockers should be initiated as first-line therapy. Calcium channel blockers reduce heart rate and cause systemic and coronary artery vasodilation, thereby reducing myocardial oxygen demand and increasing myocardial oxygen supply. Calcium channel blockers are the preferred therapy over β-blockers when quality of life, preserved exercise capacity, and normal sexual function are the primary treatment goals. Because they cause coronary artery vasodilation, calcium channel blockers are also first-line therapy for patients with vasospastic (Prinzmetal) angina. In the setting of continued angina despite optimal doses of β-blockers and nitrates, calcium channel blockers can be added. Side effects of calcium channel blockers include peripheral edema, dizziness, headache, and constipation. Bradycardia and heart block can occur in patients with significant conduction system disease. In those with severe systolic dysfunction, calcium channel blockers can worsen or precipitate heart failure.

Ranolazine is a novel antianginal agent that causes selective inhibition of the late sodium channel. It should be considered in patients who remain symptomatic despite optimal doses of β-blockers, calcium channel blockers, and nitrates. Ranolazine prolongs the QT interval but the risk of arrhythmias is unclear. It should be used with caution in patients with significant kidney or liver disease.

Cardiovascular-Protective Medications

Aspirin reduces the risk of stroke, MI, and vascular death in patients with CAD and a dose of 75 to 162 mg/d should be prescribed for these patients unless there are contraindications. Clopidogrel may be an alternative in patients in whom aspirin is contraindicated. Combination therapy with aspirin and clopidogrel is indicated only in patients with recent MI or stent placement.

For patients with normal left ventricular ejection fraction, ACE inhibitors reduce cardiovascular and all-cause mortality by 17% and 13%, respectively. For patients with reduced left ventricular systolic function, ACE inhibitors provide greater benefit, reducing death or MI and all-cause mortality by 23% and 20%, respectively. ACE inhibitors should therefore be used in CAD patients with diabetes mellitus, reduced left ventricular ejection fraction, or hypertension. In all other subgroups of patients with chronic stable angina, ACE inhibitors should be considered. ACE inhibitors are contraindicated in pregnant women and should be avoided in women who may become pregnant while receiving treatment. ACE inhibitors must be used with caution in patients with advanced chronic kidney disease.

In patients with established CAD, statins reduce future cardiovascular events, including MI and death, by approximately 25% to 30%. The benefits of statins are proportional to the level of LDL cholesterol reduction. The LDL cholesterol goal for patients with CAD is below 100 mg/dL (2.59 mmol/L), with an optional goal of below 70 mg/dL (1.81 mmol/L) for those with a very high risk of a coronary event. Statins are generally well tolerated but require monitoring of liver enzymes at the initiation of therapy and with any change in dose. A moderate elevation in liver enzymes, defined as greater than three times normal, occurs in approximately 3% of patients treated with a high-dose statin. Serious side effects (myositis, rhabdomyolysis) are extremely rare. Ezetimibe reduces LDL cholesterol through inhibition of cholesterol

absorption. Although studies have found dramatic reductions in LDL cholesterol levels, ezetimibe has not been shown to reduce the progression of atherosclerosis or future cardiovascular events.

Additional treatments such as vitamin C, vitamin E, and chelation therapy have not been shown to provide benefit to patients at risk for or those with established CAD.

KEY POINTS

- Most patients with chronic stable angina require β-blockers and nitrates to control angina.

- All patients with chronic stable angina should receive daily low-dose aspirin unless there are contraindications.

- An ACE inhibitor should be prescribed in patients with coronary artery disease and reduced left ventricular function, diabetes, or hypertension.

- Patients with chronic stable angina should receive statin therapy unless contraindicated.

Coronary Revascularization

Patients who benefit from coronary revascularization are those with more extensive and severe disease, those with continued symptoms despite optimal medical therapy, those with reduced left ventricular systolic function, and those with multivessel or left main disease. The decision to proceed with percutaneous coronary intervention (PCI) versus surgical revascularization depends upon the coronary anatomy, comorbid conditions that may increase operative risk (underlying cerebrovascular or lung disease), and patient preference.

Percutaneous Coronary Intervention

Although PCI reduces the frequency and severity of angina and improves overall quality of life, it does not reduce future cardiovascular events nor improve survival. In recent years, dramatic advances have been made in the percutaneous management of CAD (newer anticoagulants, such as bivalirudin; drug-eluting stents; vascular closure devices) and in medical therapy (clopidogrel, statins, β-blockers, ACE inhibitors). Several large trials have compared revascularization with optimal medical therapy. The COURAGE trial found that contemporary PCI combined with aggressive medical therapy was not superior to aggressive medical therapy alone in reducing death or MI. The BARI-2D trial randomized patients with type 2 diabetes with class I or II angina to revascularization (PCI or surgery) or medical therapy and found no difference in all-cause mortality or MI at 5 years. However, a significant number of patients initially randomized to medical therapy had progressive angina and crossed over to revascularization. Based on these studies, current guidelines recommend that coronary angiography and PCI be reserved for patients who remain symptomatic despite optimal medical therapy, patients unable to tolerate the side effects of medications, and those with high-risk findings on noninvasive imaging (see "criteria for markedly positive test" in Figure 8).

PCI of the left main coronary artery is an evolving area in interventional cardiology. Although left main disease was previously considered a strict indication for surgery, recent studies indicate excellent outcomes with drug-eluting stents in lesions involving the ostium and proximal and mid vessel (so-called "noncomplex" lesions) of the left main coronary artery. In patients with reduced left ventricular function, left main coronary stenting may require the use of an intra-aortic balloon pump or percutaneously placed ventricular assist device during the procedure.

Surgical Revascularization

Surgical revascularization is indicated for patients with left main disease and multivessel disease (two or three vessels) with involvement of the proximal left anterior descending artery and reduced systolic function. Patients who undergo traditional coronary artery bypass grafting (CABG) with median sternotomy and cardiopulmonary bypass may experience excessive pain, a prolonged hospital stay, and postoperative neurologic dysfunction. Off-pump surgery avoids the cardiopulmonary bypass machine, and experienced surgeons can achieve similar graft patency rates despite the technical challenges of operating on a beating heart. However, a recent randomized trial found that off-pump surgery was associated with a higher rate of adverse cardiovascular events at 1 year and poor graft patency compared with traditional on-pump surgery. Off-pump surgery may be combined with a minimally invasive approach that uses stabilizers to allow construction of graft anastomoses through small thoracotomy windows, thus reducing the need for a complete sternotomy. For patients with significant comorbid conditions, off-pump and minimally invasive surgical techniques may reduce operative risk and shorten recovery times. Hybrid coronary revascularization refers to the combination of minimally invasive surgery and PCI and attempts to further reduce operative risk by taking advantage of both surgical and percutaneous techniques.

> **KEY POINTS**
> - Percutaneous coronary intervention improves chronic stable angina symptoms but does not improve survival or reduce future cardiovascular events.
> - In chronic stable angina, percutaneous coronary intervention is reserved for patients who remain symptomatic despite optimal medical therapy, patients unable to tolerate adverse effects of medications, and those with high-risk findings on noninvasive imaging.
> - Surgical revascularization is indicated for chronic stable angina patients with left main or multivessel disease with involvement of the proximal left anterior descending artery and reduced systolic function.

Follow-up Care

After Percutaneous Coronary Intervention

Neither routine stress testing nor routine ECGs are advocated by current guidelines for patients following successful PCI. For patients unable to exercise and those with possible silent ischemia (patients with diabetes), pharmacologic stress testing may be useful. Restenosis following successful PCI usually presents as recurrent angina 6 to 9 months after the index procedure and has been dramatically reduced with the use of drug-eluting stents.

For patients with stable angina who underwent PCI, clopidogrel should be continued without interruption for a minimum of 1 year following placement of a drug-eluting stent and for 1 month following placement of a bare-metal stent (**Table 8**). Aspirin should be continued indefinitely. Consideration for extended use of clopidogrel should be individualized, taking into account the overall risk profile (extent and severity of CAD) and underlying bleeding risk. The risk of stent thrombosis increases with the premature discontinuation of dual antiplatelet therapy (aspirin and clopidogrel), and is associated with an in-hospital mortality rate of approximately 40%.

The need for elective noncardiac surgery in patients with established CAD and a coronary stent is a common problem

TABLE 8. Clopidogrel Duration of Therapy Based on Clinical Presentation				
Condition	**No Stent**	**Bare-Metal Stent**	**Drug-Eluting Stent**	**CABG**
Chronic stable CAD	Only if aspirin is contraindicated	1 month	1 year	Not indicated[a]
UA/NSTEMI	1 year	1 year	1 year	1 year
STEMI	1 year	1 year	1 year	1 year

CABG = coronary artery bypass grafting; CAD = coronary artery disease; NSTEMI = non–ST-elevation myocardial infarction; STEMI = ST-elevation myocardial infarction; UA = unstable angina.

[a]Preliminary data suggest clopidogrel improves patency of bypass grafts after CABG.

Note: Extended clopidogrel therapy can be considered if the risk-benefit ratio is favorable.

in clinical practice. If possible, surgery should be delayed for at least 6 weeks following placement of a bare-metal stent and for at least 1 year following placement of a drug-eluting stent.

After Surgical Revascularization

Following surgical revascularization, patients should be restarted on their preoperative antiplatelet, lipid-lowering, and antianginal therapy. Aspirin should be continued life-long because it reduces future cardiovascular events and improves bypass graft patency. Clopidogrel should be continued for 1 year for patients who presented with unstable angina or non–ST-elevation myocardial infarction (NSTEMI) prior to surgery. Recent studies also suggest that clopidogrel combined with aspirin may improve venous bypass graft patency compared with aspirin alone. Statin therapy should be adjusted to achieve an LDL cholesterol level of less than 70 mg/dL (1.81 mmol/L). In the setting of complete revascularization, antianginal therapy can be reduced or discontinued. β-Blockers should be continued indefinitely for patients with reduced left ventricular systolic function, previous MI, or acute coronary syndrome.

Exercise stress testing can be considered in symptomatic patients following surgery to distinguish between cardiac and noncardiac causes of chest pain. In asymptomatic patients following surgery, the development of vein graft disease remains a problem. Stress imaging may be useful to identify this problem prior to the occurrence of graft occlusion.

KEY POINT

- Patients with stable angina who undergo percutaneous coronary intervention should receive clopidogrel for 1 year following placement of a drug-eluting stent and for 1 month following placement of a bare-metal stent; aspirin should be continued indefinitely.

Acute Coronary Syndromes

Clinical Presentation and Classification

Acute coronary syndromes (ACSs) comprise unstable angina, NSTEMI, and ST-elevation MI (STEMI) (**Figure 10**). The pathophysiology involves rupture (75% of cases) or erosion (25% of cases) of a coronary plaque with exposure of the subendothelial matrix to circulating blood and subsequent platelet adhesion, platelet activation, and platelet aggregation. A thrombus (clot) forms, resulting in partial or complete occlusion of the lumen of the coronary artery. Most patients with a STEMI have complete occlusion of the coronary artery at the time of coronary angiography, whereas most patients with unstable angina or NSTEMI have only partial occlusion of the vessel.

Although atherosclerosis is the most common cause of an ACS, several unusual diseases may also present with anginal chest pain, transient ECG changes, and elevated cardiac biomarkers. Coronary spasm, or vasospastic angina, mainly occurs at rest, is associated with transient ST-segment elevation or depression, and usually occurs in normal or near-normal coronary artery segments. Coronary spasm can also occur following intranasal cocaine or methamphetamine use. Apical ballooning syndrome (takotsubo or stress cardiomyopathy) is a newly recognized reversible cardiomyopathy that may present similarly to a MI, with chest pain, transient ECG changes, and elevated cardiac biomarkers. Wall motion abnormalities of the mid and apical segments of the left ventricle are present, with sparing of the basal segments. Obstructive coronary lesions are absent. Patients typically present following a recent stressful event or critical illness.

Patients who present with presumed ischemic chest pain can initially be classified to either unstable angina, NSTEMI, or STEMI based on the initial ECG and the results of serum

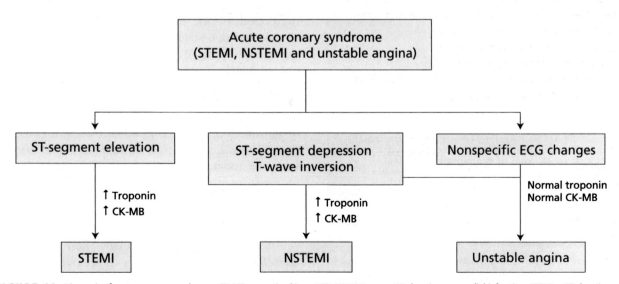

FIGURE 10. Diagnosis of acute coronary syndromes. CK-MB = creatine kinase MB; NSTEMI = non–ST-elevation myocardial infarction; STEMI = ST-elevation myocardial infarction.

cardiac biomarker assays (troponin and creatine kinase MB). Although the initial ECG is nondiagnostic in up to 50% of patients presenting with chest pain, it is a critical part of the evaluation. A simple yet effective approach to initiating therapy applies the distinction between STEMI and NSTEMI/unstable angina. Patients with ischemic chest pain and STEMI benefit from reperfusion therapy, either thrombolytic therapy or primary angioplasty. Patients with NSTEMI or unstable angina represent a heterogeneous group and require risk stratification (determination of their risk for death or nonfatal MI) to direct therapy. Although patients with unstable angina may have similar ECG findings to those with NSTEMI, they can be differentiated by the lack of elevation in serum cardiac biomarkers.

Non–ST-Elevation Myocardial Infarction and Unstable Angina

Risk Stratification

The TIMI risk score is used to estimate the short-term risk for death and nonfatal MI in patients presenting with unstable angina or NSTEMI (**Table 9**). A low TIMI risk score is associated with a rate of recurrent MI or death at 14 days of 8%, whereas a high score is associated with an event rate of approximately 31%.

In addition to predicting clinical outcome, the TIMI risk score also is used to determine which patients will derive the greatest benefit from aggressive medical therapy (including glycoprotein IIb/IIIa inhibitors) and an early invasive treatment approach (**Figure 11**). The patients who benefit most from an early invasive approach are those at highest risk for future cardiovascular events (TIMI risk scores of 3 or more).

TABLE 9. TIMI Risk Score for Unstable Angina/Non–ST-Elevation Myocardial Infarction
Prognostic Variables
Age ≥65 years
≥3 Traditional CAD risk factors[a]
Documented CAD with ≥50% diameter stenosis
ST-segment deviation
≥2 Anginal episodes in the past 24 hours
Aspirin use in the past week
Elevated cardiac biomarkers (creatine kinase MB or troponin)
TIMI Risk Score (Sum of Prognostic Variables)
0-2 Low risk
3-4 Intermediate risk
5-7 High risk

CAD = coronary artery disease.

[a]Family history of CAD, hypertension, hypercholesterolemia, diabetes mellitus, being a current smoker.

Adapted from Antman EM, Cohen M, Bernink PJ, et al. The TIMI risk score for unstable angina/non-ST elevation MI: a method for prognostication and therapeutic decision making. JAMA. 2000;284(7):835-842. [PMID: 10938172]

A conservative approach may be considered for stable patients with a TIMI score of 0 to 2.

Medical Therapy

Antianginal Medications

All patients presenting with ischemic chest pain and presumed unstable angina or NSTEMI should be treated with aspirin, β-blockers, and nitrates. Oral β-blockers should be given to all patients without a contraindication (decompensated heart failure, advanced atrioventricular block, or severe reactive airways disease). Intravenous β-blockers can be considered, but caution should be used in the elderly and in those with heart failure, hypotension, or hemodynamic instability.

The form of nitrates used depends on the clinical presentation—intravenous nitroglycerin should be used for ongoing chest pain; transdermal or oral routes should be used for recent episodes of chest pain but no active symptoms at presentation. Nitrates are contraindicated in patients who have taken a phosphodiesterase inhibitor (sildenafil, vardenafil, tadalafil) within the past 24 hours.

Calcium channel blockers, with the exception of nifedipine, can be used in patients with contraindications to β-blockers and in those with continued angina despite optimal doses of β-blockers and nitrates.

After the initiation of standard antianginal therapy (aspirin, β-blockers, and nitrates), patients should be classified as low, intermediate, or high risk using the TIMI risk score and additional therapy applied based on patient risk.

Antiplatelet Medications

Aspirin at a dose of 325 mg/d should be initiated as soon as a diagnosis of unstable angina or NSTEMI is considered. For patients who subsequently progress to an invasive strategy and undergo coronary stent placement, aspirin should be continued at this dosage for at least 1 month following placement of either a bare metal stent or a drug-eluting stent; for all patients with unstable angina/NSTEMI, the dose can be decreased to 81 mg/d after 1 month and should be continued indefinitely. In patients who are unable to tolerate aspirin because of gastrointestinal distress or a documented allergy, clopidogrel should be initiated at hospital presentation.

Clopidogrel should be given as a 300-mg loading dose to all patients on background aspirin therapy, regardless of their TIMI risk score, unless an increased risk of bleeding exists. It is unclear whether a higher loading dose (600 or 900 mg) provides any additional benefit without increasing bleeding events. Patients with a low TIMI risk score who receive a conservative treatment approach should continue taking clopidogrel for at least 1 year (see Table 8).

Patients undergoing coronary stent placement following an ACS should take clopidogrel for at least a full year, regardless of whether the stent is bare metal or drug-eluting. In patients who undergo coronary angiography and are found to have multivessel CAD requiring surgical revascularization, clopidogrel should be stopped and surgery delayed for 5 to 7 days to avoid excessive intraoperative and postoperative bleeding.

Prasugrel is a recently approved oral thienopyridine that does not require hepatic conversion to its active form and is more potent with a faster onset than clopidogrel. Prasugrel may decrease cardiac events compared with clopidogrel but at an increased risk of major bleeding; the role of prasugrel in the treatment of an ACS is yet to be defined.

Glycoprotein IIb/IIIa inhibitors block the final common pathway of platelet aggregation. Three glycoprotein IIb/IIIa inhibitors are approved (tirofiban, eptifibatide, abciximab) and each has different pharmacodynamic and pharmacokinetic properties. The main adverse effect of these agents is increased bleeding events, usually occurring at the site of vascular access (in patients who undergo coronary angiography) or at mucocutaneous locations (for example, gingival bleeding).

Patients with an intermediate or high TIMI risk score derive the most benefit from glycoprotein IIb/IIIa inhibitors, as well as patients who undergo an early invasive approach and receive PCI. Glycoprotein IIb/IIIa inhibitors should also be considered in patients with ongoing angina after the initiation of standard medical therapy (aspirin, β-blockers, and intravenous nitroglycerin) and in those with dynamic ECG changes, diabetes, or heart failure. The benefit of glycoprotein IIb/IIIa inhibitors in patients who receive conservative medical therapy is unclear, however, and most physicians would choose these agents only if the bleeding risk were low or in a patient with an intermediate or high TIMI risk score who is not deemed a candidate for early angiography because of comorbid conditions (elderly age, malignancy). The optimal timing for initiation of glycoprotein IIb/IIIa inhibitors has been evaluated in several trials in an attempt to clarify whether early use (so-called "upstream" use in the emergency department) is more beneficial than selective use (so-called "delayed" use at the time of angiography and PCI). The ACUITY and the EARLY ACS trials found increased bleeding events and no clinical benefit for patients receiving routine early use of glycoprotein IIb/IIIa inhibitors in the emergency department.

Anticoagulants

Anticoagulants used for the treatment of unstable angina/NSTEMI include unfractionated heparin, low-molecular-weight heparin (LMWH), and the direct thrombin inhibitor bivalirudin. The decision to use a particular agent is

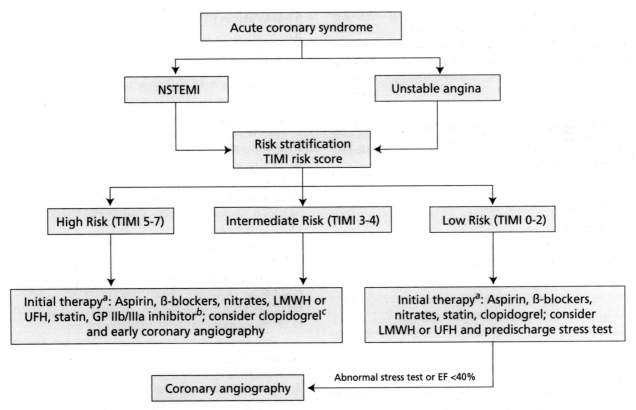

FIGURE 11. Initial management of unstable angina and non–ST-elevation myocardial infarction. EF = ejection fraction; GP = glycoprotein; LMWH = low-molecular-weight heparin; NSTEMI = non–ST-elevation myocardial infarction; UFH = unfractionated heparin.

[a]For patients with continued symptoms despite initial medical therapy, consider GP IIb/IIIa inhibitor and emergent coronary angiography.

[b]Indications for GP IIb/IIIa inhibitor include ongoing chest pain, dynamic electrocardiographic changes, elevated troponin on presentation, heart failure, and diabetes mellitus.

[c]Clopidogrel can be given prior to coronary angiography. If coronary artery bypass grafting is required, clopidogrel should be stopped and surgery delayed for at least 5 days.

based on the TIMI risk score, whether a patient undergoes an early invasive or conservative treatment approach, timing of coronary angiography, consideration of the bleeding risk, renal status, and physician preference.

Heparin can be considered in patients with a low TIMI risk score but provides more benefit to those in the intermediate- and high-risk TIMI groups. Unfractionated heparin is preferable for patients being considered for an early invasive approach, those with increased bleeding risk, and in the setting of kidney disease. Advantages of LMWH include twice-daily subcutaneous administration and achievement of predictable levels of anticoagulation without the need for laboratory monitoring. LMWH is preferred in the absence of kidney disease, in planned surgical revascularization, and in those undergoing an early invasive approach.

For patients undergoing elective PCI, the direct thrombin inhibitor bivalirudin is an acceptable alternative to unfractionated heparin. The ACUITY trial evaluated patients with moderate- and high-risk unstable angina/NSTEMI undergoing an early angiography invasive strategy. Rates of death, MI, and repeat revascularization in patients receiving bivalirudin as monotherapy were similar to those receiving unfractionated heparin combined with a glycoprotein IIb/IIIa inhibitor. Based on these findings, bivalirudin can be initiated in the emergency department, instead of unfractionated heparin or LMWH, and continued as the primary anticoagulant for patients undergoing an early invasive approach with PCI.

Lipid-Lowering Medications

Although the benefits of lipid lowering in post-ACS patients are known, the benefit of intensive lipid lowering in the early phases of an ACS (before discharge) is still being established. The MIRACL and PROVE IT trials found that high-dose statin therapy initiated soon after an ACS reduced cardiovascular events at 18 months and 2 years, respectively. The current consensus for patients with unstable angina/NSTEMI is that early treatment with high-dose statins is beneficial. Current guidelines recommend a target LDL cholesterol level lower than 100 mg/dL (2.59 mmol/L), with an optional goal of below 70 mg/dL (1.81 mmol/L).

Invasive versus Conservative Management

Following the initiation of medical therapy, management options for patients with unstable angina and NSTEMI include a conservative approach of continued medical therapy and noninvasive stress testing before hospital discharge versus an early invasive approach of coronary angiography and subsequent revascularization (PCI or surgical revascularization). The majority of contemporary trials evaluating these two alternatives show a benefit for early angiography and revascularization (invasive approach).

Timing of Coronary Angiography

Although patients with intermediate or high-risk features should undergo early angiography, the optimal timing for angiography remains unclear. In the TIMACS trial, 3031 patients with an ACS were randomized to angiography within 24 hours or angiography 36 hours or longer after randomization. No significant difference was seen in the clinical outcome of death, recurrent MI, or stroke at 6 months. The ISAR-COOL study found that immediate angiography was superior to a strategy of angiography delayed 3 to 5 days in reducing death or MI at 1 month. In summary, for clinically stable patients, there is conflicting evidence as to the optimal timing to perform angiography.

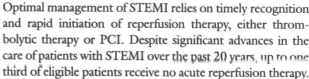

KEY POINTS

- All patients with presumed unstable angina or non–ST-elevation myocardial infarction should receive aspirin, β-blocker, nitrates, a statin, and a thienopyridine (clopidogrel or prasugrel); additional medical therapy depends on the TIMI risk score.

- Most patients with unstable angina or non–ST-elevation myocardial infarction should undergo early angiography, especially those at highest risk for future cardiovascular events (TIMI risk score of 3 or more).

ST-Elevation Myocardial Infarction
Recognition
Optimal management of STEMI relies on timely recognition and rapid initiation of reperfusion therapy, either thrombolytic therapy or PCI. Despite significant advances in the care of patients with STEMI over the past 20 years, up to one third of eligible patients receive no acute reperfusion therapy.

In the patient presenting with a presumed STEMI, several diseases should be considered in the differential diagnosis and rapidly excluded. These include pericarditis, pulmonary embolism, and acute aortic dissection. An acute type A aortic dissection will occasionally present as an inferior wall STEMI if the dissection plane extends into the origin of the right coronary artery.

A focused history should include the duration of pain; history of CAD, PCI, or CABG; and any conditions associated with increased bleeding risks (previous stroke, recent gastrointestinal bleeding). Elderly patients and those with diabetes may present with atypical symptoms such as shortness of breath without pain; heart failure; or confusion.

The physical examination should focus on conditions that can mimic a STEMI such as aortic dissection (asymmetric blood pressures) and pericarditis (pericardial rub), potential contraindications to thrombolytic therapy (neurologic deficit, guaiac-positive stool), and associated conditions that will influence treatment options and management decisions (heart failure, coagulopathy, acute kidney failure).

High-risk features in patients with STEMI include cardiogenic shock, new (or presumed new) left bundle branch block, anterior wall MI, heart failure, extensive ST-segment elevation, systolic blood pressure less than 100 mm Hg, heart rate greater than 100/min, and age older than 75 years.

Reperfusion Therapy
Reperfusion for patients with STEMI can be achieved by thrombolytic therapy or primary PCI (**Figure 12**). The decision to use one strategy over the other is based on the ability to provide a timely PCI, time from onset of symptoms, the presence of high-risk features, and contraindications to thrombolytic therapy. Many patients with STEMI in the United States present to non–PCI-capable hospitals, thus rendering thrombolytic therapy or transfer for primary PCI the available treatment options.

In the presence of high-risk STEMI features, onsite PCI is preferred over thrombolytic therapy. For patients at high risk who initially present to a non–PCI-capable facility, either immediate transfer to a PCI facility or full-dose thrombolytic therapy followed by immediate transfer to a PCI facility are the best options. Recent studies have found that if a high-risk patient presents to a non–PCI-capable facility and receives thrombolytic therapy, immediate transfer to a PCI-capable facility is preferred to waiting to determine if reperfusion has occurred. For patients with cardiogenic shock who present to a non–PCI-capable facility, thrombolytic therapy, placement of an intra-aortic balloon pump, and immediate transfer to a PCI facility may be superior to direct transfer for PCI.

The time to achieve balloon inflation is a major determinant of the benefits of PCI versus thrombolytic therapy. If inherent delays to performing PCI are present, thrombolytic therapy should be considered. Randomized trials indicate a benefit of transfer for primary PCI compared with onsite thrombolytic therapy, despite transfer delays in some studies exceeding 1 hour. However, observational data from community hospitals within the United States have found that fewer than 5% of patients achieve the guideline-suggested door-to-balloon time of less than 90 minutes. Nationwide efforts are underway to develop regionalized PCI centers where patients with STEMI are rapidly transported by emergency medical services in an attempt to improve treatment times.

For patients with absolute contraindications to thrombolytic therapy (**Table 10**), PCI should be performed. If the patient has relative contraindications to thrombolytic therapy and the time to PCI will not be delayed, most physicians advocate primary PCI. Patients older than 75 years represent a unique high-risk subgroup with an increased risk for bleeding complications with thrombolytic therapy, and treatment options must be individualized.

Rescue PCI is PCI performed in the setting of failed thrombolytic therapy and provides a benefit over conservative medical therapy or the repeat administration of thrombolytics. *Facilitated PCI* is a strategy of planned, immediate PCI after full- or half-dose thrombolytic therapy alone or in combination with a glycoprotein IIb/IIIa inhibitor. Trials have demonstrated that facilitated PCI is associated with an increase in adverse events and routine use should be avoided.

Vascular complications occur in fewer than 6% of patients undergoing PCI and include hematoma, arterial pseudoaneurysm, arteriovenous fistula, and retroperitoneal bleeding (see Diagnostic Testing in Cardiology).

Thrombolytic Therapy
Characteristics of four commonly used thrombolytic agents are shown in **Table 11**. The main side effect of thrombolytic therapy is bleeding complications. Intracerebral hemorrhage occurs in fewer than 1% of patients but is associated with a mortality rate of 50% to 65%. Risk factors for intracerebral hemorrhage include older age, lower body weight, female sex, previous stroke, and systolic blood pressure above 160 mm Hg at presentation. Streptokinase has the lowest rate of intracerebral hemorrhage among available thrombolytic agents. Additional bleeding complications include bruising at venous puncture sites, hematuria, and gastrointestinal bleeding. For life-threatening bleeding events, blood transfusions, cryoprecipitate, and fresh frozen plasma may be required.

Thrombolytic therapy failure, which occurs in up to 30% of patients, remains difficult to diagnose. Chest pain resolution, ST-segment elevation improvement, and reperfusion arrhythmias (most commonly an accelerated idioventricular rhythm) indicate successful thrombolysis. Although complete ST-segment elevation resolution is associated with coronary patency, it occurs in a minority of patients. Improvement in ST-segment elevation greater than 50% on an ECG obtained 60 minutes after the administration of thrombolytic therapy is the most commonly used criterion to indicate successful reperfusion. Continued chest pain, lack of improvement in ST-segment elevation, hemodynamic instability, and the absence of reperfusion arrhythmias most likely indicate failure of thrombolytic therapy and indicate the need for rescue PCI.

Initial Medical Therapy for STEMI
In addition to prompt reperfusion, initial medical therapy for patients with STEMI includes general treatment measures (aspirin, analgesics, nitrates, and oxygen), therapy to reduce infarct size (β-blockers and ACE inhibitors), antithrombotic agents (unfractionated heparin or LMWH), and antiplatelet therapy (clopidogrel).

The initial dose of aspirin should be 325 mg, and patients should be instructed to chew the tablet to rapidly achieve therapeutic blood levels. Control of chest pain with analgesics such as morphine sulfate suppresses the heightened sympathetic response that occurs during a STEMI. Nitrates reduce preload by increasing venous capacitance and improve coronary blood flow by coronary vasodilation. Sublingual nitroglycerin should be given to all patients except those with an inferior STEMI and presumed right ventricular infarction. Following sublingual nitroglycerin and in the absence of

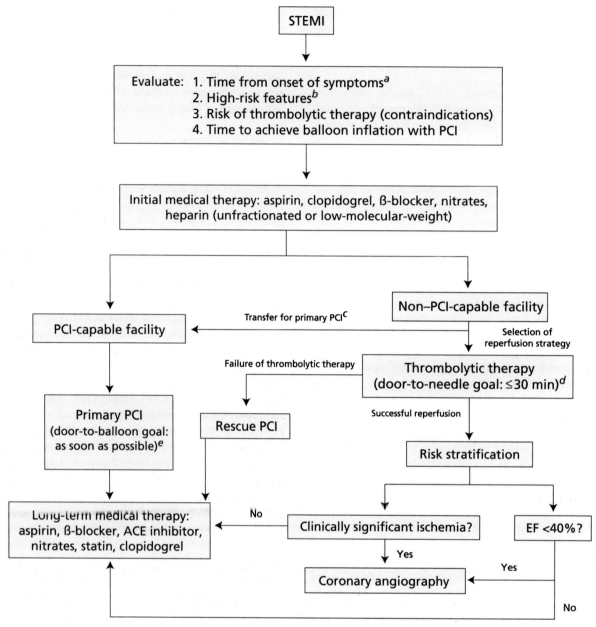

FIGURE 12. Management of ST-elevation myocardial infarction. EF = ejection fraction; PCI = percutaneous coronary intervention; STEMI = ST-elevation myocardial infarction.

[a]If 4 or more hours have elapsed since symptom onset, PCI is preferred.

[b]High-risk features such as cardiogenic shock and heart failure favor PCI.

[c]Door-to-balloon goal for patients being transferred for primary PCI is ≤90 minutes.

[d]STEMI patients presenting to a hospital without PCI capability and who cannot be transferred to a PCI center and undergo PCI within 90 minutes of first medical contact ("door-to-balloon time") should be treated with thrombolytic therapy within 30 minutes of hospital presentation ("door-to-needle time") as a systems goal unless thrombolytic therapy is contraindicated.

[e]STEMI patients presenting to a hospital with PCI capability should be treated with primary PCI as soon as possible as a systems goal (previous goal: door-to-balloon time ≤90 minutes).

Recommendations based on Kushner FG, Hand M, Smith SC Jr, King SB 3rd, et al. 2009 Focused Updates: ACC/AHA guidelines for the management of patients with ST-elevation myocardial infarction (updating the 2004 guideline and 2007 focused update) and ACC/AHA/SCAI guidelines on percutaneous coronary intervention (updating the 2005 guideline and 2007 focused update): a report of the American College of Cardiology Foundation/American Heart Association Task Force on Practice Guidelines [erratum in Circulation. 2010;121(12):e257]. Circulation. 2009;120(22):2271-2306. [PMID: 19923169]

TABLE 10. Contraindications to Thrombolytic Therapy for ST-Elevation Myocardial Infarction
Absolute Contraindications
Any previous intracerebral hemorrhage
Known cerebrovascular lesion (e.g., arteriovenous malformation)
Ischemic stroke within 3 months
Suspected aortic dissection
Active bleeding or bleeding diathesis (excluding menses)
Significant closed head or facial trauma within 3 months
Relative Contraindications
History of chronic, severe, poorly controlled hypertension
Severe uncontrolled hypertension on presentation (SBP >180 mm Hg or DBP >110 mm Hg)[a]
History of ischemic stroke (>3 months), dementia, or known intracranial pathology
Traumatic or prolonged (>10 minutes) CPR or major surgery (<3 weeks)
Recent (within 2-4 weeks) internal bleeding
Noncompressible vascular puncture site
For streptokinase/anistreplase: previous exposure (>5 days) or previous allergic reaction to these agents
Pregnancy
Active peptic ulcer disease
Current use of anticoagulants: the higher the INR, the higher the bleeding risk

CPR = cardiopulmonary resuscitation; DBP = diastolic blood pressure; SBP = systolic blood pressure.

[a]Thrombolytic therapy can be considered if SBP can be reduced to <140 mm Hg and DBP to <90 mm Hg with initial medical therapy.

hypotension, intravenous nitroglycerin should be initiated for patients with continued chest pain. Although it is common practice to give supplemental oxygen to all patients, the main benefit is seen in those with arterial hypoxemia.

β-Blockers reduce mortality and should be given to all patients except those with heart failure, systolic blood pressure below 90 mm Hg, bradycardia (<50/min), or second-degree atrioventricular block. Metoprolol is commonly given three times as 5-mg intravenous bolus doses, each over 3 to 5 minutes, for a total dose of 15 mg. If the systolic blood pressure remains greater than 90 mm Hg, metoprolol, 25 mg or 50 mg orally every 6 hours, should be given. For patients with relative contraindications to β-blockers, such as reactive airways disease, a short-acting intravenous agent such as esmolol can be considered.

ACE inhibitors inhibit postinfarction remodeling, helping to preserve ventricular function. Initiation of an ACE inhibitor within 24 hours in those with a systolic blood pressure greater than 100 mm Hg and without clinically significant kidney failure provides the most benefit. For patients intolerant of an ACE inhibitor or in those with contraindications, an angiotensin receptor blocker can be considered.

Antithrombotic Therapy

For patients receiving thrombolytic therapy with fibrin-specific agents such as reteplase and tenecteplase, unfractionated heparin is thought to prevent reocclusion of the infarct-related artery. More recently, LMWH has been used in combination with thrombolytic agents and appears to yield improved outcomes compared with unfractionated heparin.

For patients undergoing primary PCI, unfractionated heparin is preferable to LMWH because of the ease with

TABLE 11. Characteristics of Thrombolytic Agents Used in the Treatment of STEMI				
Characteristic	**Streptokinase**	**Alteplase**	**Reteplase**	**Tenecteplase**
Dose	1.5 million units over 30-60 min	Up to 100 mg in 90 min[a]	10 units × 2 (30 min apart) each over 2 min	30-50 mg[a]
Bolus administration	No	No	Yes	Yes
Allergic reaction possible on repeat exposure	Yes	No	No	No
TIMI flow grade 2/3[b]	~55%	~75%	~83%	~83%
Rate of intracerebral hemorrhage	~0.4%	~0.4-0.7%	~0.8%	~0.9%
Fibrin specificity	None	+++	+	++++

STEMI = ST-elevation myocardial infarction.

[a]Based on body weight.

[b]TIMI flow grade 2/3 refers to mildly impaired flow through the coronary artery involved in the myocardial infarction. The higher the percentage of TIMI 2/3 flow, the more effective the thrombolytic agent.

Adapted from Boden WE, Eagle K, Granger CB. Reperfusion strategies in acute ST-segment elevation myocardial infarction: a comprehensive review of contemporary management options. J Am Coll Cardiol. 2007;50(10):917-929. [PMID: 17765117]

which the degree of anticoagulation can be assessed in the catheterization laboratory during PCI by measuring the activated clotting time. The direct thrombin inhibitor bivalirudin is an alternative to unfractionated heparin and LMWH for patients undergoing PCI and is associated with fewer bleeding events.

Antiplatelet Therapy

The addition of clopidogrel to standard medical therapy and thrombolytic therapy further reduces cardiovascular events without a significant increase in bleeding. For patients undergoing primary PCI, clopidogrel should be given at the time of hospital presentation because the majority of patients will subsequently receive a coronary stent, and pretreatment appears to be beneficial.

Glycoprotein IIb/IIIa inhibitors are beneficial in selected patients undergoing primary PCI. Recent studies found no clear benefit of early administration in the emergency department compared with initiation at the time of PCI.

Glucose Control

Intensive glucose control has been a topic of active research in recent years as several retrospective studies found that hyperglycemia was associated with worse outcome after MI. The recent NICE-SUGAR randomized trial found that intensive glucose control (target plasma glucose range 81-108 mg/dL [4.5-6.0 mmol/L]) increased mortality compared with conventional glucose control (target plasma glucose range <180 mg/dL [10.0 mmol/L]). This study included patients admitted to the intensive care unit with medical and surgical conditions and did not specifically target patients with an acute MI.

In persons with diabetes presenting with an ACS, including those with previously undiagnosed diabetes, higher plasma glucose concentrations are highly predictive of worse outcome in the hospital and after discharge. The DIGAMI study demonstrated an 11% absolute reduction (28% relative reduction) in mortality at 1 year in the patients randomized to aggressive glucose control. (Glucose in the control groups was managed at the discretion of the physician.) The DIGAMI-2 trial did not show a reduction in mortality with insulin treatment but did confirm that good glycemic control was highly predictive for the 2-year mortality rate.

Recommendations from the American Diabetes Association and the American College of Endocrinology suggest less aggressive control of hyperglycemia. In patients with an ACS admitted to an intensive care unit, glucose levels should be monitored closely, with consideration for intensive glucose control in patients with significant hyperglycemia (plasma glucose >180 mg/dL [10.0 mmol/L]), regardless of previous diabetes history. In patients hospitalized in the non–intensive care unit setting, efforts should be directed at maintaining plasma glucose levels below 180 mg/dL (10.0 mmol/L) with subcutaneous insulin regimens, with the avoidance of hypoglycemia.

Complications Following STEMI

Complications that may occur during the early-management period of STEMI include arrhythmias, heart failure, and vascular complications related to arterial access from PCI. Up to 75% of patients with a STEMI will have some type of arrhythmia during the peri-infarction period. In an inferior STEMI with successful reperfusion, sinus bradycardia and hypotension may occur secondary to the Bezold-Jarisch reflex. Treatment includes intravenous fluids and possibly atropine or dopamine. Sinus bradycardia without significant hypotension is common with an inferior MI, and sinus tachycardia is common with an anterior wall infarction. Persistent sinus tachycardia that occurs several days following a STEMI may be an early manifestation of heart failure and is a poor prognostic sign. Transient atrial fibrillation may occur in patients with associated pericarditis.

Complete heart block may be associated with an anterior or inferior wall MI. In an inferior infarction, complete heart block is usually transient but may require temporary transvenous pacing. In an anterior wall infarction, complete heart block usually indicates a large infarction and is a poor prognostic sign. Permanent pacing is commonly required.

Ventricular tachycardia that occurs in the first 24 hours following MI is usually self-limited and not associated with a worse clinical outcome. In contrast, ventricular tachycardia that occurs later in the hospital course is usually associated with a larger MI and carries a higher short- and long-term mortality risk.

Increased injury to the myocardium (larger infarcts) increases the probability for left ventricular dysfunction and heart failure. The severity of left ventricular dysfunction is directly related to mortality. Patients who develop heart failure in the early period benefit from preload reduction with diuretics and afterload reduction with ACE inhibitors and nitrates. For patients with progressive symptoms despite aggressive medical therapy, invasive hemodynamic monitoring with a pulmonary artery catheter may be useful.

Mechanical complications that may occur in the first several days of a STEMI include cardiogenic shock, right ventricular infarction, ventricular septal defect, papillary muscle rupture with secondary severe mitral regurgitation, left ventricular free wall rupture, and left ventricular thrombus (**Table 12**). Cardiogenic shock can occur from extensive damage to the myocardium (contractile dysfunction), right ventricular infarction, or one of several mechanical complications (see Heart Failure). Inpatient mortality for cardiogenic shock approaches 60%, with half of the deaths occurring in the first 48 hours of hospitalization.

Right ventricular infarction should be considered in the setting of an inferior wall infarction complicated by hypotension. Occlusion of the right coronary artery proximal to the

TABLE 12. Potential Mechanical Complications of Myocardial Infarction

Complication	Physical Examination Findings	Electrocardiography Findings	Echocardiography Findings	Pulmonary Artery Catheter Findings
Right ventricular infarction	Hypotension, jugular venous distention, clear lung fields	>1 mm ST-segment elevation in leads V$_3$R and V$_4$R	Dilated right ventricle with reduced systolic function	Elevated right atrial and right ventricular pressures, low wedge pressure
Extensive left ventricular infarction	Systolic blood pressure <90 mm Hg	Extensive ST-segment elevation, usually in anterior leads	Severe left ventricular systolic dysfunction	CI <2.0 L/min/m², wedge pressure >18 mm Hg
Ventricular septal defect	Holosystolic murmur along left sternal border, often with thrill	Nonspecific; approximately 50% of ventricular septal defects occur in anterior wall MI	High-velocity left-to-right systolic jet within ventricular septum, systolic turbulence on right ventricle side of ventricular septum	Prominent, large v waves in wedge pressure tracing; step-up in O$_2$ saturation from right atrium to right ventricle
Mitral regurgitation	Holosystolic murmur at left sternal border and apex, may radiate to axillae	Usually associated with inferior and inferior-posterior wall MI	Flail mitral valve leaflet with attached mass (papillary muscle head), severe mitral regurgitation	Prominent, large v waves in wedge pressure tracing
Left ventricular free wall rupture	Hypotension, jugular venous distention, distant heart sounds	Nonspecific	Diffuse or localized pericardial effusion with tamponade; discrete wall motion abnormality; defect in myocardium may be seen	Equalization of diastolic pressures, CI <2.0 L/min/m²

CI = cardiac index; MI = myocardial infarction.

origin of the acute marginal vessels results in ischemia to the right ventricle. Right ventricular ischemia impairs the systolic function of the right ventricle, causing limited filling to the left ventricle, which results in the clinical triad of hypotension, clear lung fields, and jugular venous distention. A right-sided ECG showing greater than 1 mm of ST-segment elevation in leads V$_3$R and V$_4$R establishes the diagnosis. Echocardiography can confirm the diagnosis and exclude other causes of cardiogenic shock (ischemic mitral regurgitation, ventricular septal defect). Treatment includes early revascularization (PCI or thrombolytic therapy) to restore blood flow to the ischemic right ventricle, aggressive volume loading to increase filling to the left ventricle, and the initiation of inotropic support with dopamine or dobutamine if hypotension persists. Even with successful revascularization, it can take up to 3 days for right ventricular function to return to normal.

A ventricular septal defect presents 3 to 7 days after the initial MI as hemodynamic compromise with a new holosystolic murmur typically heard along the left sternal border. Echocardiography is the most reliable and rapid tool to establish the diagnosis. Treatment includes stabilization with an intra-aortic balloon pump and vasopressor agents followed by urgent surgical repair. Although surgical mortality is extremely high (>50%), mortality with medical therapy alone approaches 95%. Percutaneous devices have been developed for postinfarction ventricular septal defects and may be a useful option for nonsurgical candidates.

Mechanisms of mitral regurgitation following MI include severe left ventricular dysfunction with annular dilation, worsening of preexisting mitral regurgitation, and rupture of a papillary muscle or chordae tendineae cordis. Papillary muscle rupture presents several days after infarction with acute pulmonary edema, a loud systolic murmur without a thrill, and rapid progression to cardiogenic shock. Echocardiography should be used to establish the diagnosis and can accurately differentiate between a ruptured papillary muscle and a ventricular septal defect. Treatment includes stabilization with an intra-aortic balloon pump, afterload reduction with sodium nitroprusside, diuretics, and emergent surgical intervention.

Rupture of the left ventricular free wall presents 3 to 7 days after infarction as hemopericardium with pericardial tamponade, electromechanical dissociation, and death. Risk factors include elderly age, female sex, first MI, and anterior location of MI. Mortality is uniformly high, but salvage is possible with early recognition, emergent pericardiocentesis, and surgery.

A left ventricular thrombus develops following an anterior STEMI in approximately 10% to 20% of patients despite the use of early revascularization and anticoagulation therapy. The most common location for a thrombus is at the apex of the left ventricle (**Figure 13**). It is diagnosed echocardiographically by the presence of an echo-dense structure within the left ventricle, adjacent to the area of the myocardium with impaired contractility. Anticoagulation with warfarin for 3 to

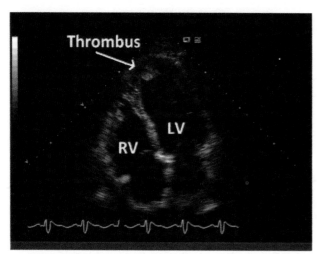

FIGURE 13. Echocardiographic image showing a left ventricular thrombus in a patient with a recent myocardial infarction. LV = left ventricle; RV = right ventricle.

6 months should be initiated after diagnosis to reduce the risk of embolization. Routine echocardiography following MI is useful to quantify left ventricular ejection fraction and, in the setting of an anterior wall infarction, to exclude a mural thrombus.

Long-Term Medical Therapy

Aspirin should be continued indefinitely following a STEMI, but the dose can be reduced to 81 mg/d after approximately 1 month. β-Blockers should be continued indefinitely in patients without contraindications. ACE inhibitors should be continued indefinitely and can be changed to angiotensin receptor blockers in those who are intolerant. Statins should be used to achieve an LDL cholesterol level below 100 mg/dL (2.59 mmol/L) (optional goal <70 mg/dL [1.81 mmol/L]) and should be continued indefinitely. Clopidogrel should be continued for at least 1 year for patients who received thrombolytic therapy in the absence of bleeding events (see Table 8). For STEMI patients with either a drug-eluting or bare metal stent, clopidogrel also should be continued for at least 1 year. Extending clopidogrel use beyond 1 year, including patients with a STEMI who have received a drug-eluting stent, is the subject of ongoing clinical trials.

Risk Stratification

Patients who undergo primary PCI are essentially risk stratified by coronary angiography, because the coronary anatomy is defined and treatment is based on the extent and severity of disease. For patients with multivessel CAD who undergo PCI of the infarct-related artery and do not have inducible ischemia or cardiogenic shock during the index hospitalization, PCI of non–infarct-related arteries should be deferred to the outpatient setting.

Patients who receive thrombolytic therapy and experience successful reperfusion require some form of risk stratification with a functional evaluation before hospital discharge. The purpose of risk stratification is to identify patients at high risk (left main or three-vessel disease) who may benefit from revascularization. Left ventricular function should be assessed by echocardiography or nuclear imaging, and those with an ejection fraction lower than 40% should be referred for coronary angiography. Episodes of chest pain during the index hospitalization, clinically significant heart failure, and ventricular arrhythmias following the first 24 hours of hospital admission also indicate the need for coronary angiography. A functional evaluation is required in all other patients before hospital discharge with either exercise or pharmacologic stress testing. Clinically significant ischemia on noninvasive testing mandates referral for coronary angiography. ◨

KEY POINTS

- Patients with an ST-elevation myocardial infarction who are elderly or have diabetes may present with atypical symptoms such as shortness of breath in the absence of pain, heart failure, or confusion.

- Patients with ST-elevation myocardial infarction should be treated with percutaneous coronary intervention (PCI) within 90 minutes of first medical contact; if PCI cannot be delivered during this time frame and in the absence of contraindications, thrombolytic therapy should be administered (within 30 minutes of presentation).

- Patients with high-risk ST-elevation myocardial infarction who receive primary thrombolytic therapy should subsequently be immediately transferred to a facility capable of performing percutaneous coronary intervention.

- The addition of clopidogrel to standard medical therapy and thrombolytic therapy in patients with ST-elevation myocardial infarction further reduces cardiovascular events without a significant increase in bleeding.

- Current guidelines suggest less aggressive control of hyperglycemia in patients hospitalized with an acute coronary syndrome, with a target plasma glucose range less than 180 mg/dL (10.0 mmol/L) and the avoidance of hypoglycemia.

Coronary Artery Disease in Patients with Diabetes Mellitus

Diagnostic Issues

Noninvasive stress testing in patients with symptoms of CAD who have diabetes has similar diagnostic accuracy as in the general population. Exercise testing offers prognostic information and should be encouraged if possible. Additionally, exercise testing permits evaluation for variables related to autonomic dysfunction, such as heart rate recovery after exercise and chronotropic response to exercise.

Assessment of CAD in asymptomatic patients with diabetes remains controversial. The AHA recommends stress testing prior to the initiation of an exercise program in patients with diabetes with known CAD without a recent stress test (in the past 2 years) or with symptoms of chest pain, known peripheral arterial disease, abnormal resting ECG, or plans for a vigorous exercise program; the American Diabetes Association recommends stress testing only for those persons with diabetes with cardiac symptoms or an abnormal resting ECG.

Invasive Approaches

The higher risk of cardiovascular events in persons with diabetes undergoing either surgical revascularization or PCI, in the setting of an ACS as well as stable CAD, relates to many factors, such as the greater likelihood of concomitant cardiovascular risk factors (dyslipidemia, hypertension, obesity), the more frequent involvement of small vessels, multivessel and multilesion disease, and the proinflammatory state that characterizes diabetes.

CABG has traditionally been the treatment of choice for multivessel CAD in patients with diabetes, based on observations from the BARI and EAST trials. These studies randomized high-risk patients (multivessel CAD or in the setting of ACS) to CABG or PCI. The benefit of CABG was primarily related to a greater need for repeat revascularization in the PCI group. The BARI 2D trial randomized 2386 patients with stable CAD and type 2 diabetes to prompt revascularization with either CABG or PCI versus optimal medical treatment. After 5 years, no significant difference was seen in rates of death or major cardiovascular complications in patients undergoing prompt revascularization versus medical therapy. In the CABG arm, the rate of major adverse cardiac events was significantly lower in the revascularization group (22.4%) than the medical therapy group (30.5%), but in the PCI arm, there were no significant differences between the two groups. CABG cannot be concluded to be superior to PCI, because the method of revascularization was assigned prior to randomization.

Current American College of Cardiology/AHA guidelines allow a great deal of flexibility in choice of PCI or CABG for patients with diabetes, although CABG may be preferred for those with multivessel disease and left ventricular systolic dysfunction. In patients undergoing PCI, randomized trials, meta-analyses of trials, and epidemiologic studies in patients with diabetes have shown superiority of drug-eluting stents over bare-metal stents in terms of reducing need for late repeat revascularization.

Pharmacologic Treatment and Secondary Prevention

Treatment of concomitant cardiovascular risk factors in patients with diabetes is essential. All patients with diabetes should have aggressive lipid modification. The goals for patients with diabetes without established CAD are the same as those for patients with CAD but without diabetes—that is, targeted therapy (preferably with a statin) to lower the LDL cholesterol level to less than 100 mg/dL (2.59 mmol/L). For patients with CAD and diabetes, even more aggressive treatment is suggested, targeting LDL cholesterol to less than 70 mg/dL (1.81 mmol/L). Diabetic patients with elevated triglycerides and low HDL cholesterol level may benefit from the addition of nicotinic acid or a fibrate. Blood pressure should be treated to less than 130/80 mm Hg, or lower for those with diabetic nephropathy. The choice of agent should be individualized, but agents that block the renin-angiotensin-aldosterone system are of particular benefit, with a reduction in multiple end points including stroke, cardiovascular mortality, and acute MI. Although β-blockers and thiazide diuretics may increase risk for developing diabetes, it is not known whether these agents have any adverse effect in patients with established diabetes and cardiovascular disease.

Cardiovascular risks associated with thiazolidinediones, specifically rosiglitazone, have been raised. An FDA advisory panel and a scientific advisory from the AHA and the American College of Cardiology have issued warnings regarding the potential risk of myocardial ischemia, particularly in patients with existing heart disease. Although a direct causal link cannot be proved, other medications are available to treat diabetes, and there is little justification to continue to use rosiglitazone. The thiazolidinediones are considered unsafe in patients with New York Heart Association functional class III or IV heart failure.

Metformin should be used with caution in patients with heart failure or recent MI, as it can increase homocysteine levels, leading to potentially fatal lactic acidosis.

Women and Cardiovascular Disease

Epidemiology

In general, women develop cardiovascular disease later in life than men, although the prevalence is similar between sexes. Although mortality from cardiovascular disease has decreased overall in recent years, the gains for women have been less impressive, and in younger women, an increase in mortality has been noted. Overall, mortality is greater for women than for men with NSTEMI or STEMI.

Differences in prevalence and death rates between sexes may be attributed to multiple factors. Women tend to present later in life and later in the disease process, with additional comorbidities. Lack of patient and physician awareness of symptoms may result in delays in diagnosis. Women presenting at a younger age are more likely to have diabetes or smoke, further increasing risk. The average lifetime risk for a woman to develop cardiovascular disease is one in two, with one of three dying of it. Comparatively, 1 in 10 women will develop breast cancer, and 1 in 30 will die of a cause related to breast cancer. Despite this, fewer than one in five women are aware that cardiovascular disease is the leading cause of death in women, and most women perceive breast cancer as their major health risk.

Clinical Presentation

Although chest pain is the most common presenting symptom for an acute MI, women are more likely to have atypical angina symptoms such as fatigue, dyspnea, and nausea. Mechanisms of angina may be different than in men; this may in part be why women are more likely to have symptoms without significant obstructive coronary disease and, conversely, are more likely to demonstrate normal coronary vessels in an ACS. Coronary microvascular dysfunction refers to both endothelial-dependent and endothelial-independent dysfunction in coronary vessels too small to be assessed visually. Endothelial function, which can be assessed peripherally by flow measurement of the brachial artery, is impaired in postmenopausal women, smokers, and persons with diabetes. Although women with normal coronary arteries but abnormal stress tests were previously considered to have a benign prognosis, recent findings from the Women's Ischemia Syndrome Evaluation Study (WISE) suggest otherwise. This study compared 540 women with suspected ischemia but no angiographic evidence of obstructive CAD with 1000 age- and race-matched asymptomatic cohorts. The 5-year annualized event rate for cardiovascular events was 16% in women with nonobstructive CAD (stenosis in any coronary artery of 1%-49%), 7.9% in those with normal coronary vessels (no stenosis in any coronary artery), and 2.4% in the asymptomatic cohort ($P < 0.002$).

The occurrence of CAD later in women than in men may relate to the grouping of risk factors that occur after menopause: obesity, hypertension, and dyslipidemia. Women with diabetes have a greater than threefold increase in cardiovascular risk compared with women without diabetes. The Framingham Heart Study was the first to suggest that women with diabetes seem to lose the relative age protection against CAD compared with men. H

Evaluation

Exercise testing has a lower overall sensitivity and specificity in women than in men for the evaluation of chest pain and other anginal symptoms. Despite this, data obtained through exercise testing (exercise capacity, hemodynamic response) offer important prognostic information. The recommendations for stress testing in women are, in general, the same as for men. Myocardial perfusion imaging has the most data to support its use but can be inaccurate because of issues regarding spatial resolution and breast artifact. Stress echocardiography is less effective for predicting single-vessel disease but has a very good negative predictive value. In women with objective ischemia but normal results of coronary angiography, findings such as wall motion abnormalities, perfusion abnormalities, and ECG changes may not represent a false-positive test but may in fact relate to microvascular dysfunction or endothelial dysfunction.

The Framingham score may be suboptimal in risk assessment in younger women because about 90% of women are classified as low risk; very few are classified as high risk before 70 years of age. The Reynolds risk score is a sex-specific tool that includes factors not present in the Framingham calculation, including family history and hsCRP. Compared with the Framingham score, use of the Reynolds score resulted in risk reclassification of about 40% of women with intermediate Framingham scores (www.reynoldsriskscore.org).

Risk Reduction

As in men, aggressive risk factor reduction is important for secondary prevention in women with cardiovascular disease. Although earlier observational studies found lower rates of cardiovascular events in women taking estrogen compared with those who did not, it is now well established that women should not use postmenopausal hormone replacement therapy for prevention of future cardiovascular events. The use of hormone replacement therapy for those women with significant perimenopausal symptoms and CAD should be individualized based on discussions between patient and physician.

The role of aspirin for primary prevention in women remains controversial. Although a mortality benefit is not apparent, ischemic strokes are reduced, most notably in women older than 65 years.

Women benefit from the same aggressive treatment of cardiovascular disease as do men. Some data, however, suggest that women with an ACS are generally treated less aggressively than men.

KEY POINTS

- Women with an acute myocardial infarction are more likely than men to have atypical angina symptoms such as fatigue, dyspnea, and nausea.
- Although exercise testing has a lower overall sensitivity and specificity in women than in men for the evaluation of angina symptoms, the recommendations for stress testing are generally the same for both sexes.

Heart Failure

Diagnosis and Evaluation of Heart Failure

Clinical Evaluation

Heart failure is a clinical syndrome characterized by dyspnea, effort intolerance, orthopnea, paroxysmal nocturnal dyspnea or nocturnal cough, and edema (manifesting as lower extremity

TABLE 13. Clinical Signs of Heart Failure

Cardiac Abnormality	Sign	Sensitivity[a]	Specificity[a]
Elevated cardiac filling pressures and fluid overload	Jugular venous distention	0.39	0.92
	S_3 gallop	0.13	0.99
	Pulmonary crackles	0.60	0.78
	Hepatojugular reflux	0.24	0.96
	Ascites	0.01	0.97
	Edema	0.50	0.78
Cardiac enlargement	Laterally displaced or prominent apical impulse	?	?
Reduced cardiac output	Narrow pulse pressure	?	?
	Cool extremities	?	?
	Tachycardia with pulsus alternans	?	?
Arrhythmia	Irregular pulse suggestive of atrial fibrillation or frequent ectopy	0.26[b]	0.93[b]

? = No large systematic evaluation published of sensitivity/specificity in diagnosing heart failure.

[a]Among patients presenting with dyspnea to the emergency department.

[b]For atrial fibrillation on electrocardiogram.

Reprinted from Journal of Cardiac Failure. 16(6). Heart Failure Society of America. Lindenfeld J, Albert NM, Boehmer JP, et al. HFSA 2010 Comprehensive Heart Failure Practice Guideline. e1-e194. Copyright 2010, with permission from Elsevier. [PMID: 16234501].

edema, ascites, or scrotal edema). Less specific symptoms of heart failure include early satiety, nausea and vomiting, abdominal discomfort, wheezing or coughing, and unexplained fatigue. Signs to evaluate in patients suspected of having heart failure are listed in **Table 13**. Initial evaluation should include assessing the clinical severity of heart failure, assessing cardiac structure and function, determining etiology of heart failure with particular attention to reversible causes, and evaluating risk for life-threatening arrhythmias. Evaluation should also include identification of any potential exacerbating factors, comorbidities that might influence therapy, and barriers to adherence to treatment.

Initial and serial evaluations for heart failure focus on assessing functional capacity and volume status. Functional status influences prognosis and treatment options and is typically graded by New York Heart Association (NYHA) functional class (**Table 14**). Volume status influences medical therapy and can be assessed by symptoms (shortness of breath, orthopnea, paroxysmal nocturnal dyspnea), physical examination findings, daily body weight monitoring, and diagnostic studies (such as B-type natriuretic peptide [BNP] level).

Diagnostic Testing

Echocardiography can be used to determine whether heart failure is caused by left ventricular systolic dysfunction, to suggest etiology (for example, regional wall motion abnormalities suggest ischemic etiology, whereas marked ventricular hypertrophy may suggest an infiltrative or hypertrophic

cardiomyopathy), and to identify comorbid conditions (valvular abnormalities, pericardial effusion, pulmonary hypertension). Echocardiography can also provide prognostic information; for example, in systolic heart failure, a restrictive diastolic filling pattern (measured by Doppler flow across the mitral valve) suggests more advanced disease and a poorer prognosis.

Electrocardiography (ECG) may aid in determining heart failure etiology. Evidence of previous myocardial infarction (MI) suggests an ischemic cause, whereas a rapid heart rate may raise suspicion for tachycardia-mediated cardiomyopathy. Low voltage on ECG in a patient with left ventricular dysfunction and in the absence of physical features that would insulate the heart from the chest wall leads (for example, obesity or emphysema) may suggest an infiltrative

TABLE 14. New York Heart Association (NYHA) Functional Class

Class	Description
I	No limitations of physical activity
II	Slight limitation of physical activity
III	Marked limitation of physical activity
IIIA	Symptoms with less than ordinary activity
IIIB	Symptoms with minimal exertion
IV	Unable to carry on any physical activity without symptoms

cardiomyopathy. ECG may also be used to assess for arrhythmias or electrical dyssynchrony (prolonged QRS interval) if cardiac resynchronization therapy is being considered and to monitor the QT interval during treatment with specific medications.

Radiography is inaccurate for measuring cardiac chamber enlargement, which should be assessed with echocardiography; also, absence of overt pulmonary edema on chest radiograph does not preclude elevated intracardiac and intravascular filling pressures, particularly in patients with long-standing heart failure, likely owing to increased efficiency of mediastinal lymphatic drainage.

Cardiopulmonary exercise testing includes assessment of respiratory gas exchange during treadmill or bicycle exercise for a more detailed assessment of functional capacity and differentiation between potential causes of exercise limitation (cardiac, pulmonary, or deconditioning, versus volitional). Cardiopulmonary exercise testing can be used to objectively measure functional capacity for exercise prescription or in the context of cardiac transplantation evaluation and is generally not otherwise needed for routine initial evaluation of heart failure.

Endomyocardial biopsy is generally not indicated for the initial evaluation of heart failure unless a specific diagnosis that would influence management or prognosis is suspected based on clinical data or noninvasive testing.

Cardiovascular magnetic resonance (CMR) imaging can be helpful for diagnosis of cardiomyopathies or for more exact definition of cardiac structure and function. Examples of the latter indication include presence of discrepancy in ejection fraction measurements by other imaging methods and assessment of extent of scarring for viability determination in ischemic cardiomyopathy. Right heart catheterization may be useful for more definitive assessment of volume status and cardiac output if these are not clear based on usual assessment by examination or laboratory testing, and if management hinges on more exact assessment of these parameters.

Laboratory Evaluation

Standard laboratory evaluation for initial assessment of heart failure includes serum electrolytes, blood urea nitrogen, creatinine, glucose, calcium, magnesium, fasting lipid profile, complete blood count, albumin, uric acid, liver chemistry tests, urinalysis, and thyroid function studies. BNP or N-terminal proBNP levels should be assessed in patients suspected of having heart failure, particularly when the diagnosis or relative contribution of heart failure to symptoms is uncertain. BNP is especially helpful in differentiating dyspnea due to heart failure versus that due to pulmonary disease. Among patients presenting to the emergency department with dyspnea of undetermined etiology, a BNP below 100 pg/mL accurately excluded decompensated heart failure as an etiology. However,

among ambulatory patients with established heart failure, "normal" ranges for BNP during periods of clinical stability may be as high as 500 pg/mL. In patients with chronic heart failure, change in BNP from their usual range may be more valuable diagnostically than the absolute value. Additional laboratory testing may be useful to assess for unusual causes of heart failure, as clinically indicated, if the initial evaluation is not revealing.

Evaluation for Ischemia

Evaluation for ischemia should be pursued in patients with new left ventricular dysfunction in whom a clinical suspicion for coronary disease exists and in patients with known coronary disease and worsening symptoms. Coronary angiography should be performed when the pretest probability for ischemic cardiomyopathy is high, unless the patient is not a candidate for revascularization. In patients with new-onset heart failure and symptoms less typical for angina, coronary angiography would be reasonable if the patient has not had a previous assessment of coronary anatomy. Noninvasive stress testing can be performed if the pretest probability for coronary disease is intermediate or, in select patients, to help guide anticipated percutaneous coronary intervention.

KEY POINTS

- Echocardiography is essential in the evaluation of heart failure and can help determine etiology, evaluate current clinical status, identify comorbidities, and provide prognostic information.
- B-type natriuretic peptide level is useful to help distinguish acute dyspnea caused by decompensated heart failure from other, non–heart failure causes.

Medical Therapy for Systolic Heart Failure

Indications for specific medications for systolic heart failure are generally based on the patient's functional status as measured by NYHA functional class. In the absence of contraindications or intolerance, treatment with an ACE inhibitor and a β-blocker is indicated for all patients with systolic heart failure regardless of functional status or symptom status. Treatment with spironolactone and hydralazine–isosorbide dinitrate (the latter specifically for black patients) in addition to standard therapy with an ACE inhibitor and a β-blocker is indicated for patients with more severe heart failure (NYHA class III-IV) (**Table 15**).

There are currently no definitive data to support routine anticoagulation with warfarin or antiplatelet agents for low left ventricular ejection fraction alone, in the absence of more established indications, such as previous thromboembolism or presence of atrial fibrillation.

TABLE 15.	Medical Therapy for Systolic Heart Failure	
Agent	**Initial Daily Dose**	**Target Dose**
ACE inhibitors		
Captopril	6.25 mg TID	50 mg TID
Enalapril	2.5 mg BID	10-40 mg BID
Fosinopril	5-10 mg daily	40-80 mg daily
Lisinopril	2.5-5 mg daily	20-40 mg daily
Perindopril	2 mg daily	8-16 mg daily
Quinapril	5 mg BID	20-80 mg BID
Ramipril	1.25-2.5 mg daily	10 mg daily
Trandolapril	1 mg daily	4 mg daily
Angiotensin receptor blockers		
Candesartan	4-8 mg daily	32 mg daily
Losartan	12.5-25 mg or 25-50 mg daily	50-200 mg daily
Valsartan	20-40 mg BID	160 mg BID
β-Blockers		
Bisoprolol	1.25 mg daily	10 mg daily
Carvedilol	3.125 mg BID	25 mg BID; 50 mg BID for patients >85 kg (187 lb)
Carvedilol (sustained release)	10 mg daily	80 mg daily
Metoprolol succinate (extended release)	12.5-25 mg daily	200 mg daily
Aldosterone antagonists		
Spironolactone	12.5-25 mg daily	25 mg daily or BID
Eplerenone	25 mg daily	50 mg daily
Other vasodilators		
Fixed-dose hydralazine–isosorbide dinitrate	37.5/20 mg TID	75/40 mg TID
Hydralazine	37.5 mg four times daily	75 mg four times daily
Isosorbide dinitrate	20 mg four times daily	40 mg four times daily

BID = twice daily; TID = three times daily.

Data from Heart Failure Society of America; Lindenfeld J, Albert NM, Boehmer JP, et al. HFSA 2010 comprehensive heart gailure practice guideline. J Card Fail. 2010;16(6):e1-e194.[PMID 20610207]; and Hunt SA, Abraham WT, Chin MH, et al. 2009 Focused update incorporated into the ACC/AHA 2005 Guidelines for the diagnosis and management of heart failure in adults a report of the American College of Cardiology Foundation/American Heart Association Task Force on Practice Guidelines developed in collaboration with the International Society for Heart and Lung Transplantation. J Am Coll Cardiol 2009;53:e1-e90 [PMID: 19358937].

ACE Inhibitors and Angiotensin Receptor Blockers

ACE inhibitors provide a hemodynamic benefit by reducing afterload and a neurohormonal benefit by blocking adverse activation of the renin-angiotensin-aldosterone system. ACE inhibitors reduce the risk for death by roughly 30% to 40% compared with placebo, with mortality reduction primarily for death due to progressive heart failure. Treatment with ACE inhibitors also reduces rates of hospitalizations, progression of left ventricular dysfunction, and development of left ventricular dysfunction after MI. A higher dose versus a lower dose of ACE inhibitor has not been shown to significantly affect survival but may reduce hospitalizations for heart failure.

Angiotensin receptor blockers (ARBs) appear to have morbidity and mortality benefits comparable to ACE inhibitors for management of systolic heart failure although less information is available. The primary reason to use an ARB instead of an ACE inhibitor is to avoid the side effect of cough. The risks for hyperkalemia or kidney disease are comparable between ARBs and ACE inhibitors (about 3% and 2% incidence, respectively, in one recent large trial). In a recent trial in patients intolerant to ACE inhibitors, higher versus lower doses of ARBs (losartan 150 mg/d versus 50 mg/d) resulted in a 10% reduction in combined mortality or heart failure hospitalization. Routine combination of ACE inhibitor and ARB therapy is not recommended because of the increased risk for adverse effects, including kidney disease, hyperkalemia, and hypotension, without definitively proven clinical benefit.

β-Blockers

β-Blockers ameliorate adverse effects of chronic neurohormonal activation on ventricular remodeling and cardiac myocyte function. In addition, newer-generation β-blockers, such as carvedilol, also have vasodilating effects resulting from additional α_1-receptor blocking properties. In general, β-blocker treatment reduces mortality by about 30%, including mortality from progressive heart failure and sudden death. Rates of hospitalization and progression of left ventricular dysfunction are also reduced. Cardiac remodeling and neurohormonal and clinical benefits of β-blockers may take several months to manifest, unlike with ACE inhibitors, which provide rapid hemodynamic benefit in addition to the long-term benefits. The survival benefit associated with β-blocker therapy appears associated with the degree of heart rate reduction rather than the absolute dose achieved. Not all β-blockers are of proven benefit in treatment of heart failure; those that have shown morbidity and mortality benefit in heart failure treatment trials include metoprolol succinate extended release, carvedilol, and bisoprolol. β-Blockers with intrinsic sympathomimetic activity, such as pindolol or acebutolol, should be avoided.

Initiating and Managing ACE Inhibitor and β-Blocker Therapy

If the patient is reasonably euvolemic and clinically stable, ACE inhibitors and β-blockers can generally be started simultaneously. Unless hypertension is present, low doses should be used initially to avoid significant hypotension. No definitive data support starting one agent first over the other, although most trials examining the effect of β-blockers studied them as additive therapy to ACE inhibitors. Starting either a β-blocker or an ACE inhibitor (or ARB) should not be delayed to achieve target doses of the other agent first. In volume-overloaded or low-output states, initiating β-blockers should be avoided because of their negative inotropic effects; specifically, β-blockers should not be initiated in the setting of heart failure decompensation. ACE inhibitors should not be initiated in patients with hypovolemia to avoid exacerbating or precipitating hypotension. Ideally, inpatients should be taking both agents before hospital discharge.

Routine laboratory monitoring for hyperkalemia and kidney function is indicated after initiating or increasing the dose of the ACE inhibitor. ACE inhibitors should generally be titrated, as tolerated, to those doses shown to reduce the risk of death and cardiovascular events in clinical trials, with the awareness that there are modest differences in outcomes with treatment with low- versus high-dose ACE inhibitors. After starting or increasing the dose of β-blocker, patients may experience a period of fatigue that generally resolves after several days to a few weeks. β-Blockers should be titrated to target doses shown to reduce morbidity and mortality in clinical trials. ⊞

Diuretics

With increasing severity of heart failure, greater amounts of diuretics are typically needed to control volume status. Loop diuretics are the most frequently used type of diuretic. If an additional diuretic effect is needed, the loop diuretic can be augmented with a thiazide diuretic. Undesirable effects of diuretics include electrolyte imbalances (in particular, hypokalemia and hypomagnesemia), kidney disease, and reactive neurohormonal activation due to relative loss of hypotonic fluid.

Diuretic use and higher doses of diuretics are frequently associated with adverse outcomes in retrospective population analyses; however, this relationship likely reflects an association with the need for a diuretic and the use of higher doses of diuretics for sicker patients, rather than a causative effect.

Digoxin

Besides the standard indication for atrial fibrillation rate control, digoxin is used for symptom reduction in systolic heart failure. Digoxin is not associated with a survival benefit but does decrease rates of hospitalization. Withdrawal of digoxin in stable patients is generally not recommended because it may precipitate heart failure decompensation. When used to treat heart failure, digoxin should be dosed at low levels (serum level 0.5-0.8 ng/mL) because higher serum levels have been associated with an increased risk for mortality. Unlike ACE inhibitors and diuretics, digoxin is not useful in the treatment of patients with acutely decompensated heart failure. Digoxin is renally cleared and must be used with caution in patients with kidney disease.

Aldosterone Antagonists

The addition of spironolactone to ACE inhibitor and β-blocker therapy is indicated for patients with severe systolic heart failure (NYHA class III-IV) and is associated with a 30% reduction in mortality (including death from progressive heart failure and sudden death), reduction in hospitalizations, and improved NYHA functional class. Because of its antiandrogen activity, some patients experience gynecomastia. This can be circumvented by using the selective aldosterone antagonist eplerenone; however, eplerenone is substantially more expensive than spironolactone. Although eplerenone is currently approved only for treatment of heart failure after MI or for hypertension, a recent study has demonstrated reduced risk of death or hospitalization for patients with mild systolic heart failure (NYHA class II symptoms, ejection fraction ≤35%) treated with eplerenone in addition to standard therapy of an ACE inhibitor or ARB plus β-blocker. Care should be taken to prescribe spironolactone according to evidence-based guidelines (NYHA class III-IV symptoms, serum potassium <5 meq/L [5 mmol/L], and creatinine <2.5 mg/dL [221 mmol/L]), and should include close clinical and laboratory follow-up, paying particular attention to serum potassium levels.

Hydralazine and Isosorbide Dinitrate

There are two situations in which combined hydralazine and isosorbide dinitrate are indicated for treatment of systolic heart failure: when ACE inhibitor or ARB therapy is contraindicated because of kidney disease or hyperkalemia and in black patients with severe systolic heart failure (NYHA class III-IV) in addition to standard ACE inhibitor and β-blocker therapy.

Early studies with vasodilator treatment for heart failure demonstrated that although treatment with an ACE inhibitor provided the greatest reduction in morbidity and mortality, treatment with the combination of hydralazine and isosorbide dinitrate was still superior to placebo regarding reduction in morbidity and mortality (36% mortality risk reduction versus placebo, tested when standard therapy for heart failure included only diuretics and digoxin). More recently, a randomized, placebo-controlled trial showed that addition of hydralazine and isosorbide dinitrate to standard therapy for severe heart failure (NYHA class III-IV) in black patients, including ACE inhibitor, β-blocker, and spironolactone, results in a 43% reduction in all-cause death, as well as reduction in heart failure hospitalizations and improvement in quality of life. It is likely the benefits seen with the hydralazine–isosorbide dinitrate combination are related to increased nitric oxide availability, because hydralazine possesses antioxidant properties and isosorbide dinitrate acts as a nitrate donor. Thus, it is preferable to use the short-acting isosorbide dinitrate formulation at the same time as hydralazine, rather than the sustained-release isosorbide mononitrate, to maximize vasodilatory action.

Calcium Channel Blockers

Calcium channel blockers are not preferred agents for treatment of systolic heart failure. These agents are not associated with any outcomes benefits and have been implicated in heart failure decompensations (13% in one study). These results are likely related to negative inotropic effects, particularly the older-generation agents. Amlodipine and felodipine are the only two calcium channel blockers tested in large clinical trials to have neutral effects on mortality in patients with systolic heart failure. These agents would be acceptable to use for treatment of conditions such as hypertension or angina that are not adequately controlled with the other, evidence-based medications. They are not indicated for the treatment of systolic heart failure itself.

KEY POINTS

- In the absence of contraindications or intolerance, treatment with an ACE inhibitor and a β-blocker is indicated for all patients with systolic heart failure regardless of functional status or symptoms.

- The addition of spironolactone to standard ACE inhibitor and β-blocker therapy is indicated for patients with severe systolic heart failure (New York Heart Association class III-IV).

- The addition of combined hydralazine and isosorbide dinitrate to standard ACE inhibitor and β-blocker therapy is indicated for treatment of black patients with severe systolic heart failure.

Heart Failure With Preserved Ejection Fraction

Heart failure with preserved ejection fraction (HFPEF) can present similarly to systolic heart failure, with dyspnea, effort intolerance, and congestion, although in acutely decompensated states, HFPEF is more often associated with uncontrolled hypertension. An echocardiogram is essential in the evaluation for specific causes of heart failure symptoms. Neither physical examination nor BNP measurement alone can distinguish between heart failure due to systolic dysfunction and HFPEF. In addition, evaluation of HFPEF includes ruling out other cardiac and noncardiac causes of dyspnea, effort intolerance, and congestion (**Figure 14**). Common risk factors for HFPEF include older age, female sex, hypertension, obesity, diabetes, coronary artery disease, and chronic kidney disease.

Therapy for HFPEF focuses on managing exacerbating factors (including hypertension, tachycardia, and ischemia) and factors predisposing patients to progression of left ventricular hypertrophy, in particular hypertension and diabetes. Compared with systolic heart failure, there are relatively few published randomized controlled trials to guide medical therapy for HFPEF. Trials have studied the use of ACE inhibitors or ARBs and have generally shown reductions in morbidity and combined cardiovascular end points but have not consistently demonstrated reduced mortality. It is likely that mechanisms underlying ventricular remodeling differ between

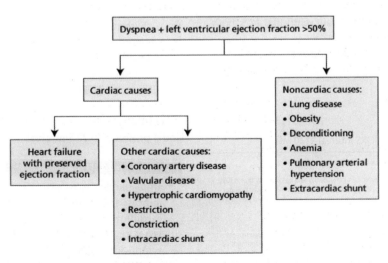

FIGURE 14. Differential diagnosis of heart failure with preserved ejection fraction.

Reprinted from Journal of the American College of Cardiology. 53(11). Maeder MT, Kaye DM. Heart failure with normal left ventricular ejection fraction. 905-918. Copyright 2009, with permission from Elsevier. [PMID: 19281919]

heart failure with reduced ejection fraction versus HFPEF; thus, medications such as ACE inhibitors and β-blockers, which robustly improve outcomes in heart failure with reduced ejection fraction, have not been associated with similar degrees of benefit in HFPEF. Part of the difficulty in establishing evidence-based therapy for treatment of HFPEF is nonuniform criteria for diagnosis and study entry criteria, resulting in varying study population characteristics. Medications that have been studied in large trials for treatment of HFPEF include ACE inhibitors (perindopril), ARBs (candesartan, irbesartan), and β-blockers (nebivolol), and it would be reasonable to preferentially use these agents for treatment.

Device Therapy

Implantable Cardioverter-Defibrillator for Prevention of Sudden Cardiac Death

Criteria for implantable cardioverter-defibrillator (ICD) placement for primary prevention of sudden death are shown in **Table 16**. ICD placement in patients meeting these criteria is associated with a roughly 30% reduction in all-cause mortality. Data are less robust in support of ICD placement for primary prevention in NYHA class I (asymptomatic) patients with nonischemic cardiomyopathy. ICD placement is also reasonable for patients with nonischemic cardiomyopathy with severely reduced systolic function and unexplained syncope. Placement of an ICD is generally not recommended for NYHA class IV patients because of the associated poor prognosis and likely lack of significant survival benefit conferred.

Cardiac Resynchronization Therapy

The aim of cardiac resynchronization therapy (CRT, or biventricular pacing) is to improve or restore myocardial electromechanical coupling and effective ventricular contraction. Up to one third of patients with systolic heart failure have a prolonged QRS interval, a marker for ventricular dyssynchrony or dysfunctional ventricular electromechanical coordination. A biventricular pacemaker can be implanted as a stand-alone device but is frequently combined in a generator with ICD capabilities. Patients who meet criteria for CRT (see Table 16) usually also meet criteria for ICD placement, and thus a combined ICD/CRT device should be considered in most instances. In addition, patients who are ventricularly paced or are undergoing pacemaker implantation may benefit from CRT if they meet other criteria, such as NYHA class of ejection fraction even in the absence of a prolonged QRS interval. Demonstrated benefits in selected patients include improved symptoms, quality of life, and exercise capacity; increases in ejection fraction; and reduction in functional mitral regurgitation. CRT is associated with up to 50% reduction in mortality from progressive heart failure compared with placebo, approximately 30% reduction in hospitalizations, and a trend toward reduced all-cause mortality. However, up to one third of patients who meet these criteria still show no benefit; thus, research into refining these criteria is ongoing. Although the largest trials studying CRT have primarily examined patients with sinus rhythm and left bundle branch block, current guidelines suggest it is acceptable to pursue CRT for patients with atrial fibrillation or right bundle branch block who meet other criteria for CRT. A recent trial has shown that addition of CRT to an ICD reduced mortality and hospitalization rates in patients with mild to moderate systolic heart failure (NYHA class II-III) with an ejection fraction of 30% or less and a prolonged QRS interval.

TABLE 16. Indications for Device Therapy in Heart Failure

Implantable Cardioverter-Defibrillator (for primary prevention)

NYHA class II or III while taking optimal medical therapy[a] *and*

Expectation of survival >1 year *and*

Either of the following:

Ischemic cardiomyopathy ≥40 days post MI or nonischemic cardiomyopathy with ejection fraction ≤35% (primary prevention)

History of hemodynamically significant ventricular arrhythmia or cardiac arrest (secondary prevention)

Biventricular Pacemaker (cardiac resynchronization therapy)

All of the following:

NYHA class III or IV

Ejection fraction ≤35%

Ventricular dyssynchrony (QRS interval ≥120 msec)

MI = myocardial infarction; NYHA = New York Heart Association.

[a]Also NYHA class I in patients with ischemic cardiomyopathy and ejection fraction <30% (MADIT-II criteria: Moss AJ, Zareba W, Hall WJ, et al; Multicenter Automatic Defibrillator Implantation Trial II Investigators. Prophylactic implantation of a defibrillator in patients with myocardial infarction and reduced ejection fraction. N Engl J Med. 2002;346(12):877-883. [PMID: 11907286]).

Recommendations from Hunt SA, Abraham WT, Chin MH, et al. 2009 Focused update incorporated into the ACC/AHA 2005 Guidelines for the diagnosis and management of heart failure in adults a report of the American College of Cardiology Foundation/American Heart Association Task Force on Practice Guidelines developed in collaboration with the International Society for Heart and Lung Transplantation. J Am Coll Cardiol. 2009;53:e1-e90 [PMID: 19358937]

KEY POINTS

- Implantable cardioverter-defibrillator placement is indicated for patients with ischemic and nonischemic cardiomyopathy and an ejection fraction of 35% or less with New York Heart Association class II or III symptoms; and for patients with ischemic cardiomyopathy, ejection fraction 30% or less, and New York Heart Association class I-III symptoms.

- Current criteria for cardiac resynchronization therapy include left ventricular ejection fraction of 35% or less, evidence for ventricular dyssynchrony on electrocardiogram, sinus rhythm, and New York Heart Association class III or IV symptoms, while receiving optimal medical therapy.

Follow-up Management of Chronic Heart Failure

Serial Assessment

Follow-up management of heart failure involves continued reassessment of symptoms, functional capacity, prognosis, and therapeutic effectiveness, and continued evaluation for potentially exacerbating comorbidities. Routine evaluation of serum electrolytes and kidney function is recommended a minimum of every 6 months in clinically stable patients and more frequently with changes in therapy or clinical status. More frequent assessment of electrolytes and kidney function is indicated in patients with severe heart failure or who are clinically unstable and in patients on high-dose diuretics or aldosterone antagonists.

Serial Natriuretic Peptide Assessment

In response to increased wall stress due to volume or pressure overload, the cardiac ventricles secrete proBNP, which is then cleaved into BNP and NT-proBNP. Both natriuretic peptides are useful for assessing prognosis and guiding treatment. A meta-analysis suggests outpatient management guided by targeting specific BNP goals may reduce all-cause mortality by almost 25%, although individual studies lacked statistically significant findings. This benefit appears greatest in younger patients (<75 years). The benefits of natriuretic peptide–guided therapy for outpatients are driven in part by the optimization of doses of evidence-based medical therapy (such as ACE inhibitors and β-blockers) and more frequent clinical follow-up initiated by responding to BNP laboratory values. As suggested in consensus guidelines, the value of serial BNP measurements to guide therapy is not well established. For patients hospitalized with heart failure, an elevated BNP level at admission is predictive of in-hospital mortality, and an elevated predischarge BNP level (>700 pg/mL in one study) was associated with increased risk for death or rehospitalization.

Echocardiography in Chronic Heart Failure

Serial echocardiography is generally not indicated for assessment of chronic heart failure in the absence of changes in clinical status. Follow-up echocardiography can be considered for patients with marked clinical improvement, which may indicate resolution of cardiomyopathy. There are currently no definitive data regarding whether or how long medications for treatment of heart failure should be continued if cardiomyopathy significantly resolves.

Assessing Prognosis

Assessing prognosis for patients with systolic heart failure is important for determining appropriate therapy and providing a context in which to discuss expected course of disease and treatment options with patients. Individual risk factors that correlate with poorer prognosis include poor functional capacity as measured by NYHA functional class or peak oxygen uptake (VO_2) on exercise testing, hyponatremia, hypotension, and inability to tolerate ACE inhibitor or β-blocker treatment because of hypotension.

Various composite risk scores have been developed to try to assess prognosis in ambulatory heart failure patients. With the Heart Failure Survival Score, worse prognosis is associated with ischemic etiology, higher resting heart rate, lower blood pressure, lower left ventricular ejection fraction, presence of intraventricular conduction delay on ECG, lower peak VO_2, and lower serum sodium level. The Seattle Heart Failure Model components include age, sex, NYHA class, weight, ejection fraction, systolic blood pressure, ischemic etiology, medication use (ACE inhibitor, β-blocker, ARB, statin, allopurinol, aldosterone blocker, diuretics), laboratory data (hemoglobin, lymphocyte percentage, uric acid, total cholesterol, sodium), and devices (ICD, biventricular pacemaker alone or combined with ICD, left ventricular assist device). An interactive template for the Seattle Heart Failure Model is available online at www.SeattleHeartFailureModel.org, which allows health care providers and patients to quickly estimate 1-, 2-, and 5-year survival and to see what effect medical and device interventions have on estimated survival.

KEY POINTS

- Routine evaluation of serum electrolytes and kidney function is recommended a minimum of every 6 months in clinically stable patients with heart failure and more frequently with changes in therapy or clinical status.
- Follow-up echocardiography is not indicated in patients with chronic heart failure in the absence of changes in clinical status.

Inpatient Management of Heart Failure

Acute Decompensated Heart Failure

In community-based populations, about half of patients admitted with acute decompensated heart failure have heart failure with preserved ejection fraction, frequently associated with uncontrolled hypertension. Acute decompensated systolic heart failure is generally characterized by hypotension. Either form can be associated with varying degrees of volume overload and evidence of end-organ hypoperfusion.

Understanding of the pathophysiology, precipitants, and optimal treatment for acute decompensated heart failure is continually evolving, making well-designed, controlled clinical trials difficult to perform. Suggested criteria from the Heart Failure Society of America for hospitalization for acute decompensated heart failure include:

- Evidence of severe acute decompensated heart failure, including hypotension, worsening kidney function, or altered mentation
- Dyspnea at rest
- Hemodynamically significant arrhythmia, including rapid atrial fibrillation
- Acute coronary syndrome
- Major electrolyte disturbance
- Associated comorbid condition, such as pneumonia, pulmonary embolism, transient ischemic attack, or stroke
- Repeated ICD firing

For patients admitted with volume overload, initial therapy is generally intravenous loop diuretics, dosed to achieve enough diuresis to relieve signs and symptoms of congestion but not so rapid as to induce hypotension, kidney disease, or marked electrolyte depletion. The initial dose of loop diuretic should be at least equivalent to, but preferably greater than, the dose of the patient's chronic outpatient diuretic. Volume status should be monitored serially by evaluating clinical signs of volume overload and measuring intake and output and daily weights. If response is not adequate, the diuretic dose should be increased, an additional synergistic diuretic should be added (usually a thiazide), or the dose of the loop diuretic should be changed to a continuous infusion. If at any time there is evidence for hypoperfusion or hypotension, inotropic agents should be considered.

For patients already on chronic ACE inhibitor or ARB therapy, these agents can generally be continued during acute decompensated heart failure unless a contraindication such as significant hypotension or acute kidney failure arises. Unless contraindications are present, abrupt withdrawal of ACE inhibitors should be avoided as this may result in clinical deterioration. Similarly, chronic β-blocker therapy also can frequently be continued through the acute decompensated episode unless a contraindication such as significant hypotension or low-output state (that is, impending or actual cardiogenic shock) is present. If these medications are stopped during the hospitalization, they should be resumed when the patient is clinically stable, prior to discharge.

Ultrafiltration is an option for fluid removal and can be performed in the setting of diuretic failure but before overt need for kidney replacement therapy. Trials of early ultrafiltration for patients hospitalized with acute decompensated heart failure with volume overload did not demonstrate any definitive effects on mortality.

Two vasopressin antagonists are used to treat euvolemic or hypovolemic hyponatremia: intravenous conivaptan, a nonselective V_{1a}/V_2 receptor blocker, and oral tolvaptan, a selective V_2 receptor blocker. These agents are generally well tolerated and improve hyponatremia, but no definitive effects on important clinical outcomes have been demonstrated.

Cardiogenic Shock

Cardiogenic shock is present when there is systemic hypotension and evidence for end-organ hypoperfusion, primarily due to inadequate cardiac output. Cardiogenic shock usually requires treatment with intravenous vasoactive medications and, in severe cases, device-based hemodynamic support. Manifestations of end-organ hypoperfusion may include acute kidney failure, elevated aminotransferases or hyperbilirubinemia, cool extremities, and decreased mental status. Cardiogenic shock is defined by persistent hypotension (systolic blood pressure <80-90 mm Hg or mean arterial pressure 30 mm Hg lower than baseline) with severe reduction in cardiac index (<1.8 L/min/m² without hemodynamic support or <2.0-2.2 L/min/m² with support) and adequate or elevated filling pressure (for example, left ventricular end-diastolic pressure >18 mm Hg or right ventricular end-diastolic pressure >10-15 mm Hg).

Early identification of specific treatable causes of cardiogenic shock is critical. These treatable diagnoses primarily include MI, which should be treated with reperfusion, and related mechanical complications, including ventricular septal or free-wall rupture or papillary muscle rupture, which require urgent surgical correction.

Echocardiography is crucial to rapidly identifying potential mechanical causes for cardiogenic shock. A pulmonary artery catheter is usually needed to assess filling pressures and cardiac output to guide therapy, although in studies of slightly different patient populations (patients in medical intensive care units and patients hospitalized with acute decompensated heart failure), use of a pulmonary artery catheter was not associated with survival benefit.

Intravenous vasoactive medications are needed in the treatment of cardiogenic shock to augment cardiac output (inotropic agents) and, if that strategy is not sufficient, to raise systemic blood pressure through peripheral vasoconstriction (vasopressors) (**Table 17**). When systemic blood pressure is acceptable, some patients may also benefit from the addition of an intravenous vasodilator, such as sodium nitroprusside, to further increase cardiac output by reducing afterload. Use of these agents is generally limited to hours or days until shock resolves or more definitive therapy such as an intra-aortic balloon pump is instituted.

Mechanical therapy for cardiogenic shock should be considered in patients with end-organ dysfunction that does not rapidly show signs of improvement (within the first 12-24 hours) with intravenous vasoactive medications and correction of volume overload. Options for mechanical therapy include intra-aortic balloon pump and percutaneous or surgically implanted ventricular assist devices (VADs). An intra-aortic balloon pump is timed to inflate during diastole,

TABLE 17. Intravenous Vasoactive Medications Used for Treatment of Cardiogenic Shock

Medication	Mechanism	Inotropy	Vasodilation
Milrinone	Phosphodiesterase inhibitor	++	+
Dobutamine	β_1, β_2 receptors	++	(+) (at low dose) – (vasoconstriction, at high dose)
Nesiritide	Natriuretic peptide receptors	0	++
Sodium nitroprusside	Nitric oxide	0	++
Nitroglycerin	Nitric oxide	0	++ (mainly venous)
Vasopressin	V receptor	–	– (vasoconstriction)
Dopamine	D receptor β_1 receptors at intermediate dose α_1 receptor at high dose	+	– (vasoconstriction, at high dose)
Norepinephrine	Affinity for α_1, α_2 receptors greater than for β_1 receptors	+	– (vasoconstriction)

Strength of effect: ++ indicates very strong; + indicates strong; (+) indicates weak; 0 indicates neutral, – indicates opposite effect.

augmenting coronary and systemic perfusion, and deflate during systole, reducing left ventricular afterload.

Strategies to Prevent Readmission

Despite reductions in hospital length of stay and in-hospital mortality since the early 1990s for patients admitted with heart failure, 30-day readmission rates have increased, to more than 20% in the current era. Most readmissions have preventable causes, including diet, medication nonadherence, or delayed medical attention to address signs and symptoms of clinical deterioration. Risk of death is highest in the 30 days following hospital discharge. Early physician follow-up, within 7 days after discharge from heart failure hospitalization, reduced 30-day all-cause readmission by 10% to 15%. The clinical and public health importance of heart failure readmissions is highlighted by Centers for Medicare and Medicaid Services (CMS) core measures for discharge of patients hospitalized with heart failure (**Table 18**).

Patients generally benefit from being followed by a multidisciplinary disease management program. Such a comprehensive approach has been demonstrated to improve patient satisfaction with care and reduce hospitalizations and mortality, although the optimal strategies are still not well defined. A heart failure management program typically includes regular telephone monitoring of signs and symptoms and adjustment of medications, in particular diuretics, by specialty nurses and the ability to have patients evaluated in the clinic for unscheduled visits if telephone management is not sufficient to reverse evidence for impending heart failure decompensation.

Although consensus guidelines recommend exercise training as an adjunct to medical therapy to improve the clinical status of ambulatory patients with heart failure, cardiac rehabilitation in the form of a structured, supervised exercise program has not been shown to reduce all-cause mortality or hospitalizations for patients with systolic heart failure.

KEY POINTS

- In patients hospitalized for acute decompensated heart failure, the initial dose of loop diuretic should be at least equivalent to, but preferably greater than, the chronic outpatient diuretic dose.

- Most hospital readmissions for heart failure have preventable causes, and early physician follow-up has been shown to substantially reduce 30-day readmission rates.

TABLE 18. CMS Hospital Core Measures for Heart Failure

Left ventricular function assessment
ACE inhibitor or ARB for left ventricular systolic dysfunction
Discharge instructions: symptom reporting, review of home medications, activity guidelines, diet guidelines, follow-up appointment, weight monitoring instructions
Adult smoking cessation advice/counseling

ARB = angiotensin receptor blocker; CMS = Centers for Medicare and Medicaid Services.

Advanced Refractory Heart Failure

Mechanical Circulatory Support

Some patients with severe refractory heart failure will need additional therapy beyond standard treatment because of progressive clinical deterioration and very high risk of death. Many mechanical devices have been developed to assist

CONT.

cardiac functioning primarily by taking over a portion of the cardiac output. Percutaneous VADs, placed in the cardiac catheterization laboratory, can be inserted through the femoral artery and advanced to the left ventricle to provide partial circulatory support. Percutaneous VADs are temporary (days to weeks), whereas surgically implanted VADs can be used longer (weeks to months or years).

Indications for VAD placement include awaiting recovery from cardiogenic shock (usually after cardiotomy or fulminant myocarditis), as a bridge to cardiac transplantation, and as "destination therapy," meaning the VAD is implanted as the ultimate therapy for the patient's advanced heart failure until death. For a left VAD, an inflow cannula in the left ventricular apex takes blood to the pump portion of the VAD, which returns blood to the aorta. End-organ perfusion, quality of life, functional status, and survival are improved with VAD support for patients with end-stage heart failure. Complications of VADs include device malfunction, thromboembolism, infection, bleeding (with models requiring systemic anticoagulation), and hemolysis (in the continuous-flow model VAD).

Management of Posttransplant Patients

In the absence of contraindications, cardiac transplantation is currently the best therapy available for treatment of end-stage heart failure in patients whose estimated prognosis is poor. One-year survival after cardiac transplantation is about 85%, with a linear annual decline in survival of 3.5% thereafter; median survival is roughly 10 years after transplantation. Common problems encountered in cardiac transplant patients include diabetes, hypertension, dyslipidemia, and kidney disease, usually as side effects from transplant medications. Many transplant medications also have potentially significant drug interactions with common medications. Most patients are treated with calcineurin inhibitors (usually cyclosporine or tacrolimus). Concurrent use of statins is associated with an increased risk for myositis. Azole antifungal agents and some calcium channel blockers (notably diltiazem and verapamil) increase serum levels of calcineurin inhibitor, whereas rifampin, isoniazid, and some antiseizure medications (phenytoin, phenobarbital) reduce levels. As a consequence of chronic immunosuppression, patients are at increased risk for infections (usual and opportunistic) and cancer, frequently skin cancer and lymphoproliferative disease. Even high-grade rejection of the cardiac allograft may be asymptomatic or may present with nonspecific findings such as atrial tachyarrhythmia (typically atrial flutter). Overt left ventricular dysfunction and clinical heart failure are generally late findings and require more intense inpatient immunosuppressive treatment.

Cardiac allograft vasculopathy (CAV) is coronary disease of the cardiac allograft and is frequently the limiting factor in allograft longevity. CAV is characterized by diffuse intimal thickening of large epicardial and small terminal coronary branches, rather than focal stenoses, and is frequently not amenable to standard revascularization interventions such as percutaneous coronary intervention or coronary artery bypass surgery. Because of denervation that occurs with the transplant surgery, patients who have had a cardiac transplant usually do not experience typical angina. Symptoms concerning for CAV in patients with a cardiac transplant include syncope, new heart failure symptoms, decreased exercise tolerance, dyspnea, and varying degrees of heart block. New-onset heart failure symptoms should prompt concern for acute rejection or CAV. In select candidates, another cardiac transplantation is the only possible treatment, but outcomes are generally not as good as with first-time transplants.

KEY POINTS

- Indications for ventricular assist device placement include awaiting recovery from cardiogenic shock, as a bridge to cardiac transplantation, and as destination therapy.

- Symptoms concerning for cardiac allograft vasculopathy in a cardiac transplant patient include syncope, new heart failure symptoms, decreased exercise tolerance, dyspnea, and varying degrees of heart block; transplant patients often do not experience typical angina.

Specific Cardiomyopathies

Takotsubo Cardiomyopathy

Takotsubo (stress-induced) cardiomyopathy is characterized by transient cardiac dysfunction with ventricular apical ballooning, usually triggered by intense emotional or physical stress, although in several published cases, no trigger was identifiable. Most patients are women, although recent reports suggest a higher prevalence among men than initially thought. The presenting clinical picture may mimic an acute coronary syndrome, with chest pain, (mildly) elevated cardiac enzymes, and ECG changes consistent with ischemia. The diagnosis is made by an echocardiogram or ventriculogram showing a typical pattern of apical ballooning and dysfunction together with the absence of significant coronary disease on coronary angiography. One recent large series found a 2% in-hospital mortality rate and a 5% subsequent nonfatal recurrence rate. Ejection fraction generally normalizes quickly, although a small percentage of patients may have delayed recovery (>2 months). Treatment is supportive; β-blocker therapy may not be protective against recurrence.

Acute Myocarditis

Myocarditis is inflammation of the myocardium, which may result from a wide range of potential causes, including toxins or infections, with the most common types likely related to viral infections. The exact pathophysiology leading from viral infection to myocarditis is not well defined, but it may involve direct and autoimmune myocardial injury. The clinical presentation of acute myocarditis ranges from minor symptoms to cardiogenic shock. Although an autoimmune mechanism may contribute to myocardial dysfunction, routine treatment with immunosuppressants is not recommended because trials have not demonstrated definitive clinical or survival benefit. Treatment is based on supportive care and standard therapy for systolic heart failure. Patients with fulminant myocarditis, manifesting with severe hemodynamic compromise, rapid onset of symptoms, and fever, appear to have a better long-term prognosis than patients with acute (nonfulminant) myocarditis.

Tachycardia-Mediated Cardiomyopathy

A variety of tachyarrhythmias can produce cardiomyopathy if present for sustained periods, generally months to years. The tachyarrhythmias may be atrial (fibrillation, flutter, tachycardia) or ventricular (extremely frequent premature ventricular contractions—in excess of several thousand per day, or ventricular tachycardia) in origin. Rate control or elimination of the arrhythmia will generally improve or resolve the cardiomyopathy, although recurrence of the tachyarrhythmia may result in rapid recurrence of cardiomyopathy.

Giant Cell Myocarditis

Giant cell myocarditis is a rare, usually fatal form of myocarditis characterized by rapid (days to months) onset of fulminant heart failure. A substantial minority of patients (about 15% in one series) have refractory ventricular arrhythmias. There is no sex predominance, and presentation typically occurs in the relatively young (in the 40s). The exact underlying mechanism is not known but is thought to be autoimmune. However, therapies to suppress or modulate the immune system (such as corticosteroids or other immunosuppressing agents) have not been shown to improve outcomes, and patients frequently must be considered for VAD implantation and cardiac transplantation. Giant cell myocarditis can also recur in the transplanted heart.

Myocardial Disease

Hypertrophic Cardiomyopathy

Hypertrophic cardiomyopathy (HCM) is a primary myocardial disease characterized by diffuse or focal left ventricular hypertrophy that occurs in the absence of conditions that increase afterload. Prevalence is 0.2% in adults. Familial autosomal dominant disease occurs in 50% of patients. The course is benign in most patients, but it can cause significant morbidity, including syncope, arrhythmia, ischemia, heart failure, and stroke. Mortality is as high as 3% to 6% annually in high-risk patients.

Clinical Presentation and Diagnosis

HCM is typically asymptomatic in childhood and adolescence. Symptoms that develop in HCM include angina, dyspnea, palpitations, fatigue, dizziness, and syncope. Symptoms may be caused by diastolic dysfunction, myocardial ischemia, outflow obstruction with or without associated mitral regurgitation, or atrial fibrillation. The most common pattern of hypertrophy is asymmetric septal hypertrophy. In this type, a midsystolic murmur caused by left ventricular outflow tract (LVOT) obstruction, may be evident. Maneuvers that decrease preload (Valsalva maneuver) enhance the murmur, and those that augment venous return (leg elevation) diminish the murmur.

Electrocardiography is typically abnormal, showing increased QRS voltage and abnormalities of the ST-T waves (**Figure 15**). Prominent Q waves may simulate a myocardial infarction; in the case of septal hypertrophy, Q waves are seen particularly in the inferolateral leads. T waves are upright in the leads with Q waves; inverted T waves suggest an alternative diagnosis (such as myocardial infarction). If apical hypertrophy is predominant, anterior T waves may be deeply inverted and symmetric. Echocardiography delineates the protean abnormalities, including increased left ventricular mass, disproportionate hypertrophy (particularly of the septum), hyperdynamic or preserved ejection fraction, diastolic dysfunction, small left ventricular cavity, and atrial enlargement (**Figure 16**). Left ventricular obstruction may occur in the outflow tract or mid cavity in more than 25% of patients during rest, a feature that is confirmed with Doppler echocardiography and has prognostic importance. LVOT obstruction is dynamic and often labile, with 50% to 60% of patients who lack an outflow gradient at rest developing obstruction during exercise. Although outflow obstruction may account for chest pain, dizziness, syncope, and fatigue, increasing gradient severity does not correlate with symptom severity. Systolic anterior motion of the mitral valve caused by outflow obstruction can result in regurgitation and contribute to symptoms.

Exercise echocardiography is useful to unmask labile obstruction (**Figure 17**). Valsalva maneuver can unmask outflow obstruction. Sensitivity of this maneuver is low (40%), however, and it underestimates the gradient's maximum severity. Pharmacologic modes of provoking obstruction (amyl nitrite, dobutamine) do not simulate exercise and are nonphysiologic. Gradients greater than 30 mm Hg are hemodynamically significant and those greater than 50 mm Hg are severe.

Echocardiography is useful in differentiating HCM from other diseases with similarly increased wall thickness. Compared with HCM, athlete's heart is more apt to manifest concentric hypertrophy, less marked hypertrophy (wall thickness ≤15 mm), an enlarged left ventricular cavity (>55 mm end-diastolic diameter), lack of marked left atrial enlargement, and normal diastolic function. In hypertension and Fabry disease, the phenotypic morphology is typically concentric wall thickening, whereas HCM is usually asymmetric. Disproportionate focal areas of thickening may occur in these conditions, however, making morphologic distinctions difficult.

Tissue Doppler echocardiography measures velocity of myocardial contraction and relaxation and may allow disease detection before development of hypertrophy. This is particularly valuable in younger athletes, in whom it may be difficult to differentiate HCM from the left ventricular hypertrophy of exercise.

Cardiovascular magnetic resonance (CMR) imaging adds incremental diagnostic information if HCM cannot be confirmed or differentiated from other etiologies. CMR imaging detects focal areas of hypertrophy and fibrosis.

KEY POINT
- Maneuvers that decrease preload (Valsalva maneuver) enhance the murmur of hypertrophic cardiomyopathy, and those that augment venous return (leg elevation) diminish the murmur.

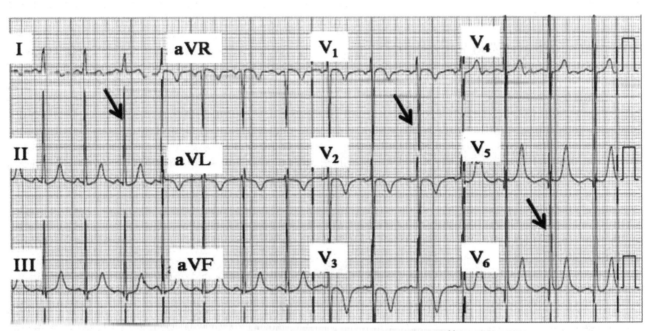

FIGURE 15. 12-Lead electrocardiogram demonstrating hypertrophic cardiomyopathy. QRS voltage is increased in several leads (*arrows*), indicative of left ventricular hypertrophy, a common feature of hypertrophic cardiomyopathy. Nonspecific ST-segment shifts also are present.

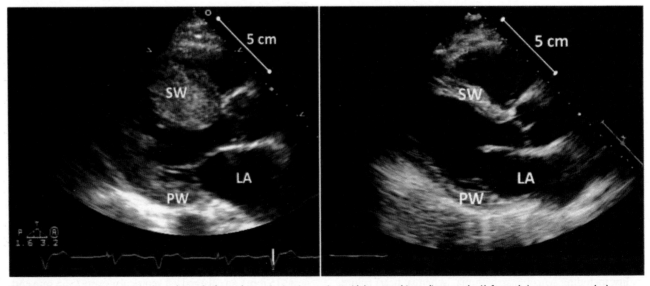

FIGURE 16. Two-dimensional echocardiography from a long-axis view in a patient with hypertrophic cardiomyopathy (*left panel*) demonstrates marked asymmetric septal wall hypertrophy. For comparison, the *right panel* shows normal left ventricular wall thicknesses (<1.1 cm) in a patient without hypertrophic cardiomyopathy. LA = left atrium; PW = posterior wall; SW = septal wall.

Clinical Course and Risk Stratification

Within 10 years of diagnosis, 25% of patients with HCM with no or mild symptoms will develop debilitating symptoms. Atrial fibrillation is present in 5% of patients at diagnosis, and develops in 10% to 22% of patients over the ensuing 5 to 9 years after diagnosis. Atrial fibrillation may precipitate heart failure or stroke. HCM progresses to dilated cardiomyopathy in 5% to 10% of patients as a result of fibrosis and ventricular remodeling. As this occurs, left ventricular obstruction, if originally present, is lost.

Causes of cardiovascular death in patients with HCM include sudden death, heart failure, and stroke. Sudden death is infrequent but is more common in the young (aged 15 to 35 years). Risk factors for sudden death are designated "major" or "possible in individual patients" (**Table 19**).

Management

Drug Treatment

Most patients with HCM can be divided into one of several overlapping groups, which dictate the focus of management (**Table 20**). In asymptomatic patients with no risk factors for sudden death, management focuses on identifying emergence of risk factors. In asymptomatic patients with a genetic mutation but no phenotypic features of HCM, no empiric treatment is recommended. In asymptomatic patients with phenotypic features of HCM but no major risk factors for sudden death, β-blockers may be considered. It is unknown whether β-blockers will lower the risk of sudden death in this subset. Vigorous exercise should be avoided in patients with phenotypic features of HCM because of risk for sudden death. In asymptomatic persons with genetic mutation for HCM but without phenotypic features, family history of sudden death, or presence of a "malignant" gene unique to the family, avoidance of vigorous exercise is controversial.

For patients with heart failure symptoms and preserved systolic function, β-blockers, verapamil, and disopyramide can be beneficial. β-Blockers and verapamil may decrease outflow obstruction and are effective for exertional dyspnea due to LVOT obstruction; they are less effective with outflow obstruction at rest. Verapamil may worsen outflow tract obstruction by vasodilation and should be avoided in patients with outflow obstruction and severe symptoms. Disopyramide can be effective in patients with obstruction but its use is complex. The QT interval must be monitored during disopyramide therapy, as prolongation may portend torsades de pointes or ventricular tachycardia; in addition, disopyramide may increase heart rate in patients with atrial fibrillation and require concomitant use of a β-blocker for rate control. In patients without outflow obstruction, disopyramide may worsen heart failure and should be avoided. Digoxin and vasodilators worsen outflow gradients and should be avoided when obstruction is present. Excessive diuresis should also be avoided as it predisposes to orthostatic hypotension, LVOT obstruction, and syncope. A pacemaker may be needed in some patients to avoid excessive bradycardia during up-titration of medications (β-blockers, verapamil).

For patients with reduced systolic function and no outflow obstruction, standard treatment for heart failure is appropriate. An implantable cardioverter-defibrillator (ICD) should be placed in patients with a left ventricular ejection fraction of 35% or below. Heart transplantation may be considered for HCM patients with advanced heart failure.

In patients with HCM and atrial fibrillation, an aggressive approach to maintaining sinus rhythm using cardioversion and antiarrhythmic therapy (amiodarone) is appropriate, as is rate control when atrial fibrillation is persistent. β-Blockers, verapamil, or digoxin (if no outflow obstruction is present) are used for rate control. If cardioversion and antiarrhythmic therapy fail to maintain sinus rhythm, percutaneous pulmonic vein isolation should be considered in select patients (young, paroxysmal atrial

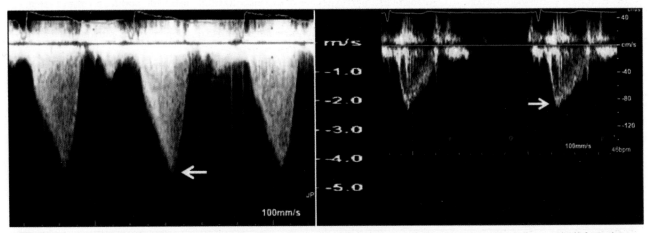

FIGURE 17. Continuous-wave Doppler echocardiography obtained after exercise stress testing in a patient with hypertrophic cardiomyopathy (*left panel*) demonstrates a high-velocity late-peaking systolic waveform (*arrow*) across the left ventricular outflow tract from an exercise-provoked dynamic obstruction. Peak velocity is 4.48 M/sec, indicative of a peak gradient of 80 mm Hg. For comparison, the *right panel* shows pulsed Doppler echocardiography across the left ventricular outflow tract in a patient without hypertrophic cardiomyopathy. There is an earlier-peaking systolic waveform (*arrow*) with a normal velocity of 0.9 M/sec, indicative of no outflow gradient. Note the difference in velocity scales.

fibrillation, absence of marked left atrial enlargement) because it maintains sinus rhythm in 67% of such patients with HCM at 29 months after treatment. Long-term anticoagulation with warfarin reduces cardioembolic risk and is recommended in patients with a CHADS$_2$ score of 2 or more. Available data support warfarin use in patients with HCM with a CHADS$_2$ score of 0 or 1 but are less definitive.

Interventional Treatment

Patients with HCM with major risk factors of previous cardiac arrest, sustained ventricular tachycardia, or ventricular fibrillation (see Table 19) are at high risk for sudden death and should receive an ICD. In this subset of patients, appropriate ICD discharges are reported during follow-up at approximately 11% per year. In patients with HCM but no definitive history of cardiac

TABLE 19. Risk Factors for Sudden Death in Patients with Hypertrophic Cardiomyopathy

Risk Factors	Comments
Major[a]	
Cardiac arrest (ventricular fibrillation)	Portends high rate of recurrence or death (47% over 10 years)
Spontaneous sustained VT	Portends high rate of recurrence
Family history of premature sudden death	Most predictive if occurs in a close relative or multiple relatives
Unexplained syncope	Most predictive if occurs in young patients, is exertional, or is recurrent
Left ventricular diastolic wall thickness ≥30 mm	Most predictive if occurs in adolescents or young adults
	Occurs in approximately 10% of patients
	May not be predictive unless it occurs in combination with unexplained syncope, blunted blood pressure with exercise, nonsustained VT, or family history of sudden death
	Wall thickness <20 mm and no major risk factors portends a favorable prognosis
Blunted increase (<20 mm Hg) or decrease in systolic blood pressure on exercise	More predictive in patients <50 years of age
	Most useful as an arbitrator of risk when risk stratification by history and echocardiography is ambiguous
Nonsustained spontaneous VT	Heart rates of at least 120/min are more predictive
Heart failure that has progressed to dilated cardiomyopathy with ejection fraction ≤35% and NYHA class II or III symptoms	Occurs in 5% to 10% of patients with hypertrophic cardiomyopathy
Possible in Individual Patients[a]	
Atrial fibrillation	
Myocardial ischemia	May be a trigger for sustained ventricular arrhythmia in select patients
Left ventricular outflow obstruction	Gradient ≥30 mm Hg is not an independently strong predictor; positive predictive value only 7%
High-risk gene mutation	Useful in families with history of sudden death (e.g., young patients with normal wall thickness)
Intense physical exertion	Although most episodes of sudden cardiac death occur at rest, during sleep, or with mild activity, risk of triggering an episode is increased with strenuous physical exertion
Factors Not Predictive	
Ventricular arrhythmias inducible by electrophysiologic stimulation	In general of no value
	May be considered appropriate in selected patients (e.g., unexplained syncope)
Chest pain	May be caused by numerous factors, including microvascular disease, ischemia, and obstruction
Dyspnea	Caused by diastolic dysfunction and obstruction
Moderate or severe mitral regurgitation	Due to left ventricular outflow obstruction and secondary systolic anterior motion of mitral valve

NYHA = New York Heart Association; VT = ventricular tachycardia.

[a]Risk factors from Zipes DP, Camm AJ, Borggrefe M, et al; American College of Cardiology/American Heart Association Task Force; European Society of Cardiology Committee for Practice Guidelines; European Heart Rhythm Association and the Heart Rhythm Society. ACC/AHA/ESC 2006 guidelines for management of patients with ventricular arrhythmias and the prevention of sudden cardiac death—executive summary. A report of the American College of Cardiology/American Heart Association Task Force and the European Society of Cardiology Committee for Practice Guidelines (Writing Committee to Develop Guidelines for Management of Patients with Ventricular Arrhythmias and the Prevention of Sudden Cardiac Death) developed in collaboration with the European Heart Rhythm Association and the Heart Rhythm Society. Eur Heart J. 2006;27(17):2099-2140. [PMID: 16923744]

arrest or malignant arrhythmia, family history of sudden cardiac death in multiple relatives younger than 40 years portends a high risk for sudden death—in excess of 40%—and therefore an ICD should be considered. Reliance on emergence of symptoms, such as presyncope, before potential sudden death is not endorsed. The presence of other major risk factors listed in Table 19 has relatively low positive predictive accuracy (15% to 30%) but supports the need for ICD in select patients with HCM (unexplained syncope in the young, left ventricular diastolic wall thickness ≥30 mm in young adults, or blunted blood pressure response during exercise in patients <50 years with otherwise ambiguous risk). Absence of any of the major risk factors has a high negative predictive accuracy (>95%).

For patients with preserved systolic function and LVOT obstruction whose symptoms of heart failure are refractory to medications (New York Heart Association functional class III or IV heart failure), alleviation of the obstruction often results in marked symptomatic improvement. Septal myectomy is the most effective method for alleviating LVOT obstruction, although surgery is not curative and patients may worsen. Alcohol septal ablation may be a better choice for patients at high surgical risk. Mortality is similar with surgery and alcohol ablation (≤3%).

Role of Genetic Testing and Screening

Twenty genes and more than 450 mutations that affect sarcomeric protein have been associated with HCM. The frequency of

TABLE 20. Management of Patients with Hypertrophic Cardiomyopathy	
Group (or predominant management issue)	**Management**
No major risk factors for sudden cardiac death	Annual screening for risk factors
Asymptomatic; genetic mutation; no phenotypic cardiac features	Annual follow-up (includes echocardiography)
	Reassurance
	No empiric medications
	Genetic counseling when appropriate
	Restriction of vigorous exercise is controversial in the absence of symptoms, family history of sudden death, or identification of a "malignant" gene unique to the family
Asymptomatic; phenotypic cardiac features but no major risk factors for sudden cardiac death	Annual follow-up (includes echocardiography, ambulatory monitoring for VT, upright exercise stress test for BP response)
	Empiric use of medications (e.g., β-blockers) to delay disease progression or prevent sudden death is unproved but can be considered on an individual basis
	Avoid vigorous exercise
Stable heart failure symptoms, preserved systolic function	β-Blockers
	Verapamil
	Disopyramide
	Diuretics if needed
	Permanent pacemaker if needed to allow up-titration of medications with negative chronotropic properties
Progressive heart failure symptoms refractory to medications, preserved systolic function, outflow tract obstruction	Septal myectomy or alcohol septal ablation
Progressive heart failure symptoms refractory to medications, reduced systolic function, no outflow tract obstruction	Vasodilators
	β-Blockers
	Digoxin
	Spironolactone
	Heart transplant
	ICD for ejection fraction ≤35%
One or more of following major risk factors for sudden cardiac death: previous cardiac arrest, sustained VT, ventricular fibrillation	ICD, β-blockers; avoid vigorous exercise

BP = blood pressure; ICD = implantable cardioverter-defibrillator; VT = ventricular tachycardia.

Recommendations from Maron BJ, McKenna WJ, Danielson GK, et al; Task Force on Clinical Expert Consensus Documents. American College of Cardiology; Committee for Practice Guidelines. European Society of Cardiology. American College of Cardiology/European Society of Cardiology clinical expert consensus document on hypertrophic cardiomyopathy. A report of the American College of Cardiology Foundation Task Force on Clinical Expert Consensus Documents and the European Society of Cardiology Committee for Practice Guidelines. J Am Coll Cardiol. 2003;42(9):1687-1713. [PMID: 14607462]

any given causal mutation is low, and specific mutations, which may portend poor or good prognosis for a specific family, do not predict a similar course in unrelated individuals. Multiple mutations may coexist in a patient. Thus, genetic testing to identify causative genes in an individual patient is daunting. In patients with HCM, routine genetic testing is not recommended to predict risk and outcome.

The Heart Failure Society of America supports genetic screening of the most affected person in a family with HCM. When a causative mutation is identified, genetic testing can establish a diagnosis in clinically ambiguous but suspected cases. However, a "negative" test does not exclude HCM. In patients with established HCM, it can allow genetic counseling for families and identify the need for serial clinical surveillance for disease emergence in first-degree relatives who share the causative mutation. Children are screened for the specific gene defect identified in the parent with the disease, and absence of the parental genetic defect excludes the disease in the child. In affected offspring, long-term follow-up is advisable.

First-degree relatives of patients with HCM who share the causative mutation identified in the patient should undergo echocardiography screening at 3- to 5-year intervals for adults, and annually for adolescents.

KEY POINTS

- Patients with hypertrophic cardiomyopathy at high risk for sudden death should receive an implantable cardioverter-defibrillator regardless of the presence or absence of symptoms.
- First-degree relatives of patients with hypertrophic cardiomyopathy should undergo periodic echocardiographic screening.

Restrictive Cardiomyopathy

Restrictive cardiomyopathy is a disease characterized by reduced or normal diastolic ventricular cavity volume and stiff ventricular myocardium that causes intracavitary pressures to markedly rise with only small amounts of filling volume. Early in its course, biventricular systolic function is normal but may deteriorate as the disease progresses. Most cases are idiopathic, but specific etiologies exist (**Table 21**). Mutations in sarcomeric proteins account for heritable forms of restrictive cardiomyopathy. Some of the mutations that cause HCM also cause restrictive cardiomyopathy or a type of HCM with a restrictive phenotype.

Clinical Presentation and Evaluation

Restrictive cardiomyopathy presents with biventricular diastolic failure. Right-sided failure often predominates, with fatigue, edema, and anorexia. Progressive disease may cause hepatomegaly, ascites, and anasarca. Exertional dyspnea is common, and pulmonary edema may occur. Right-sided heart failure may be evident on physical examination. An S_3 gallop is typically present, but unlike in systolic heart failure or constrictive pericarditis, the apical impulse is forceful.

Echocardiography shows restrictive ventricular filling, normal ejection fraction, severe biatrial enlargement, and normal wall thickness with increased central venous pressure.

Idiopathic restrictive cardiomyopathy is more common in the elderly, and occurs more often in women. Evaluation for a secondary cause of restrictive cardiomyopathy is guided by history and examination findings that suggest a specific etiology. Amyloidosis is suggested in patients with neuropathy, proteinuria, and macroglossia. Low QRS voltage on electrocardiography (≤ 10 mV in all precordial leads or ≤ 5 mV in all limb leads) despite thick ventricular walls on echocardiography is consistent with an infiltrative restrictive cardiomyopathy, such as amyloidosis. Gingival biopsy or an abdominal fat pad aspirate can confirm amyloidosis. If nondiagnostic, endomyocardial biopsy should be done to confirm diagnosis.

Cardiac sarcoidosis should be suspected in patients with concomitant pulmonary disease. Cardiac involvement can be confirmed by CMR imaging, which detects focal myocardial areas of high intensity indicative of sarcoid. Endocardial biopsy is insensitive for diagnosis.

Hemochromatosis, an iron overload and storage disorder, is typically diagnosed before cardiac manifestations occur; in 15% of patients, however, cardiac symptoms are the initial presentation. Echocardiography shows a restrictive cardiomyopathy. CMR imaging can confirm cardiac involvement by demonstrating very low signal intensity from iron deposits. Transferrin saturation and serum ferritin level are useful screening tests. Hereditary hemochromatosis is autosomal recessive. Genetic testing can be performed to confirm diagnosis.

Differentiating Restrictive Cardiomyopathy from Constrictive Pericarditis

Restrictive cardiomyopathy may be difficult to distinguish from constrictive pericarditis, a disease that may be treated with pericardiectomy. Left ventricular filling on Doppler echocardiography is "restrictive" in both diseases, whereby early diastole shows an elevated peak filling rate and is shortened. Additional echocardiographic features of constrictive pericarditis not seen in restrictive cardiomyopathy, however, allow these diseases to be distinguished (see Pericardial Disease). Plasma B-type natriuretic peptide levels show marked elevations in restrictive cardiomyopathy (mean >800 pg/mL).

Management

The prognosis with restrictive cardiomyopathy is generally poor. In a cohort of patients with idiopathic restrictive cardiomyopathy and a mean age of 64 years, survival was 64% at 5 years and 37% at 10 years from diagnosis. Treatment is directed toward specific etiologies whenever possible (**Table 22**) with additional therapy guided by symptoms. The goal is to reduce pulmonary and systemic congestion. Dyspnea and volume overload are treated with diuretics. Excessive diuresis can lower filling pressures too much, leading to reduced stroke volume, orthostatic hypotension, and syncope. Serial monitoring of serum creatinine and blood urea nitrogen levels is necessary to guard against volume depletion and renal hypoperfusion.

β-Blockers, verapamil, and diltiazem are useful adjuncts to diuretics, enhancing diastolic filling. In some patients, maximal diastolic filling is relatively fixed, and bradycardia can reduce cardiac output and worsen symptoms of low output, such as weakness and fatigue. Underlying conduction abnormalities predispose to heart block. Pacemakers may be needed for bradyarrhythmias.

Cardiac Tumors

Tumor Types
Seventy-five percent of primary cardiac tumors are benign; the remaining 25% are malignant. Myxoma is the most common primary tumor, 80% of which originate in the left atrium. Other benign tumors include papillary fibroelastoma and lipoma. Malignant cardiac tumors are frequently sarcomas.

Secondary tumors reach the heart by metastasis or direct extension and are 20 times more common than primary cardiac tumors. The most common secondary tumors originate from lung and breast carcinomas. Any structure of the heart can be affected. Renal, hepatocellular, and adrenal carcinomas may grow within the inferior vena cava and extend to the right atrium.

Clinical Presentation and Evaluation
Cardiac tumors may cause nonspecific constitutional symptoms or symptoms of heart failure or pericardial constriction, or may present in more dramatic fashion (syncope, stroke, heart block, ventricular tachycardia, sudden death).

TABLE 21. Characteristics of Selected Causes of Restrictive Cardiomyopathy		
Type	**Etiology**	**Notes**
Noninfiltrative Myocardial Conditions		
Idiopathic	Unknown	Diagnosis of exclusion
		Most common form
Familial	Mutations in genes encoding troponin I and T, α-actin, and β-myosin heavy chain	Rare
Scleroderma	Patchy myocardial fibrosis often associated with contraction band necrosis	May result from recurrent vasospasm of small vessels
Infiltrative Myocardial Conditions		
Amyloidosis	Commonly associated with transthyretin gene mutation	Most common identifiable underlying cause of restrictive cardiomyopathy
		Amyloid heart involvement occurs more in primary (50%) vs. secondary (<5%) amyloidosis
Sarcoidosis	Noncaseating granulomas, inflammation, and fibrosis	Clinical manifestations uncommon but may include ventricular arrhythmias, conduction block, and sudden death
Hemochromatosis	Iron deposits may be associated with myocardial or endocardial fibrosis	Most often presents as dilated cardiomyopathy but may present as restrictive form
Myocardial Storage Conditions		
Fabry disease	X-linked deficiency of α-galactosidase causing accumulation of globotriaosylceramide	Has some features of hypertrophic cardiomyopathy
Endomyocardial Disorders		
Endomyocardial fibrosis	Unknown cause but may relate to nutritional deficiencies, eosinophilia, or genetics	Endocardial fibrosis of the right and left ventricular apices, occurring mainly in west and central Africa
Eosinophilic cardiomyopathy (Löffler endocarditis)	Hypereosinophilia, organ infiltration, and release of toxic mediators	Fibrosis of the endomyocardium
Toxic effect of anthracyclines	Doxorubicin, daunorubicin, idarubicin, epirubicin, and mitoxantrone (an anthraquinone) are the most frequently implicated	Can cause dilated or restrictive disease
		Risk increases with concomitant irradiation
Radiation	Diffuse fibrosis in the interstitium of the myocardium	May occur years or decades after exposure

To diagnose and determine the extent of a cardiac tumor, transthoracic echocardiography is the initial procedure of choice. Transesophageal echocardiography (**Figure 18**), CT, or CMR imaging are complementary. Biopsy or surgically derived tissue samples provide a specific histologic diagnosis.

Management

Myxomas should be surgically removed, particularly if left-sided, to avoid systemic embolic events even in asymptomatic patients. The appropriate treatment for left-sided papillary fibroelastomas remains controversial. Surgical removal is curative and should be considered in patients with systemic emboli or if the fibroelastoma is highly mobile. If surgical risk is high, anticoagulation or antiplatelet therapy is reasonable.

Malignant tumors are not amenable to curative surgery. Surgical resection may be needed to confirm diagnosis and to exclude a benign tumor amenable to curative surgery. Prognosis of malignant primary or metastatic tumors is poor. Treatment may entail chemotherapy, radiation therapy, and palliative measures.

KEY POINT

- A myxoma should be surgically removed, particularly if left-sided, to avoid systemic embolic events even in asymptomatic patients.

Arrhythmias

Approach to the Patient with Bradycardia

Clinical Presentation

Patients with bradycardia (heart rate <60/min) can have diverse and nonspecific symptoms. The most concerning is syncope; other symptoms include lightheadedness, fatigue, dyspnea, exercise intolerance, and bradycardia-induced ventricular arrhythmias. Bradycardia can be due to dysfunction of the sinus node, the atrioventricular (AV) node, or the His-Purkinje system. Some causes of bradycardia, such as Lyme disease, drugs, hyperkalemia, and thyroid disease, may be reversible.

It is important that symptoms are correlated with bradycardic episodes. Evaluation begins with a 12-lead electrocardiogram (ECG); a 24-hour continuous ambulatory ECG monitor or event recorder may also be used, depending on the frequency of symptoms (see Diagnostic Testing in Cardiology).

Sinus Bradycardia

Sinus bradycardia is not necessarily pathologic; athletes and other highly conditioned persons may have resting heart rates

TABLE 22. Treatment Approaches for Specific Causes of Restrictive Cardiomyopathy		
Cause	**Medical Therapy**	**Surgical Therapy**
Amyloidosis		
Familial/mutant transthyretin		Heart/liver transplant
AL (primary)	Chemotherapy	Heart transplant (controversial)
		Untreated median survival after heart failure <6 months
AA (secondary)	Specific for cause of inflammation or infection	
Granulomatous		
Sarcoidosis	First-line therapy: corticosteroids	Heart transplant
	Second-line therapy: chloroquine, hydroxychloroquine, cyclosporine, methotrexate	
Hemochromatosis		
Hereditary	Phlebotomy	Heart transplant
Acquired	Iron chelation	
Endomyocardial diseases		
Endomyocardial fibrosis	Warfarin (for documented cardiac thrombus)	Endomyocardectomy (palliative)
Hypereosinophilia syndrome (Löffler endocarditis)	First-line therapy: corticosteroids	Endomyocardectomy (palliative)
	Second-line therapy: tyrosine kinase inhibitor, interferon, cyclosporine, chemotherapeutic drugs	Bone marrow transplant (for treatment-resistant disease)
	Warfarin (for documented cardiac thrombus)	
Storage diseases		
Fabry disease	α-Galactosidase A replacement	
AA = amyloid associated; AL = amyloid light chain.		

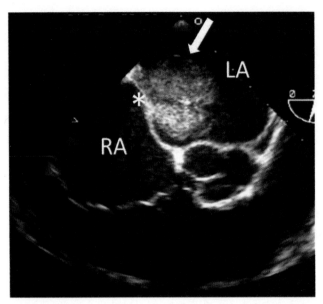

FIGURE 18. Transesophageal echocardiography across the right atrium (*RA*) and left atrium (*LA*) demonstrates a large mass (*arrow*) attached to the atrial septum in proximity of the fossa ovalis (*asterisk*); the mass was surgically removed and proved to be a left atrial myxoma.

of 40/min and sleeping heart rates as low as 30/min. The underlying cause of pathologic sinus bradycardia in most patients is fibrotic replacement of the sinus node associated with aging. Other causes include node damage secondary to infarction or cardiac surgery, infiltrative processes such as amyloidosis and sarcoidosis, increased vagal tone secondary to a Valsalva maneuver or vomiting, medications such as β-blockers and calcium channel blockers, and, rarely, genetic diseases. Sinus node dysfunction may manifest as sick sinus syndrome, sinus arrest, or chronotropic incompetence (heart rate does not increase in response to hemodynamic need).

Atrioventricular Block

Three types of heart block exist, all representing dysfunction of the AV node or the His-Purkinje system. First-degree AV block, characterized by a PR interval of greater than 200 msec, does not represent true conduction block but rather a delay in impulse conduction in the AV node. Although first-degree AV block is typically asymptomatic, recent data suggest an increased risk of atrial fibrillation, pacemaker implantation, and all-cause mortality over long-term follow-up.

Second-degree AV block is divided into two types: Mobitz type 1 (Wenckebach) and Mobitz type 2. Mobitz type 1 block is usually caused by disease within the AV node, characterized by progressive lengthening of the PR interval until a QRS complex is absent because of conduction failure (**Figure 19**). The first return beat has a shorter PR interval than the last conducted beat. The ECG may have the appearance of grouped beating because of a relatively fixed interval between nonconducted beats.

Mobitz type 2 second-degree AV block, characterized by a dropped QRS complex with no change in preceding PR intervals, is more worrisome, suggesting His-Purkinje disease. This lesion has a high risk of progressing to complete heart block. In patients with 2:1 AV block, it is impossible to differentiate between Mobitz type 1 and 2 AV block. Advanced second-degree heart block, or high-grade heart block, occurs when two or more nonconducted P waves occur for each QRS complex.

Third-degree block (complete heart block) occurs when there is no relationship between P waves and the QRS escape rhythm (**Figure 20**). This is usually caused by conduction block in the His bundle or below. Reversible causes of complete heart block include medications (β-blockers, calcium channel blockers, digoxin) and Lyme disease.

In acute coronary syndromes, the incidence of heart block due to infarction has decreased owing to more rapid revascularization achieved with thrombolytic therapy and percutaneous coronary intervention, limiting the extent of myocardial injury. Anterior myocardial infarctions are more likely to have permanent conduction defects because of larger infarct sizes, whereas inferior myocardial infarctions may have only transient heart block that resolves in a few days. If persistent heart block develops, there is increased risk for in-hospital mortality from ventricular arrhythmias and cardiogenic shock. The decision to implant a permanent pacemaker should only be made after several days to determine if the heart block is transient or permanent.

Pacemakers

The treatment for symptomatic sinus bradycardia or heart block without reversible causes is a permanent pacemaker (**Table 23**). These devices are usually placed in the left pectoral area with leads inserted through a vein into the heart. Permanent pacemakers are generally not indicated for

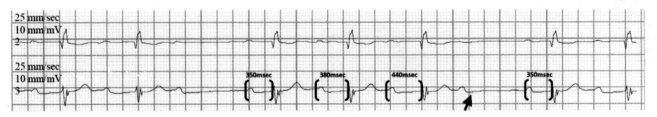

FIGURE 19. An electrocardiogram demonstrating second-degree, type 1 atrioventricular block (Wenckebach block). Note the progressively longer PR interval (*brackets*) followed by a P wave with no QRS complex (*arrow*). The first return PR interval is shorter than the last conducted PR interval.

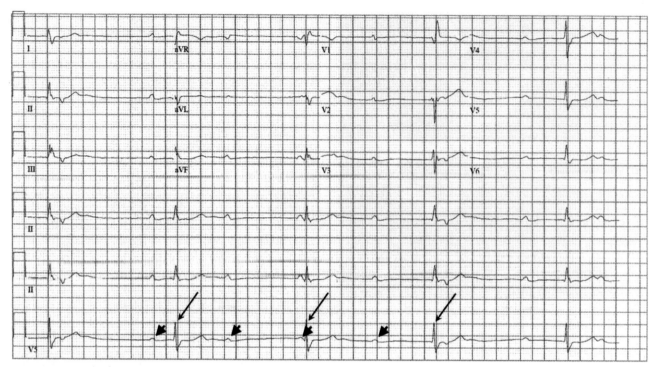

FIGURE 20. In this electrocardiogram, the P waves (*short arrows*) and QRS complexes (*long arrows*) are not associated with each other, indicating the presence of a complete heart block.

TABLE 23. Selected Indications for Permanent Pacing
Symptomatic bradycardia (heart rate <40/min) or sinus pauses
Symptomatic complete heart block or second-degree heart block (type 1 or 2)
Asymptomatic complete heart block or advanced second-degree heart block
Atrial fibrillation with pauses of ≥5 seconds
Alternating bundle branch block

Information from Epstein AE, DiMarco JP, Ellenbogen KA, et al; American College of Cardiology/American Heart Association Task Force on Practice Guidelines (Writing Committee to Revise the ACC/AHA/NASPE 2002 Guideline Update for Implantation of Cardiac Pacemakers and Antiarrhythmia Devices); American Association for Thoracic Surgery; Society of Thoracic Surgeons. ACC/AHA/HRS 2008 Guidelines for device-based therapy of cardiac rhythm abnormalities: a report of the American College of Cardiology/American Heart Association Task Force on Practice Guidelines (Writing Committee to Revise the ACC/AHA/NASPE 2002 Guideline Update for Implantation of Cardiac Pacemakers and Antiarrhythmia Devices): developed in collaboration with the American Association for Thoracic Surgery and Society of Thoracic Surgeons. Circulation. 2008;117(21):e350-e408. [PMID: 18483207]

bradycardia or first- or second-degree heart block in the absence of symptoms.

Electrocautery during surgery can inhibit pacemaker function; therefore, if a pacemaker-dependent patient undergoes surgery, the device should be reprogrammed to an asynchronous pacing mode. It is reasonable to place a magnet over the pacemaker, as this will also change it to an asynchronous mode. MRI is currently contraindicated for most patients with pacemakers, although FDA-approved MRI-conditional pacemakers are now being implanted.

In some patients, right ventricular apical pacing can lead to atrial fibrillation and left ventricular dysfunction by inducing mechanical dyssynchrony. Newer algorithms have been developed that can reduce the amount of ventricular pacing and reduce these adverse effects.

KEY POINTS

- Mobitz type 2 second-degree atrioventricular block has a high risk of progressing to complete heart block.

- A pacemaker is indicated for symptomatic bradycardia from sinus node dysfunction, advanced second-degree heart block, or complete heart block.

Approach to the Patient With Tachycardia

Evaluation

Sinus tachycardia is the most common tachycardia (heart rate >100/min) and is usually a secondary rhythm. Common underlying causes include pain, fever, anxiety, and anemia. In younger persons, paroxysmal supraventricular tachycardias (SVTs) are more common. Older persons are more likely to have atrial fibrillation, atrial flutter, or ventricular tachycardia (VT). Persons of any age may have premature atrial contractions (PACs) or premature ventricular contractions (PVCs).

Palpitations are often felt during tachycardia, although other symptoms, such as chest pain, shortness of breath, syncope, or presyncope, may be experienced. Hemodynamic stability does not help distinguish the mechanism of tachycardia. Patients with VT may be stable with a normal blood pressure, especially if cardiac function is normal. On the other hand, onset of atrial fibrillation in diastolic dysfunction often produces dyspnea owing to loss of the atrial "kick" needed for left ventricular filling.

The best method for determining the cause of palpitations is to capture the rhythm using an ECG, continuous ambulatory ECG monitor, event recorder, or implantable loop recorder (see Diagnostic Testing in Cardiology). A baseline ECG should be obtained in all patients, because abnormalities on the ECG may suggest the mechanism of the arrhythmia. For example, a delta wave indicating ventricular preexcitation suggests AV reciprocating tachycardia, whereas evidence of ischemic heart disease, including Q waves or T-wave abnormalities, points to a ventricular arrhythmia as the likely cause.

 Antiarrhythmic Medications

Antiarrhythmic medications can have more than one mechanism of action but are grouped by their main effect using the Vaughan-Williams classification (**Table 24**). Class II and class IV agents (β-blockers and calcium channel blockers) are used frequently but should be avoided in patients with decompensated systolic heart failure or in whom Wolff-Parkinson-White syndrome is suspected. Class I and class III agents (sodium channel and potassium channel blockers) have greater antiarrhythmic effects but may cause ventricular arrhythmias and have toxicities that limit their use. Class IC medications are often prescribed for atrial fibrillation and flutter. These agents are contraindicated in those with coronary artery disease, especially after myocardial infarction, because they increase the risk of polymorphic VT. They also slow down the atrial flutter rate, which may predispose to rapid 1:1 AV nodal conduction. Therefore, an AV nodal blocker is often concurrently given with class IC medications.

Class III agents are used for atrial and ventricular arrhythmias but can lengthen the QT interval; for this reason, they are often initiated in an inpatient setting over 3 days to monitor for torsades de pointes. If the corrected QT (QTc) interval becomes greater than 500 msec or increases by more than 15% or 60 msec, the dose should be decreased or discontinued. Amiodarone, which affects multiple pathways, is the preferred agent in patients with heart failure or left ventricular hypertrophy, although it has several side

TABLE 24.	Antiarrhythmic Medications			
Vaughan-Williams Classification	Mechanism of Action	Examples	Effect	Use
Class IA	Sodium channel blockade, some potassium channel blockade	Quinidine, procainamide, disopyramide	Slows conduction and prolongs repolarization	Preexcited atrial fibrillation, SVT, ventricular arrhythmias
Class IB	Sodium channel blockade	Lidocaine, mexiletine, phenytoin	Slows conduction in diseased tissues, shortens repolarization	Ventricular arrhythmias
Class IC	Sodium channel blockade	Flecainide, propafenone	Markedly slows conduction, slightly prolongs repolarization	Atrial fibrillation, atrial flutter, SVT, ventricular arrhythmias
Class II	β-blockade	Metoprolol, propranolol, atenolol	Suppresses automaticity and slows AV nodal conduction	Rate control of atrial arrhythmias, SVT, ventricular arrhythmias
Class III	Potassium channel blockade	Sotalol, amiodarone, dofetilide, dronedarone	Prolongs action potential duration	Atrial fibrillation, atrial flutter, ventricular arrhythmias
Class IV	Calcium channel blockade	Verapamil, diltiazem	Slows sinoatrial node automaticity and AV nodal conduction	SVT, rate control of atrial arrhythmias, triggered arrhythmias
—	A₁ receptor agonist	Adenosine[a]	Slows or blocks sinoatrial and AV nodal conduction	Termination of SVT
—	Increasing vagal activity	Digoxin[a]	Slows AV nodal conduction	Rate control of atrial arrhythmias

AV = atrioventricular; SVT = supraventricular tachycardia.

[a]These agents do not fall into the Vaughan-Williams classification scheme.

effects, including thyroid dysfunction, liver toxicity, pulmonary fibrosis, and skin hypersensitivity. Intravenous loading of amiodarone may lead to hypotension. Amiodarone can prolong the QT interval but has not been shown to cause torsades de pointes and does not have to be initiated as an inpatient. Dronedarone, the newest agent, can reduce the incidence of hospitalization for cardiovascular events or death in patients with atrial fibrillation or flutter, and it does not have the side effect profile of amiodarone. Dronedarone may lead to an increase in measured serum creatinine level through inhibition of tubular secretion, but it does not actually change the glomerular filtration rate. It should not be used in patients with New York Heart Association (NYHA) functional class II or III heart failure with recent decompensation or with class IV heart failure; in addition, it should not be used as a rate control agent in those with permanent atrial fibrillation.

Digoxin and adenosine are antiarrhythmic agents that do not fit into the Vaughan-Williams classification. Digoxin functions as a sodium-potassium exchange blocker and also increases vagal activity to the heart. It is most beneficial in patients with heart failure to provide additional inotropy and in sedentary patients because the AV nodal blocking effect is less effective during activity. Adenosine blocks the A_1 receptors in the AV node and can terminate reentrant SVTs. It has a half-life of less than 6 seconds and must be rapidly pushed through an intravenous line.

Atrial Fibrillation and Atrial Flutter

Atrial fibrillation is caused by rapid and uncoordinated electrical activation within the atria. The ECG demonstrates an absence of P waves and an irregular ventricular response (**Figure 21**).

Atrial fibrillation is common, affecting approximately 2.2 million people in the United States. Men are more likely to have atrial fibrillation, and prevalence increases with age, to almost 10% in persons older than 80 years. Although rate-controlled atrial fibrillation itself is not life threatening, blood stasis in the left atrium may cause clot formation and is the leading cause of embolic stroke. Atrial fibrillation is also associated with increased risk for heart failure and all-cause mortality.

Clinical Presentation

Symptoms of atrial fibrillation include palpitations, dyspnea, chest discomfort, fatigue, dizziness, and syncope. Patients can be asymptomatic, especially if the arrhythmia has persisted for a long period of time. If atrial fibrillation terminates on its own, it is defined as paroxysmal. If the rhythm sustains for longer than 7 days, it becomes persistent. When atrial fibrillation is continuous and cardioversion has failed or is no longer attempted, the rhythm is classified as permanent.

Atrial fibrillation is associated with other conditions, including heart failure, hyperthyroidism, hypertension,

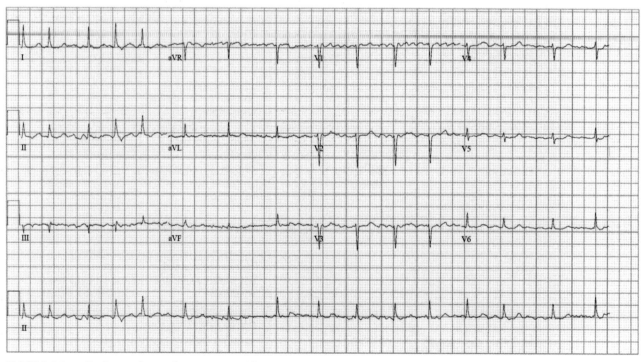

FIGURE 21. In this electrocardiogram demonstrating atrial fibrillation, no clear P waves are seen and the ventricular response is irregular.

Wolff-Parkinson-White syndrome, cardiac surgery, myocardial infarction, myocarditis, pericarditis, and acute pulmonary disease. Patients with mitral valvular disease, especially rheumatic mitral stenosis, have a high rate of developing atrial fibrillation. When atrial fibrillation occurs in the absence of structural heart disease in a patient younger than 60 years, it is designated as lone atrial fibrillation.

Acute Management

Evaluation of atrial fibrillation starts with an ECG. A thorough history of symptoms should be obtained, and laboratory testing for thyroid, renal, and hepatic abnormalities should be ordered. Transthoracic echocardiography should be performed to evaluate for valvular disease, pulmonary hypertension, left ventricular hypertrophy, and other cardiac abnormalities.

Acute Anticoagulation

If direct-current cardioversion is not planned, it is usually not necessary to anticoagulate acutely with heparin unless the patient has high thromboembolic risk factors. It is sufficient to start oral anticoagulation. However, anticoagulation must be considered in the acute setting before either electrical or pharmacologic cardioversion. For patients who have been in atrial fibrillation for less than 48 hours, anticoagulation is not mandatory because clot formation during that time is unlikely. If the patient has been in atrial fibrillation for more than 48 hours or for an unknown duration, two equivalent treatment strategies are available, based on the patient's symptom tolerance. The first strategy is to medicate with warfarin for 3 weeks and then perform cardioversion. In the second strategy, the patient is fully anticoagulated and undergoes transesophageal echocardiography (TEE) to assess for an intracardiac thrombus. If the TEE shows no clot, then cardioversion can proceed immediately. Although electrical atrial activity is normalized following cardioversion, atrial mechanical stunning and a higher risk of stroke may persist for up to 4 weeks, and warfarin (goal INR, 2.0-3.0) must be continued during this time.

Cardioversion and Acute Rate Control

Approximately 50% of patients who present to the emergency department with atrial fibrillation convert spontaneously. If the patient has hypotension, angina, or heart failure, cardioversion should be emergently performed, regardless of atrial fibrillation duration. It is important to ensure R-wave synchronization by the cardioverter to prevent an "R-on-T" shock and induction of ventricular fibrillation (VF).

If the patient is hemodynamically stable, the initial goal is to maintain a heart rate of 60/min to 110/min with a rate control agent. Intravenous options include diltiazem, verapamil, metoprolol, or esmolol. Digoxin can be used as a second agent, especially in those with heart failure or systolic dysfunction, but takes up to 6 hours to see a peak effect. In those with rapid atrial fibrillation with only minimal or mild symptoms, oral agents may be used.

Long-term Management

Anticoagulation

Validated risk factors for thromboembolism in patients with atrial fibrillation include mitral stenosis, previous thromboembolism, heart failure, systolic dysfunction, diabetes, hypertension, presence of a mechanical heart valve, and older age. In patients without significant valvular disease, the most commonly used method to determine choice of thromboprophylaxis is the CHADS$_2$ score (**Table 25**). One point each

TABLE 25. Long-Term Anticoagulation Based on CHADS$_2$ Score

CHADS$_2$ Score[a]	Adjusted Annual Incidence of Stroke Not Treated with Anticoagulation (per 100 patient-years)[b]	Anticoagulation Therapy[c]
0	1.9	Aspirin or no therapy
1	2.8	Aspirin or warfarin
2	4.0	Warfarin
3	5.9	Warfarin
4	8.5	Warfarin
5	12.5	Warfarin
6	18.2	Warfarin

[a]One point is given for heart failure, hypertension, age ≥75 years, and diabetes. Two points are given for previous stroke or transient ischemic attack.

[b]Data from: Gage BF, Waterman AD, Shannon W, Boechler M, Rich MW, Radford MJ. Validation of clinical classification schemes for predicting stroke: results from the National Registry of Atrial Fibrillation. JAMA. 2001;285(22):2864-2870. [PMID: 11401607]

[c]Aspirin dosage: 81-325 mg/d; warfarin to INR 2.0-3.0.

is given for heart failure, hypertension (even if treated), age 75 years or older, and diabetes; two points are given for previous stroke or transient ischemic attack. Patients with zero points have a low stroke risk, and aspirin or no treatment is used. Those with a score of 1 have an intermediate stroke risk, and it is physician and patient preference whether to use warfarin or aspirin. A score of 2 or higher is high risk, and warfarin with a goal INR of 2.0 to 3.0 is preferred. Rheumatic mitral stenosis also increases risk, and goal INR in patients with rheumatic mitral stenosis and atrial fibrillation is 2.0 to 3.0. If a mechanical heart valve is present in a patient with atrial fibrillation, the level of anticoagulation is based on the type of valve, with a minimum INR of 2.5.

In patients who are not candidates for warfarin, adding clopidogrel to aspirin can reduce stroke risk more than aspirin alone, although risk for major bleeding events is increased. In patients who are able to take warfarin, however, clopidogrel plus aspirin is inferior for preventing ischemic strokes. There is currently no role for prasugrel for stroke prophylaxis in atrial fibrillation.

A new class of anticoagulation agents is the direct thrombin inhibitors, which include dabigatran. In the RE-LY trial, dabigatran was shown to be superior to warfarin in preventing ischemic and hemorrhagic stroke, with a reduced risk of life-threatening bleeding but a higher risk of gastrointestinal bleeding. Laboratory monitoring is not needed with direct thrombin inhibitors, but also no laboratory test can measure the extent of anticoagulation. Additionally, no reversal agent is available in the event of major bleeding. Dabigatran is an alternative to warfarin in those with a $CHADS_2$ score of 1 or higher in those with nonvalvular atrial fibrillation.

Rivaroxaban, an oral factor Xa inhibitor, also has been approved for prevention of stroke and systemic embolism in atrial fibrillation. It is noninferior to warfarin for stroke prevention with no difference in major bleeding, but demonstrates a reduction in intracranial hemorrhage. The risk of thrombotic events is increased within the first 28 days after rivaroxaban is stopped, so overlapping with another anticoagulant during this time should be considered.

Interruption of oral anticoagulation in patients with atrial fibrillation is sometimes needed for invasive procedures, and it must be determined whether bridging with heparin is indicated. If the patient has a low short-term risk ($CHADS_2$ score of 0-2) and the duration of interruption is less than 1 week, then bridging is not needed. If the patient has a higher short-term risk ($CHADS_2$ score of 5-6, recent stroke, mechanical or rheumatic mitral valve) or if the interruption is more than 1 week, then use of a bridging agent should be considered more strongly. In patients who have undergone cardioversion, continuous therapeutic anticoagulation must be maintained for at least 4 weeks following the cardioversion. Elective procedures should be postponed until this time period has been completed.

Rate versus Rhythm Control

No mortality or stroke reduction benefit is associated with restoration of sinus rhythm, even in those with heart failure. Asymptomatic patients, therefore, can be managed with rate control, with a resting heart rate goal of less than 110/min, as long as left ventricular ejection fraction is over 40%. Agents that can control heart rate include β-blockers, nondihydropyridine calcium channel blockers, and digoxin. It may be reasonable to perform an exercise test or ambulatory monitoring to assess whether rate control medications are working appropriately.

In patients with symptoms despite adequate rate control, a rhythm control strategy should be considered. This involves use of antiarrhythmic agents and cardioversion if necessary. The choice of antiarrhythmic agent is determined by comorbidities and risk of adverse effects. Patients receiving rhythm control remain at risk for systemic embolism because episodic atrial fibrillation may still occur; therefore, regardless of whether a rate control or a rhythm control strategy is pursued, anticoagulation should be given based on the $CHADS_2$ score.

Another strategy for patients with symptomatic paroxysmal atrial fibrillation is a "pill-in-the-pocket" approach with flecainide or propafenone, as long as there is no sinus or AV node dysfunction, bundle branch block, structural heart disease, or long QT syndrome. Patients should take a short-acting β-blocker or calcium channel blocker 30 minutes before taking the antiarrhythmic agent or use background rate control therapy. Because of concern of a postconversion pause, patients should be monitored the first time a "pill-in-the-pocket" antiarrhythmic agent is used.

Nonpharmacologic Strategies

Atrial fibrillation ablation is an option in patients who are symptomatic and have been treated unsuccessfully with at least one antiarrhythmic agent. The procedure entails electrical isolation of the pulmonary veins so that premature atrial contractions, which frequently originate in the pulmonary veins, cannot initiate atrial fibrillation. In all patients, warfarin should be continued for 2 to 3 months after an atrial fibrillation ablation. Thereafter, anticoagulation should be guided by the $CHADS_2$ score. Although the procedure has a success rate of up to 84%, it must sometimes be repeated, and complications, including stroke, atrial-esophageal fistula, pulmonary vein stenosis, cardiac tamponade, and death, may occur in up to 4.5% of patients.

In those who are not candidates for an atrial fibrillation ablation and have tachycardia despite medical therapy, AV node ablation is an option. A pacemaker is inserted at the time of ablation so the ventricular rate is controlled by the device. AV node ablation carries a small risk for polymorphic VT afterward, which can be reduced by increasing the paced heart rate for a few months after the procedure.

Another option is maze surgery, which is usually performed concurrent with open cardiac surgery. The procedure involves several incisions or ablations in the right and left atria to interrupt potential reentrant pathways required for atrial fibrillation maintenance.

KEY POINTS

- Patients with atrial fibrillation with hypotension, angina, or acute heart failure should undergo emergent direct-current cardioversion.

- Following cardioversion for atrial fibrillation, patients must receive 4 weeks of anticoagulation with warfarin, with a goal INR of 2.0 to 3.0.

Atrial Flutter

Typical atrial flutter is a macro-reentrant circuit in the right atrium that usually loops at 250 to 350/min. The ECG pattern for typical flutter has negative sawtooth flutter waves in the inferior leads and a positive flutter wave in lead V_1 (**Figure 22**). Atypical atrial flutter may also occur, usually revolving around a scar in the atria in a patient with a history of cardiac surgery, previous atrial fibrillation ablation, or congenital heart disease. Atypical atrial flutter appears differently on ECG compared with typical atrial flutter, but management is similar.

Atrial flutter is conducted through the AV node at a multiple of the atrial rate and can also conduct with grouped

beating. Occasionally, 1:1 conduction of atrial flutter with a very rapid ventricular rate occurs, especially if the flutter rate is slow (200-250/min).

Atrial flutter is managed similarly to atrial fibrillation, including appropriate thromboprophylaxis. Rate or rhythm control is acceptable. The threshold for recommending ablation for atrial flutter is lower than for atrial fibrillation, because the success rate is higher and complication risk is lower. Typical flutter ablation is completed by ablating in the isthmus between the inferior vena cava and the tricuspid valve.

Supraventricular Tachycardias

SVTs are rapid heart rhythms that require atrial tissue or the AV node for initiation and maintenance. The QRS complex is usually narrow, but may be wide if there is a bundle branch block or there is conduction down a bypass pathway. Although atrial fibrillation and atrial flutter are technically SVTs, the term generally describes the most frequent paroxysmal SVTs: AV nodal reentrant tachycardia (AVNRT), AV reciprocating tachycardia (AVRT), and atrial tachycardia. Paroxysmal SVT occurs in 0.2% to 0.8% of the population, usually in those with no structural heart disease.

Clinical Presentation

Patients with SVT present with palpitations, presyncope or syncope, dyspnea, chest pain, or fatigue. Elevated atrial

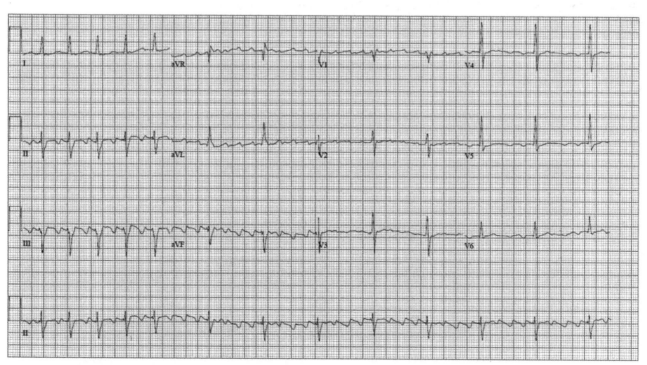

FIGURE 22. In this electrocardiogram demonstrating typical atrial flutter, negative sawtooth waves are seen in the inferior leads and positive waves are seen in lead V_1. In the bottom rhythm strip, 2:1 and 4:1 conduction patterns are seen.

pressure and release of atrial natriuretic peptide may cause polyuria. Patients with AVNRT may describe neck pounding or have visible neck pulsations, caused by atrial contraction against a closed tricuspid valve.

SVTs can be categorized on the basis of the P wave relationship to the preceding QRS complex. If the P wave is closer to the preceding QRS complex, it is called a *short-RP tachycardia*. If the P wave is closer to the following QRS complex, it is a *long-RP tachycardia*. Short-RP tachycardias include AVNRT, AVRT, and junctional tachycardia. Long-RP tachycardias include atrial tachycardia, sinus tachycardia, atypical AVNRT, and the permanent form of junctional reciprocating tachycardia.

Patients can sometimes terminate SVT on their own using the Valsalva maneuver, carotid sinus massage, or facial dunking into ice water. Adenosine can be used to diagnose and treat SVT. By transiently blocking AV nodal conduction, adenosine interrupts the reentrant circuit and usually terminates AVNRT and AVRT. In other supraventricular arrhythmias (such as atrial fibrillation, sinus tachycardia, and atrial tachycardia), adenosine may slow the ventricular rate and demonstrate clear P waves.

Atrioventricular Nodal Reentrant Tachycardia

The most common paroxysmal SVT is AVNRT, which involves a slow and a fast pathway within the AV node (**Figure 23**). The slow pathway conducts slowly but repolarizes quickly, whereas the fast pathway conducts quickly but repolarizes slowly.

Typical AVNRT (slow-fast) often has an RP interval so short that the P wave is buried within the QRS complex, but it may be seen as a pseudo R' in lead V$_1$ and a pseudo S wave in the inferior leads. This is because conduction during AVNRT goes down the slow pathway but quickly up the fast pathway. Atypical AVNRT occurs when the signal goes down the fast pathway and up the slow pathway (fast-slow AVNRT) or travels through two slow pathways (slow-slow AVNRT).

AVNRT can be treated with vagal maneuvers, adenosine, β-blockers, nondihydropyridine calcium channel blockers, antiarrhythmic agents, or cardioversion. If medical therapy is not successful or the patient does not desire it, catheter ablation has a high success rate.

Atrioventricular Reciprocating Tachycardia

AVRT is a reentrant circuit that includes a bypass pathway and the AV node. The bypass pathways are accessory connections (Kent bundles) between the atrium and ventricle. If a bypass pathway conducts antegrade, a preexcitation pattern may be seen on the ECG. This includes a short PR interval (because the bypass pathway conducts rapidly and faster than the AV node) and a delta wave, which is a slurred initial segment of the QRS complex resulting from slow conduction through ventricular tissue instead of the His-Purkinje system. Left-sided bypass pathways, which are farther away from the sinus

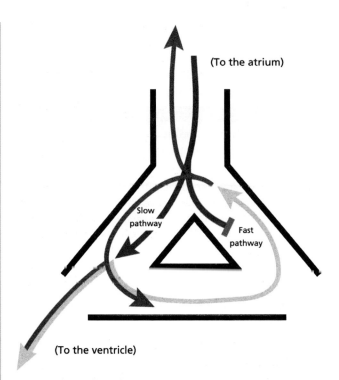

FIGURE 23. Mechanism of typical atrioventricular nodal reentrant tachycardia. The slow pathway has a short refractory period and the fast pathway has a long refractory period. The *blue line* represents antegrade conduction down the slow pathway; conduction does not occur down the fast pathway because it is refractory. The *yellow line* represents impulse conduction into the ventricle and retrograde up the fast pathway, which is no longer refractory. The *red line* represents completion of the circuit with activation of the atria and ventricles.

node, may not show as much preexcitation because the AV node can conduct earlier than the bypass pathway.

In AVRT, the signal usually travels down the AV node and up the bypass pathway, resulting in a narrow QRS complex on ECG (orthodromic conduction; about 90%-95% of patients); the signal may also conduct down the bypass tract and up the AV node, resulting in a wide QRS complex (antidromic conduction; about 5%-10% of patients).

A preexcitation pattern on the ECG is known as the Wolff-Parkinson-White (WPW) pattern; when this pattern is accompanied by a symptomatic tachycardia, it is termed WPW syndrome. Many bypass pathways only conduct retrograde, and delta waves are not seen on ECG. About one third of patients with a WPW pattern develop atrial fibrillation. If atrial fibrillation conducts rapidly down the bypass pathway, it can degenerate into VF. Risk factors for VF in patients with WPW syndrome include a history of AVRT, a rapidly conducting bypass pathway, multiple bypass pathways, and Ebstein anomaly.

The management of an asymptomatic patient with a WPW pattern on ECG is under debate. If a bypass pathway disappears during rest or on a treadmill, risk for sudden death is thought to be low, and no further evaluation or treatment is needed. For persons in high-risk professions (airplane pilot, school bus driver), an electrophysiology study should be completed to assess how fast the bypass pathway can conduct, with ablation if the pathway is high risk.

In patients with symptoms and preexcitation, especially if there is a history of rapid atrial fibrillation, catheter ablation should be performed as first-line therapy. In addition to curing AVRT, ablation reduces the risk of future atrial fibrillation. If the patient does not want an ablation, antiarrhythmic agents should be used. AV nodal blocking medications should not be given to patients with preexcitation. If the patient develops atrial fibrillation and is taking an AV nodal blocker, conduction will preferentially occur down the bypass pathway and increase the ventricular rate. Procainamide and amiodarone will slow conduction down the bypass pathway acutely and are the preferred agents.

In patients with AVRT in the absence of preexcitation on an ECG, depending on symptom severity, catheter ablation, β-blockers or antiarrhythmic agents are acceptable. Calcium channel blockers are thought to be less effective.

Premature Atrial Contractions and Atrial Tachycardia

PACs are single early atrial beats often found on continuous ambulatory ECG monitoring. If PACs are symptomatic, they can be treated with β-blockers or calcium channel blockers, but usually only reassurance is needed.

Atrial tachycardia is caused by an ectopic focus or area of micro-reentry that fires faster than the sinus rate. It can be treated with β-blockers, calcium channel blockers, digoxin, or antiarrhythmic agents. Catheter ablation is an option, although the success rate is lower than for AVNRT or AVRT.

Multifocal atrial tachycardia is an irregular tachycardia that demonstrates three or more P waves of different morphologies and is usually associated with underlying pulmonary disease. Treatment usually centers on treating the pulmonary disease, electrolyte repletion, and, occasionally, β-blockers or calcium channel blockers.

KEY POINT

- Atrioventricular nodal blockers are contraindicated in patients with Wolff-Parkinson-White syndrome and atrial fibrillation as they may increase conduction down the accessory pathway.

Ventricular Arrhythmias

Premature Ventricular Contractions

PVCs occur in up to 75% of healthy persons. Persons usually report a sensation of skipped or extra strong beats because of the compensatory pause after the PVC. In the absence of structural heart disease, a family history of early sudden cardiac death (SCD), or syncope, reassurance is all that is needed. Very frequent PVCs carry a risk of developing a cardiomyopathy that may be reversible with treatment. PVCs are more common in persons with hypertension, left ventricular hypertrophy, heart failure, and myocardial ischemia or infarction.

If the patient is very symptomatic, treatment should begin with a β-blocker or calcium channel blocker. Antiarrhythmic agents may rarely be required. Catheter ablation is an option for patients in whom medical therapy has failed.

Ventricular Tachycardia with Structural Heart Disease

VT is a rhythm greater than 100/min that originates in the ventricles. It is sustained when it lasts for more than 30 seconds or produces hemodynamic collapse. In persons with structural heart disease, such as from previous myocardial infarction or cardiomyopathy, VT is usually regular and monomorphic, traversing small pathways of viable myocardium within areas of scar. In patients with low ejection fraction and rapid tachycardia, hypotension and syncope may progress to sudden cardiac arrest. Patients with near-normal cardiac function or with a slow VT may have only minimal symptoms, such as palpitations, dizziness, chest pain, or dyspnea. Patients with structural heart disease who develop VT are at an increased risk of SCD. Prevention begins with β-blockers, which have been shown to reduce mortality and SCD in those with heart failure and ischemic heart disease.

In patients with a history of VF, hemodynamically unstable VT, or stable VT with structural heart disease, implantable cardioverter-defibrillators (ICDs) have been shown to improve survival. Antiarrhythmic agents are beneficial in the prevention of ICD shocks but have not been shown to reduce mortality. In patients with heart failure, amiodarone has the best efficacy. Sotalol can be used in those intolerant of amiodarone, but because of its greater β-blocking properties, may precipitate heart failure decompensation.

An electrophysiology study can be useful in patients with syncope, dizziness, or palpitations if the diagnosis of VT is in question. If a patient has a history of recurrent VT, catheter ablation can be performed to reduce ICD shocks, although this does not affect mortality.

Idiopathic Ventricular Tachycardia

Idiopathic VT, which occurs in normal hearts, carries a much better prognosis than VT with structural heart disease. Patients report palpitations; syncope is unusual. The rhythm often occurs in salvos and can be provoked by exercise or emotional stress. It occurs more frequently in women than in men and usually between the ages of 20 and 40 years. Idiopathic VT is monomorphic and usually originates from the right ventricular outflow tract. The ECG demonstrates runs of VT with a left bundle branch block pattern that is positive in the inferior leads (**Figure 24**). The main differential diagnosis is arrhythmogenic right ventricular cardiomyopathy/dysplasia (ARVC/D).

A baseline ECG should be obtained in all patients to examine for evidence of previous infarction, T-wave inversions,

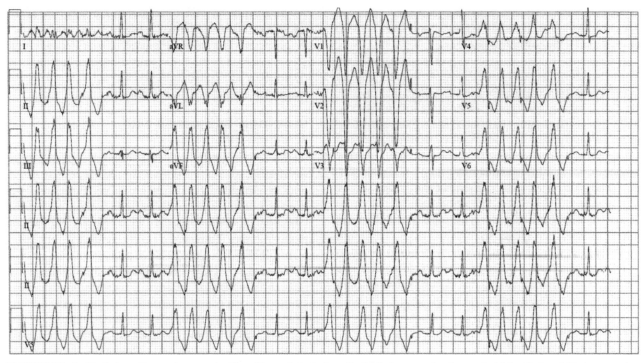

FIGURE 24. In this electrocardiogram demonstrating idiopathic ventricular tachycardia, the rhythm occurs in salvos, and a left bundle branch block pattern that is positive in the inferior leads is seen.

or epsilon waves suggestive of ARVC/D. Continuous ambulatory ECG monitoring demonstrates a wide-complex tachycardia. The rhythm should be documented on a 12-lead ECG if possible, and a treadmill test should be completed to attempt to provoke the tachycardia. The treadmill test also can evaluate for ischemia, which is most beneficial in those with intermediate risk factors for coronary disease. Echocardiography should be performed to look for structural heart disease.

In patients with mild symptoms, no treatment is necessary. If symptoms are frequent or severe, calcium channel blockers or β-blockers should be started. If these are ineffective, class I or III antiarrhythmic agents can be used, or, alternatively, catheter ablation, which has a high rate of success, can be performed. An ICD is not indicated for idiopathic VT because of the benign prognosis and efficacy of other therapies.

> **KEY POINT**
> - Patients with highly symptomatic premature ventricular contractions can be treated with β-blockers or calcium channel blockers; catheter ablation is an option if symptoms are refractory to medication.

Inherited Arrhythmia Syndromes

Recent advances in genetic diagnoses have led to a greater understanding of the molecular origin of cardiovascular disease. This has been especially true in the case of channelopathies, conditions in which no morphologic abnormalities are obvious but the risk for SCD is increased. Characteristics of inherited arrhythmia syndromes are summarized in **Table 26**.

Long QT syndrome is the most common channelopathy and is thought to affect 1 in 5000 persons. Patients usually have syncope related to polymorphic VT. Most of the mutations identified as causing long QT syndrome are in genes that affect ion channels. Depending on the specific channel affected, various triggers can precipitate cardiac arrest, including exercise, sudden loud noises, or sleep. Factors conferring the highest risk for SCD include a history of sudden cardiac arrest, recent syncope, and QTc interval greater than 500 msec.

β-Blockers are the mainstay of therapy in long QT syndrome. Drugs that can prolong the QT interval, such as haloperidol, sotalol, and erythromycin, must be avoided, and Web sites such as www.qtdrugs.org list drugs that can prolong the QT interval. ICDs are reasonable for patients with a history of sudden cardiac arrest or those who have syncope or VT while taking β-blockers and can also be considered for those with a strong family history of SCD.

Drug-induced QT prolongation may develop in the absence of a genetic channelopathy, and these patients can be at risk for torsades de pointes when exposed to QT-prolonging medications. This is seen more frequently in the hospital

TABLE 26. Inherited Arrhythmia Syndromes

Disease	Characteristic Findings	Treatment
Long QT syndrome	Syncope, QTc interval usually >460 msec, torsades de pointes	β-Blockers, ICD
Short QT syndrome	Syncope, QTc interval usually <350 msec, atrial fibrillation, VT, VF	ICD
Brugada syndrome	Syncope, VF, coved ST-segment elevation in leads V_1-V_3	ICD
Catecholaminergic polymorphic VT	Syncope, polymorphic or bidirectional VT during exercise or emotional stress	β-Blockers, ICD
ARVC/D	Syncope, T-wave inversions from lead V_1 to at least V_3, monomorphic VT, epsilon waves, abnormal signal-averaged electrocardiogram, frequent PVCs, abnormal right ventricular size and function on echo/CMR imaging	ICD, β-blockers, sotalol, amiodarone

ARVC/D = arrhythmogenic right ventricular cardiomyopathy/dysplasia; ICD = implantable cardioverter-defibrillator; CMR = cardiovascular magnetic resonance; PVC = premature ventricular contractions; QTc = corrected QT interval; VF = ventricular fibrillation; VT = ventricular tachycardia.

setting, in which patients may receive several QT-prolonging drugs simultaneously.

Short QT syndrome is less common than long QT syndrome. The QTc interval is often below 350 msec. Patients can develop atrial fibrillation, syncope, polymorphic VT, and VF. Quinidine may be an effective therapy by prolonging the QT interval. Because of the high risk of SCD, patients with short QT syndrome should be offered an ICD.

Brugada syndrome is a pattern of 2 mm or greater J-point elevation, coved ST-segment elevation, and T-wave inversions in leads V_1 to V_3 with an increased risk of syncope, VF, and sudden cardiac arrest (**Figure 25**). ECG findings can be intermittent; infusion with a sodium channel blocker can sometimes elicit the pattern. Those with spontaneous ECG findings are at a higher risk for cardiac events. There is debate regarding the best management of patients with the Brugada

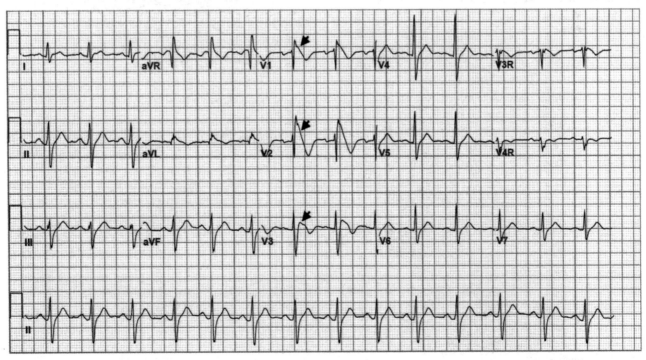

FIGURE 25. In this electrocardiogram demonstrating a type 1 Brugada pattern, ≥2 mm J-point elevation, coved ST-segment elevation (*arrowheads*), and T-wave inversions are seen in leads V_1 to V_3.

pattern in the absence of symptoms, as the pattern may be elicited in some patients by fever, hypo- and hyperkalemia, tricyclic antidepressants, and cocaine and alcohol use. Medical therapy is limited, although recent data suggest quinidine may be effective. An ICD should be implanted in patients at high risk.

Catecholaminergic polymorphic VT usually affects patients younger than 20 years. It is characterized by VT during times of high adrenergic tone, carrying a high risk of SCD. The ECG is normal at baseline, but demonstrates polymorphic VT or bidirectional VT during exercise or emotional stress, with the QRS complex alternating between two morphologies on every other beat. Exercise should be avoided in these patients. β-Blockers should be used to reduce syncopal events and the risk of SCD. An ICD is usually implanted if β-blockers are not effective.

ARVC/D is characterized by fibrofatty infiltration of the right ventricle resulting from dysfunction of the desmosome. The disease is often heralded by syncope or sudden cardiac arrest caused by VT originating from the right ventricle. As the disease progresses, right ventricular dysfunction and, eventually, left ventricular dysfunction can occur. ECG demonstrates T-wave inversions from lead V_1 until at least V_3 and may show an epsilon wave, which is a high-frequency signal at the end of the QRS complex. Continuous ambulatory ECG monitoring shows VT or more than 500 PVCs in a 24-hour period. Signal-averaged ECG may demonstrate abnormal late potentials, and echocardiogram can demonstrate enlarged right ventricular size and dysfunction. Cardiovascular magnetic resonance (CMR) imaging can better image the right ventricle, and should be performed if ARVC/D is suspected. If the diagnosis is in doubt, right ventricular biopsy shows a reduction in myocyte number with fibrotic replacement. Because of the high risk of VT and accelerated progression of disease, patients are strongly discouraged from exercise and, if risk factors such as previous sudden cardiac arrest, syncope, family history of sudden cardiac arrest, sustained VT, or extensive right ventricular or any left ventricular involvement are present, an ICD is indicated. There is no medical therapy to delay progression of the disease. β-Blockers, sotalol, amiodarone, and catheter ablation can be used to reduce ICD shocks.

A large subset of patients have idiopathic VF, with no identifiable cause. Some of these patients have evidence of inferolateral early repolarization on ECG. This ECG pattern is a common benign finding, especially in young men, and no further evaluation or treatment is needed in the absence of symptoms. In those with a history of VF of unknown cause, an ICD should be implanted. Limited studies have suggested class IA antiarrhythmic agents and β-blockers can be used to reduce ICD shocks.

Sudden Cardiac Arrest

Epidemiology

Sudden cardiac arrest is the abrupt absence of coordinated cardiac activity; progression to death (SCD) is imminent without rapid treatment. Sudden cardiac arrest affects approximately 300,000 to 450,000 persons in the United States annually. The predominant mechanism is ventricular tachyarrhythmias. Most patients with sudden cardiac arrest have a history of coronary disease, but other cardiomyopathies, coronary artery spasm, congenital heart disease, and myocarditis are also risk factors. Conditions associated with sudden cardiac arrest include older age, family history of SCD, male sex or postmenopausal women, obesity, hypertension, hyperlipidemia, diabetes, cigarette smoking, and inherited arrhythmia syndromes.

Acute Management

If a person sustains a cardiac arrest, emergency medical services should be activated immediately and cardiopulmonary resuscitation (CPR) administered. In the most recent guidelines for advanced cardiac life support, the mnemonic for the initial management of cardiac arrest has been changed from ABC (Airway, Breathing, Circulation) to CAB, for Chest compressions, Airway, and Breathing, to emphasize the importance of early chest compressions. Thirty chest compressions should be given, followed by two rescue breaths, for five cycles. Chest compressions must be of adequate depth (>2.0 in [5.1 cm]) and should allow sufficient time for chest recoil, with a rate of about 100/min. It is imperative that any breaks in chest compression be of short duration. After an endotracheal tube has been placed, quantitative waveform capnography should be used to confirm placement, and one breath should be delivered every 6 to 8 seconds.

CPR should be administered for 2 minutes before a rhythm check is completed. If the rhythm is shockable, defibrillation should occur. After a shock is given, CPR should be continued for five cycles before reassessing rhythm, even if the ECG suggests sinus rhythm. If the rhythm is still VT or VF, another shock may be given and CPR continued. Epinephrine should be given every 3 to 5 minutes, but the first or second dose may be replaced with vasopressin. After the third shock, amiodarone may be given. The process of repeating shocks with CPR is then continued.

If the rhythm is asystole or pulseless electrical activity, shocks are not indicated and CPR and epinephrine should be used. Atropine is no longer recommended.

"Hands-only CPR" is now advocated by the American Heart Association for untrained rescuers providing CPR. In hands-only CPR, compressions are delivered without ventilations. The impetus is to enhance the amount of time compressions are given and to prevent excessive positive pressure ventilation. In addition, because many people are unwilling to perform mouth-to-mouth breathing, compression-only CPR increases bystander involvement.

If the presenting rhythm is symptomatic bradycardia, atropine should be given first. If this is ineffective, dopamine and epinephrine can be given until transcutaneous or transvenous pacing is initiated.

For comatose patients surviving cardiac arrest, therapeutic hypothermia of 32.0 °C to 34.0 °C (89.6 °F–93.2 °F) for 12 to 24 hours should be started as soon as possible (achieved with cooled intravenous fluids and cooling blankets). Appropriate sedation and neuromuscular blockade may be needed to prevent shivering. Electrolytes, glucose, volume status, and risk for bleeding should be monitored during cooling.

Device Therapy for Prevention of Sudden Death

The ICD has dramatically changed management of ventricular arrhythmias. ICDs are indicated for use in those who have suffered a hemodynamically significant or sustained (>30 sec) ventricular tachyarrhythmic event (secondary prevention) and in those who are at high risk for SCD (primary prevention; see Heart Failure).

Surgical electrocautery may generate electromagnetic interference sensed by an ICD as VT or VF. When a patient undergoes a procedure using electrocautery, the ICD shock function must be turned off. If a magnet is placed over an ICD, it turns off shock therapy but does not affect the pacing capabilities.

Biventricular pacemakers, which can improve mortality and symptoms in certain patients with heart failure, can also be incorporated into ICDs.

> **KEY POINT**
> - In the most recent guidelines for advanced cardiac life support, the sequence for cardiopulmonary resuscitation is CAB, for Chest compressions, Airway, and Breathing, to emphasize the importance of early chest compressions with only a short delay to the first ventilation.

Device Infection

Infections of cardiac devices (including ICDs and pacemakers) may present with localized pocket erosion or abscess, a vegetation on a lead, or an unexplained bloodstream infection. It is important to not attempt aspiration of the device site because this can damage the leads.

If cardiac device infection is suspected, blood cultures should be obtained and transthoracic echocardiography performed. If blood cultures are positive, transesophageal echocardiography should be completed to examine the leads and cardiac valves. When a device is infected, the best way to treat the infection is with extraction of the entire system, including the leads, followed by antibiotic therapy. The decision when to reimplant a device is guided by whether the patient still has indications for the device and the risk of reinfection.

> **KEY POINTS**
> - If a cardiac device infection is suspected, it is important not to attempt aspiration of the device site.
> - The optimal treatment of an infected cardiac device is to extract the entire system, including the leads, followed by antibiotic therapy.

Pericardial Disease

Pericarditis

Clinical Presentation

Acute Pericarditis

Viral infection is the most common known cause of acute pericarditis, but there are many others (**Table 27**). Chest pain is the most frequent symptom, accounting for 5% of emergency department evaluations of patients with chest pain unrelated to an acute coronary syndrome. Diagnosis is most often made by confirming two of three classic findings: chest pain, often with a pleuritic component; friction rub; and diffuse ST-segment elevation on electrocardiography (ECG). If pericardial effusion is evident on echocardiography and unexplained, only one of these findings is necessary. Pericardial effusion is present in 60% of patients with pericarditis, but absence of effusion does not exclude pericarditis.

The chest pain of pericarditis is sharp and severe, and acute pericarditis must be distinguished from other potentially life-threatening illnesses, such as myocardial infarction (MI), pulmonary embolism, or aortic dissection (**Table 28, Table 29**). Acute pericarditis may follow MI in early (1-3 days) or delayed (>1 week to several months) forms. Acute pericarditis after acute MI may contribute to ECG changes (ST-segment elevation and/or T-wave inversions) and to postinfarction pain. A unique feature of chest pain in acute pericarditis is that it may worsen in the recumbent position, which helps to rule out other causes of pain.

A pericardial friction rub is virtually pathognomonic of acute pericarditis. It is best auscultated at the left lower sternal border during suspended respiration while the patient is leaning forward. The classic rub has three components and can be squeaky, scratchy, or swooshing. It is often transient. A single-component rub may be confused with a murmur and is not diagnostic. In acute pericarditis, epicardial inflammation causes upwardly concave ST-segment elevation in all leads except aVR (**Figure 26, page 64**). An ST-segment

(Text continued on page 65)

TABLE 27. Causes of Acute Pericarditis and Pericardial Effusion

Cause	Comments
Idiopathic	
Presumed viral or autoimmune etiology in most cases	40% of all cases with conventional diagnostic tests
	5% of all cases with specialized pericardial fluid testing (tumor marker analysis, polymerase chain reaction, immunochemistry)
Infection	
Viruses: coxsackievirus A and B, echovirus, adenovirus, HIV, hepatitis B virus, others	20% of all cases
	Cultures and titers low yield
	HIV test indicated in patients at risk and those with tuberculous pericarditis
Bacteria: *Staphylococcus, Streptococcus, Haemophilus*, pneumococcus, others	7% of all cases
	Suspect in cases of bacteremia, pneumonia, endocarditis
	Pericardial drainage is essential
Mycobacterium tuberculosis	Infrequent in developed countries
	Treatment effective, but poor outcome if diagnosis missed
	Consider diagnosis in all cases
Fungi: *Histoplasma, Aspergillus, Candida*	Occurs primarily in immunocompromised patients
	Pericardial drainage is essential
Autoimmune	
Rheumatic diseases: SLE, rheumatoid arthritis, scleroderma	20% to 40% of patients with SLE will have acute pericarditis during their lifetime
Nonrheumatic diseases: Ulcerative colitis, giant cell arteritis, polyarteritis nodosa	
Radiation	
Thoracic irradiation	Modern methods of shielding the heart have lowered frequency from 25% to 2%
	Occurs on average 5 months after irradiation
Myocardial Infarction–Related	
AMI	Occurs within 1-3 days of AMI, presumably due to inflammation mediated from healing myocardium
	AMI typically ST-elevation type (transmural)
	Less frequent after thrombolytics or PCI
	Friction rub is evanescent, lasting for ≤3 days after AMI
Postmyocardial infarction: Dressler syndrome	Occurs several weeks to months after AMI; not necessarily transmural
	Mediated by autoimmune mechanism; associated with signs of systemic inflammation (fever, polyserositis)
	Now infrequently occurs, presumably as a consequence of revascularization treatment leading to smaller AMI and less release of immunologic stimulants
Neoplasm	
Lung, breast, lymphoma, leukemia	7% of all cases
	15%-25% of moderate or large pericardial effusions
	History of malignancy, large effusion, or inadequate response to anti-inflammatory agents raises suspicion of malignancy
Cardiac Injury	
Blunt and penetrating chest trauma	May develop cardiac tamponade
	Usually associated with cardiac contusion; uncomplicated cases of traumatic pericarditis usually resolve
Postpericardiotomy	Occurs >7 days after cardiac surgery
	Tamponade may occur
Iatrogenic	Catheter-based cardiac perforation

(Continued on the next page)

TABLE 27. Causes of Acute Pericarditis and Pericardial Effusion *(continued)*

Cause	Comments
Medications	
Antiarrhythmic agents	Procainamide, amiodarone (rare)
Antihypertensive agents	Hydralazine
Antibiotics	Penicillin
Chemotherapeutic agents	Doxorubicin, daunorubicin
Metabolic Disorders	
Uremia	6% of all cases
Aortic Disease	
Thoracic aortic dissection: leakage or rupture into pericardial space	Pericardial effusion present in 17%-48% of patients Causes cardiac tamponade Life-threatening emergency requiring surgery
Thoracic aortic penetrating ulcer	Rare
Newly Recognized Causes	
Radiofrequency catheter ablation of atrial fibrillation	Pericardial effusions common Occurs in absence of perforation Tamponade uncommon but occurs
Takotsubo cardiomyopathy	Pericarditis may occur in recovery phase of takotsubo (case reports) Alternatively, viral pericarditis may cause takotsubo cardiomyopathy

AMI = acute myocardial infarction; PCI = percutaneous coronary intervention; SLE = systemic lupus erythematosus.

TABLE 28. Differentiation of Chest Pain Caused by Acute Pericarditis, Myocardial Ischemia, Acute Pulmonary Embolism, and Aortic Dissection

Characteristics of Chest Pain	Acute Pericarditis	Myocardial Ischemia	Pulmonary Embolism	Aortic Dissection
Quality	Sharp, pleuritic	Pressure, heaviness, tightness, constricting	Sharp, stabbing, pleuritic	Ripping, tearing
Location	Left precordial or retrosternal	Retrosternal	Precordial	Retrosternal
Radiation pattern	Left trapezius ridge	Neck, jaw, arm(s), shoulder(s)	Variable	Upper back
Duration/pattern	Hours or days; persistent	Stable angina: 1-15 min Unstable angina: >20 min; may wax and wane Myocardial infarction: Hours; may wax and wane	Hours or days	Hours; persistent
Relation to exercise	Unrelated	Stable angina: Related Unstable angina or myocardial infarction: Unrelated	Unrelated	May be precipitated by isometric exercise
Relation to position	Relieved by leaning forward Aggravated by assuming a recumbent position	Unrelated	Unrelated	Unrelated

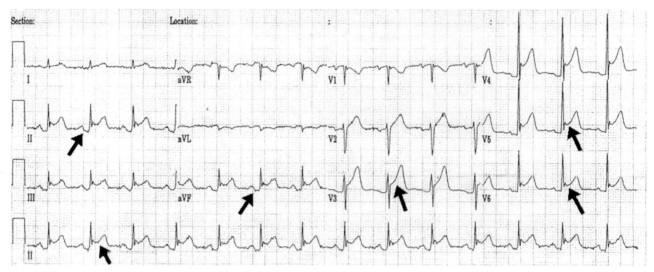

FIGURE 26. 12-Lead electrocardiogram demonstrating acute pericarditis shows diffuse upwardly concave ST-segment elevation (*leftward arrows*) and PR-segment depression (*rightward arrows*) indicative of acute pericarditis.

TABLE 29. Differentiation of Electrocardiographic and Echocardiographic Findings of Acute Pericarditis, Myocardial Ischemia, Acute Pulmonary Embolus, and Aortic Dissection

Test Component	Acute Pericarditis	Myocardial Ischemia	Pulmonary Embolism	Aortic Dissection
ECG Component				
ST segment	ECG changes accompany onset of chest pain: ST-segment elevation is upwardly concave and diffuse (occurs in all leads except aVR and V_1); ST- segment elevation seen within hours to days.	ST-segment elevation is downwardly concave and localized; or ST-segment depression; ST- segment elevation seen within minutes to hours.	ST-segment elevation in leads III and/or aVF (not specific for pulmonary embolism)	None if uncomplicated; findings of myocardial ischemia if dissection occludes coronary artery
T wave	T waves invert after ST-segment elevation resolves and are not associated with loss of R-wave voltage or Q waves (occurs several days after onset of chest pain); may eventually normalize or remain persistently inverted.	T waves invert while ST-segment elevation is present; may be associated with loss of R-wave voltage or appearance of Q waves.	T waves invert while ST-segments elevated in leads II, aVF, V_1 to V_4 (not specific for pulmonary embolism)	
PR segment	PR-segment depression present in 80% of patients (may occur in any of the limb or precordial leads except aVR) and accompanies initial ST-segment elevation. Reciprocal PR-segment elevation may occur in aVR. PR-segment deviations are very specific, but not sensitive findings.	PR-segment depression rarely present. Atrial ischemia is a cause.		
Q wave	Q waves absent	Q waves may be present	Q waves in lead III and/or aVF (not specific for pulmonary embolism)	
Echocardiography				
Findings	No LV regional wall motion abnormality; pericardial effusion may be present	LV regional wall motion abnormality in distribution of coronary artery	May show RV enlargement and pressure overload if the embolism is significant	No LV wall motion abnormality; dissection flap may be visible, especially on TEE

ECG = electrocardiography; LV = left ventricular; RV = right ventricular; TEE = transesophageal echocardiography.

CONT.

elevation–to–T-wave amplitude ratio of 0.24 or greater in lead V_6 is reliable in distinguishing pericarditis from early repolarization, a common and benign condition. PR-segment depression in the limb leads (particularly lead II) or precordial leads, and elevation in lead aVR, may accompany ST-segment elevation. PR-segment shifts are highly specific but not sensitive findings.

The clinical course of viral and idiopathic acute pericarditis is generally good and most patients recover; a subset develop tamponade or recurrent or constrictive pericarditis.

Myopericarditis

Acute pericarditis often coexists with mild myocarditis. When clinical findings confirm myocardial injury unrelated to MI, myopericarditis is diagnosed, occurring in 15% of patients with pericarditis. The ECG in myopericarditis shows regional concave downward ST-segment elevation akin to MI (**Figure 27**), new segmental or global left ventricular dysfunction, and elevated cardiac markers. Most patients with myopericarditis do well unless substantial myocardial involvement and heart failure are present. Sequelae are similar to those of pericarditis.

Recurrent Pericarditis

Recurrent pericarditis, which is likely autoimmune, is characterized by recurring bouts of acute pericarditis over 2 to 5 years, rarely as long as 15 years. It develops in up to 30% of patients with acute pericarditis. Features that confer a high risk of recurrent pericarditis include failure of an acute episode to respond to aspirin or NSAIDs and previous treatment of acute pericarditis with corticosteroids. Diagnosis is made by recurrent chest pain and one of the following: fever, friction rub, characteristic ECG changes, pericardial effusion, or an elevated inflammatory marker.

KEY POINTS

- The absence of a pericardial effusion on echocardiogram does not rule out acute pericarditis.
- Lack of response in acute pericarditis to NSAIDs and treatment of the initial episode of acute pericarditis with corticosteroids increase the likelihood of recurrence.

Evaluation

In acute pericarditis and myopericarditis, physical examination should include assessment for cardiac tamponade and heart failure. Echocardiography is an essential adjunct to physical examination. In acute pericarditis, serial ECG to monitor evolution of ST-segment and T-wave changes aids in differentiation from MI (see Table 29) but may be less helpful in myopericarditis. Chest radiography has limited diagnostic utility but helps to exclude other causes of pleuritic chest pain. Inflammatory markers are elevated; normal results of these tests should raise doubt about the diagnosis. Cardiac markers are elevated in myopericarditis.

Additional tests are appropriate when specific etiologies of pericarditis are suspected, such as uremia, bacterial infection, autoimmune disease, HIV, and tuberculosis. Generally, viral titers have low diagnostic yield and are not indicated in most patients. Chest CT and cardiovascular magnetic resonance (CMR) imaging are useful to evaluate the pericardium, such as when malignancy is suspected.

Management

Treatment directed at the specific etiology of pericarditis should be provided. If myopericarditis is suspected on the basis of left ventricular dysfunction or elevated cardiac markers, patients should be hospitalized. The goals of treating

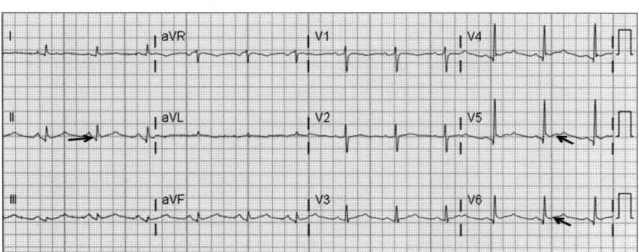

FIGURE 27. 12-Lead electrocardiogram demonstrating acute myopericarditis shows downwardly concave ST-segment elevation (*leftward arrows*) and PR-segment depression (*rightward arrow*).

acute pericarditis or myopericarditis are pain relief as well as prevention of recurrence, tamponade, and constrictive pericarditis. Outpatient treatment is safe and feasible in adult patients with small pericardial effusions (<1 cm) uncomplicated by myocarditis, pyogenic infection, sepsis, tamponade, recent trauma, suspicion of malignancy, coagulopathy, or hemodynamic instability. If outpatient treatment fails, hospitalization may be required.

Anti-inflammatory medications are the primary treatment for acute pericarditis, with the goal of relieving chest pain, fever, and inflammation. Aspirin or NSAIDs should be initiated at high doses and then tapered weekly over a span of 3 to 4 weeks (**Table 30**). A concurrent proton pump inhibitor should be considered for gastric protection. In acute pericarditis due to MI, NSAIDs should be used with caution as these agents impair fibrosis formation and may promote ventricular rupture after infarction. Aspirin is the medication of choice in this setting. Chest pain from acute pericarditis usually responds within 24 hours of starting anti-inflammatory medications. In refractory cases, colchicine should be added. Nonrandomized and nonblinded studies support the use of colchicine as an alternative first-line agent or as an adjunctive treatment for acute pericarditis. The COPE trial, a prospective, randomized, nonblinded study, supports colchicine as an adjunctive agent to conventional treatment of acute pericarditis; recurrence rate at 18 months was decreased from 32% without colchicine to 10.7% with 3 months of colchicine.

In the absence of a specific indication for their use, corticosteroids should only be used in refractory cases of acute pericarditis or in patients with contraindications to aspirin, NSAIDs, and colchicine. Corticosteroids increase risk for recurrent pericarditis and are contraindicated in pyogenic etiologies.

Anticoagulation is permissible to treat acute MI in patients who develop acute pericarditis, provided pericardial effusion does not develop or, if previously present, does not increase in size.

For recurrent pericarditis, studies support colchicine with aspirin or NSAID as the treatment of choice to reduce recurrences and the need for corticosteroids (**Table 31**). Although generally safe, colchicine often causes gastrointestinal side effects and rarely bone marrow suppression. It should be used with caution in patients with chronic kidney injury. The multicenter CORP trial demonstrated that colchicine as an adjunct to conventional therapy for recurrent pericarditis is safe and effective. Idiopathic cases of recurrent pericarditis do not warrant etiologic evaluation with each recurrence if specific causes are not suspected. Pericardiectomy is not effective for acute pericarditis or recurrent pericarditis.

TABLE 30. Pharmacologic Treatment of Acute Pericarditis

Treatment Phase	First-line Agents		Alternative or Added to First-line Agent	Third-line Agent (for refractory cases)
	Aspirin	**NSAID**	**Colchicine**	**Corticosteroid**[a]
Initiation	650 mg every 4-6 h	Ibuprofen 400-800 mg every 6-8 h	Body weight <70 kg: 0.6 mg every 12 h (use for 1 day only if combined with aspirin or NSAID) Body weight ≥70 kg: 0.6 mg every 8 h (use for 1 day only if combined with aspirin or NSAID)	Prednisone 60 mg/d until improved
Taper	↓650-975 mg weekly until off	After 2 weeks, begin taper to maintenance dose	NA	↓5 mg every 3 days until 20-mg/d dose reached
Maintenance	NA	Variable: 200 to 300 mg three times daily	Body weight <70 kg: 0.6 mg/d Body weight ≥70 kg: 0.6 mg twice daily	Taper slowly after reaching 20-mg/d dose
Duration	3-4 weeks	3-4 weeks	3 months	Months

NA = not applicable.

[a]Contraindicated in acute myocardial infarction. Preferred in systemic inflammatory diseases or uremia.

Recommendations based on: Maisch B, Seferovic PM, Ristic AD, et al; Task Force on the Diagnosis and Management of Pericardial Disease of the European Society of Cardiology. Guidelines on the diagnosis and management of pericardial diseases executive summary: the Task Force on the Diagnosis and Management of Pericardial Diseases of the European Society of Cardiology. Eur Heart J. 2004;25(7):587-610. [PMID: 15120056] *and* Spodick DH. Acute pericarditis: current concepts and practice. JAMA. 2003;289(9):1150-1153. [PMID: 12622586] *and* Imazio M, Bobbio M, Cecchi E, et al. Colchicine in addition to conventional therapy for acute pericarditis: results of the COlchicine for acute PEricarditis (COPE) trial. Circulation. 2005;112(13):2012-2016. [PMID: 16186437]

- Anti-inflammatory drugs are the primary treatment for acute pericarditis.
- Corticosteroids should be used only in refractory cases of acute pericarditis or in patients with contraindications to aspirin, NSAIDs, and colchicine.

Pericardial Effusion Without Cardiac Compression

Clinical Presentation and Evaluation

Pericardial effusion is caused by many of the same entities that cause pericarditis (see Table 27); it is also associated with hypothyroidism. If intrapericardial pressure is not increased and pericarditis is absent, patients are typically asymptomatic. If an effusion is large, nonspecific findings of muffled heart sounds and dullness percussible beyond the apex may be evident. ECG is nonspecific, but QRS voltage may be reduced compared with previous tracings or electrical alternans may be present with a large effusion. Echocardiography is diagnostic (**Figure 28**); it is helpful in determining the hemodynamic significance of the effusion and in following resolution or accumulation. CT and CMR imaging may identify a pericardial effusion but should not be used for diagnosis unless a

more detailed investigation of the anatomy is necessary (suspected pericardial malignancy or constriction).

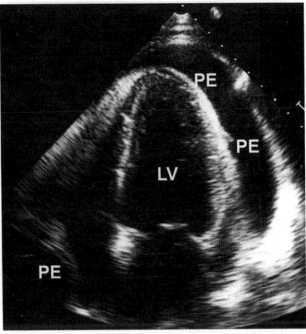

FIGURE 28. Two-dimensional echocardiographic image demonstrates a large circumferential pericardial effusion (*PE*) surrounding the left ventricle (*LV*).

TABLE 31. Pharmacologic Treatment of Recurrent Pericarditis

Treatment Phase	First-line Agents			Corticosteroid (second-line agent for refractory cases)
	Colchicine (+ aspirin or NSAID)	Aspirin added to colchicine	NSAID added to colchicine	
Initiation	Body weight <70 kg: 0.6 mg every 12 h Body weight ≥70 kg: 0.6 mg every 8 h	812 mg every 8 h for 7-10 days	Ibuprofen 600 mg every 6-8 h for 7-10 days	Prednisone 1-1.5 mg/kg daily for 1 month
Taper	NA	Gradual tapering over 3-4 weeks	NA	Taper over 3 months; for recurrent symptoms during taper, return to previous dose for 2-3 weeks and then resume taper
Maintenance	Body weight <70 kg: 0.6 mg/d Body weight ≥70 kg: 0.6 mg twice daily	NA	400 mg three to four times daily over 3-4 weeks	Add aspirin, NSAID, or azathioprine near end of taper and continue this agent for additional 3 months
Duration	6 months	4-5 weeks	4-5 weeks	≥4 months

NA = not applicable.

Recommendations based on: Maisch B, Seferovic PM, Ristic AD, et al; Task Force on the Diagnosis and Management of Pericardial Diseases of the European Society of Cardiology. Guidelines on the diagnosis and management of pericardial disease executive summary: the Task Force on the Diagnosis and Management of Pericardial Diseases of the European Society of Cardiology. Eur Heart J. 2004;25(7):587-610. [PMID: 15120056] and Imazio M, Bobbio M, Cecchi E, et al. Colchicine as first-choice therapy for recurrent pericarditis: results of the CORE (COlchicine for REcurrent pericarditis) trial. Arch Intern Med. 2005;165(17):1987-1991. [PMID: 16186468] and Artom G, Koren-Morag N, Spodick DH, et al. Pretreatment with corticosteroids attenuates the efficacy of colchicine in preventing recurrent pericarditis: a multi-centre all-case analysis. Eur Heart J. 2005;26(7):723-727. [PMID: 15755753] and Imazio M, Brucato A, Cemin R, et al. Colchicine for Recurrrent Pericarditis (CORP): a randomized trial. Ann Intern Med. 2011;155:409-414. [PMID: 21873705]

If clinical assessment fails to reveal an obvious cause, it is unlikely that extensive laboratory tests will yield a diagnosis. In this circumstance, it is reasonable to perform a complete blood count, electrolyte panel, and tests for blood urea nitrogen and serum creatinine, thyroid-stimulating hormone, antinuclear antibodies, and tuberculin skin response. Pericardiocentesis aids in diagnosing serious causes of pericardial effusion, such as bacterial infection, malignancy, and tuberculosis; accordingly, pericardial fluid should be sent for culture, cytology, and adenosine deaminase activity. Tests of the pericardial fluid for cell counts, lactate dehydrogenase, total protein, and glucose are rarely helpful. Diagnostic yield is enhanced by surgical pericardial biopsy to assess for malignancy and systemic inflammatory disease, but nondiagnostic results are common.

Management

In stable patients, no specific therapy is needed for chronic idiopathic pericardial effusion. Occult hypothyroidism should be excluded. Echocardiography is useful to monitor for regression or progression of the effusion and for signs of increasing intrapericardial pressure as a harbinger of cardiac tamponade. In patients with idiopathic pericardial effusion that has not resolved by 3 months, pericardiocentesis should be performed. In these patients, pericardiocentesis may be curative as well as diagnostic. Pericardial biopsy should be considered to increase diagnostic yield whenever malignancy or tuberculosis is suspected. Hemopericardium is a worrisome complication of pericardiocentesis, and anticoagulants should be avoided in the postprocedure time period.

Drainage of an infected pericardial effusion is essential. Intravenous antibiotic therapy is initially empiric but is later guided by organism identification. Malignant pericardial effusions are likely to reaccumulate, and a variety of therapies may be needed to prevent this, such as prolonged catheter drainage, pericardial sclerosis, surgical decompression, and percutaneous balloon pericardiotomy. Life expectancy is typically short in patients with a malignant pericardial effusion.

KEY POINT

- In patients with an idiopathic pericardial effusion that has not resolved by 3 months, pericardiocentesis should be performed.

Cardiac Tamponade

Clinical Presentation and Evaluation

Cardiac tamponade is caused by an increase in intrapericardial pressure from accumulation of pericardial fluid. Clinically, it is characterized by dyspnea, tachycardia, jugular venous distention, hemodynamic instability, and hypotension. The heart chambers are extrinsically compressed, preventing filling and reducing venous return, stroke volume, and cardiac output. The rapidity of fluid accumulation, rather than the absolute size of an effusion, is the major determinant of clinical tamponade. Tamponade is typically caused by circumferential effusions, but loculated effusion also can cause focal tamponade and may be difficult to diagnose. Tamponade usually presents acutely and must be urgently differentiated from other life-threatening conditions (MI or pulmonary embolism). It sometimes presents subacutely, when fluid accumulates slowly, allowing time for the pericardium to stretch. Occasionally, tamponade occurs with near-normal pericardial pressure if intracavitary pressures are low from severe hypovolemia, so-called low-pressure tamponade. In such cases, jugular venous distention may be absent.

Pulsus paradoxus supports a diagnosis of tamponade but is not pathognomonic or always present. For example, it may be caused by respiratory distress, and it may be absent if tamponade coexists with atrial septal defect, pulmonary hypertension, or significant aortic regurgitation.

Echocardiography is diagnostic. Echocardiographic findings that indicate an elevated intrapericardial pressure and support a diagnosis of tamponade include diastolic invagination ("collapse") of the right atrial or ventricular wall, accentuated respiratory fluctuations in peak transvalvular velocities, and distended inferior vena cava.

Management

In early or subacute tamponade, hemodynamic compromise may be mild. In such circumstances, conservative therapy may be undertaken with serial hemodynamic monitoring and echocardiography, volume resuscitation, and treatment of cause. Patients with hypotension require prompt and aggressive treatment, beginning with volume resuscitation and vasopressors for immediate stabilization. If ventricular function is impaired, inotropic support or an intra-aortic balloon pump may be needed. Pericardiocentesis or surgery is performed to drain the effusion. Surgical drainage is preferred for malignant effusions to slow reaccumulation. In tamponade caused by an aortic dissection that ruptures into the pericardial space, the dissection is essentially being contained by the tamponade; pericardiocentesis would exacerbate the condition, and surgical drainage is therefore preferable.

In patients with tamponade and respiratory distress, mechanical ventilation and deep sedation may potentiate hemodynamic compromise and should be avoided whenever possible. Mechanical ventilation with high positive end-expiratory pressure reduces venous return, and deep sedation reduces compensatory sympathetic drive, further lowering blood pressure. Cardiac tamponade may cause pulseless electrical activity; prompt pericardiocentesis is indicated. **H**

KEY POINTS

- Jugular venous distention is present in many patients with cardiac tamponade, but may be absent in those with severe hypovolemia.

- If drainage of an effusion is needed to treat cardiac tamponade, surgical drainage rather than pericardiocentesis should be performed for patients with a malignant effusion and for those with aortic dissection.

Constrictive Pericarditis

Clinical Presentation and Evaluation

Constrictive pericarditis is a rare but disabling condition characterized by impaired filling resulting from restraint of ventricular diastolic expansion by a stiff pericardium. Patients present with dyspnea, fatigue, and peripheral edema. Atrial fibrillation is present in 20% of patients. Examination may show jugular venous distention with Kussmaul sign (jugular vein engorgement with inspiration), pericardial knock, hepatomegaly, and ascites. Pulmonary congestion is absent. Any cause of pericarditis can lead to the condition; common causes in the United States are viruses, cardiac surgery, mediastinal irradiation, and connective tissue disease. Effusive-constrictive pericarditis is a hybrid disease with features of both tamponade and constriction. This disorder is often unmasked when drainage of the pericardial effusion does not result in decrease in right-sided pressures as the constriction becomes manifest.

It is important to distinguish constrictive pericarditis from restrictive cardiomyopathy (**Table 32**) because surgical pericardiectomy may be curative in constrictive pericarditis. Transthoracic echocardiography is most useful in the differentiation, but other modalities (transesophageal echocardiography, CMR imaging, CT, catheterization) are complementary (**Figure 29**). An occult form of constrictive pericarditis has been described, in which patients present with nonspecific chest pain, dyspnea, and fatigue, but have unremarkable examination and catheterization findings at rest. A saline bolus during right heart catheterization may unmask hemodynamic characteristics consistent with constriction.

TABLE 32. Differentiation of Constrictive Pericarditis from Restrictive Cardiomyopathy

Findings	Constrictive Pericarditis	Restrictive Cardiomyopathy
Physical Examination		
Point of maximal impulse	Not detectable	Often detectable
Electrocardiography		
Presence of left or right bundle branch block	Not supportive	Supportive
Presence of left or right ventricular hypertrophy	Not supportive	Supportive
Chest Radiography		
Pericardial calcification	May be present	Absent
Echocardiography		
Presence of left ventricular hypertrophy	Absent	Present
Reduced tissue Doppler velocities	Absent	Present
Accentuated drop in peak left ventricular filling during inspiration	Present	Absent
To-and-fro diastolic motion of ventricular septum	Present	Absent
CMR Imaging/CT		
Increased pericardial thickness	Present in 80%	Absent
Hemodynamic Right and Left Heart Catheterization		
Elevated and equalized diastolic left and right ventricular pressures (within 5 mm Hg)	Present	Absent
Left and right ventricular systolic pressure changes with respiratory cycle	Discordant	Concordant
Laboratory Testing		
B-type natriuretic peptide	Normal or minimally elevated[a]	Markedly elevated

CMR = cardiovascular magnetic resonance.

[a]Applies to idiopathic constrictive pericarditis, but not constrictive pericarditis due to cardiac surgery or previous thoracic irradiation. In the latter etiologies, B-type natriuretic peptide is more often significantly elevated and, when present, does not allow constrictive pericarditis to be excluded in favor of a diagnosis of restrictive cardiomyopathy.

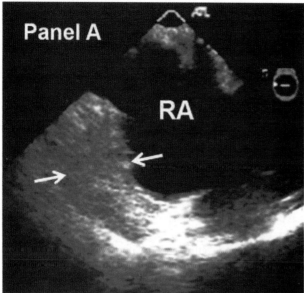

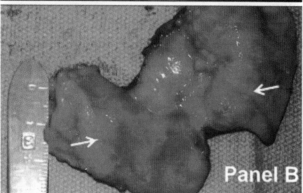

FIGURE 29. Constrictive pericarditis. Panel A shows a transesophageal echocardiogram of thickening pericardium (*arrows*) surrounding the right atrium (*RA*) in a patient with radiation-induced constrictive pericarditis. Panel B shows the operative confirmation of thickened pericardium (*arrows*) that surrounded the right atrium.

Management

Judicious use of loop diuretics is important in patients with constrictive pericarditis to reduce dyspnea and edema, but because higher filling pressures are needed to maintain stroke volume, overly aggressive diuresis can reduce cardiac output, causing dizziness and orthostatic hypotension. Rate response in atrial fibrillation should be controlled with conventional medications, but bradycardia should be avoided because a compensatory increase in heart rate is expected.

A transient form of constrictive pericarditis occurs and may resolve spontaneously or after anti-inflammatory therapy, typically within 6 months. Causes include viral infection, connective tissue disease, trauma, malignancy, and pericardiotomy. In stable patients, a 2- to 3-month trial of anti-inflammatory therapy is warranted before proceeding to surgical pericardiectomy. Constrictive pericarditis from tuberculosis resolves within 6 months in most patients treated with antituberculosis drugs.

Pericardiectomy is the only effective treatment for chronic constrictive pericarditis. It is indicated in patients with chronic constrictive pericarditis with New York Heart Association (NYHA) functional class II or III heart failure. Pericardiectomy does not always lead to immediate improvement and may require several months. In relatively asymptomatic patients, surgery should be postponed. In end-stage disease (NYHA class IV), the benefit of surgery is marginal and operative mortality is 6% to 19%; surgery should not be pursued in most patients.

KEY POINT

- Pericardiectomy is the only effective treatment for chronic constrictive pericarditis and is indicated in patients with New York Heart Association functional class II or III heart failure.

Valvular Heart Disease

Pathophysiology of Valvular Heart Disease

Abnormal function of the cardiac valves can be categorized as stenotic, regurgitant, or combined lesions. Stenotic lesions result in pressure overload of the cardiac chamber (atrium or ventricle) proximal to the diseased valve, whereas regurgitant lesions result in volume overload of both chambers proximal and distal to the valve (for example, mitral regurgitation results in volume overload of the left atrium and left ventricle).

Ventricular remodeling in response to loading conditions of pure stenotic or regurgitant lesions leads to the major clinical sequelae of these conditions. In stenotic, semilunar, or outflow valve conditions (such as aortic stenosis), increased afterload to the left ventricle results in *concentric* left ventricular hypertrophy. This pattern of hypertrophy is adaptive to the increased wall stress of the left ventricle and helps maintain normal systolic function of the left ventricle. However, as severity of stenosis and left ventricular remodeling progresses, abnormal diastolic function typically occurs (before systolic dysfunction), resulting in increased left ventricular filling pressures and symptoms of angina and dyspnea.

In contrast, pure regurgitant lesions (such as mitral valve regurgitation) cause volume overload to the left ventricle. The left ventricular remodeling pattern involves *eccentric* hypertrophy, a compensatory mechanism that maintains ventricular compliance (allowing increased left ventricular volume without increased left ventricular filling pressure). With progression of regurgitation and left ventricular dilation, left ventricular contractility or systolic function is impaired. Patients with mixed stenotic and regurgitant lesions (for example, combined aortic stenosis and regurgitation) may develop concentric and eccentric hypertrophy, with the dominant lesion determining left ventricular remodeling, clinical presentation, and management. The clinical presentation of these valve lesions is discussed later.

These compensatory, hypertrophic changes to the left ventricle occur gradually, with a progressive increase in ventricular loading. The gradual and progressive nature of degenerative or functional valve lesions means that these lesions may not be associated with symptoms, even in the setting of severe valve dysfunction. These compensatory changes are not present in acute valvular (regurgitant) lesions and as a result, acute left-sided valvular regurgitation causes sudden volume overload in the left ventricle with limited compliance. Cardiac chamber size is generally preserved, with normal or hyperdynamic systolic function, but diastolic filling pressure is increased and heart failure, pulmonary edema, respiratory failure, and hypotension may ensue. Patients are symptomatic and often hemodynamically unstable.

Diagnostic Evaluation

History and Physical Examination

The most common symptom associated with severe valve regurgitation or stenosis is dyspnea with exertion, but symptom onset may be subtle and slowly progress with insidious curtailment of activities. A careful history to evaluate current functional status compared with recent levels may elicit this slow progression. Right-sided valve lesions more commonly are associated with systemic venous congestion, resulting in lower extremity edema, abdominal distention, or ascites. These symptoms may also occur when left-sided valve lesions cause either left ventricular systolic dysfunction or pulmonary hypertension. Aortic valve lesions, either stenosis or regurgitation, may also be associated with exertional symptoms of angina (due to reduced coronary flow reserve through the hypertrophied myocardium, causing subendocardial ischemia) or pre-syncope or syncope (due to reduced cardiac output reserve). Mitral valve stenosis and regurgitation are both strongly associated with a higher incidence of atrial fibrillation, causing palpitations, fatigue, and acute onset of dyspnea. Other symptoms of heart failure, specifically orthopnea and paroxysmal nocturnal dyspnea, are not commonly present in valvular heart lesions unless left ventricular systolic dysfunction is present. During conditions associated with increased left ventricular preload or cardiac output (sepsis, anemia, pregnancy) or tachycardia (such as atrial fibrillation), symptoms may develop acutely to a severe degree in patients with previously asymptomatic severe valve regurgitation or stenosis.

The heart murmur is the hallmark of valvular dysfunction on physical examination. Murmurs should be described based on characteristics of intensity, duration, location, radiation, timing in the cardiac cycle, and response to bedside maneuvers, such as changes in position, Valsalva maneuver, and isometric handgrip maneuver.

Maneuvers such as standing from a seated or squatting position or the Valsalva maneuver acutely reduce cardiac preload; these maneuvers may be useful when mitral valve prolapse is suspected; if prolapse is present, these maneuvers shorten the duration between S_1 and the mitral valve click, with an earlier initiation and longer duration of the systolic murmur. Maneuvers that reduce preload can also help to differentiate dynamic left ventricular outflow obstruction from fixed valvular or subvalvular stenosis; if stenosis is fixed, these maneuvers result in decreased intensity of the systolic murmur.

Isometric handgrip maneuver results in an acute increase in arterial afterload, which increases left ventricular systolic pressure and, thus, the intensity of a mitral regurgitation murmur.

Additional findings that may help identify the specific valve lesion and its effect on ventricular function include an enlarged or displaced apical impulse, abnormal peripheral pulses, and timing and intensity of heart sounds (including extra heart sounds such as an S_3 or S_4 or a systolic ejection click). The common valve lesions and heart murmurs are described in **Table 33**.

Laboratory and Imaging Tests

Transthoracic echocardiography is the primary test for diagnosis and assessment of valvular disease severity as well as for identification of coexistent lesions, diagnosis of pulmonary hypertension, and assessment of ventricular size and function. The appropriateness of this test is guided by history and physical examination, and is indicated in symptomatic patients, in those with a systolic murmur grade 3/6 intensity or greater, and in those with any continuous murmur (a murmur that begins after S_1 and extends beyond S_2) or diastolic murmur (**Figure 30**). Transesophageal echocardiography is recommended in some patients with valve disease, including those with severe mitral valve disease, prosthetic valves, and infective endocarditis, or in patients in whom transthoracic imaging is not informative.

For stenotic lesions, Doppler-derived velocities across the affected valve allow calculation of pressure gradients across the valve and the valve area and are the strongest predictors of clinical outcome (**Table 34, page 74**). For regurgitant lesions, the assessment of severity includes color Doppler jet size, the width of the narrowest segment of the regurgitant jet (vena contracta), and jet signal strength. Quantitative measurements of the size of the regurgitant orifice (regurgitant orifice area) and volume of regurgitant flow (regurgitant volume), although technically more demanding to acquire, are increasingly routinely reported and are strongly associated with prognosis (**Figure 31, page 75**). As a result, the 2006 American College of Cardiology/American Heart Association (ACC/AHA) valvular heart disease guidelines now emphasize quantitative measures in reporting regurgitation severity.

(Text continued on page 74)

TABLE 33. Valvular and Other Cardiac Lesions and Their Associated Examination Findings

Cardiac Condition	Characteristic Murmur	Location	Radiation	Associated Findings	Severity and Pitfalls
Aortic stenosis	Mid-systolic; crescendo-decrescendo	RUSB	Right clavicular, carotid, apex	Enlarged, nondisplaced apical impulse; S_4; bicuspid valve without calcification will have systolic ejection click followed by murmur	Severe aortic stenosis may include decreased A_2; high-pitched, late peaking murmur; diminished and delayed carotid upstroke Radiation of murmur down the descending thoracic aorta may mimic mitral regurgitation
Aortic regurgitation	Diastolic; decrescendo	LLSB (valvar) or RLSB (dilated aorta)	None	Enlarged, displaced apical impulse; S_3 or S_4; increased pulse pressure; bounding carotid and peripheral pulse	Acute, severe regurgitation murmur may be masked by tachycardia, short duration of murmur Severity in chronic regurgitation is difficult to assess by murmur
Mitral stenosis	Diastolic; low pitched, decrescendo	Apex (heard best in left lateral decubitus position)	None	Opening snap after S_2 if leaflets mobile; irregular pulse if atrial fibrillation present	Interval between S_2 and opening snap is short in severe mitral stenosis Intensity of murmur correlates with transvalvar gradient P_2 may be loud if pulmonary hypertension present
Mitral regurgitation	Systolic; holo- or late systolic	Apex	To axilla or back; occasionally anteriorly to precordium	Systolic click in mitral valve prolapse; S_3; apical impulse hyperdynamic and may be displaced if dilated left ventricle; in mitral valve prolapse, Valsalva maneuver moves onset of murmur closer to S_1; handgrip increases murmur intensity	Acute, severe regurgitation may have soft or no holosystolic murmur, mitral inflow rumble, S_3
Tricuspid stenosis	Diastolic; low pitched, decrescendo; increased intensity during inspiration	LLSB	Nonradiating	Elevated central venous pressure with prominent *a* wave, signs of venous congestion (hepatomegaly, ascites, edema)	Low-pitched frequency may be difficult to auscultate, especially at higher heart rate
Tricuspid regurgitation	Holosystolic	LLSB	LUSB	Merged and prominent *c* and *v* waves in jugular venous pulse; murmur increases during inspiration	Right ventricular impulse below sternum Pulsatile, enlarged liver with possible ascites May be higher pitched if associated with severe pulmonary hypertension
Pulmonary stenosis	Systolic; crescendo-decrescendo	LUSB	Left clavicle	Pulmonic ejection click after S_1 (diminishes with inspiration)	Increased intensity of murmur with late peaking
Pulmonary regurgitation	Diastolic; decrescendo	LLSB	None	Loud P_2 if pulmonary hypertension present	Murmur may be minimal or absent if severe due to minimal difference in pulmonary artery and right ventricular diastolic pressures

(Continued on the next page)

TABLE 33. Valvular and Other Cardiac Lesions and Their Associated Examination Findings *(continued)*

Cardiac Condition	Characteristic Murmur	Location	Radiation	Associated Findings	Severity and Pitfalls
Innocent flow murmur	Midsystolic; grade 1/6 or 2/6 in intensity	RUSB	None	Normal intensity of A₂; no radiation to left clavicle	May be present in conditions with increased flow (e.g., pregnancy, fever, anemia, hyperthyroidism)
Hypertrophic obstructive cardiomyopathy	Systolic; crescendo-decrescendo	LLSB	None	Enlarged, hyperdynamic apical impulse; bifid carotid impulse with delay; increased intensity during Valsalva maneuver or with squatting to standing	Harsh murmur with increased intensity; murmur may not be present in nonobstructive hypertrophic cardiomyopathy
Atrial septal defect	Systolic; crescendo-decrescendo	RUSB	None	Fixed, split S₂; right ventricular heave; rarely, tricuspid inflow murmur	May be associated with pulmonary hypertension, including increased intensity of P₂ heart sound, pulmonary valve regurgitation
Ventricular septal defect	Holosystolic	LLSB	None	Palpable thrill; murmur increases with hand-grip, decreases with amyl nitrite	Murmur intensity and duration decrease as pulmonary hypertension develops (Eisenmenger syndrome)
					Cyanosis if Eisenmenger syndrome develops

A₂ = aortic valve component of S₂; LLSB = left lower sternal border; LUSB = left upper sternal border; P₂ = pulmonic valve component of S₂; RLSB = right lower sternal border; RUSB = right upper sternal border.

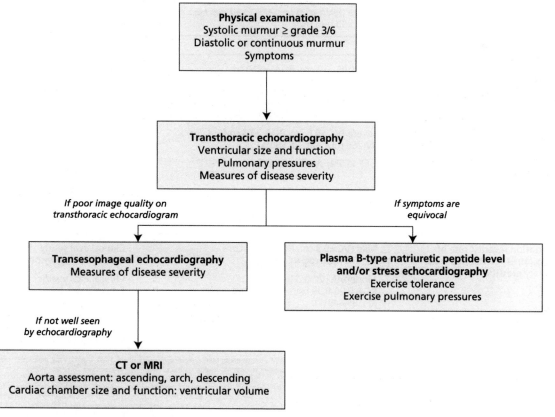

FIGURE 30. Diagnostic evaluation of valvular heart disease.

After the initial diagnosis of a valve lesion and assessment of its severity, clinical follow-up of the patient is recommended every 6 to 12 months (more frequently when the lesion is severe). Repeat echocardiography may be indicated at intervals dependent on the specific lesion and its severity. Mild, asymptomatic valvular disease may be followed clinically with close monitoring of patients for symptoms and may not require routine periodic echocardiography. In left-sided, severe regurgitant lesions (aortic or mitral regurgitation), more frequent assessment (every 6 months) is recommended to monitor for the possible development of asymptomatic left ventricular systolic dysfunction.

Electrocardiography may be performed to evaluate for adverse effects of valvular lesions, such as left ventricular hypertrophy, ischemia, or atrial fibrillation, but is insensitive for evaluation of ventricular function.

The B-type natriuretic peptide (BNP) level has been associated with the presence and severity of symptoms

TABLE 34. Serial Evaluation of Asymptomatic Patients with Left-Sided Valvular Conditions		
Factors Considered	**Lesion Severity**	**Frequency**
Aortic Stenosis		
Stenosis severity; rate of progression	Mild (mean gradient <25 mm Hg, V_{max} <3 m/s, AVA >1.5 cm^2)	Clinical eval yearly Echo every 3-5 y
	Moderate (mean gradient 25-40 mm Hg, V_{max} 3-4 m/s, AVA 1.0-1.5 cm^2)	Clinical eval yearly Echo every 1-2 y
	Severe (mean gradient >40 mm Hg, V_{max} >4 m/s, AVA <1.0 cm^2)	Clinical eval yearly Echo yearly
Mitral Stenosis		
Stenosis severity; rate of progression	Mild (MVA >1.5 cm^2, MPG <5 mm Hg, PASP <30 mm Hg)	Clinical eval yearly Echo every 3-5 y
	Moderate (MVA 1.0-1.5 cm^2, MPG 5-10 mm Hg, PASP 30-50 mm Hg)	Clinical eval yearly Echo every 1-2 y
	Severe (MVA <1.0 cm^2, MPG >10 mm Hg, PASP >50 mm Hg)	Clinical eval yearly Echo yearly
Aortic Regurgitation		
Regurgitation severity; rate of progression; EF; LV chamber size; ascending aorta dilation	Mild (VC <0.3 cm, ROA <0.10 cm^2, RV <30 mL/beat); normal EF	Clinical eval yearly Echo every 2-3 y
	Moderate (VC 0.3-0.6 cm, ROA 0.10-0.29 cm^2, RV 30-59 mL/beat, RF 30%-49%)	Clinical eval yearly Echo every 1-2 y
	Severe (VC >0.6 cm, ROA ≥0.3 cm^2, RV ≥60 mL/beat, RF >50%)	
	EF >50%; LV size normal	Clinical eval every 6-12 mo Echo yearly
	EF >50%; LV size increased	Clinical eval every 6 mo Echo every 6-12 mo
Mitral Regurgitation		
Regurgitation severity; rate of progression; EF; LV chamber size; pulmonary pressure	Mild (VC <0.3 cm, ROA <0.20 cm^2, RV <30 mL/beat; RF <30%)	Clinical eval yearly Echo only if symptomatic
	Moderate (VC 0.3-0.69 cm, ROA 0.20-0.39 cm^2, RV 30-59 mL/beat, RF 30%-49%)	Clinical eval yearly Echo every 1-2 y
	Severe (VC ≥0.7 cm, ROA ≥0.4 cm^2, RV ≥60 mL/beat, RF >50%)	Clinical eval every 6-12 mo Echo every 6-12 mo

AVA = aortic valve area; echo = echocardiography; EF = ejection fraction; eval = evaluation; LV = left ventricle; MPG = mean pressure gradient; MVA = mitral valve area; PASP = pulmonary artery systolic pressure, RF = regurgitant fraction; ROA = regurgitant orifice area; RV = regurgitant volume; VC = vena contracta width; V_{max} = maximum aortic jet velocity.

Recommendations based on American College of Cardiology/American Heart Association Task Force on Practice Guidelines; Society of Cardiovascular Anesthesiologists; Society for Cardiovascular Angiography and Interventions; Society of Thoracic Surgeons, Bonow RO, Carabello BA, Kanu C, et al. ACC/AHA 2006 guidelines for the management of patients with valvular heart disease: a report of the American College of Cardiology/American Heart Association Task Force on Practice Guidelines (writing committee to revise the 1998 Guidelines for the Management of Patients With Valvular Heart Disease): developed in collaboration with the Society of Cardiovascular Anesthesiologists: endorsed by the Society for Cardiovascular Angiography and Interventions and the Society of Thoracic Surgeons. Circulation. 2006;114(5):e84-e231. [PMID: 16880336]

(dyspnea) in various heart conditions, including aortic stenosis and mitral regurgitation, and has been found to have adverse prognostic implications if elevated. However, this test is not routinely indicated for patients with valvular disease, as a positive test is unlikely to change patient management. The BNP is most useful when it is negative in a patient with atypical symptoms, suggesting a noncardiac etiology. There is no role for serial BNP measurements in patients with valvular heart disease.

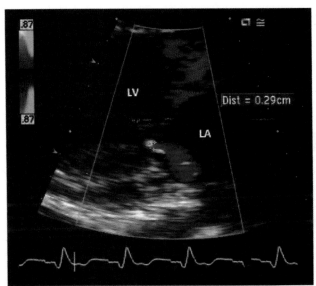

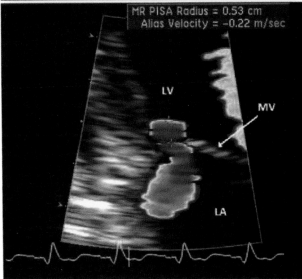

FIGURE 31. Quantitative measurement of valvular regurgitation. In the *top panel*, color Doppler echocardiography of the mitral valve shows the narrowest segment of the regurgitant jet (the vena contracta). In this image, the vena contracta is measured at 0.29 cm, consistent with mild mitral regurgitation. In the *bottom panel*, measurement of the acceleration of blood flow on the ventricular side of the valve (the proximal isovelocity surface area, or PISA) is shown. Using these two measurements, the regurgitant orifice area (ROA) may be calculated. LA = left atrium; LV = left ventricle; MV = mitral valve.

Exercise testing may provide additional prognostic information, such as exercise capacity and blood pressure response. Cardiac catheterization is not recommended for primary evaluation of valvular disease except in patients with discrepant determination of severity. Preoperative assessment for significant coronary artery disease in patients with atherosclerotic risk factors is indicated to determine whether concurrent bypass grafting is needed at the time of surgery.

> **KEY POINTS**
>
> - The most common symptom associated with severe valve regurgitation is dyspnea with exertion, but symptom onset may be subtle and slowly progress with insidious curtailment of activities.
> - Transthoracic echocardiography is indicated for diagnosis and assessment of valvular disease in symptomatic patients, in those with a systolic murmur grade 3/6 intensity or greater, and in those with any continuous murmur or diastolic murmur.

General Principles of Management of Valvular Disease

The timing of intervention for valvular heart disease is primarily based on the presence of cardiopulmonary symptoms attributable to the lesion or evidence of adverse hemodynamic consequences, particularly ventricular dilation or systolic dysfunction (**Table 35**). In the setting of severe valvular disease, the onset of symptoms or the development of ventricular systolic dysfunction generally portends a poor prognosis without definitive intervention. Cardiopulmonary symptoms in a patient with a valve lesion of mild or moderate degree should prompt evaluation for other superimposed or primary disease processes.

Even in severe valvular disease, compensatory mechanisms over time may provide several years before symptoms or ventricular dysfunction develops. In the absence of symptoms, known exertional arrhythmia, or severe valve stenosis, patients with valvular heart disease can usually participate in competitive sports. Most asymptomatic patients with significant valvular disease who need noncardiac surgery can be managed conservatively by a team experienced in the care of patients with valvular heart disease with careful intraoperative attention to perioperative hemodynamics and fluid status.

When symptoms develop, intervention is indicated regardless of preserved ventricular systolic function because of a significantly increased risk of adverse outcomes after symptom onset. Although medical therapy to reduce pulmonary congestion, treat arrhythmia, and improve hemodynamics may improve symptoms for a short duration, no medical interventions have been shown to improve the long-term natural history of these progressive conditions, and adverse events, including irreversible left ventricular dysfunction, pulmonary hypertension, or death, may occur.

Surgical valve repair or replacement, indicated in severe valve dysfunction with symptoms or abnormal ventricular function, is the only definitive intervention for valvular heart disease. In patients with mitral or congenital pulmonic valve stenosis with favorable valve morphology, balloon valvotomy may be performed with excellent initial and long-term results, but restenosis of rheumatic mitral stenosis may occur. Surgical treatment of valvular disease in the absence of these adverse effects should be reserved for patients with rapid progression of valvular dysfunction or those undergoing other cardiac surgery with an acceptable operative risk. After valve surgery, patients require routine evaluation of the prosthetic or repaired valve function over time.

Acute valvular regurgitation is a medical emergency, regardless of the cause. Afterload reduction and inotropic medications may initially help stabilize the patient by increasing forward flow but do not usually supplant the need for urgent surgical intervention before refractory cardiogenic shock ensues.

KEY POINTS

- The timing of intervention for valvular heart disease is primarily based on the presence of cardiopulmonary symptoms attributable to the lesion or evidence of adverse hemodynamic consequences, particularly ventricular dilation or systolic dysfunction.
- Surgical valve repair or replacement, indicated in severe valve dysfunction with symptoms or abnormal ventricular function, is the only definitive intervention for valvular heart disease as medical therapy alone does not prolong survival.

TABLE 35. Indications for Interventions for Valvular Heart Conditions

Valve Lesion	Indications to Intervene	Intervention
Aortic stenosis	Symptoms	Aortic valve replacement
	LVEF <50%	
	Moderate stenosis at time of other cardiac surgery	
	Abnormal blood pressure response (decrease in systolic blood pressure) during exercise	
	Rapidly progressive stenosis	
Aortic regurgitation	Symptoms	Aortic valve replacement with ascending aorta graft replacement if enlarged
	LVEF <50%	
	LV dilatation (end-systolic dimension >55 mm or end-diastolic dimension >75 mm)	
Mitral stenosis	Symptoms	Percutaneous balloon valvotomy (if anatomy favorable by echocardiography with less than moderate mitral regurgitation and no left atrial thrombus)[a]
	Pulmonary hypertension (PA systolic pressure ≥50 mm Hg at rest or ≥60 mm Hg during exercise)	Mitral valve replacement
Mitral regurgitation	Symptoms	Mitral valve repair if anatomy favorable (presence of annular dilation, mitral leaflet prolapse, or myxomatous changes without calcification or stenosis)
	LVEF <60%	
	LV end-systolic diameter >40 mm	
	Pulmonary hypertension (PA systolic pressure ≥50 mm Hg at rest or ≥60 mm Hg during exercise)	Mitral valve replacement
	New-onset atrial fibrillation	
Tricuspid regurgitation	Refractory right-sided heart failure	Tricuspid valve repair if anatomy favorable
	Right ventricular enlargement, systolic dysfunction	Tricuspid valve replacement (bioprosthetic)
	Moderate or severe regurgitation at time of mitral valve surgery	

LV = left ventricle; LVEF = left ventricular ejection fraction; PA = pulmonary artery.

[a]All patients considered for percutaneous balloon mitral valvotomy should undergo transesophageal echocardiography to assess for left atrial appendage clot and mitral regurgitation severity regardless of whether patient has sinus rhythm or atrial fibrillation.

Recommendations from: Bonow RO, Carabello BA, Chatterjee K, et al; 2006 Writing Committee Members; American College of Cardiology/American Heart Association Task Force. 2008 Focused update incorporated into the ACC/AHA 2006 guidelines for the management of patients with valvular heart disease: a report of the American College of Cardiology/American Heart Association Task Force on Practice Guidelines (Writing Committee to Revise the 1998 Guidelines for the Management of Patients With Valvular Heart Disease): endorsed by the Society of Cardiovascular Anesthesiologists, Society for Cardiovascular Angiography and Interventions, and Society of Thoracic Surgeons. Circulation. 2008;118(15):e523- e661. [PMID: 18820172]

Aortic Stenosis

Pathophysiology and Natural History

Calcific degeneration of a trileaflet aortic valve is the most common cause of aortic stenosis. Along with mitral annular calcification, this degenerative process is now recognized as an active process of atherosclerotic-like changes in the valve as a calcific response to endocardial injury. Congenital bicuspid aortic valve is the second most common cause of aortic stenosis, with a younger age of presentation and need for surgical intervention (see Bicuspid Aortic Valve, later). Rheumatic heart disease is a relatively uncommon cause of aortic stenosis. The initial changes in aortic valve structure result in aortic sclerosis, apparent as thickening of the aortic leaflets without obstruction or stenosis. Aortic sclerosis affects about 25% of adults older than 65 years. An early peaking systolic murmur is often detected, and echocardiography demonstrates thickening of the aortic leaflets but without an elevated velocity or pressure gradient across the valve. Associated with risk factors for atherosclerosis, these sclerotic changes progress to aortic stenosis in a minority of patients. In patients with progressive stenosis, natural history studies have shown an average annual rate of increase in mean aortic transvalvular gradient of 7 mm Hg and average annual rate of reduction in effective orifice area of 0.1 cm^2, but these estimates cannot predict progression in the individual patient, necessitating regular follow-up of patients with aortic sclerosis.

Progression of aortic stenosis may lead to left ventricular hypertrophy and diastolic dysfunction, causing dyspnea. In addition, the hypertrophic process and high intraventricular pressure may result in subendocardial ischemia and angina. Because of the relatively fixed left ventricular stroke volume, cardiac output may be limited during exertion, resulting in syncope. Loss of atrial contribution to left ventricular filling and reduced diastolic filling time (such as during atrial fibrillation with rapid ventricular rate) may lead to acute clinical deterioration.

Asymptomatic patients with aortic stenosis, even severe, have survival times similar to age-matched healthy controls. However, the likelihood of valve-related symptoms developing is related to the severity of stenosis. The development of symptoms may be insidious and subtle. Exercise testing, which is relatively safe with direct physician supervision in asymptomatic patients with severe stenosis, may be useful to assess functional status or adverse prognostic features (such as blunted or reduced blood pressure response during exercise) when the presence of symptoms is indeterminate. Uncommonly, patients with left ventricular systolic dysfunction and reduced cardiac output may have a moderate transvalvular gradient but severe stenosis by calculated valve area (so-called "low-gradient aortic stenosis"). In this situation, dobutamine stress echocardiography may be useful to differentiate true aortic stenosis (severe valve stenosis persists despite a dobutamine-induced increase in stroke volume) from pseudostenosis (calculated valve area increases in response to dobutamine-induced increase in myocardial contractility).

Mitral valve regurgitation is frequently present in combination with significant aortic stenosis owing to mitral annular calcification and increased left ventricular systolic pressure and may contribute to dyspnea when regurgitation is moderate or severe.

Management

No pharmacologic therapies, including statins, have been shown to reduce or delay the progression of aortic stenosis. Other common coexisting conditions, such as hypertension and hypercholesterolemia, should be treated to reduce the risk of cardiovascular events, particularly because of the high prevalence of concomitant coronary artery disease. In patients with aortic stenosis and decompensated heart failure, cautious diuresis may improve symptoms, but acute reduction in preload may result in reduced stroke volume and arterial blood pressure. Although diuresis may result in improvement or resolution of heart failure symptoms, this improvement does not obviate the indication for surgical intervention once symptoms have occurred. Afterload reduction may be used in patients with acute pulmonary edema or left ventricular systolic dysfunction with some improvement in symptoms and hemodynamics, but it should be titrated carefully to avoid hypotension.

Decreased exercise tolerance and dyspnea on exertion may be the earliest symptoms. The onset of the cardinal symptoms of aortic stenosis, angina, syncope, or heart failure, heralds an expected average survival of only 2 to 3 years without intervention. Surgical aortic valve replacement is the only treatment of aortic stenosis associated with a survival benefit and durable symptom relief. For patients with acceptable operative risk, perioperative mortality is low (1%-4%). Considering this low operative mortality rate, consideration for elective aortic valve replacement may be extended to asymptomatic patients with severe, rapidly progressive stenosis or to patients with moderate stenosis undergoing other cardiac surgery. In patients with risk factors for coronary artery disease (most patients with degenerative calcific stenosis), cardiac catheterization is indicated prior to aortic valve replacement.

In patients with severe, symptomatic aortic stenosis who are poor operative candidates, balloon valvuloplasty may be utilized as a temporary bridge toward improved hemodynamics and clinical status, but with a high likelihood of short-term restenosis and without beneficial effect on the natural history of aortic stenosis. Transcatheter aortic valve implantation is a recently approved therapy for patients with severe, symptomatic aortic stenosis who are not candidates for surgical valve replacement because of other severe medical conditions. Ongoing clinical trials continue to evaluate these novel therapies for lower-risk operative candidates.

- The onset of angina, syncope, or heart failure in a patient with aortic stenosis heralds an expected average survival of 2 to 3 years without intervention, and surgical aortic valve replacement is the only treatment of aortic stenosis associated with a survival benefit and durable symptom relief.

Aortic Regurgitation

Pathophysiology and Natural History

Acute aortic regurgitation may result from aortic dissection, infective endocarditis, or trauma. Chronic, progressive aortic regurgitation may result from valve leaflet abnormalities (bicuspid aortic valve, calcific degeneration, or myxomatous degeneration), ascending aortic pathology (Marfan syndrome or ascending aortic dilation, aortitis due to ankylosing spondylitis or giant cell aortitis), or subvalvular abnormalities (subaortic stenosis or ventricular septal defect causing damage to aortic valve leaflets).

Aortic regurgitation leads to volume and pressure overload of the left ventricle. Both eccentric hypertrophy (due to increased preload) and concentric hypertrophy (due to increased afterload or ventricular wall stress) occur as compensatory mechanisms, which may be ongoing for decades. Chronic, severe aortic regurgitation is a gradually progressive process, with development of symptoms or left ventricular systolic dysfunction (ejection fraction <50%) in approximately 4% of patients annually. Progressive left ventricular dilation may lead to impaired contractility and global systolic function even in the absence of symptoms. As left ventricular dilation progresses, the annual risk of symptoms, systolic dysfunction, and death increases to as high as 19% among patients with left ventricular end-systolic diameter greater than 50 mm. Similarly, in patients who develop asymptomatic left ventricular systolic dysfunction, the annual rate of cardiac symptom development exceeds 25%. Although left ventricular systolic dysfunction can occur without symptoms, it is uncommon, and recovery of systolic function is likely after aortic valve replacement. Severe left ventricular dilatation represents impaired contractility and is an indication for surgery to prevent irreversible left ventricular dysfunction. When symptoms develop (dyspnea, angina, presyncope or syncope), the mortality rate increases significantly, to 10% to 20% per year.

Management

As with aortic stenosis, surgical aortic valve replacement is the only definitive therapy for aortic regurgitation that improves the natural history of the condition. Aortic valve replacement is indicated when either symptoms or evidence of left ventricular systolic dysfunction or severe dilatation develops (see Table 35). Pharmacologic vasodilators have theoretical benefits of lowered afterload, reduced regurgitant volume, and

positive ventricular remodeling. However, results of small, randomized trials have not shown definitive benefit on the rate of progression of aortic regurgitation. As a result, the strongest indications for vasodilator therapy in severe aortic regurgitation include acute, severe aortic regurgitation for short-term hemodynamic improvement before surgery; aortic regurgitation with left ventricular systolic dysfunction in patients who are not surgical candidates; and concomitant hypertension. Intra-aortic balloon counterpulsation is contraindicated in moderate or severe aortic regurgitation as it will increase diastolic flow and regurgitant volume.

- It is uncommon for patients with aortic regurgitation to have left ventricular systolic dysfunction without symptoms, and recovery of systolic function is likely after aortic valve replacement.
- Surgical aortic valve replacement is the only definitive therapy for aortic regurgitation that improves the natural history of the condition.

Bicuspid Aortic Valve

Bicuspid aortic valve disease is the most common congenital heart lesion, occurring in approximately 1% of persons. Bicuspid aortic valve has an increased prevalence associated with congenital lesions such as coarctation of the aorta, interrupted aortic arch, and Turner syndrome. More than 70% of patients with a bicuspid valve will require surgical intervention for a stenotic or regurgitant valve or aortic pathology over the course of a lifetime.

Progressive degenerative changes with premature calcification of the bicuspid valve generally lead to aortic valve stenosis rather than regurgitation, and intervention is required at an earlier age than intervention for degenerative tricuspid valve stenosis. In patients undergoing aortic valve replacement, bicuspid aortic valve disease may be found by pathologic examination in nearly 50% of excised valve specimens. Although natural history studies have not reported a higher overall mortality rate than in age-matched control subjects without aortic valve disease, patients with a bicuspid aortic valve do have a higher rate of valve-related complications, with approximately 2% annually developing symptoms or needing cardiac surgery (particularly aortic valve and root replacements). This event rate is largely predicted by older age of the patient and the degree of valve dysfunction, either stenosis or regurgitation, at the time of diagnosis. Bicuspid aortic valve is also associated with a higher overall risk of infective endocarditis, approximately 2% during long-term follow-up.

In addition to the indications for intervention as defined by the primary aortic valve lesion (stenosis or regurgitation), ascending aortic dilation may occur in persons with a bicuspid aortic valve, in combination with aortic valve disease or as an independent condition. Previously considered a secondary event due to abnormal aortic valve function, the aortopathy associated with a bicuspid aortic valve is now recognized to result from intrinsically abnormal connective tissue. As a result, serial evaluation of ascending aortic diameter should be performed by transthoracic echocardiography (or by CT angiography or magnetic resonance angiography if not adequately visualized by echocardiography).

In severe bicuspid aortic valve stenosis, balloon valvotomy in patients younger than 30 years without significant valvular calcification may offer intermediate-term benefit, thus delaying eventual aortic valve replacement. At the time of aortic valve replacement surgery, surgery to replace the ascending aorta is indicated if its diameter is greater than 4.5 cm because of the likelihood of progressive dilation. Furthermore, surgery to replace the ascending aorta is recommended in patients with a bicuspid aortic valve if the diameter of the aortic root or ascending aorta is greater than 5.0 cm regardless of valve function. After aortic valve replacement for bicuspid aortic valve disease, serial evaluation of the ascending aorta is still warranted.

KEY POINTS

- Most patients with a bicuspid aortic valve will require surgical intervention for a stenotic or regurgitant valve or aortic pathology over the course of a lifetime.

- Aortic root dilation is common in patients with a bicuspid aortic valve, and root repair or replacement may be required at the time of valve replacement surgery.

Mitral Stenosis

Pathophysiology and Natural History

The major cause of mitral stenosis is rheumatic heart disease. Although rheumatic heart disease may affect other valves, including aortic and tricuspid, the mitral valve is the predominant lesion. Rheumatic mitral stenosis predominantly affects women, with clinical presentation in the fourth or fifth decades of life. In patients from endemic regions, clinical presentation is earlier, likely because of recurrent attacks of rheumatic fever. Rarely, calcific degeneration may cause mitral stenosis. This typically is associated with mitral annulus calcification and occurs in the elderly.

In contrast to other left-sided valvular lesions, the loading conditions of the left ventricle are not significantly altered in mitral stenosis. Rather, progressive stenosis of the mitral valve increases left atrial, pulmonary vein, and pulmonary artery pressure, resulting in exertional dyspnea. In some patients, acute pulmonary edema may occur during states of high flow (such as pregnancy) or other impairment to left ventricular filling (such as atrial fibrillation leading to loss of atrial contraction and tachycardia). Atrial fibrillation is a common sequela of mitral stenosis, occurring in more

than 30% of symptomatic patients, and is associated with a very high risk for persistent or chronic atrial fibrillation and thromboembolism.

Management

In severe mitral stenosis, negative chronotropic drugs such as β-blockers allow increased diastolic filling time of the left ventricle and may improve symptoms. Rate control of atrial fibrillation is therefore important. If atrial fibrillation develops (even if paroxysmal), chronic anticoagulation therapy with warfarin is indicated to reduce the risk of thromboembolism, which is much higher than in nonvalvular atrial fibrillation. Rhythm control of atrial fibrillation is not likely to be durable if mitral stenosis is not treated because of the enlarged left atrium with elevated pressure. In addition, diuretic therapy may improve pulmonary congestion.

Indications for intervention are outlined in Table 35. In patients with mild mitral stenosis but significant symptoms, exercise echocardiography may be useful to estimate the pulmonary artery systolic pressure. Significant elevation of the pulmonary artery pressure at rest or during exercise is an indication for intervention.

In patients with moderate or severe mitral stenosis, the presence of symptoms or pulmonary hypertension should prompt intervention. If the mitral valve morphology is favorable, less than moderate mitral regurgitation is present, and if no left atrial thrombus is seen by transesophageal echocardiography, percutaneous balloon valvotomy may be performed as the procedure of choice. The procedure, when performed by experienced operators, is associated with a high acute procedural success rate (only mild residual stenosis and moderate or less regurgitation) and good intermediate-term freedom from limiting symptoms or repeat intervention, but restenosis gradually occurs. In patients with unfavorable anatomy (significant mitral leaflet thickening, calcification, immobility, or subvalvular thickening) or unsuccessful balloon valvotomy, mitral valve replacement is the appropriate intervention if the patient has an acceptable operative risk profile.

KEY POINTS

- Progressive stenosis of the mitral valve increases left atrial, pulmonary vein, and pulmonary artery pressure, resulting in exertional dyspnea.

- Atrial fibrillation is a common sequela of mitral stenosis and carries a much higher risk of thromboembolism than nonvalvular atrial fibrillation; chronic anticoagulation therapy with warfarin is indicated in these patients.

- In patients with moderate or severe mitral stenosis, the presence of symptoms or pulmonary hypertension should prompt intervention.

Mitral Regurgitation

Pathophysiology and Natural History

Causes of mitral regurgitation can broadly be classified as organic (mitral valve prolapse, rheumatic heart disease, infective endocarditis, collagen vascular disease) or functional (resulting from left ventricular systolic dysfunction causing mitral annular dilation or restricted leaflet mobility). Mitral regurgitation due to coronary artery disease and myocardial ischemia may be caused by acute degeneration (for example, papillary muscle dysfunction or rupture) or chronic functional changes (for example, left ventricular dilation and systolic dysfunction, causing mitral leaflet tethering and malcoaptation).

Mitral regurgitation is generally progressive in nature and increases left ventricular preload, whereas afterload is unchanged or reduced because of the low impedance of flow into the left atrium. The process of eccentric hypertrophy accommodates the increased left ventricular filling volume (initially without increasing diastolic filling pressure) and maintains forward stroke volume. Eventually, however, increased left atrial pressure results in dyspnea and pulmonary hypertension, and progressive left atrial dilation may result in atrial fibrillation. In addition, progressive left ventricular dilation may lead to systolic dysfunction. In asymptomatic patients with chronic severe mitral regurgitation, either symptoms or left ventricular dysfunction develops within 6 to 10 years. In patients with acute severe mitral regurgitation, the lack of compensatory eccentric hypertrophy commonly results in fulminant symptoms of heart failure and possible cardiogenic shock.

Patients with mitral regurgitation due to mitral valve prolapse, a condition present in 1% to 2.5% of the population, are heterogeneous regarding their spectrum of disease and associated manifestations. Mitral valve prolapse is diagnosed by echocardiography with visualization of a displaced coaptation level of the anterior and posterior mitral leaflets 2 mm or more above the mitral annulus. Patients with mitral valve prolapse generally have a benign prognosis, with age-adjusted survival similar to nonaffected persons. Some patients have symptoms of "mitral valve prolapse syndrome," which include palpitations, nonanginal chest pain, fatigue, and dyspnea; the link between symptoms and the valvular abnormality, however, is unclear. Patients with thickened mitral leaflets (≥5 mm) are at higher risk for progressive severe regurgitation and complications. In patients with flail mitral leaflets (lack of coaptation), the annual mortality rate is significantly higher than that for mitral valve prolapse with regurgitation, and earlier intervention should be considered.

Management

Medical therapy has a limited role in organic mitral regurgitation. Symptomatic patients with acute severe mitral regurgitation should be promptly referred for cardiac surgery. In this situation, afterload reduction with vasodilators (intravenous nitroprusside) and stroke volume enhancement with inotropic agents may stabilize the patient before urgent cardiac surgery. Alternatively, intra-aortic balloon counterpulsation offers mechanical ventricular unloading. In patients with chronic severe mitral regurgitation that is asymptomatic, no studies have demonstrated a clinical benefit with medical therapy.

In patients with functional or chronic ischemic mitral regurgitation with left ventricular systolic dysfunction, treatment of the underlying heart failure with an ACE inhibitor or β-blocker may reduce severity of regurgitation, improve left ventricular function, and reduce cardiovascular events.

Indications for surgical treatment of severe mitral regurgitation are described in Table 35. When surgery is indicated for organic mitral regurgitation, mitral valve repair is associated with a smaller decrement in left ventricular ejection fraction than mitral valve replacement and potentially avoids the need for chronic anticoagulation. Referral to an experienced surgeon and high-volume center increases the likelihood of successful repair. The reoperation rate after successful mitral valve repair, owing to failure of the initial operation or progressive valve disease, is similar to that after mitral valve replacement (approximately 1% per year).

Importantly, whereas mitral valve surgery has proven clinical benefits for patients with severe organic mitral regurgitation, the effect of surgery for functional mitral regurgitation (that is, mitral regurgitation secondary to left ventricular dilatation and dysfunction) on outcome is unclear. For chronic ischemic mitral regurgitation, revascularization by coronary artery bypass surgery or percutaneous coronary intervention has been associated with improved outcome in observational studies; however, concomitant mitral valve surgery has not been associated with additional survival benefit, and randomized studies are ongoing.

KEY POINTS

- Mitral regurgitation is generally progressive in nature; in patients with chronic severe mitral regurgitation, either symptoms or left ventricular dysfunction develops within 6 to 10 years.

- Patients with mitral valve prolapse generally have a benign prognosis, with age-adjusted survival similar to that of nonaffected persons.

- Mitral valve surgery has proven clinical benefits for patients with severe organic mitral regurgitation; however, the effect of surgery for functional mitral regurgitation on outcome is unclear.

Tricuspid Valve Disease

Tricuspid stenosis is an uncommon condition caused predominantly by rheumatic heart disease. Severe stenosis leads to right atrial pressure elevation, atrial flutter, and systemic venous congestion (edema, hepatomegaly, ascites). Causes of tricuspid regurgitation associated with abnormal leaflets include rheumatic heart disease, infective endocarditis, carcinoid tumor, congenital Ebstein anomaly, radiation therapy, connective tissue disease, prolapse, and trauma (particularly permanent pacemaker or implantable cardioverter-defibrillator leads). In addition, tricuspid regurgitation commonly is present in patients with pulmonary hypertension, due to the increased right ventricular systolic pressure and right ventricular dilatation. The appropriate timing of surgical intervention (repair or replacement) for severe tricuspid regurgitation is controversial, but is generally considered for patients with right-sided heart failure symptoms refractory to medical therapy or is performed concomitantly with mitral valve surgery.

Infective Endocarditis

Infective endocarditis is a bacterial or fungal infection of the endocardium, including native or prosthetic valves, the endocardial surface, or an implanted cardiac device. Endocarditis generally is caused by bacteremia with adherence of bacteria to a preexisting endocardial, particularly valvular, lesion. Whereas streptococcal infection was the predominant cause in earlier eras, staphylococcal infection is now the leading cause of native valve, prosthetic valve, and cardiac device infections, largely owing to the increase in health care–related invasive procedures and intravascular access. As a result, duration of symptoms before presentation is shorter. Despite advancements in the diagnosis and therapy for endocarditis, the in-hospital mortality rate remains high, at nearly 20%.

Diagnosis and Management

Infective endocarditis should be suspected in any patient with a new or increased regurgitant heart murmur along with signs or symptoms of infection or bacteremia. Blood cultures may not demonstrate growth if antibiotics are administered before cultures are taken or if the infection is caused by fastidious organisms.

Echocardiography has a primary role in the diagnosis of endocarditis. The modified Duke criteria for diagnosis of endocarditis (**Table 36**) include typical bacteriologic evidence in blood cultures or valve specimens, clinical findings, and echocardiographic evidence of endocardial involvement (new or worsening valve regurgitation, vegetation, paravalvular abscess, or leaflet perforation). Transthoracic echocardiography has less than optimal sensitivity (50%-80%) for the detection of such endocardial involvement; in contrast, transesophageal echocardiography has very high sensitivity and specificity for these diagnostic findings and complications of endocarditis (intracardiac abscess, fistula). Although transesophageal echocardiography requires greater operator training and sedation of the patient, it should be regarded as an acceptable primary diagnostic test without previous transthoracic echocardiography in certain clinical situations: intermediate or high pretest probability of endocarditis, particularly in patients with *Staphylococcus aureus* bacteremia; patients with prosthetic heart valves; and evaluation for complications of endocarditis, such as intracardiac abscess, valve perforation, or fistula formation.

Initiation of empiric antibiotic therapy is appropriate after multiple blood cultures have been drawn when clinical suspicion for endocarditis is intermediate or high. Tailored antibiotic therapy is guided by the causative organism and its microbiologic susceptibilities. In addition to a prolonged course of parenteral antibiotic therapy, surgery during the index hospitalization is performed in nearly 50% of patients with valvular infective endocarditis and a higher percentage of those with cardiac device infective endocarditis. Indications for surgery include: (1) severe hemodynamic perturbation, particularly related to severe left-sided valvular regurgitation or fistula formation and resultant heart failure; (2) evidence

---

TABLE 36. Clinical Criteria for the Diagnosis of Endocarditis

Definite Endocarditis

Presence of any pathologic criteria[a] *or*
2 major criteria *or*
1 major and 3 minor criteria *or*
5 minor criteria

Major Criteria	Minor Criteria
Persistently positive blood cultures of organisms typical for endocarditis[b]	Predisposing condition or injection drug use
	Fever
Endocardial involvement (new valvular regurgitation or positive echocardiogram)	Embolic vascular phenomena
	Immunologic phenomena (e.g., glomerulonephritis, rheumatoid factor)
	Positive blood cultures not meeting major criteria

[a]Organisms demonstrated by culture or histologic examination of a vegetation, a vegetation that has embolized, or an intracardiac abscess specimen; or a vegetation or abscess showing active endocarditis.

[b]Or a single positive culture for *Coxiella burnetii* or IgG antibody titer >1:800.

Information from Li JS, Sexton DJ, Mick N, et al. Proposed modifications to the Duke criteria for the diagnosis of infective endocarditis. Clin Infect Dis. 2000;30(4):633-638. [PMID: 10770721]

CONT.

or likelihood of persistent infection despite appropriate antibiotic therapy (including persistent bacteremia or intracardiac abscess, or involvement of a prosthetic surface); and (3) evidence or high risk of recurrent embolic event because of a large vegetation. In patients with endocarditis complicated by these events, surgery has been found to improve mortality compared with antibiotic therapy alone.

Prophylaxis

Guidelines for antibiotic prophylaxis before elective procedures that may be associated with transient bacteremia have become more conservative for several reasons. A strong association between these procedures and developing infective endocarditis has not been demonstrated, and other, nonmedical routine events may cause transient bacteremia. Also, evidence that antibiotic prophylaxis reduces the risk of endocarditis is inconclusive. As a result, prophylaxis is recommended only for dental procedures associated with a higher rate of transient bacteremia, in patients in whom infective endocarditis would be associated with a higher risk of a complicated course or adverse events. Indications for prophylaxis and recommended prophylactic regimens are discussed in MKSAP 16 Infectious Disease. In the absence of previous infective endocarditis, antibiotic prophylaxis is not recommended for patients with native valvular lesions, including mitral valve prolapse with regurgitation, bicuspid aortic valve, or rheumatic valve disease.

KEY POINTS

- Staphylococcal infection is now the leading cause of native valve, prosthetic valve, and cardiac device infections.

- If clinical suspicion for endocarditis is intermediate or high, initiation of empiric antibiotic therapy is appropriate after multiple blood cultures have been drawn.

- Antibiotic prophylaxis is not recommended for patients with native valvular lesions, including mitral valve prolapse with regurgitation, bicuspid aortic valve, or rheumatic valve disease, unless there is a history of previous endocarditis.

Prosthetic Valves

For patients requiring valve replacement surgery, options for the type of prosthetic valve are biologic (xenograft or homograft) or mechanical valves. The major consideration regarding these types of valves is structural valve deterioration of biologic valves versus the need for life-long anticoagulation for mechanical valves. Biologic valve durability is dependent on the position of implantation, with greatest durability in right-sided valve replacements, followed by aortic and mitral positions. In the most common aortic location, the anticipated duration is 14 to 20 years before significant structural deterioration occurs. Other factors in this choice include hemodynamic performance and patient preference. Current recommendations for the type of prosthesis for left-sided valve replacement are shown in **Table 37**.

After implantation of either a biologic or mechanical prosthetic valve, anticoagulation with warfarin is recommended for at least 3 months to allow endothelialization of the prosthetic material. In addition, all patients should receive aspirin (75-100 mg/d) to further reduce the risk for thromboembolic events. After 3 months, patients with a biologic valve replacement who are at low risk for thromboembolic events (that is, with no other conditions such as atrial fibrillation or a previous thromboembolic event) can discontinue warfarin but must remain on aspirin indefinitely; patients with a mechanical valve replacement should continue taking low-dose aspirin and warfarin indefinitely (goal INR range 2.0-3.0 for aortic valve replacement and 2.5-3.5 for mitral valve replacement).

Patients with mechanical prosthetic valves, particularly in the mitral position, are at higher risk for valve thrombosis. Additional risk factors for thrombosis include the presence of atrial fibrillation, previous thromboembolism, left ventricular systolic dysfunction, hypercoagulable conditions, older-generation mechanical valves, mechanical tricuspid valve, or more than one mechanical valve. As a result, patients with a mechanical mitral valve or a mechanical aortic valve with additional risk factors for thromboembolism (including a prosthetic aortic valve that is not a bileaflet mechanical valve) undergoing an elective surgical procedure requiring warfarin cessation should

---

TABLE 37. Recommendations for Type of Prosthetic Valve Replacement

Position of Prosthetic Valve	Mechanical Prosthesis Recommended	Biologic Prosthesis Recommended
Aortic	Mechanical valve present in other valve location Age <65 years in the absence of contraindications to anticoagulation	Age ≥65 years without other risks for thromboembolism Contraindication to anticoagulation Patient preference
Mitral	Age <65 years	Age ≥65 years Contraindication to anticoagulation Patient preference

Recommendations from Bonow RO, Carabello BA, Chatterjee K, et al; 2006 Writing Committee Members; American College of Cardiology/American Heart Association Task Force. 2008 Focused update incorporated into the ACC/AHA 2006 guidelines for the management of patients with valvular heart disease: a report of the American College of Cardiology/American Heart Association Task Force on Practice Guidelines (Writing Committee to Revise the 1998 Guidelines for the Management of Patients With Valvular Heart Disease): endorsed by the Society of Cardiovascular Anesthesiologists, Society for Cardiovascular Angiography and Interventions, and Society of Thoracic Surgeons. Circulation. 2008;118(15):e618-e620. [PMID: 18820172]

be bridged with unfractionated heparin intravenously or low-molecular-weight heparin subcutaneously before and after the procedure until therapeutic INR is achieved.

Notably, the definition of a patient with a mechanical aortic prosthetic valve at low risk of thromboembolism differs between the ACC/AHA and the American College of Chest Physician guidelines, with the latter recommending bridging for patients with diabetes mellitus or hypertension or who are older than 75 years (similar to risk factors for stroke in atrial fibrillation).

For patients with heparin-induced thrombocytopenia, bivalirudin may be used for bridging of anticoagulation. In patients at low risk of valve thrombosis (bileaflet mechanical aortic valve replacement with no risk factors for thrombosis), warfarin may be stopped 48 to 72 hours before the elective procedure and restarted within 24 hours after the procedure. Thrombosis of a mechanical valve is an emergent situation associated with a high risk for pulmonary edema and thromboembolism, and therapeutic options include repeat cardiac surgery or intravenous fibrinolytic therapy.

For baseline assessment, all patients undergoing valve replacement surgery should have annual clinical evaluation and transthoracic echocardiography performed 2 to 3 months after implantation. Subsequently, however, routine annual echocardiography is not indicated if no change in clinical status has occurred.

All patients with prosthetic valves are at increased risk for infective endocarditis (approximately 1% annual risk), and antibiotic prophylaxis is recommended for dental procedures.

KEY POINTS

- After implantation of either a biologic or mechanical prosthetic valve, anticoagulation with warfarin is recommended for at least 3 months, and aspirin should be continued indefinitely.

- Patients with a mechanical valve replacement require lifelong anticoagulation with warfarin and aspirin.

- Patients with a mechanical prosthetic valve with a low risk of valve thrombosis (bileaflet mechanical aortic valve replacement with no risk factors for thrombosis) do not require bridging anticoagulation for elective surgical procedures requiring warfarin cessation.

- All patients with prosthetic valves are at increased risk for infective endocarditis, and antibiotic prophylaxis is recommended for dental procedures.

Adult Congenital Heart Disease

Introduction

Marked improvement in the care of congenital heart disease has resulted in a growing population of affected adults. With more adults than children living with congenital heart diseases in North America, education about these conditions is critical to the medical community and to the patients and their families.

Adolescents and young adult patients with congenital heart disease should transition their medical care from a pediatric to an adult congenital practice. The time for transition usually occurs in the mid teens to mid 20s. Cardiovascular residua are common in patients with previous operative or percutaneous intervention for congenital cardiac lesions, underscoring the importance of periodic follow-up by an adult congenital cardiac specialist. In addition, patients with congenital heart disease are at risk for endocarditis and often require antimicrobial prophylaxis prior to nonsterile procedures (see MKSAP 16 Infectious Disease). Patients with cyanotic or complex congenital heart disease are at high risk for perioperative cardiac complications and should have elective operations performed at centers that care for such patients with a coordinated multidisciplinary team approach to the perioperative care.

Patent Foramen Ovale

In gestation, the foramen ovale allows transfer of oxygenated placental blood to the fetal circulation. The communication usually closes shortly after birth, but remains patent in 25% to 30% of the general population (**Figure 32**). A patent foramen ovale (PFO) is often incidentally noted by transthoracic echocardiography.

Most patients with a PFO are asymptomatic; however, risk may be increased for stroke caused by paradoxical embolism. Presence of an atrial septal aneurysm with a PFO further increases the risk of stroke versus a PFO alone.

In a patient with cryptogenic stroke, a PFO may be diagnosed by visualizing the interatrial septum. During echocardiography, agitated saline is injected intravenously. The heart is observed during normal respiration, with cough, and during a Valsalva maneuver. In a patient with a PFO, this procedure will often demonstrate a right-to-left shunt of the saline bubbles at the atrial level with cough or during Valsalva release, which transiently increases right atrial pressure. If transthoracic echocardiography is nondiagnostic, transesophageal echocardiography provides improved visualization of the atrial septum.

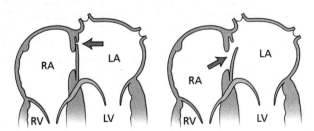

FIGURE 32. Patent foramen ovale. The *arrows* demonstrate the mechanism of right-to-left shunt through the patent foramen ovale. LA = left atrium; LV = left ventricle; RA = right atrium; RV = right ventricle.

Redrawn from original supplied courtesy of Dr. William D. Edwards, Department of Laboratory Medicine and Pathology, Mayo Clinic, Rochester, MN.

There is no indication for PFO closure in asymptomatic patients. Data are insufficient to make a recommendation regarding closure for secondary stroke prevention after a first stroke. Antiplatelet therapy should be considered for patients with PFO and cryptogenic stroke. Closure may be considered for patients with recurrent cryptogenic stroke despite medical therapy; there are several ongoing clinical trials assessing this option. Rarely, a PFO may be associated with the orthodeoxia-platypnea syndrome (postural dyspnea and cyanosis). In addition, patients with severe tricuspid valve regurgitation may develop cyanosis because of the direction of the tricuspid regurgitation across the PFO. Device closure in these patients may be clinically beneficial.

Observational studies have suggested an association between PFO and migraine headaches. However, evidence to support a causal link is insufficient. PFO closure should not be performed for the prophylaxis of migraine headaches.

KEY POINTS

- The foramen ovale remains patent in 25% to 30% of the general population and is often incidentally noted by transthoracic echocardiography.

- There is no indication for patent foramen ovale closure in asymptomatic patients; data are insufficient to make a recommendation regarding closure for secondary stroke prevention after a first stroke.

- Patent foramen ovale closure may be considered for patients with recurrent cryptogenic stroke despite medical therapy.

Atrial Septal Defect

Pathophysiology and Genetics

An atrial septal defect (ASD) is a communication between the atria. A left-to-right shunt causes right-sided cardiac chamber dilatation. Defects are classified according to location (**Figure 33**). Ostium secundum ASDs are located in the middle portion of the atrial septum near the fossa ovalis membrane (75% of cases of ASDs); ostium primum defects are located in the lowest portion of the atrial septum near the cardiac crux (15%-20% of cases); sinus venosus defects are usually located near the superior vena cava (5%-10% of cases) or rarely near the inferior vena cava. A coronary sinus defect (or unroofed coronary sinus) is a communication between the coronary sinus and the left atrium (<1% of cases).

Most ASDs occur sporadically; however, several genetic syndromes are recognized. The Holt-Oram syndrome involves bilateral upper extremity abnormalities and congenital heart defects, most commonly an ASD. Down syndrome is commonly associated with ostium primum or secundum ASDs or ventricular septal defects. Familial occurrence of ostium secundum ASD is recognized and linked to chromosome 5. In some families, ASD is an autosomal dominant trait.

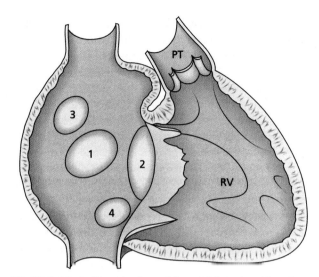

FIGURE 33. Positions of various atrial septal defects viewed from the right side of the heart. (1) ostium secundum; (2) ostium primum; (3) sinus venosus; (4) inferior vena cava. PT = pulmonary trunk; RV = right ventricle.

Redrawn from original supplied courtesy of Dr. William D. Edwards, Department of Laboratory Medicine and Pathology, Mayo Clinic, Rochester, MN.

Clinical Presentation

Unrepaired ASDs are commonly identified in adulthood; the age of presentation depends on the shunt size and the presence or absence of associated defects. Patients generally present with symptoms of fatigue, exertional dyspnea, atrial fibrillation, or paradoxical embolism. Rarely, patients with isolated ASDs present with pulmonary arterial hypertension; this usually occurs in women, suggesting the possible coexistence of idiopathic pulmonary arterial hypertension.

Ostium secundum ASDs are generally isolated abnormalities and present with right-sided cardiac chamber enlargement. Ostium primum ASDs (most common in Down syndrome) are commonly associated with cleft mitral and tricuspid valves, ventricular septal defects, and subaortic stenosis, a collection of abnormalities termed "endocardial cushion defect." Sinus venosus ASDs are commonly associated with partial anomalous pulmonary venous drainage, particularly involving the right upper pulmonary vein. The coronary sinus ASD or unroofed coronary sinus is commonly associated with complex congenital heart lesions.

Clinical findings include jugular venous distention, a parasternal impulse, and a systolic flow murmur at the second left intercostal space. Fixed splitting of the S_2 is the characteristic auscultatory finding in patients with ASDs, although this is variable. Large shunts with increased right-sided volume may cause a diastolic flow rumble across the tricuspid valve.

Diagnostic Evaluation

The diagnostic imaging modality of choice for ASDs is transthoracic echocardiography, which is highly accurate in the diagnosis of ostium primum and secundum ASDs. Sinus venosus and coronary sinus ASDs are less readily diagnosed by transthoracic imaging in adults and often require transesophageal echocardiography or cardiovascular magnetic resonance (CMR) imaging. Additional findings on echocardiography include right-sided cardiac chamber enlargement, variable tricuspid regurgitation related to tricuspid annular dilatation, and increased right ventricular systolic pressure. Agitated saline contrast injection may help identify a right-to-left atrial shunt if advanced disease or Eisenmenger syndrome is suspected. Cardiac catheterization is the only reliable method to calculate the pulmonary–to–systemic blood flow ratio (Qp:Qs) but is rarely required for this reason alone.

The electrocardiogram (ECG) and chest radiograph findings in patients with ASDs are outlined in **Table 38**. Complete heart block may occur in familial ASD. CMR imaging can be used to noninvasively quantify right ventricular volumes and ejection fraction. CT, CMR imaging, and transesophageal echocardiography are useful for identifying anomalous pulmonary veins. In equivocal cases, CMR imaging may provide improved cardiac tomographic images for localization of defects. Exercise testing is used to document exercise limitation in patients with ASDs and to aid in decisions regarding management. Diagnostic catheterization is not required for uncomplicated ASDs; it may, however, be recommended in the patient with an ASD and pulmonary arterial hypertension to aid in determining whether closure is indicated.

Treatment

The main indications for ASD closure are the presence of symptoms and a Qp:Qs ratio greater than 1.5 to 2.0 to avoid long-term complications. Other considerations include patient age, defect size and location, associated abnormalities, and hemodynamic impact. Percutaneous intervention should be considered in patients who have ostium secundum ASDs with right-sided cardiac chamber enlargement or paradoxical embolism, related to the intracardiac shunt, but no other associated cardiovascular abnormality that requires operative intervention. Surgical closure is indicated for non–ostium secundum ASDs or for patients with any type of ASD when coexistent cardiovascular disease requires operative intervention, such as coronary artery disease or severe tricuspid valve regurgitation. Closure is also recommended for patients who have documented orthodeoxia-platypnea syndrome. A very small ostium secundum ASD without associated right-sided cardiac enlargement can be followed clinically. Closure of an ASD should be considered in patients with intracardiac shunt before pacemaker placement because of the two-fold increased risk for systemic thromboembolism in patients with shunts compared with those without.

Patients with severe pulmonary arterial hypertension and an ASD may be considered for closure providing there is persistent left-to-right shunt and no evidence of fixed pulmonary vascular disease. Standard medical therapy for pulmonary arterial hypertension should also be prescribed.

Patients with isolated anomalous pulmonary venous connections may present with clinical and echocardiographic features similar to an ASD, but with a transthoracic echocardiogram demonstrating no atrial-level shunt during agitated saline contrast study. A high clinical index of suspicion should prompt focused imaging with transesophageal echocardiography, thoracic CT, or CMR imaging.

Patients with small ASDs do not need any limitation of physical activity. In patients with large left-to-right shunts, exercise is often self-limited owing to decreased cardiopulmonary function.

Reproductive Considerations

Pregnancy in patients with ASD is generally well tolerated in the absence of pulmonary arterial hypertension. The risk of congenital heart disease transmission in patients with sporadic ASD is estimated to be 8% to 10%. Genetic syndromes will have variable inheritance; Holt-Oram syndrome is inherited in an autosomal dominant fashion. Careful family history should be taken for all patients with ASD due to recognized familial inheritance.

Follow-up After Atrial Septal Defect Closure

Clinical follow-up is recommended for all adult patients after ASD closure. Atrial fibrillation is often present after closure. A small residual shunt is common early after percutaneous closure of an ASD; warfarin anticoagulation is recommended following closure in select patients. Rare complications after device closure include device dislocation or migration, device erosion into the aorta or pericardium, and sudden death. Chest pain or syncope after device closure warrants urgent echocardiographic evaluation for device erosion. The frequency of follow-up should be individualized.

KEY POINTS

- Clinical findings suggesting atrial septal defect include fixed splitting of the S_2, jugular venous distention, a parasternal impulse, and a systolic flow murmur at the second left intercostal space.

- The diagnostic imaging modality of choice for an atrial septal defect is transthoracic echocardiography.

Ventricular Septal Defect

Pathophysiology

Ventricular septal defects (VSDs) are the most common congenital heart defects at birth, but the frequency decreases substantially by adulthood because of spontaneous closure of small defects. Four types of VSD are defined according to their location on the ventricular septum (**Figure 34**). Perimembranous VSD is the most common (80% of cases); these are usually isolated abnormalities, but occasionally tricuspid or aortic valve regurgitation or aneurysms of the ventricular septum coexist. Subpulmonary VSDs (also called outlet or supracristal VSD) account for approximately 6% of defects in the non-Asian population (33% in Asians). These defects are often associated with progressive aortic valve regurgitation, and spontaneous closure is uncommon. Muscular VSDs, rarely seen in adults, can be located anywhere in the ventricular septum. They may be single or multiple but commonly close spontaneously. Inlet defects occur in the superior-posterior portion of the ventricular septum adjacent to the tricuspid valve. These defects are also rare in adults but do

TABLE 38. Imaging Findings and Late Complications in Adult Congenital Heart Disease

Lesion	ECG and CXR Findings	Late Complications
Patent foramen ovale	Normal	Paradoxical embolism, orthodeoxia-platypnea syndrome
Ostium secundum ASD	ECG: Incomplete RBBB, RA enlargement, right axis deviation	Right heart enlargement, atrial fibrillation, PAH (rare)
	CXR: Right heart enlargement, prominent pulmonary artery, increased pulmonary vascularity	
Ostium primum ASD	ECG: Left axis deviation, 1st-degree atrioventricular block	Right heart enlargement, atrial fibrillation, mitral regurgitation (from mitral valve cleft), PAH (rare)
	CXR: Right heart enlargement, prominent pulmonary artery, increased pulmonary vascularity	
Sinus venosus ASD	ECG: Abnormal P axis	Right heart enlargement, atrial fibrillation, PAH (rare)
	CXR: Right heart enlargement, prominent pulmonary artery, increased pulmonary vascularity	
Small VSD	Normal	Endocarditis
Large VSD	ECG: RV or RV/LV hypertrophy	Left heart enlargement, PAH
	CXR: LA and LV enlargement, increased pulmonary vascular markings; with PAH: prominent central pulmonary arteries, reduced peripheral pulmonary vascular markings	
Small PDA	Normal	Endocarditis
Large PDA	ECG: LA enlargement, LV hypertrophy; with PAH: RV hypertrophy	Endocarditis, heart failure
	CXR: Cardiomegaly, increased pulmonary vascular markings; calcification of PDA (occasional); with PAH: prominent central pulmonary arteries, reduced peripheral pulmonary vascular markings	
Pulmonary valve stenosis	ECG: Normal when RV systolic pressure <60 mm Hg; if RV systolic pressure >60 mm Hg: RA enlargement, right axis deviation, RV hypertrophy	Risk of severe pulmonary valve regurgitation after pulmonary valvuloplasty
	CXR: Pulmonary artery dilatation, calcification of pulmonary valve (rare); RA enlargement may be noted	
Aortic coarctation	ECG: LV hypertrophy and ST-T wave abnormalities	Hypertension (75% of cases), bicuspid aortic valve (>50% of cases), increased risk of aortic aneurysm and intracranial aneurysm
	CXR: Dilated ascending aorta, figure 3 sign beneath transverse arch, rib notching from collateral vessels	
		Post repair: Recoarctation, hypertension
Repaired tetralogy of Fallot	ECG: RBBB, increased QRS duration (QRS duration reflects degree of RV dilatation)	Post repair: Increased atrial and ventricular arrhythmia risk
	CXR: Cardiomegaly with pulmonary or tricuspid valve regurgitation; right aortic arch in 25% of cases	QRS >180 msec increases risk of ventricular tachycardia and sudden death
Eisenmenger syndrome	ECG: Right axis deviation, RA enlargement, RV hypertrophy	Right heart failure
	CXR: RV dilatation, prominent pulmonary artery, reduced pulmonary vascularity	

ASD = atrial septal defect; CXR = chest radiograph; ECG = electrocardiogram; LA = left atrium; LV = left ventricle; PAH = pulmonary arterial hypertension; PDA = patent ductus arteriosus; RA = right atrium; RBBB = right bundle branch block; RV = right ventricle; VSD = ventricular septal defect.

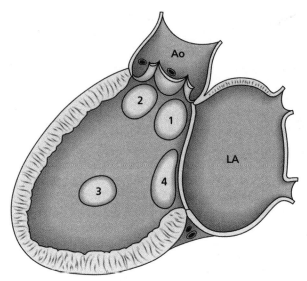

FIGURE 34. Positions of various ventricular septal defects viewed from the left side of the heart. (1) perimembranous; (2) subpulmonary; (3) muscular; (4) inlet. Ao = aorta; LA = left atrium.

Redrawn from original supplied courtesy of Dr. William D. Edwards, Department of Laboratory Medicine and Pathology, Mayo Clinic, Rochester, MN.

occur as part of the atrioventricular septal defect complex and are most commonly seen in patients with Down syndrome.

Clinical Presentation

Clinical presentation of an isolated VSD depends on the size of the defect and the amount of pulmonary vascular resistance. Patients with a small VSD have a small left-to-right shunt, no pulmonary arterial hypertension, and present with a loud holosystolic murmur located at the left lower sternal border that often obliterates the S_2 and may even be palpable. Small VSDs do not cause left heart enlargement or pulmonary arterial hypertension.

A moderate-sized VSD with a moderate left-to-right shunt may cause left ventricular volume overload and eventually pulmonary arterial hypertension. Patients may remain asymptomatic for many years but eventually present with symptoms of heart failure. On clinical examination, the left ventricular impulse is displaced; when present, it is an indicator of volume overload. A holosystolic murmur is noted at the left lower sternal border; the duration and quality depend on the pressure gradient between the left and right ventricles. With progressive pulmonary arterial hypertension, the murmur becomes an early peaking shorter systolic murmur. A mitral diastolic rumble occurs in patients with a moderate or large left-to-right shunt related to increased flow across the mitral valve.

Large VSDs associated with moderate or large left-to-right shunts are usually detected in childhood through the presence of a murmur, heart failure, and failure to thrive. Without closure early in life, fixed pulmonary arterial hypertension will occur within several years, resulting in Eisenmenger syndrome and reversal of the shunt (changing to a right-to-left shunt).

Diagnostic Evaluation

Transthoracic echocardiography is the primary diagnostic technique for patients with a suspected VSD. The location, size, and hemodynamic impact of the VSD can be readily identified, as can the presence or absence of associated tricuspid or aortic valve regurgitation, pulmonary arterial hypertension, and left heart enlargement. CMR imaging has been used in select cases to help delineate cardiac anatomy in patients with limited echocardiographic images and allows measurement of right ventricular volumes.

The ECG and chest radiograph findings in patients with VSDs are outlined in Table 38. Cardiac catheterization is rarely performed to confirm the diagnosis but is helpful in delineating pulmonary vascular disease and the Qp:Qs ratio.

Treatment

Closure of a VSD is indicated when there is a Qp:Qs ratio of 2.0 or greater and evidence of left ventricular volume overload or a history of endocarditis. VSD closure is reasonable when net left-to-right shunting is present at a Qp:Qs ratio greater than 1.5 with pulmonary artery pressure less than two thirds of systemic pressure and pulmonary vascular resistance less than two thirds of systemic vascular resistance; or when net left-to-right shunting is present at a Qp:Qs ratio greater than 1.5 in the presence of left ventricular systolic or diastolic failure.

Small VSDs with a small left-to-right shunt and no left heart enlargement or valvular disease can be observed through periodic clinical evaluation and imaging.

At this time, percutaneous device closure is possible for select VSDs, but most patients are treated surgically. Large VSDs with reversal of the cardiac shunt (becoming a right-to-left shunt) and pulmonary arterial hypertension (Eisenmenger syndrome) should not be closed; closure will result in clinical deterioration.

Patients with a small VSD require no activity restrictions. If pulmonary vascular disease is present, patients should be advised against isometric or competitive exercise.

Reproductive Considerations

Pregnancy in patients with VSDs is generally well tolerated in the absence of pulmonary arterial hypertension. Women with VSDs and associated pulmonary arterial hypertension should be counseled against pregnancy.

Follow-up After Ventricular Septal Defect Closure

Periodic cardiovascular evaluation is recommended for all patients with previous VSD closure. Complications following repair include residual or recurrent VSD, heart block, arrhythmias, pulmonary arterial hypertension, and aortic or tricuspid valve regurgitation.

Patent Ductus Arteriosus

Pathophysiology

During fetal life, the aorta and pulmonary artery are connected by the arterial duct. Maternal rubella and neonatal prematurity predispose the fetus to persistence of the ductus arteriosus after birth. The patent arterial duct may be an isolated abnormality or associated with other congenital cardiac defects such as VSD or ASD.

Clinical Presentation

A tiny patent ductus arteriosus (PDA) may be inaudible. A small PDA produces an arteriovenous fistula with a continuous murmur that envelops the S_2; this murmur is best heard beneath the left clavicle. Patients with a moderate PDA may present with symptoms of heart failure and a continuous "machinery" murmur heard best beneath the left clavicle. Bounding pulses and a wide pulse pressure will also be noted. The differential diagnosis on examination should include any type of arteriovenous fistula, ruptured sinus of Valsalva aneurysm, or VSD with aortic regurgitation.

A large PDA may cause pulmonary arterial hypertension with shunt reversal from right-to-left with Eisenmenger syndrome. A characteristic clinical feature of an Eisenmenger duct is reduced oxygen saturation and clubbing affecting the feet but not the hands owing to desaturated blood reaching the lower part of the body preferentially (differential cyanosis).

Diagnostic Evaluation

Transthoracic echocardiography with color flow Doppler imaging will often confirm the suspected presence of a PDA; however, in patients with severe pulmonary arterial hypertension, the PDA may be very difficult to visualize. Cardiac CT and CMR imaging may identify PDA, but the diagnostic roles of these procedures are to provide ancillary information. The ECG and chest radiograph findings in patients with PDA are outlined in Table 38. Cardiac catheterization is reserved for patients with a moderate-sized PDA with elevated pulmonary artery pressures or for patients with severe pulmonary arterial hypertension to determine reversibility. Angiography confirms the size and shape of the PDA and helps to determine whether percutaneous intervention will be feasible.

Treatment

Closure of a PDA either percutaneously or surgically is indicated for left atrial or left ventricular enlargement in the absence of pulmonary arterial hypertension, or in the presence of net left-to-right shunting. Surgical closure of a PDA, particularly when calcification is present, may be challenging and referral to a congenital cardiac center for consideration of percutaneous versus surgical closure is appropriate.

A tiny PDA can be observed clinically. Transcatheter closure of a small PDA should be considered in patients with a history of endocarditis. A moderate-sized PDA can be closed by percutaneous intervention. A large PDA with associated severe pulmonary arterial hypertension should be observed; closure may be detrimental. Medical therapy for pulmonary arterial hypertension should then be considered.

Patients with a small PDA without pulmonary arterial hypertension do not need any limitation of physical activity.

Pulmonary Valve Stenosis

Pathophysiology

Pulmonary valve stenosis causes obstruction to right ventricular outflow and is usually an isolated lesion. Isolated pulmonary valve stenosis is often associated with Noonan syndrome, an autosomal dominant disorder characterized by short stature, variable intellectual impairment, unique facial features, neck webbing, hypertelorism, and congenital heart disease.

Clinical Presentation

Most patients with pulmonary valve stenosis are asymptomatic; rarely, symptoms of exertional dyspnea occur. Mild stenosis is characterized by a normal jugular venous pulse, absence of a right ventricular impulse, and a pulmonary ejection click that decreases with inspiration. A prominent a wave on the jugular venous pressure waveform and a right ventricular lift resulting from right ventricular hypertrophy are common in patients with moderate or severe pulmonary valve stenosis. An ejection click is common, but as the severity of pulmonary valve stenosis progresses, the click eventually disappears owing to loss of valve pliability. A systolic murmur is present, which increases in intensity and duration as the severity of pulmonary valve stenosis worsens. The pulmonic component of S_2 is delayed and eventually disappears with increasing severity; eventually a right ventricular S_4 is heard.

Diagnostic Evaluation

The ECG and chest radiograph findings in patients with pulmonary valve stenosis are outlined in Table 38. Transthoracic echocardiography confirms the diagnosis of pulmonary valve stenosis by identifying a pressure gradient across the right ventricular outflow tract. Pulmonary valve mobility and the effects of obstruction on the right ventricle may impact treatment options. Right heart enlargement in patients with pulmonary valve stenosis suggests an associated lesion such as pulmonary regurgitation or an ASD. CMR imaging and CT are not routinely used in the assessment of patients with known or suspected pulmonary valve stenosis. It is sometimes difficult to differentiate pulmonary valve stenosis from subpulmonic or supravalvular stenosis. In these patients, CMR imaging may be useful. Cardiac catheterization is primarily used when intervention is considered.

Treatment

The treatment of choice for pulmonary valve stenosis is pulmonary balloon valvuloplasty. Balloon valvuloplasty is indicated for asymptomatic patients with appropriate pulmonary valve morphology who have a peak instantaneous Doppler gradient of at least 60 mm Hg or a mean gradient greater than 40 mm Hg and pulmonary valve regurgitation that is less than moderate. Balloon valvuloplasty is also recommended for symptomatic patients with appropriate valve morphology who have a peak instantaneous Doppler gradient of greater than 50 mm Hg or a mean gradient greater than 30 mm Hg. Operative intervention is recommended when pulmonary valve stenosis is associated with a small pulmonary annulus, more than moderate pulmonary regurgitation, or subvalvar or supravalvar pulmonary stenosis.

Patients with previous balloon or surgical pulmonary valvuloplasty are at increased risk for the development of pulmonary valve regurgitation. Long-term follow-up (clinical and imaging) is required for patients with pulmonary stenosis after pulmonary balloon valvuloplasty. Residual pulmonary stenosis is uncommon after balloon or surgical pulmonary valvuloplasty.

Patients with mild or moderate pulmonary valve stenosis (peak gradient <50 mm Hg) do not require exercise restriction; those with more severe stenosis should participate only in low-intensity sports.

Reproductive Considerations

Women with pulmonary valve stenosis generally tolerate pregnancy unless the lesion is severe. Percutaneous valvotomy has been performed during pregnancy.

KEY POINTS

- Transthoracic echocardiography confirms the diagnosis of pulmonary valve stenosis by identifying a pressure gradient across the right ventricular outflow tract.
- The treatment of choice for pulmonary valve stenosis is pulmonary balloon valvuloplasty.

- Operative intervention is recommended when pulmonary valve stenosis is associated with a small pulmonary annulus, more than moderate pulmonary regurgitation, or subvalvar or supravalvar pulmonary stenosis.

Aortic Coarctation

Pathophysiology

Aortic coarctation is a discrete narrowing in the descending aorta, most commonly located just beyond the left subclavian artery, causing high blood pressure proximal to the narrowing and reduced blood pressure distal to the narrowing.

Clinical Presentation

Patients with aortic coarctation may present with symptoms of exertional headaches, leg fatigue, or claudication. Findings include upper extremity hypertension with reduced blood pressure and pulses in the lower extremities, resulting in a radial artery–to–femoral artery pulse delay. A bicuspid aortic valve is present in more than 50% of patients with aortic coarctation.

Aortic coarctation is common in Turner syndrome, a chromosomal abnormality (45,X) that typically occurs in females and is characterized by short stature with a broad chest, widely spaced nipples, webbed neck, and cardiac defects. Additional cardiovascular associations with aortic coarctation include subaortic stenosis, parachute mitral valve, VSD, and cerebral artery aneurysms.

Aortic coarctation should be suspected if a systolic murmur is heard in the left infraclavicular region or over the back. When coarctation is severe, the murmur may be continuous, and a murmur from collateral intercostal vessels may also be audible and palpable over the anterior or posterior chest. In the presence of collateral vessels, the femoral pulses may be less diminished, and the measured systolic gradients may not reflect the severity of aortic coarctation. If a bicuspid aortic valve is present, patients may have an ejection click or a systolic murmur. An S_4 is often audible.

Diagnostic Evaluation

Transthoracic echocardiography is often the initial diagnostic test and usually confirms the presence of coarctation and associated features such as bicuspid aortic valve and left ventricular hypertrophy. The ECG and chest radiograph findings in patients with aortic coarctation are outlined in Table 38. The "figure 3 sign" on chest radiograph (**Figure 35**) is caused by dilatation of the aorta above and below the area of coarctation. Dilatation of intercostal arteries may also result in the characteristic radiographic appearance of "rib notching."

CMR imaging and CT are useful in delineating the coarctation severity, the presence of collateral vessels, and associated abnormalities such as aortic dilatation. Cardiac

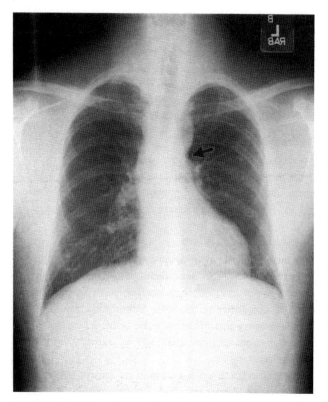

FIGURE 35. Chest radiograph of a patient with aortic coarctation exhibiting the figure 3 sign, caused by dilatation of the aorta above and below the area of coarctation (*arrow*).

catheterization is primarily performed in patients who are being considered for percutaneous intervention.

Treatment

Unoperated severe aortic coarctation is associated with reduced survival. Cardiovascular concerns such as systemic hypertension, accelerated coronary artery disease, stroke, aortic dissection, and heart failure are common causes of morbidity and mortality.

Intervention for coarctation is recommended when the systolic peak-to-peak gradient (peak pressure gradient across the coarctation) is 20 mm Hg or higher. Intervention may be indicated in patients with peak-to-peak coarctation gradient less than 20 mm Hg when radiologic evidence of significant coarctation with collateral flow is found. Surgical treatment is often preferred for patients with primary coarctation and percutaneous intervention preferred for patients with recoarctation.

Patients with residual or unrepaired coarctation, associated aortic stenosis, or a dilated aorta should be counseled to avoid contact sports and isometric exercise.

Reproductive Considerations

Patients without recoarctation after repair generally tolerate pregnancy well. A comprehensive prepregnancy evaluation is warranted to assess for residua. Operative intervention is generally recommended for patients with coarctation because of a concern about tissue integrity of the paracoarctation region during pregnancy.

Follow-up After Aortic Coarctation Repair

Hypertension is the most common cardiovascular problem following coarctation repair, occurring in up to 75% of patients; meticulous blood pressure control is indicated to prevent hypertension-related morbidity. Additional cardiovascular complications often require intervention; these include bicuspid aortic valve, aortic aneurysm affecting the coarctation repair site or the ascending aorta, aortic dissection, recoarctation, coronary artery disease, systolic or diastolic heart failure, and intracranial aneurysm.

Age at the time of repair is the most important predictor of long-term survival. Life-long follow-up is important and should include regular evaluation with a congenital cardiologist.

KEY POINTS

- Patients with aortic coarctation typically exhibit upper extremity hypertension with reduced blood pressure and pulses in the lower extremities, resulting in a radial artery–to–femoral artery pulse delay.

- Patients with residual or unrepaired coarctation, associated aortic stenosis, or a dilated aorta should be counseled to avoid contact sports and isometric exercise.

- Intervention for aortic coarctation is recommended when the systolic peak-to-peak gradient is 20 mm Hg or higher.

Tetralogy of Fallot

The anatomic features of tetralogy of Fallot include a large subaortic VSD, obstruction to pulmonary blood flow with infundibular or valvular pulmonary stenosis, aortic override, and right ventricular hypertrophy (**Figure 36**). Tetralogy of Fallot is the most common cyanotic congenital cardiac lesion, but adult patients who have not undergone surgery are rarely encountered.

Approximately 15% of all patients with tetralogy of Fallot have the chromosome 22q11.2 microdeletion, which increases the chance of congenital heart disease in the offspring to approximately 50% compared with approximately 5% in offspring of patients without the microdeletion. Dysmorphic facial features may not be present and genetic screening is recommended for all patients planning reproduction. Tetralogy of Fallot is also commonly seen in Down syndrome.

Successful surgical repair of tetralogy of Fallot results in near normal survival; however, because of the high risk of residua, annual follow-up by an adult congenital cardiologist is recommended. Surgical repair involves patch closure of the VSD and relief of right ventricular outflow tract obstruction,

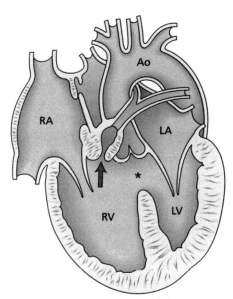

FIGURE 36. Tetralogy of Fallot. A subarterial ventricular septal defect (*asterisk*) and pulmonary stenosis (*arrow*) are associated with secondary aortic override and right ventricular hypertrophy. Ao = aorta; LA = left atrium; LV = left ventricle; RA = right atrium; RV = right ventricle.

Redrawn from original supplied courtesy of Dr. William D. Edwards, Department of Laboratory Medicine and Pathology, Mayo Clinic, Rochester, MN.

most commonly using a transannular patch, which disrupts the integrity of the pulmonary valve, causing pulmonary valve regurgitation. Pulmonary valve regurgitation is the most common residua after repair, causing progressive right heart enlargement, tricuspid regurgitation with resultant right heart enlargement, exercise limitation, and increased risk for atrial and ventricular arrhythmias. Pulmonary valve regurgitation is the most common reason for reoperation in patients after repair of tetralogy of Fallot.

Diagnostic Evaluation after Repair of Tetralogy of Fallot

The ECG and chest radiograph findings in patients with repaired tetralogy of Fallot are outlined in Table 38. Atrial flutter or fibrillation suggests hemodynamic or anatomic residua such as pulmonary valve regurgitation. The QRS duration reflects the degree of right ventricular dilatation: a QRS duration of 180 msec or longer and nonsustained ventricular tachycardia are risk factors for sudden cardiac death.

Transthoracic echocardiography should be performed regularly after repair and can confirm residua of pulmonary or tricuspid valve regurgitation, right ventricular outflow tract obstruction, or VSD. Aortic regurgitation may also occur after repair and is usually related to aortic dilatation. CMR imaging is often performed in the assessment of right ventricular size and function; the information obtained is helpful in deciding appropriate timing for pulmonary valve replacement. CMR imaging, CT, or catheterization may be required to evaluate anatomy of the pulmonary arteries and coronary arteries. Diagnostic catheterization is occasionally required in patients with previous tetralogy of Fallot repair to assess hemodynamics, delineate coronary artery anatomy, and assess residual shunts.

Treatment of Tetralogy of Fallot Residua

Treatment of tetralogy of Fallot residua depends on the residual lesion identified. Pulmonary valve replacement is generally recommended in patients with repaired tetralogy of Fallot who have severe pulmonary valve regurgitation with symptoms, decreased exercise tolerance, moderate or greater right heart enlargement or dysfunction, or development of atrial or ventricular arrhythmias. Long-standing pulmonary valve regurgitation may eventually result in tricuspid regurgitation, and repair or replacement of the tricuspid valve may also be needed. Percutaneous pulmonary valve replacement is now available for select patients with previous operative intervention for tetralogy of Fallot. For patients with atrial fibrillation undergoing open-heart valve surgery, the maze procedure is a treatment option.

Patients with repaired tetralogy of Fallot and important residual sequelae should be cautioned regarding participation in contact sports, isometric exercise, and heavy weight lifting.

> **KEY POINTS**
> - Tetralogy of Fallot is the most common cyanotic congenital cardiac lesion, but adult patients who have not undergone surgery are rarely encountered.
> - Pulmonary valve regurgitation is the most common reason for reoperation after repair of tetralogy of Fallot.

Adults with Cyanotic Congenital Heart Disease

General Management

Right-to-left intracardiac or extracardiac shunts result in hypoxemia, erythrocytosis, and cyanosis. Examples include unrepaired or palliated complex congenital heart disease such as tetralogy of Fallot, truncus arteriosus, or tricuspid atresia. Eisenmenger syndrome is another form of cyanotic congenital heart disease. The increase in the erythrocyte mass in patients with cyanosis is a compensatory response to improve oxygen transport. The resulting physical features include central cyanosis and digital clubbing. Patients with cyanotic congenital heart disease are predisposed to hemostatic problems, scoliosis, arthropathy and arthritis, gallstones, pulmonary hemorrhage or thrombus, paradoxical cerebral emboli or cerebral abscess, and kidney dysfunction. Because of these problems, an adult congenital cardiac specialist should evaluate patients with cyanotic congenital heart disease at least annually.

Hospitalization of patients with right-to-left shunt should prompt consideration of filters on intravenous lines to prevent paradoxical air embolism. Consultation with a congenital cardiac specialist should be considered when patients with cyanotic congenital heart disease are hospitalized for medical or surgical problems. In the hospital, early ambulation or pneumatic compression devices are recommended for prevention of venous stasis and potential venous thrombosis and paradoxical embolism.

Most cyanotic patients have compensated erythrocytosis and stable hemoglobin levels. Rarely, hyperviscosity symptoms occur and are manifested by headaches and reduced concentration. Dehydration should be excluded before considering therapeutic phlebotomy. Phlebotomy for hyperviscosity is recommended for a hemoglobin level greater than 20 g/dL and a hematocrit level greater than 65% associated with hyperviscosity symptoms in the absence of dehydration. The procedure should be followed by fluid administration and should be performed no more than two or three times per year. Repeated phlebotomies deplete iron stores and may result in the production of iron-deficient erythrocytes or microcytosis. Microcytes are rigid, inefficient in oxygen transport, and increase the risk of stroke. The treatment for iron deficiency in a patient with destabilized erythropoiesis is oral iron therapy for a short time. The hemoglobin and serum ferritin levels should be monitored. After the serum ferritin and transferrin saturation are within the normal range, iron therapy is discontinued.

Maternal cyanosis is a recognized handicap to normal fetal growth and development, with an increased risk of intrauterine growth retardation and miscarriage. Maternal and fetal morbidity and mortality are increased and related to the degree of cyanosis, ventricular function, and pulmonary pressures.

Eisenmenger Syndrome

Eisenmenger syndrome is a form of cyanotic congenital heart disease characterized by a long-standing intracardiac shunt (caused by VSD, PDA, or, less commonly, ASD) that eventually reverses to a right-to-left shunt. This is infrequent today because of medical screening, availability of echocardiography early in life, and appropriate interventional options.

Conservative medical management is recommended for patients with Eisenmenger syndrome. Women with Eisenmenger syndrome should be cautioned to avoid pregnancy because of the 30% to 50% risk for maternal mortality. Persons with Eisenmenger syndrome should also be cautioned regarding dehydration, moderate or severe strenuous or isometric exercise, acute exposure to excess heat, chronic altitude exposure (which causes further reduction in oxygen saturation), and iron deficiency.

Annual evaluation by an adult congenital cardiac specialist is recommended for all patients with Eisenmenger syndrome. Noncardiac surgery should be performed at centers with expertise in the care of patients with complex congenital cardiac disease whenever possible. Meticulous care of intravenous lines is imperative, with filters to avoid paradoxical air embolism. Patients with Eisenmenger syndrome have improved survival compared with patients with pulmonary arterial hypertension from other causes. Pulmonary vasodilator therapy for patients with Eisenmenger syndrome with progressive symptoms may result in clinical improvement.

Patients with Eisenmenger syndrome should be advised against strenuous exercise or travel to altitudes above 1524 meters (5000 feet). Long-distance air travel should be approached with caution. Select patients may benefit from supplemental oxygen with prolonged air travel.

KEY POINTS

- Right-to-left intracardiac or extracardiac shunts result in hypoxemia, erythrocytosis, and cyanosis.
- Hospitalization of patients with right-to-left shunt should prompt consideration of filters on intravenous lines to prevent paradoxical air embolism.
- Women with Eisenmenger syndrome should be cautioned to avoid pregnancy because of the 30% to 50% risk for maternal mortality.

Diseases of the Aorta

Introduction

Aortic disease accounts for approximately 45,000 deaths annually within the United States. Appropriate surveillance and treatment of aortic disease are crucial to preventing catastrophic vascular events. Aneurysm, dissection, intramural hematoma, and atheromatous disease leading to embolism or penetrating ulcer are all processes that can affect the aorta.

Imaging of the Thoracic Aorta

There are no current recommendations for screening asymptomatic patients with imaging for abnormalities of the thoracic aorta, except in patients with underlying vascular pathology (Marfan syndrome, giant cell arteritis) or a positive family history for aortic disease. Abnormalities of the thoracic aorta are sometimes discovered incidentally on chest radiographs or CT scans of patients performed for other purposes. If an abnormality is found, additional noninvasive imaging of the aorta with CT, MRI, or echocardiography can be used to determine aortic cross-sectional area, which may predict the risk of acute aortic events such as aneurysm rupture and dissection. There is substantial variance in measured aortic dimension according to image technique, and comparison of measurements derived by different techniques is difficult. Current recommendations for elective aortic surgery take into account this variability. Additionally, measurement must be performed perpendicular to the long axis of the aorta, as oblique or tangential measurements may yield an overestimate of true aortic diameter. CT, MRI, and echocardiography have similar sensitivity and specificity for diagnosis of acute thoracic aorta disease, although each has advantages and disadvantages (**Table 39**). Invasive imaging of the aorta by angiography is

TABLE 39. Comparison of Thoracic Aortic Imaging Modalities		
Modality	**Screening**	**Acute Disease**
Echocardiography	Good visualization of aortic root/proximal ascending aorta	Allows definition of valvular pathology, myocardial function, pericardial disease
	No exposure to radiation or contrast dye	Bedside diagnosis
	Limited visualization of aortic arch	No exposure to radiation or contrast dye
		Limited visualization of aortic arch and great vessels
		Requires experienced operator
CT	Visualization of entire aorta and side branches	Visualization of entire aorta and side branches
	Exposes patient to radiation, iodinated contrast dye	Exposes patient to radiation, iodinated contrast dye
		Rapid imaging
		Multiplanar reconstruction
MRI	Visualization of entire aorta and side branches	Visualization of entire aorta and side branches
	No exposure to radiation or iodinated contrast dye	No exposure to radiation or iodinated contrast dye
		Prolonged image acquisition away from acute care area
		Contraindicated in patients with implanted pacemaker or defibrillator
		Gadolinium contrast dye contraindicated in patients with renal insufficiency

not indicated for screening and is rarely necessary for the diagnosis of acute disease; this modality should be reserved for patients in whom a percutaneous intervention is planned.

Thoracic Aortic Aneurysm

Thoracic aortic aneurysms may arise in relation to heritable or acquired disease. Heritable disorders include Marfan syndrome, other associated diseases that affect the aortic tissue, and the aortopathy associated with congenital heart disease. The latter is most common in association with bicuspid aortic valves. Thoracic aortic aneurysms associated with genetic mutations are at higher risk of dissection or rupture at a smaller size than those associated with degenerative disease.

Most acquired aortic disease is degenerative and related to hypertension, smoking, and atherosclerosis. Most remaining cases are attributable to acquired infections and inflammatory conditions, such as syphilis and Takayasu arteritis. Untreated syphilis is associated with an arteritis of the vasa vasorum within the aortic media, leading to ascending aortic aneurysm. Takayasu arteritis produces scarring and stenosis within the subclavian arteries, or, less commonly, the descending thoracic aorta (see MKSAP 16 Rheumatology). Pregnancy has also been associated with an increased risk for aortic dissection for unclear reasons, and specifically increases the risk in women with Marfan syndrome at aortic diameters that are smaller than would usually be considered for elective repair.

Most thoracic aortic aneurysms are detected incidentally, but a few are discovered in relation to compressive symptoms, such as hoarseness, stridor, or dysphagia. In some patients, phenotypic expression of genetic disease is recognizable and should prompt aortic imaging (**Table 40**). In other patients, a family history of thoracic aortic aneurysm or dissection should prompt imaging in first-degree family members and genetic counseling with possible DNA sequencing for relevant mutations. Regular surveillance is needed for determining the timing of elective repair. The type of surveillance and indications for repair differ depending on etiology (**Table 41**). Compressive symptoms and chest or back pain referable to aneurysm expansion should prompt urgent repair regardless of aortic size.

In patients with Marfan syndrome, several studies support the role of β-blockers in reducing the rate of aneurysm expansion. All patients with Marfan syndrome and associated aneurysm should receive β-blockers in the absence of a contraindication. In animal models of Marfan syndrome, angiotensin receptor blockade has demonstrated significant prevention of aneurysm expansion, which appears to be independent of hemodynamic effects. Preliminary pediatric studies support this result in humans, but large group, long-term comparative studies of angiotensin receptor blockade versus β-blockade are not yet completed. It is reasonable to prescribe an angiotensin receptor blocker for patients with Marfan syndrome unless contraindicated.

In all patients with thoracic aortic aneurysm, blood pressure elevation should be aggressively treated. Patients with degenerative atherosclerotic aneurysms should undergo appropriate aggressive risk factor modification. Although there is no evidence that this prevents aneurysm expansion, it

TABLE 40. Recognizable Clinical Features of Genetic Aortic Disease

Clinical Syndrome	External Phenotypic Features
Marfan syndrome	Superior lens dislocation
	Arm span greater than height
	Joint hypermobility
	Arachnodactyly
	Scoliosis
	Tall stature
	Sternal deformity (carinatum type)
	Thumb sign (distal phalanx protrudes beyond border of clenched fist)
	Wrist sign (thumb and fifth digit overlap when around wrist)
	High palate
	Mitral valve prolapse (auscultation)
Loeys-Dietz syndrome	Bifid uvula or cleft palate
	Hypertelorism
	Craniosynostosis
	Skeletal features similar to Marfan syndrome
	Thin, translucent skin[a]
Ehlers-Danlos syndrome, vascular form	Thin, translucent skin

[a]In transforming growth factor–β receptor 2 (TGFBR2) type.

will help decrease the risk of coexisting coronary, peripheral, and cerebral vascular disease.

Repair of ascending aortic and aortic arch aneurysms requires surgery and may include aortic valve replacement in patients with significant annular dilatation or associated aortic valve pathology. Endovascular stent grafts have been approved by the FDA for the treatment of descending thoracic aortic aneurysms. Endovascular stent repair has been associated with shorter hospital stays and lower hospital morbidity and has the potential advantages of avoiding thoracotomy, aortic cross-clamping, and extracorporeal support. However, no randomized data are available comparing such treatment with open surgical repair or with medical therapy, and no evidence shows that spinal cord injury (related to the anterior spinal artery) is less common with endovascular repair. Stroke rates between 2.5% and 8% have been reported with endovascular repair, most likely due to catheter and guide wire manipulation within an atherosclerotic aorta. Additionally, "endoleaks" are not uncommon, whereby there is incomplete exclusion of the aneurysm sac by the endograft with continued blood flow into the area. Endoleaks may require subsequent surgical repair. Some anatomic considerations limit the use of endovascular repair, including the availability of appropriate "landing zones" for the stent and peripheral arteries large enough and free enough of atherosclerosis to accept the large catheters employed. There is no routine need for warfarin or antiplatelet therapy after aortic endograft placement, although many patients have other associated indications for antiplatelet agents. Given the large diameter of these stents, graft thrombosis is a rare event. Additionally, there is no indication for antibiotic prophylaxis after endovascular aortic repair prior to dental procedures.

KEY POINTS

- Compressive symptoms and chest or back pain referable to thoracic aortic aneurysm expansion should prompt urgent repair regardless of aortic size.
- Stroke rates between 2.5% and 8% have been reported with endovascular repair of thoracic aortic aneurysms.
- There is no routine need for warfarin or antiplatelet therapy after thoracic aortic endograft placement.
- Antibiotic prophylaxis is not indicated after endovascular thoracic aortic aneurysm repair prior to dental procedures.

TABLE 41. Asymptomatic Thoracic Aortic Aneurysm Surveillance and Timing of Repair

Etiology	Preferred Imaging Modality and Surveillance Schedule	Indication for Repair[a]
Marfan syndrome	TTE at diagnosis and at 6 months, then annually if aortic size is stable	≥5 cm external diameter (CT or MRI) (similar internal diameter by echocardiography likely to be 4.6-4.8 cm) ≥4 cm in women considering pregnancy
Loeys-Dietz syndrome	MRI of entire arterial system from head to pelvis annually	4.4 to 4.6 cm external diameter (MRI or CT) or ≥4.2 cm internal diameter by TEE
Familial TAAD	CT or MRI at diagnosis and at 6 months, then annually if aortic size is stable	Repair should be considered at dimensions <5 cm
Degenerative disease	CT or MRI: annual surveillance for 3.5-4.4 cm, semiannual surveillance for 4.5-5.0 cm	≥5.5 cm

TAAD = thoracic aortic aneurysm/dissection; TEE = transesophageal echocardiography; TTE = transthoracic echocardiography.

[a]Rapid expansion (>0.5 cm/year) may be an indication for repair regardless of absolute diameter.

Acute Aortic Syndromes

Diagnosis and Evaluation

Acute aortic syndromes include aortic dissection, intramural hematoma, and penetrating atherosclerotic ulcer (**Figure 37**). A tear in the aortic intima with formation of a flap and migration of a column of blood into the media is characteristic of dissection. Intramural hematomas may result from rupture of the vasa vasorum or "microtears" in the intima, resulting in a crescent of hematoma within the media without identifiable

Acute aortic dissection

Acute intramural hematoma

Penetrating atherosclerotic ulcer

FIGURE 37. Cross-sectional representation of acute aortic syndromes. Acute aortic dissection: interruption of intima (*blue*) with creation of an intimal flap and false lumen formation within the media (*red*). Color flow by Doppler echocardiography or intravenous (IV) contrast by CT is present within the false lumen in the acute phase. Acute intramural hematoma: crescent-shaped hematoma contained within the media without interruption of the intima (*blue*). No color flow by Doppler echocardiography or IV contrast by CT within crescent. Penetrating atherosclerotic ulcer: atheroma (*yellow*) with plaque rupture disrupting intimal integrity; blood pool contained within intima-medial layer (pseudoaneurysm). Color flow by Doppler echocardiography or IV contrast by CT enters the ulcer crater.

interruption of the intima. These may progress to typical dissection with intimal flap or aneurysmal dilatation, or they may resolve with time and treatment. Penetrating atherosclerotic ulcers occur in the setting of severe aortic atherosclerosis and hypertension. Plaque rupture and erosion of blood into (and sometimes through) the aortic media result in a contained pseudoaneurysm.

The acute aortic syndromes present similarly, with the abrupt onset of severe thoracic pain. Classic descriptions of ripping or tearing pain are present in approximately half of patients with aortic dissection, and more than half of patients with dissection demonstrate widening of the mediastinum on a chest radiograph. Migratory pain, significant differences in arm blood pressures, palpated pulse discrepancies or deficits, and the murmur of aortic insufficiency are important features of the history and physical examination. However, these classic elements of the history, physical examination, and chest radiograph are often ephemeral or absent, and therefore an acute aortic syndrome must be considered in any patient with new onset of unexplained severe thoracic pain. The diagnosis of an acute aortic syndrome is confirmed by imaging.

Treatment

Patients with suspected acute aortic syndrome who are not in shock should receive medical therapy aimed at reducing heart rate and blood pressure. An intravenous β-blocker should be administered to a target heart rate of 60 to 80/min. Following this, a rapidly titratable antihypertensive medication, such as sodium nitroprusside or fenoldopam, should be given intravenously, with a goal of decreasing the mean arterial pressure to the lowest level that still allows visceral and cerebral perfusion.

Decisions regarding optimal therapy are dependent on the location of the origin of the injury. The Stanford classification describes type A dissections as originating within the ascending aorta or arch, whereas type B dissections originate distal to the left subclavian artery. This nomenclature has been generalized to all of the acute aortic syndromes, although most intramural hematomas and penetrating ulcers are type B.

Type A aortic dissection is a surgical emergency, and surgery provides a survival benefit compared with medical therapy. No current application of endovascular therapy is accepted for type A aortic dissection. Type A intramural hematoma carries a high mortality risk, similar to that of dissection, and most authorities favor early surgical correction. The risks for early complications and death appear to be higher with large hematomas (>11 mm) and in patients with associated root dilatation (>4.8 cm).

Most type B aortic syndromes should be treated medically. Medical treatment includes tight blood pressure control with β-blockers being the initial agent of choice, as described above.

Indications for interventional therapy in type B aortic syndromes are as follows:

CONT.

- Occlusion of a major aortic branch with visceral or limb ischemia
- Progressive dilation or extension despite appropriate medical therapy
- Contained rupture of type B aortic dissection
- Penetrating atherosclerotic ulcer ≥20 mm in diameter and >10 mm in depth
- Penetrating atherosclerotic ulcer with associated intramural hematoma

For complicated type B syndromes, open surgical revascularization has largely been replaced by endovascular percutaneous techniques. Although not FDA-approved other than for aneurysm repair, interventional strategies using stent grafts include fenestration of a dissection flap, stenting of malperfused side branches, occlusion of the origin of a dissection, and exclusion of a pseudoaneurysm or penetrating ulcer. There is currently no accepted role for prophylactic endovascular stent grafting of type B aortic lesions to prevent extension, dilation, and malperfusion syndromes.

KEY POINTS

- An acute aortic syndrome must be considered in any patient with unexplained abrupt onset of severe chest or back pain.
- Patients with a suspected acute aortic syndrome who are not in shock should immediately receive medical therapy aimed at reducing heart rate and blood pressure.
- Acute aortic syndromes involving the ascending aorta or arch are surgical emergencies.

Aortic Atheroma

Atherosclerotic changes within the aorta are common in adults and may be detected incidentally during imaging procedures or as part of a directed search for the cause of a stroke. In patients with stroke, an atheroma within the ascending aorta or arch measuring 4 mm or more has been associated with increased risk of recurrent stroke. Plaques that are highly mobile, ulcerated, and particularly those that are not calcified may also be associated with higher risk. Plaques are commonly seen on transesophageal echocardiography (**Figure 38**), although visualization of the distal aortic arch is relatively limited compared with CT or MRI imaging.

No prospective data exist regarding the treatment of asymptomatic patients with an aortic atheroma. However, because of primary and secondary stroke prevention data that have accrued with the use of statins, it is reasonable to consider statin therapy when an aortic arch atheroma is discovered. One observational study of patients with aortic atheromas demonstrated significant reduction of stroke risk in patients treated with statins. In addition to a statin, patients with an unexplained cerebrovascular event with an aortic

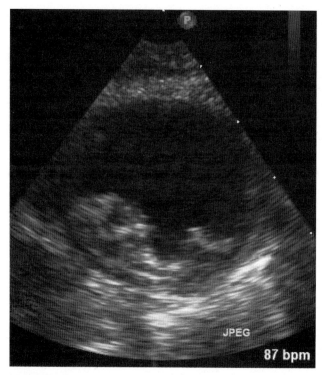

FIGURE 38. An aortic atheroma is demonstrated on a transverse view of the descending thoracic aorta on transesophageal echocardiogram. A complex atheroma is seen projecting 1 cm into the aortic lumen.

atheroma should be treated with warfarin (to an adjusted INR of 2.0-3.0) or antiplatelet therapy. No comparative data exist to conclusively answer which option is superior, but a large trial is under way (ARCH trial).

Data regarding surgery for aortic arch atheromas are isolated to prophylactic arch endarterectomy in patients undergoing other cardiovascular operations. An unacceptably high stroke risk was associated with the procedure.

KEY POINTS

- An aortic atheroma larger than 4 mm proximal to the left subclavian artery is a risk factor for recurrent stroke.
- Patients with an unexplained cerebrovascular event with an aortic atheroma should be treated with a statin and antiplatelet therapy or warfarin (to an adjusted INR of 2.0-3.0).

Abdominal Aortic Aneurysm

Screening and Surveillance

The greatest risk factors for the development of abdominal aortic aneurysm (AAA) are age, male sex (men outnumber women by up to 6:1), and a history of smoking (duration being more important than total number of cigarettes smoked). A family history of AAA appears to significantly raise the risks for first-degree relatives, although genetic markers of disease susceptibility have not been established (with the exception of the vascular form of Ehlers-Danlos syndrome). Current guidelines from the U.S. Preventive Services Task Force recommend a one-time ultrasonographic screening in men aged 65 to 75 years who have ever smoked. The sensitivity and specificity of ultrasonography for detection of AAA are excellent.

After AAA has been identified, surveillance imaging results determine the timing of repair (**Table 42**). Elective repair of asymptomatic AAA is recommended at 5.5 cm or if expansion of greater than 0.5 cm/year is noted. Symptomatic AAA, heralded by otherwise unexplained lower back or abdominal pain, should be treated urgently regardless of the absolute aneurysm dimension.

Treatment

Because of the high associated incidence of cardiovascular disease, all patients with AAA should be screened and treated for comorbid hypertension and hyperlipidemia. Continued smoking correlates with increased risk of AAA expansion, and patients should be counseled to quit.

Medical therapy for small AAAs is controversial regarding its ability to delay expansion. Several prospective studies of β-blockade have failed to demonstrate an effect relative to placebo, but these studies were hampered by poor adherence to treatment. Statin therapy reduces atherosclerotic risks, has anti-inflammatory effects, and may reduce the activity of matrix metalloproteinases; however, no conclusive data in humans show that statins reduce aneurysm expansion. Similarly, there is no convincing evidence that ACE inhibitors decrease the rate of aneurysm expansion. Several small studies have shown the use of macrolide antibiotics may slow AAA expansion in patients with serologic evidence of *Chlamydia pneumoniae* infection, but further study is needed before adoption of this treatment.

Open surgical or endovascular aneurysm repair (EVAR) may be considered for the treatment of symptomatic or asymptomatic large AAAs in patients with a life expectancy greater than 2 years. The interventional choice is determined by anatomic considerations, operative risks, and availability of regular patient follow-up, which is necessary for surveillance of EVAR. EVAR is associated with shorter hospital stays and lower hospital morbidity. In large trials, however,

no long-term difference has been noted in total mortality or aneurysm-related mortality. EVAR is associated with more graft-related complications and more repeat procedures. In patients with severe comorbid disease considered not eligible for open surgical correction, a trial of EVAR versus conventional medical therapy demonstrated no difference in all-cause mortality and, as expected, greater cost and complications associated with endovascular repair. A trial of EVAR versus open surgical repair for ruptured AAA has demonstrated significant reduction (25%) in perioperative mortality for the EVAR group, and this difference was still present at 6 months, suggesting that EVAR may be the treatment of choice for extremely high-risk patients.

KEY POINTS

- Current guidelines recommend a one-time ultrasonographic screening for abdominal aortic aneurysm in men aged 65 to 75 years who have ever smoked.
- Elective repair of asymptomatic abdominal aortic aneurysm is recommended at 5.5 cm or if expansion of greater than 0.5 cm/year is noted.
- Open surgical or endovascular repair may be considered for the treatment of symptomatic or asymptomatic large abdominal aortic aneurysms in patients with a life expectancy greater than 2 years.

Peripheral Arterial Disease

Epidemiology and Screening

Peripheral arterial disease (PAD) is physiologically significant atherosclerosis of the aortic bifurcation or the arteries of the lower limbs. It is strongly associated with smoking, diabetes mellitus, and aging, and shares all risk factors common to atherosclerosis. PAD is defined noninvasively by calculation of the ankle-brachial index (ABI). PAD is common, with an estimated unselected adult incidence of 3% to 10% and an even greater incidence (15% to 20%) in patients older than 70 years. Most patients with PAD are asymptomatic; approximately 25% have symptoms referable to circulatory compromise.

Patients with an abnormal ABI have an annual event rate of 5% to 7% for myocardial infarction (MI), ischemic stroke, or vascular death, and most patients with PAD die from cardiovascular causes. The severity of PAD correlates with risk, with an estimated increase of 10% in major cardiovascular events for every decrease of the ABI by 0.1. Patients with critical limb ischemia have a 25% risk of death within the first year of presentation. Screening for PAD in asymptomatic patients remains controversial, but should be considered in patients at high risk (**Table 43**).

TABLE 42. Recommended Surveillance Imaging for Abdominal Aortic Aneurysm by Diameter	
Aneurysm Diameter (cm)	**Surveillance Interval**
2.6-2.9	5 years
3.0-3.4	3 years
3.5-4.4	1 year
≥4.5	6 months

TABLE 43. Indications for Peripheral Arterial Disease Screening

Age ≥50 years and a history of diabetes or smoking
Age ≥65 years
Exertional leg symptoms
Nonhealing leg ulcers

Recommendations from Rooke TW, Hirsch AT, Misra S, et al. 2011 ACCF/AHA Focused Update of the Guideline for the Management of Patients With Peripheral Artery Disease (Updating the 2005 Guideline): A Report of the American College of Cardiology Foundation/American Heart Association Task Force on Practice Guidelines. Circulation. 2011;124(18):2020-2045. [PMID: 21959305]

KEY POINT

- Most patients with peripheral arterial disease are asymptomatic; screening using the ankle-brachial index should be considered in patients at high risk.

Evaluation

History and Physical Examination

Patients with atherosclerotic risk factors should be screened for symptoms consistent with PAD; specifically, frequency, duration, and length of walking; frequency and location of any symptoms; and the effects of limb and body position relative to symptoms. Classic claudication (reproducible exertional muscle cramping relieved by rest) is uncommon but provides clues regarding the site of stenosis. Claudication is most often experienced just distal to the level of obstruction: aortoiliac disease results in buttock or thigh pain, superficial femoral disease leads to upper calf pain, and popliteal disease is associated with lower calf pain. Patients commonly describe vague symptoms of leg fatigue, pain, or difficulty walking; such symptoms in patients with risk factors should raise suspicion of PAD. Symptoms that may reflect etiologies other than PAD should be identified (**Table 44**).

All patients at risk for PAD should undergo a directed physical examination including palpation of the femoral, popliteal, dorsalis pedis, and posterior tibial pulses. Weak, absent, or asymmetric pulses suggest disease. Auscultation may reveal abdominal or femoral bruits associated with "inflow" lesions to the lower extremities. Shiny skin and hair loss below the knee suggest PAD. Shoes and socks must be removed and the feet inspected for skin discoloration, breakdown, or ulceration.

Diagnostic Testing

The ABI is the ratio of lower extremity systolic pressure to upper extremity systolic pressure. The ABI is sensitive and specific for the diagnosis of PAD and has excellent reproducibility when obtained by trained personnel. Patients are examined in the fully supine position after a period of rest. A hand-held Doppler probe is used to locate the dorsalis pedis and posterior tibial pulses on each side. A manually operated blood pressure cuff is applied above the malleolus and inflated to occlude blood flow. As the cuff is slowly deflated, the blood pressure at which the first arterial flow is detected is recorded for both arteries. The procedure is then repeated in the opposite lower extremity, and the same technique is applied to record the systolic pressure in both brachial arteries. The ABI for each leg is the highest ankle

TABLE 44. Differential Diagnosis of Peripheral Arterial Disease

Disease	Notes
Osteoarthritis	Pain locates to the hips and knees; pain with variable activity and certain positions; common in the same age group as PAD
Sensory neuropathy	Pain not dependent on activity, more often position-related; symptoms include numbness or burning pain; patients often younger than those with PAD; association with diabetes mellitus
Musculoskeletal disease	Diffuse muscle pains, unrelated to activity; typical in patients with fibromyalgia and systemic autoimmune diseases
Venous disease	Limb pain worsens with activity and standing; limb elevation relieves the pain; usually associated with edema; patients younger and may have history of DVT; leg pruritus, hyperpigmentation, and medial malleolar ulcers may be present
Lumbar radiculopathy	Pain may be burning and localized to the back of the leg; history of back problems or pain in the setting of back injury
Popliteal entrapment syndrome	Pain affects the calves and worsens with physical activity; drop in the ABI occurs with dorsiflexion; occurs in young athletes
Chronic compartment syndrome	Pain affects calves and is worse after a long duration of physical activity; ABI is not affected; occurs primarily in young athletes
Lumbar spinal stenosis	Pain is bilateral, involving thighs and/or buttocks; not necessarily related to exertion; may be provoked by prolonged standing. Pain relieved with sitting, lying down, or leaning forward

ABI = ankle-brachial index; DVT = deep venous thrombosis; PAD = peripheral arterial disease.

TABLE 45. Interpretation of the Ankle-Brachial Index

Ankle-Brachial Index	Interpretation
>1.40	Noncompressible (calcified) vessel (uninterpretable result)
1.00-1.40	Normal
0.91-0.99	Borderline
0.41-0.90	Mild to moderate PAD
0.00-0.40	Severe PAD

PAD = peripheral arterial disease.

pressure for that side divided by the highest brachial pressure (regardless of side). An ABI of 0.90 or lower establishes a diagnosis of PAD; an ABI of 0.40 or less is associated with severe PAD (Table 45).

An ABI greater than 1.40 is associated with calcified vessels and is not an interpretable result. Because great toe vessels are less commonly calcified, a toe-brachial index may provide a useful alternative measure. A toe-brachial index less than 0.70 is considered diagnostic of PAD. Alternatively, a great toe systolic pressure greater than 40 mm Hg is considered normal. In patients with borderline or normal ABI and symptoms highly suggestive of PAD, an exercise test may be performed. A decrease of the ABI by 20% after exercise suggests significant PAD.

Noninvasive angiography is performed for anatomic delineation of PAD in patients requiring surgical or endovascular intervention. CT angiography (CTA) is rapid and easily available but requires the administration of intravenous contrast dye. The risk of dye-induced nephropathy must be considered in patients with chronic kidney disease, especially if an endovascular repair is being contemplated, because it would entail repeat administration of iodinated contrast dye. Magnetic resonance angiography (MRA) requires intravenous gadolinium for PAD definition; gadolinium has been associated with nephrogenic systemic fibrosis in patients with chronic kidney disease. Additionally, MRA may be contraindicated in patients with implanted pacemakers and cardioverter-defibrillators. Both CTA and MRA compare favorably with digital subtraction (invasive) angiography for the detection of occlusive arterial disease. CTA has additional benefits of demonstrating vascular calcification, has higher spatial resolution than MRA, and allows visualization of adjacent soft tissues and of endovascular stent grafts. Invasive angiography, in most instances, is used only as part of an interventional procedure.

KEY POINT

- An ankle-brachial index (ABI) of 0.90 or lower establishes a diagnosis of peripheral arterial disease; an ABI of 0.40 or less is associated with severe peripheral arterial disease.

Medical Therapy

Cardiovascular Risk Reduction

Smoking cessation is imperative for patients with PAD. Patients who quit smoking have a lower risk for PAD progression, critical limb ischemia, and amputation. Smokers with PAD who quit have lower risks for MI and stroke and greater long-term survival compared with smokers. Additionally, peripheral arterial surgical bypass graft patency rates are lower in smokers.

PAD is considered equivalent to coronary disease in guidelines for lipid-lowering therapy. All patients with PAD should use a statin to lower their LDL cholesterol level to less than 100 mg/dL (2.59 mmol/L). In patients with diabetes mellitus, multiple risk factors, or previous peripheral revascularization procedures, an LDL cholesterol goal of below 70 mg/dL (1.81 mmol/L) has been recommended by some advisory panels. Although no prospective statin trials have focused singularly on PAD, the Heart Protection Study (HPS) included 6748 patients with PAD in the study group. This large-scale study of statin versus placebo in patients at high risk demonstrated a 24% relative risk reduction for cardiovascular events in treated patients, and the subgroup with PAD shared similar benefits (even in patients without a history of MI or coronary artery disease). Additionally, high-dose statin use modestly improves pain-free walking distance in patients with claudication.

Hypertension is commonly associated with PAD. In one large international registry, more than 80% of patients with PAD had hypertension. In the INVEST trial, patients with hypertension, coronary artery disease, and PAD had a 26% increased risk of death, MI, or stroke compared with those without PAD. Controversy exists regarding the importance of specific classes of medication used for blood pressure control. Current guidelines state a blood pressure goal of less than 140/90 mm Hg for patients with PAD. In patients with diabetes or kidney disease, a lower target (<130/80 mm Hg) may be considered. Data from several recent trials suggest that evaluation of the blood pressure goal for patients with PAD deserves further study and that evidence is insufficient to recommend use of one class of antihypertensive agent over another. β-Blockers do not worsen PAD and should be used when appropriate for a cardiac indication.

The Antithrombotic Trialists' Collaboration meta-analysis found a 22% odds reduction (1.3% absolute risk reduction) for adverse cardiovascular events in patients with PAD treated with antiplatelet therapy compared with those not receiving such treatment. Aspirin doses of 75 to 150 mg/d were as effective as higher dosing. Clopidogrel at a dose of 75 mg/d may be used in patients who cannot tolerate aspirin, but it is more expensive. Cilostazol has effects on platelet aggregation and is a direct arterial vasodilator that has been shown to significantly increase pain-free walking distance in patients with claudication, but it has not been evaluated in comparison with other antiplatelet strategies.

Antiplatelet therapy is indicated for all patients with symptomatic PAD, previous lower extremity revascularization, or amputation due to PAD. Antiplatelet therapy is reasonable in patients with asymptomatic PAD, particularly if they have evidence of atherosclerosis elsewhere (coronary or cerebral arteries). Combination treatment with an antiplatelet agent and warfarin, and warfarin monotherapy (adjusted to an INR of 2.0-3.0), is no more effective than antiplatelet therapy alone and carries a higher risk of life-threatening bleeding.

Although diabetes mellitus is strongly associated with PAD and tight glycemic control decreases microvascular complications, no prospective studies have demonstrated that intensive diabetic control (hemoglobin A_{1c} <7%) reduces macrovascular complications.

Symptom Relief

Exercise and cilostazol are effective therapies for patients with stable symptomatic PAD. Patients must be motivated to engage in a regular supervised exercise program, which should include a minimum of 30 to 45 minutes of exercise at least three times weekly for at least 12 weeks. This exercise regimen leads to substantial gains in pain-free walking time and maximal walking time, exceeding the gains demonstrated with any pharmacotherapy. Studies evaluating patients instructed to engage in self-directed, home-based exercise programs have not demonstrated the same degree of benefit as supervised programs, although unsupervised exercise may be beneficial if a supervised program is not possible.

Cilostazol is a phosphodiesterase inhibitor with antiplatelet activity and vasodilatory properties. Cilostazol is contraindicated in patients with chronic heart failure because of its structural association with milrinone, which increases mortality in patients with heart failure. Compared with placebo, cilostazol significantly increases pain-free walking time and maximal walking time, although the gains with exercise are two- to three-fold greater than with cilostazol alone. Cilostazol also showed significant benefit regarding these metrics compared with pentoxifylline, a methylxanthine derivative. The maximal benefits of cilostazol may take weeks to months to emerge, and lack of apparent benefit with short-term treatment should not connote failure of the drug.

Pentoxifylline is approved for claudication, but data regarding significant benefits are lacking. It should be reserved for patients who cannot take cilostazol. Alternative therapies, such as L-arginine, carnitine, *Ginkgo biloba* extract, and chelation therapy have not shown benefit.

KEY POINTS

- Smoking cessation, blood pressure control, and lipid lowering are important for cardiovascular risk reduction in patients with peripheral arterial disease.

- Antiplatelet therapy is indicated for all patients with symptomatic peripheral arterial disease (PAD) and should be considered in patients with asymptomatic PAD to reduce cardiovascular risk.

- Exercise and cilostazol are effective therapies to alleviate symptoms in patients with stable symptomatic peripheral arterial disease.

Interventional Therapy

Patients with stable claudication progress to critical limb ischemia and limb loss at a rate of less than 5% annually. For most symptomatic patients, therefore, noninvasive therapy with exercise and medication is appropriate. If conservative therapy fails or patients have symptoms limiting their lifestyle or employment, revascularization should be considered.

Endovascular treatment has become the revascularization modality of choice for aortoiliac disease in all but the most complex lesions (**Figure 39**). This reflects high procedural success, low restenosis rates, and decreased morbidity and mortality compared with open surgical repair. American College of Cardiology/American Heart Association guidelines recommend primary stent placement as opposed to angioplasty with provisional stenting as needed. Primary stenting is associated with a 43% reduction in long-term failure compared with angioplasty alone.

Stent placement within the common femoral artery is generally avoided. A theoretical concern of flexion-related stent fracture exists because of the location immediately above the hip joint. Additionally, the common femoral artery is the most common site of arterial access for diagnostic angiography and interventional procedures, which may be limited by stent placement. Endarterectomy with possible surgical patch repair is the preferred technique for revascularization of the common femoral artery.

Revascularization of the deep femoral artery has traditionally required open surgical therapy. Recently, small studies have demonstrated safety and feasibility of endovascular repair, but large group studies and long-term follow-up are lacking.

Revascularization strategies of the superficial femoral artery for claudication are numerous and have included surgery, cryotherapy, brachytherapy, laser-assisted angioplasty, bare metal and drug-eluting stents, as well as debulking strategies using atherectomy or cutting balloons. No comprehensive comparative trials have addressed all of these approaches. TASC II guidelines for the treatment of superficial femoral artery claudication recommend an endovascular approach for short stenoses (<3 cm) and an open surgical approach for stenoses longer than 5 cm. No conclusions were drawn regarding the preferred therapy for intermediate lesions. A randomized trial has demonstrated improvement in ABI and walking distance, and showed significantly lower restenosis rates, when a strategy of primary stent placement was compared with angioplasty and provisional

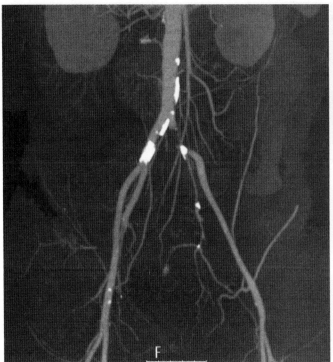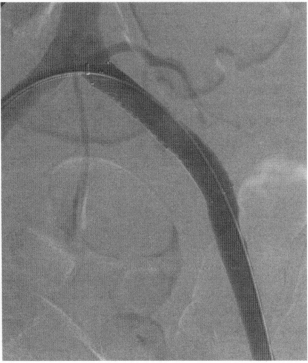

FIGURE 39. Iliac artery stenosis and intervention. Left panel: CT angiogram demonstrating occlusive common iliac artery disease and associated vascular calcification. Right panel: Successful stenting of the common iliac artery.

stenting. Additionally, the recent RESILIENT trial demonstrated excellent acute procedural and 1-year patency rates achieved with primary stenting in long lesions (mean length in the stent group was 71 mm). The results with primary stenting were superior to balloon angioplasty.

> **KEY POINTS**
>
> - For most symptomatic patients with peripheral arterial disease, noninvasive therapy with exercise and medication is appropriate.
>
> - Endovascular treatment with primary stent placement has become the revascularization modality of choice in patients with aortoiliac disease who fail conservative treatment.
>
> - Endarterectomy with possible surgical patch repair is the preferred technique for revascularization of the common femoral artery.

Acute Limb Ischemia

Acute limb ischemia (ALI) results from progression of severe atherosclerotic disease, superimposed thrombosis, or embolization. Embolization may occur spontaneously in patients with atrial fibrillation, left ventricular thrombus, or left-sided endocarditis. Cholesterol embolization may occur after arterial instrumentation and is heralded by systemic illness, kidney dysfunction, eosinophilia, and livedo reticularis. Treatment for cholesterol embolization syndrome is supportive.

Patients with ALI present with resting limb pain, weakness, or sensory deficits. The physical examination may demonstrate a pallid and cool limb. Rapid evaluation of arterial pulses and pressures, muscle strength, and sensory deficits is necessary in determining appropriate therapy.

Patients with ALI can be divided into four categories (**Table 46**). Patients with a viable limb should receive combined antiplatelet and systemic heparin therapy. Early consultation with a vascular specialist is appropriate, along with planned noninvasive arteriography. Limb salvage is achieved in most patients with appropriate therapy.

Patients with either a marginally or immediately threatened limb require emergent hospitalization and consultation with a vascular specialist along with antiplatelet and antithrombotic therapy. Emergent intervention and revascularization are necessary if the limb is to be saved. In some patients, intra-arterial thrombolytic therapy may be employed. However, in patients with muscle weakness or persistent sensory loss, urgent surgical or endovascular therapy is generally necessary.

Patients with findings signifying irreversible ischemia have a nonviable limb, and major tissue loss is inevitable. Prompt amputation is required.

The benefits of bypass surgery versus angioplasty for severe limb ischemia were evaluated in the United Kingdom

TABLE 46.	Categories and Prognosis of Acute Limb Ischemia			
Category	**Sensory Loss**	**Muscle Weakness**	**Arterial Doppler Signals**	**Prognosis**
Viable	None	None	Audible	Not immediately threatened
Marginally threatened	None to minimal (toes)	None	Inaudible	Salvageable with prompt treatment
Immediately threatened	More than toes	Mild to moderate	Inaudible	Salvageable only with immediate revascularization
Irreversible	Profound anesthesia	Profound/paralysis	Inaudible	Not viable; major tissue loss inevitable

Reprinted with permission. Circulation. 2006;113:e464-e654. ©2006, American Heart Association, Inc. [PMID: 16549646]

CONT.

BASIL trial. No difference was noted between these strategies in overall survival or amputation-free survival at 2 years from randomization; beyond 2 years, however, bypass surgery appeared to be most advantageous. The authors concluded that in patients expected to live more than 2 years, a strategy of bypass surgery is preferred to balloon angioplasty.

Recently, the PaRADISE trial evaluated drug-eluting stents for critical limb ischemia below the knee. High immediate procedural success was coupled with a 3-year survival of 71% and amputation-free survival of 68%. Although the populations differ slightly, patients in the BASIL trial had an amputation-free survival of 55% at 3 years. The results of the PaRADISE trial suggest that primary drug-eluting stent implantation for ALI below the knee is safe, effective, and associated with improved survival and freedom from amputation compared with historic controls. Within this study, all patients received dual preprocedural antiplatelet therapy with aspirin and a thienopyridine, and the continuation of both was advised indefinitely afterwards. **H**

KEY POINTS

- Acute limb ischemia results from progression of severe atherosclerotic disease, superimposed thrombosis, or embolization.

- Patients with either a marginally or immediately threatened limb require emergent hospitalization and consultation with a vascular specialist along with antiplatelet and antithrombotic therapy.

Cardiovascular Disease in Cancer Survivors

Cardiotoxicity of Radiation Therapy to the Thorax

Manifestations and Monitoring of Cardiotoxicity After Completion of Radiation Therapy

Breast cancer, Hodgkin lymphoma, and malignancies of the chest are commonly managed with radiation therapy. Such therapy can be cardiotoxic. Cardiovascular complications may present shortly or years after therapy (**Table 47**).

The risk for cardiotoxicity increases with higher total radiation dose, dose per fraction, and volume of heart in the field. No single threshold dose exists below which cardiotoxicity cannot occur. Treatment with cardiotoxic chemotherapeutic medications potentiates the risk of developing cardiac injury. Although modern methods of reducing radiation doses to the heart are likely to substantially lessen the frequency and severity of cardiotoxicity, this remains to be established.

Cancer survivors exposed to thoracic radiation therapy require a life-long strategy of monitoring because radiation-related cardiotoxicity may progress without clinical manifestations. Although no specific guidelines have been adopted, a reasonable approach includes annual cardiovascular evaluation, including history, clinical examination, and electrocardiography. A fasting lipid profile and glucose testing every 3 to 5 years is suggested because of the risk of premature coronary atherosclerosis, and counseling for smoking cessation should be provided.

For asymptomatic patients, echocardiography 10 years after irradiation may be beneficial for the detection of occult pericardial constriction and assessment of cardiac and valvular function. In patients with coronary artery disease (CAD) before radiation treatment or with atherosclerotic risk factors, a surveillance nuclear perfusion stress test 5 years after therapy should be considered.

Management of Radiation-Induced Coronary Artery Disease

In patients with radiation-induced CAD, management is similar to native disease; however, important differences exist. Coronary artery bypass surgery for radiation-induced CAD is associated with more frequent complications because of concomitant mediastinal fibrosis. Bare-metal stenting of radiation-induced CAD has a restenosis rate of 80%. Whether use of drug-eluting stents will lower this high restenosis rate is unknown.

Pericardiectomy for pericardial constriction is higher risk because of adherent epicardial fibrosis, and outcomes may not

TABLE 47. Cardiotoxicity of Radiation Therapy to the Thorax

Manifestations	Clinical Onset After Radiation Therapy	Comments
Acute pericarditis or pericardial effusion	As early as 2 months, but 5 months on average	A common cardiac complication historically (25%), less common now (2%) owing to methods minimizing mediastinal irradiation
Pericardial fibrosis and constriction	As early as 1.5 years, but often more than 10 years	Risk persists for >25 years
		RV more extensively involved, leading to marked findings of RV failure
Accelerated coronary atherosclerosis	Average onset 7 years	Predilection for involvement of ostia or proximal segments of coronaries
		Patients with traditional risk factors for CAD are at higher risk
		May occur in absence of traditional risk factors for CAD
		May manifest as myocardial infarction
		Sudden death may occur rarely
Valvular fibrosis and regurgitation	10 to 25 years or more	Frequency greater in left- vs. right-sided valves
		Clinically significant aortic regurgitation may occur in ≥25% of long-term survivors
		Slowly progressive and requires lifelong monitoring
		Concomitant anthracycline use increases risk
Myocardial fibrosis, diastolic dysfunction, and restrictive cardiomyopathy	Years	Concomitant anthracycline use increases risk for heart failure
Fibrosis of conduction pathways leading to bradycardia, dysrhythmias, or heart block	Years or decades	

CAD = coronary artery disease; RV = right ventricle.

always be favorable (**Figure 40**); however, pericardiectomy remains the only effective treatment.

Cardiotoxicity of Chemotherapy

Manifestations and Monitoring of Cardiotoxicity After Completion of Chemotherapy

Chemotherapeutic agents can cause myocardial necrosis, leading to dilated cardiomyopathy. Cancer survivors previously treated with chemotherapeutic drugs remain at long-term risk from adverse and potentially fatal cardiotoxic effects (**Table 48**).

Cardiotoxicity of anthracycline and anthracycline-like agents may manifest at any time during treatment or years after therapy. Risk factors include dose exposure (>550 mg/m^2 for doxorubicin), advanced age (>70 years), radiation therapy of the thorax, administration of additional cardiotoxic agents, hypertension, and possibly coexistent myocardial or coronary disease. Incidence of heart failure has been estimated to be 26% with cumulative doses of doxorubicin of more than 550 mg/m^2. Incidence decreases to 3% to 5% with cumulative doses of 400 mg/m^2.

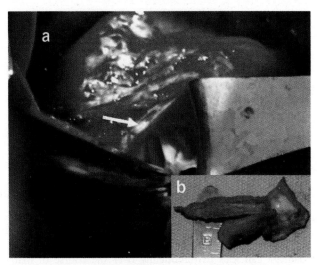

FIGURE 40. Pericardiectomy for radiation-induced pericardial constriction. Intraoperative view showing an opened pericardial sac (*arrow*) in panel A; marked thickening is apparent (panel B). This patient developed pericardial constriction 15 years after radiation therapy for Hodgkin lymphoma.

TABLE 48. Late-Onset Cardiotoxicity of Chemotherapeutic Agents[a]

Drug	Cardiotoxicity
Anthracyclines	Synergistic toxicity when administered with nonanthracycline agents
Doxorubicin	Heart failure (1.6%-5%)
	Higher in elderly women
	Typically irreversible
	Improved by aggressive treatment (resynchronization therapy)
	Left ventricular dysfunction (progression slowed by standard treatment)
	Dilated cardiomyopathy (odds ratio: 6.25[b])
	Cardiac death (odds ratio: 4.94[b])
Daunorubicin	Presumably similar to doxorubicin
Epirubicin	Heart failure (<5% with appropriate dosing)
Mitoxantrone	Heart failure
	Incidence significantly increased with dose >160 mg/m^2
	Survival improved by standard treatment
	Left ventricular dysfunction
Alkylating agents	
Cyclophosphamide	Heart failure (dose dependent)
	Left ventricular dysfunction (3%-5% with dose >100 mg/kg)
Cisplatin	Heart failure
Mitomycin	Cardiomyopathy
5-Fluorouracil	Heart failure (rare) from myocardial infarction occurring during treatment
Paclitaxel	Heart failure (if given with doxorubicin)
Trastuzumab	Heart failure
	0.6% (NYHA class III or IV)
	1.5% (NYHA class II at 2 y)
	Left ventricular dysfunction (3%; asymptomatic)
Interleukin-2	Heart failure from previous cardiomyopathy, myocarditis, or myocardial infarction occurring during treatment (rare)
Interferon-α	Heart failure from previous myocardial infarction during treatment (rare)

NYHA = New York Heart Association.

[a]Cardiotoxicity emerging 1 year or more after chemotherapy.

[b]When anthracycline is added to chemotherapy regimen.

Nonanthracycline and monoclonal antibody drugs can impair ventricular function. Unlike cardiomyopathy caused by anthracyclines, trastuzumab-induced ventricular dysfunction is largely reversible and not typically progressive.

Heart failure presenting years after cessation of cardiotoxic chemotherapy typically manifests as a dilated cardiomyopathy. Incidence is not clearly defined and diagnosis may be obscured by competing alternative potential causes, such as CAD. Late-developing anthracycline-induced cardiomyopathy and heart failure have a high mortality.

Myocardial damage from chemotherapeutic agents is not always demonstrable during therapy. Occult myocardial damage can lead to remodeling over the course of many years, whereby the left ventricle dilates with a decrease in ejection fraction, ultimately progressing to a dilated cardiomyopathy. This process is often subclinical, and although most authorities agree monitoring is necessary, no published guidelines for adult cancer survivors exist. A suggested schema for monitoring is presented in **Figure 41**. Left ventricular ejection fraction is most commonly measured using radionuclide ventriculography or echocardiography; however, systolic dysfunction is a late manifestation of cardiotoxicity. Development of diastolic dysfunction is an earlier sign and can be confirmed using echocardiography.

Reduced contractile reserve is an earlier feature of cardiotoxicity that can be detected by lack of significant increase in ejection fraction during stress echocardiography. This assessment should be considered if cardiotoxicity is suspected despite normal resting ejection fraction and diastolic function. Strain imaging assessed with echocardiography or cardiovascular magnetic resonance imaging may detect myocardial toxicity at even earlier stages and is reasonable to consider in the symptomatic

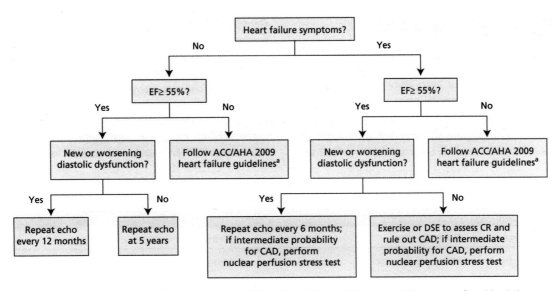

FIGURE 41. Suggested monitoring for myocardial toxicity after completion of chemotherapy with agents with late-onset cardiotoxicity. CAD = coronary artery disease; CR = contractility reserve; DSE = dobutamine stress echocardiography; Echo = two-dimensional, Doppler, and tissue Doppler echocardiography; EF = left ventricular ejection fraction.

[a]Hunt SA, Abraham WT, Chin MH, et al. 2009 Focused Update Incorporated into the ACC/AHA 2005 Guidelines for the Diagnosis and Management of Heart Failure in Adults. A Report of the American College of Cardiology Foundation/American Heart Association Task Force on Practice Guidelines. Circulation. 2009;119:e391-e479. [PMID:19324966]

patient with suspected cardiotoxicity but preserved ejection fraction and resting diastolic function. However, expertise in these advanced modalities is not yet widely available.

In the cancer survivor who develops systolic heart failure, alternative causes should also be sought, including CAD, uncontrolled hypertension, obstructive sleep apnea, and excessive alcohol ingestion.

Management of Chemotherapy-Induced Cardiotoxicity

It is unknown whether early detection and treatment of chemotherapy-induced myocardial toxicity before ejection fraction is reduced will result in improved outcome. However, this should not prohibit instituting appropriate treatment. As soon as patients develop new or worsening diastolic or systolic dysfunction they should be treated aggressively with medical therapy for heart failure. The prognosis for cancer survivors with dilated cardiomyopathy is poor.

In all patients who have had chemotherapy, particularly with chest radiotherapy, conventional risk factors for CAD must be identified and aggressively treated.

KEY POINTS

- Unlike cardiomyopathy caused by anthracyclines, trastuzumab-induced ventricular dysfunction is largely reversible and not typically progressive.

- It is unknown whether early detection and treatment of chemotherapy-induced myocardial toxicity results in improved outcomes, and no guidelines exist for monitoring adult cancer survivors for myocardial toxicity.

- In all patients who have had chemotherapy, particularly in association with chest radiotherapy, conventional risk factors for atherosclerotic coronary artery disease must be identified and aggressively treated.

Pregnancy and Cardiovascular Disease

Cardiovascular Changes During Pregnancy

Knowledge of the normal physiology of pregnancy is important in the interpretation of signs and symptoms in the pregnant patient (**Table 49**). Important hemodynamic changes that occur during a normal pregnancy include an increase in plasma volume and a lesser increase in erythrocyte mass, resulting in increased total blood volume and relative anemia. The systemic vascular resistance decreases substantially during pregnancy, although the heart rate and cardiac output rise; as a result, there is only a modest drop in mean arterial pressure. By the 32nd week of pregnancy, maternal cardiac output is approximately 40% above the prepregnancy level and stays at this level until term. During delivery, additional increases in heart rate and blood pressure lead to an increase in cardiac output to as much as 80% above the prepregnancy level.

Prepregnancy Evaluation

Prepregnancy clinical evaluation is recommended for all women anticipating pregnancy who have structural heart disease. Patients with congenital heart disease should consult with a specialist in adult congenital heart disease to evaluate the risks of future pregnancy and to develop a plan for management of labor and the postpartum period, including consideration of appropriate responses to potential complications.

Genetic counseling is recommended for patients with genetic syndromes who anticipate pregnancy.

The CARPREG index identifies women with cardiovascular disease who are at high risk for cardiovascular complications during pregnancy (**Table 50**). Independent predictors of maternal outcome and pregnancy-related complications identified in the CARPREG study were a previous cardiac event or arrhythmia, New York Heart Association (NYHA) functional class III or IV heart failure

TABLE 49.	Normal Versus Abnormal Cardiac Symptoms and Signs in Pregnancy	
Symptom or Sign	**Normal**	**Pathologic**
Shortness of breath	Mild, with exertion	Orthopnea, PND, cough
Palpitations	Atrial and ventricular premature beats	Atrial fibrillation or flutter; ventricular tachycardia
Chest pain	No	Chest pressure, heaviness, or pain
Murmur	Basal systolic murmur grade 1/6 or 2/6 present in 80% of pregnant women	Systolic murmur grade ≥3/6; any diastolic murmur
Tachycardia	Heart rate increased by 20%-30%	Heart rate >100/min
Low blood pressure	Blood pressure typically is modestly decreased (~10 mm Hg)	Low blood pressure associated with symptoms
Edema	Mild peripheral	Pulmonary edema
Gallop	S_3	S_4

PND = paroxysmal nocturnal dyspnea.

TABLE 50.	
Risk Factor (Predictor)	**Operational Definition**
Previous cardiac event or arrhythmia	Heart failure, transient ischemic attack, stroke, arrhythmia
Baseline NYHA class III or IV or cyanosis	Mild symptoms (mild shortness of breath and/or angina pain) and slight limitation during ordinary activity
Left-sided heart obstruction	Mitral valve area <2 cm²; aortic valve area <1.5 cm² or resting peak left ventricular outflow tract gradient >30 mm Hg
Reduced systemic ventricular systolic function	Ejection fraction <40%

Estimated Risk for Cardiac Events[a]		
No. of Predictors	**Estimated Risk (%)**	**Recommendation**
0	4	Consider preconception cardiac intervention for specific lesions; increase frequency of follow-up; delivery at community hospital
1	31	Consider preconception cardiac intervention for specific lesions; refer to regional center for ongoing care
>1	69	Consider preconception cardiac intervention for specific lesions; refer to regional center for ongoing care

NYHA = New York Heart Association.

[a]Pulmonary edema, tachyarrhythmia, embolic stroke, cardiac death.

Data and recommendations from Siu SC, Sermer M, Colman JM, et al. Cardiac Disease in Pregnancy (CARPREG) Investigators. Prospective multicenter study of pregnancy outcomes in women with heart disease. Circulation. 2001;104(5):515-521. [PMID: 11479246]

symptoms, cyanosis, left-sided heart obstruction, and systemic ventricular systolic dysfunction (with or without symptoms). Women with severe pulmonary hypertension (pulmonary artery pressure ≥ two-thirds of the systemic pressure) are at very high risk for cardiovascular complications during pregnancy, with an estimated maternal mortality between 30% and 50%. In the CARPREG study, however, pulmonary hypertension alone was not an independent risk factor because of its association with left-sided heart obstruction and poor functional class. Systemic ventricular systolic dysfunction (ejection fraction below 40%) associated with NYHA class III or IV heart failure carries a high risk of maternal and fetal complications and is generally considered a contraindication to pregnancy.

KEY POINTS

- Women with severe pulmonary hypertension (pulmonary artery pressure ≥ two-thirds of the systemic pressure) have an estimated maternal mortality between 30% and 50%.

- Women with an ejection fraction below 40% associated with NYHA class III or IV heart failure have a high risk of maternal and fetal complications.

Management of Cardiovascular Disease During Pregnancy

When a woman with cardiovascular disease becomes pregnant, special attention should be paid to her cardiovascular response to the hemodynamic changes that occur during pregnancy. In general, patients with obstructive cardiac lesions develop symptoms during pregnancy, whereas patients with regurgitant valve lesions tolerate pregnancy reasonably well. Vaginal delivery is generally preferred for all patients; however, cesarean delivery is recommended for obstetric reasons, in patients anticoagulated with warfarin (to reduce the risk of fetal intracranial hemorrhage), and in select patients with severe pulmonary hypertension or a markedly dilated ascending aorta.

Peripartum Cardiomyopathy

Peripartum cardiomyopathy is previously unrecognized left ventricular systolic dysfunction identified toward the end of pregnancy or in the months following delivery in the absence of another identifiable cause. Peripartum cardiomyopathy occurs with increased frequency in women who are multiparous, older than 30 years, or black; and in those with multifetal pregnancy, gestational hypertension, preeclampsia, or who have been treated with tocolytic agents. Half of women who develop peripartum cardiomyopathy show improvement in left ventricular systolic function within 6 months of delivery. Peripartum cardiomyopathy is the leading cause of pregnancy-related maternal death in North

America; deaths are related to heart failure, thromboembolic events, and arrhythmias.

Medical therapy should be started promptly in patients with peripartum cardiomyopathy and includes standard proven therapies for systolic dysfunction (β-blockers, digoxin, hydralazine, nitrates, and diuretics) as normally indicated. ACE inhibitors, angiotensin receptor blockers, and aldosterone antagonists should be avoided until after delivery. In women with a left ventricular ejection fraction below 35%, anticoagulation with warfarin is recommended owing to the increased risk of thromboembolism.

Therapies that have been demonstrated to have potential benefit in peripartum cardiomyopathy include intravenous immune globulin (related to the possible immune pathogenesis) and pentoxifylline, which inhibits tumor necrosis factor α. Most recently, bromocriptine, which blocks prolactin secretion, has been shown to improve left ventricular ejection fraction and composite clinical outcome in patients with acute severe peripartum cardiomyopathy when added to heart failure therapy.

For women with refractory severe heart failure related to peripartum cardiomyopathy, referral for a ventricular assist device or heart transplantation should be considered.

Subsequent pregnancy in women with peripartum cardiomyopathy is often associated with recurrent or further reduction of left ventricular function, which can result in clinical deterioration or even death. Thus, additional pregnancies should be discouraged in women with a history of peripartum cardiomyopathy with persistent left ventricular dysfunction.

Medication Use During Pregnancy

Data are limited on the safety of most cardiovascular medications during pregnancy, and most are not FDA-approved for use during pregnancy (**Table 51**). Although the desired therapeutic effect may outweigh the risk, medications should be used only when necessary. Some general guidelines for the use of several cardiovascular drugs during pregnancy are provided in **Table 52**.

β-Blockers cross the placenta and are present in human breast milk, causing significant levels in the fetus and newborn infant. When β-blockers are used during pregnancy or lactation, fetal and newborn heart rate and newborn blood glucose monitoring are indicated. Atenolol use during early pregnancy has been reported to cause small fetal size for

TABLE 51.	FDA Classification of Drugs in Pregnancy
Class	**Fetal Effect of Drug During Pregnancy**
A	No disclosed fetal effects
B	Animal studies suggest fetal risk
C	Animal studies suggest adverse fetal effects
D	Evidence of human fetal risk
X	Documented fetal abnormalities

gestational age, early delivery, and low birth weight and is therefore usually avoided during pregnancy. Patients taking this medication are usually transitioned to a different β-blocker. Adenosine is the treatment of choice for acute treatment of symptomatic supraventricular tachycardia during pregnancy. Recurrent symptoms are often treated with β-blockers and digoxin; sotalol and flecainide have also been safely used. Rarely (owing to toxicity concerns), amiodarone is used for refractory symptoms.

ACE inhibitors, angiotensin receptor blockers, and aldosterone antagonists should be avoided during pregnancy because of teratogenicity. These medications can be restarted after delivery. Some ACE inhibitors are safe to use while breastfeeding, but evidence is inconclusive to determine infant risk when angiotensin receptor blockers are used during breastfeeding. Spironolactone is considered compatible with breastfeeding; although spironolactone and the active metabolite, canrenone, appear in breast milk, the concentrations are too low to be pharmacologically significant.

Anticoagulation Therapy During Pregnancy

Pregnancy is a hypercoagulable state, and anticoagulation during pregnancy is indicated for women with atrial fibrillation, mechanical valve prosthesis, antiphospholipid antibody syndrome, and venous thromboembolism; regimens and level of anticoagulation depend on the specific indication (**Table 53**). Prepregnancy counseling is recommended for all women receiving chronic anticoagulation with warfarin to enable them to make an informed decision regarding which anticoagulation regimen is preferred during their pregnancy and to understand maternal and fetal risk.

Unfractionated heparin, low-molecular-weight heparin (LMWH), and warfarin can all be used for anticoagulation

TABLE 52.	Drugs for Cardiac Disorders in Pregnancy				
Drug	**Use Justified When Indicated**[a]	**Use Justified in Some Circumstances**[b]	**Use Rarely Justified**[c]	**Compatible with Breastfeeding**	**Comments**
ACE inhibitors					
Captopril, enalapril			✓	Y	Teratogenic in first trimester; cause fetal/neonatal kidney failure with second or third trimester exposure; scleroderma renal crisis is only indication
Lisinopril			✓	?	Same as above
ARBs			✓	?	Teratogenic in first trimester; cause fetal/neonatal kidney failure with second or third trimester exposure
Adenosine	✓			?	No change in fetal heart rate when used for supraventricular tachycardia
Amiodarone			✓	Not recommended	Fetal hypothyroidism, prematurity
Antiplatelet agents					
Dipyridamole, clopidogrel		✓		?	No evidence of harm in animal studies; no human data
Aspirin (≤81 mg)	✓			Y	
β-Blockers					
Atenolol		✓		N	Low birth weight, intrauterine growth restriction
Esmolol		✓		?	More pronounced bradycardia
Labetalol	✓			Y	Preferred drug in class
Metoprolol	✓			Y	Shortened half-life
Propranolol		✓		Y	Intrauterine growth restriction
Sotalol		✓		?	Insufficient data; reserve use for arrhythmia not responding to alternative agent

(Continued on the next page)

TABLE 52. Drugs for Cardiac Disorders in Pregnancy *(continued)*					
Drug	**Use Justified When Indicated[a]**	**Use Justified in Some Circumstances[b]**	**Use Rarely Justified[c]**	**Compatible with Breastfeeding**	**Comments**
Calcium channel blockers					
Diltiazem, verapamil		✓		Y	Maternal hypotension with rapid intravenous infusion; used for fetal supraventricular tachycardia.
Digoxin		✓		Y	Shortened half-life
Disopyramide		✓		Y	Case reports of preterm labor
Diuretics		✓		Y	Use when needed for maternal volume overload only
Flecainide		✓		?	Inadequate data but used for fetal arrhythmia; case report of fetal hyperbilirubinemia
Hydralazine	✓			Y	Vasodilator of choice
Lidocaine	✓			Y	Treatment of choice for ventricular arrhythmias
Sodium nitroprusside			✓	N	Potential fetal thiocyanate toxicity
Organic nitrates	✓			?	No apparent increased risk
Phenytoin			✓	Y	Known teratogenicity and bleeding risk; last resort for arrhythmia
Procainamide	✓			Y	Used for fetal arrhythmia
Propafenone		✓		?	Used for fetal arrhythmia
Quinidine	✓			Y	Preferred drug in class; increases digoxin levels

ARB = angiotensin receptor blocker; N = no; Y = yes; ? = unknown.

[a]Data or extensive experience support the safety of the drug for the indication.

[b]Less extensive or desirable data are reported, but the drug is reasonable as a second-line agent or is indicated based on the severity of maternal disease.

[c]Use only when alternatives supported by experience or better safety data are not available or for life-threatening indications.

Adapted from Rosene-Montella K, Keely EJ, Lee RV, Barbour LA. Medical Care of the Pregnant Patient. 2nd Edition. Philadelphia, PA: American College of Physicians; 2008. p 356-357. Copyright 2008, American College of Physicians.

during pregnancy. Warfarin is often avoided during the first trimester owing to concerns about warfarin embryopathy and is stopped before delivery owing to the risk for fetal intracranial hemorrhage if spontaneous labor occurs while the mother (and thus also the fetus) is anticoagulated with warfarin. Meticulous monitoring and dose adjustment are recommended for all anticoagulation regimens during pregnancy. The dosages of LMWH, unfractionated heparin, and warfarin may change during pregnancy, emphasizing the importance of regular monitoring. Maternal and fetal well-being also should be closely observed when anticoagulation is administered during pregnancy.

Pregnant women with mechanical valve prostheses represent a high-risk subset of patients, with increased risk of valve thrombosis, bleeding, and fetal risk. The literature is controversial, and the best anticoagulation regimen for pregnant women with mechanical valve prostheses has not been established. Warfarin anticoagulation during pregnancy poses an increased fetal risk, with possible teratogenicity, miscarriage, and fetal loss due to intracranial hemorrhage. Data suggest, however, that warfarin may be the safest agent to prevent maternal prosthetic valve thrombosis. LMWH and unfractionated heparin are safer for the fetus; however, these therapies increase maternal risk by increasing the risk of prosthetic valve thrombosis.

The latest guidelines from the American College of Cardiology/American Heart Association on the management of anticoagulation during pregnancy conclude that unfractionated heparin, LMWH, or warfarin may be used for anticoagulation of pregnant women with mechanical heart valves. A best practice regimen has not been delineated.

TABLE 53. Anticoagulation Regimens During Pregnancy	
Weeks of Gestation	**Recommended Regimen**
Venous Thromboembolism	
Pregnancy – week 6	Warfarin
Week 6-12	UFH (IV or SQ; aPTT 2 × control)
	Weight-based LMWH
Week 13-37	UFH (SQ; aPTT 2 × control)
	Weight-based LMWH
	Warfarin (INR 2-3)
Week 37 to term	UFH (IV; aPTT 2 × control)
Atrial Fibrillation	
Pregnancy – week 6	Warfarin
Week 6-12	UFH (IV or SQ; aPTT 2 × control)
	Weight-based LMWH
Week 13-37	UFH (SQ; aPTT 2 × control)
	Weight-based LMWH
	Warfarin (INR 2-3)
Week 37 to term	UFH (IV; aPTT 2 × control)
Mechanical Valve Prosthesis	
Pregnancy – week 6	Warfarin
Week 6-12	UFH (IV or SQ; aPTT 2 × control)
	Anti-Xa adjusted LMWH
	Warfarin (INR 2.5-3.5)
Week 13-37	UFH (IV or SQ; aPTT 2 × control)
	Anti-Xa adjusted LMWH
	Warfarin (INR 2.5-3.5)
Week 37 to term	UFH (IV; aPTT 2 × control)
Ventricular Dysfunction	
Pregnancy – week 6	Warfarin
Week 6-12	UFH (IV or SQ; aPTT 2 × control)
	Weight-based LMWH
Week 13-37	UFH (SQ; aPTT 2 × control)
	Weight-based LMWH
	Warfarin (INR 2-3)
Week 37 to term	UFH (IV; aPTT 2 × control)

aPTT = activated partial thromboplastin time; IV = intravenous; LMWH = low-molecular-weight heparin; SQ = subcutaneous; UFH = unfractionated heparin.

Recommendations from Bonow RO, Carabello BA, Canu C, et al; American College of Cardiology/American Heart Association Task Force on Practice Guidelines; Society of Cardiovascular Anesthesiologists; Society for Cardiovascular Angiography and Interventions; Society of Thoracic Surgeons. ACC/AHA 2006 guidelines for the management of patients with valvular heart disease: report of the American College of Cardiology/American Heart Association Task Force on Practice Guidelines (Writing Committee to Develop Guidelines for the Management of Patients With Valvular Heart Disease). Circulation. 2006;114(5): e84-e231. [PMID: 16880336] and Bates SM, Greer IA, Pabinger I, Sofaer S, Hirsh J; American College of Chest Physicians. Venous thromboembolism, thrombophilia, antithrombotic therapy, and pregnancy: American College of Chest Physicians Evidence-Based Clinical Practice Guidelines (8th Edition). Chest. 2008;133(6 Suppl):844S-886S. [PMID:18574280] and Furie KL, Kasner SE, Adams RJ, et al; on behalf of the American Heart Association Stroke Council, Council on Cardiovascular Nursing, Council on Clinical Cardiology, and Interdisciplinary Council on Quality of Care and Outcomes Research. Guidelines for the prevention of stroke in patients with stroke or transient ischemic attack: a guideline for healthcare professionals from the American Heart Association/American Stroke Association. Stroke. 2011;42(1):227-276. [PMID: 20966421]

Bibliography

Epidemiology of Cardiovascular Disease

Forouhi NG, Sattar N. CVD risk factors and ethnicity—a homogeneous relationship? Atheroscler Suppl. 2006;7(1):11-19. [PMID: 16500156]

Knockaert DC. Cardiac involvement in systemic inflammatory diseases. Eur Heart J. 2007;28(15):1797-1804. [PMID: 17562669]

Lloyd-Jones D, Adams RJ, Brown TM, et al; American Heart Association Statistics Committee and Stroke Statistics Subcommittee. Executive summary: heart disease and stroke statistics—2010 update: a report from the American Heart Association. Circulation. 2010;121(7):948-954. [PMID: 20177011]

National Heart, Lung, and Blood Institute. Morbidity and mortality: 2009 chart book on cardiovascular and lung diseases. Bethesda, MD: National Institutes of Health; 2009. www.nhlbi.nih.gov/resources/docs/2009_ChartBook.pdf

Parikh NI, Hwang S-J, Larson MG, Levy D, Fox CS. Chronic kidney disease as a predictor of cardiovascular disease (from the Framingham Heart Study). Am J Cardiol. 2008;102(1):47-53. [PMID: 18572034]

Petri MA, Kiani AN, Post W, Christopher-Stine L, Magder LS. Lupus Atherosclerosis Prevention Study (LAPS). Ann Rheum Dis. 2011;70(5):760-765. [PMID: 21177297]

Yusuf S, Hawken S, Ounpuu S, et al; INTERHEART Study Investigators. Effect of potentially modifiable risk factors associated with myocardial infarction in 52 countries (the INTERHEART study): case-control study. Lancet. 2004;364(9438):937-952. [PMID: 15364185]

Diagnostic Testing in Cardiology

American College of Cardiology Foundation Task Force on Expert Consensus Documents; Hundley WG, Bluemke DA, Finn JP, et al. ACCF/ACR/AHA/NASCI/SCMR 2010 expert consensus document on cardiovascular magnetic resonance: a report of the American College of Cardiology Foundation Task Force on Expert Consensus Documents. J Am Coll Cardiol. 2010;55(23):2614-2662. [PMID: 20513610]

American College of Cardiology Foundation Task Force on Expert Consensus Documents; Mark DB, Berman DS, Budoff MJ, et al. ACCF/ACR/AHA/NASCI/SAIP/SCAI/SCCT 2010 expert consensus document on coronary computed tomographic angiography: a report of the American College of Cardiology Foundation Task Force on Expert Consensus Documents. J Am Coll Cardiol. 2010;55(23):2663-2699. [PMID: 20513611]

Bonow RO, Maurer G, Lee KL, et al; STICH Trial Investigators. Myocardial viability and survival in ischemic left ventricular dysfunction. N Engl J Med. 2011;364(17):1617-25. [PMID: 21463153]

Douglas PS, Khandheria B, Stainback RF, et al; American College of Cardiology Foundation Quality Strategic Directions Committee Appropriateness Criteria Working Group; American Society of Echocardiography; American College of Emergency Physicians; American Society of Nuclear Cardiology; Society for Cardiovascular Angiography and Interventions; Society of Cardiovascular Computed Tomography; Society for Cardiovascular Magnetic Resonance; American College of Chest Physicians; Society of Critical Care Medicine. ACCF/ASE/ACEP/ASNC/SCAI/SCCT/SCMR 2007 appropriateness criteria for transthoracic and transesophageal echocardiography: a report of the American College of Cardiology Foundation Quality Strategic Directions Committee Appropriateness Criteria Working Group, American Society of Echocardiography, American College of Emergency Physicians, American Society of Nuclear Cardiology, Society for Cardiovascular Angiography and Interventions, Society of Cardiovascular Computed Tomography, and the Society for Cardiovascular Magnetic Resonance endorsed by the American College of Chest Physicians and the Society of Critical Care Medicine. J Am Coll Cardiol. 2007;50(2):187-204. [PMID: 17616306]

Douglas PS, Khandheria B, Stainback RF, et al; American College of Cardiology Foundation Quality Strategic Directions Committee Appropriateness Criteria Working Group; American Society of Echocardiography; American College of Emergency Physicians; American Heart Association; American Society of Nuclear Cardiology; Society for Cardiovascular Angiography and Interventions; Society of Cardiovascular Computed Tomography; Society for Cardiovascular Magnetic Resonance; Heart Rhythm Society; Society of Critical Care Medicine. ACCF/ASE/ACEP/AHA/ASNC/SCAI/SCCT/SCMR 2008 appropriateness criteria for stress echocardiography: a report of the American College of Cardiology Foundation Quality Strategic Directions Committee Appropriateness Criteria Working Group, American Society of Echocardiography, American College of Emergency Physicians, American Heart Association, American Society of Nuclear Cardiology, Society for Cardiovascular Angiography and Interventions, Society of Cardiovascular Computed Tomography, and Society for Cardiovascular Magnetic Resonance endorsed by the Heart Rhythm Society and the Society of Critical Care Medicine. J Am Coll Cardiol. 2008;51(11):1127-1147. [PMID: 18342240]

Greenland P, Bonow RO, Brundage BH, et al; American College of Cardiology Foundation Clinical Expert Consensus Task Force (ACCF/AHA Writing Committee to Update the 2000 Expert Consensus Document on Electron Beam Computed Tomography); Society of Atherosclerosis Imaging and Prevention; Society of Cardiovascular Computed Tomography. ACCF/AHA 2007 clinical expert consensus document on coronary artery calcium scoring by computed tomography in global cardiovascular risk assessment and in evaluation of patients with chest pain: a report of the American College of Cardiology Foundation Clinical Expert Consensus Task Force (ACCF/AHA Writing Committee to Update the 2000 Expert Consensus Document on Electron Beam Computed Tomography) developed in collaboration with the Society of Atherosclerosis Imaging and Prevention and the Society of Cardiovascular Computed Tomography. J Am Coll Cardiol. 2007;49(3):378-402. [PMID: 17239724]

Zimetbaum PJ, Josephson ME. The evolving role of ambulatory arrhythmia monitoring in general clinical practice. Ann Intern Med. 1999;130(10):848-856. [PMID: 10366376]

Coronary Artery Disease

Antithrombotic Trialists' (ATT) Collaboration; Baigent C, Blackwell L, Collins R, et al. Aspirin in the primary and secondary prevention of vascular disease: collaborative meta-analysis of individual participant data from randomised trials. Lancet. 2009;373(9678):1849-1860. [PMID: 19482214]

BARI 2D Study Group; Frye RL, August P, Brooks MM, et al. A randomized trial of therapies for type 2 diabetes and coronary artery disease. N Engl J Med. 2009;360(24):2503-2515. [PMID: 19502645]

Cantor WJ, Fitchett D, Borgundvaag B, et al; TRANSFER-AMI Trial Investigators. Routine early angioplasty after fibrinolysis for acute myocardial infarction. N Engl J Med. 2009;360(26):2705-2718. [PMID: 19553646]

Chaitman BR, Hardison RM, Adler D, et al; Bypass Angioplasty Revascularization Investigation 2 Diabetes (BARI 2D) Study Group. The Bypass Angioplasty Revascularization Investigation 2 Diabetes randomized trial of different treatment strategies in type 2 diabetes mellitus with stable ischemic heart disease: impact of treatment strategy on cardiac mortality and myocardial infarction [erratum in Circulation. 2010;121(12):e254]. Circulation. 2009;120(25):2529-2540. [PMID: 19920001]

Di Mario C, Dudek D, Piscione F, et al; CARESS-in-AMI (Combined Abciximab RE-teplase Stent Study in Acute Myocardial Infarction) Investigators. Immediate angioplasty versus standard therapy with rescue angioplasty after thrombolysis in the Combined Abciximab REteplase Stent Study in Acute Myocardial Infarction (CARESS-in-AMI): an open, prospective, randomised, multicentre trial. Lancet. 2008;371(9612):559-568. [PMID: 18280326]

Fraker TD Jr, Fihn SD, Gibbons RJ, et al. 2007 chronic angina focused update of the ACC/AHA 2002 Guidelines for the management of patients with chronic stable angina: a report of the American College of Cardiology/American Heart Association Task Force on Practice Guidelines Writing Group to develop the focused update of the 2002 Guidelines for the management of patients with chronic stable angina [erratum in Circulation. 2007;116(23):e558]. Circulation. 2007;116(23):2762-2772. [PMID: 17998462]

Giugliano RP, White JA, Bode C, et al; EARLY ACS Investigators. Early versus delayed, provisional eptifibatide in acute coronary syndromes. N Engl J Med. 2009;360(21):2176-2190. [PMID: 19332455]

Gulati M, Cooper-DeHoff RM, McClure C, et al. Adverse cardiovascular outcomes in women with nonobstructive coronary artery disease: a report from the Women's Ischemia Syndrome Evaluation Study and the St James Women Take Heart Project. Arch Intern Med. 2009;169(9):843-850. [PMID: 19433695]

Kaul S, Bolger AF, Herrington D, Giugliano RP, Eckel RH; American Heart Association; American College of Cardiology Foundation. Thiazolidinedione drugs and cardiovascular risks: a science advisory from the American Heart Association and the American College of Cardiology Foundation. J Am Coll Cardiol. 2010;55(17):1885-1894. [PMID: 20413044]

Kushner FG, Hand M, Smith SC Jr, King SB 3rd, et al. 2009 Focused Updates: ACC/AHA Guidelines for the management of patients with ST-elevation myocardial infarction (updating the 2004 Guideline and 2007 Focused Update) and ACC/AHA/SCAI Guidelines on percutaneous coronary intervention (updating the 2005 Guideline and 2007 Focused Update): a report of the American College of Cardiology Foundation/American Heart Association Task Force on Practice Guidelines [erratum in Circulation. 2010;121(12):e257]. Circulation. 2009;120(22):2271-1306. [PMID: 19923169]

Lloyd-Jones D, Adams RJ, Brown TM, et al; American Heart Association Statistics Committee and Stroke Statistics Subcommittee. Executive summary: heart disease and stroke statistics—2010 update: a report from the American Heart Association. Circulation. 2010;121(7):948-954. [PMID: 20177011]

Mehta SR, Granger CB, Boden WE, et al; TIMACS Investigators. Early versus delayed invasive intervention in acute coronary syndromes. N Engl J Med. 2009;360(21):2165-2175. [PMID: 19458363]

Montalescot G, Cayla G, Collet JP, et al; ABOARD Investigators. Immediate vs delayed intervention for acute coronary syndromes: a randomized clinical trial. JAMA. 2009;302(9):947-954. [PMID: 19724041]

NICE-SUGAR Study Investigators; Finfer S, Chittock DR, Su SY, et al. Intensive versus conventional glucose control in critically ill patients. N Engl J Med. 2009;360(13):1283-1297. [PMID: 19318384]

Patel NB, Balady GJ. Diagnostic and prognostic testing to evaluate coronary artery disease in patients with diabetes mellitus. Rev Endocr Metab Disord. 2010;11(1):11-20. [PMID: 20225090]

Serruys PW, Morice MC, Kappetein AP, et al; SYNTAX Investigators. Percutaneous coronary intervention versus coronary-artery bypass grafting for severe coronary artery disease. N Engl J Med. 2009;360(10):961-972. [PMID: 19228612]

Shaw LJ, Bugiardini R, Merz CN. Women and ischemic heart disease: evolving knowledge. J Am Coll Cardiol. 2009;54(17):1561-1575. [PMID: 19833255]

Shroyer AL, Grover FL, Hattler B, et al; Veterans Affairs Randomized On/Off Bypass (ROOBY) Study Group. On-pump versus off-pump coronary-artery bypass surgery. N Engl J Med. 2009;361(19):1827-1837. [PMID: 19890125]

Sobel BE. Coronary revascularization in patients with type 2 diabetes and results of the BARI 2D trial. Coron Artery Dis. 2010;21(3):189-198. [PMID: 20308880]

Stone GW, Bertrand ME, Moses JW, et al; ACUITY Investigators. Routine upstream initiation vs deferred selective use of glycoprotein IIb/IIIa inhibitors in acute coronary syndromes: the ACUITY Timing trial. JAMA. 2007;297(6):591-602. [PMID: 17299194]

Heart Failure

Heart Failure Society of America; Lindenfeld J, Albert NM, Boehmer JP, et al. HFSA 2010 Comprehensive Heart Failure Practice Guideline. J Card Fail. 2010;16(6):e1-e194. [PMID: 20610207]

Hernandez AF, Greiner MA, Fonarow GC, et al. Relationship between early physician follow-up and 30-day readmission among Medicare beneficiaries hospitalized for heart failure. JAMA. 2010;303(17):1716-1722. [PMID: 20442387]

Hunt SA, Abraham WT, Chin MH, et al; American College of Cardiology Foundation; American Heart Association. 2009 Focused update incorporated into the ACC/AHA 2005 Guidelines for the Diagnosis and Management of Heart Failure in Adults: A report of the American College of Cardiology Foundation/American Heart Association Task Force on Practice Guidelines Developed in Collaboration With the International Society for Heart and Lung Transplantation. J Am Coll Cardiol. 2009;53(15):e1-e90. [PMID: 19358937]

Konstam MA, Neaton JD, Dickstein K, et al; HEAAL Investigators. Effects of high-dose versus low-dose losartan on clinical outcomes in patients with heart failure (HEAAL study): a randomised, double-blind trial [erratum in Lancet. 2009;374(9705):1888]. Lancet. 2009;374(9704):1840-1848. [PMID: 19922995]

O'Connor CM, Whellan DJ, Lee KL, et al; HF-ACTION Investigators. Efficacy and safety of exercise training in patients with chronic heart failure: HF-ACTION randomized controlled trial. JAMA. 2009;301(14):1439-1450. [PMID: 19351941]

Phillips CO, Kashani A, Ko DK, Francis G, Krumholz HM. Adverse effects of combination angiotensin II receptor blockers plus angiotensin-converting enzyme inhibitors for left ventricular dysfunction: a quantitative review of data from randomized clinical trials. Arch Intern Med. 2007;167(18):1930-1936. [PMID: 17923591]

Porapakkham P, Porapakkham P, Zimmet H, Billah B, Krum H. B-type natriuretic peptide-guided heart failure therapy: a meta-analysis. Arch Intern Med. 2010;170(6):507-514. [PMID: 20308637]

Reynolds HR, Hochman JS. Cardiogenic shock: current concepts and improving outcomes. Circulation. 2008;117(5):686-697. [PMID: 18250279]

Tang AS, Wells GA, Talajic M, et al; Resynchronization-Defibrillation for Ambulatory Heart Failure Trial Investigators. Cardiac-resynchronization therapy for mild-to-moderate heart failure. N Engl J Med. 2010;363(25):2385-95. [PMID: 21073365]

Zannad F, McMurray JJ, Krum H, et al; EMPHASIS-HF Study Group. Eplerenone in patients with systolic heart failure and mild symptoms. N Engl J Med. 2011;364(1):11-21. [PMID: 21073363]

Myocardial Disease

Alam M, Dokainish H, Lakkis NM. Hypertrophic obstructive cardiomyopathy—alcohol septal ablation vs. myectomy: a meta-analysis. Eur Heart J. 2009;30(9):1080-1087. [PMID: 19233857]

Elbardissi AW, Dearani JA, Daly RC, et al. Embolic potential of cardiac tumors and outcome after resection: a case-control study. Stroke. 2009;40(1):156-162. [PMID: 18948602]

Fifer MA, Vlahakes GJ. Management of symptoms in hypertrophic cardiomyopathy. Circulation. 2008;117(3):429-439. [PMID: 18212300]

Leonardi S, Raineri C, De Ferrari GM, et al. Usefulness of cardiac magnetic resonance in assessing the risk of ventricular arrhythmias and sudden death in patients with hypertrophic cardiomyopathy. Eur Heart J. 2009;30(16):2003-2010. [PMID: 19474054]

Marian AJ. Hypertrophic cardiomyopathy: from genetics to treatment. Eur J Clin Invest. 2010;40(4):360-369. [PMID: 20503496]

Seward JB, Casaclang-Verzosa G. Infiltrative cardiovascular diseases: cardiomyopathics that look alike. J Am Coll Cardiol. 2010;55(17):1769-1779. [PMID: 20413025]

Vaglio JC Jr, Ommen SR, Nishimura RA, Tajik AJ, Gersh BJ. Clinical characteristics and outcomes of patients with hypertrophic cardiomyopathy with latent obstruction. Am Heart J. 2008;156(2):342-347. [PMID: 18657666]

Arrhythmias

ACTIVE Investigators; Connolly SJ, Pogue J, Hart RG, et al. Effect of clopidogrel added to aspirin in patients with atrial fibrillation. N Engl J Med. 2009;360(20):2066-2078. [PMID: 19336502]

Blomström-Lundqvist C, Scheinman MM, Aliot EM, et al; American College of Cardiology; American Heart Association Task Force on Practice Guidelines; European Society of Cardiology Committee for Practice Guidelines. Writing Committee to Develop Guidelines for the Management of Patients with Supraventricular Arrhythmias. ACC/AHA/ESC guidelines for the management of patients with supraventricular arrhythmias–executive summary: a report of the American College of Cardiology/American Heart Association Task Force on Practice Guidelines and the European Society of Cardiology Committee for Practice Guidelines (Writing Committee to Develop Guidelines for the Management of Patients With Supraventricular Arrhythmias). Circulation. 2003;108(15):1871-1909. [PMID: 14557344]

Connolly SJ, Ezekowitz MD, Yusuf S, Eikelboom J, Oldgren J, Parekh A, et al. Dabigatran versus warfarin in patients with atrial fibrillation [erratum in N Engl J Med. 2010;363(19):1877]. N Engl J Med. 2009;361(12):1139-1151. [PMID 19717844]

Douketis JD, Berger PB, Dunn AS, Jaffer AK, Spyropoulos AC, Becker RC, et al. The perioperative management of antithrombotic therapy: American College of Chest Physicians Evidence-Based Clinical Practice Guidelines (8th Edition). Chest. 2008;133(6 Suppl):299S-339S. [PMID 18574269]

European Heart Rhythm Association; Heart Rhythm Society; Zipes DP, Camm AJ, Borggrefe M, et al. ACC/AHA/ESC 2006 guidelines for management of patients with ventricular arrhythmias and the prevention of sudden cardiac death: a report of the American College of Cardiology/American Heart Association Task Force and the European Society of Cardiology Committee for Practice Guidelines (Writing Committee to Develop Guidelines for Management of Patients With Ventricular Arrhythmias and the Prevention of Sudden Cardiac Death). J Am Coll Cardiol. 2006;48(5):e247-e346. [PMID: 16949478]

Goldenberg I, Moss AJ. Long QT syndrome. J Am Coll Cardiol. 2008;51(24):2291-2300. [PMID: 18549912]

Hohnloser SH, Crijns HJ, van Eickels M, et al; ATHENA Investigators. Effect of dronedarone on cardiovascular events in atrial fibrillation [errata in N Engl J Med. 2009;360(23):2487 and N Engl J Med.

2011;364(15):1481]. N Engl J Med. 2009;360(7):668-678. [PMID: 19213680]

Neumar RW, Otto CW, Link MS, et al. Part 8: adult advanced cardiovascular life support: 2010 American Heart Association Guidelines for Cardiopulmonary Resuscitation and Emergency Cardiovascular Care. Circulation. 2010;122(18 suppl 3):S729-S767. [PMID 20956224]

Van Gelder IC, Groenveld HF, Crijns HJ, et al; RACE II Investigators. Lenient versus strict rate control in patients with atrial fibrillation. N Engl J Med. 2010;362(15):1363-1373. [PMID: 20231232]

Wann LS, Curtis AB, January CT, et al. 2011 ACCF/AHA/HRS Focused Update on the Management of Patients With Atrial Fibrillation (Updating the 2006 Guideline): A Report of the American College of Cardiology Foundation/American Heart Association Task Force on Practice Guidelines. Circulation. 2011;123(1):104-23.[PMID: 21173346]

Pericardial Disease

Apodaca-Cruz A, Villarreal-Garza C, Torres-Avila B, et al. Effectiveness and prognosis of initial pericardiocentesis in the primary management of malignant pericardial effusion. Interact Cardiovasc Thorac Surg. 2010;11(2):154-161. [PMID: 20504889]

Imazio M, Brucato A, Cemin R, et al; on behalf of the CORP (COlchicine for Recurrent Pericarditis) Investigators. Colchicine for Recurrent Pericarditis (CORP) a randomized trial. Ann Intern Med. 2011;155(7):409-414. [PMID: 21873705.]

Imazio M, Cecchi E, Ierna S, Trinchero R; ICAP Investigators. Investigation of colchicine for acute pericarditis: a multicenter randomized placebo-controlled trial evaluating the clinical benefits of colchicine as adjunct to conventional therapy in the treatment and prevention of pericarditis; study design and rationale. J Cardiovasc Med. 2007;8(8):613-617. [PMID: 17667033]

Imazio M, Trinchero R. Myopericarditis: etiology, management, and prognosis. Int J Cardiol. 2008;127(1):17-26. [PMID: 18221804]

Imazio M, Trinchero R. Triage and management of acute pericarditis. Int J Cardiol. 2007;118(3):286-294. [PMID: 17049636]

Maruyama T, Hanaoka T, Nakajima H. Acute pericarditis in the recovery phase of transient left ventricular apical ballooning syndrome (takotsubo cardiomyopathy). Intern Med. 2007;46(22):1857-1860. [PMID: 18025768]

Schwefer M, Aschenbach R, Heidemann J, Mey C, Lapp H. Constrictive pericarditis, still a diagnostic challenge: comprehensive review of clinical management. Eur J Cardiothorac Surg. 2009;36(3):502-510. [PMID:19394850]

Valvular Heart Disease

Bonow RO, Carabello BA, Chatterjee K, et al; 2006 Writing Committee Members; American College of Cardiology/American Heart Association Task Force. 2008 Focused update incorporated into the ACC/AHA 2006 guidelines for the management of patients with valvular heart disease: a report of the American College of Cardiology/American Heart Association Task Force on Practice Guidelines (Writing Committee to Revise the 1998 Guidelines for the Management of Patients With Valvular Heart Disease): endorsed by the Society of Cardiovascular Anesthesiologists, Society for Cardiovascular Angiography and Interventions, and Society of Thoracic Surgeons. Circulation. 2008;118(15):e523- e661. [PMID: 18820172]

Chan KL, Teo K, Dumesnil JG, Ni A, Tam J; ASTRONOMER Investigators. Effect of lipid lowering with rosuvastatin on progression of aortic stenosis: results of the aortic stenosis progression observation: measuring effects of rosuvastatin (ASTRONOMER) trial. Circulation. 2010;121(2):306-314. [PMID 20048204]

Douglas PS, Khandheria B, Stainback RF, et al; American College of Cardiology Foundation Quality Strategic Directions Committee Appropriateness Criteria Working Group; American Society of Echocardiography; American College of Emergency Physicians; American Society of Nuclear Cardiology; Society for Cardiovascular Angiography and Interventions; Society of Cardiovascular Computed

Tomography; Society for Cardiovascular Magnetic Resonance; American College of Chest Physicians; Society of Critical Care Medicine. ACCF/ASE/ACEP/ASNC/SCAI/SCCT/SCMR 2007 appropriateness criteria for transthoracic and transesophageal echocardiography: a report of the American College of Cardiology Foundation Quality Strategic Directions Committee Appropriateness Criteria Working Group, American Society of Echocardiography, American College of Emergency Physicians, American Society of Nuclear Cardiology, Society for Cardiovascular Angiography and Interventions, Society of Cardiovascular Computed Tomography, and the Society for Cardiovascular Magnetic Resonance endorsed by the American College of Chest Physicians and the Society of Critical Care Medicine. J Am Coll Cardiol. 2007;50(2):187-204. [PMID: 17616306].

Douketis JD, Berger PB, Dunn AS, et al. The perioperative management of antithrombotic therapy: American College of Chest Physicians evidence-based clinical practice guidelines (8th edition). Chest 2008;133:299S-339S. [PMID: 18574269]

Foster E. Clinical practice. Mitral regurgitation due to degenerative mitral valve disease. N Engl J Med. 2010;363(2):156-165. [PMID: 20647211]

Li JS, Sexton DJ, Mick N, et al. Proposed modifications to the Duke criteria for the diagnosis of infective endocarditis. Clin Infect Dis. 2000;30(4):633-638. [PMID: 10770721]

Murdoch DR, Corey GR, Hoen B, et al; International Collaboration on Endocarditis-Prospective Cohort Study (ICE-PCS) Investigators. Clinical presentation, etiology, and outcome of infective endocarditis in the 21st century: the International Collaboration on Endocarditis-Prospective Cohort Study. Arch Intern Med. 2009;169(5):463-473. [PMID: 19273776]

Rahimtoola SH. Choice of prosthetic heart valve in adults: an update. J Am Coll Cardiol. 2010;55(22):2413-2426. [PMID: 20510209]

Tzemos N, Therrien J, Yip J, et al. Outcomes in adults with bicuspid aortic valves. JAMA. 2008;300(11):1317-1325. [PMID: 18799444]

Adult Congenital Heart Disease

Garg P, Servoss SJ, Wu JC, et al. Lack of association between migraine headache and patent foramen ovale: results of a case-control study. Circulation. 2010;121(12):1406-1412. [PMID: 20231534]

Kaemmerer H, Bauer U, Pensl U, et al. Management of emergencies in adults with congenital cardiac disease. Am J Cardiol. 2008;101(4):521-525. [PMID: 18312770]

Warnes CA, Williams RG, Bashore TM, et al. ACC/AHA 2008 guidelines for the management of adults with congenital heart disease: a report of the American College of Cardiology/American Heart Association Task Force on Practice Guidelines (Writing Committee to Develop Guidelines on the Management of Adults With Congenital Heart Disease). Developed in collaboration with the American Society of Echocardiography, Heart Rhythm Society, International Society for Adult Congenital Heart Disease, Society for Cardiovascular Angiography and Interventions, and Society of Thoracic Surgeons. J Am Coll Cardiol. 2008;52(23):e1-e121. [PMID: 19038677]

Diseases of the Aorta

Baxter BT, Terrin MC, Dalman RL. Medical management of small abdominal aortic aneurysms. Circulation. 2008;117(14):1883-1889. [PMID: 18391122]

Ferguson CD, Clancy P, Bourke B, et al. Association of statin prescription with small abdominal aortic aneurysm progression. Am Heart J. 2010;159(2):307-313. [PMID: 20152231]

De Bruin JL, Baas AF, Buth J, et al; DREAM Study Group. Long-term outcome of open or endovascular repair of abdominal aortic aneurysm. N Engl J Med. 2010;362(20):1881-1889. [PMID: 20484396]

Hiratzka LF, Bakris GL, Beckman JA, et al; American College of Cardiology Foundation/American Heart Association Task Force on Practice Guidelines; American Association for Thoracic Surgery; American College of Radiology; American Stroke Association; Society

of Cardiovascular Anesthesiologists; Society for Cardiovascular Angiography and Interventions; Society of Interventional Radiology; Society of Thoracic Surgeons; Society for Vascular Medicine. 2010 ACCF/AHA/AATS/ACR/ASA/SCA/SCAI/SIR/STS/SVM Guidelines for the diagnosis and management of patients with thoracic aortic disease. A Report of the American College of Cardiology Foundation/American Heart Association Task Force on Practice Guidelines, American Association for Thoracic Surgery, American College of Radiology, American Stroke Association, Society of Cardiovascular Anesthesiologists, Society for Cardiovascular Angiography and Interventions, Society of Interventional Radiology, Society of Thoracic Surgeons, and Society for Vascular Medicine. J Am Coll Cardiol. 2010;55(14):e27-e129. [PMID: 20359588]

Hirsch AT, Haskal ZJ, Hertzer NR, et al; American Association for Vascular Surgery; Society for Vascular Surgery; Society for Cardiovascular Angiography and Interventions; Society for Vascular Medicine and Biology; Society of Interventional Radiology; ACC/AHA Task Force on Practice Guidelines; American Association of Cardiovascular and Pulmonary Rehabilitation; National Heart, Lung, and Blood Institute; Society for Vascular Nursing; TransAtlantic Inter-Society Consensus; Vascular Disease Foundation. ACC/AHA 2005 guidelines for the management of patients with peripheral arterial disease (lower extremity, renal, mesenteric, and abdominal aortic): executive summary a collaborative report from the American Association for Vascular Surgery/Society for Vascular Surgery, Society for Cardiovascular Angiography and Interventions, Society for Vascular Medicine and Biology, Society of Interventional Radiology, and the ACC/AHA Task Force on Practice Guidelines (Writing Committee to Develop Guidelines for the Management of Patients With Peripheral Arterial Disease) endorsed by the American Association of Cardiovascular and Pulmonary Rehabilitation; National Heart, Lung, and Blood Institute; Society for Vascular Nursing; TransAtlantic Inter-Society Consensus; and Vascular Disease Foundation. J Am Coll Cardiol. 2006;47(6):1239-1312. [PMID: 16545667]

Ten Bosch JA, Teijink JAW, Willigendael EM, Prins MH. Endovascular aneurysm repair is superior to open surgery for ruptured abdominal aortic aneurysms in EVAR-suitable patients. J Vasc Surg. 2010;52(1):13-18. [PMID: 20471775]

United Kingdom EVAR Trial Investigators; Greenhalgh RM, Brown LC, Powell JT, Thompson SG, Epstein D. Endovascular repair of aortic aneurysm in patients physically ineligible for open repair. N Engl J Med. 2010;362(20):1872-1880. [PMID: 20382982]

United Kingdom EVAR Trial Investigators; Greenhalgh RM, Brown LC, Powell JT, Thompson SG, Epstein D, Sculpher MJ. Endovascular versus open repair of abdominal aortic aneurysm. N Engl J Med. 2010;362(20):1863-1871. [PMID: 20382983]

Peripheral Arterial Disease

Bavry AA, Anderson RD, Gong Y, et al. Outcomes among hypertensive patients with concomitant peripheral and coronary artery disease: findings from the INternational VErapamil-SR/Trandolapril STudy. Hypertension. 2010;55(1):48-53. [PMID: 19996066]

Feiring AJ, Krahn M, Nelson L, Wesolowski A, Eastwood D, Szabo A. Preventing leg amputations in critical limb ischemia with below-the-knee drug-eluting stents. The PaRADISE (PReventing Amputations using Drug eluting StEnts) trial. J Am Coll Cardiol. 2010;55(15):1580-1589. [PMID: 20378075]

Laird JR, Katzen BT, Scheinert D, et al. Nitinol stent implantation versus balloon angioplasty for lesions in the superficial femoral artery and proximal popliteal artery: twelve-month results from the RESILIENT randomized trial. Circ Cardiovasc Interv. 2010;3(3):267-276. [PMID: 20484101]

Norgren L, Hiatt WR, Dormandy JA, Nehler MR, Harris KA, Fowkes FG; TASC II Working Group. Inter-Society Consensus for the management of peripheral arterial disease (TASC II). J Vasc Surg. 2007;45(Suppl S):S5-S67. [PMID: 17223489]

Schillinger M, Sabeti S, Loewe C, et al. Balloon angioplasty versus implantation of nitinol stents in the superficial femoral artery. N Engl J Med. 2006;354(18):1879-1888. [PMID: 16672699]

Warfarin Antiplatelet Vascular Evaluation Trial Investigators; Anand S, Yusuf S, Xie C, et al. Oral anticoagulant and antiplatelet therapy and peripheral arterial disease. N Engl J Med. 2007;357(3):217-227. [PMID: 17634457]

Cardiovascular Disease in Cancer Survivors

Barbetakis N, Xenikakis T, Paliouras D, et al. Pericardiectomy for radiation-induced constrictive pericarditis. Hellenic J Cardiol. 2010;51(3):214-218. [PMID: 20515853]

Curigliano G, Mayer EL, Burstein HJ, Winer EP, Goldhirsch A. Cardiac toxicity from systemic cancer therapy: a comprehensive review. Prog Cardiovasc Dis. 2010 Sep-Oct;53(2):94-104. [PMID: 20728696]

Darby SC, Cutter DJ, Boerma M, et al. Radiation-related heart disease: current knowledge and future prospects. Int J Radiat Oncol Biol Phys. 2010;76(3):656-665. [PMID: 20159360]

Heidenreich PA, Kapoor JR. Radiation induced heart disease: systemic disorders in heart disease. Heart. 2009 Mar;95(3):252-8. Review. [PMID: 19144884]

Heidenreich PA, Schnittger I, Strauss HW, et al. Screening for coronary artery disease after mediastinal irradiation for Hodgkin's disease. J Clin Oncol. 2007;25(1):43-9. Erratum in: J Clin Oncol. 2007 Apr 20;25(12):1635. [PMID:17194904]

Myrehaug S, Pintilie M, Tsang R, et al. Cardiac morbidity following modern treatment for Hodgkin lymphoma: supra-additive cardiotoxicity of doxorubicin and radiation therapy. Leuk Lymphoma. 2008;49(8):1486-1493. [PMID: 18608873]

Wethal T, Lund MB, Edvardsen T, et al. Valvular dysfunction and left ventricular changes in Hodgkin's lymphoma survivors. A longitudinal study. Br J Cancer. 2009;101(4):575-581. [PMID: 19623176]

Pregnancy and Cardiovascular Disease

Siu SC, Sermer M, Colman JM, et al; Cardiac Disease in Pregnancy (CARPREG) Investigators. Prospective multicenter study of pregnancy outcomes in women with heart disease. Circulation. 2001;104(5):515-521. [PMID: 11479246]

Sliwa K, Blauwet L, Tibazarwa K, et al. Evaluation of bromocriptine in the treatment of acute severe peripartum cardiomyopathy: a proof-of-concept pilot study. Circulation. 2010;121(13):1465-1473. [PMID: 20308616]

Sliwa K, Hilfiker-Kleiner D, Petrie MC, et al; Heart Failure Association of the European Society of Cardiology Working Group on Peripartum Cardiomyopathy. Current state of knowledge on aetiology, diagnosis, management, and therapy of peripartum cardiomyopathy: a position statement from the Heart Failure Association of the European Society of Cardiology Working Group on peripartum cardiomyopathy. Eur J Heart Fail. 2010;12(8):767-778. [PMID: 20675664]

Warnes CA, Williams RG, Bashore TM, et al; America College of Cardiology; American Heart Association Task Force on Practice Guidelines; American Society of Echocardiography; Heart Rhythm Society; International Society for Adult Congenital Heart Disease; Society for Cardiovascular Angiography and Interventions; Society of Thoracic Surgeons. ACC/AHA 2008 guidelines for the management of adults with congenital heart disease: a report of the American College of Cardiology/American Heart Association Task Force on Practice Guidelines. J Am Coll Cardiol. 2008;52(23):e1-e121. [PMID: 19038677]

Yinon Y, Siu SC, Warshafsky C, et al. Use of low molecular weight heparin in pregnant women with mechanical heart valves. Am J Cardiol. 2009;104(9):1259-1263. [PMID: 19840573]

Cardiovascular Medicine Self-Assessment Test

This self-assessment test contains one-best-answer multiple-choice questions. Please read these directions carefully before answering the questions. Answers, critiques, and bibliographies immediately follow these multiple-choice questions. The American College of Physicians is accredited by the Accreditation Council for Continuing Medical Education (ACCME) to provide continuing medical education for physicians.

The American College of Physicians designates MKSAP 16 Cardiovascular Medicine for a maximum of 18 *AMA PRA Category 1 Credits*™. Physicians should claim only the credit commensurate with the extent of their participation in the activity.

Earn "Same-Day" CME Credits Online

For the first time, print subscribers can enter their answers online to earn CME credits in 24 hours or less. You can submit your answers using online answer sheets that are provided at mksap.acponline.org, where a record of your MKSAP 16 credits will be available. To earn CME credits, you need to answer all of the questions in a test and earn a score of at least 50% correct (number of correct answers divided by the total number of questions). Take any of the following approaches:

➤ Use the printed answer sheet at the back of this book to record your answers. Go to mksap.acponline.org, access the appropriate online answer sheet, transcribe your answers, and submit your test for same-day CME credits. There is no additional fee for this service.

➤ Go to mksap.acponline.org, access the appropriate online answer sheet, directly enter your answers, and submit your test for same-day CME credits. There is no additional fee for this service.

➤ Pay a $10 processing fee per answer sheet and submit the printed answer sheet at the back of this book by mail or fax, as instructed on the answer sheet. Make sure you calculate your score and fax the answer sheet to 215-351-2799 or mail the answer sheet to Member and Customer Service, American College of Physicians, 190 N. Independence Mall West, Philadelphia, PA 19106-1572, using the courtesy envelope provided in your MKSAP 16 slipcase. You will need your 10-digit order number and 8-digit ACP ID number, which are printed on your packing slip. Please allow 4 to 6 weeks for your score report to be emailed back to you. Be sure to include your email address for a response.

If you do not have a 10-digit order number and 8-digit ACP ID number or if you need help creating a username and password to access the MKSAP 16 online answer sheets, go to mksap.acponline.org or email custserv@acponline.org.

CME credit is available from the publication date of July 31, 2012, until July 31, 2015. You may submit your answer sheets at any time during this period.

Directions

*Each of the numbered items is followed by lettered answers. Select the **ONE** lettered answer that is **BEST** in each case.*

Item 1

A 60-year-old man is evaluated for chest pain of 4 months' duration. He describes the pain as sharp, located in the left chest, with no radiation or associated symptoms, that occurs with walking one to two blocks and resolves with rest. Occasionally, the pain improves with continued walking or occurs during the evening hours. He has hypertension. Family history does not include cardiovascular disease in any first-degree relatives. His only medication is amlodipine.

On physical examination, he is afebrile, blood pressure is 130/80 mm Hg, pulse rate is 72/min, and respiration rate is 12/min. BMI is 28. No carotid bruits are present, and a normal S_1 and S_2 with no murmurs are heard. Lung fields are clear, and distal pulses are normal.

Electrocardiogram is shown.

Which of the following is the most appropriate diagnostic test to perform next?

(A) Adenosine nuclear perfusion stress test
(B) Coronary angiography
(C) Echocardiography
(D) Exercise treadmill stress test

Item 2

A 52-year-old man is evaluated in the office during a routine visit. Medical history is significant for type 2 diabetes mellitus, hypertension, hypercholesterolemia, and obesity. Medications are lisinopril, insulin glargine, insulin aspart, aspirin, and pravastatin (20 mg/d).

On physical examination, he is afebrile, blood pressure is 128/80 mm Hg, pulse rate is 73/min, and respiration rate is 18/min. BMI is 35. The lungs are clear to auscultation, and no murmurs are heard.

Laboratory studies:

Hemoglobin A_{1c}	7.2%
Total cholesterol	168 mg/dL (4.35 mmol/L)
LDL cholesterol	109 mg/dL (2.82 mmol/L)
HDL cholesterol	40 mg/dL (1.04 mmol/L)
Triglycerides	95 mg/dL (1.07 mmol/L)

Which of the following is the most appropriate management?

(A) Increase statin dose
(B) Start bile acid sequestrant
(C) Start fibrate
(D) Start niacin

Item 3

A 38-year-old man is evaluated during a routine health examination. He exercises 2 or 3 days each week by jogging for 30 minutes without shortness of breath or chest discomfort. During stressful emotional situations, he occasionally feels "skipped heart beats" but has not had prolonged palpitations, presyncope, or syncope. He generally feels in good health. He has no history of medical problems and takes no medications. He has not had fever or chills.

Physical examination shows normal temperature, blood pressure is 124/68 mm Hg, pulse rate is 64/min and regular, and respiration rate is 14/min. BMI is 23. Cardiac examination

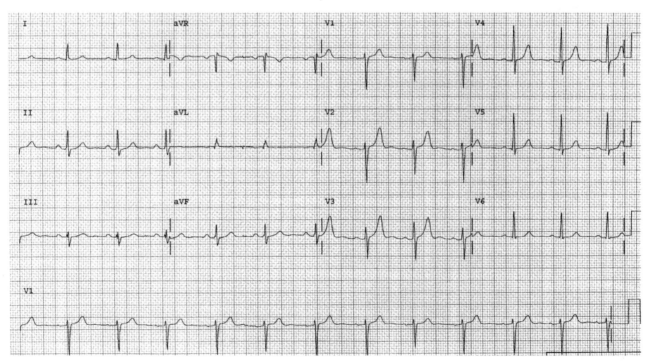

ITEM 1

demonstrates a grade 2/6 early systolic crescendo-decrescendo murmur heard best at the lower left sternal border without radiation. Lungs are clear. Peripheral pulses are normal.

Electrocardiogram is normal.

Which of the following is the most appropriate next test?

(A) Ambulatory electrocardiography
(B) Transesophageal echocardiography
(C) Transthoracic echocardiography
(D) No additional testing

Item 4

A 58-year-old man is evaluated for 3 to 4 months of progressive aching pain in the left buttock and hip; the pain is experienced during walking and is relieved with rest. The patient has been experiencing erectile dysfunction over a similar period. He has a 30-pack-year history of smoking and quit 1 year ago. He has hypercholesterolemia and type 2 diabetes mellitus. His medications are aspirin, lisinopril, simvastatin, metformin, and metoprolol.

On physical examination, his temperature is normal, blood pressure is 112/72 mm Hg, pulse rate is 68/min, and respiration rate is 16/min. BMI is 25. Femoral, popliteal, and foot pulses are diminished. There is no distal ulceration or skin breakdown. Ankle-brachial index on the left side is 0.7. Hemoglobin A_{1c} is 6.1% and LDL cholesterol level is 70 mg/dL (1.81 mmol/L).

Which of the following is the most likely site of this patient's arterial disease?

(A) Aortoiliac system
(B) Common femoral artery
(C) Popliteal artery
(D) Superficial femoral artery

Item 5

A 62-year-old man is evaluated during a routine examination. Medical history is significant for a myocardial infarction 3 years ago, dyslipidemia, hypertension, tobacco use, and drinking two alcoholic drinks per day. Medications are an ACE inhibitor, a statin, a β-blocker, and aspirin. He participates in cardiac rehabilitation, exercising four to five times per week.

On physical examination, he is afebrile, blood pressure is 128/80 mm Hg, pulse rate is 83/min, and respiration rate is 18/min. BMI is 31. The patient has an obese abdomen.

Laboratory studies show a serum LDL cholesterol level of 68 mg/dL (1.76 mmol/L), HDL cholesterol level of 43 mg/dL (1.11 mmol/L), and triglyceride level of 150 mg/dL (1.70 mmol/L).

Which of the following interventions offers the greatest cardiac risk reduction in this patient?

(A) Increase physical activity
(B) More aggressive blood pressure lowering
(C) More aggressive lipid modification
(D) Reduce alcohol consumption
(E) Smoking cessation

Item 6

A 27-year-old woman is admitted to the hospital with a 1-week history of worsening exertional substernal chest pressure relieved by rest. She was admitted after 30 minutes of chest pain relieved with sublingual nitroglycerin tablets. Medical history is significant for Hodgkin lymphoma 7 years ago, treated with high-dose (90 *Gy*) chest radiation therapy. She reports a history of cocaine use. There is no history of fever or rash. She takes no medications.

On physical examination, temperature is normal, blood pressure is 110/50 mm Hg, pulse rate is 98/min, and respiration rate is 14/min. Cardiopulmonary and peripheral vascular examinations are normal.

Serum toxicology screen is negative. Serum troponin I level is 0.01 ng/mL (0.01 µg/L). Prothrombin and activated partial thromboplastin time are normal.

Electrocardiogram during chest pain at the time of admission indicates ST-segment depression in leads V_1 to V_4. Cardiac catheterization shows 60% ostial narrowing of the left main coronary artery and 60% narrowing of the proximal left anterior descending coronary artery.

Which of the following is the most likely cause of this patient's chest pain?

(A) Antiphospholipid syndrome
(B) Cocaine-induced coronary artery vasospasm
(C) Coronary artery disease
(D) Kawasaki disease

Item 7

A 50-year-old man is evaluated for a 3-month history of fatigue, shortness of breath, early satiety and nausea, weight loss, lower extremity edema, and easy bruising. Medical and family histories are unremarkable, and he takes no medications.

On physical examination, the patient is afebrile, blood pressure is 95/70 mm Hg, and pulse rate is 95/min. BMI is 18. Cardiac and pulmonary examinations are normal. He has elevated central venous pressure, hepatomegaly, and bilateral edema to the shins.

Laboratory studies:

Hemoglobin	11 g/dL (110 g/L)
Albumin	3.2 g/dL (32 g/L)
B-type natriuretic peptide	300 pg/mL
Creatinine	2.3 mg/dL (203 µmol/L)
Urinalysis	3+ protein, no erythrocytes or leukocytes

Electrocardiogram is shown (see next page). Echocardiogram shows increased left ventricular wall thickness, ejection fraction of 65%, and no regional wall motion abnormalities. Chest radiograph shows no acute pulmonary process and a normal cardiac/pericardial silhouette.

Which of the following is the most likely diagnosis?

(A) Amyloidosis
(B) Coronary artery disease
(C) Giant cell myocarditis
(D) Sarcoidosis

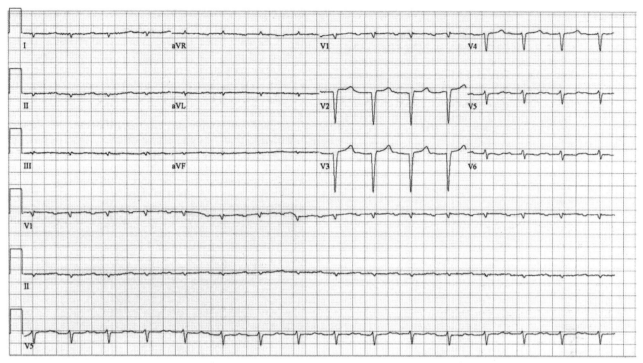

ITEM 7

Item 8

A 38-year-old man is evaluated for progressive dyspnea and edema. He has a history of injection drug use, which he discontinued 7 years ago. For the past several months, he has noted worsening dyspnea with his daily activities. During the same period, he has had worsening lower extremity edema and abdominal fullness.

On physical examination, temperature is normal, blood pressure is 124/84 mm Hg, pulse rate is 75/min, and respiration rate is 16/min. There is jugular venous distention to the jaw with a prominent *v* wave. Heart rhythm is regular. The apical impulse and heart sounds are normal. There is a grade 2/6 low-pitched, holosystolic murmur along the left sternal border that increases during inspiration. Lung examination is normal. The liver span is increased. There are ascites and edema to the thigh level.

Electrocardiogram shows atrial flutter with 4:1 conduction with a right bundle branch block. Transthoracic echocardiogram shows normal left ventricular dimensions and systolic function. The right ventricle is dilated with reduced systolic contraction. There is poor coaptation of the tricuspid valve leaflets with mobile, thickened leaflets and severe tricuspid regurgitation. The right atrium is also dilated. The estimated right ventricular systolic pressure is 25 mm Hg by Doppler velocity. Blood cultures are negative.

Which of the following is the most appropriate treatment?

(A) Cardioversion of atrial flutter
(B) Digoxin
(C) Nafcillin intravenously for 4 weeks
(D) Tricuspid valve replacement surgery

Item 9

A 66-year-old woman is evaluated in the emergency department for the abrupt onset of severe pain in her chest and back that has persisted for 2 hours. She has no abdominal pain, leg pain, or neurologic symptoms. She has hypertension. Medications are sustained-release diltiazem and hydrochlorothiazide.

On physical examination, temperature is normal, blood pressure is 180/100 mm Hg in both arms, pulse rate is 98/min, and respiration rate is 18/min. Oxygen saturation is 96% on 2 L oxygen by nasal cannula. Cardiac auscultation discloses an S_4 gallop but no murmur. Pulmonary examination is normal. Pulses are symmetric and equal in all extremities.

Pertinent laboratory results are a D-dimer level of 1.2 µg/mL (1.2 mg/L) and a serum creatinine level of 1.4 mg/dL (124 µmol/L). Initial cardiac troponin I level is less than 0.5 ng/mL (0.5 µg/L).

Electrocardiogram demonstrates left ventricular hypertrophy with repolarization abnormalities. Chest radiograph is consistent with left ventricular hypertrophy. A chest CT scan with intravenous contrast demonstrates intramural hematoma distal to the left subclavian artery.

Which of the following is the most appropriate management?

(A) Emergency cardiac catheterization
(B) Emergency cardiothoracic surgery
(C) Endovascular stent grafting
(D) Intravenous β-blockade followed by intravenous sodium nitroprusside
(E) Intravenous heparin

Item 10

A 76-year-old woman is evaluated in the emergency department for dizziness, shortness of breath, and palpitations that began acutely 1 hour ago. She has a history of hypertension and heart failure with preserved ejection fraction. Medications are hydrochlorothiazide, lisinopril, and aspirin.

On physical examination, she is afebrile, blood pressure is 80/60 mm Hg, pulse rate is 155/min, and respiration rate is 30/min. Oxygen saturation is 80% with 40% oxygen by face mask. Cardiac auscultation reveals an irregularly irregular rhythm, tachycardia, and some variability in S_1 intensity. Crackles are heard bilaterally one-third up in the lower lung fields.

Electrocardiogram demonstrates atrial fibrillation with a rapid ventricular rate.

Which of the following is the most appropriate acute treatment?

(A) Adenosine
(B) Amiodarone
(C) Cardioversion
(D) Diltiazem
(E) Metoprolol

Item 11

A 48-year-old man arrives at the emergency department with a 2-day history of increasing shortness of breath. Medical history is significant for nonischemic cardiomyopathy and hypertension. Medications are hydrochlorothiazide, enalapril, and metoprolol.

Temperature is normal, blood pressure is 130/70 mm Hg, pulse rate is 110/min, and respiration rate is 22/min. BMI is 45. Oxygen saturation is 91% on ambient air. Central venous pressure is elevated to 15 cm H_2O. Crackles are heard bilaterally at the lung bases. Cardiac examination reveals a regular rhythm and an S_3. Edema bilaterally to the knees is observed.

Laboratory studies reveal a B-type natriuretic peptide level of 170 pg/mL and creatinine level of 1.1 mg/dL (97.2 µmol/L). Hemoglobin level and leukocyte count are normal.

Chest radiograph and electrocardiogram are shown. Echocardiogram shows left ventricular hypertrophy, an enlarged left ventricle, ejection fraction of 35%, normal right ventricle size and function, mild tricuspid regurgitation, and a right ventricular systolic pressure of 45 mm Hg.

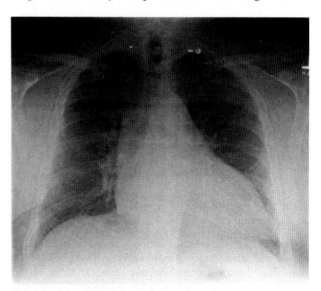

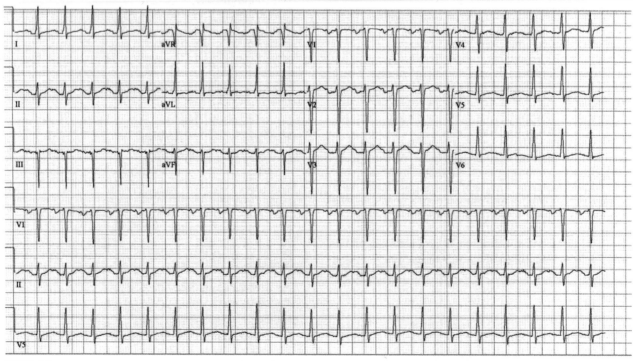

ITEM 11

H
CONT.

Which of the following is the most appropriate treatment?

(A) Inhaled iloprost
(B) Intravenous furosemide
(C) Oral azithromycin and intravenous ceftriaxone
(D) Subcutaneous enoxaparin

H ## Item 12

A 73-year-old man is evaluated in the hospital following a non–ST-elevation myocardial infarction. He has type 2 diabetes mellitus and dyslipidemia. Medications are aspirin, simvastatin, metoprolol, lisinopril, clopidogrel, and metformin. He is nearing discharge.

On physical examination, temperature is normal. Blood pressure is 110/80 mm Hg and pulse rate is 52/min. Heart sounds are normal, lung fields are clear, and there is no peripheral edema.

Laboratory studies:

Total cholesterol	112 mg/dL (2.90 mmol/L)
HDL cholesterol	42 mg/dL (1.09 mmol/L)
LDL cholesterol	55 mg/dL (1.42 mmol/L)
Triglycerides	73 mg/dL (0.82 mmol/L)
Creatinine	1.2 mg/dL (106 μmol/L)
Potassium	4.2 meq/L (4.2 mmol/L)
Fasting plasma glucose	110 mg/dL (6.1 mmol/L)

Electrocardiogram demonstrates sinus rhythm and nonspecific ST-T wave changes. Echocardiogram demonstrates an ejection fraction of 30% and no evidence of left ventricular thrombus.

Which of the following is the most appropriate adjustment to his discharge medications?

(A) Discontinue clopidogrel
(B) Increase metoprolol dose
(C) Start eplerenone
(D) Start warfarin

Item 13

A 68-year-old woman is seen for an evaluation. Medical history is significant for ischemic cardiomyopathy and hypertension. She had an implantable cardioverter-defibrillator placed 5 years ago. She has good functional capacity and is able to walk three blocks without limitations. Medications are lisinopril, carvedilol, aspirin, and pravastatin.

On physical examination, she is afebrile, blood pressure is 137/70 mm Hg, pulse rate is 82/min, and respiration rate is 18/min. BMI is 23. The remainder of the examination is normal.

Laboratory studies:

Hemoglobin A_{1c}	6.9%
Total cholesterol	115 mg/dL (2.98 mmol/L)
LDL cholesterol	53 mg/dL (1.37 mmol/L)
HDL cholesterol	40 mg/dL (1.04 mmol/L)
Triglycerides	112 mg/dL (1.27 mmol/L)

Which of the following clinical measures is most important to target in this patient to reduce her risk of a cardiovascular event?

(A) Blood pressure
(B) Hemoglobin A_{1c}
(C) LDL cholesterol level
(D) Triglyceride level

Item 14

A 33-year-old woman is evaluated for a recent increase in exertional dyspnea. She has self-diagnosed asthma, but has never been evaluated for this condition. She is otherwise in good health. There is no significant family history. She takes no medications.

Blood pressure is 110/80 mm Hg in both upper extremities. Estimated central venous pressure is 5 cm H_2O. The apical impulse is normal and there is a left parasternal impulse. The S_1 is normal and there is fixed splitting of the S_2. A grade 2/6 midsystolic murmur is noted at the second left intercostal space and a grade 2/6 diastolic rumble is noted at the left sternal border. There is no cyanosis or clubbing. The pulses are symmetric and full.

The electrocardiogram demonstrates sinus rhythm with incomplete right bundle branch block. The chest radiograph demonstrates right-sided cardiac chamber enlargement, an enlarged pulmonary artery, and increased pulmonary vascularity.

Which of the following is the most likely diagnosis?

(A) Eisenmenger physiology
(B) Idiopathic pulmonary arterial hypertension
(C) Ostium secundum atrial septal defect
(D) Rheumatic mitral stenosis

Item 15

A 67-year-old woman is evaluated for a 1-month history of shortness of breath and lower extremity edema. Review of systems is negative for chest pain, palpitations, and syncope. Medical history is notable for hypertension. Her only medication is hydrochlorothiazide, which is switched to furosemide during this visit in response to symptoms and physical examination findings.

On physical examination, blood pressure is 170/90 mm Hg and pulse rate is 65/min. BMI is 30. Estimated central venous pressure is 12 cm H_2O. Cardiac examination reveals a regular rate and rhythm with no murmurs. Crackles are heard bilaterally in the lung bases. Pitting edema to the midshin bilaterally is present.

The electrocardiogram is shown (see next page). Echocardiogram demonstrates moderate concentric left ventricular hypertrophy, no significant valvular abnormalities, and no pericardial effusion. Left ventricular ejection fraction is 60%.

Which of the following is the most appropriate treatment?

(A) Candesartan
(B) Digoxin

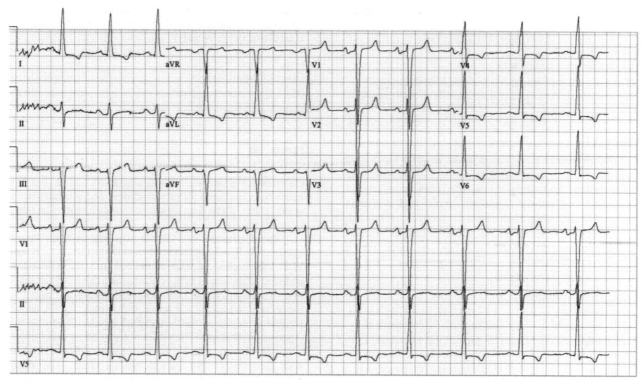

ITEM 15

(C) Disopyramide

(D) Verapamil

Item 16

A 16-year-old girl is evaluated for primary amenorrhea. She has no cardiovascular or other concerning symptoms.

Her general features are striking for short stature, webbed neck, and shield-shaped chest. Blood pressure is 100/70 mm Hg bilaterally. The jugular and carotid examinations are normal. There is an ejection click and early systolic murmur noted at the second right intercostal space. All pulses are palpable and normal. The remainder of the examination is unremarkable.

A transthoracic echocardiogram demonstrates a bicuspid aortic valve with a mean transvalvular gradient of 20 mm Hg. There is mild aortic valve regurgitation. The remainder of the echocardiographic examination is unremarkable.

Which of the following is the most likely genetic diagnosis?

(A) Down syndrome

(B) Holt-Oram syndrome

(C) Marfan syndrome

(D) Turner syndrome

Item 17

A 70-year-old man was admitted to the hospital 1 week ago with acute decompensated heart failure. Currently, he can walk about 200 yards around the hospital ward before stopping because of fatigue and shortness of breath. Medical history is significant for nonischemic cardiomyopathy, with an implantable cardioverter-defibrillator placed 1 year ago. He has mild (stage 1) chronic obstructive pulmonary disease. Medications while in the hospital are lisinopril, bumetanide, digoxin, spironolactone, and an albuterol inhaler, used as needed.

On physical examination, blood pressure is 90/70 mm Hg and pulse rate is 80/min. A grade 2/6 holosystolic murmur is heard at the left sternal border radiating to the apex. No jugular venous distention is present, lungs are clear to auscultation, no S₃ is heard, and there is no edema.

The electrocardiogram shows a QRS duration of 110 msec and normal sinus rhythm. Echocardiogram shows ejection fraction of 20%, left ventricular enlargement, and moderate mitral regurgitation but otherwise no anatomic abnormalities of the mitral valve (unchanged from previous echocardiogram 1 year ago).

Which of the following is the most appropriate treatment?

(A) Refer for mitral valve repair

(B) Replace spironolactone with eplerenone

(C) Start metoprolol succinate

(D) Upgrade to biventricular pacemaker with implantable cardioverter-defibrillator

Item 18

A 65-year-old man asks for advice on cardiac risk assessment during a routine evaluation. He is asymptomatic, does not smoke cigarettes, has no pertinent medical or family history, and takes no medications.

On physical examination, blood pressure is 148/90 mm Hg, pulse rate is 83/min, and respiration rate is 18/min. The remainder of the physical examination is normal. The patient's Framingham risk score predicts a 15% chance of a myocardial infarction or coronary death in the next 10 years.

Laboratory studies:

Total cholesterol	217 mg/dL (5.62 mmol/L)
LDL cholesterol	125 mg/dL (3.24 mmol/L)
HDL cholesterol	48 mg/dL (1.24 mmol/L)
Triglycerides	269 mg/dL (3.04 mmol/L)

Which of the following is the most appropriate test to perform next?

(A) B-type natriuretic peptide
(B) Cardiac CT angiography
(C) High-sensitivity C-reactive protein
(D) Stress echocardiography

Item 19

A 54-year-old woman is evaluated for dyspnea. She has experienced gradually progressive dyspnea with exertion. Her medical history is noncontributory.

On physical examination, blood pressure is 158/68 mm Hg, pulse rate is 92/min, and respiration rate is 20/min. Jugular venous distention is visible 2 cm above the clavicle in the upright position. There is a regular rhythm with normal S_1 and S_2. There is a grade 2/6 early-peaking systolic murmur at the right upper sternal border and a grade 3/6 diastolic decrescendo murmur at the left lower sternal border. Lungs are clear to auscultation.

Transthoracic echocardiogram shows a dilated and mildly hypertrophied left ventricle (end-diastolic diameter 58 mm, end-systolic diameter 46 mm) with estimated left ventricular ejection fraction of 50%. There is a bicuspid aortic valve with moderate calcification of the leaflets. The peak aortic valve gradient is 35 mm Hg, and the calculated aortic valve area is 1.3 cm². There is severe aortic regurgitation. The ascending aortic maximum diameter is 47 mm.

Which of the following is the most appropriate treatment?

(A) Aortic valve replacement
(B) Aortic valve replacement and ascending aortic graft placement
(C) Begin carvedilol and reassess in 3 months
(D) Begin losartan and reassess in 3 months

Item 20

A 35-year-old woman is evaluated for a 2-day history of myalgia and malaise. She was prescribed fluconazole for a vaginal yeast infection 1 week ago, and those symptoms resolved. Medical history is remarkable for a heart transplant 3 years ago for nonischemic cardiomyopathy. Medications are cyclosporine, prednisone, atorvastatin, and aspirin.

On physical examination, temperature is normal, blood pressure is 130/80 mm Hg, and pulse rate is 70/min.

Lungs are clear to auscultation. Cardiac examination reveals a regular rate and rhythm. Her arms and legs are tender to palpation. Strength is normal and symmetric.

Laboratory studies show a serum creatine kinase level of 800 units/L, troponin I of less than 0.1 ng/mL (0.1 µg/L), and normal liver chemistry tests and complete blood count.

Electrocardiogram shows a normal sinus rhythm and is otherwise unremarkable. Echocardiogram displays a normal ejection fraction, no regional wall motion abnormalities, and no pericardial effusion.

Which of the following is the most likely diagnosis?

(A) Acute rejection
(B) Cytomegalovirus viremia
(C) Drug-induced myositis
(D) Transplant vasculopathy

Item 21

A 62-year-old woman comes in for evaluation of her pacemaker generator, which has been visible for the past 3 days. She reports no fevers, presyncope, or syncope. Medical history is significant for complete heart block; a permanent pacemaker was placed 8 years ago, and the generator was replaced 2 months ago because the battery was nearing the end of its life. She takes no medications.

On physical examination, her temperature is 37.2 °C (99.0 °F), blood pressure is 128/82 mm Hg, and pulse rate is 60/min. A corner of the pacemaker is seen eroding through the skin. Minimal erythema is seen surrounding the exit site. No drainage or pus is present.

Electrocardiogram shows atrial sensing and ventricular pacing. Transthoracic echocardiogram shows the two leads with no vegetations on the leads or valves. Blood cultures are negative.

Which of the following is the principal therapy in the treatment of this patient?

(A) Extraction of the pacemaker and leads
(B) Intravenous vancomycin for 4 weeks
(C) Oral cephalexin for 4 weeks
(D) Surgical closure of the skin wound

Item 22

A 68-year-old woman is evaluated during a routine examination. She went through menopause 16 years ago. She is obese. Family history is significant for a paternal aunt with ovarian cancer at age 64 years. She takes no medications.

Blood pressure is 148/90 mm Hg, pulse rate is 83/min, and respiration rate is 18/min. BMI is 35. Waist measurement is 100 cm (39.3 in).

Which of the following diseases poses the greatest risk of death in this patient?

(A) Breast cancer
(B) Coronary artery disease
(C) Diabetes mellitus
(D) Ovarian cancer

Item 23

A 75-year-old man with hypertension is evaluated during his first outpatient visit after an acute myocardial infarction. He is now asymptomatic and reports no chest pain or symptoms of heart failure since discharge. He had a lateral infarction, and a drug-eluting stent was placed in the left circumflex artery. He had two episodes of symptomatic atrial fibrillation during the hospitalization associated with presyncope, and a rhythm control approach was chosen; his left ventricular ejection fraction was normal. His medications at the time of discharge were metoprolol, aspirin, dronedarone, clopidogrel, warfarin, and atorvastatin. Serum creatinine level on the day of discharge was 1.1 mg/dL (97.2 µmol/L) and his ejection fraction was 55%.

On physical examination, he is afebrile, blood pressure is 130/78 mm Hg, pulse rate is 68/min and regular, respiration rate is 12/min. There is an S_4 but the remainder of the cardiac examination is normal. Lungs are clear and there is no peripheral edema.

Laboratory studies are normal except for a serum creatinine level of 1.5 mg/dL (133 µmol/L).

Which of the following medications is most likely to have caused the increase in serum creatinine level?

(A) Atorvastatin
(B) Clopidogrel
(C) Dronedarone
(D) Metoprolol

Item 24

A 64-year-old woman is evaluated during a routine appointment. She has nonischemic cardiomyopathy, and her symptoms have been stable for several months. She reports dyspnea on exertion with ascending less than one flight of stairs; she has no symptoms at rest, no edema, and her weight is stable. Her most recent ejection fraction of 25% was measured 6 months ago, and an implantable cardioverter-defibrillator was placed at that time. Medications are lisinopril, carvedilol, and bumetanide.

On physical examination, blood pressure is 90/70 mm Hg and pulse rate is 65/min. Cardiac examination reveals a regular rhythm, normal S_1 and S_2, an S_3, and a grade 2/6 holosystolic murmur at the left sternal border radiating to the left axilla. No jugular venous distention or edema is present, and lungs are clear to auscultation.

Laboratory studies:

B-type natriuretic peptide	300 pg/mL (200-400 pg/mL during previous year)
Blood urea nitrogen	30 mg/dL (10.7 mmol/L)
Creatinine	1.4 mg/dL (124 µmol/L) (1.2-1.6 mg/dL during previous year [106-141 µmol/L])
Sodium	134 meq/L (134 mmol/L)
Potassium	4.7 meq/L (4.7 mmol/L)

Electrocardiogram shows normal sinus rhythm and a QRS interval of 100 msec.

Which of the following is the most appropriate treatment?

(A) Add candesartan
(B) Add spironolactone
(C) Increase bumetanide
(D) Increase carvedilol

Item 25

A 72-year-old woman presents to the emergency department for evaluation of neck and shoulder pain. These symptoms have been present intermittently for 2 weeks, occurring with activity, lasting 5 to 10 minutes, and resolving with rest. During the episodes of pain, she notes associated shortness of breath and diaphoresis. She had episodes yesterday and today; today's episode occurred at rest and has continued for approximately 30 minutes. Medical history is significant for hypertension and type 2 diabetes mellitus. Her sister underwent coronary artery bypass surgery at age 62 years. Medications are aspirin, hydrochlorothiazide, and metformin.

On physical examination, temperature is 37.3 °C (99.2 °F), blood pressure is 130/86 mm Hg, pulse rate is 80/min, and respiration rate is 12/min. A normal carotid upstroke without carotid bruits is noted, normal jugular venous pulsations are present, and normal S_1 and S_2 are heard without murmurs. Lung fields are clear, distal pulses are normal, and no peripheral edema is present.

Serum troponin I level is 2.0 ng/mL (2.0 µg/L). INR is 1.0. Other laboratory findings are within normal limits.

Electrocardiogram shows normal sinus rhythm, isolated premature ventricular contractions, bigeminy, 2-mm ST-segment depression in leads II, III, and aVF, and no Q waves.

She is given aspirin, unfractionated heparin, clopidogrel, metoprolol, and sublingual nitroglycerin.

Which of the following is the most appropriate additional drug therapy?

(A) Atorvastatin
(B) Atorvastatin and eptifibatide
(C) Lidocaine
(D) Tenecteplase

Item 26

A 63-year-old man is evaluated for pleuritic left-sided anterior chest pain, which has persisted intermittently for 1 week. The pain lasts for hours at a time and is not provoked by exertion or relieved by rest but is worse when supine. He reports transient relief with acetaminophen and codeine and occasionally when leaning forward. He has had a low-grade fever for 3 days, without cough or chills. Medical history is significant for acute pericarditis 7 months ago. He was treated at that time with ibuprofen and had rapid resolution of his symptoms. His only current medications are acetaminophen and codeine.

On physical examination, temperature is 37.8 °C (100.0 °F), blood pressure is 132/78 mm Hg, pulse rate is 98/min, and respiration rate is 16/min. No jugular venous distention is noted. A two-component pericardial friction rub is heard over the left side of the sternum. Pulsus paradoxus of 6 mm Hg is noted. Lung auscultation reveals normal breath sounds with no wheezing. No pedal edema is present.

Electrocardiogram demonstrates sinus rhythm and no ST-segment shift.

Which of the following is the most appropriate management?

(A) Azathioprine
(B) Chest CT
(C) Colchicine and aspirin
(D) Pericardiectomy
(E) Prednisone

Item 27

A 19-year-old woman is evaluated during a physical examination prior to entering college. She is asymptomatic and her medical and family histories are unremarkable. She takes no medications.

On physical examination, temperature is normal, blood pressure is 110/50 mm Hg, pulse rate is 60/min, and respiration rate is 12/min. There is no palpable lymphadenopathy. Cardiac examination reveals a grade 2/6 diastolic murmur at the apex; heart sounds are otherwise normal.

Echocardiogram reveals a 3.5-cm smooth and circular mobile left atrial mass that is attached along the middle aspect of the atrial septum and prolapses into the mitral valve orifice during diastole. Chamber sizes are normal, and there are no septal defects.

Which of the following is the most appropriate management?

(A) Catheter-based biopsy of atrial mass
(B) Factor V Leiden testing
(C) Surgical resection of atrial mass
(D) Warfarin

Item 28

A 55-year-old woman presents for evaluation of sharp, localized, left-sided chest pain for the past 3 weeks. The pain is unrelated to exertion and is associated with mild dyspnea and fatigue. Typically it lasts for 5 to 10 minutes and abates spontaneously. The pain is not pleuritic, positional, or related to eating. She has hypertension and hypercholesterolemia. Her father had a myocardial infarction at age 54 years. Her daily medications consist of hydrochlorothiazide, simvastatin, and aspirin.

On physical examination, her blood pressure is 135/78 mm Hg, pulse rate is 78/min, and respiration rate is 14/min. Her BMI is 28. Cardiac auscultation reveals only an S_4; no carotid or femoral bruits are heard.

Electrocardiogram demonstrates sinus rhythm with a rate of 75/min; QRS axis is −20°; no ST-segment or T-wave abnormalities are noted.

Which of the following is the most appropriate diagnostic study?

(A) Coronary angiography
(B) Exercise echocardiography
(C) Exercise electrocardiography
(D) Pharmacologic stress test

Item 29

A 66-year-old man is admitted to the hospital with a 2-month history of progressive dyspnea and worsening pedal edema. Medical history is significant for coronary artery bypass surgery 3 years ago. He has a 10-year history of hypertension. Medications are metoprolol, atorvastatin, and aspirin.

On physical examination, temperature is normal, blood pressure is 118/64 mm Hg, pulse rate is 120/min, and respiration rate is 26/min. Jugular venous distention that increases with inspiration is noted. Cardiac examination reveals no murmur, rub, or gallop. Pulsus paradoxus of 5 mm Hg is present. Lungs are clear to auscultation. Hepatojugular reflux is present. Pedal edema of 2+ is noted.

Electrocardiogram shows sinus rhythm with increased voltage in precordial leads. Echocardiogram shows left ventricular ejection fraction of 70%, restrictive left ventricular filling, increased ventricular wall thickness, biatrial enlargement, a small pericardial effusion, and abnormal diastolic to-and-fro ventricular septal motion consistent with ventricular interdependence. Cardiac CT shows diffuse pericardial thickening. Chest radiograph shows no infiltrates and no diaphragmatic elevation.

Which of the following is the most likely diagnosis?

(A) Cardiac amyloidosis
(B) Cardiac tamponade
(C) Constrictive pericarditis
(D) Severe tricuspid regurgitation

Item 30

A 56-year-old man is evaluated in the hospital for paroxysmal episodes of atrial fibrillation. The patient develops increasing shortness of breath during these episodes. Five days ago, he was admitted for an acute myocardial infarction and cardiogenic shock and received a drug-eluting stent in the left anterior descending coronary artery. Medications are lisinopril, digoxin, furosemide, aspirin, clopidogrel, eplerenone, simvastatin, and unfractionated heparin.

On physical examination, the patient is afebrile, blood pressure is 92/65 mm Hg, and pulse rate is 75/min. Oxygen saturation is 95% with 3 L oxygen by nasal cannula. Cardiac examination reveals estimated central venous pressure of 12 cm H_2O. Heart sounds are distant and regular. There is a grade 2/6 holosystolic murmur at the cardiac apex. A summation gallop is present. Crackles are auscultated bilaterally in the lower lung fields.

Transthoracic echocardiogram shows left ventricular ejection fraction of 32%.

Which of the following is the most appropriate treatment for this patient's atrial fibrillation?

CONT.

(A) Amiodarone
(B) Disopyramide
(C) Dronedarone
(D) Flecainide
(E) Sotalol

Item 31

A 46-year-old man is evaluated in the emergency department for acute onset of severe chest and back pain 1 hour ago, which has been unremitting. The patient had one episode of loss of consciousness early after the onset of pain. His medical history is significant for a murmur detected in adolescence that has been present through adulthood, a bicuspid aortic valve, and hypertension. His medications are valsartan and hydrochlorothiazide.

On physical examination, the patient is conscious and in pain. He is afebrile, blood pressure is 90/50 mm Hg, pulse rate is 118/min and regular, and respiration rate is 18/min. His pulse rate and blood pressure are equal in both arms. Heart sounds are distant, regular, and rapid. A very faint early diastolic decrescendo murmur is heard at the right upper sternal border. Estimated central venous pressure is 12 cm H_2O.

An electrocardiogram indicates sinus tachycardia. A chest CT scan with intravenous contrast is shown.

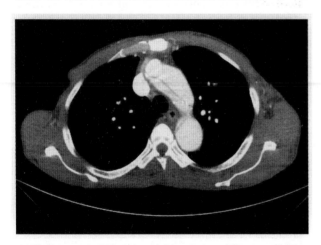

Which of the following is the most appropriate management?

(A) Chest magnetic resonance angiography
(B) Emergency surgical intervention
(C) Endovascular stenting
(D) Insertion of intra-aortic balloon pump
(E) Transesophageal echocardiography

Item 32

A 59-year-old woman is evaluated before beginning an exercise program. She works in an office and is sedentary at home. She is able to do light housework without chest discomfort or dyspnea. She has hypertension and type 2 diabetes mellitus. Daily medications are lisinopril, aspirin, and metformin.

On physical examination, her blood pressure is 134/70 mm Hg and her BMI is 28. The remainder of her physical examination is normal.

Laboratory studies:

Hemoglobin A_{1c}	7.2%
Total cholesterol	196 mg/dL (5.08 mmol/L)
LDL cholesterol	106 mg/dL (2.75 mmol/L)
HDL cholesterol	50 mg/dL (1.30 mmol/L)
Triglycerides	200 mg/dL (2.26 mmol/L)

Because of her cardiovascular risk factors and sedentary lifestyle, she undergoes exercise stress testing before beginning her exercise program. Following a markedly abnormal stress test result, cardiac catheterization is performed, which demonstrates 80% stenosis in the mid-left anterior descending coronary artery. Left ventricular ejection fraction is 59%. There is minor stenosis in other coronary arteries.

Which of the following treatment options will offer this patient the greatest reduction in her risk of myocardial infarction?

(A) Add a statin
(B) Add clopidogrel to aspirin
(C) Coronary artery bypass graft surgery
(D) Percutaneous coronary intervention

Item 33

A 68-year-old woman is evaluated for palpitations. Her symptoms occur daily during both rest and exertion. She describes the palpitations as intermittent "hard" beats that "take her breath away." Her symptoms are made worse by caffeine consumption. She reports no dizziness or syncope. Medical history is significant for hypertension and hyperlipidemia. Medications are an ACE inhibitor and a statin.

On physical examination, she is afebrile, blood pressure is 138/80 mm Hg, pulse rate is 83/min, and respiration rate is 18/min. On cardiac examination, the rhythm is regular. There are no murmurs or extra sounds. The lungs are clear. The remainder of the general physical examination is normal.

The electrocardiogram shows normal sinus rhythm with minor ST-segment abnormalities.

Which is the most appropriate testing option to utilize next in this patient?

(A) Electrophysiologic study
(B) 24-Hour continuous ambulatory electrocardiographic monitor
(C) Implantable loop recorder
(D) Postsymptom event recorder

Item 34

A 56-year-old asymptomatic woman is evaluated during a routine physical examination. She has a history of a "mild heart murmur" since adolescence, but no prior echocardiography has been performed. She has hypertension, treated with chlorthalidone. She has a very active lifestyle, including exercising on a treadmill for 40 minutes several times a week.

On physical examination, vital signs are normal. Her lungs are clear to auscultation. Her apical impulse is not displaced or enlarged, but there is a palpable thrill. There is a regular rhythm with a systolic click heard after S_1, followed by a grade 4/6 late systolic murmur heard best at the apex. During Valsalva maneuver, the interval between the S_1 and systolic click shortens, and the murmur is prolonged. Electrocardiogram is normal.

Which of the following is the most appropriate management for this patient?

(A) Measure B-type natriuretic peptide level
(B) Transesophageal echocardiography
(C) Transthoracic echocardiography
(D) Continued observation annually unless symptoms ensue

Item 35

A 72-year-old man is evaluated in the emergency department for worsening shortness of breath for several weeks, orthopnea, and bilateral lower extremity edema. He has had chest heaviness with exertion, but no presyncope or syncope.

Physical examination shows a diaphoretic man in mild distress. Blood pressure is 118/74 mm Hg, pulse rate is 96/min, respiration rate is 20/min. Oxygen saturation is 88% on ambient air. Estimated central venous pressure is 10 cm H_2O. There is a regular rhythm and S_2 is diminished in intensity. There is a grade 3/6 late-peaking systolic murmur at the left lower sternal border. An S_3 is audible. Lung examination demonstrates bibasilar crackles. There is bilateral lower extremity edema to the knees.

Chest radiograph shows cardiomegaly and increased bilateral interstitial markings.

Electrocardiogram shows sinus rhythm and left ventricular hypertrophy. Transthoracic echocardiogram shows left ventricular dilatation with mild concentric hypertrophy. The ejection fraction is 30% with global hypocontractility. The aortic valve leaflets are thickened with reduced mobility and severe calcification. The aortic valve peak instantaneous gradient is 54 mm Hg and mean gradient is 38 mm Hg. The calculated aortic valve area is 0.8 cm².

The patient is treated with intravenous furosemide with symptomatic improvement in dyspnea and oxygen saturation.

Which of the following is the most appropriate treatment for this patient?

(A) Balloon aortic valvuloplasty
(B) Intravenous nitroprusside
(C) Surgical aortic valve replacement
(D) Transcatheter aortic valve implantation

Item 36

A 35-year-old woman is evaluated for follow-up of heart failure secondary to peripartum cardiomyopathy. Symptoms began in her third trimester and therapy was begun at that time. She gave birth to a healthy baby 3 weeks ago but remains symptomatic; she can walk approximately one block on level ground. More than 3 months ago, she had no functional limitations. Medical history is otherwise unremarkable; medications are carvedilol, spironolactone, and hydrochlorothiazide

On physical examination, she is afebrile, blood pressure is 100/70 mm Hg, and pulse rate is 50/min. No jugular venous distention is present. The point of maximal impact is enlarged. Cardiac examination reveals a regular rhythm, normal S_1 and S_2, no S_3, and a grade 2/6 holosystolic murmur radiating to the apex. Lungs are clear to auscultation. No hepatomegaly or edema is present.

Electrocardiogram is shown (see next page). Echocardiogram shows left ventricular ejection fraction of 25%.

Which of the following is the most appropriate management?

(A) Cardiac resynchronization therapy
(B) Endomyocardial biopsy
(C) Increase carvedilol
(D) Start enalapril

Item 37

A 60-year-old man with paroxysmal atrial fibrillation is scheduled to undergo a screening colonoscopy. Warfarin must be discontinued in case a biopsy is needed. When the patient is in atrial fibrillation, he is asymptomatic. He also has hypertension and type 2 diabetes mellitus. He has never had a stroke, transient ischemic attack, or history of venous thromboembolic disease. Medications are metoprolol, metformin, and warfarin.

On physical examination, pulse rate is 65/min. Other vital signs are normal. Cardiac rhythm is irregularly irregular.

Laboratory studies reveal an INR of 2.3.

In addition to discontinuing warfarin, which of the following is the most appropriate treatment?

(A) Switch to aspirin
(B) Switch to clopidogrel
(C) Switch to intravenous unfractionated heparin
(D) Switch to therapeutic doses of low-molecular-weight heparin
(E) No bridging agent is needed

Item 38

A 54-year-old man is evaluated in the emergency department for an acute coronary syndrome that began 30 minutes ago. He has type 2 diabetes mellitus and hypertension. He reports no history of bleeding or stroke. He has a remote history of peptic ulcer disease for which he takes no medications. Medications are lisinopril and glipizide.

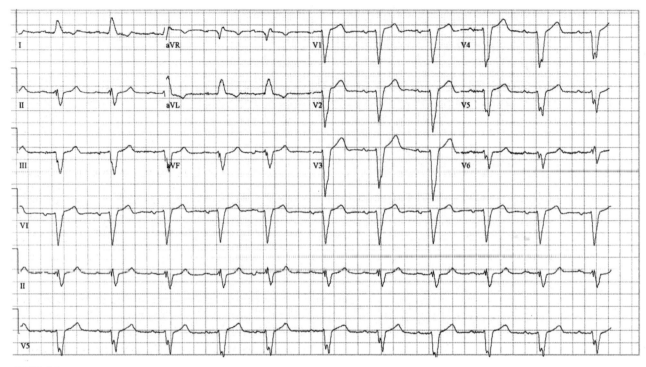

ITEM 36

On physical examination, he is afebrile, blood pressure is 160/90 mm Hg, pulse rate is 80/min, and respiration rate is 12/min. Cardiovascular examination reveals a normal S_1 and S_2 without an S_3, and no murmurs. Lung fields are clear.

Serum troponin and creatine kinase levels are pending. Hematocrit is 42% and platelet count is 220,000/µL (220 × 10^9/L).

Electrocardiogram shows 3-mm ST-segment elevation in leads V_2 through V_4 and a 1-mm ST-segment depression in leads II, III, and aVF. A chest radiograph is normal.

There is no cardiac catheterization laboratory present at the hospital, and it would take approximately 1.5 hours to transfer the patient to the closest facility that performs percutaneous coronary interventions (PCI). β-Blockers, unfractionated heparin, clopidogrel, and aspirin are initiated.

Which of the following is the most appropriate management?

(A) Abciximab and thrombolytic therapy
(B) Await the results of troponin and creatine kinase testing
(C) Thrombolytic therapy
(D) Transfer for primary PCI

Item 39

A 27-year-old man is admitted to the hospital with a 1-week history of progressive shortness of breath, fatigue, lower extremity edema, and orthopnea.

On physical examination, temperature is 37.2 °C (99.0 °F), systolic blood pressure is 65 mm Hg by Doppler examination, and pulse rate is 110/min. The patient is somnolent but arousable and oriented. Estimated central venous pressure is elevated and there are crackles bilaterally in the lung bases. Cardiac examination reveals a regular rhythm, an S_3 gallop, and no murmurs. The extremities are cool.

Laboratory studies:

Alanine aminotransferase	900 units/L
Aspartate aminotransferase	800 units/L
Creatinine	3.1 mg/dL (274 µmol/L)
Sodium	134 meq/L (134 mmol/L)
Troponin I	<0.1 ng/mL (0.1 µg/L)

The drug screen is negative, thyroid-stimulating hormone level is normal, leukocyte count is normal, blood cultures are negative, and urinalysis is normal.

Electrocardiogram shows sinus tachycardia. Echocardiogram shows ejection fraction of 20%, global hypokinesis, no pericardial effusion, and no valvular abnormalities.

A dobutamine infusion is started and uptitrated to 10 µg/kg/min. Because no clinical improvement is seen and volume status and cardiac output are uncertain, a pulmonary artery catheter is placed.

Pulmonary artery catheterization measurements:

Right atrium pressure	20 mm Hg
Pulmonary artery pressure	38/28 mm Hg
Pulmonary capillary wedge pressure	28 mm Hg
Cardiac output	3.4 L/min
Cardiac index	1.7 L/min/m²

Which of the following is the most appropriate treatment?

(A) Intra-aortic balloon pump
(B) Intravenous conivaptan
(C) Intravenous furosemide
(D) Intravenous nesiritide

Item 40

A 41-year-old man is evaluated for progressive shortness of breath over several months. Medical history is significant for Hodgkin lymphoma, diagnosed when he was a teenager. At that time, he received doxorubicin, bleomycin, vinblastine, and dacarbazine with mantle radiation. He is currently in remission and takes no medications.

On physical examination, he is afebrile, blood pressure is 128/70 mm Hg, and pulse rate is 74/min and regular. Estimated central venous pressure is 6 cm H_2O. An inspiratory decline in central venous pressure is noted. The S_1 is regular, with respiratory variation of S_2. A grade 2/6 mid-peaking systolic murmur is heard. The lungs are clear.

Given the patient's symptoms, transthoracic echocardiography is ordered and shows normal biventricular size and systolic function. Diastolic indices show impaired left ventricular relaxation with normal left ventricular filling pressure. Pulmonary systolic pressure is 25 to 30 mm Hg. The inferior vena cava is of normal diameter, with full inspiratory collapse. Mild thickening of the aortic valve and mitral valve is observed. Electrocardiogram shows normal sinus rhythm with first-degree atrioventricular block and is otherwise unremarkable.

Which of the following is the most appropriate diagnostic test to perform next?

(A) Cardiac CT
(B) Exercise electrocardiographic stress testing

(C) Right heart catheterization
(D) Transesophageal echocardiography

Item 41

A 45-year-old man is evaluated for a 6-week history of progressive exertional dyspnea. He has had minor exercise limitation due to dyspnea for approximately 5 months but now he has difficulty climbing a flight of stairs. He has no other cardiovascular symptoms.

The blood pressure is 110/70 mm Hg bilaterally. The estimated central venous pressure is elevated; jugular pulsations include a large *a* wave. There is no digital clubbing or cyanosis. A parasternal impulse is present at the left sternal border. There is fixed splitting of the S_2, and a soft systolic murmur is noted at the second left intercostal space that increases with inspiration. A separate holosystolic murmur is noted at the apex that does not change with respiration. The pulses are full without radial artery–to–femoral artery pulse delay. There is no edema.

The electrocardiogram is shown. The chest radiograph demonstrates mild cardiac enlargement and prominence of the proximal pulmonary arteries.

Which of the following is the most likely diagnosis?

(A) Aortic coarctation
(B) Ostium primum atrial septal defect
(C) Pulmonary valve stenosis
(D) Small perimembranous ventricular septal defect

Item 42

A 67-year-old man is seen for preoperative evaluation before elective total hip replacement. He has a mechanical bileaflet aortic valve and takes warfarin. He has no history of stroke.

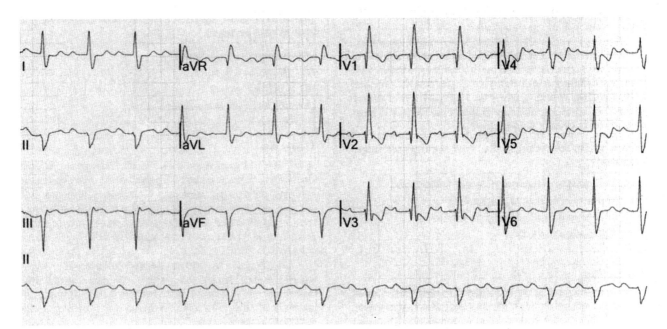

ITEM 41

Physical examination shows normal vital signs. There is a regular rhythm with mechanical S_1. There is a grade 2/6 early peaking systolic ejection murmur at the right upper sternal border without radiation. Lungs are clear to auscultation bilaterally.

Which of the following is the most appropriate perioperative recommendation regarding anticoagulation for this patient?

(A) Discontinue warfarin 3 days before surgery and bridge with heparin before and after surgery

(B) Discontinue warfarin 3 days before surgery and restart on evening of the surgery

(C) Do not discontinue warfarin

(D) Reverse anticoagulation with fresh frozen plasma transfusion 1 hour before surgery; restart warfarin on evening of surgery

Item 43

A 50-year-old man is evaluated for dyspnea on exertion. He has had a murmur for many years. He has not been evaluated recently from either a general medical or cardiovascular standpoint.

The blood pressure is 120/80 mm Hg and the heart rate is 75/min. The estimated central venous pressure is 7 cm H_2O; there is a prominent a wave. A left parasternal impulse and thrill are present. A grade 4/6 early systolic murmur that increases with inspiration is noted at the left sternal border and second left intercostal space. The pulmonic component of the S_2 is delayed and soft. An S_4 is noted along the left sternal border. There is no cyanosis or clubbing. Lower extremity pulses are intact and there is no delay between the radial and femoral artery impulses.

The electrocardiogram demonstrates normal sinus rhythm. There is evidence of right axis deviation, as well as right atrial and right ventricular hypertrophy with a strain pattern.

The chest radiograph demonstrates a normal cardiac silhouette. There is dilatation of the main pulmonary artery with normal pulmonary vascularity.

A transthoracic echocardiogram demonstrates normal left heart chambers and valves. The right ventricular size is normal with a marked increase in right ventricular wall thickness. The estimated right ventricular systolic pressure is 80 mm Hg. A peak gradient of 70 mm Hg is obtained across the pulmonary valve by Doppler calculations. There is mild tricuspid valve regurgitation.

Which of the following is the most appropriate management?

(A) Percutaneous pulmonary balloon valvuloplasty

(B) Pulmonary vasodilator therapy

(C) Surgical pulmonary valve replacement

(D) Observation and follow-up

Item 44

A 70-year-old woman is hospitalized for an ST-elevation myocardial infarction involving the anterior wall. Her symptoms initially began 3 days prior to admission. The pain resolved spontaneously before to reaching the hospital.

Two hours after presentation to the emergency department, she develops acute onset of dyspnea and hypotension and requires emergent intubation. A portable chest radiograph shows cardiomegaly and pulmonary edema. Dopamine is initiated to support her blood pressure.

On physical examination, blood pressure is 90/60 mm Hg, pulse rate is 120/min, and respiration rate is 12/min. She has a grade 4/6 harsh holosystolic murmur at the right and left sternal borders associated with a palpable thrill. No S_3 or S_4 is heard. Crackles are heard bilaterally at the lung bases.

Which of the following is the most likely diagnosis?

(A) Aortic dissection

(B) Free wall rupture

(C) Right ventricular infarction

(D) Ventricular septal defect

Item 45

A 47-year-old woman is evaluated during a routine examination. Medical history is significant only for a 40-pack-year history of cigarette smoking. She was born and raised in the United States. Her father had a myocardial infarction at age 46 years, and her mother died of a myocardial infarction last month, at the age of 64 years. She has no medical problems and takes no medications.

Blood pressure is 148/90 mm Hg, pulse rate is 83/min, and respiration rate is 18/min.

Laboratory studies:

Total cholesterol	201 mg/dL (5.21 mmol/L)
LDL cholesterol	100 mg/dL (2.59 mmol/L)
HDL cholesterol	45 mg/dL (1.17 mmol/L)
Total cholesterol/HDL cholesterol ratio	4.4
Glucose	89 mg/dL (4.9 mmol/L)

Which of the following risk assessment tools would provide the most accurate prediction of cardiovascular risk in this patient?

(A) Framingham risk score

(B) Reynolds risk score

(C) QRISK2 system

(D) SCORE risk assessment

Item 46

A 54-year-old man is evaluated in the emergency department for a 2-hour history of palpitations. He reports no syncope, presyncope, chest pain, or shortness of breath, and has had no previous episodes of palpitations. Medical history is significant for nonischemic cardiomyopathy; ejection fraction was most recently measured at 38%. Medications are carvedilol and candesartan.

On physical examination, he is afebrile, blood pressure is 125/86 mm Hg, and pulse rate is 110/min. Cardiac evaluation reveals a regular rate and rhythm, although the intensity of the S_1 is variable. Cannon a waves are seen in the jugular venous pulsation.

The electrocardiogram is shown (see next page).

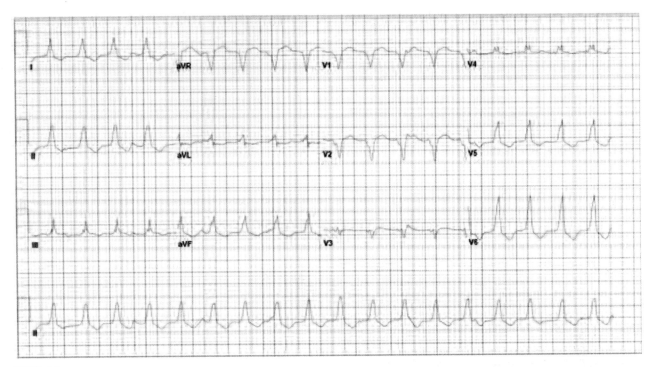

ITEM 46

 Which of the following is the most appropriate treatment?

CONT.

(A) Immediate cardioversion
(B) Intravenous adenosine
(C) Intravenous amiodarone
(D) Intravenous verapamil

Item 47

A 31-year-old woman with cyanotic congenital heart disease is evaluated during a routine examination. She has Down syndrome and is accompanied by her guardian. She has never had cardiac surgery and has no symptoms.

Her blood pressure is 110/80 mm Hg bilaterally. The cardiac apex is displaced. A left parasternal impulse is present. There is a normal S_1. The pulmonic component of the S_2 is increased. A grade 1/6 to 2/6 holosystolic murmur is noted at the left sternal border. There is no change with respiration. Digital cyanosis and clubbing are present. The rest of the examination is unremarkable.

The electrocardiogram demonstrates normal sinus rhythm with right axis deviation and right atrial enlargement. There is also right ventricular hypertrophy with a strain pattern. The chest radiograph demonstrates mild cardiac enlargement as well as enlargement of the central pulmonary arteries with reduced pulmonary vascularity.

Which of the following is the most likely diagnosis?

(A) Aortic coarctation
(B) Ebstein anomaly
(C) Eisenmenger syndrome
(D) Tetralogy of Fallot

Item 48

A 63-year-old woman is evaluated during a routine examination. She has hypertension and depression, and she smokes cigarettes. Her father had a nonfatal myocardial infarction at age 54 years. Medications are an ACE inhibitor and a selective serotonin reuptake inhibitor.

On physical examination, she is afebrile, blood pressure is 128/70 mm Hg, pulse rate is 92/min, and respiration rate is 18/min. BMI is 30. Lungs are clear to auscultation. There are no murmurs or extra heart sounds.

Laboratory studies:

Total cholesterol	160 mg/dL (4.14 mmol/L)
LDL cholesterol	98 mg/dL (2.54 mmol/L)
HDL cholesterol	45 mg/dL (1.17 mmol/L)
Glucose, fasting	78 mg/dL (4.3 mmol/L)

Which of the following components of this patient's presentation is associated with the greatest risk for an acute myocardial infarction?

(A) Current smoking
(B) Depression
(C) Family history
(D) Hypertension
(E) Obesity

Item 49

A 35-year-old woman is evaluated during the 14th week of pregnancy. This is her first pregnancy and the first medical appointment during the pregnancy. She has a history of rheumatic mitral stenosis and had a mechanical mitral valve replacement 2 years ago. She has no cardiovascular symptoms. She is taking warfarin.

Blood pressure is 110/72 mm Hg and heart rate is 70/min. She has normal prosthetic valve heart sounds and no extra sounds or murmurs. The remainder of the examination is normal.

Which of the following is the most appropriate anticoagulation regimen for this patient at this time?

(A) Aspirin, 325 mg/d
(B) Clopidogrel, 75 mg/d
(C) Therapeutic warfarin
(D) Unfractionated heparin, 5000 units subcutaneously twice daily

Item 50

A 66-year-old man is evaluated in the emergency department for chest pain. He describes a sharp pain in the mid-chest that does not radiate. The pain began suddenly at rest and has persisted for approximately 40 minutes. He has hypertension treated with amlodipine.

Temperature is 37.4 °C (99.3 °F), blood pressure is 180/80 mm Hg in the left arm and 200/80 mm Hg in the right arm, pulse rate is 110/min, and respiration rate is 18/min. BMI is 32. Pulse oximetry shows oxygen saturation of 98% on ambient air. A normal carotid upstroke without carotid bruits is noted, jugular venous pulsations are normal, and normal S_1 and S_2 are heard. A grade 2/6 early diastolic murmur is heard at the left sternal border. Lung fields are clear, distal pulses are normal, and no peripheral edema is present.

Laboratory studies:

Hematocrit	40%
Platelet count	220,000/μL (220 × 10⁹/L)
Creatine kinase	100 units/L
Creatinine	1.6 mg/dL (141 μmol/L)
Troponin I	0.05 ng/mL (0.05 μg/L)
Myoglobin	40 ng/mL (40 μg/L) (normal range, 0-90 ng/mL [0-90 μg/L])

Electrocardiogram shows sinus tachycardia at 110/min, with nonspecific ST- and T-wave changes in the lateral leads. Chest radiograph (portable film) is shown.

Which of the following is the most appropriate diagnostic test to perform next?

(A) Chest CT
(B) Electrocardiography with posterior leads
(C) Transthoracic echocardiography
(D) Ventilation-perfusion scanning

Item 51

A 21-year-old man is evaluated during a medical examination for health insurance. The patient is a weight lifter. He has no medical problems and takes no medications or illicit drugs.

On physical examination, blood pressure is 128/73 mm Hg, pulse rate is 56/min, and respiration rate is 16/min; BMI is 30. Increased skeletal muscle mass is noted. There is no jugular venous distention. Carotid

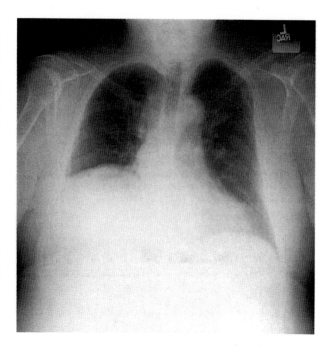

ITEM 50

upstrokes are brisk. There is a grade 2/6 early systolic murmur along the left lower sternal border that is accentuated by a Valsalva maneuver and decreases with a hand-grip maneuver. An S_4 gallop is also noted. Electrocardiogram shows sinus bradycardia and left ventricular hypertrophy by voltage. Echocardiogram shows left ventricular hypertrophy with marked septal hypertrophy and an associated 46 mm Hg outflow tract obstruction, small left ventricular cavity size, normal systolic function with an ejection fraction of 65%, marked left atrial enlargement, and reduced early diastolic filling.

Which of the following is the most likely diagnosis?

(A) Dilated cardiomyopathy
(B) Hypertensive cardiomyopathy
(C) Hypertrophic cardiomyopathy
(D) Restrictive cardiomyopathy

Item 52

A 61-year-old man is evaluated during a follow-up examination. He has a 4-year history of atrial fibrillation and underwent atrial fibrillation ablation 6 months ago. He has had no symptoms of palpitations, fatigue, shortness of breath, or presyncope since the procedure. He has hypertension and type 2 diabetes mellitus. Medications are lisinopril, atenolol, metformin, and warfarin.

Blood pressure is 124/82 mm Hg and pulse rate is 72/min. Cardiac examination discloses regular rate and rhythm. The rest of the physical examination is normal.

Electrocardiogram demonstrates normal sinus rhythm.

Which of the following is the most appropriate treatment?

(A) Continue warfarin
(B) Switch to aspirin

(C) Switch to clopidogrel

(D) Switch to aspirin and clopidogrel

Item 53

A 68-year-old man was admitted to the hospital 3 days ago for a non–ST-elevation myocardial infarction and underwent cardiac catheterization via the right groin. Today, the patient reports pain in his left toes and diffuse soreness in the left calf. Medical history is significant for hyperlipidemia and hypertension. Medications are aspirin, atorvastatin, metoprolol, and lisinopril.

On physical examination, temperature is 37.8 °C (100.1 °F), blood pressure is 132/82 mm Hg, pulse rate is 68/min, and respiration rate is 14/min. BMI is 22. Dorsalis pedis and posterior tibial pulses in both feet are normal; femoral and popliteal pulses are intact. No femoral bruit is present.

A photograph of the left foot is shown.

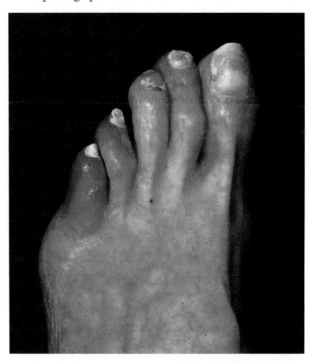

At admission, serum creatinine level was 1.2 mg/dL (106 μmol/L); it is now 2.2 mg/dL (194 μmol/L). Leukocyte count was 5000/μL (5.0×10^9/L) and is now 9000/μL (9.0×10^9/L) with 6% eosinophils. Erythrocyte sedimentation rate is 63 mm/h. Hansel stain of urine sediment demonstrates eosinophils.

Which of the following is the most likely diagnosis?

(A) Acute interstitial nephritis

(B) Cholesterol embolization syndrome

(C) Contrast-induced nephropathy

(D) Delayed hypersensitivity reaction

Item 54

A 52-year-old woman is evaluated for a 1-year history of nonischemic cardiomyopathy. She reports feeling shortness of breath with exertion when walking up one flight of stairs or walking one city block. Medical and family histories are unremarkable. Medications are carvedilol, lisinopril, digoxin, spironolactone, and furosemide.

On physical examination, she is afebrile, blood pressure is 112/74 mm Hg, and pulse rate is 82/min. Cardiac evaluation reveals a regular rate and rhythm, positive S_3, and a grade 2/6 holosystolic murmur heard best at the apex and radiating to the axilla.

An electrocardiogram demonstrates sinus rhythm and left bundle branch block with QRS interval of 155 msec. Echocardiogram shows a moderately dilated left ventricle and severely depressed left ventricular systolic function, with an ejection fraction of 25%.

Which of the following is the most appropriate treatment?

(A) Biventricular pacemaker with implantable cardioverter-defibrillator (ICD)

(B) Dual-chamber (right atrial and right ventricular leads) ICD

(C) Dual-chamber (right atrial and right ventricular leads) pacemaker

(D) Single-chamber (right ventricular lead) ICD

Item 55

A 32-year-old man is evaluated in the emergency department for palpitations and dyspnea of 1 week's duration. His medical history is remarkable for tetralogy of Fallot that was repaired in childhood. He has had not recent cardiovascular follow-up.

Blood pressure is 110/70 mm Hg bilaterally, and pulse rate is 100/min. Estimated central venous pressure is 10 cm H_2O; jugular pulsations include a large v wave. The apical impulse is displaced. A parasternal impulse is present and there is a single S_2. A grade 2/6 holosystolic murmur and a grade 2/6 diastolic murmur are noted at the left sternal border that increase with inspiration. Pulsatile hepatomegaly and lower extremity edema are present.

The electrocardiogram demonstrates atrial fibrillation and right bundle branch block. The chest radiograph demonstrates cardiomegaly and a right aortic arch. Transthoracic echocardiography demonstrates marked right-sided cardiac chamber enlargement and severe pulmonary and tricuspid valve regurgitation. There is no evidence of pulmonary hypertension. The ventricular septum is intact.

The patient is started on intravenous unfractionated heparin therapy and is treated with intravenous diltiazem that controls the heart rate response. Atrial fibrillation persists.

Which of the following is the most appropriate management?

(A) Cardioversion, warfarin, and amiodarone

(B) Pulmonary valve replacement, tricuspid valve repair, and maze procedure

(C) Radiofrequency atrial fibrillation ablation

(D) Referral for heart transplantation

Item 56

A 54-year-old man visits to discuss his risk of having a heart attack. He currently runs 3 to 4 miles daily without limitation. He has no history of chest pain or shortness of breath. He reports no cardiac history. He has a 4-year history of hypertension. His father experienced a myocardial infarction at age 50 years, and his brother underwent angioplasty at age 49 years. His only medication is losartan.

Temperature is 37.0 °C (98.6 °F), blood pressure is 130/80 mm Hg, pulse rate is 60/min, and respiration rate is 10/min. BMI is 20. The general physical examination is normal.

Laboratory studies:

High-sensitivity C-reactive protein	0.4 mg/dL (4.0 mg/L)
Total cholesterol	180 mg/dL (4.66 mmol/L)
LDL cholesterol	110 mg/dL (2.85 mmol/L)
HDL cholesterol	30 mg/dL (0.78 mmol/L)

The Framingham risk score predicts an 11% probability of a coronary event in the next 10 years.

In addition to aspirin, which of the following is the most appropriate treatment?

(A) β-Carotene
(B) Folic acid
(C) Rosuvastatin
(D) Vitamin E

Item 57

A 64-year-old man is evaluated in the emergency department for chest pain. He describes the chest pain as pressure located in the midchest that is nonradiating and not associated with any symptoms. The chest pain began at rest and has lasted approximately 15 minutes. He reports no history of similar chest pain. Medical history is remarkable for hypertension, type 2 diabetes mellitus, hyperlipidemia, asthma, and a 20-pack-year history of smoking, which he quit 2 years ago. Medications are hydrochlorothiazide, metformin, simvastatin, isosorbide mononitrate, albuterol, and corticosteroid metered-dose inhalers. The patient admits to difficulty in adhering to his medical regimen.

On physical examination, he is afebrile, blood pressure is 140/80 mm Hg, pulse rate is 62/min, and respiration rate is 16/min. BMI is 32. Inspiratory and expiratory wheezes are heard bilaterally. A normal carotid upstroke without carotid bruits is noted, jugular venous pulsations are normal, and normal S_1 and S_2 are heard without murmurs. Distal pulses are normal, and no peripheral edema is present.

Laboratory findings, including cardiac biomarkers, are within normal limits.

Electrocardiogram shows a normal sinus rhythm and a T-wave inversion in leads V_2 through V_6 with no Q waves.

He is given aspirin, clopidogrel, and low-molecular-weight heparin.

Which of the following medications should be added to his treatment regimen?

(A) Carvedilol
(B) Diltiazem
(C) Metoprolol
(D) Nifedipine

Item 58

A 68-year-old man is admitted to the hospital with a 1-week history of progressive shortness of breath, lower extremity edema, and weight gain of 4.5 kg (10 lb). He has ischemic cardiomyopathy and type 2 diabetes mellitus complicated by nephropathy. Medications are insulin, lisinopril, metoprolol, aspirin, and atorvastatin.

On physical examination, temperature is normal, blood pressure is 130/80 mm Hg, and pulse rate is 80/min. Estimated central venous pressure is 15 cm H_2O. Cardiac examination reveals a regular rhythm, an S_3, and a grade 2/6 holosystolic murmur radiating to the apex. Lower extremity edema with bilateral pitting to the knees is present.

Laboratory studies:

Hemoglobin	9.5 g/dL (95 g/L) (10.5 g/dL [105 g/L] 3 months ago)
Creatinine	3.7 mg/dL (327 μmol/L) (1.9 mg/dL [168 μmol/L] 3 months ago)
Sodium	136 meq/L (136 mmol/L)
Troponin I	<0.1 ng/mL (0.1 μg/L)

An echocardiogram shows a left ventricular ejection fraction of 30%, mild to moderate mitral regurgitation, anterior wall akinesis, and left ventricular enlargement.

Which of the following is the most appropriate treatment?

(A) Erythrocyte transfusion
(B) Intravenous bumetanide
(C) Intravenous milrinone
(D) Low-dose dopamine

Item 59

A 34-year-old woman comes to the emergency department after the acute onset of palpitations approximately 1 hour ago. She reports no shortness of breath, chest pain, presyncope, or syncope. Her medical history is unremarkable, and there is no family history of sudden cardiac death. She takes no medications.

On physical examination, she is afebrile, blood pressure is 118/64 mm Hg, and pulse rate is 165/min. Other than a regular, rapid heart rate, the cardiopulmonary examination is normal.

Baseline electrocardiogram demonstrates a narrow complex tachycardia at 165/min. Adenosine is given as a rapid intravenous push; simultaneous electrocardiogram is shown (see next page).

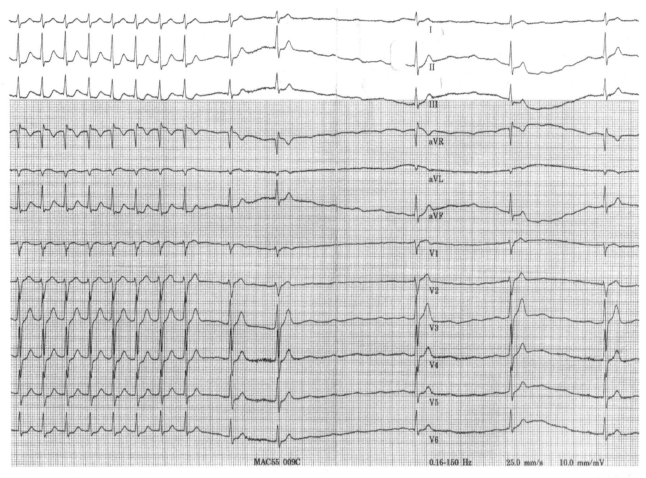

ITEM 59

CONT.

Which of the following is the most likely diagnosis?

(A) Atrial tachycardia
(B) Atrioventricular nodal reentrant tachycardia
(C) Atrioventricular reciprocating tachycardia
(D) Junctional tachycardia

Item 60

A 72-year-old man is evaluated for bilateral thigh pain with walking 3 to 4 blocks. He feels better if he can stop and rest, but symptoms recur when he resumes walking. Symptoms have been present for 6 to 8 months and have been stable. Medical history is significant for hypertension and hyperlipidemia; he was a cigarette smoker, but quit 12 years ago. Medications are atorvastatin and lisinopril.

On physical examination, blood pressure is 132/84 mm Hg, pulse rate is 78/min and regular, and respiration rate is 16/min. BMI is 22. Deep tendon reflexes are symmetric and normal at the knees and at the ankles. Lower extremity muscle strength is normal. No abdominal or femoral bruit is present. Hair is absent and the skin is shiny below the knees bilaterally. Distal pulses are faintly palpable bilaterally. Resting ankle-brachial index (ABI) is 0.94 on both sides.

Which of the following is the most appropriate diagnostic test to perform next?

(A) Contrast CT aortofemoral angiography
(B) Exercise ABI testing
(C) MRI of the lumbar spine
(D) Segmental lower extremity plethysmography

Item 61

A 60-year-old man with a history of coronary artery disease undergoes a preoperative assessment prior to cholecystectomy following a single episode of biliary colic that occurred 3 weeks ago. Ultrasonography documented cholelithiasis without gallbladder edema. Six months ago, a drug-eluting stent was placed in the left anterior descending coronary artery. He also has hypertension. Medications are lisinopril, aspirin, clopidogrel, and metoprolol. He has modified his diet and has not had any additional abdominal discomfort since the episode 3 weeks ago.

On physical examination, temperature is normal, blood pressure is 125/80 mm Hg, pulse rate is 60/min, and respiration rate is 12/min. BMI is 26. A normal carotid upstroke without carotid bruits is noted, jugular venous pulsations are normal, and normal S_1 and S_2 are heard without murmurs.

Lung fields are clear, distal pulses are normal, and no peripheral edema is present.

Which of the following is the most appropriate management?

(A) Postpone surgery for 6 months
(B) Stop aspirin and proceed with surgery
(C) Stop aspirin and clopidogrel and proceed with surgery
(D) Stop aspirin and clopidogrel, begin unfractionated heparin, and proceed with surgery

Item 62

A 72-year-old woman is evaluated during a routine examination. Medical history is significant for hypertension, type 2 diabetes mellitus, and dyslipidemia. Medications are lisinopril, metformin, and pravastatin. She exercises daily; ingests a diet high in fruits, nuts, and vegetables; and does not smoke. She has no allergies.

Blood pressure is 118/70 mm Hg, pulse rate is 73/min, and respiration rate is 16/min. The remainder of the physical examination, including cardiovascular, pulmonary, and neurologic examinations, is normal.

Laboratory studies:

Hemoglobin A_{1c}	6.5%
Total cholesterol	116 mg/dL (3.00 mmol/L)
LDL cholesterol	51 mg/dL (1.32 mmol/L)
HDL cholesterol	57 mg/dL (1.48 mmol/L)
Triglycerides	40 mg/dL (0.45 mmol/L)

Which of the following is the most appropriate treatment?

(A) Start aspirin
(B) Start aspirin and clopidogrel
(C) Start aspirin and dipyridamole
(D) Start clopidogrel

Item 63

A 45-year-old woman is evaluated in the emergency department for acute severe shortness of breath. She has a history of mitral valve prolapse for more than 30 years. Before today, she has been able to swim for 1 hour without symptoms. Two hours ago while moving furniture she experienced acute dyspnea and chest discomfort. She has had no fever or chills.

Physical examination shows a thin woman with labored breathing. Temperature is 37.2 °C (99.0 °F), blood pressure is 115/76 mm Hg, heart rate is 120/min and regular, and respiration rate is 20/min. Oxygen saturation is 88% on ambient air. There is no jugular venous distention, and carotid upstrokes are brisk. The apical impulse is not displaced. S_1 is reduced and there is a grade 2/6 early systolic murmur at the apex with radiation to the back. An S_3 is present. Her lungs have bilateral crackles. Extremities are cool.

Electrocardiogram shows sinus tachycardia and prominent QRS voltage. Chest radiograph shows normal cardiac size and pulmonary edema. Urgent transthoracic echocardiogram shows normal left and right ventricular size and

systolic function, left ventricular ejection fraction of 70%, and partial flail of the anterior mitral valve leaflet with severe mitral regurgitation. The left atrium is not dilated and no other valve abnormalities are detected.

In addition to supplemental oxygen and diuretic therapy, which of the following is the most appropriate next treatment of this patient?

(A) Captopril
(B) Esmolol
(C) Mitral valve surgery
(D) Vancomycin and gentamicin after blood cultures are drawn

Item 64

A 64-year-old woman is evaluated in the emergency department for chest pain and shortness of breath. The chest pain began earlier in the day after she received news that her younger sister had died in a motor vehicle accident. She reports no similar episodes of chest pain before today. She takes no medications.

On physical examination, temperature is 37.3 °C (99.1 °F), blood pressure is 150/80 mm Hg, pulse rate is 90/min, and respiration rate is 11/min. BMI is 24. A normal carotid upstroke without carotid bruits is noted, jugular venous pulsations are normal, and normal S_1 and S_2 are heard without murmurs.

Serum troponin level is 1.4 ng/mL (1.4 µg/L).

Electrocardiogram displays a sinus rhythm at 90/min, 1-mm ST-segment elevation in leads V_1 through V_4, and no Q waves. An echocardiogram shows reduced wall motion of the anterior and apical portion of the heart, hyperdynamic wall motion of the basal segments, no significant valvular heart disease, and no pericardial effusion. She undergoes emergent coronary angiography, which shows normal coronary arteries. Ventriculography shows no movement of the apical portion of the heart and hyperdynamic wall motion of the basal segments of the heart.

Which of the following is the most likely diagnosis?

(A) Non–ST-elevation myocardial infarction
(B) Pericarditis
(C) ST-elevation myocardial infarction
(D) Stress cardiomyopathy

Item 65

A 90-year-old woman is admitted to the hospital for the evaluation of chest pain. She describes the pain as pressure within the midchest with radiation to the neck. During the past week, she has had several episodes at rest, with two episodes in the last 24 hours for which she took aspirin. She is currently free of pain. Last week she met with her general internist to discuss end-of-life issues and decided upon do-not-resuscitate (DNR) status and does not want invasive procedures performed to prolong her life. She is amenable to medical therapy for potentially reversible conditions. Her medications are aspirin, a multivitamin, and docusate.

CONT.

On physical examination, temperature is normal, blood pressure is 140/80 mm Hg, pulse rate is 72/min, and respiration rate is 11/min. BMI is 20. A normal carotid upstroke without carotid bruits is noted, jugular venous pulsations are normal, and normal S_1 and S_2 are heard without murmurs. Distal pulses are normal and no peripheral edema is present.

Serum troponin level is elevated. Electrocardiogram displays a sinus rhythm at 70/min, T-wave inversion in leads V_4 through V_6, and no Q waves.

In addition to aspirin and low-molecular-weight heparin, which of the following is the most appropriate treatment?

(A) Diltiazem
(B) Diltiazem, atorvastatin, and clopidogrel
(C) Metoprolol
(D) Metoprolol, atorvastatin, and clopidogrel

Item 66

An 18-year-old man is evaluated during a sports physical examination. He was diagnosed with a ventricular septal defect early in life. He has had no operative intervention or recent cardiovascular evaluation. He is an athlete without any limitations.

The blood pressure is 110/70 mm Hg in both upper extremities. The jugular and carotid examinations are normal. There is no clubbing or cyanosis. The apical impulse is at the midclavicular line in the fifth intercostal space. No parasternal impulse is present. A blowing grade 3/6 holosystolic murmur is noted at the lower left sternal border and obliterates the S_2. There is no diastolic murmur and no extra heart sounds. The remainder of the examination is unremarkable.

Laboratory studies, chest radiograph, and electrocardiogram are normal.

A transthoracic echocardiogram demonstrates a small perimembranous ventricular septal defect. The left and right heart size and function are normal. The right ventricular systolic pressure is normal. The cardiac valves are normal.

Which of the following is the most appropriate management?

(A) Cardiovascular magnetic resonance (CMR) imaging
(B) Closure of the defect
(C) Hemodynamic cardiac catheterization
(D) Observation and follow-up

Item 67

A 54-year-old woman is evaluated for palpitations. For the past week, she has noted an irregular heart rhythm. She has not experienced chest discomfort, lightheadedness, syncope, orthopnea, paroxysmal nocturnal dyspnea, or edema.

She has a history of chronic severe mitral regurgitation due to myxomatous mitral valve degeneration. Her annual transthoracic echocardiogram 2 months ago showed left ventricular ejection fraction of 65% with left ventricular end-diastolic diameter of 53 mm and end-systolic diameter

of 38 mm. The left atrium was dilated, with an area of 28 cm². The mitral valve leaflets were thickened and redundant, with posterior prolapse and severe, anteriorly directed mitral regurgitation (effective regurgitant orifice area of 0.4 cm²). The estimated right ventricular systolic pressure was 38 mm Hg.

On physical examination, temperature is 37.4 °C (99.3 °F), blood pressure is 132/74 mm Hg, pulse rate is 95/min and irregular, and respiration rate is 15/min. Estimated central venous pressure and carotid upstrokes are normal. The apical impulse is not palpable. There is a grade 3/6 holosystolic murmur at the apex radiating to the right upper sternal border. Lungs are clear to auscultation.

Electrocardiogram shows atrial fibrillation with a ventricular rate of 95/min with left axis deviation and normal intervals.

In addition to starting warfarin, which of the following is the most appropriate management at this time?

(A) Amiodarone
(B) Direct-current cardioversion
(C) Exercise echocardiography
(D) Mitral valve repair surgery

Item 68

A 56-year-old man is admitted to the hospital with new-onset substernal chest pressure. Medical history is remarkable for hyperlipidemia. He is a cigarette smoker. His medications are aspirin and atorvastatin; upon admission to the hospital, he began receiving metoprolol, clopidogrel, and intravenous heparin.

On physical examination, the patient is afebrile, blood pressure is 132/78 mm Hg, pulse rate is 82/min and regular, and respiration rate is 14/min. No jugular venous distention is noted, the lungs are clear to auscultation, no murmur or gallop is heard, and no peripheral edema is noted.

On admission, cardiac troponin I level was 1.2 ng/mL (1.2 µg/L); on hospital day 2 it peaks at 8.4 ng/mL (8.4 µg/L). An electrocardiogram on arrival to the emergency department demonstrated a nonspecific ST-T wave abnormality, but no ST-segment elevation or depression. Cardiac catheterization demonstrates overall preserved left ventricular systolic function with diffuse severe disease of the distal portion of all three major epicardial vessels. No catheter-based intervention is performed.

Which of the following is the most appropriate management of this patient's clopidogrel therapy?

(A) Stop clopidogrel
(B) Continue clopidogrel therapy for 2 weeks
(C) Continue clopidogrel therapy for 1 year
(D) Continue clopidogrel therapy lifelong

Item 69

A 30-year-old man is evaluated during a routine examination to establish care. He jogs several times per week and is now training for his first marathon. He has recently noted leg cramping during longer runs, which resolves with rest. Review of systems reveals no angina, dyspnea, fatigue, or edema.

On physical examination, he is afebrile and blood pressure is 160/80 mm Hg bilaterally. BMI is 24. On cardiac examination, the point of maximal impulse is undisplaced. The S_1 is normal and the S_2 is physiologically split. An S_4 is heard. There is an early systolic click and a grade 2/6 early systolic murmur at the upper right sternal border. A midsystolic murmur can be heard from the back at the left paravertebral area. Distal pulses in the radial arteries are prominent. Dorsalis pedis and posterior tibial pulses are difficult to palpate. The rest of the physical examination is unrevealing.

Which of the following is the most likely diagnosis?

(A) Aortic coarctation
(B) Atrial septal defect
(C) Mitral valve prolapse
(D) Ventricular septal defect

Item 70

A 74-year-old man with a 10-year history of coronary artery disease with multiple interventions is evaluated for continuing angina. He is able to walk a quarter of a block and is limited by angina and bilateral calf claudication. The angina is relieved with rest and 1 or 2 sublingual nitroglycerin tablets. He has not had episodes of angina at rest. There are no options for additional bypass surgery or percutaneous coronary intervention. He has established peripheral vascular disease. Medications are aspirin, metoprolol, isosorbide mononitrate extended release, diltiazem, simvastatin, and sublingual nitroglycerin.

On physical examination, temperature is 37.2 °C (99.0 °F), blood pressure is 110/80 mm Hg, pulse rate is 52/min, and respiration rate is 12/min. BMI is 20. A normal carotid upstroke without carotid bruits is noted, jugular venous pulsations are normal, and S_1 and S_2 are heard without murmurs. Distal pulses are diminished bilaterally, and no peripheral edema is present.

Laboratory results are within normal limits. Electrocardiogram shows sinus rhythm at 50/min, left ventricular hypertrophy, and Q waves in leads II, III, and aVF. QT interval is normal.

Which of the following is the most appropriate management?

(A) Carvedilol
(B) External enhanced counterpulsation
(C) Ranolazine
(D) Spinal cord stimulation

Item 71

A 62-year-old woman is awaiting a procedure in the presurgical area. She has a single-chamber implantable cardioverter-defibrillator (ICD) and is about to undergo a hemicolectomy for colon cancer. Medical history is pertinent for ischemic cardiomyopathy, chronic atrial fibrillation, complete heart block, and pacemaker dependence. Medications are aspirin, carvedilol, lisinopril, digoxin, warfarin (withheld), and rosuvastatin. Perioperative anticoagulation is provided with unfractionated heparin.

Which of the following is the most appropriate perioperative management of the patient's ICD?

(A) Insert a temporary pacemaker
(B) Place a magnet over the ICD
(C) Turn shock therapy off and change to asynchronous mode
(D) No programming changes needed to ICD

Item 72

A 78-year-old man is evaluated in the emergency department with chest pain. The patient reports that the pain, which is present in the left substernal area, began at rest, and has been present for 12 hours. He reports no similar episodes of chest pain. Medical history is significant for hypertension and a 30-pack-year history of ongoing tobacco use. His only medication is nifedipine.

On physical examination, temperature is 37.9 °C (100.3 °F), blood pressure is 130/80 mm Hg, pulse rate is 72/min, and respiration rate is 12/min. BMI is 28. A normal carotid upstroke without carotid bruits is noted, jugular venous pulsations are normal, and S_1 and S_2 are heard without murmurs. Lung fields are clear, distal pulses are normal, and no peripheral edema is present.

Serum creatine kinase level is 500 units/L and troponin I level is 26 ng/mL (26 µg/L). Laboratory findings are otherwise normal.

Electrocardiogram shows sinus rhythm at 70/min; 2-mm ST-segment elevation in leads II, III and aVF; and 1-mm ST-segment depression in leads V_2 and V_3. He is taken to the cardiac catheterization laboratory and found to have single-vessel coronary artery disease with a severe stenosis of the proximal left anterior descending coronary artery.

Which of the following is the most appropriate treatment?

(A) Coronary artery bypass surgery
(B) Intracoronary thrombolytic therapy
(C) Medical therapy
(D) Primary percutaneous coronary intervention

Item 73

An 87-year-old woman is recovering in the hospital from a hip fracture, which was surgically repaired 3 days ago. She has developed a urinary tract infection and episodes of rapid atrial fibrillation. She also has had episodes of delirium. Medical history is significant for paroxysmal atrial fibrillation. Before hospitalization, her only medication was aspirin; she is currently also taking digoxin, diltiazem, trimethoprim, haloperidol, and enoxaparin.

On physical examination, she is afebrile, blood pressure is 135/88 mm Hg, and pulse rate is 63/min.

Her baseline and current electrocardiograms are shown (see next page).

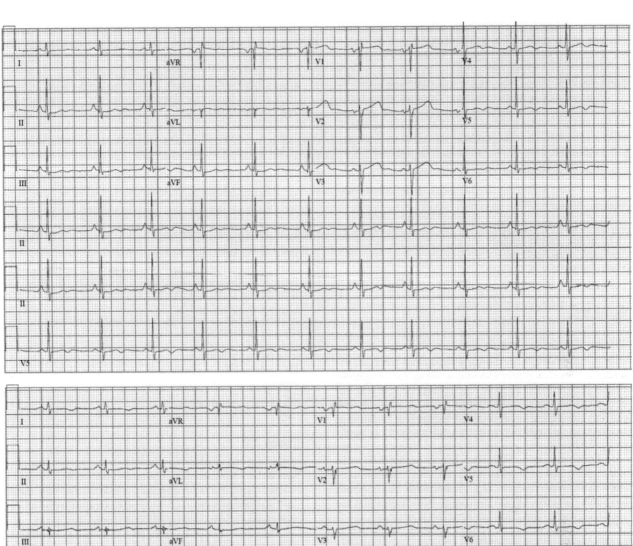

ITEM 73. Baseline electrocardiogram (top); current electrocardiogram (bottom).

CONT.

Which of the following medications is most likely to have caused the change in the electrocardiograms?

(A) Digoxin
(B) Diltiazem
(C) Enoxaparin
(D) Haloperidol
(E) Trimethoprim

Item 74

A 55-year-old man is evaluated during a routine examination. He has a history of aortic coarctation that was repaired in childhood. He is asymptomatic and has not had a recent cardiovascular evaluation. He takes no medications.

Blood pressure is 180/100 mm Hg bilaterally. A systolic murmur and ejection click are noted at the left sternal border and second right intercostal space. The aortic component of the S_2 is reduced. The lower extremity pulses are normal. The rest of the examination is unremarkable.

Left ventricular hypertrophy is noted on the electrocardiogram. The chest radiograph demonstrates no evidence of rib notching; the cardiac silhouette is normal.

A transthoracic echocardiogram demonstrates a bicuspid aortic valve with aortic stenosis; the mean gradient across the aortic valve is 40 mm Hg. The ascending aorta is normal dimension; the descending thoracic aorta is incompletely visualized.

Antihypertensive medication is initiated.

Which of the following is the most appropriate next step in management?

(A) Aortic valve replacement
(B) Cardiac catheterization
(C) MRI of the aorta
(D) Percutaneous stent placement in the aorta

Item 75

A 58-year-old man with heart failure is evaluated during a routine examination. He has ischemic cardiomyopathy with no revascularizable lesions. He has had three admissions for heart failure in the past 6 months, each requiring short-term inotropic support. He is disabled and severely symptomatic with minimal exertion. He has an implanted cardioverter-defibrillator (ICD). Medications are aspirin, atorvastatin, carvedilol, furosemide, spironolactone, lisinopril, and digoxin.

Blood pressure is 90/60 mm Hg, pulse rate is 68/min and regular, and respiration rate is 16/min. Estimate central venous pressure is 9 cm H_2O. Crackles are heard at both lung bases. There is a grade 2/6 holosystolic murmur at the apex radiating to the axilla. An S_3 gallop is present.

Laboratory studies reveal a blood urea nitrogen level of 32 mg/dL (11.4 mmol/L), serum potassium level of 5.4 meq/L (5.4 mmol/L), and serum creatinine level of 1.6 mg/dL (141 µmol/L). Electrocardiogram shows normal sinus rhythm, with a rate of 68/min. There are extensive Q waves and a QRS interval of 110 msec. Echocardiography reveals extensive severe anterior, apical, and inferior hypokinesis; left ventricular ejection fraction of 20%; and moderate mitral regurgitation.

Which of the following is the most appropriate treatment?

(A) Add hydralazine and isosorbide dinitrate
(B) Increase lisinopril
(C) Referral for cardiac transplantation evaluation
(D) Upgrade ICD to combined biventricular pacer/ICD

Item 76

A 38-year-old man is admitted to the hospital for fever and shortness of breath. He reports a 4-week history of malaise, recurrent fevers with chills, myalgia, and decreased appetite.

On physical examination, temperature is 39.0 °C (102.2 °F), blood pressure is 138/60 mm Hg, and pulse rate is 112/min. Oxygen saturation on ambient air is 92%.

Jugular venous distention is increased. The carotid upstrokes are brisk. There is an early systolic ejection click after S_1 followed by a grade 3/6 midpeaking systolic ejection murmur at the right upper sternal border. S_2 is normal but is followed by a grade 3/6 decrescendo diastolic murmur at the left lower sternal border. An S_3 and bibasilar crackles are heard.

Laboratory findings include a hemoglobin level of 9.0 g/dL (90 g/L) and a leukocyte count of 17,500/µL (17.5×10^9/L) with a left shift. He is empirically treated with vancomycin and gentamicin intravenously.

Blood cultures are positive for viridans streptococci, susceptible to penicillin.

Transesophageal echocardiogram shows normal left ventricular size and systolic function. The aortic valve is bicuspid with fusion of the right and left cusps. There is mild aortic stenosis. There is severe aortic valve regurgitation, with a leaflet perforation. An oscillating vegetation is found on the aortic valve, and echolucency (fluid) is seen around the aortic annulus posterior to this region.

Which of the following is the most appropriate next step in management?

(A) Add rifampin
(B) Aortic valve replacement
(C) Cardiac catheterization
(D) Heparin intravenously

Item 77

A 43-year-old woman is evaluated for a 3-month history of substernal exertional chest pain and a 2-month history of worsening dyspnea on exertion. Medical history is significant for breast cancer 13 years ago, treated with lumpectomy and radiation therapy that involved the thorax.

On physical examination, temperature is normal, blood pressure is 155/43 mm Hg, pulse rate is 80/min, and respiration rate is 14/min. Carotid upstrokes are rapid and accentuated with a rapid decline. She has no jugular venous distention or retrograde waves. The S_2 is diminished; there is no S_3 gallop. A grade 2/6 high-pitched blowing diastolic decrescendo murmur is heard to the left of the sternum at the third intercostal space. The apical point of maximal impulse is displaced inferiorly and laterally. Hepatojugular reflux is absent.

Which of the following is the most likely cause of her symptoms?

(A) Aortic valve regurgitation
(B) Constrictive pericarditis
(C) Restrictive cardiomyopathy
(D) Severe tricuspid regurgitation

Item 78

A 41-year-old woman is evaluated for worsening exertional dyspnea and lightheadedness. She has a history of heart murmur since birth. She takes no medications.

On physical examination, her blood pressure is 120/75 mm Hg and pulse rate is 72/min and regular. The jugular venous pulsation demonstrates a prominent *a* wave; carotid pulsations are normal. There is a palpable parasternal impulse and systolic thrill. The apical impulse is normal. An ejection click is heard in close proximity to S_1 at the left sternal border in the second intercostal space. This click decreases in intensity with inspiration. A grade 4/6 systolic crescendo-decrescendo murmur that increases during inspiration is heard in the second left intercostal space and radiates to the left clavicular region.

Chest radiograph shows a normal cardiac silhouette but a dilated main pulmonary artery; lung fields are normal.

Which of the following is the most likely diagnosis?

(A) Atrial septal defect
(B) Bicuspid aortic valve
(C) Mitral valve prolapse and regurgitation
(D) Pulmonary valve stenosis
(E) Ventricular septal defect

Item 79

A 36-year-old woman is evaluated for 3 months of generalized malaise with fevers and 3.6 kg (8 lb) weight loss. She has noted cramping in her arms over the last month during exercise that she previously accomplished without difficulty. She has had no chest or back pain or discomfort. She has previously been healthy. She is a lifelong nonsmoker and has never had hypertension or hyperlipidemia.

On physical examination, temperature is 37.9 °C (100.2 °F). Systolic blood pressures are 62 mm Hg in the right arm and 80 mm Hg in the left arm. Pulse rate is 86/min and respiration rate is 16/min. BMI is 20. Bruits are present below both clavicles. There is tenderness upon palpation of both carotid arteries. There is no cardiac murmur, gallop, or rub. The brachial pulses are faintly palpable; radial pulses are absent. Femoral, popliteal, dorsalis pedis, and posterior tibialis pulses are full and symmetric. No abdominal or femoral bruit is present.

Pertinent laboratory findings include normal complete blood count and basic metabolic profile. Erythrocyte sedimentation rate is 82 mm/h, serum LDL cholesterol level is 68 mg/dL (1.76 mmol/L), HDL cholesterol level is 45 mg/dL (1.17 mmol/L), and triglyceride level is 92 mg/dL (1.04 mmol/L).

Chest radiographs are normal.

Which of the following is the most likely diagnosis?

(A) Aortic dissection
(B) Buerger disease
(C) Kawasaki disease
(D) Takayasu arteritis

Item 80

A 43-year-old man is evaluated in the hospital prior to discharge. He has nonischemic cardiomyopathy and was admitted to the hospital 4 days ago with volume overload. He was treated with intravenous furosemide with significant improvement in his symptoms. He has been hospitalized three times in the past 4 months for acute decompensated

heart failure. He has an implanted biventricular pacemaker/cardioverter-defibrillator. He is stable with his oral medications, which are metoprolol, lisinopril, furosemide, and spironolactone.

Blood pressure is 100/70 mm Hg and pulse rate is 60/min. Estimated central venous pressure is 6 cm H_2O. Cardiac examination reveals a regular rhythm and no S_3 or murmurs. The lungs are clear to auscultation.

Which of the following is the most appropriate management to reduce the risk of hospital readmission?

(A) Follow-up appointment within 1 week
(B) Follow-up appointment within 10 days
(C) Follow-up appointment within 2 weeks
(D) Visiting nurse within 1 week

Item 81

An 86-year-old man is evaluated in the hospital for progressive weakness of 1 month's duration. His medical history is significant for hypertension, hyperlipidemia, chronic obstructive pulmonary disease, and heart failure (New York Heart Association functional class III; left ventricular ejection fraction, 30%). Two months ago, he received a drug-eluting stent in the left anterior descending coronary artery following an acute anterior myocardial infarction. He uses home oxygen (2 L/min continuous flow). He has unintentionally lost 9.1 kg (20 lb) in 6 months. His medications are lisinopril, carvedilol, atorvastatin, aspirin, clopidogrel, and furosemide.

On physical examination, the patient appears ill and frail. He is afebrile, blood pressure is 138/80 mm Hg, pulse rate is 68/min and regular, and respiration rate is 16/min. BMI is 17. Jugular venous distention is present. Crackles are heard in the lower quarter of both lung fields, and an S_3 gallop is present. The abdomen is scaphoid, a pulsatile mass is palpable above the umbilicus, and a soft bruit is present in the same location. Rectal examination is normal.

Which of the following is the most appropriate next test to evaluate this patient's abdominal mass?

(A) Abdominal ultrasound
(B) CT of abdomen with contrast
(C) Magnetic resonance angiography
(D) No diagnostic testing

Item 82

A 55-year-old man is evaluated for a 2-month history of dyspnea on exertion without chest pain. Medical history is significant for type 2 diabetes mellitus, hypertension, and hyperlipidemia. Medications are metformin, lisinopril, pravastatin, and aspirin.

On physical examination, blood pressure is 110/75 mm Hg and pulse rate is 60/min. BMI is 35. Jugular venous distention is noted, and trace lower extremity edema is present. The point of maximal impulse is normal in size and location. Cardiac examination reveals a regular rate and rhythm, and the chest is clear to auscultation.

Laboratory studies show a serum B-type natriuretic peptide level of 110 pg/mL.

Electrocardiogram is shown. Echocardiogram shows inferior wall hypokinesis and ejection fraction of 35%.

Which of the following is the most appropriate diagnostic test to perform next?

(A) Adenosine thallium stress test
(B) Cardiac magnetic resonance (CMR) imaging
(C) Cardiopulmonary exercise test
(D) Coronary angiography

Item 83

A 70-year-old woman is evaluated in the coronary care unit for right groin pain 8 hours after undergoing angioplasty and stent placement for an inferior wall ST-elevation myocardial infarction. During the procedure, she developed transient bradycardia and required placement of a temporary transvenous pacemaker through the right femoral vein. Medical history is significant for gout treated with allopurinol and type 2 diabetes mellitus treated with glyburide. Additional medications are aspirin, eptifibatide, clopidogrel, and simvastatin.

Blood pressure is 130/80 mm Hg, heart rate is 72/min, and respiration rate is 12/min. Physical examination is notable for a 12- by 12-cm area of fullness at the right groin puncture site that is tender to palpation. Auscultation over the groin puncture site is notable for a continuous bruit. The dorsalis pedis and posterior tibial pulses are 2+ bilaterally and the right foot is warm. A stat hematocrit is 39%.

Which of the following is the most appropriate management?

(A) Ankle-brachial index
(B) CT
(C) Duplex ultrasonography
(D) Lower-extremity angiography

Item 84

A 64-year-old woman with constrictive pericarditis is evaluated during a follow-up appointment. She was diagnosed with acute idiopathic pericarditis 3 months ago. She was treated with ibuprofen for 4 weeks with resolution of chest pain. Six weeks ago, she presented with a 1-week history of dyspnea on exertion. Her symptoms had decreased from New York Heart Association (NYHA) functional class I to class III. Echocardiogram showed a trace pericardial effusion and new findings of restrictive filling and ventricular interdependence. Ibuprofen was restarted, and colchicine was added. At a visit 2 weeks ago, functional class had improved to NYHA class II. Repeat echocardiogram showed resolution of restrictive filling, ventricular interdependence, and pericardial effusion. The patient is now NYHA class II. She has no history of chest irradiation, connective tissue disease, kidney failure, malignancy, or tuberculosis. Medications are ibuprofen and colchicine.

On physical examination, temperature is normal, blood pressure is 120/70 mm Hg, pulse rate is 85/min, and respiration rate is 14/min. She has no pedal edema, but does have mild hepatojugular reflux. No jugular venous distention is noted. Lungs are clear to auscultation. Cardiac examination shows no rub.

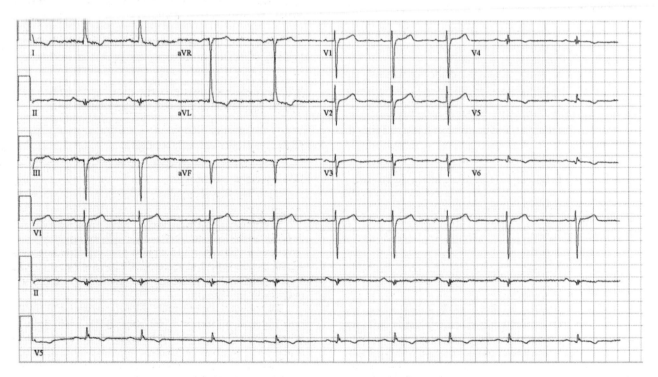

ITEM 82

Laboratory studies show a rheumatoid factor level of 15 units/mL (15 kU/L) and a thyroid-stimulating hormone level of 2 µU/mL (2 mU/L); the antinuclear antibody titer is negative.

Which of the following is the most appropriate management?

(A) Endomyocardial biopsy

(B) Pericardiectomy

(C) Right and left heart hemodynamic cardiac catheterization

(D) Continue current management

Item 85

A 68-year-old woman is evaluated in the emergency department because she cannot move her right foot. She has a 1-year history of progressive cramping in the right calf associated with decreasing levels of exertion. One week ago, she developed unremitting and severe rest pain in her right foot that has now resolved. She has a 20-year history of type 2 diabetes mellitus. Medications are metformin, losartan, and hydrochlorothiazide.

On physical examination, she is afebrile, blood pressure is 140/90 mm Hg, pulse rate is 84/min and regular, and respiration rate is 16/min. The right foot is cool and pale. No capillary refill is noted in the nail beds. The dorsalis pedis and posterior tibialis pulses are not palpable, and arterial Doppler ultrasound signals are absent. Sensation of light touch and pin prick is absent to the midshin. The patient is unable to actively move the foot or digits. The right popliteal pulse is faint but present. No right femoral or abdominal bruits are noted. The right femoral pulse is intact.

Which of the following is the most appropriate management?

(A) Calculate ankle-brachial index

(B) Intra-arterial thrombolytic therapy

(C) Magnetic resonance angiography

(D) Prompt surgical amputation

(E) Urgent angiography and endovascular repair

Item 86

A 60-year-old asymptomatic man is evaluated during a routine examination. He has a long history of heart murmur. With normal daily activities, he has not experienced shortness of breath, chest discomfort, or palpitations.

Blood pressure is 138/78 mm Hg, pulse rate is 82/min and regular, and respiration rate is 16/min. BMI is 27. Cardiac examination shows normal jugular venous pressure with hepatojugular reflux. There is a regular rhythm and a grade 3/6 holosystolic murmur at the apex that radiates to the axilla. An S₄ is heard. Lungs are clear to auscultation bilaterally.

Electrocardiogram shows sinus rhythm with late R/S transition in the precordial leads. Transthoracic echocardiogram shows mild left ventricular hypertrophy with an ejection fraction of 65%. The left ventricular end-diastolic diameter is 52 mm and end-systolic diameter is 38 mm.

There is bileaflet mitral valve prolapse without calcification but severe mitral regurgitation is present. The left atrium is moderately dilated. There is mild tricuspid valve regurgitation with an estimated right ventricular systolic pressure of 60 mm Hg.

Which of the following is the most appropriate treatment for this patient?

(A) Begin bosentan

(B) Begin lisinopril

(C) Mitral valve repair surgery

(D) Mitral valve replacement surgery

Item 87

A 60-year-old man is admitted to the hospital for a 3-week history of progressive fatigue and dyspnea. Medical history is remarkable for cardiac transplantation 6 years ago for idiopathic myocarditis; cellular rejection occurred early after transplantation, but the rejection resolved, and the patient has done well in the intervening years. The patient has hyperlipidemia and hypertension. Medications are tacrolimus, mycophenolate, pravastatin, and lisinopril.

On physical examination, the patient is afebrile, blood pressure is 148/92 mm Hg, pulse rate is 114/min and regular, and respiration rate is 18/min. BMI is 30. The estimated central venous pressure is 8 cm H₂O, and crackles are present at both lung bases. An S₃ gallop is auscultated.

Laboratory studies reveal a normal complete blood count and immunosuppressant level. Chest radiograph shows cardiomegaly and fine interstitial infiltrates bilaterally. Electrocardiogram shows sinus tachycardia and left bundle branch block. Echocardiography reveals a left ventricular ejection fraction of 35% with anterior hypokinesis and no effusion. Right-sided heart size, function, and pressure are normal.

Which of the following is the most likely diagnosis?

(A) Cardiac allograft vasculopathy

(B) Chronic cellular rejection

(C) *Pneumocystis jirovecii* pneumonia

(D) Recurrent idiopathic myocarditis

Item 88

A 41-year-old man is admitted to the hospital for acute onset of severe pain in the chest and back beginning 6 hours ago. He does not regularly see a physician and takes no medications.

On physical examination, temperature is 37.6 °C (99.6 °F), blood pressure is 190/110 mm Hg in both arms, pulse rate is 100/min and regular, and respiration rate is 18/min. His oxygen saturation is 98% on ambient air. An S₄ gallop is heard. Pulses are equal and full throughout; no murmur is heard.

Toxicology screen is pending. Electrocardiogram demonstrates sinus tachycardia, left ventricular hypertrophy by voltage criteria, and early repolarization abnormality. A chest CT scan with intravenous contrast is shown (see next page).

Medical therapy with intravenous morphine, labetalol, and sodium nitroprusside is initiated.

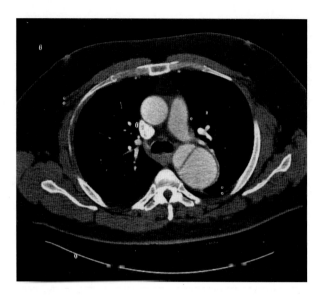

CONT.

Which of the following is the most appropriate treatment?

(A) Catheter-based fenestration
(B) Endovascular stenting
(C) Urgent surgical repair
(D) No additional therapy

Item 89

A 38-year-old woman is evaluated during a follow-up visit for two syncopal episodes experienced in the past 2 years. The first episode occurred 18 months ago at rest. The second episode occurred 5 months ago while she was walking. The patient describes an "uneasy" sensation preceding the events, but reports no dyspnea, chest discomfort, palpitations, or loss of bowel or bladder control. A looping event recorder worn for 30 days did not reveal arrhythmia. She is employed as a school bus driver. She takes no medications.

On physical examination, she is afebrile, blood pressure is 120/60 mm Hg, and pulse rate is 60/min and regular. The remainder of the examination is normal.

Baseline electrocardiogram is normal.

Which of the following is the most appropriate testing option?

(A) Continuous ambulatory electrocardiographic monitor
(B) Implantable loop recorder
(C) Postsymptom event recorder
(D) No further testing

Item 90

A 72-year-old woman is evaluated during a routine follow-up appointment for aortic stenosis. She does not have any symptoms, including chest pain or dyspnea. She feels that she is in good health "for her age."

On physical examination, vital signs are normal. Estimated central venous pressure is normal. Carotid upstrokes are diminished and delayed. The apical impulse is sustained but not displaced. S_1 is normal, but S_2 is decreased in intensity. There is a grade 3/6 late-peaking, systolic, crescendo-decrescendo murmur at the right upper sternal border which radiates to the right carotid. Lungs are clear to auscultation.

Transthoracic echocardiogram shows normal left ventricular ejection fraction (62%) with moderate concentric hypertrophy (septal and posterior wall thickness 1.4 cm). The aortic valve leaflets are calcified with poor mobility. There is severe aortic stenosis with a peak aortic valve gradient of 65 mm Hg, mean gradient of 42 mm Hg, and calculated aortic valve area of 0.8 cm^2.

Which of the following is the most appropriate management of this patient?

(A) Aortic valve replacement surgery
(B) Balloon aortic valvuloplasty
(C) Dobutamine stress echocardiography
(D) Repeat echocardiography in 12 months

Item 91

A 68-year-old man is evaluated for a 6-month history of right lower calf pain with exertion. The pain develops gradually after walking 2 blocks and limits the patient to walking 3 to 4 blocks. Upon stopping, the discomfort resolves within 5 to 10 minutes. He has New York Heart Association functional class II heart failure symptoms with a left ventricular ejection fraction of 35%. He also has hypertension, hyperlipidemia, and a 40-pack-year history of cigarette smoking; he quit 3 years ago. Medications are aspirin, lisinopril, atorvastatin, and metoprolol.

On physical examination, blood pressure is 132/68 mm Hg and pulse rate is 66/min and regular. BMI is 24. Skin is shiny, with associated hair loss below the knees bilaterally; distal pulses are diminished. No areas of skin breakdown or necrosis are noted. Ankle-brachial index testing demonstrates a right-side value of 0.72 and a left-side value of 0.90. No abdominal or femoral bruit is present, and femoral pulses are normal.

Which of the following is the most appropriate treatment?

(A) Chelation therapy
(B) Cilostazol
(C) Femoral-popliteal bypass
(D) Supervised exercise program

Item 92

A 68-year-old woman is evaluated for a 3-week history of intermittent exertional chest pain. She walks several days per week. She has type 2 diabetes mellitus and hypertension. Her father had a myocardial infarction at age 54 years. Medications are aspirin, metformin, glyburide, and lisinopril.

On physical examination, she is afebrile, blood pressure is 128/90 mm Hg, pulse rate is 83/min, and respiration rate is 18/min. BMI is 35. Cardiac sounds are distant but otherwise unremarkable, without extra sounds or murmur.

An electrocardiogram (ECG) is shown (see next page).

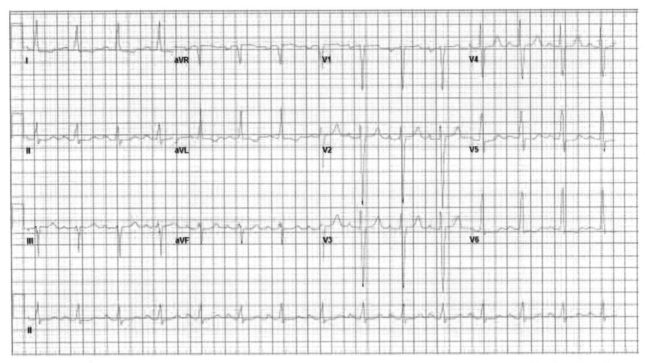

ITEM 92

Which of the following is the most appropriate diagnostic test to perform next?

(A) Cardiovascular magnetic resonance (CMR) imaging with gadolinium enhancement

(B) Exercise ECG stress test

(C) Exercise stress echocardiography

(D) Pharmacologic perfusion imaging study

Item 93

A 74-year-old woman is evaluated for a 2-year history of dyspnea on exertion. She has had progressively worsening dyspnea and fatigue for 4 weeks, and increasing pedal edema, abdominal girth, and right upper quadrant abdominal discomfort for 2 weeks. Medical history is significant only for hypertension. Medications are furosemide, metoprolol, and amlodipine.

On physical examination, temperature is 36.4 °C (97.5 °F), blood pressure is 110/60 mm Hg, pulse rate is 110/min, and respiration rate is 22/min. Jugular venous distention is present and increases with inspiration. Point of maximal impulse is enlarged and displaced leftward. An S_4 is present; there are no murmurs or rubs. Lungs have bibasilar crackles. The abdomen is distended, with shifting dullness. She has 3+ lower extremity edema to the level of the ankles.

Laboratory studies:

Hemoglobin	14 g/dL (140 g/L)
Alanine aminotransferase	45 units/L
Aspartate aminotransferase	65 units/L
B-type natriuretic peptide	2300 pg/mL
Creatinine	1.2 mg/dL (106 μmol/L)
Iron	80 μg/dL (14 μmol/L)

Electrocardiogram shows sinus tachycardia with normal QRS voltage. Echocardiogram reveals severe biatrial enlargement; normal left ventricular systolic function, cavity size, and wall thicknesses; restrictive ventricular filling; and moderate pulmonary hypertension.

Which of the following is the most likely diagnosis?

(A) Cardiac hemochromatosis

(B) Constrictive pericarditis

(C) Hypertrophic cardiomyopathy

(D) Restrictive cardiomyopathy

Item 94

A 19-year-old man is evaluated after the recent sudden death of his father at age 45 years. He reports no chest pain, shortness of breath, palpitations, dizziness, or syncope. He does not smoke or take illicit drugs and is not hypertensive. The patient has no siblings. He takes no medications.

On physical examination, he is afebrile, blood pressure is 120/60 mm Hg, pulse rate is 60/min, and respiration rate is 14/min. No jugular venous distention is present. A grade 2/6 midsystolic murmur that increases during the strain phase of the Valsalva maneuver is heard; brisk carotid upstrokes are present. The lungs are clear to auscultation.

Electrocardiogram shows sinus rhythm and increased QRS voltage of precordial leads. Echocardiogram shows asymmetric basal and midseptal hypertrophy, a 36-mm left ventricular end-diastolic wall thickness of the septum, and peak left ventricular outflow tract gradient of 50 mm Hg.

Which of the following is the most appropriate management?

(A) Alcohol septal ablation
(B) Electrophysiology testing
(C) Measurement of blood pressure response to exercise
(D) Placement of implantable cardioverter-defibrillator
(E) Start amiodarone

Item 95

An 83-year-old woman is admitted to the hospital with a 3-month history of progressively worsening dyspnea on exertion. Medical history is significant for a 13-year history of chronic obstructive pulmonary disease and left breast carcinoma 10 years ago, which was treated with mastectomy, chemotherapy that included doxorubicin (cumulative dose of 600 mg/m²) and cyclophosphamide, and radiation. Medications are ipratropium bromide–albuterol metered-dose inhaler.

On physical examination, temperature is normal, blood pressure is 90/54 mm Hg, pulse rate is 110/min, and respiration rate is 24/min. There is minimal jugular venous distention. A pulsus paradoxus of 6 mm Hg is present. Lung examination discloses crackles one third of the way up the posterior lung fields. Cardiac examination reveals an S_3 gallop.

Laboratory studies reveal a B-type natriuretic peptide level of 3500 pg/mL.

Electrocardiogram shows sinus tachycardia with diffuse low voltage. Chest radiograph shows an enlarged cardiac silhouette.

Which of the following is the most likely diagnosis?

(A) Cardiac tamponade
(B) Chronic obstructive pulmonary disease exacerbation
(C) Doxorubicin-induced dilated cardiomyopathy
(D) Radiation-induced constrictive pericarditis

Item 96

A 40-year-old woman was admitted to the hospital with a 5-day history of intermittent sharp substernal chest pain that worsened with deep breathing. She reported a fever and sore throat for 7 days with no cough. Initial examination was notable for a precordial rub and clear lungs.

Electrocardiogram (ECG) on admission showed 2 mm of concave downward ST-segment elevation in leads V_1 through V_4, aVR, and aVL. Cardiac catheterization showed hypokinesis of the mid and distal anterior wall and the anterolateral wall and apex, left ventricular ejection fraction of 45%, and no coronary artery obstruction. Peak serum troponin I level during the first 24 hours after admission was 45 ng/mL. Over the subsequent 3 days of hospitalization she developed progressively worsening dyspnea.

On day 3 of hospitalization, she is evaluated for progressive dyspnea. On physical examination, temperature is normal, blood pressure is 92/54 mm Hg, pulse rate is 123/min, and respiration rate is 33/min. No jugular venous distention is present. Cardiac examination reveals a summation gallop, diminished heart sounds, and no rub.

Pulsus paradoxus of 7 mm Hg is noted. Bilateral crackles are heard one quarter of the way up the posterior lung fields.

Repeat ECG shows 0.5-mm ST-segment elevation and T-wave inversions in the same leads as the initial ECG. Chest radiograph demonstrates pulmonary edema. Echocardiogram demonstrates akinesis of the mid and distal anterior wall and anterolateral wall and apex, left ventricular ejection fraction of 30%, left ventricular enlargement, and small circumferential pericardial effusion.

Which of the following is the most likely diagnosis?

(A) Cardiac tamponade
(B) Myopericarditis
(C) Post–myocardial infarction syndrome
(D) Takotsubo cardiomyopathy

Item 97

A 52-year-old man is evaluated in the hospital for 1 week of persistent shortness of breath and lower extremity edema; previously, he could walk and ascend stairs without limiting symptoms. He has hypertension. Medications on admission were enalapril and hydrochlorothiazide. Stress echocardiogram on admission showed a globally hypokinetic left ventricle with an ejection fraction of 35%, no significant valvular abnormalities, and no inducible ischemia. He underwent diuresis with intravenous furosemide with resolution of his symptoms. Medications in the hospital are enalapril and oral furosemide.

The patient is a black man. Blood pressure is 110/80 mm Hg and pulse rate is 70/min. No jugular venous distention is present, and no S_3 is heard. The lungs are clear, and no peripheral edema is present.

Laboratory results include a normal thyroid-stimulating hormone level. Electrocardiogram discloses normal sinus rhythm without Q waves.

Which of the following is the most appropriate medication to add to this patient's regimen?

(A) Amlodipine
(B) Carvedilol
(C) Hydralazine–isosorbide dinitrate
(D) Spironolactone

Item 98

A 75-year-old woman is evaluated in the emergency department for a 7-day history of nausea, poor oral intake, and confusion. Medical history is significant for persistent atrial fibrillation and hypertension. Medications are metoprolol, digoxin, and warfarin.

On physical examination, temperature is normal, blood pressure is 105/74 mm Hg, and pulse rate is 49/min. She is oriented to name, but does not know the date or that she is in the emergency department. The remainder of the examination is normal.

Laboratory studies reveal a serum creatinine level of 3.2 mg/dL (283 µmol/L), potassium level of 4.8 meq/L (4.8 mmol/L), and INR of 2.3.

The electrocardiogram is shown (see next page).

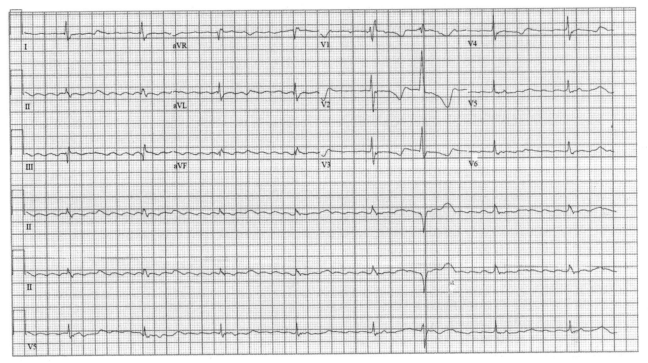

ITEM 98

Which of the following is the most appropriate management?

(A) Direct-current cardioversion
(B) Insert a temporary pacemaker
(C) Measure the digoxin level
(D) Start dobutamine

Item 99

A 68-year-old man is evaluated for exertional chest pain of 3 months' duration. He describes the chest pain as pressure in the midsternal area with no radiation that occurs with walking one to two blocks and resolves with rest or sublingual nitroglycerin. No symptoms have occurred at rest. Medical history is significant for myocardial infarction 3 years ago, hypertension, and hyperlipidemia. Medications are aspirin, metoprolol 25 mg twice daily, simvastatin, isosorbide dinitrate, and sublingual nitroglycerin as needed for chest pain.

On physical examination, temperature is normal, blood pressure is 150/85 mm Hg, pulse rate is 80/min, and respiration rate is 12/min. BMI is 26. No carotid bruits are present, and a normal S_1 and S_2 with no murmurs are heard. Lung fields are clear, and distal pulses are normal.

Electrocardiogram shows normal sinus rhythm, no left ventricular hypertrophy, no ST- or T-wave changes, and no Q waves.

Which of the following is the most appropriate management?

(A) Add diltiazem
(B) Add ranolazine

(C) Coronary angiography
(D) Increase metoprolol dosage

Item 100

A 22-year-old woman is evaluated for a murmur noted on physical examination. The patient was born prematurely, and a murmur was noted early in life. She is asymptomatic and her medical history is otherwise unremarkable.

On physical examination, blood pressure is 110/80 mm Hg bilaterally. The jugular and carotid examinations are normal. The cardiac apex is not displaced, and there is no parasternal impulse. A grade 3/6 continuous machinery-type murmur that envelops the S_2 is noted along the left sternal border and second left intercostal space. The murmur is best heard under the left clavicle. The remainder of the examination is normal, including normal lower extremity pulses and no evidence of pulse delay between the radial and femoral arteries. There is no digital clubbing or cyanosis.

The electrocardiogram and chest radiograph are normal.

Which of the following is the most likely diagnosis?

(A) Aortic coarctation
(B) Atrial septal defect
(C) Patent ductus arteriosus
(D) Pulmonary valve stenosis
(E) Ventricular septal defect

Item 101

A 35-year-old woman is evaluated for a systolic murmur noted during a physical examination. The patient has no cardiovascular symptoms.

On physical examination, vital signs are normal. The S_2 is widely split. There is a grade 2/6 midsystolic murmur heard best at the upper left sternal border and a grade 2/6 holosystolic murmur at the lower left sternal border that increases with inspiration. Lungs are clear and there is no peripheral edema.

An electrocardiogram demonstrates normal sinus rhythm with incomplete right bundle branch block. The chest radiograph demonstrates mild right-sided cardiac chamber enlargement with prominent central pulmonary arteries and increased pulmonary vascular markings.

The transthoracic echocardiogram demonstrates a 1.5-cm ostium secundum atrial septal defect with moderate right-sided cardiac chamber enlargement. Right ventricular systolic pressure is 38 mm Hg. There is mild tricuspid valve regurgitation.

Which of the following is the most appropriate treatment?

(A) Aspirin therapy
(B) Closure of the atrial septal defect
(C) Warfarin anticoagulation therapy
(D) Observation and follow-up

Item 102

A 67-year-old man is evaluated during a follow-up appointment. He was recently diagnosed with ischemic cardiomyopathy not amenable to revascularization. Left ventricular ejection fraction was 35%. He was started on enalapril, carvedilol, isosorbide dinitrate, aspirin, and pravastatin. He is feeling well, with minimal dyspnea on exertion.

On physical examination, blood pressure is 110/75 mm Hg and pulse rate is 60/min. Cardiac examination reveals a regular rate and rhythm with no S_3. No jugular venous distention is present, no crackles are heard, and no edema is observed.

At the time of diagnosis, laboratory studies showed serum potassium level of 3.9 meq/L (3.9 mmol/L) and creatinine level of 0.9 mg/dL (79.6 µmol/L). Now, serum potassium level is 5.5 meq/L (5.5 mmol/L) and creatinine level is 1.9 mg/dL (168 µmol/L). Enalapril is stopped. Seven days later, the serum potassium level is 4.5 meq/L (4.5 mmol/L) and creatinine level is 1.2 mg/dL (106 µmol/L).

Which of the following is the most appropriate treatment?

(A) Amlodipine
(B) Candesartan
(C) Hydralazine
(D) Spironolactone

Item 103

A 60-year-old man is evaluated during an initial care visit. He walks 2 to 3 miles on a daily basis without any symptoms. Medical history is notable for type 2 diabetes mellitus and a myocardial infarction 5 years ago that was previously treated

with medical therapy. The patient discontinued follow-up with physicians.

On physical examination, blood pressure is 150/80 mm Hg, pulse rate is 72/min, and respiration rate is 12/min. BMI is 30. A normal carotid upstroke without carotid bruits is noted, normal jugular venous pulsations are present, and normal S_1 and S_2 are heard without murmurs. Lung fields are clear, distal pulses are normal, and no peripheral edema is present.

Laboratory studies show a total cholesterol level of 220 mg/dL (5.70 mmol/L), an LDL cholesterol level of 160 mg/dL (4.14 mmol/L), and a serum creatinine level of 1.0 mg/dL (88.4 µmol/L).

Electrocardiogram shows normal sinus rhythm; Q waves in leads II, III, and aVF; and upright T waves in leads II, III, and aVF.

In addition to therapy for diabetes, which of the following is the most appropriate treatment?

(A) Aspirin
(B) Aspirin and simvastatin
(C) Aspirin, simvastatin, and metoprolol
(D) No additional medical therapy

Item 104

A 31-year-old woman is evaluated in the emergency department for shortness of breath, palpitations, and dizziness of 30 minutes' duration. Medical history is remarkable for asthma. Her only medication is albuterol as needed.

On physical examination, she is afebrile, blood pressure is 110/65 mm Hg, and pulse rate is 174/min. The patient is alert and her extremities are warm. A tachycardic, irregularly irregular rhythm is auscultated. There is no jugular venous distention or crackles on pulmonary examination.

The patient's electrocardiogram is shown (see next page).

Which of the following is the most likely diagnosis?

(A) Atrial fibrillation
(B) Atrial flutter
(C) Multifocal atrial tachycardia
(D) Polymorphic ventricular tachycardia

Item 105

A 42-year-old woman is evaluated in the emergency department for progressive shortness of breath for 3 weeks. Medical history is noncontributory. She takes no medications.

On physical examination, temperature is 37.4 °C (99.3 °F), blood pressure is 112/64 mm Hg, pulse rate is 62/min, and respiration rate is 20/min. Estimated central venous pressure and carotid upstrokes are normal. Cardiac auscultation discloses an opening snap, a grade 2/6 diastolic low-pitched murmur at the apex, and a grade 2/6 holosystolic murmur at the apex radiating to the axilla.

Electrocardiogram demonstrates sinus tachycardia, left atrial enlargement, and right axis deviation. Transthoracic echocardiogram demonstrates normal biventricular size and function; a dilated left atrium; reduced posterior mitral leaflet excursion without leaflet calcification or significant

ECG Rensor: ARRYTHMIA

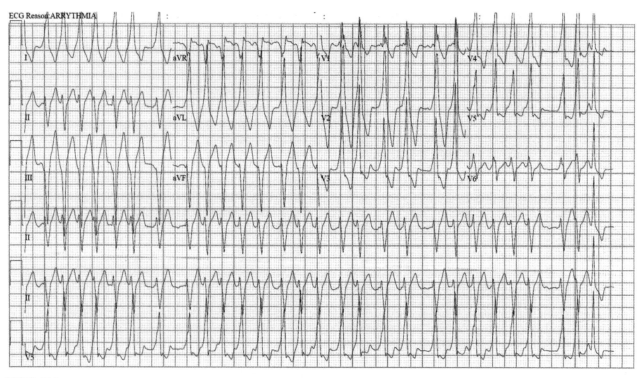

ITEM 104

thickening; severe mitral stenosis with mean gradient 15 mm Hg; mild mitral regurgitation; and mild tricuspid regurgitation. Estimated pulmonary artery systolic pressure is 58 mm Hg.

Which of the following is the most appropriate treatment?

(A) Balloon mitral valvuloplasty
(B) Metoprolol
(C) Mitral valve replacement
(D) Open surgical commissurotomy

Item 106

A 33-year-old man is evaluated the emergency department after being involved in a motor vehicle accident 30 minutes ago. He was confused at the scene, with a forehead laceration. On arrival, blood pressure is 165/90 mm Hg and pulse rate is 80/min. Head CT is unremarkable. Over the course of 1 hour, blood pressure decreases to 80/45 mm Hg, pulse rate increases to 100/min. Blood pressure increases to 86/50 mm Hg after a normal saline bolus. Despite dopamine, blood pressure progressively declines. A medical alert bracelet notes a history of hypertrophic cardiomyopathy. Further medical and family histories and medications are unobtainable.

On physical examination, he is afebrile, blood pressure is 70/40 mm Hg, pulse rate is 125/min, and respiration rate is 20/min. Estimated central venous pressure is 5 cm H_2O. A grade 3/6 midsystolic murmur is heard at the left sternal border. Lungs are clear to auscultation. No focal neurologic abnormalities are seen.

Hemoglobin level is normal. Electrocardiogram shows sinus rhythm, increased QRS voltage, and inverted T waves. Echocardiogram reveals small left and right ventricular cavities, hyperdynamic left ventricular function, asymmetric basilar septal hypertrophy, prolonged systolic anterior motion of the mitral valve, moderate mitral regurgitation, and no pericardial effusion.

In addition to saline boluses and discontinuing dopamine, which of the following is the most appropriate treatment?

(A) Dobutamine
(B) Epinephrine
(C) Milrinone
(D) Phenylephrine

Item 107

A 72-year-old man undergoes a preoperative evaluation prior to left hip replacement surgery. He describes intermittent, sharp, left-sided chest discomfort that spontaneously occurs at rest and after physical activity, occasionally radiating toward the right side of the chest. These symptoms have been present for 1 to 2 years. The symptoms have been stable and have not been associated with dyspnea, palpitations, or syncope. Medical history is remarkable for chronic obstructive pulmonary disease and osteoarthritis. He used to smoke but quit 10 years ago. Medications are albuterol and ipratropium bromide metered dose inhalers.

On physical examination, he is afebrile, blood pressure is 118/60 mm Hg, and pulse rate is 80/min and regular. No jugular venous distention is observed. Heart sounds are distant, with regular S$_1$ and S$_2$; no murmurs are heard. Breath sounds are distant. No pedal edema is noted. Baseline electrocardiogram shows sinus rhythm with nonspecific ST-T wave changes in the lateral leads.

Which of the following is the most appropriate diagnostic test to perform next?

(A) Coronary angiography

(B) Dobutamine stress echocardiography

(C) Exercise electrocardiographic stress testing

(D) Vasodilator myocardial perfusion single photon emission CT (SPECT)

(E) No further testing is indicated

Item 108

A 30-year-old woman with sarcoidosis is evaluated for a 3-month history of progressively worsening dyspnea on exertion, reaching New York Heart Association functional class II to III. She was diagnosed with sarcoidosis 5 years ago, and has had involvement of the skin, joints, and lungs. She has corticosteroid-induced hypertension. Medications are prednisone, furosemide, and hydralazine. Previous pulmonary function tests were stable, and CT of the chest was normal.

On physical examination, temperature is 36.4 °C (97.6 °F), blood pressure is 133/65 mm Hg, pulse rate is 98/min, and respiration rate is 16/min. A yellow maculopapular rash on the cheeks is noted. Jugular venous distention is present. No cardiac murmur is heard. Lung auscultation reveals bibasilar crackles. Hepatojugular reflux and 2+ pedal edema are present.

Laboratory studies reveal B-type natriuretic peptide level of 830 pg/mL.

Electrocardiogram shows sinus rhythm and normal conduction. Echocardiogram shows normal left and right ventricular cavity size, moderate biatrial enlargement, left ventricular ejection fraction of 65%, estimated peak pulmonary systolic pressure of 35 mm Hg, restrictive left ventricular diastolic filling, and reduced peak early diastolic annular velocity by tissue Doppler echocardiography. Chest radiograph reveals hilar prominence but no acute pulmonary infiltrates.

Which of the following is the most appropriate test to perform next to diagnose the cause of her dyspnea?

(A) Cardiac magnetic resonance (CMR) imaging

(B) CT angiography of coronary arteries

(C) Endomyocardial biopsy

(D) Transesophageal echocardiography

Item 109

A 55-year-old man is admitted to the hospital with a 3-week history of intermittent fevers and shortness of breath. He has a mechanical aortic valve. He takes warfarin and no other medications.

On physical examination, he has a temperature of 40.0 °C (104.0 °F), blood pressure is 148/50 mm Hg, pulse rate is 93/min, and respiration rate is 22/min. A grade 2/6 early systolic murmur and early diastolic murmur are noted at the cardiac base.

Electrocardiogram shows sinus tachycardia with a new first-degree atrioventricular block (prolonged PR interval). Blood cultures obtained on admission demonstrate gram-positive cocci in clusters. Serum creatinine level is 2.3 mg/dL (203 µmol/L).

Which of the following is the most appropriate initial study to obtain?

(A) Cardiac CT angiography

(B) Cardiovascular magnetic resonance (CMR) imaging

(C) Transesophageal echocardiography

(D) Transthoracic echocardiography

Item 110

A 65-year-old man is evaluated for episodic dyspnea and cyanosis 1 month after a right pneumonectomy for lung cancer. The patient has severe dyspnea and cyanosis with sitting; these symptoms are relieved when supine.

Physical examination is unremarkable except for his recent pneumonectomy. Pulse oximetry oxygen saturation is normal when the patient is supine but drops to 82% when he sits up. Laboratory studies and electrocardiogram are normal. The chest radiograph demonstrates features of previous right pneumonectomy. An echocardiogram demonstrates a patent foramen ovale but no pulmonary hypertension. The right heart chambers appear normal. The valves are normal. A peripheral vein injection of agitated saline demonstrates brisk filling of the right-sided and left-sided cardiac chambers with the patient sitting. No shunting is identified when the patient is supine.

Which of the following is the most appropriate treatment?

(A) Ambulatory oxygen therapy

(B) Anticoagulation with warfarin

(C) Furosemide

(D) Percutaneous device closure of the patent foramen ovale

Item 111

A 21-year-old male student is evaluated for a murmur heard during an athletic preparticipation physical examination. He is asymptomatic. His medical and family history is unremarkable and he takes no medications.

On physical examination, the patient is afebrile, blood pressure is 118/76 mm Hg, pulse rate is 68/min, and respiration rate is 14/min. BMI is 18. He wears corrective lenses for myopia. Mild thoracic scoliosis is noted. He has long, thin fingers and a mild pectus excavatum deformity. His height is 188 cm (6 ft 2 in) and arm span is 200 cm from fingertip to fingertip. On cardiac auscultation, a soft early diastolic decrescendo murmur is heard, and is best heard along the left sternal border during expiration with the patient seated and leaning forward slightly.

A transthoracic echocardiogram demonstrates dilatation of the aortic root of 6.2 cm.

Which of the following is the most appropriate treatment?

(A) Admit to hospital; begin metoprolol and intravenous sodium nitroprusside

(B) Begin oral losartan and metoprolol

(C) Plan urgent surgery

(D) Repeat echocardiogram in 6 months

Item 112

A 58-year-old woman is evaluated in the emergency department for pleuritic chest pain with shortness of breath that began 4 hours ago. She reports intermittent fever, chills, sore throat, and muscle aches for the past week. Her history is significant for hypertension treated with hydrochlorothiazide and metoprolol.

On physical examination, temperature is normal. Blood pressure is 125/76 mm Hg in the right arm and 120/74 mm Hg in the left arm. Pulse rate is 112/min and respiration rate is 22/min. The chest pain is accentuated when the patient assumes a recumbent position. Estimated central venous pressure is less than 5 cm H_2O. There is an S_3 gallop but no murmur or friction rub. The lungs are clear.

Pertinent laboratory findings include serum troponin I level of 1.2 ng/mL (1.2 µg/L). The electrocardiogram demonstrates sinus tachycardia and 2 mm of concave downward ST-segment elevation in leads V_1 through V_3. Urgent cardiac catheterization with coronary angiography is normal. Left ventriculogram shows hypokinesis of the anteroapical wall and normal contraction otherwise. Subsequent chest radiograph demonstrates no infiltrates.

Which of the following is the most likely diagnosis?

(A) Acute aortic dissection

(B) Acute myocardial infarction

(C) Acute myopericarditis

(D) Acute pleuritis

(E) Acute pulmonary embolism

Item 113

A 45-year-old woman with unrepaired ventricular septal defect and Eisenmenger syndrome is evaluated for worsening fatigue and exertional dyspnea over the past 6 months. She has had recent menopausal symptoms with associated menorrhagia.

On physical examination, blood pressure is 110/70 mm Hg, heart rate is 85/min, and respiration rate is 20/min. There is digital clubbing and cyanosis affecting fingers and toes equally. The cardiac apex is palpated at the midclavicular line in the fifth intercostal space, and a parasternal impulse is present. The S_1 is normal and the pulmonic component of the S_2 is increased. A grade 2/6 holosystolic murmur is noted at the left sternal border that increases with inspiration. No diastolic murmur is appreciated. No S_3 or S_4 is present. The remainder of the examination is unremarkable.

Laboratory studies:

Ferritin	10 ng/mL (10 µg/L)
Hematocrit	52%
Hemoglobin	15.5 g/dL (155 g/L)
Transferrin saturation	13%

Which of the following is the most appropriate treatment?

(A) Atrial septostomy

(B) Heart/lung transplantation

(C) Iron therapy

(D) Phlebotomy

(E) Pulmonary vasodilator therapy

Item 114

A 28-year-old woman is evaluated for exertional dyspnea. During college, she played on an intramural women's soccer team. Recently, she has noted a decrease in exercise tolerance with easy fatigability. Medical history is unremarkable and she takes no medications.

On physical examination, vital signs are normal. No jugular venous distention is observed. A regular S_1 with fixed splitting of the S_2 is heard. A grade 3/6 holosystolic murmur is heard over the lower right sternal border that increases with inspiration. Lungs are clear. No pedal edema is noted.

Transthoracic echocardiography shows normal left ventricular size and function and mild dilatation of the right ventricle with mildly decreased function. Pulmonary systolic pressure is 35 to 40 mm Hg. Mild to moderate tricuspid regurgitation is present. Chest radiography is normal.

Which of the following is the most appropriate cardiac imaging test to perform next?

(A) Coronary angiography with iodine radiocontrast

(B) Dobutamine stress echocardiography with transpulmonary microbubble contrast

(C) Nuclear perfusion single-photon emission CT (SPECT) with technetium

(D) Transthoracic echocardiography with agitated saline contrast

Item 115

A 60-year-old man is evaluated for chest pain. The patient reports the chest pain is present in the left side of the chest, has a burning quality, is nonradiating, occurs at times with activity and resolves with rest, and has been present intermittently for 4 months. He has also noted episodes of similar pain in the evening, after eating dinner. Other than occasional chest pain with exertion, he can walk without limitation. Medical history is significant for hypertension. His only medication is hydrochlorothiazide.

On physical examination, temperature is 36.8 °C (98.3 °F), blood pressure is 140/80 mm Hg, pulse rate is 80/min, and respiration rate is 14/min. BMI is 30. The general physical examination is normal.

Electrocardiogram displays a sinus rhythm at 70/min, nonspecific 1-mm ST-segment changes in the anterior and lateral leads, left atrial enlargement, and left ventricular hypertrophy.

Which of the following is the most appropriate diagnostic test to perform next?

(A) Coronary artery calcium score
(B) Exercise electrocardiographic stress test
(C) Exercise perfusion stress test
(D) Pharmacologic stress test

Item 116

A 68-year-old woman is assessed for a 6-month history of progressive exertional leg discomfort, described as a "heaviness" involving both calves. The symptoms are relieved within 5 to 10 minutes of rest. She has noted the same limiting heaviness with bicycling. Medical history is significant for hypertension, type 2 diabetes mellitus, and hyperlipidemia; she does not smoke cigarettes. Medications are valsartan, hydrochlorothiazide, metformin, and rosuvastatin.

On physical examination, the patient is afebrile. Blood pressure is 130/84 mm Hg in both arms. The highest right foot systolic pressure is 184 mm Hg; the highest left foot systolic pressure is 186 mm Hg. Pulse rate is 78/min and regular, and respiration rate is 14/min. BMI is 30. Distal pulses are diminished but equal bilaterally. Sensation to light touch is diminished bilaterally in the toes extending to the midfoot. No abdominal or femoral bruits are present. Deep tendon reflexes at the knees and ankles are 2+ and symmetric. Strength is 5/5 throughout in the lower extremities.

Which of the following is the most appropriate diagnostic test to evaluate her exertional leg pain?

(A) Electromyography and nerve conduction studies
(B) Exercise ankle-brachial index
(C) Great toe pressure measurement
(D) Lumbar MRI

Item 117

An 80-year-old woman is evaluated for intermittent episodes of an irregular heartbeat that last a few minutes in duration. She has had several episodes of presyncope, which occur once or twice a month. It is unclear whether her irregular heartbeat episodes correlate with her presyncope. She has no history of coronary artery disease. She has hypertension treated with lisinopril.

On physical examination, blood pressure is 128/70 mm Hg, and pulse rate is 50/min and regular. No jugular venous distention is observed. Heart sounds are normal. A grade 2/6 midpeaking systolic murmur is heard at the cardiac base, which does not radiate. Lungs are clear. No pedal edema is noted.

A 12-lead electrocardiogram is shown.

Which of the following is the most appropriate diagnostic testing option?

(A) 24-Hour continuous ambulatory electrocardiographic monitor
(B) Electrophysiology testing
(C) Looping event recorder
(D) Postsymptom event recorder

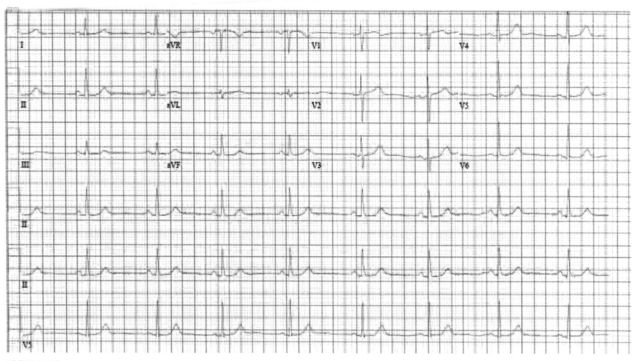

ITEM 117

Item 118

A 74-year-old man hospitalized for a heart failure exacerbation goes into ventricular fibrillation and is administered cardiopulmonary resuscitation (CPR). An external defibrillator is attached and he receives a 200 J shock.

Which of the following is the most appropriate management immediately after the defibrillator shock?

(A) Continue CPR
(B) Give amiodarone
(C) Give epinephrine
(D) Give vasopressin
(E) Reassess rhythm

Item 119

A 31-year-old man is evaluated in the emergency department after experiencing a syncopal event while playing basketball. A friend playing with him reported that he was unconsciousness for about 15 seconds with no evidence of seizure-like activity. Medical history is significant for arrhythmogenic right ventricular cardiomyopathy/dysplasia. His only medication is atenolol.

On physical examination, the patient is afebrile, blood pressure is 128/76 mm Hg, and pulse rate is 64/min.

Electrocardiogram shows normal sinus rhythm with T-wave inversions in leads V_1 to V_3 with an epsilon wave. Echocardiogram demonstrates moderate right ventricular dysfunction and enlargement. Cardiovascular magnetic resonance (CMR) imaging of the heart shows dilatation and akinesia of the right ventricular outflow tract.

Which of the following is the most appropriate management?

(A) Electrophysiology study
(B) 24-Hour continuous ambulatory electrocardiographic monitoring
(C) Implantable cardioverter-defibrillator placement
(D) Looping event recorder implantation
(E) Sotalol administration

Item 120

A 55-year-old man is evaluated during a routine examination. He has a 2-year history of nonischemic cardiomyopathy. (Echocardiogram 2 years ago demonstrated a left ventricular ejection fraction of 35%.) He is feeling well and reports no shortness of breath; he walks 2 miles daily without symptoms. Medical history is remarkable for hypertension. Medications are lisinopril, carvedilol, and chlorthalidone.

On physical examination, blood pressure is 150/90 mm Hg and pulse rate is 50/min. No jugular venous distention is present. Cardiac examination reveals a regular rhythm with no murmurs or gallops. Lungs are clear to auscultation. No edema is present.

Laboratory studies show serum creatinine level of 1.5 mg/dL (133 µmol/L), sodium level of 138 meq/L (138 mmol/L), and potassium level of 4.0 meq/L (4.0 mmol/L).

Electrocardiogram shows a normal sinus rhythm and left ventricular hypertrophy.

Which of the following calcium channel blockers should be added to this patient's medical regimen?

(A) Amlodipine
(B) Diltiazem
(C) Nifedipine
(D) Verapamil

Answers and Critiques

Item 1   Answer: D

Educational Objective: Evaluate chest pain in a patient with an intermediate pretest probability of coronary artery disease.

The most appropriate test to establish a diagnosis of coronary artery disease (CAD) in this patient is an exercise treadmill stress test. The description of chest pain has both typical and atypical features. Based on the patient's age and sex, the pretest likelihood that his symptoms represent angina are increased, giving him an intermediate pretest probability for CAD. The patient is able to exercise and has a normal baseline electrocardiogram (ECG). In this setting, an exercise treadmill stress test is the most appropriate noninvasive imaging study.

A pharmacologic stress test such as an adenosine nuclear perfusion stress test is useful when a patient cannot exercise because of physical limitations such as arthritis, physical deconditioning, or advanced lung disease and in the setting of an abnormal baseline ECG. Pharmacologic stress agents include dobutamine, dipyridamole, and adenosine. Given that the patient has a normal baseline ECG and is able to exercise, a pharmacologic stress test would not be the correct choice.

Coronary angiography has a small but inherent risk of vascular complications and is therefore usually not the initial diagnostic test used to evaluate a patient presenting with chest pain. For patients with lifestyle-limiting angina despite optimal medical therapy, high-risk criteria on noninvasive stress testing, or successful resuscitation from sudden cardiac death, coronary angiography may be useful.

An echocardiogram would be useful to evaluate left ventricular systolic function (ejection fraction), assess for wall motion abnormalities (that may indicate a previous myocardial infarction), and exclude significant valvular heart disease. A normal echocardiogram, however, would not exclude the presence of underlying CAD and therefore would not be the best test to establish a diagnosis in this patient.

KEY POINT

- For a patient who is able to exercise and has a normal baseline electrocardiogram, an exercise treadmill stress test is the most appropriate noninvasive study to evaluate for coronary artery disease.

Bibliography

Chou TM, Amidon TM. Evaluating coronary artery disease noninvasively–which test for whom? West J Med. 1994;161(2):173-180. [PMID: 7941543]

Item 2   Answer: A

Educational Objective: Manage elevated cholesterol level in a patient with diabetes mellitus.

The most appropriate modification of this patient's treatment regimen is to increase the statin dose. The National Cholesterol Education Program (NCEP) Adult Treatment Panel III LDL cholesterol treatment target for all patients at high risk is below 100 mg/dL (2.59 mmol/L). High risk is defined as the presence of coronary heart disease (CHD) or CHD risk equivalents, which include peripheral arterial disease, abdominal aortic aneurysm, carotid artery disease, transient ischemic attacks or stroke of carotid origin or 50% obstruction of a carotid artery, diabetes mellitus, and 10-year risk for cardiovascular disease of 20% or greater. For patients in the very-high-risk category, such as those with coronary artery disease and diabetes mellitus, as well as in the setting of an acute coronary syndrome, an LDL cholesterol level below 70 mg/dL (1.81 mmol/L) is a therapeutic option.

Patients with diabetes show similar relative risk reductions compared with those without diabetes, but as the absolute risk in these patients is higher, the number needed to treat (to prevent a cardiovascular event) is lower. Several studies have demonstrated the benefits of statin therapy. In ad hoc analyses involving patients with diabetes from the Scandinavian Simvastatin Survival Study, simvastatin therapy was associated with a 55% reduction in major coronary events. In analyses of the 8000 patients in the diabetic subgroup from the Heart Protection Study, there was a 22% reduction (20.2% vs. 25.1%) in major vascular events in the group receiving simvastatin.

Statins remain the first-line therapy for the treatment of hyperlipidemia and for the primary and secondary prevention of CHD. Trials of nonstatin drugs in the primary prevention of CHD have been associated with reductions in coronary events but not mortality. In this patient, an increase from a low dose (20 mg) of pravastatin to a moderate dose (40 mg) is the best approach, both in terms of tolerability and effectiveness.

KEY POINT

- The presence of diabetes mellitus is considered a cardiovascular disease risk equivalent in the assessment of cardiovascular risk.

Bibliography

Rydén L, Standl E, Bartnik M, et al; Task Force on Diabetes and Cardiovascular Diseases of the European Society of Cardiology (ESC); European Association for the Study of Diabetes (EASD). Guidelines on diabetes, pre-diabetes, and cardiovascular diseases: executive summary. The Task Force on Diabetes and Cardiovascular Diseases of the European Society of Cardiology (ESC) and of the European Association for the Study of Diabetes (EASD). Eur Heart J. 2007;28(1):88-136. [PMID: 17220161]

Item 3   Answer: D

Educational Objective: Evaluate a low-intensity heart murmur.

No additional testing is needed for this patient. He has an asymptomatic benign systolic ejection murmur. The benign characteristics of the murmur include its intensity or grade (<3/6), timing (early and brief systolic), lack of radiation of the murmur, and the absence of additional abnormal heart sounds. The remainder of the physical examination and the electrocardiogram are normal, without any evidence of cardiac enlargement or dysfunction. In this common situation, the patient should be reassured, and no additional diagnostic testing is indicated.

Ambulatory electrocardiography, either continuously for 24 to 48 hours or as event-activated recordings, is not indicated. The patient's brief episodes of palpitations are sporadic and not associated with hemodynamic abnormalities. In patients with repetitive, frequent palpitations, ambulatory electrocardiography may be diagnostically useful.

Transesophageal echocardiography may be useful in patients with poor imaging by transthoracic study or to evaluate the feasibility of surgical repair when surgery is planned but is not indicated in this patient.

Transthoracic echocardiography is recommended for diagnosis of systolic murmurs grade 3/6 or greater in intensity, diastolic murmurs, continuous murmurs, holosystolic murmurs, late systolic murmurs, murmurs associated with ejection clicks, or murmurs that radiate to the neck or back. This patient's murmur does not have any of these characteristics.

KEY POINT

- Echocardiography is not indicated for patients with brief, early systolic, low-intensity murmurs detected by physical examination without symptoms or associated findings of valvular or cardiac dysfunction.

Bibliography

Etchells E, Bell C, Robb K. Does this patient have an abnormal systolic murmur? JAMA. 1997;277(7):564-571. [PMID: 9032164]

Item 4   Answer: A

Educational Objective: Localize peripheral arterial disease.

This patient most likely has aortoiliac disease. Symptoms often give important clues as to the likely site of peripheral arterial disease. This patient presents with buttock and hip claudication, diminished femoral pulses, and erectile dysfunction, sometimes referred to as Leriche syndrome. This presentation most commonly represents atherosclerotic disease within the aortoiliac system.

Claudication as a result of aortoiliac disease often results in greater disability compared with more distal disease.

Additionally, aortoiliac disease increases the risk for distal embolization. Accordingly, a more aggressive approach to aortoiliac disease is typically taken that may include either endovascular intervention or aortoiliac surgery.

Common femoral arterial occlusive disease may cause thigh pain with effort, but it would not result in erectile dysfunction. Because of the location of the common femoral artery with respect to the hip joint, surgical therapy or angioplasty, but not stenting, would be considered as part of therapy.

Occlusive disease within the popliteal artery would produce pain within the lower calf. Disease in this location should be managed primarily with an exercise program and medical therapy. Patients who do not benefit from such conservative management should be considered for femoral-popliteal bypass.

Occlusive disease within the superficial femoral artery usually produces effort-related discomfort in the upper calf. Angioplasty may be appropriate for patients with superficial femoral artery–related symptoms who have not benefited from medical therapy or who are extremely limited despite medical therapy.

KEY POINT

- Buttock and hip claudication, diminished femoral pulses, and erectile dysfunction (Leriche syndrome) suggest atherosclerotic disease within the aortoiliac system.

Bibliography

Mohler E 3rd, Giri J; ACC; AHA. Management of peripheral arterial disease patients: comparing the ACC/AHA and TASC-II guidelines. Curr Med Res Opin. 2008;24(9):2509-2522. [PMID: 18664318]

Item 5   Answer: E

Educational Objective: Manage risk factors in a patient with coronary artery disease.

Smoking cessation may have a greater effect on reducing mortality among patients with coronary artery disease (CAD) than any other intervention or treatment. One half of all smokers will die prematurely from consequences of tobacco abuse, and it is a principal contributor to the development of CAD, sudden cardiac death, acute myocardial infarction (MI), and heart failure.

A meta-analysis of 12 cohort studies of the effect of smoking cessation after myocardial infarction found the combined odds ratio for death in patients who quit was 0.54 compared with patients who continued, equivalent to a number needed to treat of 13. Similar mortality rate benefits have been observed in persons who quit smoking after coronary artery bypass surgery, following coronary angioplasty, and among patients with angiographically documented coronary stenosis. Another cohort study found that mortality among patients who quit smoking after MI approached that of nonsmokers within 3 years.

The benefits of cessation are seen early after cessation and have a significant effect on disease progression, hospital readmission, and mortality. Smokers should be educated to the fact that the relationship between MI and cigarette smoking is dose related and linear. There is an eight-fold elevation in the odds ratio for persons who smoke more than 40 cigarettes per day.

The benefits of pharmacologic therapy have made it the prime means of successful smoking cessation. There are multiple forms available, including nicotine replacement, bupropion, and varenicline.

Persons with CAD without demonstrable ischemia are recommended by the American College of Cardiology and the American Heart Association (ACC/AHA) to exercise at least 3 times weekly for at least 20 minutes per session. This patient already meets that goal.

Based on recommendations from the ACC/AHA, the target blood pressure for persons with CAD is below 130/80 mm Hg; in those with left ventricular systolic dysfunction, below 120/80 mm Hg. This patient does not have left ventricular systolic dysfunction and his antihypertensive therapy is sufficient.

The National Cholesterol Education Panel (NCEP) Adult Treatment Panel III (ATP III) LDL cholesterol goal for persons at high cardiovascular risk is below 100 mg/dL (2.59 mmol/L). An optional LDL cholesterol goal for persons at very high cardiovascular risk, which includes those with established CAD and continued smoking, is below 70 mg/dL (1.81 mmol/L). This patient's LDL cholesterol level is already below 70 mg/dL (1.81 mmol/L).

Although moderate alcohol consumption (approximately one to three drinks daily) is associated with a lower risk of CAD, excessive alcohol intake accounts for approximately 4% of cases of dilated cardiomyopathy. The level of ingestion has been estimated to be 8 to 21 drinks per day for at least 5 years before abnormalities in cardiac structure and function occur. Reducing this patient's current level of alcohol consumption will not reduce his risk of CAD.

KEY POINT

- Mortality among patients who quit smoking following a myocardial infarction approaches that of nonsmokers within 3 years.

Bibliography

Pipe AL, Papadakis S, Reid RD. The role of smoking cessation in the prevention of coronary artery disease. Curr Atheroscler Rep. 2010;12(2):145-150. [PMID: 20425251]

Item 6   Answer: C

Educational Objective: Diagnose premature coronary artery disease in a cancer survivor with previous radiation therapy.

This young woman's chest pain is most likely caused by coronary artery disease (CAD). She has chest pain consistent with unstable angina. In a patient with a history of chest irradiation who is young and free from conventional risk factors, CAD can be attributed to the effects of the irradiation. Coronary obstructions from previous chest radiation typically occur in ostial or proximal sites. Pathologic examination of the coronary vessels shows intimal proliferation that consists of fibrous tissue without extracellular lipid deposits. The fibrous nature of radiation-induced coronary lesions makes them poor candidates for interventional dilatation procedures.

The antiphospholipid antibody typically prolongs the activated partial thromboplastin time or the prothrombin time. These antibodies are paradoxically associated with an increased risk for venous and arterial thromboembolism and pregnancy loss. The antiphospholipid syndrome is unlikely in a patient with normal coagulation and a more compelling alternative reason for CAD.

Cocaine-induced coronary artery vasospasm is a reasonable consideration in this patient with a history of cocaine use. However, the negative screen for cocaine makes it an unlikely cause of her chest pain. In addition, vasospasm of epicardial coronary vessels is more apt to cause ST-segment elevation than depression.

Kawasaki disease is characterized by fever, conjunctivitis, erythema of the oral mucous membranes, erythema or edema of the extremities, cervical lymphadenopathy, coronary aneurysms, and coronary artery thrombosis and occlusion. It occurs mainly in childhood. However, coronary artery aneurysms from the disease may be seen in adulthood. This patient has no history of Kawasaki disease and no angiographic findings of coronary aneurysms.

KEY POINT

- The fibrous nature of radiation-induced coronary lesions makes them poor candidates for interventional dilatation procedures.

Bibliography

Darby SC, Cutter DJ, Boerma M, et al. Radiation-related heart disease: current knowledge and future prospects. Int J Radiat Oncol Biol Phys. 2010;76(3):656-665. [PMID: 20159360]

Item 7   Answer: A

Educational Objective: Diagnose amyloidosis in a patient with heart failure.

The most likely diagnosis in this patient is amyloidosis. His constellation of signs and symptoms suggests a systemic disease (heart failure, hepatomegaly, proteinuria, bruising). In addition, low voltage on the electrocardiogram (ECG) despite increased ventricular wall thickness suggests an infiltrative process involving the myocardium. Further diagnostic testing would include serum and urine protein electrophoresis and abdominal fat pad or gingival biopsy. If cardiac involvement is suspected, endomyocardial biopsy can confirm the diagnosis. Cardiac involvement is associated with a worse prognosis.

Although Q waves are present in the anteroseptal leads of the ECG, there is no evidence for prior myocardial infarction on his echocardiogram (focal hypokinesis). In addition, coronary artery disease would not account for the global low voltage on ECG or the patient's noncardiac findings.

Giant cell myocarditis generally presents with significant heart failure or even cardiogenic shock and has a high mortality rate. A significant proportion of patients also have refractory ventricular arrhythmias. Although patients may develop symptoms over several months, many present fulminantly, over several days. Giant cell myocarditis is not typically associated with the systemic symptoms, such as nausea, weight loss, and bruising, found in this patient.

Although sarcoidosis may also affect the myocardium, cardiac involvement is characterized by patchy areas of inflammation and fibrosis related to granuloma formation. Because the myocardium is not being replaced or displaced by an infiltrative process (as in amyloidosis), low voltage on ECG is not typically present. In addition, the patient does not exhibit noncardiac signs typical of sarcoidosis, such as pulmonary disease or skin lesions; conversely, proteinuria and bleeding abnormalities are not characteristic of sarcoidosis.

KEY POINT

- Low voltage on the electrocardiogram in a patient with increased ventricular wall thickness and manifestations of systemic disease suggests an infiltrative cardiomyopathy such as amyloidosis.

Bibliography

Seward JB, Casaclang-Verzosa G. Infiltrative cardiovascular diseases: cardiomyopathies that look alike. J Am Coll Cardiol. 2010;55(17):1769-1779. [PMID: 20413025]

Item 8   Answer: D

Educational Objective: Treat symptomatic severe tricuspid valve regurgitation.

This patient with severe tricuspid regurgitation should undergo tricuspid valve replacement surgery. He has evidence of right ventricular volume overload, including dilation and reduced systolic function. He has severe right-sided heart failure as well as dyspnea, possibly related to reduced forward output. Tricuspid regurgitation is commonly present in the setting of pulmonary hypertension, which increases right ventricular pressure and leads to functional regurgitation. Functional tricuspid regurgitation may also occur in cardiomyopathy involving right ventricular dilation. In this patient, however, the normal estimated right ventricular systolic pressure by Doppler echocardiography suggests regurgitation caused by leaflet or myocardial dysfunction.

The only definitive therapy for severe, symptomatic tricuspid valve regurgitation is surgery, either tricuspid annuloplasty or replacement. The timing of tricuspid valve surgery is challenging but should be considered in patients with severe regurgitation and either symptoms or evidence of progressive right ventricular enlargement or dysfunction.

Cardioversion of atrial flutter is unlikely to be maintained because of underlying severe tricuspid regurgitation and resulting right atrial dilation.

Although there is evidence of right ventricular dysfunction, no studies conclusively demonstrate a benefit for digoxin or other inotropic therapy for right-sided heart failure, particularly if it is secondary to tricuspid regurgitation.

The patient does not have clinical symptoms of infective endocarditis, such as fever, or echocardiographic evidence, such as vegetation; empiric antibiotic therapy for endocarditis is therefore not indicated.

KEY POINT

- Tricuspid valve surgery should be considered in patients with severe tricuspid regurgitation and either symptoms or evidence of progressive right ventricular enlargement or dysfunction.

Bibliography

Bruce CJ, Connolly HM. Right-sided valve disease deserves a little more respect. Circulation. 2009;119(20):2726-2734. [PMID: 19470901]

Item 9   Answer: D   H

Educational Objective: Treat descending aortic intramural hematoma.

This patient should receive intravenous β-blockade followed by intravenous sodium nitroprusside to control blood pressure. The CT scan (shown) shows a type B aortic intramural hematoma. Type A dissections or intramural hematomas involve the ascending aorta or aortic arch, whereas type B syndromes begin distal to the left subclavian artery. In this CT scan, a descending aortic intramural hematoma (*asterisks*) is seen as a circumferential aortic

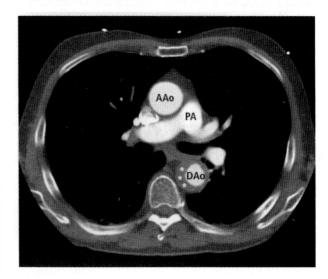

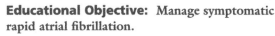

CONT.

soft-tissue density without contrast enhancement and without an identifiable dissection flap. The ascending aorta (AAo) is normal in contour and is not involved. (DAo = descending aorta; PA = pulmonary artery.)

Elevation of D-dimer level frequently accompanies acute aortic syndromes, although it is usually higher in classic dissection compared with intramural hematoma or penetrating atherosclerotic ulcer. Within the International Registry of Acute Aortic Dissection, a D-dimer value below 0.5 μg/mL (0.5 mg/L) measured within the first 24 hours of symptoms had a negative predictive value of 95% for acute aortic dissection.

Chest pain is a common presenting symptom in the emergency department, and physicians evaluating such patients must rapidly exclude three potentially lethal causes: acute myocardial infarction, acute pulmonary embolism, and an acute aortic syndrome. In this patient, the electrocardiogram does not confirm an ST-elevation myocardial infarction, but a non–ST-elevation myocardial infarction cannot be excluded based on the electrocardiogram. However, although a single troponin level does not exclude infarction, troponin I would likely be elevated after 2 hours of ongoing chest pain. The patient has an elevated D-dimer level but this value does not confirm the diagnosis of pulmonary embolism, and the patient has an alternative explanation for her symptoms.

Malperfusion syndromes are uncommon with aortic intramural hematoma but could occur with transformation to classic dissection. In such cases, endovascular fenestration or stenting may be necessary. This patient shows no evidence of lower limb or visceral malperfusion, and catheterization with endovascular repair is not indicated.

Emergency surgery is indicated for type A (proximal) aortic intramural hematoma, but acute surgical intervention is rarely indicated for type B aortic syndromes. Indications for surgical or endovascular intervention in a type B syndrome include malperfusion syndromes and significant aneurysmal dilatation.

Aortic intramural hematoma may progress to classic dissection or undergo aneurysmal dilatation; however, endovascular stent grafting to prevent such transformation is not indicated.

The hematoma is contained within the aortic media and does not present a risk of distal embolization; anticoagulation is not indicated.

KEY POINT

- Uncomplicated type B aortic intramural hematoma is best treated medically, initially with β-blockade followed by a parenteral arterial vasodilator to control blood pressure.

Bibliography
Suzuki T, Distante A, Zizza A, et al; IRAD-Bio Investigators. Diagnosis of acute aortic dissection by D-dimer: the International Registry of Acute Aortic Dissection Substudy on Biomarkers (IRAD-Bio) experience. Circulation. 2009;119(20):2702-2707. [PMID: 19433758]

Item 10   Answer: C

Educational Objective: Manage symptomatic rapid atrial fibrillation.

This patient with atrial fibrillation is hemodynamically unstable and should undergo immediate cardioversion. She has hypotension and pulmonary edema in the setting of rapid atrial fibrillation. In patients with heart failure with preserved systolic function, usually due to hypertension, the loss of the atrial "kick" with atrial fibrillation can sometimes lead to severe symptoms. The best treatment in this situation is immediate cardioversion to convert the patient to normal sinus rhythm. Although there is a risk of a thromboembolic event since she is not anticoagulated, she is currently in extremis and is at risk of imminent demise if not aggressively treated. In addition, she acutely became symptomatic 1 hour ago, and while this is not proof that she developed atrial fibrillation very recently, her risk of thromboembolism is low if the atrial fibrillation developed within the previous 48 hours.

Adenosine can be useful for diagnosing a supraventricular tachycardia and can treat atrioventricular node–dependent tachycardias such as atrioventricular nodal reentrant tachycardia, but it is not useful in the treatment of atrial fibrillation.

Amiodarone can convert atrial fibrillation to normal sinus rhythm as well as provide rate control, but immediate treatment is needed and amiodarone may take several hours to work. Oral amiodarone may be a reasonable option for long-term atrial fibrillation prevention in this patient given the severity of her symptoms, especially if she has significant left ventricular hypertrophy.

Metoprolol or diltiazem would slow her heart rate; however, she is hypotensive and these medications could make her blood pressure lower. In addition, she is in active heart failure, and metoprolol or diltiazem could worsen the pulmonary edema.

KEY POINT

- Patients with atrial fibrillation who are hemodynamically unstable should undergo immediate cardioversion.

Bibliography
Zimetbaum P. In the clinic. Atrial fibrillation. Ann Intern Med. 2010;153(11):ITC6-1-ITC6-16. [PMID: 21135291]

Item 11   Answer: B

Educational Objective: Interpret B-type natriuretic peptide level in an obese patient with acute heart failure.

This patient has decompensated diastolic heart failure with evidence for volume overload, including elevated central venous pressure, pulmonary crackles, lower extremity edema, and pulmonary edema on chest radiograph (diffuse increased interstitial opacities, including Kerley B lines;

CONT.

prominent and indistinct pulmonary vasculature; tiny pleural effusions). He would most appropriately be treated with an intravenous diuretic such as furosemide. The electrocardiogram shows sinus tachycardia with left ventricular hypertrophy and left axis deviation.

The patient's B-type natriuretic peptide (BNP) level is disproportionately low in the setting of acute heart failure owing to his obesity. The exact mechanism for lower BNP levels seen in patients with obesity is not fully established but may involve the presence of natriuretic peptide clearance receptors in adipose tissue. BNP levels are elevated in patients with chronic kidney disease and tend to be elevated in older patients and in women. In addition, conditions other than acute heart failure that cause ventricular strain increase BNP, including acute myocardial infarction, pulmonary embolism, and acute tachycardia.

Inhaled iloprost is therapy for pulmonary arterial hypertension. This patient has evidence for pulmonary hypertension (elevated right ventricular systolic pressure) but it is likely secondary to heart failure.

Azithromycin and ceftriaxone would be appropriate treatment for community-acquired pneumonia in hospitalized patients. This patient is afebrile, with normal leukocyte count, and does not have symptoms to suggest respiratory tract infection. In addition, the chest radiograph shows bilateral symmetric pulmonary edema rather than either the reticular pattern typical of atypical pneumonia or a focal infiltrate suggestive of bacterial pneumonia.

Subcutaneous enoxaparin would be indicated for acute pulmonary embolism. However, the symmetric airspace opacities on chest radiograph indicate pulmonary edema, and symmetric lower extremity edema is present; these findings are not consistent with pulmonary embolism or deep venous thrombosis.

KEY POINT

- **In patients with acute heart failure, the expected increase in B-type natriuretic peptide level is attenuated by the presence of obesity.**

Bibliography
Mehra MR, Uber PA, Park MH, et al. Obesity and suppressed B-type natriuretic peptide levels in heart failure. J Am Coll Cardiol. 2004;43(9):1590-1595. [PMID: 15120816]

 Item 12   Answer: C

Educational Objective: Choose appropriate medical management for a patient with diabetes mellitus and coronary artery disease.

This patient with diabetes mellitus and an acute coronary syndrome would benefit from starting an aldosterone antagonist such as eplerenone. The 2007 American College of Cardiology/American Heart Association guidelines recommend the administration of an aldosterone antagonist to all patients following a non–ST-elevation myocardial infarction (NSTEMI) who are receiving an ACE inhibitor, have a left ventricular ejection fraction of 40% or below, and have either heart failure symptoms or diabetes mellitus. Contraindications to the use of an aldosterone antagonist in this setting include chronic kidney disease and hyperkalemia. Agents that block the renin-angiotensin-aldosterone system are particularly beneficial in high-risk patients, and the presence of diabetes places this patient in that category.

The EPHESUS trial randomized patients presenting with an acute coronary syndrome, left ventricular systolic dysfunction (ejection fraction ≤40%), and either heart failure or diabetes to the aldosterone antagonist eplerenone or placebo in addition to optimal medical therapy. There was a 15% relative risk reduction in all-cause mortality and a 13% relative risk reduction in cardiovascular mortality/cardiovascular complications in the eplerenone group compared with the placebo group. The aldosterone antagonist should be initiated before hospital discharge because a mortality benefit can be seen within the first 30 days of adding the medication.

Clopidogrel or another thienopyridine should be added to background aspirin therapy in all patients following a NSTEMI regardless of their TIMI risk score unless there is an elevated risk of bleeding, such as recent gastrointestinal bleeding or newly diagnosed anemia. Guidelines recommend the continuation of clopidogrel for at least 1 year following a NSTEMI.

Increasing the β-blocker is incorrect because this patient's resting heart rate is sufficiently low, and increasing the dose may result in symptomatic bradycardia.

Current guidelines recommend the use of warfarin therapy following NSTEMI only in those patients who are at high risk for embolization, such as those with atrial fibrillation and left ventricular thrombus. This patient has none of these indications.

KEY POINT

- **Agents that block the renin-angiotensin-aldosterone system are particularly beneficial in high-risk patients with an acute coronary syndrome, such those with left ventricular ejection fraction of 40% or below and either heart failure symptoms or diabetes mellitus.**

Bibliography
Pitt B, Remme W, Zannad F, et al; Eplerenone Post-Acute Myocardial Infarction Heart Failure Efficacy and Survival Study Investigators. Eplerenone, a selective aldosterone blocker, in patients with left ventricular dysfunction after myocardial infarction. N Engl J Med. 2003;348(14):1309-1321. [PMID: 12668699]

Item 13   Answer: A

Educational Objective: Identify areas for secondary prevention in a patient with coronary artery disease.

In this patient with heart failure and elevated blood pressure, aggressive blood pressure reduction should be undertaken to reduce her risk of a cardiovascular event. The American

Heart Association recommends targeting a blood pressure reduction to less than 130/80 mm Hg in patients with coronary heart disease (CHD) or a CHD risk equivalent (carotid disease, peripheral vascular disease, abdominal aortic aneurysm) and to below 120/80 mm Hg for those with heart failure or a left ventricular ejection fraction below 40%.

There is no benefit to strict glycemic control on the impact of macrovascular disease. For most patients, a reasonable goal is a hemoglobin A_{1c} value of 7.0% or below. This patient's hemoglobin A_{1c} level is at 6.9%, and reducing her blood pressure is a higher priority than further lowering her hemoglobin A_{1c}.

In patients with a high risk of a cardiovascular event, LDL cholesterol levels should be treated aggressively with lipid-lowering therapy with a target LDL goal of below 100 mg/dL (2.59 mmol/L), with a reasonable goal of further reduction to below 70 mg/dL (1.81 mmol/L) in patients at very high risk. Patients considered at very high risk include those with established cardiovascular disease plus multiple major risk factors, particularly diabetes mellitus; poorly controlled risk factors, such as continued smoking; metabolic syndrome; and those with a history of an acute coronary syndrome. This patient is in the very-high-risk category, but her LDL cholesterol level is already below 70 mg/dL (1.81 mmol/L).

Hypertriglyceridemia is a predictor of development of CHD but not after adjustment for LDL or HDL cholesterol subfractions. Treatment of moderate triglyceride elevation (200-499 mg/dL [2.26-5.64 mmol/L]) is recommended only if non–HDL cholesterol (total cholesterol minus HDL cholesterol) is elevated. The non–HDL cholesterol goal equals the patient's LDL cholesterol goal plus 30 mg/dL (0.78 mmol/L). This patient's non–HDL cholesterol is at goal and requires no further intervention.

KEY POINT

- Aggressive blood pressure lowering reduces the incidence of cardiovascular events and progression of cardiovascular disease in patients with coronary artery disease.

Bibliography

Rosendorff C, Black HR, Cannon CP, et al; American Heart Association Council for High Blood Pressure Research; American Heart Association Council on Clinical Cardiology; American Heart Association Council on Epidemiology and Prevention. Treatment of hypertension in the prevention and management of ischemic heart disease: a scientific statement from the American Heart Association Council for High Blood Pressure Research and the Councils on Clinical Cardiology and Epidemiology and Prevention [erratum in Circulation. 2007;116(5):e121]. Circulation. 2007;115(21):2761-2788. [PMID: 17502569]

Item 14   Answer: C
Educational Objective: Diagnose atrial septal defect in an adult.

This patient presents with findings consistent with an ostium secundum atrial septal defect. The characteristic features include a right ventricular or parasternal impulse, fixed splitting of the S_2, and right-sided cardiac chamber enlargement noted on chest radiograph. Right axis deviation and incomplete right bundle branch block are common findings on the electrocardiogram. The systolic murmur is related to increased flow through the pulmonary artery during systole, and the diastolic murmur is related to increased flow through the tricuspid valve; both murmurs are caused by the left-to-right shunt.

Eisenmenger physiology is the development of severe pulmonary hypertension related to congenital cardiac disease. Characteristically, patients have cyanosis and clubbing. The severe pulmonary hypertension results in pressure hypertrophy of the right ventricle. The pulmonic component of the S_2 is increased, but fixed splitting of the S_2 is not noted. The chest radiograph in Eisenmenger syndrome demonstrates enlargement of the central pulmonary arteries and reduced peripheral pulmonary vascularity, and the electrocardiogram demonstrates right axis deviation and right ventricular hypertrophy with strain.

Idiopathic pulmonary arterial hypertension commonly affects young women. A parasternal lift and increased pulmonic component of the S_2 are noted with severe pulmonary arterial hypertension. Although the pulmonary arteries may be enlarged on chest radiograph, distal pulmonary vascularity is decreased. The electrocardiogram in patients with pulmonary arterial hypertension demonstrates right axis deviation and right ventricular hypertrophy with strain.

Rheumatic mitral stenosis is characterized by a prominent apical impulse and a loud S_1. The S_2 may be increased when there is associated pulmonary hypertension, but fixed splitting of the S_2 is not expected. An opening snap is often heard when the valve is still pliable and is related to the abrupt halt in leaflet motion during early diastole. The murmur of mitral stenosis is a diastolic murmur best heard at the cardiac apex; presystolic accentuation of the diastolic murmur may be present. The chest radiograph will demonstrate features of left atrial enlargement, which include a straightened left heart border, elevation of the left bronchus, and posterior displacement of the heart on the lateral chest radiograph.

KEY POINT

- Ostium secundum atrial septal defect is characterized by a right ventricular or parasternal impulse, fixed splitting of the S_2, a systolic pulmonary flow murmur, and right-sided cardiac chamber enlargement noted on chest radiograph.

Bibliography

Baumgartner H, Bonhoeffer P, De Groot NM, et al; Task Force on the Management of Grown-up Congenital Heart Disease of the European Society of Cardiology (ESC); Association for European Pediatric Cardiology (AEPC). ESC Guidelines for the management of grown-up congenital heart disease (new version 2010). Eur Heart J. 2010;31(23):2915-2957. [PMID: 20801927]

Item 15   Answer: A

Educational Objective: Treat heart failure with preserved ejection fraction.

The most appropriate treatment for this patient is candesartan. She has heart failure with preserved ejection fraction (HFPEF; diastolic heart failure), as evidenced by signs and symptoms of heart failure (dyspnea, edema, examination findings consistent with volume overload) in the setting of a normal ejection fraction, as measured by echocardiography in this case. The electrocardiogram displays normal sinus rhythm, left axis deviation, and left ventricular hypertrophy with repolarization abnormalities.

There is not a large body of evidence to guide treatment of HFPEF; in addition, the large trials that have been published have primarily demonstrated reductions in hospitalizations or combined mortality and hospitalizations, if any benefit is demonstrated at all, rather than any effect on the more robust outcome of mortality alone. Treatment of HFPEF is thus primarily focused on managing the manifestations of heart failure (volume overload) and targeting risk factors for left ventricular hypertrophy (primarily hypertension), which is strongly associated with HFPEF. This patient's hypertension is not well controlled. In addition to reducing congestion by increased diuretics, an antihypertensive agent should be added. The angiotensin receptor blocker candesartan is an agent that has been studied in a large randomized controlled trial of HFPEF treatment and was associated with a reduction in hospitalizations.

In patients with severe systolic heart failure, digoxin can be used to reduce symptoms. However, there is no established role for digoxin in the treatment of HFPEF. Disopyramide is sometimes used to treat hypertrophic cardiomyopathy when there is left ventricular outflow tract obstruction, because negative inotropy reduces the dynamic outflow tract obstruction that occurs with systole. This patient has features suggestive of hypertensive heart disease rather than hypertrophic cardiomyopathy with obstruction (echocardiogram shows concentric rather than eccentric and severe left ventricular hypertrophy). In addition, she has mildly decompensated heart failure with evidence of volume overload, contraindicating treatment with a negative inotropic agent. For the same reasons, the negative inotropic agent verapamil would not be a good choice for controlling her hypertension.

KEY POINT

- Treatment of heart failure with preserved ejection fraction (HFPEF) is focused on managing the manifestations of heart failure and targeting risk factors for left ventricular hypertrophy, which is strongly associated with HFPEF.

Bibliography

Paulus WJ, van Ballegoij JJ. Treatment of heart failure with normal ejection fraction: an inconvenient truth! J Am Coll Cardiol. 2010;55(6):526-537. [PMID: 20152557]

Item 16   Answer: D

Educational Objective: Diagnose Turner syndrome.

This patient most likely has Turner syndrome. She has the typical physical findings of Turner syndrome, including short stature, shield-shaped chest, and a webbed neck. Primary amenorrhea is common in Turner syndrome. She also has a bicuspid aortic valve. Turner syndrome is caused by the absence of one of the X chromosomes and is generally diagnosed early in life because of characteristic physical findings. Approximately 30% of patients with Turner syndrome have a bicuspid aortic valve. Additional common cardiovascular findings in Turner syndrome include aortic coarctation and ascending aortic dilatation, which should be indexed to body surface area because of short stature. These patients are at increased risk of aortic dissection and rupture when the aortic dimension reaches 2.5 cm^2/m^2 or greater. This patient has no physical examination findings or echocardiographic findings of aortic coarctation or aortic root dilatation.

Approximately 40% of patients with Down syndrome have some form of congenital heart disease, most commonly an atrioventricular septal defect, either partial or complete. This patient does not have characteristic features of Down syndrome, the most prominent of which include cognitive impairment, upslanting palpebral fissures, epicanthic folds, open mouth and protruding tongue, and short neck.

The Holt-Oram syndrome is a developmental disorder of the heart and upper limbs, inherited in an autosomal dominant manner with near complete penetrance and variable expression; 40% of cases are sporadic. Phenotypic features include upper limb defects ranging from phocomelia to minor thumb anomalies and cardiac defects in up to 95% of patients, most often an ostium secundum atrial septal defect. This patient does not have features of Holt-Oram syndrome.

Marfan syndrome is an autosomal dominant disorder of connective tissue. Patients with Marfan syndrome generally are of tall stature due to overgrowth of the long bones; additional characteristics include arm span greater than the height, long fingers, joint hypermobility, and sternal deformity. Cardiovascular features include dilatation of the proximal ascending aorta with or without mitral valve prolapse. This patient does not have features of Marfan syndrome.

KEY POINT

- Frequent cardiac abnormalities of Turner syndrome include bicuspid aortic valve, aortic coarctation, and ascending aortic dilatation.

Bibliography

Matura LA, Ho VB, Rosing DR, Bondy CA. Aortic dilatation and dissection in Turner syndrome. Circulation. 2007;116(15):1663-1670. [PMID: 17875973]

Ⓗ Item 17   Answer: C

Educational Objective: Treat systolic heart failure with β-blocker therapy.

This patient should be started on a β-blocker, such as metoprolol succinate (long-acting form of metoprolol) or carvedilol. Treatment with a β-blocker is indicated for systolic heart failure regardless of symptom status, including asymptomatic or mildly symptomatic heart failure, although β-blocker therapy should generally not be initiated in decompensated states such as volume overload or a low-output state. Even patients with severe heart failure have shown clinical benefit from and tolerate β-blocker therapy. Many patients with pulmonary disease also tolerate β-blocker therapy without side effects, in particular the more β_1-selective agents, such as metoprolol or bisoprolol. Initiation of β-blocker therapy is usually tolerated when patients are clinically stable, prior to hospital discharge.

This patient likely has functional mitral regurgitation secondary to tethering of the mitral valve leaflets due to ventricular dilation in the setting of cardiomyopathy. There is currently no definitive evidence that surgically correcting functional mitral regurgitation in the setting of nonischemic cardiomyopathy improves survival.

Eplerenone is indicated for treatment of heart failure following myocardial infarction or for hypertension. It may also be a suitable alternative to spironolactone for treatment of severe heart failure if the patient experiences gynecomastia as a side effect. The patient does not meet any of these criteria.

Biventricular pacing together with an implantable cardioverter-defibrillator (cardiac resynchronization therapy) is indicated for patients with severe symptomatic heart failure (NYHA class III-IV), ejection fraction below 35%, and ventricular dyssynchrony as evidenced by prolonged QRS on electrocardiogram (>120 msec) while taking optimal medical therapy. This patient does not have a prolonged QRS complex and therefore would not benefit from upgrading to a biventricular device.

KEY POINT

- **Many patients with heart failure and pulmonary disease tolerate β-blocker therapy without side effects, in particular the more β_1-selective agents, such as metoprolol or bisoprolol.**

Bibliography
Sirak TE, Jelic S, Le Jemtel TH. Therapeutic update: non-selective beta- and alpha-adrenergic blockade in patients with coexistent chronic obstructive pulmonary disease and chronic heart failure. J Am Coll Cardiol. 2004;44(3):497-502. [PMID: 15358010]

Item 18   Answer: C

Educational Objective: Use additional testing for cardiac risk stratification in a patient at intermediate risk.

An appropriate test for this patient is high-sensitivity C-reactive protein (hsCRP) assessment. He has a 15% 10-year risk for myocardial infarction and coronary death as calculated by the Framingham risk score (online calculator available at http://hp2010.nhlbihin.net/atpiii/calculator.asp?usertype=prof), which is considered an intermediate level of risk. Measurement of hsCRP has been demonstrated to be clinically useful for guiding primary prevention strategies in persons with an intermediate risk of future cardiovascular events (Framingham risk score of 10%-20%), with up to 30% of these patients reclassified as either low risk or high risk based on hsCRP measurement. These patients may benefit from either initiation or intensification of pharmacologic therapies, such as with statins, to reduce risk in primary and secondary prevention.

The JUPITER trial tested the hypothesis that healthy middle-aged and older persons with elevated hsCRP but without elevated LDL cholesterol (<130 mg/dL [3.37 mmol/L]) would benefit from statin treatment. Statin treatment was associated with lowering of median LDL cholesterol level from 108 to 55 mg/dL (2.80 to 1.42 mmol/L, 50% reduction) and median hsCRP level from 0.42 to 0.22 mg/dL (4.2 to 2.2 mg/L, 37% reduction). The JUPITER trial was terminated early after a median follow-up of 1.9 years because of reduction in the primary end point rate (incidence of a first major cardiovascular event) from 1.36 to 0.77 per 100 patient-years of follow-up. The absolute reduction was relatively small at 1.2%.

B-type natriuretic peptide (BNP) is released from cardiac myocytes in response to elevated preload, afterload, or increased cardiac wall stress. It is not typically viewed as an inflammatory marker. Data are insufficient to recommend the use of BNP or its precursor, NT-proBNP, to guide intensity of treatment for primary or secondary prevention.

The patient has no cardiac symptoms. There is no role for either stress echocardiography or for CT angiography in this patient.

It is worth noting that this patient is hypertensive. At a minimum, he should return to have his blood pressure measurements repeated. He should be counseled on appropriate lifestyle modifications to help lower blood pressure as well, including limiting sodium consumption and exercising regularly. If his blood pressure remains elevated on subsequent evaluation, initiation of drug therapy may be appropriate.

KEY POINT

- **High-sensitivity C-reactive protein level may be helpful for reclassifying patients with an intermediate cardiovascular risk as either high or low risk.**

Bibliography
Corson MA. Emerging inflammatory markers for assessing coronary heart disease risk. Curr Cardiol Rep. 2009;11(6):452-459. [PMID: 19863870]

Answers and Critiques

Item 19   Answer: B

Educational Objective: Treat aortic disease in a patient with a bicuspid aortic valve.

This patient has severe symptomatic aortic regurgitation, and therefore surgical aortic valve replacement is indicated regardless of left ventricular systolic function. In patients with an ascending aortic diameter greater than 45 mm at the time of planned aortic valve surgery, repair of the ascending aorta, performed by placement of a graft conduit or homograft, is indicated and performed concomitantly.

A bicuspid aortic valve is frequently associated with dilation of the ascending aorta, which is now recognized to be caused by abnormal connective tissue or an aortopathy in patients with a bicuspid aortic valve. Many patients with a bicuspid aortic valve requiring aortic valve replacement also require aortic root surgery. In some patients, progressive aneurysmal dilation of the ascending aorta may occur with mild aortic valve dysfunction and become the primary indication for surgical intervention to reduce the risk of aortic dissection. Surgical replacement of the aortic valve without repair of the ascending aorta in this patient will likely require a future surgery owing to progression of aortic dilation.

β-Blockers such as carvedilol have been used to slow progression of ascending aortic dilation in Marfan syndrome; however, these agents have not been evaluated in aortic dilation caused by a bicuspid aortic valve, and this patient meets criteria for aortic graft placement now.

The role of vasodilator therapy to reduce the progression of chronic severe aortic regurgitation has been studied in several small trials with inconclusive results. Although vasodilator therapy with losartan may provide short-term improvement in symptoms before planned surgery, reassessment in 3 months is not appropriate because delay in surgical intervention may result in aortic dissection or worsening ventricular dysfunction.

KEY POINT

- **Many patients with a bicuspid aortic valve requiring aortic valve replacement also require aortic root surgery.**

Bibliography

Siu SC, Silversides CK. Bicuspid aortic valve disease. J Am Coll Cardiol. 2010;55(25):2789-2800. [PMID: 20579534]

H Item 20   Answer: C

Educational Objective: Diagnose a drug interaction in a cardiac transplant patient.

This patient has rhabdomyositis due to potentiation of cyclosporine and statins to cause myositis by the recent addition of fluconazole, which raises cyclosporine and tacrolimus levels. One of the difficulties in chronic management of transplant patients is the myriad potential drug interactions. Calcineurin inhibitors (commonly cyclosporine or tacrolimus) are a mainstay of immunosuppression for cardiac transplant patients but carry a risk of interaction with many commonly used drugs. When used with statins, the risk of myositis is increased. When used with azole antifungal agents or certain calcium channel blockers (diltiazem, verapamil), levels of calcineurin inhibitors are increased. When used with certain antimicrobial agents (rifampin, isoniazid) or antiseizure medications (phenytoin, phenobarbital), levels of calcineurin inhibitors are decreased. Although there is an increased risk for myositis with concurrent statin and calcineurin inhibitor use, statins have been shown to reduce the occurrence of transplant vasculopathy and improve survival; in general, dosages are low or moderate to reduce risk of myositis. Good communication between the general internist and transplant cardiologist regarding the cardiac transplant recipient's medications is important to avoid problems arising from drug interactions.

Acute rejection is frequently asymptomatic and may be incidentally detected on routine surveillance endomyocardial biopsy. Clinical manifestations include atrial tachyarrhythmias or new-onset heart failure symptoms; left ventricular dysfunction is a late finding and generally indicates more severe rejection. This patient has no heart failure symptoms and a normal echocardiogram. In addition, the clinical presentation of myalgia and elevated creatine kinase level would not be typical for acute rejection.

Cytomegalovirus infection in a solid organ transplant patient may be due to reactivation of a latent infection in the recipient. Signs and symptoms of cytomegalovirus viremia may include flu-like febrile illness, gastrointestinal symptoms (colitis), leukopenia, or elevated aminotransferases (hepatitis), which this patient does not demonstrate.

Transplant vasculopathy is coronary disease of the transplanted heart, characterized by diffuse intimal thickening. Significant transplant vasculopathy may manifest as acute myocardial infarction, high-degree atrioventricular block, heart failure, or cardiac arrest. With a normal echocardiogram and electrocardiogram and negative troponin test, it is unlikely that coronary disease is contributing to this patient's clinical presentation.

KEY POINT

- **Cardiac transplant patients are subject to potential interactions of certain immunosuppressive agents (calcineurin inhibitors) with a myriad of other drugs, including statins as well as some calcium channel blockers, antifungal agents, antimicrobial agents, and antiseizure medications.**

Bibliography

Page RL 2nd, Miller GG, Lindenfeld J. Drug therapy in the heart transplant recipient: part IV: drug-drug interactions. Circulation. 2005;111(2):230-239. [PMID: 15657387]

Item 21   Answer: A

Educational Objective: Manage implanted cardiac device infection.

This patient should undergo extraction of her pacemaker and leads. Infection is an increasingly common complication of pacemakers and other implanted cardiac devices, likely owing to an increase in comorbidities of patients receiving devices. Even though this patient has no symptoms of systemic infection, a visible generator indicates that the entire pacemaker system is infected, as microorganisms track down the leads, including the intravascular portions. Proper management of a pacemaker infection includes extracting the generator and leads. A temporary pacemaker may then be needed until the patient has received antibiotics for at least 72 hours and a new pacemaker can be implanted. Patients with pacemaker erosion and negative blood cultures should then receive a 7- to 14-day course of antibiotics based on sensitivities of the organism cultured intraoperatively from the pacemaker pocket. Coagulase-negative staphylococci and *Staphylococcus aureus* are the most common causative agents. For patients with bacteremia or endocarditis, it may be prudent to wait a longer period of time before reimplantation and extend the duration of antibiotic therapy.

In the setting of a device erosion or pocket infection, either oral or intravenous antibiotics may be used prior to explantation to prevent the development of a systemic infection, but are not enough to cure the infection and extraction is still needed. In patients with localized pocket inflammation but no erosion, pocket aspiration should not be performed because it can introduce infection and risks damaging a lead. Blood cultures should be obtained before starting antibiotics to determine if bacteremia is present. In patients with positive blood cultures or previous antibiotic treatment, transesophageal echocardiography should be performed to assess for lead or valvular vegetations.

Surgically closing the wound repairs the erosion, but does not treat the underlying infection, and it is highly likely the device will re-erode, develop signs of pocket inflammation, or lead to an endovascular infection in the future.

KEY POINT

- Management of implanted cardiac device infection includes extraction of the device and leads.

Bibliography

Baddour LM, Epstein AE, Erickson CC, et al; American Heart Association Rheumatic Fever, Endocarditis, and Kawasaki Disease Committee; Council on Cardiovascular Disease in Young; Council on Cardiovascular Surgery and Anesthesia; Council on Cardiovascular Nursing; Council on Clinical Cardiology; Interdisciplinary Council on Quality of Care; American Heart Association. Update on cardiovascular implantable electronic device infections and their management: a scientific statement from the American Heart Association. Circulation. 2010;121(3):458-477. [PMID: 20048212]

Item 22   Answer: B

Educational Objective: Recognize the risk of death from cardiovascular disease in women relative to that of other common diseases.

Coronary artery disease (CAD) poses the greatest health risk to this patient. This patient has increased risk for coronary artery disease based upon her age and postmenopausal state, presence of hypertension, obesity, and increased waist circumference. Cardiovascular disease is the leading cause of death in women and accounts for more deaths annually in women than the other listed causes combined. Cardiovascular disease includes CAD, peripheral vascular disease, and stroke. The average lifetime risk for a woman to develop CAD is 1 in 2; 1 in 3 women will die of the disease. The death rate for CAD in women increases with age, from less than 100 deaths per 100,000 population in women aged 45 to 54 years to more than 1000 per 100,000 population in women 75 years and older. Differences in prevalence and death rates between men and women may be attributed to multiple factors. Women present later in life and later in the disease process and have additional comorbidities. Lack of patient and physician awareness of symptoms may result in delays in diagnosis. In addition, women presenting at a younger age are more likely to have diabetes mellitus or smoke, further increasing risk.

Most women perceive breast cancer as their major health risk. Fewer than 1 in 5 women are aware that CAD is the leading cause of death in women. In comparison, 1 in 10 women will develop breast cancer and 1 in 30 will die of causes related to breast cancer.

Diabetes is a significant concern for many patients, including this obese woman. The primary cause of death in patients with diabetes is ischemic heart disease, however, rather than the diabetes itself. Adults with diabetes have heart disease death rates and stroke risk about 2 to 4 times higher than adults without diabetes.

Ovarian cancer is the second most common gynecologic malignancy in the United States and the fifth leading cause of cancer deaths in all women. Although ovarian cancer primarily affects postmenopausal women, this patient's risk of developing ovarian cancer is small compared with that of developing CAD, particularly because nothing in the patient's history would suggest a genetic predisposition for ovarian cancer.

KEY POINT

- Cardiovascular disease is the leading cause of death in women and accounts for more deaths annually in women than other causes combined.

Bibliography

Lloyd-Jones D, Adams RJ, Brown TM, et al; American Heart Association Statistics Committee and Stroke Statistics Subcommittee. Executive summary: heart disease and stroke statistics—2010 update: a report from the American Heart Association. Circulation. 2010;121(7):948-954. [PMID: 20177011]

Item 23   Answer: C

Educational Objective: Manage an abnormal creatinine level in a patient taking antiarrhythmic medication.

Dronedarone is most likely to have caused this patient's elevated serum creatinine level. Dronedarone is the newest antiarrhythmic agent approved for the treatment of atrial fibrillation or flutter and has been shown to reduce the combined endpoint of cardiovascular hospitalizations and mortality. It is chemically related in structure to amiodarone and exhibits properties of all four Vaughan-Williams classes of antiarrhythmic agents, but was designed to have an improved safety profile. Dronedarone, however, has been shown to cause an average decrease in creatinine clearance of 18% compared with baseline in normal subjects, and up to 5% of patients taking dronedarone will demonstrate a significant increase in measured serum creatinine level. This is due to partial inhibition of tubular transport of creatinine, but there is no change in glomerular filtration rate. Therefore, although the creatinine level is increased, kidney function is unchanged. In this patient, the measured value should be considered the new baseline, with the understanding that it is an underestimation of the glomerular filtration rate. If dronedarone is stopped, the serum creatinine will decrease to a baseline level.

Dronedarone has been issued a black box warning by the U.S. FDA. In patients with severe heart failure requiring recent hospitalization or referral to a specialized heart failure clinic for worsening symptoms, those taking dronedarone had a greater than twofold increase in mortality. Use of dronedarone is contraindicated in patients with New York Heart Association class IV heart failure or class II-III heart failure with recent decompensation requiring hospitalization or referral to a specialized heart failure clinic. In addition, dronedarone leads to higher rates of heart failure hospitalization, stroke, and death from cardiovascular causes in those with permanent atrial fibrillation.

The increase in serum creatinine level from dronedarone must be considered if ACE inhibitors are started simultaneously, because ACE inhibitors can affect serum creatinine levels as well as glomerular filtration rate. Dronedarone is metabolized primarily by the liver, so changes in kidney function should not affect dosing.

Neither atorvastatin, clopidogrel, nor metoprolol would be expected to cause an increase in serum creatinine level.

KEY POINT

- **Dronedarone may reduce creatinine clearance; however, it does not affect glomerular filtration rate and does not reduce kidney function.**

Bibliography

Patel C, Yan GX, Kowey PR. Dronedarone. Circulation. 2009;120(7):636-644. [PMID: 19687370]

Item 24   Answer: B

Educational Objective: Treat severe systolic heart failure with spironolactone.

This patient has severe systolic heart failure (New York Heart Association [NYHA] functional class III-IV symptoms) and would benefit from the addition of spironolactone to standard medical therapy for systolic heart failure (ACE inhibitor and β-blocker). The Randomized Aldactone Evaluation Study (RALES) demonstrated a substantial morbidity and mortality benefit to spironolactone in patients with NYHA class III-IV heart failure and ejection fraction 35% or below, serum potassium level 5.0 meq/L (5.0 mmol/L) or below, and creatinine level 2.5 mg/dL (221 μmol/L) or below. More recently, the Eplerenone in Mild Patients Hospitalization and Survival Study in Heart Failure (EMPHASIS-HF) trial showed reduced risk of death and of hospitalization in patients with mild systolic heart failure (NYHA class II) who were randomized to the aldosterone blocker eplerenone versus placebo.

Although some trials and meta-analyses show combined treatment with an ACE inhibitor and angiotensin receptor blocker (ARB) such as candesartan reduces hospitalizations and improves combined cardiovascular endpoints in patients with heart failure, definitive mortality reduction has not been demonstrated. In addition, the risk for adverse effects such as hyperkalemia and kidney dysfunction is increased with combined ACE inhibitor and ARB therapy.

The patient's weight has been stable, there is no jugular venous distention or edema, and the B-type natriuretic peptide level is within her chronic range, as is her creatinine level. Therefore, increasing the bumetanide would not be appropriate.

Although there is a dose-response effect with β-blocker therapy, increasing carvedilol in this patient is limited by her relative hypotension and low heart rate.

KEY POINT

- **Spironolactone, in addition to ACE inhibitor and β-blocker therapy, is indicated in the treatment of severe systolic heart failure (New York Heart Association class III-IV).**

Bibliography

Zannad F, McMurray JJ, Krum H, et al; EMPHASIS-HF Study Group. Eplerenone in patients with systolic heart failure and mild symptoms. N Engl J Med. 2011;364(1):11-21. [PMID: 21073363]

Item 25   Answer: B

Educational Objective: Initiate medical therapy in a high-risk patient with a non–ST-elevation myocardial infarction.

In addition to antianginal therapy, heparin, and clopidogrel, this patient with a non–ST-elevation myocardial infarction (NSTEMI) and high-risk features should receive a statin and a glycoprotein IIb/IIIa inhibitor. Early coronary angiography

CONT.

should also be considered. Her TIMI risk score is 6 (one point each for age ≥65 years, the presence of ≥3 traditional risk factors, ST-segment deviation, ≥2 anginal episodes in the past 24 hours, aspirin use in the past week, and elevated biomarkers), indicating a high-risk NSTEMI. Patients with a high-risk NSTEMI benefit from aggressive medical therapy and an early invasive treatment approach.

All patients with an acute coronary syndrome should receive nitrates, a β-blocker, aspirin, clopidogrel (unless an increased risk of bleeding exists), and a statin. In addition, patients with a high TIMI risk score (5-7) should receive anticoagulation therapy (unfractionated heparin, low-molecular-weight heparin [LMWH], or bivalirudin) and a glycoprotein IIb/IIIa inhibitor, such as eptifibatide. Although the benefit of intensive lipid lowering in the early phases of an acute coronary syndrome (before discharge) is still being established, current consensus recommends early intensive lipid-lowering therapy for NSTEMI and unstable angina regardless of risk score.

Heparin provides the most benefit for patients with intermediate (3-4) and high TIMI risk scores. For patients being considered for an early invasive approach, unfractionated heparin is preferred over LMWH because of the ability to monitor the level of anticoagulation with unfractionated heparin during coronary intervention. Glycoprotein IIb/IIIa inhibitors are potent antiplatelet agents that block the final common pathway of platelet aggregation and are beneficial for high-risk NSTEMI patients. Early coronary angiography and revascularization are most beneficial for patients with intermediate or high TIMI risk scores because these interventions have been shown to reduce recurrent myocardial infarction and death.

In the setting of acute coronary syndrome, prophylactic lidocaine to prevent ventricular arrhythmias is not recommended. The recommended treatment for prevention of ventricular arrhythmias is the early use of β-blockers and maintaining the serum potassium level above 4.0 meq/L (4.0 mmol/L) and magnesium level above 2.0 mg/dL (0.83 mmol/L).

Thrombolytic agents such as tenecteplase are used for patients with an ST-elevation myocardial infarction (STEMI), but are not indicated for patients with a NSTEMI. Previous clinical trials in NSTEMI patients in the early 1990s found that thrombolytic agents were associated with excessive bleeding events without an improvement in clinical outcome.

KEY POINT

- Patients with a high-risk non–ST-elevation myocardial infarction benefit from aggressive medical therapy, including anticoagulation and a glycoprotein IIb/IIIa inhibitor, and an early invasive treatment approach.

Bibliography
Kalra S, Duggal S, Valdez G, Smalligan RD. Review of acute coronary syndrome diagnosis and management. Postgrad Med. 2008;120(1):18-27. [PMID: 18467805]

Item 26   Answer: C

Educational Objective: Manage recurrent pericarditis.

This patient most likely has recurrent pericarditis, and colchicine in combination with aspirin is the first-line treatment. He has pleuritic chest pain that is worse when supine and partially relieved by leaning forward and evidence of a pericardial friction rub. These findings are consistent with pericarditis. Lack of ST-segment elevation on electrocardiography does not exclude pericarditis. Seven months ago, he was diagnosed with acute pericarditis and treated with ibuprofen.

In patients with recurrent pericarditis who have not benefited from colchicine plus aspirin and who have not benefited from or cannot tolerate corticosteroid therapy, current guidelines support the use of alternative immunosuppressive therapy with azathioprine or cyclophosphamide. However, these third-line agents are not indicated in this patient who has yet to be treated with colchicine and aspirin.

Chest CT is useful for assessment of pericardial thickness when constrictive pericarditis is suspected on the basis of right heart failure (jugular venous distention, pedal edema, hepatic congestion). This patient has no such findings, and chest CT is not required.

In patients with acute or recurrent pericarditis, pericardiectomy does not prevent recurrent disease and is only indicated in patients who develop constrictive pericarditis.

Corticosteroids should generally be avoided for both acute and recurrent pericarditis because they increase the risk for recurrences. Prednisone is indicated in selected patients with recurrent pericarditis, such as those with pericarditis related to connective tissue disease and those with pericarditis refractory to colchicine and NSAIDs.

KEY POINT

- Colchicine plus aspirin is the first-line treatment for recurrent pericarditis.

Bibliography
Lotrionte M, Biondi-Zoccai G, Imazio M, et al. International collaborative systematic review of controlled clinical trials on pharmacologic treatments for acute pericarditis and its recurrences. Am Heart J. 2010;160(4):662-670. [PMID: 20934560]

Item 27   Answer: C

Educational Objective: Manage left atrial myxoma in an asymptomatic patient.

The most appropriate management is surgical resection of the atrial mass. This asymptomatic young woman has a left atrial mass seen on echocardiography, which was performed to assess for the etiology of a diastolic murmur. The mass as described is characteristic of a left atrial myxoma, and accounts for the diastolic murmur by impeding blood flow through the mitral valve. Left atrial myxoma portends a

Answers and Critiques (sidebar)

high risk for systemic embolism and stroke. Myxomas should be surgically removed to avoid systemic embolic events, even in asymptomatic patients.

Catheter-based biopsy by a percutaneous approach of an intracardiac mass to establish a tissue diagnosis has been described. This approach is considered when the mass is within the right heart and is likely malignant, because it may allow for a diagnosis while circumventing a more invasive surgical approach. In this patient, the mass is classic for a left atrial myxoma. The risk of stroke associated with this location strongly argues against a catheter-based biopsy approach in this patient.

A hypercoagulable state is not suggested by the finding of the left atrial mass, which is most indicative of a myxoma, not a thrombus. Thus, factor V Leiden testing is not indicated.

Warfarin has been used for stroke prevention in patients with atrial myxoma, but its efficacy has not been determined. It is not an appropriate treatment for left atrial myxoma in patients who can safely undergo surgical resection of the tumor.

In young patients with a primary cardiac tumor, the Carney complex should be considered. This disorder is autosomal dominant and characterized by multiple tumors, which include cardiac and extracardiac myxomas, endocrine tumors, and schwannomas. Family history of such tumors is important to obtain in a young patient diagnosed with atrial myxoma.

KEY POINT

- Myxomas should be surgically removed to avoid systemic embolic events, even in asymptomatic patients.

Bibliography

Elbardissi AW, Dearani JA, Daly RC, et al. Embolic potential of cardiac tumors and outcome after resection: a case-control study. Stroke. 2009;40(1):156-162. [PMID: 18948602]

Item 28   Answer: C

Educational Objective: Evaluate a woman with atypical chest pain.

This patient should undergo exercise electrocardiography (ECG). She has several risk factors for coronary artery disease (CAD), including hypertension, hypercholesterolemia, and a family history of premature CAD. Her symptoms are not typical for angina (her chest discomfort is localized, sharp, and not reproducible with exertion), and the resting ECG is normal. In the presence of multiple risk factors and atypical symptoms, the pretest probability that CAD is the cause of her symptoms is intermediate. The results of exercise ECG testing, whether normal or abnormal, will significantly affect the posttest probability of CAD. Exercise testing is recommended as the initial test of choice in patients with an intermediate pretest probability of CAD based on age, sex, and symptoms, including patients with right

bundle branch block or less than 1-mm ST-segment depression at baseline. In addition, the results of the exercise ECG test will provide prognostic information regarding her risk of death and myocardial infarction on the basis of her exercise duration, presence or absence of angina, and the magnitude of ST-segment depression.

Coronary angiography is incorrect because this patient's pretest probability of CAD is intermediate, which is too low to warrant immediate coronary angiography as the initial diagnostic test.

Although exercise ECG testing in women has been found to have a lower specificity and higher false-positive rate compared with men, the routine use of exercise testing with echocardiography to assess left ventricular regional wall motion or perfusion imaging is not recommended for women or men in the absence of baseline ECG abnormalities. Although echocardiography increases the sensitivity of the ECG results, use of stress echocardiography as the initial test has not been found to reduce cardiovascular events compared with exercise ECG testing alone.

Pharmacologic stress testing is not indicated because this patient is physically able to exercise. Pharmacologic agents include dobutamine (which increases heart rate and myocardial contractility) or vasodilators (which cause relative increases in coronary blood flow in myocardial regions not supplied by stenotic vessels). Exercise is preferred over pharmacologic agents because of the additional diagnostic and prognostic information provided by exercise testing.

KEY POINT

- Despite having a higher false-positive rate in women, exercise electrocardiography is the recommended modality for noninvasive diagnostic testing in women who are able to exercise and have interpretable electrocardiograms.

Bibliography

Shaw LJ, Bugiardini R, Merz CN. Women and ischemic heart disease: evolving knowledge. J Am Coll Cardiol. 2009;54(17):1561-1575. [PMID: 19833255]

Item 29   Answer: C

Educational Objective: Diagnose constrictive pericarditis.

This patient most likely has constrictive pericarditis. He has worsening dyspnea and pedal edema with evidence of elevated right heart pressure on examination (jugular venous distention, hepatojugular reflux, pedal edema) with no evidence of left heart failure. A Kussmaul sign (jugular vein engorgement with inspiration) raises clinical suspicion for constrictive pericarditis. Constrictive pericarditis is evident on the basis of echocardiographic findings of restrictive filling and ventricular interdependence (that is, the diastolic filling of one ventricular chamber impeding that of the other, as may be manifested by a to-and-fro diastolic motion of the ventricular septum). Cardiac CT demonstrates pericardial thickening, further supporting this diagnosis. Constrictive pericarditis is a recognized potential complication following coronary artery bypass surgery.

Restrictive cardiomyopathy from cardiac amyloidosis could result in dyspnea, right-sided heart failure, restrictive ventricular filling, and increased wall thickness. However, left ventricular hypertrophy and ventricular interdependence would be unusual findings in cardiac amyloidosis.

Although cardiac tamponade could account for dyspnea and jugular venous distention, it is an unlikely diagnosis in this patient. Pulsus paradoxus greater than 10 mm Hg, a typical finding in cardiac tamponade, is absent in this patient.

Severe tricuspid regurgitation could account for dyspnea and pedal edema and findings of elevated right heart pressure on physical examination, as seen in this patient. Although a holosystolic murmur is commonly heard, a murmur may be absent with severe tricuspid regurgitation. However, tricuspid regurgitation would be evident on echocardiography.

> **KEY POINT**
> - Dyspnea, pedal edema, clear lung fields, and jugular vein engorgement with inspiration raise clinical suspicion for constrictive pericarditis.

Bibliography
Ahsan SY, Moon JC, Hayward MP, Chow AW, Lambiase PD. Constrictive pericarditis after catheter ablation for atrial fibrillation. Circulation. 2008;118(24):e834-e835. [PMID: 19064687]

Item 30   Answer: A

Educational Objective: Treat atrial fibrillation in the setting of heart failure after a myocardial infarction.

Amiodarone is the best option for managing symptomatic atrial fibrillation in the setting of heart failure. Patients with heart failure and myocardial infarction are at an increased risk of developing atrial fibrillation. Although amiodarone has many extracardiac side effects, it is the most effective agent for preventing atrial fibrillation recurrences, and it is one of the few agents proved safe in patients with heart failure, left ventricular hypertrophy, coronary artery disease, or previous myocardial infarction. In addition, amiodarone has β-blocking properties that can help with rate control. This patient is not currently taking a β-blocker because of the cardiogenic shock, but one should be started as soon as the patient's heart failure is stabilized.

Disopyramide has negative inotropic effects, which can be detrimental to someone with reduced left ventricular function and heart failure, and is contraindicated in this setting.

Dronedarone increases mortality in patients with New York Heart Association class IV heart failure or class II or III heart failure with recent decompensation, such as this patient, and thus should not be used.

Flecainide is contraindicated after a myocardial infarction because it increases the risk of polymorphic ventricular tachycardia.

Like amiodarone, sotalol is a class III antiarrhythmic agent, but because of its more potent β-blocking effects, it should not be used in the setting of acute heart failure.

While not one of the options listed, dofetilide is another medication for prevention of atrial fibrillation in the setting of heart failure, but this agent requires careful monitoring of the QT interval.

> **KEY POINT**
> - Amiodarone is the best option for managing symptomatic atrial fibrillation in the setting of structural heart disease or heart failure.

Bibliography
Deedwania PC, Lardizabal JA. Atrial fibrillation in heart failure: a comprehensive review. Am J Med. 2010;123(3):198-204. [PMID: 20193823]

Item 31   Answer: B

Educational Objective: Treat type A acute aortic dissection.

The CT scan with intravenous contrast (shown) demonstrates a dissection plane (*arrows*) extending from the proximal aorta through the arch (AA) and into the descending aorta (DAo). This is a Stanford type A dissection, which requires emergency surgical intervention.

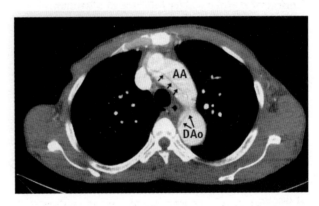

The patient has a long-standing history of a murmur associated with a documented bicuspid aortic valve. The most frequent cardiovascular finding associated with a bicuspid valve is dilation of the proximal ascending aorta, which is related to abnormalities of the aortic media. These changes in the aortic media are independent of the degree of functional stenosis of the valve and increase the risk of aneurysm formation and aortic dissection.

Abrupt onset of severe chest and back pain is typical of an acute aortic syndrome. A diastolic murmur consistent with aortic valvular insufficiency increases the clinical suspicion for a proximal aortic dissection that has disrupted normal valve leaflet coaptation. Although marked asymmetry in upper

CONT.

extremity pulses and pressures are classic findings for aortic dissection, these features were present in fewer than 10% of patients with acute dissection in the International Registry of Acute Aortic Dissection. Syncope occurs in approximately 10% of patients with an acute aortic dissection and is more commonly associated with proximal dissection. Syncope is associated with a higher coincidence of pericardial tamponade and worse in-hospital survival.

Further diagnostic imaging with coronary angiography, MRI, or transesophageal echocardiography is not necessary and would only delay critically necessary surgical repair.

There is no accepted role for endovascular treatment of an acute type A aortic dissection.

In patients with an acute aortic dissection involving the aortic valve, an intra-aortic balloon pump is contraindicated because inflation of the balloon in diastole will worsen the severity of the associated aortic regurgitation.

KEY POINT

- A dissection originating within the ascending aorta or aortic arch (Stanford type A) is a surgical emergency.

Bibliography

Siu SC, Silversides CK. Bicuspid aortic valve disease. J Am Coll Cardiol. 2010;55(25):2789-2800. [PMID: 20579534]

Item 32   Answer: A

Educational Objective: Manage secondary prevention of coronary artery disease in a woman.

The addition of a statin would offer this patient the greatest reduction of cardiovascular risk. This patient is a postmenopausal, overweight woman with asymptomatic coronary artery disease (CAD), hypercholesterolemia, and diabetes mellitus. Women presenting with CAD at a younger age are more likely than men to have diabetes, as does this patient, or smoke, increasing the risk of cardiovascular death. Cardiovascular risk in women with diabetes is more than tripled in comparison to women without diabetes. As in men, aggressive risk factor reduction is important for secondary prevention in women with cardiovascular disease.

Lowering LDL cholesterol levels with the use of a statin has resulted in the most significant reduction in myocardial infarction in both primary and secondary prevention trials of CAD in recent years. For the secondary prevention of CAD events, the goal LDL cholesterol level is less than 100 mg/dL (2.59 mmol/L), with an optional goal of less than 70 mg/dL (1.81 mmol/L) for patients deemed at very high risk. In general, patients who have CAD and multiple risk factors, such as this patient, or who have experienced an acute coronary syndrome are considered candidates for the more aggressive lower LDL cholesterol goal.

The addition of clopidogrel to aspirin therapy was studied in the CHARISMA randomized controlled trial, which involved patients with cardiovascular disease or multiple risk factors. The addition of clopidogrel did not significantly reduce the risk of myocardial infarction, stroke, or death from cardiovascular causes.

Coronary artery bypass grafting (CABG) has a survival benefit for patients with left main disease, three-vessel disease with left ventricular systolic dysfunction, or multivessel disease with involvement of the proximal left anterior descending coronary artery in comparison with medical therapy alone. However, CABG has not been shown to reduce the risk of myocardial infarction or death in patients with asymptomatic, single-vessel disease. Similarly, percutaneous coronary intervention has not been shown to reduce the risk of future myocardial infarction or mortality in the setting of asymptomatic or stable CAD.

KEY POINT

- As in men, aggressive risk factor reduction is important for secondary prevention in women with cardiovascular disease.

Bibliography

Boden WE, O'Rourke RA, Teo KK, et al; COURAGE Trial Research Group. Optimal medical therapy with or without PCI for stable coronary disease. N Engl J Med. 2007;356(15):1503-1516. [PMID: 17387127]

Item 33   Answer: B

Educational Objective: Choose appropriate evaluation for an arrhythmia.

The most appropriate test to perform next in this patient is 24-hour continuous ambulatory electrocardiographic (ECG) monitoring. When evaluating palpitations, it is important to capture the rhythm using ECG, continuous ambulatory ECG monitoring, an event recorder, or implantable loop recorder, depending on the frequency of the symptoms. This patient's symptoms occur daily, so 24- or 48-hour continuous ambulatory ECG monitoring is likely to capture an irregular rhythm during an episode of palpitations.

This patient describes symptoms consistent with premature ventricular contractions (PVCs). A PVC is followed by a compensatory pause, often described by patients as a "skipped beat." PVCs are often caused or made worse by agents such as caffeine, alcohol, and nicotine. For most patients (those without structural heart disease, a family history of early sudden cardiac death, or syncope), PVCs are benign, and simple reassurance is sufficient.

Electrophysiologic testing identifies patients with rhythm disorders or other symptoms such as syncope who are likely to have a sustained ventricular tachyarrhythmia or are at risk for sudden death. Invasive electrophysiologic studies can determine the mechanism underlying an arrhythmia, as well as the precise location of the origin of the arrhythmia. Electrophysiologic testing is reserved for patients who are stratified prior to testing to an intermediate-risk group for a ventricular arrhythmia or sudden death.

This patient is not at high risk for sudden cardiac death based upon her history, physical examination findings, and initial tests; therefore, invasive electrophysiologic testing is not indicated.

Event recorders are useful for symptoms that do not occur daily and record the heart rhythm only when triggered by the patient. A looping event recorder records several seconds of the rhythm prior to the device being triggered and is useful in patients with syncope who may not be able to trigger the recording device. A postsymptom event recorder is held to the chest when symptoms occur, and is useful to record symptomatic arrhythmias that persist long enough for the patient to activate the device. It does not record the onset of the arrhythmia. An implantable loop recorder is useful when symptoms are even less frequent than can be captured by an event recorder. This device is placed subcutaneously, similarly to a pacemaker, but there are no leads in the heart chambers. Recording parameters are set based on heart rate and QRS width, and the device can be interrogated noninvasively. This patient's symptoms are sufficiently frequent that 24- or 48-hour continuous ambulatory ECG monitoring is likely to capture the arrhythmia.

> **KEY POINT**
> - For patients with palpitations that occur on a daily basis, 24- or 48-hour continuous ambulatory electrocardiographic monitoring is appropriate to correlate symptoms with heart rhythm.

Bibliography
Zimetbaum P, Goldman A. Ambulatory arrhythmia monitoring: choosing the right device. Circulation. 2010;122(16):1629-1636. [PMID: 20956237]

Item 34   Answer: C
Educational Objective: Evaluate an asymptomatic heart murmur.

Transthoracic echocardiography is indicated for patients with a loud systolic murmur (≥3/6 in intensity) or any diastolic or continuous murmur. This asymptomatic patient has evidence of mitral valve prolapse by physical examination, including a systolic click (caused by prolapse of one or both mitral valve leaflets), followed by a systolic murmur due to mitral valve regurgitation. Increase in left ventricular volume or preload by squatting results in decreased severity of prolapse, with a delay in the systolic click and shorter duration of the murmur. Conversely, a reduction in left ventricular volume by standing or a Valsalva maneuver shortens the time interval between S_1 and the systolic click, prolonging the duration of valve regurgitation.

Echocardiography is the diagnostic test of choice for mitral valve prolapse as well as for quantification of mitral regurgitation severity and its sequelae (left atrial or ventricular dilation, left ventricular systolic dysfunction). In addition, in patients with severe mitral regurgitation, the pulmonary artery systolic pressure may be estimated from the tricuspid regurgitation jet velocity, if detected. These parameters help to determine whether mitral valve surgery is indicated.

Measurement of the B-type natriuretic peptide level may be useful to determine left ventricular myocardial stress in patients in whom the presence or cause of symptoms is unclear. However, this patient has no symptoms with a vigorous activity level, and transthoracic echocardiography will provide more useful clinical information for her management.

Transesophageal echocardiography is indicated in patients in whom transthoracic echocardiography is not diagnostic or adequate owing to image quality. In addition, transesophageal echocardiography may provide superior information regarding the anatomic cause or mechanism of mitral regurgitation if a surgical intervention is planned.

Continued observation annually without a diagnostic transthoracic echocardiogram is not appropriate because severe mitral regurgitation may lead to irreversible left ventricular systolic dysfunction or pulmonary hypertension even in the absence of symptoms.

> **KEY POINT**
> - Transthoracic echocardiography is indicated for patients with a loud systolic murmur (≥3/6 in intensity) or any diastolic or continuous murmur.

Bibliography
Foster E. Clinical practice. Mitral regurgitation due to degenerative mitral-valve disease. N Engl J Med. 2010;363(2):156-165. [PMID: 20647211]

Item 35   Answer: C

Educational Objective: Treat aortic stenosis with left ventricular systolic dysfunction.

This patient should undergo aortic valve replacement surgery. He has decompensated heart failure caused by severe aortic stenosis. Despite severe left ventricular systolic dysfunction, his cardiac output is preserved, and consequently, the transvalvular aortic gradient is high in the setting of severe aortic stenosis. In patients with severe valve dysfunction with symptoms or abnormal ventricular function, surgical valve repair or replacement is the only definitive intervention.

Balloon aortic valvuloplasty is indicated only for patients with severe aortic stenosis with hemodynamic compromise or deterioration as a bridge to eventual aortic valve replacement. Although this patient has heart failure symptoms, he is hemodynamically stable and has improved quickly with diuretic therapy. Balloon aortic valvuloplasty for calcific aortic stenosis results in only a small improvement in aortic valve area and has a high rate of restenosis at 6 months after the procedure.

Severe aortic stenosis complicated by decompensated heart failure and low cardiac output may benefit from intravenous nitroprusside. This patient does not have hemodynamic instability and has responded favorably to intravenous diuretic therapy.

Transcatheter aortic valve implantation (TAVI) is a novel therapy for aortic valve replacement in patients with very high predicted operative mortality. A recent randomized study of TAVI for patients with very high operative risk (approaching 50%) found improved survival at 1 year after TAVI compared with medical therapy, including balloon aortic valvuloplasty. This patient has an acceptable operative risk for aortic valve replacement and does not require TAVI.

> **KEY POINT**
> - In patients with severe valve dysfunction with symptoms or abnormal ventricular function, surgical valve repair or replacement is the only definitive intervention.

Bibliography

Bonow RO, Carabello BA, Chatterjee K, et al; American College of Cardiology/American Heart Association Task Force on Practice Guidelines. 2008 focused update incorporated into the ACC/AHA 2006 guidelines for the management of patients with valvular heart disease: a report of the American College of Cardiology/American Heart Association Task Force on Practice Guidelines (Writing Committee to revise the 1998 guidelines for the management of patients with valvular heart disease). Endorsed by the Society of Cardiovascular Anesthesiologists, Society for Cardiovascular Angiography and Interventions, and Society of Thoracic Surgeons. J Am Coll Cardiol. 2008;52(13):e1-e142. [PMID: 18848134]

Item 36   Answer: D

Educational Objective: Prescribe optimal medical therapy for severe systolic heart failure.

This patient with systolic heart failure due to peripartum cardiomyopathy should start enalapril. This patient appears euvolemic and reports New York Heart Association (NYHA) functional class III heart failure symptoms. The electrocardiogram (ECG) demonstrates normal sinus rhythm, first-degree atrioventricular block, left axis deviation, and left bundle branch block. Medical therapy for heart failure during pregnancy should include standard therapy for heart failure with β-blockers, digoxin, and diuretics, but ACE inhibitors and angiotensin receptor blockers should be excluded until after delivery. An ACE inhibitor, such as enalapril, should therefore be started. Because she has severe symptoms (NYHA class III), treatment with spironolactone is also indicated.

If this patient were receiving optimal medical therapy and euvolemic and had persistent moderate to severe symptoms, she would be eligible for cardiac resynchronization therapy, as her left ventricular ejection fraction is below 35% and her QRS interval is prolonged (>120 msec). However, her medical therapy is not optimal because she is not taking an ACE inhibitor.

Endomyocardial biopsy is generally indicated to assist in the diagnosis of suspected infiltrative or inflammatory cardiomyopathies in which a definitive diagnosis would impact treatment or prognosis, such as with amyloidosis, hemochromatosis, or sarcoidosis. The patient does not demonstrate any significant evidence such as increased ventricular wall thickness or low voltage on ECG to suggest an infiltrative cardiomyopathy, or systemic manifestations of illness, such as fever, to suggest an inflammatory cardiomyopathy.

Although, in general, it is desirable to titrate the β-blocker to target doses, increasing carvedilol in this patient would likely be limited by her relatively slow heart rate as well as significant fatigue.

> **KEY POINT**
> - Optimal medical therapy for severe systolic heart failure includes an ACE inhibitor, a β-blocker, and spironolactone.

Bibliography

Goldberg LR. Heart failure. Ann Intern Med. 2010;152(11):ITC6-1-ITC6-15. [PMID: 20513825]

Item 37   Answer: E

Educational Objective: Manage anticoagulation during the periprocedural period in a patient with paroxysmal atrial fibrillation.

For this patient with a CHADS$_2$ score of 2 (hypertension and diabetes mellitus), no periprocedural bridging is needed. Periprocedural management of anticoagulation in the setting of atrial fibrillation depends on the patient's risk of developing a thromboembolism and having an adverse bleeding event. The CHADS$_2$ score is one commonly used risk stratification tool for the perioperative period. The assessment of low, moderate, and high risk, however, is different in the perioperative period versus long-term use. For those with CHADS$_2$ scores of 0-2, who are at lowest perioperative risk, it is best to simply discontinue warfarin approximately 5 days before the procedure with no bridging agent. Alternatively, low-dose subcutaneous low-molecular-weight heparin (LMWH) can be used as a "bridge" to provide adequate anticoagulation when the INR is not in the therapeutic range. Therapeutic-dose subcutaneous LMWH or intravenous unfractionated heparin (UFH) is not recommended. Warfarin can then often be restarted 12 to 24 hours after the procedure if there is no active bleeding.

For atrial fibrillation patients with moderate risk features (CHADS$_2$ score of 3 or 4), a history of remote transient ischemic attack or stroke, or a mechanical aortic valve, management is individualized and bridging with therapeutic-dose LMWH or therapeutic dose intravenous UFH may be reasonable.

For those with high-risk features (CHADS$_2$ score of 5 or 6), a recent transient ischemic attack or stroke, a mechanical mitral valve, or rheumatic valvular disease, bridging anticoagulation with therapeutic-dose subcutaneous LMWH or therapeutic-dose intravenous UFH should be provided.

> **KEY POINT**
> - For atrial fibrillation patients at low perioperative risk for thromboembolism (CHADS$_2$ score ≤2 and no additional risk factors [mechanical valve, history of stroke or transient ischemic attack]), no bridging anticoagulation is needed.

Bibliography

Douketis JD, Berger PB, Dunn AS, et al; American College of Chest Physicians. The perioperative management of antithrombotic therapy: American College of Chest Physicians Evidence-Based Clinical Practice Guidelines (8th Edition). Chest. 2008;133(6 suppl):299S-339S. [PMID: 18574269]

Item 38   Answer: C

Educational Objective: Recognize absolute and relative contraindications to thrombolytic therapy in a patient with an ST-elevation myocardial infarction.

This patient should be given thrombolytic therapy. He has electrocardiographic changes consistent with an acute anterior ST-elevation myocardial infarction (STEMI). Therapy for patients with STEMI presenting within 12 hours of symptom onset should be either thrombolytic therapy or primary percutaneous coronary intervention (PCI). The decision to choose thrombolytic therapy versus primary PCI includes duration of symptoms, availability of PCI, presence of high-risk clinical features such as cardiogenic shock, and relative and absolute contraindications to thrombolytic therapy.

Absolute contraindications to thrombolytic therapy include any previous intracerebral hemorrhage, known cerebrovascular lesion, ischemic stroke within 3 months, suspected aortic dissection, and active bleeding or significant closed head or facial trauma within 3 months. Relative contraindications include a history of chronic, severe, poorly controlled hypertension or severe uncontrolled hypertension on presentation (systolic blood pressure >180 mm Hg or diastolic blood pressure >110 mm Hg); ischemic stroke more than 3 months ago; dementia or known intracranial pathology; traumatic or prolonged (>10 min) cardiopulmonary resuscitation or major surgery (<3 weeks); recent (within 2-4 weeks) internal bleeding; noncompressible vascular puncture site; previous exposure to streptokinase; pregnancy; active peptic ulcer disease; and current use of anticoagulants.

The use of a glycoprotein IIb/IIIa inhibitor, such as abciximab, with thrombolytic therapy is not recommended because it does not improve patient outcomes and is associated with an increased risk of bleeding, particularly in older patients.

Optimal management of patients with STEMI relies heavily upon timely recognition and rapid initiation of reperfusion therapy, either thrombolytic therapy or PCI.

Patients with an acute coronary syndrome and an electrocardiogram compatible with STEMI can be treated with reperfusion therapy without biomarker confirmation; early biomarker results may be normal in patients with STEMI, and waiting for the results of the troponin and creatine kinase levels would delay appropriate treatment.

Transfer for primary PCI is a reasonable alternative to thrombolytic therapy in the setting of absolute contraindications to thrombolytic therapy or high-risk clinical features and if an acceptable time to transfer the patient to a PCI-capable hospital can be achieved (door to balloon time of 90 minutes or less). This patient has no absolute contraindications to thrombolytic therapy and no high-risk clinical features, and the transfer time to receive primary PCI would be prolonged. Given these factors, thrombolytic therapy is the best reperfusion strategy.

> **KEY POINT**
> - In the absence of contraindications, patients with an acute ST-elevation myocardial infarction presenting to a facility not capable of performing percutaneous coronary interventions (PCI) should undergo thrombolytic therapy unless transfer to a PCI-capable facility can be accomplished to achieve a door-to-balloon time of 90 minutes or less.

Bibliography

Boden WE, Eagle K, Granger CB. Reperfusion strategies in acute ST-segment elevation myocardial infarction: a comprehensive review of contemporary management options. J Am Coll Cardiol. 2007;50(10):917-929. [PMID: 17765117]

Item 39   Answer: A

Educational Objective: Treat cardiogenic shock.

This patient has cardiogenic shock (likely from subacute myocarditis) and requires mechanical hemodynamic support with an intra-aortic balloon pump. He has low cardiac output and inadequate end-organ perfusion, as evidenced by cool extremities, decreased mental status, reduced kidney function, and elevated liver chemistry tests. He is also volume overloaded, as confirmed by invasive hemodynamic measurements (elevated right atrial and pulmonary capillary wedge pressures). The next appropriate intervention for hemodynamic support is an intra-aortic balloon pump, which will further reduce afterload and thus improve cardiac output.

Conivaptan is a vasopressin receptor antagonist used to treat euvolemic or hypervolemic hyponatremia. Although this patient does have hyponatremia, it is not severe, it is likely a result of the patient's severely decompensated heart failure, and it will likely correct with treatment of the patient's cardiogenic shock with hemodynamic support.

This patient's invasive hemodynamic measurements indicate that he is volume overloaded (elevated right atrial and pulmonary capillary wedge pressures) and has moderately reduced cardiac output even with high-dose dobutamine

CONT.

infusion. Although he eventually will require diuresis, it would not be appropriate to initiate diuresis at this time given his cardiogenic shock; thus, intravenous furosemide would not be an appropriate next step in management. Diuresis at this point would likely worsen his severe hypotension. The appropriate approach would be to first correct his hypotension (with intravenous vasoactive medications, and, if not effective, an intra-aortic balloon pump, as in this case) before initiating diuresis.

Nesiritide is a pure vasodilator with natriuretic and diuretic effects and without inotropic or vasopressor effects. In the setting of systemic hypotension, additional vasodilation would not be appropriate therapy and would likely worsen systemic hypotension.

> **KEY POINT**
> • Mechanical hemodynamic support should be considered in patients with cardiogenic shock that does not improve with inotropic agents.

Bibliography
Reynolds HR, Hochman JS. Cardiogenic shock: current concepts and improving outcomes. Circulation. 2008;117(5):686-697. [PMID: 18250279]

Item 40   Answer: B

Educational Objective: Select the most appropriate test for evaluating late cardiovascular complications of cancer treatment.

This patient should undergo exercise electrocardiographic (ECG) stress testing. Because of his history of Hodgkin lymphoma treated with chemotherapeutic and radiation regimens, there are multiple potential contributing factors to dyspnea present, including systolic and diastolic dysfunction, restrictive cardiomyopathy, radiation valve disease, and coronary artery disease (CAD). Of the options listed, exercise ECG stress testing would provide the most diagnostic benefit given that revascularization may relieve symptoms if ischemia due to a critical blockage is identified. CAD secondary to radiation exposure is classically proximal, most commonly affecting the left anterior descending coronary artery owing to its relatively anterior position and course in the heart.

The risk of fatal myocardial infarction in survivors of Hodgkin lymphoma is up to 7-fold greater than the general population and persists beyond 20 years after completion of treatment for Hodgkin lymphoma. Other common late cardiovascular complications, which often arise 10 to 20 years after the original treatment, include valve disorders, diastolic dysfunction, restrictive cardiomyopathy, and pericardial constriction. Increased risk for all cardiovascular complications is attributed to both the use of mediastinal radiation and exposure to potentially cardiotoxic chemotherapeutic regimens.

Cardiac CT is helpful in evaluating pericardial constriction by visualizing pericardial thickness. This patient's clinical examination is not consistent with pericardial constriction

given the absence of a Kussmaul sign (increase in jugular venous pressure with inspiration), absence of signs of right-sided heart failure, and normal central venous pressure by physical examination and echocardiography (normal inferior vena cava diameter with inspiratory collapse).

Right heart catheterization is a helpful tool in diagnosing pericardial constriction in patients with compatible physical examination findings, which are not present in this patient. During right heart catheterization, pericardial constriction would be suggested with equalization of diastolic pressures in the pulmonary artery and cardiac chambers. Additional right heart pressure tracings suggestive of constriction include an early diastolic "dip-and-plateau" pattern and a steep *y* descent.

Late-onset valvular disease associated with mediastinal radiation is slowly progressive. In this patient, the grade 2/6 midpeaking systolic murmur heard is consistent with aortic sclerosis. However, no pathologic regurgitation or stenosis of the valve was seen by transthoracic imaging; additional transesophageal echocardiography would provide little incremental diagnostic benefit given that the valves were visualized with standard transthoracic imaging.

> **KEY POINT**
> • Common late cardiovascular complications of Hodgkin disease treatment include coronary artery disease, valve disorders, diastolic dysfunction, restrictive cardiomyopathy, and pericardial constriction.

Bibliography
Ng AK. Review of the cardiac long-term effects of therapy for Hodgkin lymphoma. Br J Haematol. 2011;54(1):23-13. [PMID: 21539537]

Item 41   Answer: B

Educational Objective: Diagnose ostium primum atrial septal defect.

This patient has features of an atrial septal defect, including dyspnea, an enlarged right heart, fixed splitting of the S$_2$, and murmurs of increased right ventricular outflow as well as mitral regurgitation. The electrocardiogram demonstrates left axis deviation, first-degree atrioventricular block, and interventricular conduction delay. The combined findings of fixed splitting of the S$_2$, mitral regurgitation murmur, and left axis deviation on the electrocardiogram are most consistent with an ostium primum atrial septal defect with associated mitral cleft and mitral valve regurgitation.

Aortic coarctation may demonstrate an early systolic murmur at the second left intercostal space and occasionally a diastolic murmur. Patients with coarctation generally are hypertensive and have a pulse delay between the upper and lower extremities. The electrocardiogram would likely demonstrate left ventricular hypertrophy. The chest radiograph may demonstrate a "figure 3 sign" (shown on next page) caused by indentation of the aortic contour at

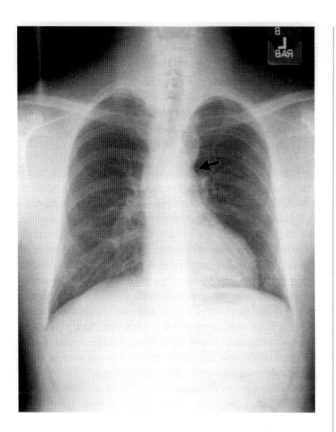

the site of coarctation with pre- and postcoarctation dilatation and rib notching, caused by collateral blood flow.

Pulmonary valve stenosis is characterized by an early systolic murmur at the second left intercostal space. The pulmonic component of the S_2 is split and the degree of splitting increases with the severity of the stenosis. There is no murmur of mitral regurgitation. The electrocardiogram in pulmonary valve stenosis demonstrates right axis deviation and right ventricular hypertrophy rather than left axis deviation.

A small perimembranous ventricular septal defect would cause a loud holosystolic murmur at the left sternal border that moves into the S_2 and is often associated with a palpable thrill. The S_2 is normal and there is no evidence of pulmonary hypertension. No electrocardiographic or chest radiographic abnormalities would be expected with a small perimembranous ventricular septal defect.

KEY POINT

- Ostium primum atrial septal defect is typically associated with a mitral regurgitation murmur and left axis deviation on the electrocardiogram.

Bibliography

Warnes CA, Williams RG, Bashore TM, et al; American College of Cardiology; American Heart Association Task Force on Practice Guidelines (Writing Committee to Develop Guidelines on the Management of Adults With Congenital Heart Disease); American Society of Echocardiography; Heart Rhythm Society; International Society for Adult Congenital Heart Disease; Society for Cardiovascular Angiography and Interventions; Society of Thoracic Surgeons. ACC/AHA 2008 guidelines for the management of adults with congenital heart disease: a report of the American College of Cardiology/American Heart Association Task Force on Practice Guidelines (Writing Committee to Develop Guidelines on the Management of Adults With Congenital Heart Disease). Developed in collaboration with the American Society of Echocardiography, Heart Rhythm Society, International Society for Adult Congenital Heart Disease, Society for Cardiovascular Angiography and Interventions, and Society of Thoracic Surgeons. J Am Coll Cardiol. 2008;52(23):e143-e263. [PMID: 19038677]

Item 42   Answer: B

Educational Objective: Manage anticoagulation for a patient with a mechanical heart valve planning elective surgery.

This patient should discontinue warfarin 3 days before his hip surgery, and restart warfarin on the evening of the surgery, provided hemostasis is maintained. Although the annual risk of a thromboembolic event in a patient with a mechanical heart valve without therapeutic anticoagulation may be as high as 20%, the short-term risk of anticoagulation discontinuation is small. In addition to valve-related characteristics, such as type of mechanical valve and its position (aortic versus mitral), other factors that increase the risk of thromboembolism include atrial fibrillation, more than one mechanical valve, left ventricular systolic dysfunction (ejection fraction <30%), a hypercoagulable state, and previous thromboembolic event, including stroke or transient ischemic attack. The current recommendation is to stop warfarin 48 to 72 hours before the procedure to reduce INR to 1.5, and restart warfarin within 24 hours after the procedure. Bridging with heparin is usually not necessary.

In patients with a mechanical valve and an increased risk of a thromboembolic event, it is recommended that unfractionated heparin is begun intravenously when INR falls below 2.0, stopped 4 to 5 hours before the procedure, and restarted as early after surgery as possible along with warfarin and continued until INR is therapeutic again. This patient does not have an increased risk for a thromboembolic event, so bridging anticoagulation is not needed.

In patients with a mechanical heart valve and therapeutic INR who require emergent surgery, reversal of anticoagulation with transfusion of fresh frozen plasma may be performed. This option is not appropriate for nonemergent surgery, however.

KEY POINT

- For patients with a mechanical valve in the aortic position and without additional risk factors, the current recommendation for periprocedural anticoagulation is to stop warfarin 48 to 72 hours before the procedure and restart it within 24 hours after the procedure; bridging with heparin is usually not necessary.

Bibliography

Bonow RO, Carabello BA, Chatterjee K, et al; American College of Cardiology/American Heart Association Task Force on Practice

Guidelines. 2008 focused update incorporated into the ACC/AHA 2006 guidelines for the management of patients with valvular heart disease: a report of the American College of Cardiology/American Heart Association Task Force on Practice Guidelines (Writing Committee to revise the 1998 guidelines for the management of patients with valvular heart disease). Endorsed by the Society of Cardiovascular Anesthesiologists, Society for Cardiovascular Angiography and Interventions, and Society of Thoracic Surgeons. J Am Coll Cardiol. 2008;52(13):e1-e142. [PMID: 18848134]

Item 43   Answer: A

Educational Objective: Manage symptomatic pulmonary valve stenosis in an adult.

This symptomatic patient with pulmonary valve stenosis meets the criteria for pulmonary balloon valvuloplasty, which carries a low risk and is highly successful. Symptomatic patients with pulmonary valve stenosis should have pulmonary balloon valvuloplasty for a peak instantaneous gradient of greater than 50 mm Hg (mean gradient >30 mm Hg) with less than moderate pulmonary valve regurgitation. For patients with severe pulmonary valve stenosis without symptoms, pulmonary balloon valvuloplasty is the treatment of choice if the pulmonary valve is pliable and the peak instantaneous pressure is greater than 60 mm Hg (mean gradient >40 mm Hg) in the absence of greater than moderate pulmonary valve regurgitation.

Pulmonary vasodilator therapy is used primarily for patients with pulmonary arterial hypertension. Although this patient does have right ventricular hypertension, the gradient across the pulmonary valve as well as the physical examination findings are consistent with pulmonary valve stenosis. Pulmonary vasodilators would not benefit this patient, and would likely be harmful.

Pulmonary valve replacement is an effective way to relieve severe pulmonary valve stenosis; however, it is reserved for patients who have a hypoplastic pulmonary annulus, subvalvular or supravalvular pulmonary stenosis, severe pulmonary valve regurgitation, or associated cardiovascular disease that mandates operative intervention. Patients who have a pliable pulmonary valve are ideally managed with pulmonary balloon valvuloplasty initially.

Observation and follow-up would not be appropriate in this patient who has symptoms, severe right ventricular hypertension, and severe right ventricular hypertrophy related to severe pulmonary valve stenosis.

KEY POINT

- **For patients with pulmonary valve stenosis requiring intervention, pulmonary balloon valvuloplasty is the preferred treatment unless the pulmonary annulus is hypoplastic or there is subvalvular or supravalvular pulmonary stenosis, severe pulmonary valve regurgitation, or associated cardiovascular disease that mandates operative intervention.**

Bibliography

Bruce CJ, Connolly HM. Right-sided valve disease deserves a little more respect. Circulation. 2009;119(20):2726-2734. [PMID: 19470901]

Item 44   Answer: D

Educational Objective: Diagnose postinfarction ventricular septal defect.

A postinfarction ventricular septal defect (VSD) is the most likely cause for this patient's condition. This patient initially presented with a delayed anterior wall ST-elevation myocardial infarction (STEMI). She then developed acute respiratory distress and is found to have a new holosystolic murmur at the left sternal border on physical examination. These findings could be consistent with either a VSD or acute ischemic mitral regurgitation. However, given the location of the murmur and its association with a thrill, a VSD is more likely. With a postinfarction VSD, shunting of oxygenated blood from the left ventricle to the right ventricle occurs. This acute volume overload to the right ventricle results in cardiogenic shock and is rapidly fatal unless emergent surgical or possibly percutaneous intervention can be performed.

An acute aortic dissection associated with a myocardial infarction is more commonly associated with an inferior wall STEMI. Physical examination findings may include asymmetric blood pressures and an early diastolic murmur of acute aortic insufficiency.

Rupture of the left ventricular free wall presents as hemopericardium with electromechanical dissociation and death. Risk factors include elderly age, female sex, first myocardial infarction, and anterior location of the infarction. The patient's loud holosystolic murmur and thrill are not compatible with a free wall rupture.

Physical examination findings of right ventricular infarction include hypotension, clear lung fields, and elevated jugular venous pulsations. It would be exceedingly unusual to develop a right ventricular infarction associated with an anterior wall infarction.

Acute ischemic mitral regurgitation is another late complication of myocardial infarction and also presents with a new holosystolic murmur. Ischemia with subsequent rupture of a papillary muscle or chordae tendineae is the most likely cause of acute ischemic mitral regurgitation and may result in a so-called "flail" mitral valve. If a pulmonary artery catheter is in place, prominent v waves may be present in the pulmonary capillary wedge pressure tracing from the increased regurgitant blood volume that travels into the left atrium. Echocardiography can accurately distinguish acute ischemic mitral regurgitation from a postinfarction VSD.

KEY POINT

- **A postinfarction ventricular septal defect is characterized by a new holosystolic murmur at the left sternal border and usually presents several days following the initial infarct.**

Bibliography

Poulsen SH, Praestholm M, Munk K, Wierup P, Egeblad H, Nielsen-Kudsk JE. Ventricular septal rupture complicating acute myocardial infarction: clinical characteristics and contemporary outcome. Ann Thorac Surg. 2008;85(5):1591-1596. [PMID: 18442545]

Item 45   Answer: B

Educational Objective: Assess cardiac risk in a younger woman.

The Reynolds risk score would provide the most accurate prediction of cardiovascular risk in this patient. Several different models are available to assess the risk of developing cardiovascular disease in patients. The most commonly used, the Framingham risk score (FRS), uses blood pressure, cholesterol, smoking status, HDL cholesterol, and age to provide a risk estimate over the next 10 years (online calculator available at http://hp2010.nhlbihin.net/atpiii/calculator.asp?usertype=prof). The FRS may be suboptimal in risk assessment in younger women, as about 90% of women are classified as low risk, and very few are classified as high risk before age 70 years. The Reynolds risk score (www.reynoldsriskscore.org) is a sex-specific tool that includes factors not present in the FRS calculation, including family history and high-sensitivity C-reactive protein. Compared with the Framingham risk score, use of the Reynolds risk score resulted in risk reclassification in about 40% of women with intermediate Framingham scores.

The QRISK2 scoring system is specifically used to predict cardiovascular risk in patients living in England and Wales. The QRISK2 includes traditional risk predictors as well as ethnicity; socioeconomic status; family history; and other conditions associated with cardiovascular disease, such as diabetes mellitus, chronic kidney disease, atrial fibrillation, and rheumatoid arthritis. The SCORE risk system was developed to provide better predictive accuracy for European patients. Risk variables include age, sex, systolic blood pressure, total cholesterol, HDL cholesterol, and cigarette smoking. A unique European aspect of SCORE is that scores were calculated for high-risk and low-risk regions of Europe. Neither the QRISK2 nor SCORE systems are validated to calculate risk for an American woman.

KEY POINT

- The Reynolds risk score is a sex-specific cardiovascular risk assessment system that is more sensitive in predicting risk in women as compared with the Framingham risk assessment system.

Bibliography

Shaw LJ, Bugiardini R, Merz CN. Women and ischemic heart disease: evolving knowledge. J Am Coll Cardiol. 2009;54(17):1561-1575. [PMID: 19833255]

Item 46   Answer: C

Educational Objective: Manage a patient with a hemodynamically stable wide-complex tachycardia.

The most appropriate treatment for this patient is amiodarone. The electrocardiogram (ECG) demonstrates a regular, monomorphic wide-complex tachycardia in a left bundle branch block pattern. The differential diagnosis is supraventricular tachycardia (SVT) with aberrancy, antidromic atrioventricular (AV) reciprocating tachycardia, and ventricular tachycardia (VT). In a patient with a wide-complex tachycardia with a history of coronary artery disease or cardiomyopathy, VT should be the assumed diagnosis. The presence of AV dissociation in this ECG (shown on next page), as demonstrated by the *arrows*, confirms the diagnosis of VT. In addition, the patient has a variable S_1 as well as cannon *a* waves, which are caused by atrial contraction against a closed tricuspid valve, confirming AV dissociation. Hemodynamic stability does not rule out a diagnosis of VT.

The first-line treatment for a hemodynamically stable VT is an intravenous antiarrhythmic agent such as amiodarone. Procainamide and sotalol are also acceptable, and lidocaine can be used as a second-line agent.

Immediate cardioversion is not necessary because this patient does not have signs of instability. If an antiarrhythmic agent is not successful, an elective cardioversion with sedation can restore normal rhythm.

Adenosine may be given for a stable wide-complex rhythm to determine whether it is SVT or VT, but in this instance, the ECG and physical examination demonstrate VT.

The administration of verapamil or β-blockers is not indicated in patients with stable VT because these drugs can cause severe hemodynamic deterioration and lead to ventricular fibrillation and cardiac arrest.

This patient should be offered an implanted cardioverter-defibrillator for long-term sudden cardiac death prevention.

KEY POINT

- In a patient with a wide-complex tachycardia with a history of coronary artery disease or cardiomyopathy, ventricular tachycardia is the most likely diagnosis.

Bibliography

Neumar RW, Otto CW, Link MS, et al. Part 8: adult advanced cardiovascular life support: 2010 American Heart Association guidelines for cardiopulmonary resuscitation and emergency cardiovascular care. Circulation. 2010;122(18 suppl 3):S729-S767. [PMID: 20956224]

Item 47   Answer: C

Educational Objective: Diagnose Eisenmenger syndrome in an adult.

The physical examination, electrocardiographic, and chest radiograph findings all suggest the presence of Eisenmenger

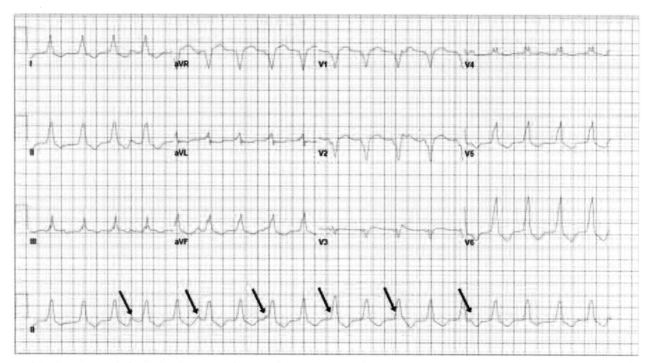

ITEM 46

syndrome. Eisenmenger syndrome is a cyanotic congenital heart disease characterized by irreversible pulmonary vascular disease due to the presence of a long-standing cardiac shunt with eventual reversal of the shunt. This diagnosis is supported by the patient's cyanosis, clubbing, evidence of right ventricular hypertrophy, and decreased pulmonary vascularity on the chest radiograph.

Approximately half of persons with Down syndrome have congenital heart disease and approximately half of these have an atrioventricular septal defect. Up to 75% of complete atrioventricular septal defects are found in persons with Down syndrome. Unoperated, patients with complete atrioventricular septal defect develop progressive pulmonary hypertension, reversal of the shunt, and, ultimately, Eisenmenger physiology with associated cyanosis and irreversible pulmonary vascular disease. Although Eisenmenger syndrome is decreasing in frequency, affected patients represent a major proportion of adults with cyanotic congenital heart disease.

Patients with aortic coarctation generally have hypertension in the upper extremities, a systolic murmur, or continuous murmur in the region of the left infraclavicular area or over the left back. Lower extremity pulses are reduced and there is generally a delay between the palpated radial artery and the femoral artery pulse. The electrocardiogram in a patient with aortic coarctation usually demonstrates left ventricular hypertrophy. The chest radiograph demonstrates a "figure 3 sign" in the region of aortic narrowing and rib notching due to collateral blood flow.

Patients with Ebstein anomaly characteristically have variable degrees of right heart enlargement and features of severe tricuspid valve regurgitation. Cyanosis can result from a right-to-left shunt at the atrial level in patients with an atrial septal defect or a patent foramen ovale and severe tricuspid valve regurgitation. The characteristic electrocardiogram in Ebstein anomaly demonstrates very tall and peaked "Himalayan" P waves. The QRS duration is usually prolonged; a right bundle branch block pattern and preexcitation may be present. The chest radiograph shows right heart enlargement with a globular cardiac contour and clear lung fields. The pulmonary arteries generally appear small.

Patients with unoperated tetralogy of Fallot may present with features of cyanosis and clubbing. However, a patient with unrepaired tetralogy of Fallot will have a loud systolic murmur due to severe right ventricular outflow tract obstruction. The absence of a loud systolic murmur makes this diagnosis unlikely in this patient.

KEY POINT

- Eisenmenger syndrome is a cyanotic congenital heart disease characterized by irreversible pulmonary vascular disease caused by a long-standing cardiac shunt with eventual reversal of the shunt.

Bibliography

Dimopoulos K, Inuzuka R, Goletto S, et al. Improved survival among patients with Eisenmenger syndrome receiving advanced therapy for pulmonary arterial hypertension. Circulation. 2010;121(1):20-25. [PMID: 20026774]

Item 48   Answer: A

Educational Objective: Identify importance of individual risk factors in the risk of acute myocardial infarction.

In this patient, her status as a current smoker is her greatest contributor of risk of a cardiovascular event. She should be counseled to quit smoking and offered medication to help her do so.

The INTERHEART study assessed the prevalence of nine potentially modifiable risk factors in more than 15,000 patients with first acute myocardial infarction (MI) and almost 15,000 asymptomatic age and sex-matched controls. Nine risk factors were strongly associated with acute MI in the 52 countries included in the trial. In descending order, these are: dyslipidemia, smoking, psychosocial stressors, diabetes mellitus, hypertension, obesity, alcohol consumption, physical inactivity, and diet low in fruits and vegetables. Results of the INTERHEART study suggest that these modifiable risk factors account for more than 90% of the risk for acute MI.

When considered on an individual basis, the two most important risk factors are smoking and dyslipidemia, accounting for about two thirds of the risk of an acute MI. Cigarette smoking results in a two- to threefold increased risk of dying of cardiovascular disease, but most of the cardiovascular risk from smoking decreases within the first 2 years after quitting. Smoking showed a graded relation with the odds of acute MI without a threshold or plateau. Thus, smoking even five cigarettes a day increases risk. Although there is no "safe" level of smoking, reducing the number of cigarettes smoked daily may reduce cardiovascular risk if quitting entirely is not possible.

> **KEY POINT**
> - The two risk factors most strongly associated with myocardial infarction are dyslipidemia and cigarette smoking.

Bibliography

Yusuf S, Hawken S, Ounpuu S, et al; INTERHEART Study Investigators. Effect of potentially modifiable risk factors associated with myocardial infarction in 52 countries (the INTERHEART Study): case-control study. Lancet. 2004;364(9438):937-952. [PMID: 15364185]

Item 49   Answer: C

Educational Objective: Provide appropriate anticoagulation during pregnancy in a woman with a mechanical prosthetic valve.

This patient should receive warfarin, with a goal INR between 2.5 and 3.5. She has a mechanical mitral valve and requires full anticoagulation. The only anticoagulation regimen listed that provides full anticoagulation coverage is warfarin.

Pregnant women with mechanical valve prostheses have an increased risk of valve thrombosis, bleeding, and fetal risk. The optimal anticoagulation regimen for this high-risk subset of patients has not been determined, and current guidelines conclude that unfractionated heparin, low-molecular-weight heparin (LMWH), or warfarin may be used. Warfarin anticoagulation during pregnancy poses an increased fetal risk, with possible teratogenicity, miscarriage, and fetal loss due to intracranial hemorrhage. Warfarin, however, may be the safest agent to prevent prosthetic valve thrombosis in the mother. LMWH and unfractionated heparin are safer for the fetus; however, these therapies increase maternal risk by increasing the risk of prosthetic valve thrombosis.

Aspirin, 325 mg/d, alone is not adequate thromboembolic prophylaxis for a patient with a mechanical mitral valve prosthesis. In addition, there is concern about the use of 325 mg/d of aspirin during pregnancy owing to the risk of premature duct closure (ductus arteriosus) in the fetus. It would be reasonable to add aspirin, 81 mg/d, to therapeutic warfarin in this patient for thromboembolic prophylaxis.

Clopidogrel, 75 mg/d, does not provide adequate thromboembolic prophylaxis for a patient with a mechanical mitral valve prosthesis. In addition, it has not been confirmed that clopidogrel is safe to use during pregnancy.

Unfractionated heparin can be safely used during pregnancy; however, a dose of 5000 units subcutaneously twice daily is not adequate to provide full anticoagulation and thus this treatment option is also not appropriate. When unfractionated heparin is used, the target activated partial thromboplastin time is at least two times control.

> **KEY POINT**
> - Current guidelines recommend unfractionated heparin, low-molecular-weight heparin, or warfarin for pregnant women with mechanical valve prostheses.

Bibliography

Bonow RO, Carabello BA, Chatterjee K, et al; American College of Cardiology/American Heart Association Task Force on Practice Guidelines. 2008 focused update incorporated into the ACC/AHA 2006 guidelines for the management of patients with valvular heart disease: a report of the American College of Cardiology/American Heart Association Task Force on Practice Guidelines (Writing Committee to revise the 1998 guidelines for the management of patients with valvular heart disease). Endorsed by the Society of Cardiovascular Anesthesiologists, Society for Cardiovascular Angiography and Interventions, and Society of Thoracic Surgeons. J Am Coll Cardiol. 2008;52(13):e1-e142. [PMID: 18848134]

Item 50   Answer: A

Educational Objective: Evaluate acute chest pain.

A CT scan of the chest should be obtained. A prudent approach to patients with acute chest pain focuses the initial evaluation on six potentially lethal conditions (the "serious six"): acute coronary syndrome, pericarditis with tamponade, pulmonary embolism, pneumothorax, aortic dissection, and esophageal rupture. Physicians must rapidly

CONT.

evaluate patients and exclude each of these conditions to initiate appropriate therapy. In this patient with acute-onset chest pain that began at rest, upper extremity blood pressures are asymmetric, there is an early diastolic murmur consistent with aortic regurgitation, and the electrocardiogram (ECG) shows no ST-segment elevation. The chest radiograph shows a widened superior mediastinum and a right pleural effusion. These findings are consistent with an acute aortic dissection. The right pleural effusion is most likely a hemothorax from the acute aortic dissection. CT of the chest would be the most efficient means to establish the diagnosis prior to proceeding to emergent surgery.

Posterior ECG leads (V_7 through V_9) can be useful in the diagnosis of an isolated posterior wall ST-elevation myocardial infarction (STEMI). An isolated posterior wall STEMI accounts for approximately 7% of all STEMIs and should be considered in patients presenting with anginal chest pain and nonspecific findings on a standard 12-lead ECG. Given that the duration of the patient's chest pain is 40 minutes, however, the normal myoglobin and troponin I levels argue against an acute coronary syndrome as a cause for the symptoms.

For a patient with a presumed ascending aortic dissection, imaging of the proximal ascending aorta can be difficult and, therefore, transthoracic echocardiography is not the imaging method of choice. In contrast, transesophageal echocardiography has high diagnostic accuracy for an ascending aortic dissection and, in some medical centers, is the imaging method of choice in unstable patients for whom transportation to the CT or MRI scanner may not be safe.

Although this patient's description of chest pain could be consistent with a pulmonary embolism, this diagnosis cannot explain the discrepant arm blood pressures or diastolic murmur; therefore, ventilation-perfusion scanning is not the most appropriate test.

KEY POINT

- In a patient presenting with acute chest pain, the life-threatening diagnoses of pulmonary embolism, acute aortic dissection, acute coronary syndrome, pericardial tamponade, pneumothorax, and esophageal rupture must be rapidly evaluated for and excluded.

Bibliography

Shiga T, Wajima Z, Apfel CC, Inoue T, Ohe Y. Diagnostic accuracy of transesophageal echocardiography, helical computed tomography, and magnetic resonance imaging for suspected thoracic aortic dissection: systematic review and meta-analysis. Arch Intern Med. 2006;166(13):1350-1356. [PMID: 16831999]

Item 51   Answer: C

Educational Objective: Diagnose hypertrophic cardiomyopathy.

The most likely diagnosis is hypertrophic cardiomyopathy. The cardiac examination is consistent with a dynamic left ventricular outflow tract obstruction, whereby the systolic murmur is accentuated during maneuvers that decrease preload (Valsalva maneuver) but attenuated by increasing afterload (hand-grip maneuver). Echocardiographic findings confirm left ventricular outflow tract obstruction and asymmetric septal hypertrophy consistent with hypertrophic cardiomyopathy.

The echocardiographic features in hypertrophic cardiomyopathy are diverse and include left ventricular hypertrophy, which may disproportionately involve the septal, anterior, lateral, or apical walls or may be concentric (particularly if marked). Dynamic left ventricular outflow tract or mid-cavity obstruction is a feature of hypertrophic cardiomyopathy, but it is not always seen nor is it a necessary finding to confirm the diagnosis. Additional echocardiographic features include a small left ventricular cavity size and significant left atrial enlargement. Although patients with hypertrophic cardiomyopathy may present with symptoms such as dyspnea, chest pain, or dizziness, many are asymptomatic.

This patient is a weight lifter, a known cause of concentric left ventricular hypertrophy (athlete's heart). Echocardiography is often useful in differentiating left ventricular hypertrophy associated with hypertrophic cardiomyopathy from that of athlete's heart. Marked hypertrophy with a small left ventricular cavity is typical of hypertrophic cardiomyopathy, whereas the cavity is often enlarged in athlete's heart. In addition, marked left atrial enlargement and diastolic dysfunction are not typical features of athlete's heart.

Dilated cardiomyopathy is easily excluded on the basis of echocardiography, which does not show an enlarged left ventricle with systolic dysfunction (ejection fraction <40%), as would be expected for this diagnosis.

Left ventricular hypertrophy, left atrial enlargement, and impaired early diastolic filling seen on the echocardiogram in this patient could be potentially explained by a hypertensive cardiomyopathy. However, a long-standing history of hypertension would need to be present. In addition, hypertensive cardiomyopathy cannot explain the patient's systolic murmur that increases in intensity with a Valsalva maneuver.

Restrictive cardiomyopathy could explain left ventricular hypertrophy. However, an accentuated rate of early diastolic filling (restrictive filling) is characteristic of this entity, and not impaired early filling, as is present in this patient. Lack of this pattern of filling virtually excludes restrictive cardiomyopathy.

KEY POINT

- Hypertrophic cardiomyopathy is characterized by a dynamic left ventricular outflow tract obstruction evidenced by a systolic murmur that is accentuated during maneuvers that decrease preload (Valsalva maneuver) but attenuated by increasing afterload (hand-grip maneuver).

Bibliography

Watkins H, Ashrafian H, Redwood C. Inherited cardiomyopathies. N Engl J Med. 2011;364(17):1643-1656. [PMID: 21524215]

Item 52   Answer: A

Educational Objective: Manage thromboembolic risk after atrial fibrillation ablation.

Warfarin should be continued in this patient. For the first 2 to 3 months after an atrial fibrillation ablation, all patients should take warfarin. The best management strategy thereafter is to provide anticoagulation as if the ablation did not occur, using a tool such as the $CHADS_2$ score to risk stratify. Although the patient has had no symptoms of atrial fibrillation since his ablation procedure, patients may have either asymptomatic episodes or a symptomatic recurrence of atrial fibrillation after the ablation and can be at risk for stroke. This patient has hypertension and diabetes mellitus and, with a $CHADS_2$ score of two, has a 4.0% risk of stroke per year. Even though his blood pressure is currently controlled, he is taking blood pressure–lowering agents and has a history of hypertension.

Switching to aspirin or clopidogrel does not provide the same protective benefit, and it is not appropriate to discontinue all anticoagulation. If the $CHADS_2$ score is zero, aspirin alone is the preferred agent. If the $CHADS_2$ score is one, either aspirin or warfarin is acceptable. If a patient is unable take warfarin, aspirin and clopidogrel provide a greater stroke reduction than aspirin alone, but this combination is less effective for stroke reduction than warfarin and carries a higher bleeding risk. New agents such as dabigatran and rivaroxaban may also be an option; however, they have not been studied in the post–atrial fibrillation ablation setting.

> **KEY POINT**
>
> - Following atrial fibrillation ablation, anticoagulation should continue for 2 to 3 months; thereafter, anticoagulation should be guided by risk stratification ($CHADS_2$ score).

Bibliography

Chowdhury P, Lewis WR, Schweikert RA, Cummings JE. Ablation of atrial fibrillation: what can we tell our patients? Cleve Clin J Med. 2009;76(9):543-550. [PMID: 19726559]

Item 53   Answer: B

Educational Objective: Diagnose cholesterol embolization syndrome.

The patient most likely has cholesterol embolization syndrome. This syndrome may present as a systemic illness, with fever, elevated leukocyte count and erythrocyte sedimentation rate, and with constitutional symptoms of fatigue and generalized muscle soreness. Patients may develop a red-purple to blue discoloration of the toes (seen in image) along with livedo reticularis, a lace-like purplish discoloration of the skin (not well visualized in the image). This patient has atherosclerotic disease documented by cardiac catheterization. Following cardiac catheterization, the patient developed pain and discoloration in the left toes, acute kidney injury, low-grade fever, elevated erythrocyte sedimentation rate, and leukocytosis with marked eosinophilia. These features are consistent with the cholesterol embolization syndrome.

Embolization of cholesterol crystals may occur spontaneously in patients with severe atherosclerotic disease or following endovascular manipulation. Embolization involves small arterioles and capillary beds, and large vessel pulses are generally not impaired by the process. Toe involvement may progress to necrosis and eschar with tissue loss. Acute kidney failure may occur with significant embolization to the kidneys.

Treatment of the cholesterol embolization syndrome is primarily supportive. Anecdotal reports have suggested a possible role for LDL apheresis, iloprost, or corticosteroids. These therapies have not been evaluated in humans in a randomized fashion or in an animal model, however, and cannot be advocated for generalized use.

Acute interstitial nephritis can result in acute kidney injury and eosinophiluria, which is best detected by Hansel stain. Acute interstitial nephritis is usually caused by a hypersensitivity reaction to a medication, most commonly β-lactam antibiotics and proton pump inhibitors; certain infections; and autoimmune conditions. Contrast-induced nephropathy is not associated with a systemic reaction such as that seen in this patient or with a painful discoloration of the toes. Similarly, a delayed hypersensitivity reaction would not cause a localized distal digital reaction.

> **KEY POINT**
>
> - Signs of cholesterol embolization syndrome include a red-purple to blue discoloration of toes, livedo reticularis, and signs of systemic illness, including elevated leukocyte count and erythrocyte sedimentation rate.

Bibliography

Kronzon I, Saric M. Cholesterol embolization syndrome. Circulation. 2010;122(6):631-641. [PMID: 20697039]

Item 54   Answer: A

Educational Objective: Treat nonischemic cardiomyopathy with device therapy.

This patient is a candidate for cardiac resynchronization therapy with a biventricular pacemaker combined with an implantable cardioverter-defibrillator (ICD). In patients with left ventricular ejection fraction of 35% or below, New York Heart Association (NYHA) functional class III or IV heart failure, a QRS interval of 120 msec or greater, and on optimal heart failure medications, a biventricular pacemaker, typically combined with an ICD, can lead to an increase in exercise capacity and 6-minute walk test with a decrease in mortality, heart failure symptoms, and heart failure hospitalizations, in about two thirds of patients. There may be improvements in left ventricular remodeling, with a decrease in left ventricular size and an increase in ejection fraction. Most patients who qualify for biventricular pacing also meet the criteria for an ICD to reduce the risk of sudden cardiac death and would therefore receive a combined device. Biventricular devices are thought to improve left ventricular dyssynchrony by coordinating contraction between the septal and lateral walls, with the greatest improvement in those with left bundle branch block pattern, QRS interval greater than or equal to 150 msec, and normal sinus rhythm. In addition, recent trials have suggested a benefit in patients with NYHA class I or II heart failure and ischemic cardiomyopathy or NYHA class II heart failure and nonischemic cardiomyopathy with left bundle branch block, QRS interval greater than or equal to 150 msec, and ejection fraction 30% or below.

A single- or dual-chamber ICD or dual-chamber pacemaker would not provide the hemodynamic benefit of biventricular pacing and could be harmful if there is excessive right ventricular–only pacing. In addition, a dual-chamber pacemaker is not appropriate for this patient because she meets criteria for an ICD for primary prevention of sudden cardiac death.

KEY POINT

- Cardiac resynchronization therapy can improve function and reduce mortality in patients on optimal heart failure medications with left ventricular ejection fraction of 35% or below, New York Heart Association functional class III or IV heart failure, and a QRS interval of 120 msec or greater.

Bibliography

Al-Majed NS, McAlister FA, Bakal JA, Ezekowitz JA. Meta-analysis: cardiac resynchronization therapy for patients with less symptomatic heart failure. Ann Intern Med. 2011;154(6):401-412. [PMID: 21320922]

Item 55   Answer: B

Educational Objective: Provide appropriate management of an adult with repaired tetralogy of Fallot.

This patient should undergo pulmonary valve replacement, tricuspid valve repair, and a maze procedure. The patient presents with symptomatic atrial fibrillation. This is related to long-standing severe pulmonary valve regurgitation and is the most common postoperative problem after tetralogy of Fallot repair due to placement of a patch across the right ventricular outflow tract. Pulmonary valve regurgitation is well tolerated for many years, but it eventually results in right-sided cardiac chamber enlargement, right ventricular dysfunction, tricuspid valve annulus dilatation, and tricuspid regurgitation. Atrial fibrillation is a common initial presenting symptom due to progressive dilatation of the right atrium. Surgical maze procedures to cure atrial fibrillation have been quite successful but require cardiopulmonary

bypass and are usually performed in concert with other cardiac surgical procedures.

Cardioversion with anticoagulation and amiodarone is not sufficient therapy for a tetralogy of Fallot patient with severe pulmonary and tricuspid valve regurgitation, severe right-sided cardiac chamber enlargement, and atrial fibrillation. Recurrent atrial fibrillation and progressive right-sided heart failure will occur if the patient does not have the pulmonary and tricuspid valve regurgitation addressed.

Radiofrequency ablation is an effective method of treatment for atrial fibrillation; however, this patient has underlying structural heart disease that has precipitated atrial fibrillation, which must be treated before considering radiofrequency ablation.

Cardiac transplantation is rarely required in a patient with repaired tetralogy of Fallot. Transplantation should be considered only if the patient has progressive severe symptoms of biventricular dysfunction that cannot be appropriately treated with other modalities.

KEY POINT

- Patients with repaired tetralogy of Fallot frequently develop pulmonary valve regurgitation, which leads to right-sided heart enlargement, tricuspid valve regurgitation, and atrial fibrillation.

Bibliography

Ammash NM, Dearani JA, Burkhart HM, Connolly HM. Pulmonary regurgitation after tetralogy of Fallot repair: clinical features, sequelae, and timing of pulmonary valve replacement. Congenit Heart Dis. 2007;2(6):386-403. [PMID: 18377431]

Item 56   Answer: C

Educational Objective: Treat an asymptomatic patient with an elevated risk for cardiovascular disease.

This patient would benefit from the addition of both aspirin and rosuvastatin to reduce his risk of a cardiovascular event.

The American Heart Association (AHA) and the Centers for Disease Control and Prevention (CDC) do not recommend routine high-sensitivity C-reactive protein (hsCRP) measurement. It may help to guide primary preventive interventions in patients with an intermediate (10%-20%) risk of future cardiovascular events based on the Framingham risk score. Measurement of hsCRP has been found to reclassify up to 30% of patients at intermediate risk as either low or high risk. This patient has an intermediate risk of a coronary event based on his Framingham score.

This patient would also benefit from rosuvastatin given that his hsCRP level is elevated in the setting of an LDL cholesterol level of below 130 mg/dL (3.37 mmol/L) based on recent findings from the JUPITER trial. The JUPITER trial found that apparently healthy individuals with an elevated CRP (defined as >0.2 mg/dL [2.0 mg/L] in JUPITER trial; >0.3 mg/dL [3.0 mg/L] in joint

AHA/CDC guidelines) and LDL cholesterol level of less than 130 mg/dL (3.37 mmol/L, approximately normal range) had reduced cardiovascular events if they received rosuvastatin compared with placebo over a mean follow-up period of 1.9 years.

Multiple randomized studies of antioxidant therapies, including vitamin E, vitamin C, folic acid, and β-carotene, in patients after myocardial infarction or at high risk of cardiovascular disease, have found no benefit for lowering the risk of cardiovascular disease morbidity or mortality. Therefore, the use of these supplements for the prevention of cardiovascular disease is not recommended.

KEY POINT

- Measurement of high-sensitivity C-reactive protein in persons at intermediate risk for a cardiovascular event (10%-20% risk over 10 years) has been found to reclassify up to 30% of patients at intermediate risk as either low or high risk.

Bibliography

Ridker PM, Danielson E, Fonseca FA, et al; JUPITER Study Group. Rosuvastatin to prevent vascular events in men and women with elevated C-reactive protein. N Engl J Med. 2008;359(21):2195-2207. [PMID: 18997196]

Item 57   Answer: B

Educational Objective: Treat unstable angina in a patient with contraindications to β-blockers.

Diltiazem should be added to this patient's therapeutic regimen. He has acute-onset chest pain, normal cardiac biomarkers, and T-wave inversions on the electrocardiogram. These findings are consistent with unstable angina. Although β-blockers are first-line therapy for patients with unstable angina, this patient has a contraindication because of bilateral wheezing consistent with active asthma. Absolute contraindications to β-blockers include symptomatic bradycardia, advanced atrioventricular block, systolic blood pressure below 80 mm Hg, cardiogenic shock, pulmonary edema, and symptomatic reactive airways disease. β-Blockers can be used in patients with mild pulmonary disease. Patients with a transient contraindication to β-blockers should be reevaluated for use at a later time. When β-blockers are contraindicated for the treatment of unstable angina, calcium channel blockers should be considered. Diltiazem is a calcium channel blocker with effective antianginal properties that should be used as first-line therapy in patients with contraindications to β-blockers.

Carvedilol is a β-blocker with both α- and β-blocker effects. Recent acute myocardial infarction trials found a benefit of carvedilol compared with standard therapy (aspirin, ACE inhibitors, and revascularization with either thrombolytic therapy or primary angioplasty) with a reduction in mortality, recurrent myocardial infarction, and heart failure. This patient has contraindications to β-blockers, however, including carvedilol.

Nifedipine is a calcium channel blocker that causes an increase in heart rate, and therefore myocardial oxygen demand, and is contraindicated in patients with an acute coronary syndrome.

KEY POINT

- Diltiazem is first-line therapy in patients with unstable angina who have contraindications to β-blockers.

Bibliography

Mehta RH, Bossone E, Eagle KA. Current concepts in secondary prevention after acute myocardial infarction. Herz. 2000;25(1):47-60. [PMID: 10713909]

Item 58   Answer: B

Educational Objective: Treat volume overload in a patient with chronic kidney disease.

This patient should receive intravenous bumetanide. Although in many clinical circumstances diuresis would not be appropriate treatment for acute kidney injury, this patient has acute-on-chronic kidney disease caused by kidney congestion in the setting of systolic heart failure with volume overload, and he should be treated with intravenous diuretics for volume reduction.

Glomerular filtration rate correlates inversely with central venous pressure, and the presence of elevated central venous pressure on examination is associated with poorer prognosis in heart failure. Successful diuresis in this patient would be expected to result in an improvement in creatinine level. Some patients who have extremely poor kidney function at baseline may not tolerate diuresis, and may need dialysis.

Anemia is common in the setting of heart failure and chronic kidney disease. Although this patient's hemoglobin level is slightly lower than his usual baseline range, it is not so low as to suggest significant blood loss as an acute problem. The slightly lower value may be related to hemodilution due to volume overload. Because this patient is clinically volume overloaded, additional volume via blood transfusion may worsen his acute heart and kidney failure.

In many patients with decompensated heart failure with acute kidney injury, the acute rise in creatinine is primarily due to hypoperfusion. In this patient, however, the blood pressure is not low and does not suggest a low-output state. Therefore, milrinone to augment inotropy would not be the best initial management.

Several studies of low-dose dopamine in critically ill patients and patients with (or at risk for) acute kidney injury have not shown clinical benefits such as reduced mortality or need for dialysis. At low doses, dopamine does not have any appreciable inotropic effect; at higher doses, dopamine has inotropic and vasoconstrictive effects, neither of which would be helpful for this patient's clinical situation.

KEY POINT

- Initial therapy for patients with acute decompensated heart failure and volume overload is diuresis with an intravenous loop diuretic.

Bibliography

Bock JS, Gottlieb SS. Cardiorenal syndrome: new perspectives. Circulation. 2010;121(23):2592-2600. [PMID: 20547939]

Item 59   Answer: A

Educational Objective: Diagnose an acute supraventricular tachycardia.

This patient's arrhythmia is atrial tachycardia. Adenosine, if pushed rapidly through an intravenous line, can be used to diagnose and treat supraventricular tachycardias. Up to 95% of reentrant atrioventricular (AV) node–dependent tachycardias, such as AV nodal reentrant tachycardia (AVNRT) and AV reciprocating tachycardia (AVRT), will terminate with adenosine if administered properly. Adenosine transiently blocks AV nodal conduction, interrupting the reentrant circuit and terminating the AV node–dependent arrhythmia. Therefore, these diagnoses are unlikely in this patient in whom adenosine failed to terminate the tachycardia. Adenosine given in the presence of other supraventricular arrhythmias, including atrial tachycardia, should only slow the ventricular rate or have no effect. In the presence of atrial tachycardia, P waves can be seen in the absence of QRS complexes owing to adenosine-induced AV block, as is seen in the electrocardiogram in this patient (shown, *arrows*).

Long-term management for this patient with atrial tachycardia starts with a β-blocker or calcium channel blocker. If these are unsuccessful, a class IC or III antiarrhythmic agent can be substituted. Catheter ablation of atrial tachycardia is also an option but has a slightly lower success rate than for AVNRT or AVRT, often because there are multiple atrial tachycardia foci.

KEY POINT

- Adenosine can be used to diagnose supraventricular tachycardias by transiently blocking atrioventricular (AV) nodal conduction and interrupting the reentrant circuit, thereby terminating AV nodal reentrant tachycardia and AV reciprocating tachycardia but not other supraventricular arrhythmias.

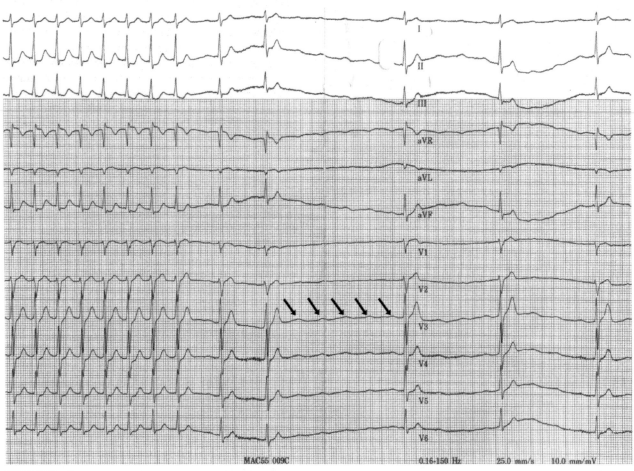

ITEM 59

MAC55 009C   0.16-150 Hz   25.0 mm/s   10.0 mm/mV

Bibliography

Colucci RA, Silver MJ, Shubrook J. Common types of supraventricular tachycardia: diagnosis and management. Am Fam Physician. 2010;82(8):942-952. [PMID: 20949888]

Item 60   Answer: B

Educational Objective: Use exercise ankle-brachial index testing to evaluate bilateral leg pain.

The most appropriate diagnostic test for this patient is to obtain an exercise ankle-brachial index (ABI). The patient has risk factors for peripheral vascular disease, including age, previous cigarette use, hypertension, and hyperlipidemia. The diminished peripheral pulses and secondary findings of hair loss and shiny skin are consistent with a diagnosis of peripheral arterial disease (PAD). The resting ABI in this patient is normal. In the setting of a normal ABI, if there is a high clinical suspicion for the presence of PAD, as in this patient, exercise testing can be useful. A decrease in the ABI of 20% measured immediately following symptom-limited exercise is diagnostic of PAD.

In patients with an established diagnosis of PAD and indications for revascularization, further vascular anatomic data can be obtained noninvasively using gadolinium-enhanced magnetic resonance angiography or contrast-enhanced multi-detector CT angiography. However, these tests should be reserved as part of planning an intervention in patients who have not benefitted from medical therapy and should not be used for the diagnosis of PAD.

Patients with lumbar spinal stenosis may report bilateral leg weakness associated with walking or with prolonged standing. Nearly half of patients have absent deep tendon reflexes at the ankles, but reflexes at the knees are usually preserved, and strength is usually preserved. MRI of the lumbar spine would be the most appropriate test for assessing the presence of lumbar spinal stenosis. In this patient with a high clinical suspicion for PAD, exercise ABI testing should be performed first.

Segmental plethysmography is useful in patients with an established diagnosis of PAD to help localize the site of stenosis. In this test, blood pressures are recorded using plethysmographic cuffs placed at the upper thigh, lower thigh, calf, and ankle. A drop of systolic pressure of 20 mm Hg identifies a zone of significant disease.

KEY POINT

- In a patient with risk factors for peripheral arterial disease (PAD) but a normal or borderline resting ankle-brachial index (ABI), an exercise ABI can be helpful, with a decrease of 20% diagnostic of PAD.

Bibliography

de Liefde II, Klein J, Bax JJ, Verhagen HJ, van Domburg RT, Poldermans D. Exercise ankle brachial index adds important prognostic information on long-term out-come only in patients with a normal resting ankle brachial index. Atherosclerosis. 2011;216(2):365-369. [PMID: 21397231]

Item 61   Answer: A

Educational Objective: Manage a patient with a recently placed coronary stent in need of elective noncardiac surgery.

This patient's elective gallbladder surgery should be postponed for 6 months. Following placement of a drug-eluting coronary stent, aspirin and clopidogrel therapy must be continued without interruption for at least 1 year. For bare metal coronary stents, aspirin and clopidogrel must be continued without interruption for 4 to 6 weeks. Early cessation of antiplatelet therapy can result in stent thrombosis, which usually results in an ST-elevation myocardial infarction and can be catastrophic.

In a patient with a recently placed coronary stent who needs noncardiac surgery, the risk of discontinuing antiplatelet therapy must be weighed against the benefits of proceeding with surgery. The safest solution for this patient is to delay surgery for at least 6 months to allow a full year of dual antiplatelet therapy and complete healing of the drug-eluting stent. Although this approach reduces the probability of stent thrombosis, it does not completely eliminate it, as recent studies have documented late stent thrombosis occurring 1 to 2 years following initial stent placement and 12 months of dual antiplatelet therapy in the setting of noncardiac surgery. This is thought to occur because the perioperative period is associated with a hypercoagulable state caused by shifts in fluid status and hemodynamic alterations, conditions that may predispose to stent thrombosis.

Proceeding to elective surgery while continuing either aspirin or clopidogrel therapy or dual antiplatelet therapy would increase the risk of bleeding complications related to surgery; furthermore, it would not completely eliminate the possibility of stent thrombosis because of the hypercoagulable state associated with the perioperative period.

Use of unfractionated or low-molecular-weight heparin in the perioperative period does not prevent stent thrombosis.

KEY POINT

- In a patient with a drug-eluting coronary stent, elective noncardiac surgery should be postponed until completion of a full year of dual antiplatelet therapy.

Bibliography

Rossini R, Capodanno D, Lettieri C, et al. Prevalence, predictors, and long-term prognosis of premature discontinuation of oral antiplatelet therapy after drug eluting stent implantation. Am J Cardiol. 2011;107(2):186-194. [PMID: 21211596]

Item 62   Answer: A

Educational Objective: Manage cardiovascular risk in an older woman.

Aspirin therapy would be reasonable for this woman with several risk factors for ischemic stroke, including advanced age, hypertension, and type 2 diabetes mellitus. The Women's Health Study evaluated the efficacy of aspirin for cardiovascular risk reduction in 40,000 healthy, low-risk women. A regimen of 100-mg aspirin on alternating days decreased the risk of stroke by 17% and ischemic stroke by 24% when compared with placebo. Notably, there was no significant reduction in the risk of cardiovascular events overall, and there was an increased bleeding risk as well. In women older than 65 years, low-dose aspirin reduced the risk of stroke, myocardial infarction, and cardiovascular death. The U.S. Preventive Services Task Force recommends the use of aspirin for women 55 to 79 years of age when the potential benefit of a reduction in ischemic strokes outweighs the potential harm of an increase in gastrointestinal hemorrhage.

For patients with a history of either transient ischemic attack (TIA) or noncardioembolic ischemic stroke associated with atherosclerosis, small vessel disease, or cryptogenic causes, antiplatelet agents are recommended to reduce the risk of recurrent stroke and other cardiovascular events. Aspirin (50-325 mg/d), the combination of aspirin (50 mg) and extended-release dipyridamole (200 mg) twice daily, and clopidogrel (75 mg/d) monotherapy are all acceptable options for initial therapy. The combination of aspirin and extended-release dipyridamole is more effective than aspirin alone, and clopidogrel may be modestly more effective than aspirin alone on the basis of direct comparison trials. The addition of aspirin to clopidogrel increases the risk of hemorrhage and is not routinely recommended for patients with a history of ischemic stroke or TIA (or for primary prevention). For patients allergic to aspirin, clopidogrel is a reasonable choice. This patient is not allergic to aspirin and does not have a history of either TIA or noncardioembolic ischemic stroke; secondary prevention strategies, therefore, are not appropriate.

KEY POINT

- Aspirin is recommended for women 55 to 79 years of age when the potential benefit of a reduction in ischemic strokes outweighs the potential harm of an increase in gastrointestinal hemorrhage.

Bibliography

Wenger NK. Preventing cardiovascular disease in women: an update. Clin Cardiol. 2008;31(3):109-113. [PMID: 17803222]

Item 63 Answer: C
Educational Objective: Treat acute severe mitral regurgitation.

This patient has acute severe mitral regurgitation, likely owing to a ruptured mitral valve chord, and requires urgent surgery to repair or replace the valve before worsening hypoxemia or cardiogenic shock ensues. In the setting of

acute severe regurgitation, the left atrium and ventricle lack the gradual, adaptive remodeling by eccentric hypertrophy that occurs in chronic regurgitation. As a result, the acute increase in regurgitant blood flow rapidly increases left ventricular diastolic and left atrial pressure, leading to pulmonary edema. In addition, the reduction in forward left ventricular stroke volume may promote additional hemodynamic instability.

Although intravenous vasodilator therapy or intra-aortic balloon counterpulsation may be beneficial for improving hemodynamics acutely for severe mitral regurgitation as a bridge to cardiac surgery, vasodilator therapy with an oral agent, such as captopril, will not improve her condition.

Esmolol is not indicated for this patient because the sinus tachycardia is compensatory. Indeed, treatment of this patient with a β-blocker may worsen her hemodynamic status.

This patient has no symptoms or signs of infective endocarditis as the cause of acute mitral regurgitation. More than 90% of patients with endocarditis have fever as a sign of endocarditis. Therefore, empiric treatment with antibiotics is not indicated for this patient.

KEY POINT

- For acute severe mitral regurgitation, urgent surgery to repair or replace the valve is indicated.

Bibliography

Stout KK, Verrier ED. Acute valvular regurgitation. Circulation. 2009;119(25):3232-3241. [PMID: 19564568]

Item 64 Answer: D
Educational Objective: Diagnose stress cardiomyopathy (takotsubo cardiomyopathy).

This patient has a clinical history and presentation consistent with stress cardiomyopathy (takotsubo cardiomyopathy). Although atherosclerosis is the most common cause of an acute coronary syndrome, other, more unusual conditions, such as coronary spasm or stress cardiomyopathy, may also present with anginal chest pain, transient electrocardiographic changes, and elevated cardiac biomarkers. Patients typically present following a stressful or emotional event, such as the loss of a loved one or a natural disaster, such as an earthquake. Accepted criteria for the diagnosis are (1) ST-segment elevation, (2) transient wall motion abnormalities of the apex and mid ventricle, (3) the absence of obstructive coronary artery disease, and (4) absence of other causes of transient left ventricular dysfunction, such as recent head trauma or myocarditis.

The images shown (see next page) were obtained during left ventriculography. In systole, the basal segments of the heart contract well, while the apical portion of the heart is dyskinetic (bulges outward as opposed to inward).

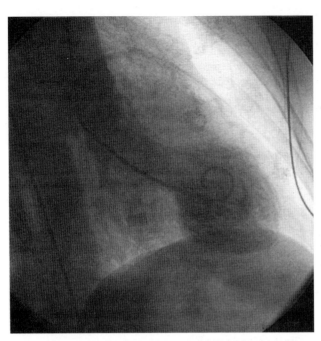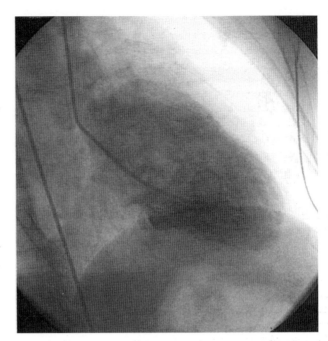

ITEM 64. Left ventriculogram during systole (left) and diastole (right).

The prognosis is excellent, with resolution of left ventricular dysfunction in several weeks with supportive care (β-blockers and ACE inhibitors). The pathophysiology remains unknown, but catecholamine-mediated myocardial stunning is thought to be the most likely mechanism.

It is often difficult to distinguish stress cardiomyopathy from a non–ST-elevation myocardial infarction (NSTEMI) or ST-elevation myocardial infarction (STEMI). Both groups of patients present with electrocardiographic changes and elevated cardiac biomarkers. The normal coronary arteries by coronary angiography suggest that this patient does not have either a NSTEMI or STEMI.

Patients with pericarditis present with pleuritic chest pain and a variety of findings on the electrocardiogram, including PR-segment depression, diffuse ST-segment elevation, and T-wave changes. Furthermore, pericarditis cannot account for the wall motion abnormalities noted on the imaging studies.

KEY POINT

- Stress cardiomyopathy (takotsubo cardiomyopathy) is an acute coronary syndrome characterized by ST-segment elevation, transient wall motion abnormalities of the apex and mid ventricle, the absence of obstructive coronary artery disease, and absence of other causes of transient left ventricular dysfunction.

Bibliography

Prasad A, Lerman A, Rihal CS. Apical ballooning syndrome (Tako-Tsubo or stress cardiomyopathy): a mimic of acute myocardial infarction. Am Heart J. 2008;155(3):408-417. [PMID: 18294473]

Item 65   Answer: D

Educational Objective: Treat a patient with a non–ST-elevation myocardial infarction who is not a candidate for invasive angiography.

This patient should begin taking a β-blocker, a statin, and clopidogrel, in addition to aspirin and low-molecular-weight heparin. Her chest pain, T-wave inversions in the lateral leads of the electrocardiogram, and elevated cardiac biomarkers are consistent with a non–ST-elevation myocardial infarction (NSTEMI). The TIMI risk score is 4 (age >65 years, elevated troponin level on presentation, aspirin use, and two angina episodes in the last 24 hours), indicating an intermediate-risk NSTEMI. She is elderly, and she recently established do-not-resuscitate (DNR) status and a request to avoid invasive procedures; therefore, she is not a candidate for invasive angiography.

Appropriate medical therapy for NSTEMI includes antiplatelet agents (aspirin and clopidogrel) and a β-blocker. In addition, patients require antithrombin therapy with either unfractionated heparin or low-molecular-weight heparin and high-dose statin therapy. Randomized trials have shown a benefit of low-molecular-weight heparin over unfractionated heparin with a reduction in death and recurrent myocardial infarction. Contraindications to low-molecular-weight heparin include kidney dysfunction, obesity, and the need for invasive procedures.

Oral β-blockers are first-line agents for treating a NSTEMI. A calcium channel blocker such as diltiazem can be used in patients with a contraindication to β-blockers and in those with continued angina despite optimal doses of β-blockers and nitrates. Contraindications to β-blockers include

CONT.

advanced heart block, heart failure, and reactive airways disease. This patient does not have contraindications to β-blockers, so diltiazem would not be the preferred treatment.

KEY POINT

- Patients with a non–ST-elevation myocardial infarction and an intermediate TIMI risk score should be treated with antiplatelet agents (aspirin and clopidogrel), a β-blocker, high-dose statin therapy, and antithrombin therapy with either unfractionated heparin or low-molec-ular-weight heparin.

Bibliography

Van Horn SE Jr, Maniu CV. Management of non-ST-segment eleva-tion myocardial infarction. Med Clin North Am. 2007;91(4):683-700. [PMID: 17640542]

Item 66   Answer: D

Educational Objective: Manage asymptomatic ventricular septal defect in an adult.

For this patient with a small perimembranous ventricular septal defect (VSD) without associated symptoms or cardiovascular problems, no intervention is needed at this time. The left heart chambers are normal and there is no evidence of pulmonary hypertension or valvular disruption related to the VSD. Cardiovascular follow-up evaluation for adults with small VSDs is generally recommended every 3 to 5 years, ideally by a cardiologist specializing in congenital disorders. Antibiotic prophylaxis is not required in the absence of previous endocarditis.

Cardiovascular magnetic resonance (CMR) imaging is an effective method for cardiovascular diagnosis. This patient, however, has had a comprehensive evaluation carried out and a CMR imaging study is unlikely to add substantially to the diagnostic and management strategy. CMR imaging may be reasonable in a patient with suboptimal transthoracic echocardiographic images and those with suspected anomalous pulmonary veins, particularly patients who are not candidates for or prefer to avoid transesophageal echocardiography. CMR imaging is not widely available.

Closure of a VSD is recommended when the pulmonary–to–systemic blood flow ratio (Qp:Qs) is 2.0 or more and there is clinical evidence of left ventricular volume overload, or the patient has a history of infective endocarditis. It may be reasonable to consider closure of a VSD when the Qp:Qs ratio is greater than 1.5 when there is net left-to-right shunting in the absence of severe pulmonary hypertension This patient has none of the features to suggest VSD closure is required.

Hemodynamic cardiac catheterization is not required in this patient given his excellent functional status as well as the echocardiographic findings, which include normal cardiac chamber size and pulmonary pressure. A calculation of the left-to-right shunt (Qp:Qs ratio) is best obtained by cardiac catheterization, but given the absence of left heart enlargement, symptoms, or increased pulmonary pressures, this would not be required in this patient. Cardiac catheterization is indicated in patients with a symptomatic VSD, findings of left heart enlargement, or pulmonary hypertension to determine feasibility of surgical closure.

KEY POINT

- Patients with a small asymptomatic ventricular septal defect without left heart enlargement, pulmonary hypertension, or valvular disruption related to the defect can be managed with periodic clinical evaluation.

Bibliography

Gabriel HM, Heger M, Innerhofer P, et al. Long-term outcome of patients with ventricular septal defect considered not to require sur-gical closure during childhood. J Am Coll Cardiol. 2002;39(6):1066-1071. [PMID: 11897452]

Item 67   Answer: D

Educational Objective: Manage chronic severe mitral regurgitation.

This patient should undergo mitral valve repair surgery. In patients with chronic severe mitral regurgitation and normal left ventricular systolic function, surgical repair is indicated in the setting of new-onset atrial fibrillation to reduce possible long-term adverse events. Pulmonary vein isolation or a maze procedure may be performed concomitantly at the time of mitral valve repair to reduce the risk of recurrent atrial fibrillation. In addition, chronic anticoagulation therapy with warfarin is indicated to reduce the risk of thromboembolism, which is much higher than in nonvalvular atrial fibrillation.

A rhythm-control strategy using an antiarrhythmic drug such as amiodarone is not likely to maintain sinus rhythm over the long term in this patient and may have a high risk of adverse effects with prolonged use.

Direct-current cardioversion (after ruling out a left atrial thrombus) is not likely to be associated with long-term maintenance of sinus rhythm given this patient's severe mitral regurgitation and left atrial dilation.

Exercise echocardiography may be useful in patients with chronic severe mitral regurgitation to evaluate the pulmonary artery pressure during exercise by Doppler imaging, but this diagnostic test does not offer additional useful information for this patient who already meets the criteria for valve repair surgery.

KEY POINT

- In patients with chronic severe mitral regurgitation and normal left ventricular systolic function, surgical repair is indicated in the setting of new-onset atrial fibrillation.

Bibliography

Foster E. Clinical practice. Mitral regurgitation due to degenerative mitral-valve disease. N Engl J Med. 2010;363(2):156-165. [PMID: 20647211]

Item 68   Answer: C

Educational Objective: Prescribe clopidogrel for a patient who has sustained a non–ST-elevation myocardial infarction.

This patient has sustained a non–ST-elevation myocardial infarction (NSTEMI), and a full year of clopidogrel therapy is recommended. In the Clopidogrel in Unstable angina to prevent Recurrent Events (CURE) trial, clopidogrel added to aspirin improved outcomes after hospitalization in patients with NSTEMI regardless of the in-hospital treatment approach. Current recommendations from the American College of Cardiology and the American Heart Association state that patients with unstable angina or NSTEMI treated medically who do not receive a stent should take clopidogrel for at least 1 month and ideally for up to 1 year.

Catheterization in this patient demonstrated significant distal coronary artery disease, but a catheter-based intervention was not performed. Patients who receive a stent require dual antiplatelet therapy with aspirin and clopidogrel until endothelialization of the foreign body is completed. For a bare metal stent placed in the absence of an acute coronary syndrome, clopidogrel should be continued for at least 1 month; for a drug-eluting stent, clopidogrel should be continued for at least 1 year. There is no general indication for life-long dual antiplatelet therapy. Clopidogrel alone may be appropriate life-long antiplatelet therapy for a patient who is unable to tolerate aspirin because of gastrointestinal distress or a documented allergy.

> **KEY POINT**
> - Patients with unstable angina or a non–ST-elevation myocardial infarction treated medically who do not receive a stent should take clopidogrel for at least 1 month and ideally for up to 1 year.

Bibliography
Yusuf S, Zhao F, Mehta SR, Chrolavicius S, Tognoni G, Fox KK; Clopidogrel in Unstable Angina to Prevent Recurrent Events Trial Investigators. Effects of clopidogrel in addition to aspirin in patients with acute coronary syndromes without ST-segment elevation [errata in N Engl J Med. 2001;345(20):1506; N Engl J Med. 2001;345(23):1716]. N Engl J Med. 2001;345(7):494-502. [PMID: 11519503]

Item 69   Answer: A

Educational Objective: Diagnose aortic coarctation.

This patient has clinical findings consistent with aortic coarctation, a congenital abnormality consisting of a discrete aortic narrowing distal to the left subclavian artery. This produces a discrepancy in blood pressure between the upper and lower extremities. The classic physical examination findings are upper extremity hypertension with diminished or delayed femoral pulses. Lower extremity claudication with physical activity is common. Coarctation may also present

with continuous murmurs from extensive collateralization. Echocardiography is diagnostic. This patient's physical examination is also consistent with a bicuspid aortic valve (early systolic click and grade 2/6 early systolic murmur at the upper right sternal border). More than 50% of patients with aortic coarctation also have a bicuspid aortic valve. Most patients are relatively asymptomatic and are identified when a murmur is auscultated on physical examination. Patients with aortic regurgitation may also have a diastolic murmur.

The classic physical examination findings with an atrial septal defect are fixed splitting of the S_2 and a holosystolic murmur due to increased volume flow across the tricuspid valve (tricuspid regurgitation). Fixed splitting of the S_2 is caused by left-to-right interatrial shunting, increased right-sided volume load, pulmonary hypertension, and a delay in the pulmonic component of the S_2.

Mitral valve prolapse is associated with a midsystolic click and late systolic murmur that decreases with passive leg elevation or squat. If significant regurgitation is present with left ventricular enlargement, the point of maximal impulse may be apically displaced.

A ventricular septal defect produces a harsh holosystolic murmur that increases with isometric exercise (increased afterload). With large or anteriorly directed ventricular septal defects, a thrill may be palpable.

> **KEY POINT**
> - Aortic coarctation is commonly associated with lower extremity claudication and upper extremity hypertension with diminished or delayed femoral pulses.

Bibliography
Tanous D, Benson LN, Horlick EM. Coarctation of the aorta: evaluation and management. Curr Opin Cardiol. 2009;24(6):509-515. [PMID: 19667980]

Item 70   Answer: C

Educational Objective: Treat a patient with chronic stable angina.

In this patient with continued symptomatic chronic stable angina despite the use of appropriate medical therapy, ranolazine may be a helpful addition for controlling his angina. He is currently taking maximally tolerated dosages of a β-blocker, a calcium channel blocker, and a long-acting oral nitrate and still requires daily sublingual nitroglycerin use. Ranolazine is a novel antianginal agent that causes selective inhibition of the late sodium channel and is approved for the treatment of chronic stable angina. Ranolazine should be considered in patients who remain symptomatic despite optimal doses of β-blockers, calcium channel blockers, and nitrates.

Ranolazine is contraindicated in patients with preexisting QT-interval prolongation because it increases the QT interval in a dose-dependent manner. Diltiazem and verapamil interfere with the metabolism of ranolazine; therefore, dose reductions and careful monitoring of the QT interval are necessary when these drugs are combined with ranolazine. Ranolazine inhibits the metabolism of digoxin and simvastatin, and dose reduction of these drugs may be necessary. Ranolazine is mainly excreted in the urine, and dosage adjustments are necessary in those with mild to moderate kidney disease. Ranolazine is contraindicated in patients with severe kidney disease (glomerular filtration rate <30 mL/min/1.73 m²) and has not been studied in those undergoing kidney replacement therapy.

The addition of a second β-blocker, such as carvedilol, for this patient would not be expected to provide any additional antianginal effects and would most likely result in adverse effects.

External enhanced counterpulsation uses pneumatic cuffs that are wrapped around the lower extremities to achieve a hemodynamic effect similar to an intra-aortic balloon pump. External enhanced counterpulsation is associated with an improvement in angina and exercise capacity but has no mortality benefit. This may be a treatment option for occasional patients with continued angina despite maximal medical therapy who are not candidates for either percutaneous or surgical revascularization. External enhanced counterpulsation is contraindicated in the presence of peripheral vascular disease. Spinal cord stimulation uses an electrocatheter within the epidural space connected to a pulse generator that stimulates the spinal cord region receiving the cardiac nerve fibers. It is a potential treatment option for medically refractory angina, although it is not recommended by current guidelines. Neither external enhanced counterpulsation nor spinal cord stimulation would be appropriate for this patient because ranolazine had not yet been initiated.

KEY POINT

- **Ranolazine should be considered in patients with chronic stable angina who remain symptomatic despite optimal doses of β-blockers, calcium channel blockers, and nitrates.**

Bibliography
Nash DT, Nash SD. Ranolazine for chronic stable angina [erratum in Lancet. 2009;373(9665):722]. Lancet. 2008;372(9646):1335-1341. [PMID: 18929905]

Item 71   Answer: C

Educational Objective: Manage a patient with an implantable cardioverter-defibrillator undergoing surgery.

In this pacemaker-dependent patient about to undergo surgery, the shock therapy function of the implantable cardioverter-defibrillator (ICD) should be turned off and the pacing function changed to an asynchronous mode. All ICDs have pacemaker capabilities. When a patient with an ICD undergoes surgery, the use of electrocautery affects what the device "thinks" is happening with cardiac activity.

When electrocautery is used, the ICD recognizes the rapid electrical signal and will treat the patient as if ventricular fibrillation is occurring, by inhibiting pacing and delivering a high-energy shock. Therefore, for a patient with an ICD who is pacemaker dependent, the best management is to reprogram the device to turn off shock therapy and change to an asynchronous mode such as VOO, which means that ventricular pacing will continue regardless of any native electrical activity or electrocautery.

A temporary pacemaker is not needed because the pacemaker function of the ICD can still be used during the surgery.

In general, placing a magnet over an ICD disables the shock function but does not affect the pacemaker settings. In a patient with a pacemaker (rather than an ICD) and complete heart block, placing a magnet over the device would be an acceptable option because it changes the pacemaker to an asynchronous pacing mode. If a patient with an ICD is not pacemaker dependent, it would be reasonable to place a magnet over the ICD to disable the shock function. In a pacemaker-dependent patient, however, if shock therapy is turned off but no changes are made to the pacemaker, the patient will not receive an ICD shock, but pacing could be inhibited during electrocautery.

After a procedure, it is imperative that the device be reprogrammed to its original settings by a knowledgeable person.

KEY POINT

- **For a patient with an implantable cardioverter-defibrillator about to undergo surgery, the device should be reprogrammed to turn off shock therapy.**

Bibliography
Crossley GH, Poole JE, Rozner MA, et al. The Heart Rhythm Society (HRS)/American Society of Anesthesiologists (ASA) expert consensus statement on the perioperative management of patients with implantable defibrillators, pacemakers and arrhythmia monitors: facilities and patient management. This document was developed as a joint project with the American Society of Anesthesiologists (ASA), and in collaboration with the American Heart Association (AHA), and the Society of Thoracic Surgeons (STS). Heart Rhythm. 2011;8(7):1114-1154. [PMID: 21722856]

Item 72   Answer: D

Educational Objective: Manage a patient presenting late with ST-elevation myocardial infarction using primary percutaneous coronary intervention.

This patient should undergo primary percutaneous coronary intervention (PCI). He is presenting with a late (12 hours) ST-elevation myocardial infarction (STEMI). Reperfusion strategies for STEMI patients include either thrombolytic therapy or primary PCI. Given the late presentation, the best option for this patient is primary PCI. Primary PCI is also useful for STEMI patients with cardiogenic shock and those with contraindications to thrombolytic therapy such as previous

CONT.

intracerebral hemorrhage, ischemic stroke within 3 months, suspected aortic dissection, or active bleeding.

Emergency coronary artery bypass graft surgery is not a routine method of revascularization in patients with STEMI. The reasons are logistical; it is nearly impossible to diagnose STEMI, perform cardiac catheterization, have access to an operating room, assemble a surgical team, and perform surgery within the time span predicted to salvage the greatest amount of myocardium.

Thrombolytic therapy has not shown a clear benefit for STEMI patients presenting more than 12 hours from symptom onset. Current guidelines emphasize that patients best suited for fibrinolytic therapy are those who present early after symptom onset with low bleeding risk, but that PCI is always preferred if the patient is in a PCI-capable facility (performed as soon as possible). Thrombolytic therapy should be given intravenously, as opposed to the intra-coronary route.

Compared with medical therapy alone, coronary reperfusion (PCI or thrombolytic therapy) improves outcomes in nearly all groups of patients with acute STEMI if performed in a timely fashion.

KEY POINT

- In patients presenting with an ST-elevation myocardial infarction and single-vessel coronary artery disease, primary percutaneous coronary intervention is recommended.

Bibliography

Armstrong PW, Westerhout CM, Welsh RC. Duration of symptoms is the key modulator of the choice of reperfusion for ST-elevation myocardial infarction. Circulation. 2009;119(9):1293-1303. [PMID: 19273730]

H Item 73   Answer: D

Educational Objective: Manage the risk for torsades de pointes in the hospital setting.

The electrocardiograms (ECGs) show a significant change in the QT interval due to haloperidol, which was being used to manage delirium. Haloperidol, along with other medications that prolong the QT interval, blocks the rapidly acting potassium channel and prolongs cardiac repolarization.

In this example, leads V_2 and V_3 most clearly demonstrate the increase in QT interval. In the baseline ECG, the QT interval, measured from the beginning of the QRS complex to the end of the T wave (without including the U wave), is 410 msec and the heart rate is 68/min (QTc = 436 msec using the Bazett formula). In the current ECG, the QT interval is 520 msec and the heart rate is 63/min (corrected QT interval [QTc] = 533 msec). If a QT-prolonging drug has been administered and the QTc is greater than 500 msec or has increased by 60 msec or more, the offending drug should be discontinued, because this is a risk factor for torsades de pointes. Potassium and

magnesium levels should be measured and supplemented as necessary.

Other risk factors for torsades de pointes include older age, female sex, use of multiple QT-prolonging agents (especially by intravenous infusion), diuretic use, impaired hepatic drug metabolism, bradycardia, frequent premature ventricular contractions, and history of long QT syndrome.

This patient should be advised to avoid QT-prolonging drugs in the future; the website www.qtdrugs.org lists QT-prolonging drugs.

Digoxin, diltiazem, enoxaparin, and trimethoprim do not affect QT interval. Excessive blood levels of digoxin may cause a variety of dysrhythmias, including accelerated junctional rhythm, asystole, atrial tachycardia, first-, second-, or third-degree heart block, premature ventricular contractions, ventricular tachycardia, and ventricular fibrillation. Diltiazem may cause may cause first-, second-, and third-degree atrioventricular block or sinus bradycardia. Enoxaparin and trimethoprim can cause hyperkalemia but do not have direct effects on cardiac conduction or rhythm.

KEY POINT

- If a QT-prolonging drug has been administered and the corrected QT interval (QTc) is greater than 500 msec or has increased by 60 msec or more, the offending drug should be discontinued, because this is a risk factor for torsades de pointes.

Bibliography

Drew BJ, Ackerman MJ, Funk M, et al; American Heart Association Acute Cardiac Care Committee of the Council on Clinical Cardiology, the Council on Cardiovascular Nursing, and the American College of Cardiology Foundation. Prevention of torsade de pointes in hospital settings: a scientific statement from the American Heart Association and the American College of Cardiology Foundation [erratum in Circulation. 2010;122(8):e440]. Circulation. 2010;121(8):1047-1060. [PMID: 20142454]

Item 74   Answer: C

Educational Objective: Manage an asymptomatic adult with repaired aortic coarctation.

This patient has a history of aortic coarctation repair. It is appropriate to assess the ascending aorta, aortic arch, and descending aorta in the region of the repair further with either MRI or CT to exclude either recurrent coarctation or aneurysm formation, which are common complications that occur late after coarctation repair. The patient also has a bicuspid aortic valve with aortic stenosis; a bicuspid aortic valve is present in more than 50% of patients with aortic coarctation. In addition, more than 50% of patients with repaired aortic coarctation have systemic hypertension and require antihypertensive therapy.

Progressive stenosis requiring surgery eventually occurs in most patients with a bicuspid aortic valve. This patient is currently asymptomatic despite a systolic mean gradient of 40 mm Hg, however, and it would be inappropriate to proceed with valve replacement at this time. Aortic valve replacement will be required in the future, and the patient should be monitored for symptoms or high-risk features that suggest valve replacement is needed. Regardless of the eventual need for valve surgery, the immediate concern is the need for aortic imaging.

Cardiac catheterization to assess the patient's aorta and aortic valve hemodynamics is not required. Echocardiography provides the hemodynamic information about the aortic valve, and the aorta can be readily assessed by MRI or CT, thus obviating the need for an invasive procedure.

There are no clinical features to suggest recurrent coarctation in this patient and no findings that suggest coarctation intervention is needed. Stent placement in the aorta is not an appropriate treatment option given the lack of demonstration of recurrent coarctation.

KEY POINT

- **In patients with repaired aortic coarctation, CT or MRI can be used to assess for recurrent coarctation or aneurysm, both of which are common late complications after repair.**

Bibliography

Tsai SF, Trivedi M, Boettner B, Daniels CJ. Usefulness of screening cardiovascular magnetic resonance imaging to detect aortic abnormalities after repair of coarctation of the aorta. Am J Cardiol. 2011;107(2):297-301. [PMID: 21211607]

Item 75   Answer: C

Educational Objective: Refer a patient with advanced heart failure for transplantation evaluation.

The patient should be referred for evaluation for cardiac transplantation. For patients with end-stage heart failure refractory to therapy, mechanical circulatory support and cardiac transplantation are potentially lifesaving options. The patient has severe symptomatic heart failure related to ischemic cardiomyopathy with systolic dysfunction. He is relatively young and has no other systemic illnesses or contraindications to transplantation. Transplantation, or mechanical support as a bridge to transplantation, are the best options for significantly extending the patient's life.

Given this patient's already low blood pressure, it is unlikely that he would tolerate significant doses of hydralazine and isosorbide dinitrate.

Although a higher dose versus a lower dose of an ACE inhibitor such as lisinopril may reduce hospitalizations for heart failure, it has not been shown to significantly affect survival.

The patient's QRS duration is normal, and available data do not support a reduction in either mortality or heart failure hospitalizations for biventricular pacing in the setting of a normal QRS interval.

KEY POINT

- **For patients with end-stage heart failure refractory to therapy, mechanical circulatory support and cardiac transplantation are potentially lifesaving options.**

Bibliography

Mancini D, Lietz K. Selection of cardiac transplantation candidates in 2010. Circulation. 2010;122(2):173-183. [PMID: 20625142]

Item 76   Answer: B

Educational Objective: Manage complicated infective endocarditis.

This patient should undergo replacement of the aortic valve. He has aortic valve endocarditis complicated by paravalvular extension resulting in an abscess and severe aortic regurgitation. Urgent surgical intervention is indicated for patients with heart failure; abscess or fistula formation; severe left-sided valvular regurgitation; refractory infection despite appropriate antibiotic therapy; or recurrent embolic events, especially with residual vegetation greater than 1.0 cm in size. There should be no delay to surgical intervention for observation of the patient's response to antibiotic therapy once surgical indications are met. In this patient, the complications of endocarditis would not likely improve or resolve without surgical therapy, and continuing antibiotic therapy alone without immediate surgical intervention may result in further decompensation of the patient's clinical status and an increased operative risk for intervention at a later time.

The addition of rifampin to the antibiotic regimen is not indicated in this patient with viridans streptococcal endocarditis and will not improve his clinical status.

Cardiac catheterization is not indicated in this patient and may increase the risk of embolization of vegetation or worsening hemodynamic status. Cardiac catheterization before planned cardiac surgery is indicated in patients with risk factors for coronary artery disease, which are not present in this patient.

Although the vegetative lesion in endocarditis is a product of both bacterial and platelet adhesion, no studies have shown a reduction in embolic events in patients treated with heparin.

KEY POINT

- **In patients with endocarditis complicated by heart failure, abscess, severe regurgitation, or hemodynamic derangements, valve replacement should be performed urgently, without delay for response to antibiotic therapy.**

Bibliography

Stout KK, Verrier ED. Acute valvular regurgitation. Circulation. 2009;119(25):3232-3241. [PMID: 19564568]

Item 77   Answer: A

Educational Objective: Diagnose radiation-induced aortic valve regurgitation.

The most likely explanation for this patient's chest pain and worsening dyspnea is aortic valve regurgitation. The direct support for this diagnosis is the presence of a diastolic murmur. Physical examination is consistent with severe aortic valve regurgitation, as evidenced by a Corrigan pulse in the carotid arteries (rapid, accentuated upstroke with a rapid decline), displaced point of maximal impulse, and widened pulse pressure (systolic pressure is elevated, pulse pressure is >50% of the systolic pressure, and diastolic pressure is <70 mm Hg).

Aortic valve disease from previous radiation therapy is the most likely cause for aortic regurgitation in this patient. The risk for cardiotoxicity, including valvular fibrosis and regurgitation, increases with higher total radiation dose. However, there is no single dose of radiation below which cardiotoxicity will not occur. The clinical onset of radiation-induced valvular regurgitation is variable and may occur 10 to 25 years or more after initial radiation therapy to the thorax. Clinically significant aortic valve regurgitation may occur in 25% or more of cancer survivors with previous radiation to the thorax. In this patient, dyspnea can be explained on the basis of elevation in left ventricular diastolic pressure from hemodynamically significant aortic regurgitation. Chest pain occurs as a result of low coronary filling pressures and subsequent myocardial ischemia from low diastolic aortic pressure induced by aortic regurgitation.

Constrictive pericarditis should be considered in a patient with prior radiation of the thorax who presents with dyspnea on exertion. The right ventricle is more extensively involved, typically leading to findings of right ventricular failure (jugular venous distention, hepatojugular reflux, peripheral edema). Physical examination in this patient showed no findings of right ventricular involvement, making constrictive pericarditis unlikely.

Restrictive cardiomyopathy may occur from previous radiation therapy but is unlikely in this patient. There are no physical examination findings of right-sided pressure overload (jugular venous distention, hepatojugular reflux), which would be expected in a patient with symptomatic restrictive cardiomyopathy.

Tricuspid regurgitation also may occur from previous radiation to the thorax. However, the physical examination does not demonstrate evidence of hemodynamically significant tricuspid regurgitation, such as jugular venous distention, large retrograde *v* waves, or hepatojugular reflux. In severe tricuspid regurgitation, a systolic murmur is usually present but may be absent. When absent, however, a large jugular vein *v* wave would be expected.

KEY POINT

- Clinically significant aortic valve regurgitation is common in cancer survivors with previous radiation to the thorax and may occur 10 to 25 years or more after initial radiation therapy.

Bibliography

Demirci S, Nam J, Hubbs JL, Nguyen T, Marks LB. Radiation-induced cardiac toxicity after therapy for breast cancer: interaction between treatment era and follow-up duration. Int J Radiat Oncol Biol Phys. 2009;73(4):980-987. [PMID: 19251085]

Item 78   Answer: D

Educational Objective: Diagnose pulmonary valve stenosis.

This patient has the characteristic physical examination findings of pulmonary valve stenosis. The jugular venous pulsations demonstrate a prominent *a* wave caused by increased right atrial pressure during contraction into a hypertrophied, less compliant right ventricle. A right ventricular lift (right ventricular hypertrophy) and systolic thrill due to high velocity of blood flow across the stenotic valve are present. An ejection click results from the rapid opening of the stenotic pulmonary valve leaflets. During inspiration, the intensity of this click is diminished because of increased flow across the pulmonary valve. Inspiration also increases the intensity of the systolic murmur. The chest radiograph shows a dilated pulmonary artery, which is associated with pulmonary valve stenosis.

In atrial septal defect, fixed splitting of the S_2 is the characteristic examination finding. In addition, a midsystolic ejection murmur is heard at the pulmonary valve or second left intercostal space.

Bicuspid aortic valve may be associated with a systolic ejection click. As aortic stenosis develops, the ejection click may be less audible. Other findings include diminished and delayed carotid pulsations (pulsus parvus et tardus), a sustained apical impulse, late-peaking systolic murmur, and a diminished closure sound (A_2). The murmur of severe aortic stenosis typically radiates to the left clavicular region as well as both carotid arteries. On chest radiograph, evidence of left ventricular hypertrophy and possibly ascending aorta dilation may be found.

In mitral valve prolapse and regurgitation, an early systolic click may be heard, followed by a midsystolic murmur. During a Valsalva maneuver, the timing of the systolic click moves closer to the S_1, and the murmur is consequently longer in duration.

The characteristic physical examination finding in ventricular septal defect is a holosystolic murmur at the left lower sternal region.

KEY POINT

- Physical examination findings characteristic of pulmonary valve stenosis include a prominent *a* wave in the jugular venous pulsations, a right ventricular lift, a systolic thrill, and an ejection click that diminishes in intensity during inspiration.

Bibliography

Etchells E, Bell C, Robb K. Does this patient have an abnormal systolic murmur? JAMA. 1997;277(7):564-571. [PMID: 9032164]

Item 79   Answer: D

Educational Objective: Diagnose Takayasu arteritis.

The most likely diagnosis is Takayasu arteritis. The patient has constitutional symptoms, laboratory evidence of an inflammatory process, and physical evidence of vascular disease involving the great vessels of the aortic arch. Takayasu arteritis is a chronic vasculitis involving the aorta and major tributaries that largely affects young women. The early symptoms are constitutional, with symptoms of vascular involvement becoming more apparent as the disease progresses. Arterial inflammation, similar pathologically to giant cell arteritis, leads to thickening, stenosis, and aneurysmal dilation of the aorta and major branches. Late manifestations include arm or leg claudication and distal ulceration. Carotid or vertebral artery involvement may provoke headache, vertigo, syncope, or visual impairment. Angina may occur with involvement of the ostial portion of the coronary arteries, and renovascular hypertension may result from mid-aortic involvement.

There are several classification schemes for establishing the diagnosis of Takayasu arteritis. The American College of Rheumatology considers the diagnosis to be supported when three or more of the following criteria are met:

- Age younger than 40 years
- Claudication, especially of the upper extremities
- Decreased pulse of one or both brachial arteries
- Difference of greater than 10 mm Hg in systolic pressures of upper extremities
- Bruit over the subclavian arteries or aorta
- Arteriographic abnormality consistent with Takayasu arteritis

The chronicity of the patient's symptoms, lack of any chest or back pain, and the normal chest radiograph strongly argue against a diagnosis of acute aortic dissection.

Buerger disease is an inflammatory thrombotic condition involving the small and medium arteries of the hands and feet that is strongly linked to tobacco use. Although the patient's age is consistent with Buerger disease, she has no history of tobacco use, and it occurs more commonly in men. Additionally, vascular involvement in the patient presented is predominantly large vessel, whereas Buerger disease predominantly affects smaller vessels.

Kawasaki arteritis is a childhood illness of unclear etiology that results in coronary artery aneurysms, but not large vessel vasculitis.

KEY POINT

- Takayasu arteritis is a chronic vasculitis involving the aorta and major tributaries that largely affects young women.

Bibliography
Mason JC. Takayasu arteritis – advances in diagnosis and management. Nat Rev Rheumatol. 2010;6(7):406-415. [PMID: 20596053]

Item 80   Answer: A

Educational Objective: Manage hospital discharge in a patient hospitalized with acute decompensated heart failure.

This patient should be scheduled for a follow-up appointment within 1 week. Physician follow-up within 7 days after discharge from hospitalization for heart failure has been shown to reduce 30-day all-cause readmission rates by 10% to 15%. The Centers for Medicare and Medicaid Services (CMS) core measures for management of heart failure include a measure regarding discharge instructions. The measure highlights the importance of giving all patients comprehensive discharge instructions that address activity level, diet, discharge medications, scheduling a follow-up appointment, weight monitoring, and what to do if symptoms worsen.

After hospital discharge, patients may benefit from visiting nurse services in conjunction with home telemonitoring and rapid clinic follow-up, but visiting nurse services alone have not been shown to reduce readmission rates.

KEY POINT

- Patients being discharged from a hospitalization for heart failure should be scheduled for a follow-up physician appointment within 1 week.

Bibliography
Hernandez AF, Greiner MA, Fonarow GC, et al. Relationship between early physician follow-up and 30-day readmission among Medicare beneficiaries hospitalized for heart failure. JAMA. 2010;303(17):1716-1722. [PMID: 20442387]

Item 81   Answer: D

Educational Objective: Manage abdominal aortic aneurysm in a patient with significant comorbidities.

No further diagnostic testing should be pursued in this patient. Elective repair of asymptomatic abdominal aortic aneurysms 5.5 cm or larger is recommended for most patients to prevent the catastrophic events associated with rupture. However, the potential benefit of surgical prevention of aneurysm-related mortality must be balanced with the risks of the operation and the patient's overall mortality risk (from any cause). This patient has had a recent myocardial infarction, has uncompensated heart failure, and has unexplained weakness and significant unintentional weight loss. The potential benefits of aneurysm repair must be weighed against the perioperative mortality risk, which is considerable in this patient with multiple comorbid conditions. This patient would not be considered for open surgical repair of the aortic aneurysm because the risk of surgery is great and unlikely to improve survival. Because of the less invasive nature and lower immediate procedural-associated morbidity and mortality, endovascular repair becomes an attractive option. However, although endovascular repair reduces the risk of aneurysm-related mortality

CONT.

in patients ineligible for open repair, it does not reduce all-cause mortality, it is costly, and it may be associated with graft-related complications and reinterventions. Treatment of the aneurysm by either means would not be recommended for this patient with multiple comorbidities.

Magnetic resonance angiography, ultrasonography, and CT with intravenous contrast are all excellent noninvasive methods of identifying an abdominal aortic aneurysm. However, because the diagnosis of an abdominal aortic aneurysm would not lead to a change in treatment in this patient, there is no reason to obtain such tests.

> **KEY POINT**
> - In patients with abdominal aortic aneurysm, the potential benefit of elective repair must be balanced with the risks of the operation and the patient's overall mortality risk.

Bibliography

United Kingdom EVAR Trial Investigators, Greenhalgh RM, Brown LC, Powell JT, Thompson SG, Epstein D. Endovascular repair of aortic aneurysm in patients physically ineligible for open repair. N Engl J Med. 2010;362(20):1872-1880. [PMID: 20382982]

Item 82   Answer: D

Educational Objective: Evaluate for ischemia in a patient with new-onset heart failure and a high pretest probability of coronary artery disease.

Coronary angiography is indicated in this patient to evaluate for coronary artery disease (CAD) as a cause for newly diagnosed left ventricular systolic dysfunction. The patient has diabetes mellitus, a risk factor for CAD, and evidence for a previous inferior wall myocardial infarction on electrocardiogram (Q waves in leads II, III, and aVF). Indications for coronary angiography for evaluation of new-onset heart failure include angina or new-onset left ventricular dysfunction in the setting of a condition, such as diabetes, that may predispose to silent ischemia. Because revascularization may improve left ventricular function, some experts recommend a low threshold for evaluation for CAD.

Noninvasive stress testing, such as with an adenosine thallium test, would likely suggest CAD in this patient, but given the relatively high pretest probability, a noninvasive stress test would not change that probability. The more relevant issue is whether the coronary anatomy is amenable to revascularization, which could improve function; thus, coronary angiography would be the most appropriate diagnostic test.

Cardiac magnetic resonance (CMR) imaging is useful for evaluating possible infiltrative or inflammatory cardiomyopathy. Given the significant evidence suggesting the presence of CAD in this patient, the likelihood of an infiltrative or inflammatory cardiomyopathy is very low, and CMR imaging would not be an appropriate first diagnostic test.

Although this patient does have some limiting symptoms (dyspnea on exertion), cardiopulmonary exercise testing to obtain more detailed information regarding exercise capacity would not address the larger underlying issue of cause of new-onset heart failure nor would it be the best method to diagnose CAD in this patient.

> **KEY POINT**
> - Coronary angiography is indicated in the evaluation of new-onset heart failure in patients with angina or new-onset left ventricular dysfunction in the setting of a condition that may predispose to silent ischemia.

Bibliography

McMurray JJ. Clinical practice. Systolic heart failure. N Engl J Med. 2010;362(3):228-238. [PMID: 20089973]

Item 83   Answer: C

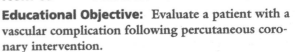

Educational Objective: Evaluate a patient with a vascular complication following percutaneous coronary intervention.

This patient who underwent a percutaneous coronary intervention (PCI) several hours ago should be evaluated with duplex ultrasonography for a possible pseudoaneurysm or arteriovenous fistula. She has pain at the site of placement of the arterial and venous sheaths. On examination, a large mass is palpated and is associated with a continuous bruit. These findings suggest either a pseudoaneurysm or an arteriovenous (AV) fistula. Vascular complications occur in fewer than 6% of patients undergoing PCI and include hematoma formation at the arterial puncture site, pseudoaneurysm, arteriovenous fistula, cholesterol emboli syndrome, and retroperitoneal bleeding. Duplex ultrasonography is the optimal method to differentiate between a pseudoaneurysm and an AV fistula and determine whether endovascular or surgical intervention is required.

An ankle-brachial index (ABI) would not add to the management of the patient presented. A normal ABI in this patient would not exclude a pseudoaneurysm or AV fistula. A low value would suggest the presence of preexisting peripheral vascular disease but would not assist in defining the problem.

CT is most often required after cardiac catheterization if there is a suspicion of a retroperitoneal bleed, which usually results from a proximal puncture of the common femoral artery in the setting of ongoing anticoagulation. Patients often present with flank or back pain and persistent hypotension. CT is useful to establish the diagnosis, but patients are often too ill to be transferred for CT scanning. Given that the patient presented has groin pain, the possibility of a retroperitoneal bleed is unlikely.

Lower-extremity angiography may occasionally be useful when complications occur following cardiac catheterization in the setting of diminished distal pulses if there is a concern for dissection of the common femoral artery or distal embolization. When this occurs, access can be obtained in a contralateral location and angiography used to confirm vessel dissection

CONT.

or occlusion of distal vessels. Angioplasty and endovascular stent placement may be required. This patient's distal pulses are normal, and lower-extremity angiography is not needed.

KEY POINT

- Duplex ultrasonography is the optimal method to differentiate between a pseudoaneurysm and an arteriovenous fistula in patients with a vascular complication following percutaneous coronary intervention.

Bibliography

Applegate RJ, Sacrinty MT, Kutcher MA, et al. Trends in vascular complications after diagnostic cardiac catheterization and percutaneous coronary intervention via the femoral artery, 1998 to 2007. JACC Cardiovasc Interv. 2008;1(3):317-326. [PMID: 19463320]

Item 84   Answer: D

Educational Objective: Manage resolving transient constrictive pericarditis.

This woman's clinical picture is consistent with transient constrictive pericarditis that is resolving, and as long as she remains stable, the current management with anti-inflammatory agents should be continued. With treatment, her functional capacity has improved, and she has demonstrated resolution of constrictive findings on echocardiogram. This clinical course is most consistent with transient constrictive pericarditis. Unlike "classic" constrictive pericarditis that is progressive and characterized by pericardial fibrosis, pericardial calcification, and refractory heart failure, a transient form of constrictive pericarditis occurs that resolves without surgical intervention. This entity is known to occur with many of the recognized causes of pericarditis, such as connective tissue diseases, infection (including tuberculosis), chemotherapy, trauma, pericardiotomy, and malignancy.

Endomyocardial biopsy and right and left heart hemodynamic cardiac catheterization are useful for differentiating constrictive pericarditis from restrictive cardiomyopathy. However, the findings of ventricular interdependence and restrictive filling are strong evidence for constrictive pericarditis, and neither an endomyocardial biopsy nor catheterization is necessary.

Pericardiectomy is indicated for progressive constrictive pericarditis in patients with New York Heart Association class II or III heart failure. In this patient who demonstrates transient constrictive pericarditis that is resolving, pericardiectomy is not indicated.

KEY POINT

- Transient constrictive pericarditis that is resolving can be treated conservatively with anti-inflammatory drugs.

Bibliography

Haley JH, Tajik AJ, Danielson GK, Schaff HV, Mulvagh SL, Oh JK. Transient constrictive pericarditis: causes and natural history. J Am Coll Cardiol. 2004;43(2):271-275. [PMID: 14736448]

Item 85   Answer: D

Educational Objective: Manage acute limb ischemia.

This patient has severe acute limb ischemia, and should be evaluated promptly for amputation. She has multiple risk factors for atherosclerotic peripheral arterial disease (PAD) and a history of symptoms consistent with effort-related claudication progressing to severe resting limb pain. Regrettably, the patient has presented late in the course of the disease. The limb is not salvageable, as marked by dense anesthesia, severe motor impairment, and lack of Doppler vascular signals. The best option is prompt amputation, and delaying this could lead to significant systemic illness as progressive limb necrosis ensues.

Given the absence of posterior tibialis and dorsalis pedis arterial Doppler signals, an ankle-brachial index cannot be obtained for the right foot. The patient should still be screened for PAD involving the left leg, but amputating the right foot is the immediate concern.

In the setting of less severe acute limb ischemia (a viable or marginally threatened limb), intra-arterial thrombolytic therapy may be considered, in combination with antiplatelet and antithrombotic therapy. In the present case, however, such therapy would put the patient at increased procedural and bleeding risk and would not restore effective perfusion to the foot.

Magnetic resonance angiography is useful for defining the anatomy of PAD and may play a staged role in planning an intervention. Further imaging in this patient is unnecessary and would only delay surgery.

If the limb were salvageable, it would be reasonable to proceed directly to invasive angiography (after institution of oral antiplatelet and intravenous antithrombotic therapy) as part of an urgent effort to save the limb.

KEY POINT

- Dense anesthesia, severe motor impairment, and lack of Doppler vascular signals indicate an acutely ischemic nonviable limb; prompt amputation is warranted.

Bibliography

Norgren L, Hiatt WR, Dormandy JA, Nehler MR, Harris KA, Fowkes FG; TASC II Working Group. Inter-society consensus for the management of peripheral arterial disease (TASC II). J Vasc Surg. 2007;45(Suppl S):S5-S67. [PMID: 17223489]

Item 86   Answer: C

Educational Objective: Manage asymptomatic severe mitral regurgitation with pulmonary hypertension.

This patient should undergo mitral valve repair surgery. He has severe asymptomatic mitral regurgitation with normal left ventricular systolic function but evidence of pulmonary hypertension. Indications for surgical intervention for mitral regurgitation include (1) left ventricular ejection fraction below 60%; (2) left ventricular end-systolic diameter greater than 40 mm; (3) severe pulmonary hypertension at rest (pulmonary artery systolic pressure >50 mm Hg) or during exercise (>60 mm Hg); or (4) new onset of atrial fibrillation. In this patient, the right ventricular systolic pressure (and therefore, the pulmonary artery systolic pressure) at rest is significantly elevated.

Although this patient has pulmonary hypertension, the presence of left-sided heart disease with elevated left atrial pressure is the likely cause, rather than idiopathic pulmonary arterial hypertension. Treatment with a pulmonary vasodilator, such as bosentan, may worsen heart failure symptoms by increasing pulmonary blood flow with fixed, elevated pulmonary venous pressure.

Lisinopril or other ACE inhibitors theoretically reduce left ventricular afterload and regurgitant volume. Acute use of afterload-reducing medications, particularly intravenously, may be beneficial in patients with severe mitral regurgitation and decompensated heart failure, if the blood pressure is acceptable. However, chronic oral treatment with ACE inhibitors or other vasodilators has not been shown to reduce progression of mitral regurgitation or cardiac events.

Mitral valve repair—rather than replacement—has important benefits, including higher left ventricular ejection fraction after surgery and better long-term survival. In addition, repair does not require long-term anticoagulation and its associated risks compared with mechanical valve replacement (commonly performed for the mitral location for its longer durability compared with a biologic valve). The likelihood of successful repair is dependent on the mitral valve anatomy as well as surgical operator and center experience.

KEY POINT

- In asymptomatic patients with severe mitral regurgitation, pulmonary hypertension at rest or during exercise is an accepted indication for mitral valve surgery.

Bibliography

Foster E. Clinical practice. Mitral regurgitation due to degenerative mitral-valve disease. N Engl J Med. 2010;363(2):156-165. [PMID: 20647211]

Item 87   Answer: A

Educational Objective: Diagnose cardiac allograft vasculopathy in a cardiac transplant patient.

This patient most likely has cardiac allograft vasculopathy (CAV). New-onset heart failure symptoms in a cardiac transplant recipient should prompt consideration of acute rejection or CAV. Other manifestations concerning for CAV include syncope and varying degrees of heart block. This patient has a recent history of progressive fatigue and dyspnea. He has evidence of heart failure on physical examination, and the echocardiogram demonstrates depressed left ventricular systolic function.

CAV is the most common cause of late ventricular dysfunction in cardiac transplant recipients. Vasculopathy is present angiographically in more than 50% of patients 5 years after transplantation; however, because of the denervation inherent in transplantation, it is uncommon for patients to present with chest discomfort. There is no specific treatment for CAV, which represents diffuse intimal hyperplasia rather than focal stenoses. Percutaneous techniques for revascularization can be considered, but they do not address the diffuse nature of the vasculopathy.

Although the patient had an episode of cellular rejection early after transplantation, he has done well since that time, and the likelihood of late cellular rejection is low. Most cellular rejection occurs early (first 6 months to 1 year), and it is rare after that time as long as immunosuppression is stable.

Opportunistic infections should always be considered in immunosuppressed patients, but *Pneumocystis jirovecii* pneumonia would not explain the cardiomegaly, jugular venous distention, S_3 gallop, or reduced left ventricular systolic function.

Recurrent idiopathic myocarditis is extremely rare clinically and is highly unlikely. In addition, acute myocarditis is often associated with pericarditis, and no pericardial effusion is noted on echocardiogram.

KEY POINT

- Cardiac allograft vasculopathy is the most common cause of late ventricular dysfunction in cardiac transplant patients and should be considered in transplant patients with new-onset heart failure.

Bibliography

Schmauss D, Weis M. Cardiac allograft vasculopathy: recent developments. Circulation. 2008;117(16):2131-2141. [PMID: 18427143]

Item 88   Answer: D

Educational Objective: Treat uncomplicated type B aortic dissection.

For this patient, medical therapy is indicated, with no further interventions at this time. The patient has an uncomplicated type B aortic dissection, which is demonstrated on the CT scan (shown on next page). The ascending aorta (AAo) appears normal in caliber and without a dissection flap separating the true and false lumen. The descending thoracic aorta (DAo) is dilated, and true and false lumens are separated by a flap (*arrows*). There is intact flow within the false lumen (contrast enhancement is equal on both sides of the dissection plane). Cocaine use is associated with increased risk for aortic dissection, and dissection has been documented with intranasal use and smoked "crack" cocaine.

Medical therapy of acute uncomplicated type B aortic dissection is preferred and is associated with a 30-day survival rate of greater than 90%. Medical therapy should consist of

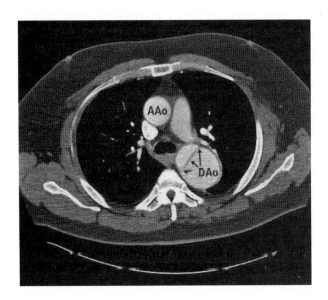

CONT. parenteral agents to lower heart rate (goal, <60/min) and blood pressure (goal, systolic blood pressure 100-120 mm Hg) to reduce the aortic shear stress. In the setting of recent cocaine use, intravenous labetalol could provide balanced α and β blockade and is a reasonable choice.

Acute aortic dissection may be associated with life-threatening organ ischemia. In these situations, emergency fenestration of the dissecting membrane is a potential intervention for patients with a type B dissection and evidence of mesenteric, renal, or peripheral ischemia. This patient has no evidence of these complications and fenestration is not indicated.

Patency of the false lumen and maximum aortic diameter of greater than 40 mm at index have been associated with greater risk of progression to malperfusion syndromes, rupture, and dissection-related death. With the availability of endovascular wall stents, there has been interest in prophylactic stenting of uncomplicated type B dissections as a means of preventing adverse outcomes. In a recent randomized controlled trial comparing medical therapy alone with medical therapy plus stenting, however, there was no difference in 2-year survival rates or aortic complications, and this type of therapy cannot be advocated for an uncomplicated type B dissection.

Complications of type B dissections that should prompt consideration of surgical or endovascular intervention include continued pain despite appropriate therapy, threatened aortic rupture, and a malperfusion syndrome.

> **KEY POINT**
> - Medical therapy to reduce heart rate and blood pressure is the preferred management for an uncomplicated type B aortic dissection.

Bibliography

Nienaber CA, Rousseau H, Eggebrecht H, et al; INSTEAD Trial. Randomized comparison of strategies for type B aortic dissection: the INvestigation of STEnt Grafts in Aortic Dissection (INSTEAD) trial. Circulation. 2009;120(25):2519-2528. [PMID: 19996018]

Item 89   Answer: B

Educational Objective: Determine the optimal cardiac monitoring device in a patient with infrequent syncopal episodes.

An implantable loop recorder (ILR) should be placed in this patient. Her physical examination and baseline electrocardiogram (ECG) do not suggest cardiovascular abnormalities. Concern for arrhythmia is significant given her previous syncopal events and her occupation, which requires driving. An ILR is placed subcutaneously under local anesthesia and has a solid state looping memory capable of storing ECG rhythm events, with a total capacity of up to 42 minutes. Battery life is approximately 3 years, a duration likely long enough to capture an event in this patient. ILRs are often useful in identifying an arrhythmia when previous, shorter-duration monitoring is not diagnostic.

A continuous ambulatory ECG monitor may detect asymptomatic arrhythmias but is typically worn for only 24 to 48 hours. External event recorders (looping event recorders and postsymptom event recorders) are used for more infrequent symptoms and record ECG tracings only when triggered by the patient. In this patient, a looping event recorder worn for 30 days did not reveal any arrhythmias. Because of the fleeting and infrequent nature of this patient's symptoms, it is unlikely that 24- or 48-hour ambulatory monitoring or an event recorder would capture an event. For arrhythmia evaluation, recent studies have shown improved diagnostic yield of mobile cardiac outpatient telemetry (MCOT) systems, another noninvasive monitoring tool, compared with looping event recorders. However, these systems are not yet widely available.

No further testing would not be appropriate in this patient who has a high-risk occupation and has experienced syncope at rest.

> **KEY POINT**
> - An implantable loop recorder is useful in identifying an infrequent arrhythmia when previous, shorter-duration monitoring is not diagnostic.

Bibliography

Parry SW, Matthews IG. Implantable loop recorders in the investigation of unexplained syncope: a state of the art review. Heart. 2010;96(20):1611-1616. [PMID: 20937748]

Item 90   Answer: D

Educational Objective: Evaluate need for aortic valve replacement.

This patient should undergo repeat echocardiography in 12 months. She has severe aortic stenosis; however, she is active and has not experienced any symptoms related to aortic stenosis, such as dyspnea, chest discomfort, or syncope. In asymptomatic patients with severe aortic stenosis, current guidelines recommend an interval examination in 6 months and an interval echocardiogram in 12 months, or sooner if symptoms develop.

In patients with severe aortic stenosis without symptoms, aortic valve replacement is indicated if left ventricular ejection fraction is abnormal (<50%), response to exercise is abnormal (hypotensive or development of symptoms), rapid progression of stenosis or very severe stenosis (mean gradient >60 mm Hg) has occurred, or if other cardiac surgery is indicated and planned. This patient does not have indications for aortic valve replacement.

Balloon aortic valvuloplasty is indicated for calcific aortic stenosis in patients with hemodynamic instability or decompensation, as a bridge to eventual aortic valve replacement. However, the degree of improvement in aortic valve area from this procedure is modest, and many patients have residual severe aortic stenosis immediately after valvuloplasty. Furthermore, balloon aortic valvuloplasty is associated with procedural risks, including stroke, myocardial infarction, vascular complications, and death, and is not indicated in this asymptomatic patient.

Dobutamine stress echocardiography may be utilized in determining the severity of aortic stenosis in the presence of severe left ventricular systolic dysfunction and a moderate aortic valve gradient (low-flow, low-gradient aortic stenosis). The assessment of the aortic valve gradient and area during higher flow rate is useful to differentiate a severe, fixed degree of stenosis from less severe stenosis. Dobutamine stress echocardiography may also be used to evaluate for possible ischemic response to suggest underlying coronary artery disease. However, this patient has no symptoms of coronary artery disease. In addition, dobutamine may result in hypotension and arrhythmias, which may have adverse consequences in a patient with severe aortic stenosis.

KEY POINT

- In patients with severe aortic stenosis without symptoms, aortic valve replacement is indicated if left ventricular ejection fraction is below 50%, exercise results in hypotension or symptoms, or rapid progression of stenosis or very severe stenosis (mean gradient >60 mm Hg) has occurred.

Bibliography

Iung B. Management of asymptomatic aortic stenosis. Heart. 2011;97(3):253-259. [PMID: 21189311]

Item 91   Answer: D

Educational Objective: Treat symptomatic peripheral arterial disease.

This patient should begin a supervised exercise program. He has typical claudication symptoms, and the physical examination supports a diagnosis of peripheral arterial disease (PAD). Several randomized trials have demonstrated that supervised exercise therapy can effectively treat claudication,

with increases in pain-free walking time and maximal walking time. To be effective, supervised exercise should be performed for a minimum of 30 to 45 minutes at least 3 times weekly for a minimum of 12 weeks. Nonsupervised exercise programs, in which patients are instructed to engage in regular walking on their own, have not demonstrated similar benefits. A recent trial evaluating supervised treadmill exercise and resistance training in patients with PAD with and without claudication symptoms demonstrated improvement in walking performance and quality of life.

Chelation therapy became a popular alternative therapy for PAD and coronary artery disease in the 1990s, but randomized trials of chelation therapy have failed to demonstrate benefit for either condition and may be harmful.

Cilostazol is an oral phosphodiesterase III inhibitor that has demonstrated increases in pain-free walking and overall walking distance in persons with claudication in randomized clinical trials. However, cilostazol is contraindicated in patients with heart failure or a left ventricular ejection fraction below 40%. This contraindication stems from cilostazol's similar pharmacologic action to the inotropic drugs milrinone and inamrinone, which demonstrated increased mortality in heart failure patients with long-term use.

Surgical intervention with femoral-popliteal bypass grafting should be reserved for patients with limb-threatening ischemia or severe lifestyle-limiting disease that has not responded to appropriate medical and exercise therapy.

KEY POINT

- Supervised exercise therapy (30 to 45 minutes at least 3 times weekly for a minimum of 12 weeks) can effectively treat claudication, with increases in pain-free walking time and maximal walking time.

Bibliography

McDermott MM, Ades P, Guralnik JM, et al. Treadmill exercise and resistance training in patients with peripheral arterial disease with and without intermittent claudication: a randomized controlled trial. JAMA. 2009;301(2):165-174. [PMID: 19141764]

Item 92   Answer: C

Educational Objective: Select the appropriate diagnostic test for a patient with chest pain and an abnormal electrocardiogram.

This woman with exertional chest pain and evidence of left ventricular hypertrophy and strain on electrocardiogram (ECG) should undergo exercise stress echocardiography to evaluate for ischemic heart disease. Based on her age, sex, and the presence of typical chest pain, she has an intermediate pretest probability of having coronary artery disease, and therefore stress testing is appropriate.

Exercise stressors are preferred to pharmacologic stressors because exercise testing can help with the reproducibility of symptoms as well as offer significant prognostic information. Those patients who cannot exercise should undergo pharmacologic testing. In addition, in the setting of left bundle branch block (LBBB), pharmacologic stress, rather than exercise stress, is preferred because stress tests that depend on increasing heart rate have an increased incidence of false-positive anteroseptal reversible defects on nuclear imaging. Patients with an abnormal resting ECG that would impair the interpretation of ischemic changes, including those with LBBB, ventricular pacing, ventricular preexcitation, or major ST-T wave abnormalities, should have imaging performed in association with the stress test. The ECG of the patient described demonstrates left ventricular hypertrophy with strain, changes that do not preclude ECG stress testing but require that imaging be obtained with it. The preferred test, therefore, is exercise stress echocardiography because she is capable of exercise.

Cardiovascular magnetic resonance (CMR) imaging with gadolinium enhancement would not provide information regarding ischemia, although it may show a previous infarct. However, exercise testing provides prognostic information not obtainable by magnetic resonance modalities alone and is preferred when possible.

> **KEY POINT**
>
> - Patients with an abnormal resting electrocardiogram that would impair the interpretation of ischemic changes, including those with left bundle branch block, ventricular pacing, ventricular preexcitation, or major ST-T wave abnormalities, should have imaging performed in association with the stress test.

Bibliography

Marwick TH, Hordern MD, Miller T, et al; Council on Clinical Cardiology, American Heart Association Exercise, Cardiac Rehabilitation, and Prevention Committee; Council on Cardiovascular Disease in the Young; Council on Cardiovascular Nursing; Council on Nutrition, Physical Activity, and Metabolism; Interdisciplinary Council on Quality of Care and Outcomes Research. Exercise training for type 2 diabetes mellitus: impact on cardiovascular risk: a scientific statement from the American Heart Association. Circulation. 2009;119(25):3244-3262. [PMID: 19506108]

Item 93   Answer: D
Educational Objective: Diagnose restrictive cardiomyopathy.

A restrictive cardiomyopathy (RCM) is the most likely explanation for this patient's presentation and echocardiographic findings. Dyspnea, edema, and fatigue can become prominent as RCM progresses. Examination may show findings of right-sided heart failure. The echocardiographic hallmark of this condition is restrictive ventricular diastolic filling. Atria are dilated, often severely. The ventricular cavities are small to normal size, systolic function is preserved, and pulmonary hypertension is often present. RCM is most often idiopathic.

Hemochromatosis can be a cause of RCM, but isolated cardiac involvement in the absence of systemic manifestations of the illness is uncommon. Serum iron levels were normal in this patient, virtually excluding hemochromatosis.

Constrictive pericarditis is a potentially treatable disorder that can be difficult to distinguish from RCM. Both entities cause restrictive filling. Atrial enlargement is often severe in RCM compared with constrictive pericarditis, and B-type natriuretic peptide level is substantially elevated in RCM but only minimally elevated or normal in constrictive pericarditis. In addition, this patient has no obvious potential cause for constrictive pericarditis, such as a history of acute pericarditis, tuberculosis, malignancy, or chest irradiation. Thus, constrictive pericarditis is less likely in this patient and is not the best choice.

Lack of left ventricular wall hypertrophy, a typical feature of hypertrophic cardiomyopathy, makes this diagnosis unlikely in this patient.

> **KEY POINT**
>
> - Restrictive cardiomyopathy is characterized echocardiographically by restrictive ventricular diastolic filling, severely dilated atria, and small- to normal-sized ventricular cavities.

Bibliography

Nihoyannopoulos P, Dawson D. Restrictive cardiomyopathies. Eur J Echocardiogr. 2009;10(8):iii23-iii33. [PMID: 19889655]

Item 94   Answer: D
Educational Objective: Manage a patient with asymptomatic hypertrophic cardiomyopathy with risk factors for sudden cardiac death.

This patient should undergo placement of an implantable cardioverter-defibrillator (ICD). Echocardiography is virtually diagnostic for hypertrophic cardiomyopathy (HCM). His current risk stratification shows the presence of two major risk factors for sudden cardiac death: family history of premature sudden death in a first-degree relative and left ventricular wall thickness of 30 mm or greater. Management in this asymptomatic patient is predominantly focused on prevention of sudden cardiac death. ICD implantation is effective for primary prevention of sudden cardiac death in patients with HCM.

In patients with outflow tract obstruction and heart failure symptoms refractory to medication, alleviation of the obstruction with septal myectomy or, in some patients, alcohol septal ablation may be indicated. This patient is asymptomatic; therefore, alcohol septal ablation is not indicated.

Electrophysiology testing is not a reliable method to risk stratify for sudden cardiac death in patients with HCM. As such, it is not an appropriate test for this patient.

A blunted blood pressure response to exercise in patients with HCM may explain dizziness and is one of the seven major risk factors for sudden cardiac death. However, this evaluation is unnecessary in this patient who already has two of the major risk factors.

Amiodarone may be used for primary prevention of sudden cardiac death in patients with HCM with one or more major risk factors, but its efficacy is not established. It may be considered when ICD implantation is not feasible.

American Heart Association consensus recommendations on physical activity in patients with HCM note that most low-level recreational activities, such as bowling or golf, are probably permissible. High-level recreational activities, such as basketball or bodybuilding, are not advised or are strongly discouraged. Recommendations on moderate-level recreational activities vary, with some activities, such as tennis, deemed probably permissible, whereas others, including weightlifting, are strongly discouraged. The 36th Bethesda Conference on Recommendations for Determining Eligibility for Competition in Athletes with Cardiovascular Abnormalities has published recommendations applicable to competitive athletes with HCM. Patients with HCM require formal counseling regarding acceptable levels of physical activities.

KEY POINT

- Patients with hypertrophic cardiomyopathy who are at high risk for sudden cardiac death should have an implantable cardioverter-defibrillator placed.

Bibliography
Maron BJ, Chaitman BR, Ackerman MJ, et al; Working Groups of the American Heart Association Committee on Exercise, Cardiac Rehabilitation, and Prevention; Councils on Clinical Cardiology and Cardiovascular Disease in the Young. Recommendations for physical activity and recreational sports participation for young patients with genetic cardiovascular diseases. Circulation. 2004;109(22):2807-2816. [PMID: 15184297]

Item 95   Answer: C
Educational Objective: Diagnose doxorubicin-induced dilated cardiomyopathy.

A doxorubicin-induced dilated cardiomyopathy is the most likely diagnosis. This elderly woman has a physical examination consistent with decompensated heart failure (S_3 gallop, pulmonary crackles). Heart failure that presents after cessation of cardiotoxic chemotherapy is typically caused by a nonischemic dilated cardiomyopathy. This may occur years to decades after chemotherapy. This patient has several clinical risk factors for its development, including a cumulative dose of doxorubicin in excess of 550 mg/m², age older than 70 years at the time of chemotherapy, and the addition of another cardiotoxic agent (cyclophosphamide) in combination with doxorubicin and radiation therapy to the thorax.

Cardiac tamponade is unlikely in this patient who lacks significant jugular venous distention and peripheral edema or a pulsus paradoxus greater than 10 mm Hg.

An exacerbation of chronic obstructive pulmonary disease (COPD) is unlikely in the absence of cough and sputum.

In addition, the increased B-type natriuretic peptide (BNP) level supports the diagnosis of cardiac decompensation, not COPD, as the cause of dyspnea.

Radiation-induced constrictive pericarditis typically manifests with right-sided findings of heart failure disproportionately greater than that of left, which was not the case in this patient. In addition, BNP is typically normal or slightly elevated in constrictive pericarditis. The striking elevation in BNP seen in this patient makes this diagnosis unlikely.

KEY POINT

- Risk factors for development of doxorubicin-induced dilated cardiomyopathy include a cumulative dose of doxorubicin in excess of 550 mg/m², age older than 70 years at time of chemotherapy, the addition of another cardiotoxic agent, radiation therapy to the thorax, and hypertension.

Bibliography
Geiger S. Lange V, Suhl P, Heinemann V, Stemmler HJ. Anticancer therapy induced cardiotoxicity: review of the literature. Anticancer Drugs. 2010;21(6):578-590. [PMID: 20375725]

Item 96   Answer: B
Educational Objective: Diagnose myopericarditis leading to heart failure.

Myopericarditis leading to heart failure is the most likely diagnosis in this patient. A diagnosis of myopericarditis can be made when acute pericarditis coexists with myocardial injury unrelated to myocardial infarction. ST-segment elevation is regional and concave-downward (akin to a myocardial infarction). A new segmental wall motion abnormality or global left ventricular dysfunction and elevated cardiac biomarkers are present, as in this patient. A subset of patients develops heart failure, as did this patient.

Cardiac tamponade as a complication of pericarditis may lead to shortness of breath. However, this patient lacks findings of cardiac tamponade, such as jugular venous distention or pulsus paradoxus. The small pericardial effusion noted on echocardiography is typical for pericarditis or myopericarditis.

Post–myocardial infarction syndrome characteristically is diagnosed as pericarditis that is preceded by cardiac injury, occurring typically from a ST-elevation myocardial infarction, which is not present in this patient. Furthermore, post–myocardial infarction syndrome does not cause heart failure.

Takotsubo cardiomyopathy could present with chest pain, ST-segment elevation, left ventricular dysfunction, normal coronary arteries, and subsequently elevated cardiac biomarkers. However, the degree of elevation in cardiac biomarkers is typically mild, versus the large rise in troponin I level in this patient. In addition, the wall motion abnormality is characteristically a ballooning apical segment of the

CONT.

left ventricle rather than the regional hypokinesis demonstrated during cardiac catheterization.

KEY POINT

- Myopericarditis, in which acute pericarditis occurs together with myocardial injury unrelated to myocardial infarction, may lead to heart failure.

Bibliography

Omar HR, Fathy A, Rashad R, Elghonemy M. Acute perimyocarditis mimicking transmural myocardial infarction. Int Arch Med. 2009;2(1):37. [PMID: 20003228]

Item 97   Answer: B

Educational Objective: Treat mildly symptomatic left ventricular dysfunction.

This patient should begin taking a β-blocker such as carvedilol. He has reduced left ventricular systolic function with mild symptoms that resolved with diuresis (New York Heart Association [NYHA] functional class I-II). Patients with left ventricular dysfunction should be treated with an ACE inhibitor and β-blocker for reduction in mortality and morbidity, regardless of symptom status. Because this patient is already taking an ACE inhibitor (enalapril), he should also begin taking a β-blocker, such as carvedilol.

Treatment with amlodipine is not associated with any morbidity or mortality benefit in systolic heart failure. First-generation calcium channel blockers have been associated with increased risk of heart failure decompensation and hospitalization; however, if a calcium channel blocker is needed in treating a patient with systolic heart failure, amlodipine would be a suitable option because it has been shown to have a neutral effect on mortality. This patient's hypertension is well controlled with his existing medical therapy, and he does not have an indication for a calcium channel blocker.

Hydralazine and isosorbide dinitrate would be appropriate therapy as an alternative for a patient with systolic heart failure who is intolerant of ACE inhibitor or angiotensin receptor blocker therapy owing to chronic kidney disease or hyperkalemia. Hydralazine and isosorbide dinitrate also are indicated for black patients with severe systolic heart failure (NYHA class III-IV). The addition of hydralazine–isosorbide dinitrate to standard therapy with an ACE inhibitor and β-blocker for black patients with severe systolic heart failure reduces mortality. This patient is not intolerant to ACE inhibitors, and although he is black, he does not have symptoms of severe heart failure (NYHA class III-IV).

Spironolactone is indicated for treatment of severe systolic heart failure (NYHA class III-IV), added to standard medical therapy of an ACE inhibitor and a β-blocker. This patient has only mild to no symptoms of heart failure (NYHA class I-II), and spironolactone is, therefore, not indicated.

KEY POINT

- Patients with left ventricular dysfunction should be treated with an ACE inhibitor and a β-blocker, regardless of symptom status.

Bibliography

McMurry JJ. Clinical practice. Systolic heart failure. N Engl J Med. 2010;362(3):228-238. [PMID: 20089973]

Item 98   Answer: C

Educational Objective: Manage a patient with bradycardia taking digoxin.

The patient's serum digoxin level should be evaluated. Manifestations of digoxin toxicity are nonspecific, and a high index of suspicion is necessary in patients taking digoxin who present with arrhythmias or constitutional symptoms. The electrocardiogram in this patient demonstrates coarse atrial fibrillation with a regularized ventricular response (in addition to a premature ventricular contraction). These findings indicate complete heart block with a junctional or ventricular escape rhythm, one of the rhythms that can be seen with digoxin toxicity. Nearly every rhythm abnormality can be seen with digoxin toxicity, although the most frequent are sinus arrest, atrial tachycardia, junctional tachycardia, atrioventricular block, premature ventricular contractions, and ventricular tachycardia. Noncardiac signs and symptoms of digoxin toxicity include nausea, anorexia, fatigue, vision abnormalities, and mental status changes. Digoxin is primarily cleared by the kidneys, and, in the setting of acute kidney injury or chronic kidney disease, the risk of toxicity is increased. Taken together, the complete heart block seen on this patient's electrocardiogram, her presenting signs and symptoms, and her increased creatinine level raise the strong possibility of digoxin toxicity.

Cardioversion would be appropriate if the patient had significant symptoms from atrial fibrillation, but that is not true in this case. In addition, cardioversion can increase intracellular calcium and possibly increase ventricular arrhythmias in the setting of digoxin toxicity. If present, some degree of hypocalcemia should be tolerated in these patients, as calcium replacement can also increase intracellular calcium.

In this patient, it is unlikely that the bradycardia is symptomatic given that the heart rate is 49/min with an acceptable blood pressure, and neither a temporary pacemaker nor dobutamine is indicated.

Treatment depends on the severity of symptoms. Digoxin cannot be removed by hemodialysis. If rapid treatment is needed, digoxin-specific Fab antibody fragments can reverse toxicity within 4 hours. Digoxin toxicity is associated with hyperkalemia because the drug interferes with Na^+,K^+-ATPase pumping of potassium into cells. Once the patient is treated with Fab fragments, the sodium-potassium pump is restored and a rapid drop in potassium may occur.

KEY POINT

- A regularized ventricular rate in the setting of atrial fibrillation is concerning for complete atrioventricular block with a junctional or ventricular escape and the possibility of digoxin toxicity.

Bibliography

Vivo RP, Krim SR, Perez J, Inklab M, Tenner T Jr, Hodgson J. Digoxin: current use and approach to toxicity. Am J Med Sci. 2008;336(5):423-428. [PMID: 19011400]

Item 99   Answer: D

Educational Objective: Treat continuing angina in a patient with chronic stable coronary artery disease.

This patient with coronary artery disease (CAD) and continuing angina should have his medical therapy optimized by increasing his dosage of β-blocker. Physical examination is notable for a blood pressure and heart rate that would allow further up-titration of the β-blocker. The β-blocker dose is adjusted to achieve a resting heart rate of approximately 55 to 60/min and approximately 75% of the heart rate that produces angina with exertion.

Calcium channel blockers are first-line antianginal therapy in patients with contraindications to β-blockers. In patients with continuing angina despite optimal doses of β-blocker and nitrates, a calcium channel blocker may be added. A calcium channel blocker such as diltiazem is not indicated in this patient because his dosage of metoprolol is not yet optimal.

Ranolazine should be considered in patients who remain symptomatic despite optimal doses of β-blockers, calcium channel blockers, and nitrates. Ranolazine is metabolized in the liver by the cytochrome P-450 system and its use is therefore contraindicated in patients with hepatic impairment, those with baseline prolongation of the QT interval, and those taking other drugs that inhibit the cytochrome P-450 system. Diltiazem and verapamil increase serum levels of ranolazine, and combined use of ranolazine with either of these agents is contraindicated.

Coronary angiography would be indicated if the patient was on maximal medical therapy with continued angina symptoms that were affecting his quality of life. Referral for coronary angiography is not indicated because the patient is not currently receiving optimal medical therapy.

KEY POINT

- In the treatment of chronic stable angina, the β-blocker dose is adjusted to achieve a resting heart rate of approximately 55 to 60 beats/min and approximately 75% of the heart rate that produces angina with exertion.

Bibliography

Boden WE, O'Rourke RA, Teo KK, et al; COURAGE Trial Research Group. Optimal medical therapy with or without PCI for stable coronary disease. N Engl J Med. 2007;356(15):1503-1516. [PMID: 17387127]

Item 100   Answer: C

Educational Objective: Diagnose asymptomatic patent ductus arteriosus in an adult.

This patient most likely has a patent ductus arteriosus. The history of prematurity and the physical examination findings are most consistent with a patent ductus arteriosus. A patent ductus arteriosus that is not associated with pulmonary hypertension usually is associated with a continuous murmur located below the left clavicle that envelops the S_2.

Patients with aortic coarctation can demonstrate a continuous murmur owing to the obstruction related to coarctation and the collateral blood flow. The murmur is usually located in the left infraclavicular region. However, the absence of both systemic hypertension and delay between radial and femoral pulses makes the diagnosis of aortic coarctation unlikely in this patient.

The physical examination in a patient with an atrial septal defect includes fixed splitting of the S_2 and a systolic murmur noted at the second left intercostal space related to increased flow through the pulmonary valve. A diastolic rumble is occasionally noted if the shunt is large. These murmurs are soft and not audible in the left subclavicular region.

Pulmonary valve stenosis is characterized by a systolic murmur noted at the second left intercostal space that increases with inspiration. A pulmonic ejection sound that decreases with inspiration is often present. A diastolic murmur is not expected unless there is associated pulmonary valve regurgitation.

A ventricular septal defect is characterized by a systolic murmur that envelops the S_2. A diastolic component of the murmur is not characteristically present unless the patient has associated aortic valve regurgitation.

KEY POINT

- A patent ductus arteriosus without pulmonary hypertension usually is associated with a continuous murmur located below the left clavicle that envelops the S_2.

Bibliography

Silversides CK, Dore A, Poirier N, et al. Canadian Cardiovascular Society 2009 Consensus Conference on the management of adults with congenital heart disease: shunt lesions. Can J Cardiol. 2010;26(3):e70-e79. [PMID: 20352137]

Item 101   Answer: B

Educational Objective: Manage asymptomatic ostium secundum atrial septal defect in an adult.

This patient should undergo closure of the atrial septal defect. Closure of an atrial septal defect is indicated in patients with right-sided cardiac chamber enlargement and no evidence of pulmonary hypertension. Additional indications for atrial septal defect closure include symptoms attributable to the atrial septal defect (dyspnea, atrial fibrillation, paradoxical embolism, or cyanosis from right-to-left shunt). The patient presented has moderate right-sided cardiac chamber enlargement and mild increase in right ventricular systolic pressure; these findings suggest atrial septal defect closure should be performed despite the absence of cardiac symptoms.

The choice of device versus surgical closure depends on the presence or absence of coexisting cardiovascular pathology as well as patient and physician preference. Generally, in the absence of associated cardiovascular disease, device closure is preferred over surgical closure because of shorter hospitalization and recovery times.

Aspirin is commonly used in an effort to prevent paradoxical embolism in patients with a patent foramen ovale or a small atrial septal defect. Data to support the use of aspirin as a method to avoid paradoxical embolism in these patients, however, are limited.

The risk of paradoxical embolism is increased in patients with an intracardiac shunt such as atrial septal defect. Despite this, warfarin anticoagulation therapy is not indicated in this patient with an atrial septal defect without a history of atrial fibrillation or paradoxical embolism.

Observation and follow-up is not appropriate in this patient because there is right-sided cardiac chamber enlargement. Delay in atrial septal defect closure increases the risk of complications, including arrhythmias. The risk of intervention is very low and the potential long-term benefits outweigh the potential risks.

KEY POINT

- Closure of an atrial septal defect is indicated in patients with right-sided cardiac chamber enlargement and no evidence of pulmonary hypertension.

Bibliography

Humenberger M, Rosenhek R, Gabriel H, et al. Benefit of atrial septal defect closure in adults: impact of age. Eur Heart J. 2011;32(5):553-560. [PMID: 20943671]

Item 102   Answer: C

Educational Objective: Treat systolic heart failure in a patient intolerant of ACE inhibitors.

The combination of hydralazine–isosorbide dinitrate is a suitable alternative for treatment of systolic heart failure in patients who are intolerant of ACE inhibitors due to hyperkalemia or chronic kidney disease (this patient is already taking isosorbide dinitrate). Although this combination is associated with a lesser reduction in mortality compared with treatment with ACE inhibitor, the benefit is still superior to placebo. Treatment with hydralazine–isosorbide dinitrate is not associated with hyperkalemia or worsening kidney function.

Amlodipine is a calcium channel blocker that has been demonstrated to have neutral effects on outcomes in systolic heart failure and thus would be an appropriate agent to use for angina or hypertension that is not adequately controlled with other medications that are associated with improved outcomes (such as ACE inhibitors and β-blockers). However, amlodipine is not associated with a reduction in mortality or morbidity and thus is not considered standard therapy for systolic heart failure.

The incidence of hyperkalemia and kidney dysfunction is similar between ACE inhibitors and angiotensin receptor blockers (ARBs), and thus switching to an ARB such as candesartan would not be helpful for this patient.

Spironolactone is indicated for treatment of severe systolic heart failure (New York Heart Association class III-IV) in addition to standard therapy of ACE inhibitor (or alternative) and β-blocker. This patient does not have severe heart failure and is not already on standard baseline therapy, and thus would not meet criteria for spironolactone. In addition, spironolactone has potential adverse effects of hyperkalemia and kidney dysfunction and so would not be an appropriate choice for this patient.

KEY POINT

- Hydralazine–isosorbide dinitrate is a suitable alternative for treatment of systolic heart failure in patients who are intolerant of ACE inhibitors owing to hyperkalemia or kidney disease.

Bibliography

Goldberg LR. Heart failure. Ann Intern Med. 2010;152(11):ITC6-1-ITC6-15. [PMID: 20513825]

Item 103   Answer: C

Educational Objective: Initiate appropriate medical therapy in a patient with established coronary artery disease.

In addition to treatment for his diabetes, this patient should start taking aspirin, a β-blocker, and a statin. He has established coronary artery disease (CAD), diabetes mellitus, hypertension, and elevated LDL cholesterol. In the absence of contraindications, all patients with CAD require lifelong aspirin for its antithrombotic effects. Because this patient experienced a previous myocardial infarction, β-blockers should also be continued lifelong in the absence of contraindications. The LDL cholesterol level should be lowered to a goal of less than 100 mg/dL (2.59 mmol/L), with an optional goal of less than 70 mg/dL (1.81 mmol/L) in high-risk patients. Because this patient has diabetes and a previous myocardial infarction, he would be a candidate for aggressive LDL cholesterol lowering.

Given the presence of diabetes, the patient's goal blood pressure should be below 130/80 mm Hg. If this blood pressure cannot be achieved after starting metoprolol, an ACE inhibitor should be considered.

The use of aspirin alone or aspirin and simvastatin would be suboptimal therapy. Although the patient is currently asymptomatic, he is at increased risk for recurrent cardiovascular events given his established diagnosis of CAD. Therefore, not initiating medical therapy at this time would not be appropriate.

KEY POINT

- Patients with established coronary artery disease and a previous myocardial infarction require long-term medical therapy, including aspirin and a β-blocker.

Bibliography

Cannon CP, Rhee KE, Califf RM, et al; REACH Registry Investigators. Current use of aspirin and antithrombotic agents in the United States among outpatients with atherothrombotic disease (from the REduction of Atherothrombosis for Continued Health [REACH] Registry). Am J Cardiol. 2010;105(4):445-452. [PMID: 20152237]

Item 104   Answer: A

Educational Objective: Diagnose an irregular wide-complex tachycardia.

This patient has atrial fibrillation. The electrocardiogram (ECG) demonstrates a rapid, irregular, wide-complex tachycardia with slight variations in the QRS morphology. No P waves are evident, and a delta wave is best seen in leads V_2 through V_5. This is most consistent with atrial fibrillation with a bypass pathway, also known as preexcited atrial fibrillation. The presence of a bypass pathway, even if it conducts retrograde only, is associated with an increased risk of atrial fibrillation.

Typical atrial flutter is characterized by rapid, regular atrial depolarizations recognized as negative "sawtooth deflections" in leads II, III, and aVF, with a positive deflection in V_1 at approximately 300 beats/min. Atrial flutter is often associated with 2:1 atrioventricular block and a resultant ventricular rate that is one-half the flutter rate. Multifocal atrial tachycardia presents with a ventricular rate of at least 90 to 100/min, three different P-wave morphologies, and differing PR and P-P intervals. The absence of P waves on this ECG rules out atrial flutter and multifocal atrial tachycardia.

Although polymorphic ventricular tachycardia can be irregular, the QRS complex on this ECG does not show the characteristic "twisting of the points" morphology—the continuously changing axis of polymorphic QRS morphologies present on the ECG in polymorphic ventricular tachycardia.

Atrioventricular nodal blockers should be avoided in patients with preexcited atrial fibrillation because these agents may lead to the atrial fibrillation conducting more rapidly down the bypass pathway and degeneration of the rhythm into ventricular fibrillation. Intravenous procainamide or amiodarone are the preferred agents to be given in the acute setting. If these are ineffective in terminating the atrial fibrillation or if the patient develops hemodynamic instability, direct-current cardioversion should be performed. An electrophysiology study should be completed to assess the conduction properties of the bypass pathway. Catheter ablation can reduce the risk of recurrent atrial fibrillation and should be offered for long-term treatment.

KEY POINT

- A rapid, irregular, wide-complex tachycardia with slight variations in the QRS morphology and presence of delta waves is consistent with preexcited atrial fibrillation.

Bibliography

Fox DJ, Tischenko A, Krahn AD, et al. Supraventricular tachycardia: diagnosis and management. Mayo Clin Proc. 2008;83(12):1400-1411. [PMID: 19046562]

Item 105   Answer: A

Educational Objective: Treat symptomatic severe mitral valve stenosis.

The most appropriate treatment for this patient is balloon mitral valvuloplasty. She has symptomatic, severe mitral stenosis (mean mitral gradient >10 mm Hg, left atrial enlargement) with pulmonary hypertension. The mitral valve morphology, although stenotic, is favorable for balloon mitral valvuloplasty in that leaflet calcification and thickening are minimal. Additional anatomic factors associated with procedural success include preserved leaflet mobility and minimal subvalvular thickening. With favorable echocardiographic features, procedural success is 85% to 90%. Risks of balloon valvuloplasty include moderate to severe mitral regurgitation, systemic embolization, cardiac perforation, tamponade, and death. If successful (mitral valve area >1.5 cm^2 with moderate or less regurgitation), freedom from death or mitral valve reintervention is approximately 75% at 5 years, with a recognized gradual process of restenosis.

β-Blocker therapy (for example, metoprolol) may also be used for symptomatic benefit to increase the diastolic filling period. However, given her resting heart rate, β-blocker therapy in this patient may result in significant bradycardia without additional benefit.

Mechanical mitral valve replacement is an effective surgical treatment of mitral stenosis but carries the risk of cardiac surgery as well as the need for long-term anticoagulation after replacement. Mitral valve replacement is generally performed in patients with combined mitral stenosis and moderate or severe regurgitation; those who are undergoing another cardiac surgical procedure (such as aortic valve replacement or coronary artery bypass surgery); and patients with an unsuccessful result after either balloon valvuloplasty or open commissurotomy.

Open surgical commissurotomy would have similar results as balloon mitral valvuloplasty but includes the risks of cardiac surgery. This treatment, which was more commonly utilized before the availability of balloon valvuloplasty, may be considered in a younger patient in whom mitral valve anatomy is not favorable for balloon valvuloplasty

KEY POINT

- Balloon mitral valvuloplasty is the treatment of choice for patients with amenable anatomy and severe symptomatic mitral stenosis.

Bibliography

Chandrashekhar Y, Westaby S, Narula J. Mitral stenosis. Lancet. 2009;374(9697):1271-1283. [PMID: 19747723]

Item 106   Answer: D

Educational Objective: Treat hypotension in a patient with hypertrophic cardiomyopathy.

The most appropriate treatment for this patient with progressively worsening hypotension is volume resuscitation, stopping dopamine, and starting phenylephrine. Echocardiogram shows findings of hypertrophic cardiomyopathy (HCM) with prolonged systolic anterior motion of the mitral valve consistent with a hemodynamically significant left ventricular outflow tract obstruction. The severity of obstruction is more severe with small ventricular volumes, low afterload, and increased contractility. Patients with HCM may present with hemodynamic collapse secondary to acute severe left ventricular outflow tract obstruction. This may occur spontaneously or be precipitated by inotropic agents (dopamine, dobutamine), withdrawal of negative inotropic agents (β-blockers, calcium channel blockers), volume depletion, vasodilators, sustained atrial arrhythmias, or sinus tachycardia. In this patient, hypotension following a motor vehicle accident was treated with dopamine, precipitating left ventricular outflow obstruction and worsening his hypotension. Phenylephrine is an α-agonist and raises afterload by peripheral vasoconstriction. Stopping dopamine and starting phenylephrine is the most appropriate treatment to reduce or ameliorate the left ventricular obstruction, and thereby raise systemic blood pressure. Intravenous β-blockers, such as esmolol, may be useful in the treatment of severe left ventricular outflow obstruction.

Dobutamine and epinephrine have positive inotropic effects, which could worsen this patient's left ventricular outflow obstruction.

Milrinone has potent vasodilator effects and would likely worsen the left ventricular outflow tract obstruction and further lower blood pressure.

KEY POINT

- In patients with left ventricular outflow tract obstruction associated with hypertrophic cardiomyopathy, inotropic agents may precipitate hemodynamic collapse and are contraindicated.

Bibliography

Fifer MA, Vlahakes GJ. Management of symptoms in hypertrophic cardiomyopathy. Circulation. 2008;117(3):429-439. [PMID: 18212300]

Item 107   Answer: B

Educational Objective: Select the appropriate cardiac stress test for a patient unable to exercise.

This patient should undergo pharmacologic stress echocardiography with dobutamine prior to hip replacement surgery. The pretest probability of coronary artery disease in an elderly man with atypical angina is intermediate, and further preoperative diagnostic testing is indicated.

The premise of stress testing is provocation of transient myocardial ischemia by a stressor. Although exercise is preferred over pharmacologic stressors because it allows for evaluation of exercise tolerance and symptom provocation, this patient is unlikely to perform to an adequate workload on a treadmill because of arthritis and COPD. Additionally, his baseline electrocardiogram abnormalities may lead to false-positive findings, and an imaging stress modality is indicated.

For stress imaging studies, images are obtained at rest and following a cardiac stressor. Induced abnormalities in myocardial function or perfusion suggest a hemodynamically significant coronary blockage. Pharmacologic stressors include agents that increase myocardial contractility and oxygen demand (such as dobutamine) and agents that induce transient regional hypoperfusion via coronary vasodilation (such as adenosine or regadenoson). Adenosine is contraindicated in patients with bronchospastic disease (present in this patient) because it can precipitate further bronchospasm. Regadenoson, a newer vasodilator, is associated with an increase in dyspnea in patients with asthma and COPD. Additional studies are needed to confirm safety in these populations, particularly in those with severe reactive airways disease. Dobutamine would be the preferred stressor in this patient.

This patient should not proceed directly to coronary angiography given the atypical features of his symptoms. A cardiac stress study should be performed.

KEY POINT

- For patients with severe reactive airways disease who require stress testing using a pharmacologic stressor, dobutamine, rather than a vasodilator, should be used as the stressor.

Bibliography

Al Jaroudi W, Iskandrian AE. Regadenoson: a new myocardial stress agent [erratum in J Am Coll Cardiol. 2009;54(17):1635]. J Am Coll Cardiol. 2009;54(13):1123-1130. [PMID: 19761931]

Item 108   Answer: A

Educational Objective: Use cardiac magnetic resonance (CMR) imaging to evaluate a patient with sarcoidosis for possible cardiac involvement.

Cardiac magnetic resonance (CMR) imaging is the most appropriate diagnostic test to perform in this patient with sarcoidosis who has signs and symptoms of heart failure.

Echocardiographic findings are indicative of restrictive cardiomyopathy (restrictive filling, reduced peak diastolic annular velocity, biatrial enlargement, normal ejection fraction). Granulomas involve the heart in nearly 25% of patients with sarcoidosis. However, such involvement is frequently subclinical, and restrictive cardiomyopathy caused by sarcoidosis is rare; therefore, a diagnostic test to confirm sarcoidosis involvement of the heart is warranted. Of the tests listed, CMR imaging offers the best means of confirming this diagnosis. CMR imaging shows delayed gadolinium hyperenhancement, typically of the mid-myocardial wall or epicardium, indicative of inflammation or fibrosis in a distribution atypical for coronary artery disease (CAD). In addition, CMR imaging can be used to exclude increased pericardial thickness, which, if present, would be indicative of possible constrictive pericarditis.

Placement of an implantable cardioverter-defibrillator would be appropriate in this patient with heart failure if cardiac sarcoidosis is confirmed on the basis of current guidelines for the prevention of sudden cardiac death. In addition to corticosteroids, additional immunosuppressive agents may be appropriate.

CT angiography of the coronary arteries is not indicated in this patient. Although CAD may occur prematurely from long-term corticosteroid use in patients with sarcoidosis, it would not account for restrictive left ventricular filling.

Endomyocardial biopsy is insensitive for the diagnosis of sarcoidosis of the heart. It may be considered if CMR imaging is nondiagnostic and incurring the risk of an invasive procedure is warranted.

Transesophageal echocardiography is a useful diagnostic test to confirm hemodynamic derangements in restrictive cardiomyopathies. However, it would only be considered for this purpose when transthoracic echocardiography (TTE) is inadequate. In this case, TTE was adequate.

KEY POINT

- **In patients with sarcoidosis, cardiac magnetic resonance (CMR) imaging can help to confirm cardiac involvement.**

Bibliography
Patel MR, Cawley PJ, Heitner JF, et al. Detection of myocardial damage in patients with sarcoidosis. Circulation. 2009;120(20):1969-1977. [PMID: 19884472]

Item 109   Answer: C

Educational Objective: Evaluate a patient with a high pretest probability of endocarditis.

This patient likely has prosthetic valve endocarditis, and transesophageal echocardiography (TEE) is the initial test of choice when there is a moderate or high pretest probability of endocarditis (for example, in patients with staphylococcal bacteremia or fungemia, a prosthetic heart valve, or an intracardiac device). There is concern for multiple

associated complications in this patient, including aortic regurgitation (widened pulse pressure and diastolic murmur) as well as aortic root abscess (prolonged PR interval). TEE is the initial imaging test in some clinical situations, such as detection of left atrial thrombus, evaluation of prosthetic mitral valve dysfunction, evaluation of suspected aortic dissection, and in patients with a moderate to high pretest probability of endocarditis. Some studies have demonstrated that TEE is 100% sensitive in the diagnosis of endocarditis compared with only 32% for transthoracic echocardiography (TTE). Patients at high risk for endocarditis and its complications should undergo early TEE rather than TTE.

Cardiac CT angiography and cardiovascular magnetic resonance (CMR) imaging may be of help in identifying the presence of an aortic root abscess; however, TEE is more apt to identify cardiac vegetations and is as likely to identify an aortic abscess. In addition, the patient presented here has an elevated serum creatinine level. These two imaging modalities should be avoided in this setting owing to risk of acute kidney injury with intravenous contrast for the CT and systemic nephrogenic fibrosis with the gadolinium used in contrast MRI.

KEY POINT

- **Transesophageal echocardiography is the initial test of choice when there is a moderate or high pretest probability of endocarditis.**

Bibliography
American College of Cardiology Foundation Appropriate Use Criteria Task Force; American Society of Echocardiography; American Heart Association; American Society of Nuclear Cardiology; Heart Failure Society of America; Heart Rhythm Society; Society for Cardiovascular Angiography and Interventions; Society of Critical Care Medicine; Society of Cardiovascular Computed Tomography; Society for Cardiovascular Magnetic Resonance; Douglas PS, Garcia MJ, Haines DE, et al. ACCF/ASE/AHA/ASNC/HFSA/HRS/SCAI/SCCM/SCCT/SCMR 2011 appropriate use criteria for echocardiography. A Report of the American College of Cardiology Foundation Appropriate Use Criteria Task Force, American Society of Echocardiography, American Heart Association, American Society of Nuclear Cardiology, Heart Failure Society of America, Heart Rhythm Society, Society for Cardiovascular Angiography and Interventions, Society of Critical Care Medicine, Society of Cardiovascular Computed Tomography, and Society for Cardiovascular Magnetic Resonance endorsed by the American College of Chest Physicians. J Am Coll Cardiol. 2011;57(9):1126-1166. [PMID: 21349406]

Item 110   Answer: D

Educational Objective: Treat patent foramen ovale.

This patient should undergo closure of the patent foramen ovale. He presents with features of platypnea-orthodeoxia, characterized by positional symptoms of cyanosis and dyspnea that generally occur when the patient is sitting and resolve in the supine position. Right-to-left shunting across an atrial septal defect or patent foramen ovale causes cyanosis and dyspnea in the upright position due to deformation of the atrial septum and redirection of shunt flow. The shunt reversal in this patient is caused by the recent pneumonectomy, which causes a change in the intracardiac flow with change in position. This uncommon condition is an indication for device closure of a documented patent foramen ovale.

Ambulatory oxygen therapy may improve the symptoms related to episodic desaturation but is not appropriate for long-term therapy and is unlikely to alleviate the positional shunting that occurs.

Anticoagulation with warfarin is not appropriate treatment for this patient. He has not had a systemic or paradoxical embolism related to his patent foramen ovale, and although this could occur, prophylactic warfarin anticoagulation is not indicated.

The patient has no features of volume overload on examination or by testing. Furosemide is not likely to improve the patient's symptoms.

KEY POINT

- Platypnea-orthodeoxia in the presence of a documented patent foramen ovale is an indication for percutaneous closure.

Bibliography
Meier B, Lock JE. Contemporary management of patent foramen ovale. Circulation. 2003;107(1):5-9. [PMID: 12515733]

Item 111   Answer: C

Educational Objective: Manage an asymptomatic thoracic aortic aneurysm in a patient with Marfan syndrome.

This patient's echocardiogram demonstrates a thoracic aortic aneurysm with an aortic root diameter of 6.2 cm, which requires urgent repair. The patient has multiple phenotypic manifestations of Marfan syndrome involving the skeleton, eyes, and heart. He is tall and thin, with an arm span greater than his height. Additional skeletal manifestations include long, thin fingers, scoliosis, and pectus deformity. Myopia is common in patients with Marfan syndrome, but is not as specific for the disease as ectopia lentis (not seen in this patient). Aortic root dilatation is typical of the disease, and the murmur heard on physical examination represents aortic regurgitation. This patient's marked aortic dilatation necessitates urgent planned surgery to prevent the risk of catastrophic dissection.

The patient has no symptoms suggesting an acute aortic syndrome, and immediate hospitalization, emergency surgery, and parenteral agents to control blood pressure or heart rate are not indicated.

Oral losartan and metoprolol have both been used as part of a strategy to reduce the rate of aortic dilation in patients with Marfan syndrome. It would be appropriate to use such therapy in a patient with Marfan syndrome

with a smaller aortic root, but initiating this therapy now would not supplant surgical treatment, and no data indicate it would decrease the risk of dissection while awaiting surgery.

Surveillance echocardiography is not indicated because the aortic root already surpasses 5 cm, a size at which surgery is indicated in asymptomatic patients with Marfan syndrome.

KEY POINT

- **In patients with Marfan syndrome, repair is indicated for an asymptomatic thoracic aortic aneurysm with a root diameter greater than 5 cm.**

Bibliography
Stout M. The Marfan syndrome: implications for athletes and their echocardiographic assessment. Echocardiography. 2009;26(9):1075-1081. [PMID: 19840071]

Item 112   Answer: C

Educational Objective: Diagnose acute myopericarditis.

The most likely diagnosis is myopericarditis, an inflammatory condition that involves pericardium and myocardium. It is characterized by pleuritic chest pain, regional concave downward ST-segment elevation, regional or global left ventricular dysfunction but no obstructive coronary artery disease, and elevated cardiac biomarkers. Although isolated pericarditis could explain this patient's pleuritic chest pain, it would not explain the concave downward ST-segment elevation, anteroapical left ventricular dysfunction, and elevated troponin I level. The absence of friction rub does not exclude myopericarditis. The etiologies of myopericarditis are the same as those for pericarditis. Given the prodromal symptoms, the likely cause in this patient is viral.

Chest pain from aortic dissection is often tearing or ripping in quality. However, there are no examination features in this patient to raise a concern for dissection, such as discrepancy in blood pressure of the arms or diastolic murmur of aortic regurgitation. Aortic dissection may occlude a coronary artery and lead to an acute myocardial infarction (MI), but cardiac catheterization would reveal findings of this complication.

In more than 80% of patients with an acute ST-elevation MI, coronary angiography demonstrates thrombotic occlusion of the culprit coronary artery. Absence of coronary artery thrombus makes this diagnosis unlikely in this patient. Coronary artery vasospasm without thrombus could cause an acute MI. However, lack of vasospasm on coronary angiography, particularly with ongoing ST-segment elevation, excludes this mechanism.

Acute pleuritis may cause pleuritic chest pain. However, it is not associated with electrocardiographic or wall motion abnormalities. Chest pain from pleuritis is not particularly accentuated in the recumbent position.

CONT.

Pulmonary embolism would not explain this patient's regional wall abnormality on ventriculography or elevated cardiac biomarkers.

KEY POINT

- Myopericarditis is characterized clinically by pleuritic chest pain, regional concave downward ST-segment elevation, regional or global left ventricular dysfunction but no obstructive coronary artery disease in the distribution of the dysfunctional myocardium, and elevated cardiac biomarkers.

Bibliography

Imazio M, Cecchi E, Demichelis B, et al. Myopericarditis versus viral or idiopathic acute pericarditis. Heart. 2008;94(4):498-501. [PMID: 17575329]

Item 113   Answer: C

Educational Objective: Manage anemia in a patient with cyanotic congenital heart disease.

Short-course iron therapy is indicated in this patient with cyanotic congenital heart disease and iron deficiency. The normal hemoglobin level for a patient with cyanotic heart disease is 18 to 20 g/dL (180-200 g/L), with a hematocrit between 60% and 65%. This patient presents with symptoms of fatigue and dyspnea, and laboratory testing demonstrates a relative reduction in hemoglobin and hematocrit for a patient with cyanotic congenital heart disease. Reduced serum ferritin and transferrin saturation levels confirm iron deficiency, which is likely from menorrhagia. Iron deficiency in patients with cyanotic congenital heart disease is undesirable because of the reduced oxygen-carrying capacity and deformability of erythrocytes (microcytes) and increased risk of stroke. Ferrous sulfate, 325 mg/d, should be administered and the hemoglobin and hematocrit rechecked after about 10 days. After ferritin or transferrin saturation has normalized, the iron therapy should be discontinued to avoid rebound erythrocytosis.

Atrial septostomy is performed for end-stage pulmonary arterial hypertension in patients without an associated intracardiac shunt. This patient has Eisenmenger syndrome with resultant mixing of venous and arterial blood related to congenital heart disease. Therefore, an atrial septostomy would not be useful.

Heart/lung transplantation has been performed for patients with end-stage Eisenmenger syndrome; however, conservative medical measures would be most appropriate initially. Despite advances in antirejection therapy, the average life expectancy of patients after lung transplantation is approximately 50% at 5 years, and generally patients with reasonable functional status related to Eisenmenger syndrome have improved survival with conservative medical care compared with transplantation.

Phlebotomy would cause further reduction in hemoglobin, hematocrit, and iron stores, which are already low for a patient with cyanotic congenital heart disease. This would adversely impact oxygen-carrying capacity and worsen symptoms.

Pulmonary vasodilator therapies have been demonstrated to be safe and to improve functional status, 6-minute walk distance, and hemodynamics in patients with Eisenmenger syndrome. This would be a reasonable option for this patient if symptoms of fatigue and exertional dyspnea persist after normalization of the patient's hematologic status.

KEY POINT

- Short-course iron therapy is indicated for patients with cyanotic congenital heart disease and relative iron deficiency (normal hemoglobin level, 18-20 g/dL [180-200 g/L]; normal hematocrit, 60%-65%).

Bibliography

Tay EL, Peset A, Papaphylactou M, et al. Replacement therapy for iron deficiency improves exercise capacity and quality of life in patients with cyanotic congenital heart disease and/or the Eisenmenger syndrome. Int J Cardiol. 2011;151(3):307-312. [PMID: 20580108]

Item 114   Answer: D

Educational Objective: Evaluate a patient for an intracardiac shunt using the agitated saline contrast study.

This patient should undergo transthoracic echocardiography (TTE) with agitated saline contrast. She has exertional dyspnea and an abnormal cardiac examination. A TTE shows mild right ventricle enlargement and mild pulmonary hypertension. The echocardiographic findings, in combination with a fixed split S_2 on physical examination, suggest an atrial septal defect. Often, right-to-left shunting, as suggested in this patient with exertional dyspnea and her echocardiographic findings, is more easily seen with the aid of an agitated saline contrast study. With agitated saline contrast, normal saline is agitated and injected intravenously. An intracardiac shunt is identified by bubbles crossing from the right heart to the left heart at the level of the shunt. The bubbles produced in an agitated saline contrast study dissipate in the pulmonary microcirculation and do not opacify the left ventricle.

Iodine radiocontrast is used for radiographic imaging studies such as CT angiography or coronary angiography and is not an initial diagnostic modality for identifying an intracardiac shunt.

Transpulmonary microbubble contrast is most commonly used to evaluate regional wall motion abnormalities when image quality is poor by standard imaging, and is particularly useful during stress echocardiography, in which rapid image acquisition is often needed. It should be used with caution in patients with decompensated heart failure or severe pulmonary hypertension. Because both sides of the heart are opacified with use of microbubble transpulmonary contrast, this modality is not useful to identify an intracardiac shunt.

Technetium-labeled erythrocytes are used to gauge coronary blood flow in nuclear perfusion single-photon emission CT (SPECT) myocardial perfusion scanning (stress testing); this test is not used for assessment for an intracardiac shunt.

> **KEY POINT**
> - An agitated saline contrast study enables the echocardiographic detection of right-to-left intracardiac shunts.

Bibliography

Mulvagh SL, Rakowski H, Vannan MA, et al; American Society of Echocardiography. American Society of Echocardiography consensus statement on the clinical applications of ultrasonic contrast agents in echocardiography. J Am Soc Echocardiogr. 2008;21(11):1179-1201. [PMID: 18992671]

Item 115   Answer: C

Educational Objective: Evaluate a patient with chest pain who has an abnormal baseline electrocardiogram.

An exercise perfusion stress test is the best option to diagnose or exclude coronary artery disease (CAD) in this patient. The decision to order a specific stress test is based on the pretest probability of CAD, the ability of the patient to exercise, findings on the resting electrocardiogram (ECG), and the presence of comorbid conditions such as reactive airways disease. His age, sex, and the atypical nature of his chest pain place his pretest probability of CAD in the intermediate range, and it would be appropriate to proceed with stress testing to establish a diagnosis. Any resting ST-segment changes reduce diagnostic accuracy, and ECG stress testing is not useful with conditions such as pre-excitation (Wolff-Parkinson-White syndrome), greater than 1-mm ST-segment depression, and left bundle branch block. Because this patient's baseline electrocardiogram is abnormal, imaging (nuclear imaging or echocardiography) would be needed to establish a diagnosis of CAD.

Coronary artery calcium (CAC) scoring uses noncontrast CT scanning to noninvasively measure the amount and extent of coronary artery calcium, which is a surrogate for atherosclerosis. It is used to help assess a patient's risk for a cardiovascular event rather than to assess the probability of CAD in a patient with chest pain. The utility of CAC scoring is highest in asymptomatic patients with an intermediate risk of a coronary event (10%-20% 10-year risk); in this patient group, a higher CAC score (>400) should prompt more intensive risk factor modification.

If this patient were unable to adequately exercise, a pharmacologic stress test would be indicated. Options for pharmacologic stress agents include adenosine, dipyridamole, dobutamine, and regadenoson. Adenosine and dipyridamole are both contraindicated in patients with bronchospastic disease.

> **KEY POINT**
> - An exercise nuclear stress test is used in patients with an indication for stress testing who are able to exercise but have baseline electrocardiographic abnormalities.

Bibliography

Anthony D. Diagnosis and screening of coronary artery disease. Prim Care. 2005;32(4):931-946. [PMID: 16326220]

Item 116   Answer: C

Educational Objective: Diagnose peripheral arterial disease in a patient with an uninterpretable ankle-brachial index.

The most appropriate test to perform in this patient is measurement of the great toe pressure. The ankle-brachial index (ABI) is obtained by measuring the systolic pressures in the dorsalis pedis and posterior tibialis arteries on both sides. The ABI for each leg is the highest ankle pressure for that side divided by the highest brachial pressure (regardless of side). An ABI of 0.90 or lower establishes a diagnosis of peripheral arterial disease (PAD). In this patient, the ABI is greater than 1.40 bilaterally. An ABI above 1.40 suggests noncompressible vessels, which may reflect medial calcification but is not diagnostic of flow-limiting atherosclerotic disease. An ABI greater than 1.40 is associated with worse cardiovascular outcomes than a normal ABI. In such cases, an appropriate next step is to either measure great toe pressure or calculate a toe-brachial index (systolic great toe pressure divided by systolic brachial pressure). Vessels within the great toe rarely become noncompressible, and a great toe systolic pressure below 40 mm Hg or a toe-brachial index of less than 0.70 is consistent with PAD.

Although the patient probably has peripheral neuropathy based on the symmetric loss of sensation to light touch, it is unlikely to be related to the patient's exertional leg pain. Therefore, electromyography and nerve conduction studies would not be helpful at this point.

An ABI obtained immediately following symptom-limited exercise is useful when a high clinical suspicion for PAD remains despite a normal (1.00-1.40) or borderline resting ABI. A decrease of the ABI by 20% compared with the resting ABI is consistent with significant PAD. This patient's ABI is above the normal range; therefore, exercise ABI would not help to establish the diagnosis.

Although spinal stenosis can produce leg discomfort with walking, patients often describe discomfort with prolonged standing. The discomfort is relieved with lying down or with waist flexion. In this patient, the physical examination does not demonstrate motor or sensory loss that would support nerve root compression as the cause of her symptoms. Additionally, the position adopted for bicycling is less likely to provoke leg pain in patients with spinal stenosis, but can result in claudication due to arterial insufficiency. Lumbar MRI, therefore, is not indicated.

Bibliography

Stein R, Hriljac I, Halperin JL, Gustavson SM, Teodorescu V, Olin JW. Limitation of the resting ankle-brachial index in symptomatic patients with peripheral arterial disease. Vasc Med. 2006;11(1):29-33. [PMID: 16669410]

Item 117   Answer: C

Educational Objective: Select the optimal ambulatory monitoring device for evaluating an arrhythmia.

The most appropriate diagnostic test for this patient is a looping event recorder. She describes symptoms of an irregular heartbeat and episodes of presyncope. The resting electrocardiogram obtained at the time of her visit is normal, without arrhythmia. The first step in evaluating a potential arrhythmia is to capture the arrhythmia and correlate it with the patient's symptoms. Sporadic symptoms can be difficult to capture on a resting electrocardiogram (ECG). Event recorders, used for more infrequent symptoms, record ECG tracings only when triggered by the patient. With a looping event recorder, the rhythm is continuously recorded but is not saved unless the patient triggers the device while experiencing symptoms. A looping event recorder also records several seconds of the presymptom rhythm.

Continuous ambulatory ECG monitoring for 24 or 48 hours is useful to detect asymptomatic arrhythmias or to correlate symptoms with rhythm if the symptoms occur frequently. It is unlikely that a 24-hour continuous ambulatory monitor would capture an arrhythmia event given the relative infrequency of this patient's symptoms.

Invasive electrophysiology testing is used to provoke an arrhythmia in a controlled setting or electrically map an arrhythmia for possible ablative intervention; it is not the first study used for diagnosis of arrhythmia.

In contrast to a looping event recorder, a postsymptom event recorder records the rhythm starting from when the device is triggered by the patient; no preceding rhythm is saved. The advantage of a postsymptom event recorder is the absence of electrode leads, making the monitor more comfortable for the patient to carry. Given the fleeting nature of this patient's symptoms, however, an arrhythmia may be resolved by the time a postsymptom event recorder is placed and triggered. Furthermore, the patient may not be able to trigger a postsymptom recorder if the symptoms are associated with a loss of consciousness.

Bibliography

Subbiah R, Gula LJ, Klein GJ, Skanes AC, Yee R, Krahn AD. Syncope: review of monitoring modalities. Curr Cardiol Rev. 2008;4(1):41-48. [PMID: 19924276]

Item 118   Answer: A

Educational Objective: Manage a patient in ventricular fibrillation.

After every shock from an external defibrillator, it is important to continue cardiopulmonary resuscitation (CPR) for 2 minutes, or five cycles of 30 compressions and two breaths, without stopping to assess the rhythm. Although the postshock rhythm may be normal sinus, there can be pulseless electrical activity or ineffective cardiac output during this time. Chest compressions should be of adequate depth (>2 in) and at a rate of 100/min, allowing for full chest recoil.

It is important to keep all interruptions to a minimum during CPR, as any break can lead to a reduction in coronary perfusion pressure and worse outcomes. The length of time that providers withhold CPR during defibrillator charging, shock, and postshock rhythm check can be more than 30 seconds. Therefore, CPR should be continued after every shock for 2 minutes, and at that point, a rhythm check should be completed. If the patient is in normal sinus rhythm, then postresuscitation care, including therapeutic hypothermia for 12 to 24 hours if the patient is comatose, should be given. If the patient is still in a shockable rhythm, a second shock should be given, followed by two more minutes of CPR.

After the second shock, an intravenous vasopressor may be given. Epinephrine may be used and repeated every 3 to 5 minutes, or, alternatively, a single dose of vasopressin can replace the first or second dose of epinephrine. If a third shock is needed, an intravenous antiarrhythmic agent such as amiodarone or lidocaine should be considered. If the patient survives the arrest, he should be offered an implantable cardioverter-defibrillator.

Bibliography

Neumar RW, Otto CW, Link MS, et al. Part 8: adult advanced cardiovascular life support: 2010 American Heart Association Guidelines for cardiopulmonary resuscitation and emergency cardiovascular care. Circulation. 2010;122(18 Suppl 3):S729-S767. [PMID: 20956224]

Item 119   Answer: C

Educational Objective: Manage syncope in a patient with arrhythmogenic right ventricular cardiomyopathy/dysplasia.

This patient with arrhythmogenic right ventricular cardiomyopathy/dysplasia (ARVC/D) who experienced a syncopal event should undergo placement of an implantable cardioverter-defibrillator (ICD). ARVC/D is a disease characterized by a disorder of the desmosome that leads to fibrofatty infiltration of the myocardium. The disease is often heralded by syncope secondary to monomorphic ventricular tachycardia originating from the right ventricle. An occurrence of syncope warrants placement of an ICD. Over time, right ventricular dysfunction, and sometimes left ventricular dysfunction, can occur. Competitive sports are strongly discouraged in patients with ARVC/D because there is a five-fold increased risk of sudden death during athletic activity owing to increased mechanical stress on the right ventricle and enhanced sympathetic tone. In addition, increased right ventricular stretch from physical activity accelerates disease progression and can hasten right ventricular dysfunction.

Induced ventricular tachycardia during an electrophysiology study has a poor predictive value for future ICD shocks and is not routinely recommended. In ARVC/D patients with multiple ICD shocks, however, intracardiac ablation, which is performed during electrophysiology study, can be used as adjunctive therapy for ventricular tachycardia.

One diagnostic criterion for ARVC/D is continuous ambulatory electrocardiographic monitoring demonstrating ventricular tachycardia or more than 500 premature ventricular contractions (PVCs) in a 24-hour period, but this patient has already been given the diagnosis of ARVC/D, so continuous ambulatory monitoring would not be useful. Likewise, a looping event recorder can record arrhythmic events should they occur but is not necessary in this patient.

A β-blocker and class III antiarrhythmic medication such as sotalol can be used to reduce the incidence of ventricular tachycardia or to reduce ICD shocks, but should not be used in place of an ICD.

KEY POINT

- Patients with arrhythmogenic right ventricular cardiomyopathy/dysplasia who experienced a syncopal event should undergo placement of an implantable cardioverter-defibrillator.

Bibliography

Basso C, Corrado D, Marcus FL, Nava A, Thiene G. Arrhythmogenic right ventricular cardiomyopathy. Lancet. 2009;373(9671):1289-1300. [PMID: 19362677]

Item 120   Answer: A

Educational Objective: Treat resistant hypertension in a patient with systolic heart failure.

This patient with resistant hypertension (blood pressure not at target with three-drug therapy of different classes of drugs, including a diuretic) and systolic heart failure should begin taking the calcium channel blocker amlodipine to improve control of his blood pressure. Although specific combinations of drugs have not been well studied in patients with resistant hypertension, many experts recommend adding a calcium channel blocker to an ACE inhibitor and a diuretic when patients are not at their target blood pressure. The diuretic chlorthalidone has a long duration of action and may be more effective than hydrochlorothiazide.

Many calcium channel blockers are relatively contraindicated in patients with systolic heart failure owing to an associated increased risk for precipitating heart failure exacerbation. Amlodipine and felodipine are newer generation agents that have been demonstrated in large-scale clinical trials to have a neutral effect on morbidity and mortality. Because they are not associated with morbidity or mortality benefits, calcium channel blockers are not first-line treatment for systolic heart failure. Use of calcium channel blockers in systolic heart failure is generally reserved for treatment of conditions such as hypertension or angina that are not optimally managed with maximal doses of evidence-based medications such as ACE inhibitors and β-blockers.

Older generation calcium channel blockers, such as diltiazem, nifedipine, and verapamil, may precipitate heart failure exacerbation owing to their negative inotropic effects. Although his symptoms are currently controlled (New York Heart Association class I), he would still be at risk of an exacerbation with one of these agents.

KEY POINT

- The calcium channel blocker amlodipine is a reasonable option for additional blood pressure control in a patient with heart failure who is already receiving optimal multidrug therapy.

Bibliography

Tsuyuki RT, McKelvie RS, Arnold JM, et al. Acute precipitants of congestive heart failure exacerbations. Arch Intern Med. 2001;161(19):2337-2342. [PMID: 11606149]

Index

A | **NAME AND ADDRESS (Please complete.)**

Last Name   First Name   Middle Initial

Address

Address cont.

City   State   ZIP Code

Country

Email address

ACP | **Medical Knowledge Self-Assessment Program® 16**
AMERICAN COLLEGE OF PHYSICIANS
INTERNAL MEDICINE | *Doctors for Adults*

TO EARN *AMA PRA CATEGORY 1 CREDITS*™ YOU MUST:

1. Answer all questions.
2. Score a minimum of 50% correct.

TO EARN *FREE* SAME-DAY *AMA PRA CATEGORY 1 CREDITS*™ ONLINE:

1. Answer all of your questions.
2. Go to **mksap.acponline.org** and access the appropriate answer sheet.
3. Transcribe your answers and submit for CME credits.
4. You can also enter your answers directly at **mksap.acponline.org** without first using this answer sheet.

To Submit Your Answer Sheet by Mail or FAX for a $10 Administrative Fee per Answer Sheet:

1. Answer all of your questions and calculate your score.
2. Complete boxes A–F.
3. Complete payment information.
4. Send the answer sheet and payment information to ACP, using the FAX number/address listed below.

B | **Order Number**
(Use the Order Number on your MKSAP materials packing slip.)

C | **ACP ID Number**
(Refer to packing slip in your MKSAP materials for your ACP ID Number.)

COMPLETE FORM BELOW ONLY IF YOU SUBMIT BY MAIL OR FAX

Last Name   First Name   MI

Payment Information. Must remit in US funds, drawn on a US bank.

The processing fee for each paper answer sheet is $10.

☐ Check, made payable to ACP, enclosed

Charge to ☐ **VISA** ☐ **MasterCard** ☐ ■ ☐ **DISCOVER**

Card Number _____

Expiration Date _____ / _____
          MM   YY

Security code (3 or 4 digit #s) _____

Signature _____

Fax to: 215-351-2799

Questions?
Go to **mskap.acponline.org** or email **custserv@acponline.org**

Mail to:
Member and Customer Service
American College of Physicians
190 N. Independence Mall West
Philadelphia, PA 19106-1572

1 Ⓐ Ⓑ Ⓒ Ⓓ Ⓔ
2 Ⓐ Ⓑ Ⓒ Ⓓ Ⓔ
3 Ⓐ Ⓑ Ⓒ Ⓓ Ⓔ
4 Ⓐ Ⓑ Ⓒ Ⓓ Ⓔ
5 Ⓐ Ⓑ Ⓒ Ⓓ Ⓔ
6 Ⓐ Ⓑ Ⓒ Ⓓ Ⓔ
7 Ⓐ Ⓑ Ⓒ Ⓓ Ⓔ
8 Ⓐ Ⓑ Ⓒ Ⓓ Ⓔ
9 Ⓐ Ⓑ Ⓒ Ⓓ Ⓔ
10 Ⓐ Ⓑ Ⓒ Ⓓ Ⓔ
11 Ⓐ Ⓑ Ⓒ Ⓓ Ⓔ
12 Ⓐ Ⓑ Ⓒ Ⓓ Ⓔ
13 Ⓐ Ⓑ Ⓒ Ⓓ Ⓔ
14 Ⓐ Ⓑ Ⓒ Ⓓ Ⓔ
15 Ⓐ Ⓑ Ⓒ Ⓓ Ⓔ
16 Ⓐ Ⓑ Ⓒ Ⓓ Ⓔ
17 Ⓐ Ⓑ Ⓒ Ⓓ Ⓔ
18 Ⓐ Ⓑ Ⓒ Ⓓ Ⓔ
19 Ⓐ Ⓑ Ⓒ Ⓓ Ⓔ
20 Ⓐ Ⓑ Ⓒ Ⓓ Ⓔ
21 Ⓐ Ⓑ Ⓒ Ⓓ Ⓔ
22 Ⓐ Ⓑ Ⓒ Ⓓ Ⓔ
23 Ⓐ Ⓑ Ⓒ Ⓓ Ⓔ
24 Ⓐ Ⓑ Ⓒ Ⓓ Ⓔ
25 Ⓐ Ⓑ Ⓒ Ⓓ Ⓔ
26 Ⓐ Ⓑ Ⓒ Ⓓ Ⓔ
27 Ⓐ Ⓑ Ⓒ Ⓓ Ⓔ
28 Ⓐ Ⓑ Ⓒ Ⓓ Ⓔ
29 Ⓐ Ⓑ Ⓒ Ⓓ Ⓔ
30 Ⓐ Ⓑ Ⓒ Ⓓ Ⓔ
31 Ⓐ Ⓑ Ⓒ Ⓓ Ⓔ
32 Ⓐ Ⓑ Ⓒ Ⓓ Ⓔ
33 Ⓐ Ⓑ Ⓒ Ⓓ Ⓔ
34 Ⓐ Ⓑ Ⓒ Ⓓ Ⓔ
35 Ⓐ Ⓑ Ⓒ Ⓓ Ⓔ
36 Ⓐ Ⓑ Ⓒ Ⓓ Ⓔ
37 Ⓐ Ⓑ Ⓒ Ⓓ Ⓔ
38 Ⓐ Ⓑ Ⓒ Ⓓ Ⓔ
39 Ⓐ Ⓑ Ⓒ Ⓓ Ⓔ
40 Ⓐ Ⓑ Ⓒ Ⓓ Ⓔ
41 Ⓐ Ⓑ Ⓒ Ⓓ Ⓔ
42 Ⓐ Ⓑ Ⓒ Ⓓ Ⓔ
43 Ⓐ Ⓑ Ⓒ Ⓓ Ⓔ
44 Ⓐ Ⓑ Ⓒ Ⓓ Ⓔ
45 Ⓐ Ⓑ Ⓒ Ⓓ Ⓔ

46 Ⓐ Ⓑ Ⓒ Ⓓ Ⓔ
47 Ⓐ Ⓑ Ⓒ Ⓓ Ⓔ
48 Ⓐ Ⓑ Ⓒ Ⓓ Ⓔ
49 Ⓐ Ⓑ Ⓒ Ⓓ Ⓔ
50 Ⓐ Ⓑ Ⓒ Ⓓ Ⓔ
51 Ⓐ Ⓑ Ⓒ Ⓓ Ⓔ
52 Ⓐ Ⓑ Ⓒ Ⓓ Ⓔ
53 Ⓐ Ⓑ Ⓒ Ⓓ Ⓔ
54 Ⓐ Ⓑ Ⓒ Ⓓ Ⓔ
55 Ⓐ Ⓑ Ⓒ Ⓓ Ⓔ
56 Ⓐ Ⓑ Ⓒ Ⓓ Ⓔ
57 Ⓐ Ⓑ Ⓒ Ⓓ Ⓔ
58 Ⓐ Ⓑ Ⓒ Ⓓ Ⓔ
59 Ⓐ Ⓑ Ⓒ Ⓓ Ⓔ
60 Ⓐ Ⓑ Ⓒ Ⓓ Ⓔ
61 Ⓐ Ⓑ Ⓒ Ⓓ Ⓔ
62 Ⓐ Ⓑ Ⓒ Ⓓ Ⓔ
63 Ⓐ Ⓑ Ⓒ Ⓓ Ⓔ
64 Ⓐ Ⓑ Ⓒ Ⓓ Ⓔ
65 Ⓐ Ⓑ Ⓒ Ⓓ Ⓔ
66 Ⓐ Ⓑ Ⓒ Ⓓ Ⓔ
67 Ⓐ Ⓑ Ⓒ Ⓓ Ⓔ
68 Ⓐ Ⓑ Ⓒ Ⓓ Ⓔ
69 Ⓐ Ⓑ Ⓒ Ⓓ Ⓔ
70 Ⓐ Ⓑ Ⓒ Ⓓ Ⓔ
71 Ⓐ Ⓑ Ⓒ Ⓓ Ⓔ
72 Ⓐ Ⓑ Ⓒ Ⓓ Ⓔ
73 Ⓐ Ⓑ Ⓒ Ⓓ Ⓔ
74 Ⓐ Ⓑ Ⓒ Ⓓ Ⓔ
75 Ⓐ Ⓑ Ⓒ Ⓓ Ⓔ
76 Ⓐ Ⓑ Ⓒ Ⓓ Ⓔ
77 Ⓐ Ⓑ Ⓒ Ⓓ Ⓔ
78 Ⓐ Ⓑ Ⓒ Ⓓ Ⓔ
79 Ⓐ Ⓑ Ⓒ Ⓓ Ⓔ
80 Ⓐ Ⓑ Ⓒ Ⓓ Ⓔ
81 Ⓐ Ⓑ Ⓒ Ⓓ Ⓔ
82 Ⓐ Ⓑ Ⓒ Ⓓ Ⓔ
83 Ⓐ Ⓑ Ⓒ Ⓓ Ⓔ
84 Ⓐ Ⓑ Ⓒ Ⓓ Ⓔ
85 Ⓐ Ⓑ Ⓒ Ⓓ Ⓔ
86 Ⓐ Ⓑ Ⓒ Ⓓ Ⓔ
87 Ⓐ Ⓑ Ⓒ Ⓓ Ⓔ
88 Ⓐ Ⓑ Ⓒ Ⓓ Ⓔ
89 Ⓐ Ⓑ Ⓒ Ⓓ Ⓔ
90 Ⓐ Ⓑ Ⓒ Ⓓ Ⓔ

91 Ⓐ Ⓑ Ⓒ Ⓓ Ⓔ
92 Ⓐ Ⓑ Ⓒ Ⓓ Ⓔ
93 Ⓐ Ⓑ Ⓒ Ⓓ Ⓔ
94 Ⓐ Ⓑ Ⓒ Ⓓ Ⓔ
95 Ⓐ Ⓑ Ⓒ Ⓓ Ⓔ
96 Ⓐ Ⓑ Ⓒ Ⓓ Ⓔ
97 Ⓐ Ⓑ Ⓒ Ⓓ Ⓔ
98 Ⓐ Ⓑ Ⓒ Ⓓ Ⓔ
99 Ⓐ Ⓑ Ⓒ Ⓓ Ⓔ
100 Ⓐ Ⓑ Ⓒ Ⓓ Ⓔ
101 Ⓐ Ⓑ Ⓒ Ⓓ Ⓔ
102 Ⓐ Ⓑ Ⓒ Ⓓ Ⓔ
103 Ⓐ Ⓑ Ⓒ Ⓓ Ⓔ
104 Ⓐ Ⓑ Ⓒ Ⓓ Ⓔ
105 Ⓐ Ⓑ Ⓒ Ⓓ Ⓔ
106 Ⓐ Ⓑ Ⓒ Ⓓ Ⓔ
107 Ⓐ Ⓑ Ⓒ Ⓓ Ⓔ
108 Ⓐ Ⓑ Ⓒ Ⓓ Ⓔ
109 Ⓐ Ⓑ Ⓒ Ⓓ Ⓔ
110 Ⓐ Ⓑ Ⓒ Ⓓ Ⓔ
111 Ⓐ Ⓑ Ⓒ Ⓓ Ⓔ
112 Ⓐ Ⓑ Ⓒ Ⓓ Ⓔ
113 Ⓐ Ⓑ Ⓒ Ⓓ Ⓔ
114 Ⓐ Ⓑ Ⓒ Ⓓ Ⓔ
115 Ⓐ Ⓑ Ⓒ Ⓓ Ⓔ
116 Ⓐ Ⓑ Ⓒ Ⓓ Ⓔ
117 Ⓐ Ⓑ Ⓒ Ⓓ Ⓔ
118 Ⓐ Ⓑ Ⓒ Ⓓ Ⓔ
119 Ⓐ Ⓑ Ⓒ Ⓓ Ⓔ
120 Ⓐ Ⓑ Ⓒ Ⓓ Ⓔ
121 Ⓐ Ⓑ Ⓒ Ⓓ Ⓔ
122 Ⓐ Ⓑ Ⓒ Ⓓ Ⓔ
123 Ⓐ Ⓑ Ⓒ Ⓓ Ⓔ
124 Ⓐ Ⓑ Ⓒ Ⓓ Ⓔ
125 Ⓐ Ⓑ Ⓒ Ⓓ Ⓔ
126 Ⓐ Ⓑ Ⓒ Ⓓ Ⓔ
127 Ⓐ Ⓑ Ⓒ Ⓓ Ⓔ
128 Ⓐ Ⓑ Ⓒ Ⓓ Ⓔ
129 Ⓐ Ⓑ Ⓒ Ⓓ Ⓔ
130 Ⓐ Ⓑ Ⓒ Ⓓ Ⓔ
131 Ⓐ Ⓑ Ⓒ Ⓓ Ⓔ
132 Ⓐ Ⓑ Ⓒ Ⓓ Ⓔ
133 Ⓐ Ⓑ Ⓒ Ⓓ Ⓔ
134 Ⓐ Ⓑ Ⓒ Ⓓ Ⓔ
135 Ⓐ Ⓑ Ⓒ Ⓓ Ⓔ

136 Ⓐ Ⓑ Ⓒ Ⓓ Ⓔ
137 Ⓐ Ⓑ Ⓒ Ⓓ Ⓔ
138 Ⓐ Ⓑ Ⓒ Ⓓ Ⓔ
139 Ⓐ Ⓑ Ⓒ Ⓓ Ⓔ
140 Ⓐ Ⓑ Ⓒ Ⓓ Ⓔ
141 Ⓐ Ⓑ Ⓒ Ⓓ Ⓔ
142 Ⓐ Ⓑ Ⓒ Ⓓ Ⓔ
143 Ⓐ Ⓑ Ⓒ Ⓓ Ⓔ
144 Ⓐ Ⓑ Ⓒ Ⓓ Ⓔ
145 Ⓐ Ⓑ Ⓒ Ⓓ Ⓔ
146 Ⓐ Ⓑ Ⓒ Ⓓ Ⓔ
147 Ⓐ Ⓑ Ⓒ Ⓓ Ⓔ
148 Ⓐ Ⓑ Ⓒ Ⓓ Ⓔ
149 Ⓐ Ⓑ Ⓒ Ⓓ Ⓔ
150 Ⓐ Ⓑ Ⓒ Ⓓ Ⓔ
151 Ⓐ Ⓑ Ⓒ Ⓓ Ⓔ
152 Ⓐ Ⓑ Ⓒ Ⓓ Ⓔ
153 Ⓐ Ⓑ Ⓒ Ⓓ Ⓔ
154 Ⓐ Ⓑ Ⓒ Ⓓ Ⓔ
155 Ⓐ Ⓑ Ⓒ Ⓓ Ⓔ
156 Ⓐ Ⓑ Ⓒ Ⓓ Ⓔ
157 Ⓐ Ⓑ Ⓒ Ⓓ Ⓔ
158 Ⓐ Ⓑ Ⓒ Ⓓ Ⓔ
159 Ⓐ Ⓑ Ⓒ Ⓓ Ⓔ
160 Ⓐ Ⓑ Ⓒ Ⓓ Ⓔ
161 Ⓐ Ⓑ Ⓒ Ⓓ Ⓔ
162 Ⓐ Ⓑ Ⓒ Ⓓ Ⓔ
163 Ⓐ Ⓑ Ⓒ Ⓓ Ⓔ
164 Ⓐ Ⓑ Ⓒ Ⓓ Ⓔ
165 Ⓐ Ⓑ Ⓒ Ⓓ Ⓔ
166 Ⓐ Ⓑ Ⓒ Ⓓ Ⓔ
167 Ⓐ Ⓑ Ⓒ Ⓓ Ⓔ
168 Ⓐ Ⓑ Ⓒ Ⓓ Ⓔ
169 Ⓐ Ⓑ Ⓒ Ⓓ Ⓔ
170 Ⓐ Ⓑ Ⓒ Ⓓ Ⓔ
171 Ⓐ Ⓑ Ⓒ Ⓓ Ⓔ
172 Ⓐ Ⓑ Ⓒ Ⓓ Ⓔ
173 Ⓐ Ⓑ Ⓒ Ⓓ Ⓔ
174 Ⓐ Ⓑ Ⓒ Ⓓ Ⓔ
175 Ⓐ Ⓑ Ⓒ Ⓓ Ⓔ
176 Ⓐ Ⓑ Ⓒ Ⓓ Ⓔ
177 Ⓐ Ⓑ Ⓒ Ⓓ Ⓔ
178 Ⓐ Ⓑ Ⓒ Ⓓ Ⓔ
179 Ⓐ Ⓑ Ⓒ Ⓓ Ⓔ
180 Ⓐ Ⓑ Ⓒ Ⓓ Ⓔ

MK1019